THE ENCYCLOPEDIA OF

TANKS

& ARMOURED FIGHTING VEHICLES

THE ENCYCLOPEDIA OF

TANKS

& ARMOURED FIGHTING VEHICLES

FROM WORLD WAR I TO THE PRESENT DAY

Grange
BOOKS

First published in 2006 for Grange Books
An imprint of Grange Books plc
The Grange
Kingsnorth Industrial Estate
Hoo, nr Rochester
Kent ME3 9ND
www.grangebooks.co.uk

A catalogue record for this book is available from the British Library.

ISBN-13: 978-1-84013-907-5
ISBN-10: 1-84013-907-2

Editorial and design by
Amber Books Ltd
Bradley's Close
74–77 White Lion Street
London N1 9PF
www.amberbooks.co.uk

Project Editor: Sarah Uttridge
Design: EQ Media

Printed in Singapore

PICTURE CREDITS

All photographs and illustrations provided by Art-Tech/ Aerospace Publishing, except the following:

9: U.S. Department of Defense

CONTENTS

INTRODUCTION   8

WORLD WAR I AND II   10

World War I Armoured Vehicles   12
World War II US Tanks   28
World War II Soviet Tanks   36
World War II German Tanks   48
World War II British Tanks   62
World War II Axis Tanks   76
World War II French Tanks   82
World War II Armoured Cars   88
World War II Special Purpose Vehicles   110
World War II Tank Destroyers   128
World War II Light Vehicles   148
World War II Amphibious Vehicles   172
World War II Halftracks   184

THE COLD WAR   202

Main Battle Tanks   204
Cold War Tracked Infantry Fighting Vehicles   240
Cold War Wheeled Armoured Personnel Carriers   256
Reconnaisance Vehicles   276

THE MODERN ERA   316

Modern Main Battle Tanks   318
Cold War Tracked Infantry Fighting Vehicles   350
Cold War Wheeled Armoured Personnel Carriers   368
Modern Light Vehicles   382
Amphibious and Oversnow Vehicles   402
Combat Engineer Vehicles   417

GLOSSARY   441
INDEX   442

A M60A3 main battle tank from the 1st Platoon, 48th Brigade, 108th Armoured Division, Georgia National Guard, moves through a recently cleared roadblock during a training exercise in Fort Steward, 1983.

Introduction

The Main Battle Tank has been the dominant force on the battlefield since the German Blitzkrieg burst onto the world stage in 1939. Although many advanced weapons systems have been developed since World War II, it is the tank, with its unique combination of firepower, mobility and protection, which remains the decisive factor in modern warfare.

The tank first saw action in World War I, when it broke the deadlock in the trenches. It could cross broken ground under fire, preparing the way for the infantry while keeping its occupants safe. Heinz Guderian, the architect of

Mainstay of Allied armoured forces in World War II, the M4 Sherman was no match for tanks like the Tiger, but it was mobile, reliable, and was available in huge numbers.

modern armoured combat, isolated the three factors that allow the tank to control the battlefield – firepower, protection, and mobility. In combination, they provide a war machine of awesome power, which has ruled the battlefield for more than 60 years.

The tank is not all-powerful. In the wrong place it can be horribly vulnerable to infantry or helicopters armed with anti-tank missiles. But in its true

terrain it is the master of any other fighting system.

It has been the decisive factor on battlefields all over the world, from the steppes of Russia through the deserts of North Africa and the Middle East, to the oilfields of Saudi Arabia and Kuwait.

The future of the tank is always open to speculation. Smart weapons attacking the thin top armour have meant a reappraisal of design philosophy. Liquid propellant

or even electromagnetic rail guns are being investigated to replace the existing guns. The balance will constantly shift, but always around the three classic factors – firepower, protection and mobility. They are the factors which have shaped the evolution of the tank since its beginning.

Armoured Fighting Vehicles
Powerful though it is, the modern tank cannot survive

on today's battlefield without the close support of infantry. In turn, infantry cannot survive without the support of the armoured fighting vehicle. The first vehicles were developed at the beginning of the 20th Century. Most were based on standard touring cars used in the cavalry role for reconnaissance. Early armoured cars were little more than modified commercial vehicles fitted with plate armour for protection, and armed with a machine-gun, but in the years after World War I they developed rapidly. Scout vehicles generally do not engage enemy armour in firefights due to their limited protection and armour and armament. They rely instead on speed and mobility to stay out of trouble. Two main types emerged: light four-wheeled vehicles for scouting ahead of armoured formations, and heavier vehicles with more powerful armament capable of acting independently.

Personnel Carriers

Germany first unleashed its Blitzkrieg on Europe in 1939. However, without infantry and light armoured support, German tank divisions would have ground to a halt. They would have had no means of holding territory once they had penetrated enemy defences. For that, they needed infantry. But infantry on foot could not keep up with the fast moving panzers, so infantry formations were mounted on trucks. To give the vehicle mounted infantry some protection, spearhead units were equipped with armoured half tracks. The Allies were slower to develop armoured personnel carriers, though by 1944 they were using old tanks with their turrets removed to carry infantry into battle.

After the war, the true armoured personnel carrier emerged. Developed in both wheeled and tracked forms, APCs were initially little more than lightly armoured 'Battle Taxis' designed to deliver infantry to the battle front from where they would fight on foot.

In the 1960s, the Soviets developed the first infantry fighting vehicles. These were more heavily armed than standard APCs, and were designed to provide close support to their infantry squads in the attack.

Modern AFVs

The battlefield has changed dramatically with the end of the Cold War. Modern military forces are expeditionary – they must be ready for deployment anywhere in the world, rapidly, and at very short notice.

Ever since World War II, the tank has put on weight. It is now so heavy that it cannot use many of Europe's small bridges. Tanks can not be

Modern Main Battle Tanks like the US Army's M1 Abrams are bigger, faster and heavier than their predecessors. Protected by incredibly tough laminated armour, their high-tech guns and fire control systems make them deadly weapons.

transported rapidly by air without considerable prior preparation.

By contrast, lighter armoured fighting vehicles, or AFVs, can be deployed rapidly, by both transport aircraft and heavy-lift helicopters. They require little or no preparation to be moved half way around the world.

Essentially armoured fighting vehicles have the same mobility as tanks, but less firepower and protection. However the gap is closing, and while the tank will always have a role in battle, that role will become increasingly limited, By contrast, the future of the armoured fighting vehicle looks extremely bright.

World War I and II

The origins of the tank date back to the Great War. Britain and France independently developed a new kind of mobile fortress – the tank. Designed to support the infantry, it could cross muddy ground and trenches while its heavy armour made it all but invulnerable to enemy fire. Mechanical reliability was more of a problem.

Between the wars, tank development took a number of different routes. Light tanks could be used for reconnaissance and to support the infantry. Medium tanks were more versatile, with heavier guns and thicker armour. Most nations also developed heavy infantry tanks, with powerful guns and thick armour. But they lacked mobility, which would be a crucial failing in World War II. In that conflict German success depended more on how tanks were used: Blitzkrieg demanded mobility and good communications more than big guns and thick armour. By the end of the war, the tank had changed beyond all recognition.

Left: British Churchill infantry tanks advance from Isola del Piano in Italy in August 1944. The introduction of Blitzkrieg tactics by the Germans at the beginning of World War II revolutionised land warfare, and it was the tank that was the spearhead of the new mobile formations.

Minerva Armoured car

The story of the Belgian **Minerva** armoured car is now little known outside Belgium. This is a pity as in many ways the Belgians were the progenitors of armoured car warfare and demonstrated to others how such vehicles could be used, so anticipating a type of mobile combat that was not to realise its full form until World War II.

Improvised armour

Almost as soon as the Germans invaded Belgium in August 1914, cavalry sweeps ahead of the main body of the German army were encountered by the Belgians. Usually the Germans heavily outnumbered the Belgians, who soon took to using the mobility of the motor car as a counter against German numbers.

By the end of the month, two Minerva touring cars were provided with improvised armour at the Cockerill works at Hoboken. These early cars were simply commercial models with sheets of 4-mm (0.16-in) armour plating around the engine and sides, and with the top left open for a Hotchkiss machine-gun mount.

Before very long the first two cars were followed by further examples with a more formal armoured hull but retaining the same basic layout. With this small force the Belgians showed what armoured cars could do: acting originally as a form of motorised cavalry they carried out long reconnaissance missions, gathered intelligence of the enemy's movements, gave fire and other support to infantry attacks when possible, and also carried out long disruption missions behind the lines of the German advance.

It was perhaps the last type of mission that attracted most attention, for at that stage of the war the Germans were advancing or marching in open order across open country or along roads. The single machine-gun of a Minerva armoured car could create havoc in such conditions, and frequently did just that.

Much-copied

However, this period did not last long. By October 1914 the line of trenches had reached the Yser region, and there the Belgian army remained until 1918. The area was too wet and boggy for armoured cars to achieve anything useful and their period of immediate action passed. However, during the few weeks they had been in action they had demonstrated to all who cared to learn what the armoured car could achieve. The Belgian example was copied directly by the British Royal Naval Air Service squadrons.

Sterling service

While the Western Front was 'out' as far as Belgian armoured car units were concerned, a special Belgian armoured car unit was formed for service in Russia against the Germans. There the Belgian cars performed sterling service until they were eventually shipped home in 1918.

Armoured turret

Once back in Belgium the units re-equipped, and in 1919 there appeared yet another version of the basic Minerva armoured car, this time with an armoured turret. The old 1914 Minervas were retained in service, however, usually for use by the Gendarmerie, with which some were still in use as late as 1933.

SPECIFICATION	
Minerva armoured car	**Dimensions:** length 4.9 m (16 ft 1 in); width 1.75 m (5 ft 9 in); height 2.3 m (7 ft 6½ in)
Crew: 3 to 6	
Weight: 4 tons	
Powerplant: one unknown petrol engine	**Performance:** maximum speed 40 km/h (25 mph); range not known

A section of Belgian Minerva armoured cars operates near Houthem in September 1917. The cars are all armed with Hotchkiss machine-guns, and the design had by 1917 been sufficiently formalised for spotlights to become standard.

Austin-Putilov Armoured cars

Although the vehicles known as the **Austin-Putilov** armoured cars had British origins they may be assumed to be Russian, as most of them were produced and used there.

In 1914 the Russian army was so short of equipment that it had to turn to the United Kingdom to supply armoured cars. Various types were involved but one of these was an Austin design, a fairly massive vehicle with twin turrets and solid-tyred wheels. Two types of hull were supplied, one of which had the armour over the driver's position arranged in such a way that it restricted the traverse of both of the gun turrets, each of which mounted a single Maxim machine-gun.

Added weight

This early arrangement was soon altered in favour of a lower cab, but on this model the weight was increased by 1.16 tons. This weight increase was brought about mainly by the use of thicker (maximum 8 mm/0.315 in) chrome-steel armour and a revision of the driving arrange-ments. The original British design could be steered from the front only, but the Russians wanted steering from the rear as well and the revisions required to accommodate this requirement added to the weight. This was not the only rearrangement demanded by the Russians, who soon found that the harsh Russian conditions were too much for the British vehicles, which broke down often.

Despite such problems, orders were placed for 200 Austin armoured cars, but not many were ever delivered. The main reason was that Austin was already stretched to the limit to supply vehicles for the British army and had few facilities to spare. Instead of complete armoured cars they supplied bare chassis direct to the Putilov

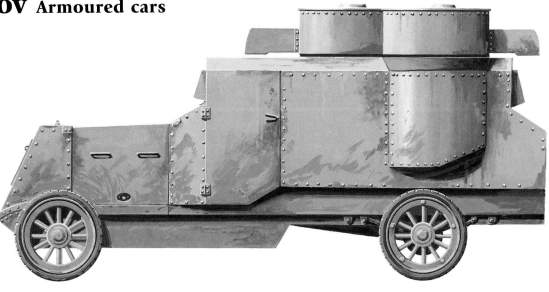

works, where the Russians added whatever strengthening they thought necessary and made some of their own modifications to the hull. This mainly involved staggering the twin turrets so that although each still covered only a 270° traverse they could together cover a slightly wider field of fire. A later innovation was the introduction of tracks in place of the rear wheels, which converted the vehicle into a half-track; eventually Putilov ceased production of the armoured cars at its St Petersburg plant and concentrated on the halftrack ver-sion. There was even a plan to produce halftracks in place of any more armoured cars but the revolution of 1917 occurred before this could be carried out.

Revolution

From 1914 to 1917 the Russians used many types of

The bulk of the Austin-Putilov is apparent in this side view. Note the riveted armoured plates and the armoured cowls over the heavy machine-gun barrel jackets. These armoured cars were among the best the Russian army had.

SPECIFICATION	
Austin-Putilov	**Dimensions:** length 4.88 m (16 ft);
Crew: 5	width 1.95 m (6 ft 4¾ in); height
Weight: 5.3 tons	2.4 m (7 ft 10½ in)
Powerplant: one 37.3-kW (50-hp)	**Performance:** max. speed 50 km/h
Austin petrol engine	(31 mph); range 200 km (125 miles)

armoured car, ranging from direct imports to local improvisations, but the most important type was the Austin-Putilov. It was numerically and mechanically the best the Russians had to hand and eventually proved to be far more suited to the rough

conditions under which the Russians had to fight. During 1917 many became involved in the internal fighting that accompanied the events leading to the October Revolution, and the type can frequently be seen in photographs of the period.

German troops examine a captured Austin-Putilov armoured car, probably in search of loot. Note the prominent Tsarist insignia and the height of these vehicles, which can be assessed by comparison with the nearby soldiers. After 1918 some of the cars were used by Poland and a few ended up in Japan.

Tank Mk I Heavy tank

The **Tank Mk I** was the production and service model of the prototype vehicle known as **'Mother'**, which was the eventual outcome of a series of development models based on the use of a Holt tractor chassis. Lieutenant W. G. Wilson was, mainly responsible for the final design of 'Mother' after a great deal of committee and experimental work, and it was he who conceived the idea of using the large and high track outline with its characteristic shape that came to be the classic tank outline of WWI.

The first 'tank'

'Mother' was demonstrated in January and February 1916, and soon after this the first production order was placed. A separate arm was established in March 1916 to use the new vehicle, which was named the 'tank' purely as a cover, though the name stuck. The first production vehicles were issued to the Heavy Section, Machine-Gun Corps in mid-1916, and the first crews were assembled.

The Tank Mk I was a large and heavy vehicle powered by a Daimler 78.3-kW (105-hp) petrol engine carried in an armoured box slung between the two massive lozenge-shaped continuous tracks. Originally it had been intended to mount a turret on the top but this would have made the design unstable so instead the main armament of two 6-pdr (57-mm; 2.24-in) guns was placed in one sponson on each side. The sponsons each had a single Lewis or Hotchkiss machine-gun, and a third such gun was fitted for extra defence. The vehicle was protected by armour plate (ranging in thickness from 6 to 12 mm; 0.24 to 0.47 in) riveted to steel joists, but in action this proved

unsatisfactory as bullet 'splash' got through the armour seams and caused casualties.

The Tank Mk I could cross trenches up to 2.44 m (8 ft) wide, and steering was at first accomplished by using external twin-wheel 'steering tails' that proved to be unnecessary: in action they were frequently damaged, yet the tanks could still be steered.

Almost as soon as the first tanks appeared in France in mid-1916 they were ordered into action, thus the first Tank Mk Is went into battle on the morning of 15 September 1916 at Flers-Courcelette in a vain attempt to provide some impetus to the flagging Somme Offensive. The tanks did manage to make some local breakthroughs and created panic when they appeared, but the sad truth was that too few actually got into action. Many of the 50 that were supposed to make the attack simply broke down or got bogged down in the mud. Individual tanks made impressions into the German line but numbers were too few to have a major impact.

Numerous versions

The Mark I was produced in two versions: the **Tank Mk I (Male)** described above, and intended

A Tank Mk I (Male) moves up into action near Thiepval in September 1916. Items to note are the anti-grenade wire mesh screen over the hull and the clumsy steering 'tail' at the rear; these steering devices were soon discarded as they proved to be of limited value.

for the primary offensive mission; and the **Tank Mk I (Female)** with larger sponsons and an armament of four Vickers and two Lewis machine-guns, and intended for the anti-infantry support of the Tank Mk I (Male). Other variants were the **Mk I Tank Tender** with steel boxes in place of the sponsons, and the **Mk I Wireless Tank** without

sponsons but with a tall aerial mast. Thus the Tank Mk I made history by being the first tank used in combat, but it was something of a fiasco as far as the action was concerned. What the type did achieve was to impress on the British military hierarchy the fact that the tank did have potential, and the 'Tank Corps' was formed in July 1917.

SPECIFICATION	
Tank Mk I (Male) **Crew:** 8 **Weight:** 28 tons **Powerplant:** one 78.3-kW (105-hp) Daimler petrol engine	**Dimensions:** length with tail 9.91 m (32 ft 6 in); length of hull 8.05 m (26 ft 5 in); width over sponsons 4.19 m (13 ft 9 in); height 2.45 m (8 ft ½ in) **Performance:** maximum speed 6 km/h (3.7 mph); range 38 km (24 miles)

A Tank Mk I (Female) emerges from battle near Flers-Courcelette on 15 September 1916 after the first-ever tank action. Note the armoured machine-gun cowls and the frame for the anti-grenade screen.

Medium Tank Mk A 'Whippet' British medium tank

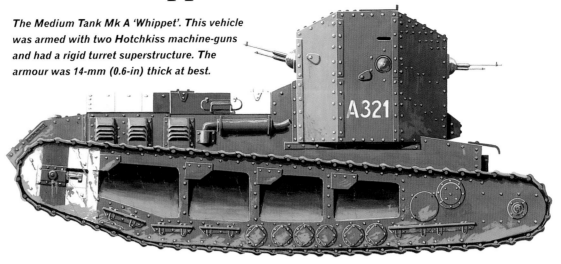

The Medium Tank Mk A 'Whippet'. This vehicle was armed with two Hotchkiss machine-guns and had a rigid turret superstructure. The armour was 14-mm (0.6-in) thick at best.

When the first tanks were designed they were intended to be little more than 'machine-gun destroyers' capable of crossing rough country. As a result they were huge lumbering beasts that could cross trenches, but could not move very fast over good ground. By 1916 the idea of using the tank as a form of cavalry began to take root; such a tank would be able to exploit the breakthroughs made in enemy lines. It was proposed that a new design of 'fast' tank with few obstacle-crossing attributes but capable of speed across good ground should be designed and built, and such a product was developed by Sir William Tritton, who had been instrumental in the development of the early landships.

The 'Whippet' arrives

The official name for the new tank was the **Medium Tank Mk A** but it was soon nicknamed **'Whippet'**. Tritton reverted to his early 'Little Willie' layout in which flat, rather than lozenge-shaped, tracks were used. A front-mounted engine bay was slung between the tracks, and this housed two Tylor 34-kW (45-hp) London bus engines, one to drive each track; steering was effected by speeding or slowing individual tracks. Towards the rear was the driver on the left, with the fighting compartment to his right. Originally this latter was to have been a turreted affair, but this was changed to a rigid superstructure mounting one Hotchkiss machine-gun in a special mounting on each face. Armour ranged in thickness from 5 mm (0.2 in) to 14 mm (0.6 in).

The prototype of the 'Whippet' was ready by February 1917, and was ordered into production in June of that year, but production took time and it was not until late 1917

that the first examples appeared. Even then they did not reach France quickly, and it was March 1918 before they saw action. The type proved to be difficult to drive as the driver had to juggle constantly with each engine clutch to control the machine, and in action many were lost when they went out of control. But the 'Whippet' soon proved to be reliable enough, and once on good ground it could notch up speeds greater than that of horsed cavalry.

The 'Musical Box'

At first the 'Whippets' were used to plug gaps in the line during the major German

advances, but it was when the time came for counter-attack that they came into their own. Some made deep forays behind enemy lines, creating havoc as they went. One example is the famous 'Muscial Box', which spent no less than nine hours cruising German rear areas and gunning down unsuspecting rear echelon troops before it was finally knocked out by a field gun.

By the time of the Armistice the 'Whippet' or Mk A was well established, but it did not remain in service long after that date. A few saw service during the Irish 'Troubles' and a batch became the first tanks exported to Japan in 1920. Additionally, prior to the Armistice the Germans had captured enough examples to take the Medium Mk A into small-scale service.

SPECIFICATION	
Medium Tank Mk A	**Dimensions:** length 6.10 m (20 ft); width 2.62 m (8 ft 7 in); height 2.74 m (9 ft)
Crew: 3 or 4	
Weight: 14 tons	
Powerplant: two 34-kW (45-hp) Tylor four-cylinder petrol engines	**Performance:** maximum speed 13.4 km/h (8.3 mph); range 64.3 km (40 miles)

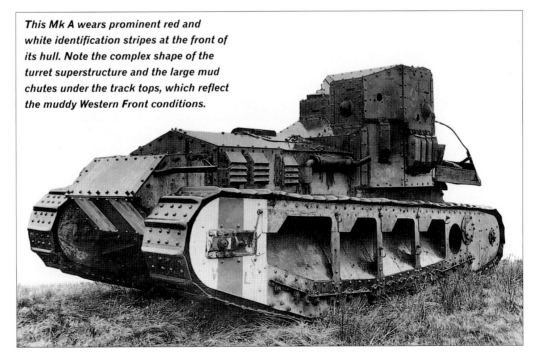

This Mk A wears prominent red and white identification stripes at the front of its hull. Note the complex shape of the turret superstructure and the large mud chutes under the track tops, which reflect the muddy Western Front conditions.

Tank Mk IV Male/Female British heavy tank

Moving barely faster than a walking soldier, the British Mk IV heavy tank had the archetype 'diamond' shape associated with the machines of this era. Although slow, the Mk IV was a potent adversary for contemporary German tanks.

The **Tank Mk IV** was the most numerous type used during World War I, and benefited from all the many design and tactical lessons that had been so desperately hard-won since the service debut of the Tank Mk I. Only relatively small numbers of the **Tank Mk II** and **Tank Mk III** had been built (50 of each), and most of these were converted to stores carriers and special duties vehicles. The Mk II featured a wider track shoe at every sixth link, and the Mk III had better armour.

When the **Mk IV** appeared in March 1917 it was the forerunner of a batch of 1,000 that had been ordered in the previous year, the design originating in October 1916.

Operational changes

The Mk IV had several changes over the previous three marks, which differed only in small detail. The main operational change was the introduction of better armour (ranging in thickness from 6 mm/0.24 in to 12 mm/0.47 in), first used on the Mk III, which had to be introduced as the Germans had quickly developed special anti-tank rifles and armour-piercing ammunition. Another change was to armament. The ex-naval 6-pdr (57-mm) guns of earlier marks were 40 calibres long, and were frequently bent or embedded into the ground when the tank was crossing trenches. They were replaced in the Mk IV by much smaller guns only 23 calibres long, and these thereafter remained standard tank guns for several years. Secondary armament was four Lewis machine-guns. The sponsons for the guns were also made smaller and for transport they could be pushed into the vehicle on rails, whereas earlier versions had the sponsons removed altogether for transport. Numerous internal mechanical changes were introduced, and an 'unditching' beam placed ready for use above the hull. This provided the extra traction required to get out of a ditch.

Keeping one eye on the enemy: the British Mk IV (Male) heavy tank demonstrates its impressive trench-crossing capabilities. Some versions were fitted with fascines to help bridge tank obstacles.

The Mk IV continued a concept that was introduced originally on the Mk I. Namely that certain tanks carried four primary machine-guns (two in each sponson) and two secondary guns, the 6-pdr guns being omitted. These were used for direct infantry support and trench-clearing, the variant being known as the **Tank Mk IV (Female)** in differentiation from the heavier-armed **Tank Mk IV (Male)**. There was also a variant with machine-guns in one sponson and a 6-pdr gun in the other; known as the **Tank Mk IV (Hermaphrodite)**.

Combat debut

The first tank 'duel' saw Mk IVs engaging German A7Vs, near Villier Bretonneux. The Mk IV was also used to good effect at Cambrai and many of the tank battles thereafter, and after 1918 the Mk IV was retained by the Tank Corps for many years. Some were used in Palestine and after the war they were used in Ireland. A few were given to the Italians, but perhaps the greatest users after the British were the Germans; almost inevitably many Mk IVs fell into the hands of the Germans, who then used them against the British, calling them **Beutepanzerwagen IV** (captured armoured vehicle IV). Other Mk IV variants were the **Mk IV Supply Tank**, the **Mk IV Tadpole Tank**, with length increased by 2.74 m (9 ft) at the rear for better trench-crossing, and the **Mk IV Fascine Tank**, fitted to carry trench-filling fascines (chainbound wood bundles some 1.37 m/ 4 ft 6 in in diameter). There was also a crane version.

SPECIFICATION	
Tank Mk IV (Male)	(26 ft 5 in); width over sponsons
Crew: 8	3.91 m (12 ft 7 in); height 2.49 m
Weight: 28 tons	(8 ft 2 in)
Powerplant: one 78 or 93-kW (105- or 125-hp) Daimler petrol engine Dimensions: length 8.05 m	**Performance:** maximum speed 6 km/h (3.7 mph); range 56 km (35 miles)

Tank Mk V Advanced British heavy tank

The **Tank Mk V** was the last of the classic lozenge-shaped tanks to serve in any numbers, and embodied all the improvements introduced on the Mk IV, together with the Wilson epicyclic gearbox that enabled the tank to be driven by one man, the earlier marks depending on the actions of two men and a great deal of team-work for steering. The Mk V also had a purpose-built engine, the 112-kW (150-hp) Ricardo, which not only gave more power but made life for the engineers inside the confines of the hull a great deal easier.

'Pigeon Post'

Another innovation was the introduction of a cupola for the commander and at long last provision was made for communication with the outside world, by the mounting of semaphore arms on the back of the hull. Until then a tank crew was virtually isolated from other troops not only by the great noise produced by the engine but by poor vision and no method of passing messages in or out. The early tanks could communicate only by sending pigeons to the rear if required. The main armament of the Male version was two 6-pdr (57-mm) guns, supplemented by four Hotchkiss machine-guns, and the armour varied in thickness from 6 mm to 14 mm (0.24 in to 0.55 in).

About 400 Mk Vs had been built in Birmingham by the time of the Armistice, and even by then the mark had begun to sprout variants. The first of these introduced a new 1.83-m (6-ft) section into the hull to improve trench-crossing capabilities and also to provide more internal space for personnel (up to 25 troops) or stores. This was the **Tank Mk V***, which was converted in the field, while the comparable, but much improved, **Tank Mk V**** was introduced on the production lines. As with the Mk IV, this improved vehicle was produced in **Tank Mk V (Male)** and **Tank Mk V (Female)** forms.

The 'American' Tank

The Mk V was also the first American tank. Enough Mk Vs were passed to the newly-arrived US Army to partially equip a battalion, together with some French FT 17s. Post-war the Mk V was used as the standard equipment of the Tank Corps, and although there were several designs based on the Mk V, none was produced or used in any numbers. The Mk V was used for all manner of experiments ranging from bridge-laying to mine-clearing with variations of the **Tank Mk V** (Tank RE)**, but never in any great numbers, as the years after 1918 were not financially conducive to such innovations. Numbers of Mk Vs were also passed to the Canadian army, where they remained in use until the early 1930s.

The Mk V never replaced the earlier Mk IV, although it arrived on the Western Front from about mid-1918 onwards. It proved to be far more reliable and easy to use than the earlier marks, but the war ended before it could take part in the massive armoured operations that had been planned for 1919. These missions called for the massed deployment of Mk Vs, along with some special tanks that never left the drawing board (supply tanks, armoured recovery vehicles and others) along chosen sectors of the front. The infantry would have little part to play as the tanks alone would advance to achieve the big 'breakthrough' sought so desperately and expensively since 1914. But the Armistice stopped 'Plan 1919'.

SPECIFICATION	
Tank Mk V (Male)	**Dimensions:** length 8.05 m (26 ft 5 in); width over sponsons 4.11 m
Crew: 8	(13 ft 6 in); height 2.64 m (8 ft 8 in)
Weight: 29 tons	**Performance:** maximum speed
Powerplant: one 112-kW (150-hp) Ricardo petrol engine	7.4 km/h (4.6 mph); range 72 km (45 miles)

Using a cable, a Tank Mk V (Male) assists another tank out of difficulties in August 1918. The Mk V carries red and white recognition stripes at the front. The rails over the top are for 'unditching' beams.

Rolls-Royce armoured car

When the Royal Naval Air Service went to war in 1914, it sent a variegated squadron of aircraft and vehicles to France and Belgium. Once there, some of the naval officers noted the way in which the Belgians were using armoured cars to harry the advancing Germans and to carry out raiding and other missions, and decided to join in. Within a few days some of the **Rolls-Royce Silver Ghost** touring cars used by the RNAS were converted in Dunkirk to carry armour plating on the sides. A single machine-gun was carried behind the driver. The Admiralty noted the success of the conversion and gave its sanction to the design of proper armoured cars based on the Silver Ghost chassis, and the first of these official designs was in France by the end of 1914.

Great success

The official Rolls-Royce armoured car, sometimes known as the **Armoured Car, Rolls-Royce (1914 Admiralty Turreted Pattern)**, was a straightforward conversion of the civilian Silver Ghost tourer with a turret and armour added. The springs were strengthened

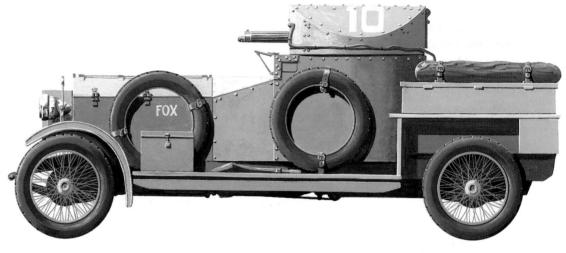

This 1914 Rolls-Royce armoured car has the original Admiralty pattern turret, mounting a Vickers 0.303 in (7.7-mm) machine-gun. These cars provided sterling service throughout the war and the type remained in use for years afterwards, especially in India and the African colonies.

to take the extra weight but that was all the modification required on the chassis. The armour extended all around the chassis, and the turret, which mounted a Vickers or Maxim machine-gun, had peculiar sloping sides rather like the shape of a bishop's mitre. The radiator had an armoured door and the roof armour on the turret could be removed if required. A small area behind the turret was left open to carry stores and a ground-mounted machine-gun. Once in service the Rolls-Royce armoured cars proved very

SPECIFICATION	
Armoured Car, Rolls-Royce (1914 Admiralty Turreted Pattern) **Crew:** 3 or 4 **Weight:** 3.5 tons **Powerplant:** 30/37.3-kW (40/50-hp) Rolls-Royce petrol engine	**Dimensions:** length 5.03 m (16 ft 6 in); width 1.91 m (6 ft 3 in); height 2.55 m (8 ft 4.5 in) **Performance:** maximum speed 95 km/h (60 mph); range 240 km (150 miles)

successful, remaining in service until 1922. Maximum armour thickness was 9 mm (0.35 in).

By March 1915 the first RNAS armoured car squadrons were in France, most of them equipped with the Rolls-Royce. Before that the RNAS armoured cars carried out some patrols and reconnaissance work along the French and Belgian coastal areas until the 'Race to the Sea' reached the Channel Coast and trench warfare became the norm. Once that was in progress there was little enough for the Rolls-Royces to do and as more squadrons were established they were used for anti-invasion patrols along the east coast of England. When the first formal armoured car squadrons were sent to France they had little to do, so eventually these RNAS armoured car squadrons were disbanded, the cars being handed over to a generally uninterested British army.

Rolls-Royce armoured cars were thereafter used on other fronts and in overseas theatres of war such as the North West Frontier in India, at Gallipoli (where they could accomplish nothing), German South West Africa (where they accomplished much during a campaign about which little is known) and in Uganda.

It was in the Western Desert and the Arabian peninsula that the Rolls-Royce armoured cars and a number of similar armoured tenders (like the armoured car but without the turret and used for carrying stores or personnel) made their greatest impact. There they proved to be remarkably reliable, fast and capable of crossing some very rough country.

The Rolls-Royce armoured cars soldiered on until 1922 when they began to be replaced by a modernised version, the **Armoured Car, Rolls-Royce (1920 Pattern)**. Even so, some of the old Pattern 1914 cars in service in India lasted until well into World War II.

A Rolls-Royce armoured car and its crew are seen at a Guards Division casualty evacuation point near Guillemont during September 1916 when the Somme Offensive was at its height. Note the anti-mud chains around the tyres of the rear wheels and the lack of front mudguards.

Lanchester armoured car

After the Rolls-Royce armoured car, the **Armoured Car, Lanchester (Admiralty Turreted Pattern)** was the most numerous in service with the Royal Naval Air Service (RNAS) armoured car squadrons that had sprung up by the end of 1914. Originally these armoured cars were supposed to provide support for the air bases and to retrieve downed airmen, but it was not long before they were used in more offensive roles. By 1915 they were being organised into formal armoured car squadrons as part of a larger Royal Naval Armoured Car Division.

Royal Navy Lanchester armoured cars in Russia during 1917. These vehicles motored thousands of miles in support of the Russians fighting the Germans and carried out scouting and raiding operations that covered many miles on all parts of the Russian front, including the Brusilov Offensive in mid-1917.

Sloping armour

In layout the Lanchester armoured car was very similar to the Rolls-Royce and also had a turret with sloping sides. However, the Lanchester had sloping armour over the front of the bonnet in place of the more angular bonnet of the Rolls-Royce. It was originally a civilian touring car but by the time the Admiralty designers had been at work, little of the original bodywork remained.

However, the engine was retained for not only did it provide a useful 44.7 kW (60 hp) but it had many advanced design features for its day, along with a very advanced epicyclic gearbox.

Spearhead

When the Royal Navy armoured cars were handed over to the army in August 1915 the latter

SPECIFICATION	
Armoured Car, Lanchester (Admiralty Turreted Pattern)	**Dimensions:** length 4.88 m (16 ft 0 in); width 1.93 m (6 ft 4 in); height 2.286 m (7 ft 6 in)
Crew: 4	
Weight: 4.8 tons	**Performance:** maximum speed 80 km/h (50 mph); range 290 km (180 miles)
Powerplant: one 45-kW (60-hp) Lanchester petrol engine	

decided that the collection of designs it received was too varied for logistic and operational comfort. It

therefore decided to standardise the Rolls-Royce design, and the Lanchesters were put to one side. They did

A Lanchester armoured car in 1914 RNAS markings. These vehicles never gained the fame accorded to the Rolls-Royce armoured cars, but at the time were just as important in service. Many with Royal Navy crews were extensively used in Russia in 1916 and 1917.

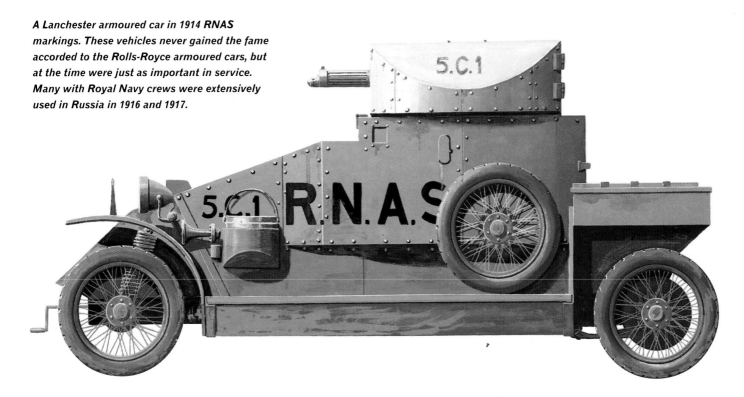

not remain neglected for long, however, for in October 1915 they were gathered together in England. The following year they were organised as No. 1 Squadron of the Royal Naval Armoured Car Division and sent to Russia. Once there, they took part in a number of campaigns about which little has been recorded. For much of the time the Lanchesters had to travel on their own wheels across a country where few roads existed. They were used in Persia, Romania and Galicia, operating in climates that varied from desert heat to near-Arctic conditions. But they kept going. For much of their operational life the Lanchesters were used in a manner that anticipated what was later to become the norm in armoured warfare. They acted as the spearhead of large motorised columns carrying troops on armoured lorries and personnel trucks that ranged far and wide over the wastes of southern Russia and the Iraq deserts. They acted as scouts, fire-support vehicles and general raiders, roles in which they proved reliable and fast. The Lanchester remained with the Russians until the final failure of the Brusilov Offensive in mid-1917. Thereafter Russia sank into the throes of internal disruption and revolution, and there was no part the Lanchester squadron could play in such conflicts. Thus they were shipped back to the UK with well over 53,000 miles added to their clocks.

Autoblindo Mitragliatrice Lancia Ansaldo IZ Armoured car

Prominent on the IZ were the twin steel rails that extended from the driver's position to a point below and in front of the wheels. These rails were intended for wire-cutting. Later versions had even more protection against wire by an extension of the armour over the wheels both at the front and rear.

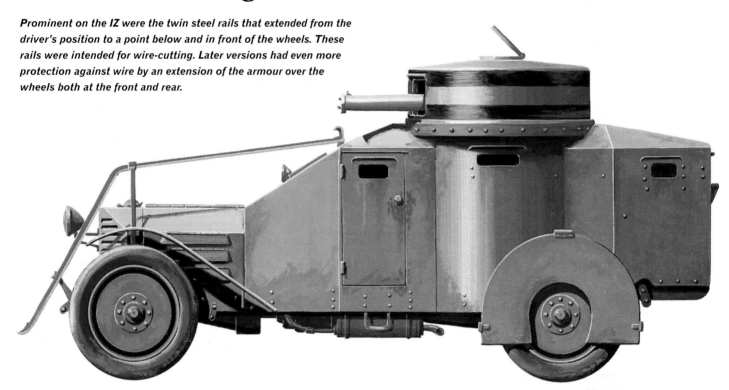

The first **Lancia modello IZ** was not an armoured car but a small truck that had a form of expanding fireman's ladder mounted on the rear, which was used by 102-mm (4-in) artillery units for the observation of fire. While this was certainly a military function it was not long after, in 1915, that the truck was drastically adapted to become an armoured car known as the **Autoblindo Mitragliatrice Lancia Ansaldo IZ**.

For its day the IZ was quite an advanced design. Its layout was conventional, with the engine forward and the main driver's position behind a fully armoured sloping plate. The main fighting compartment was in a box structure at the rear, which mounted a squat round turret with a single machine-gun. On some later versions this turret arrangement was revised to accommodate a second but smaller turret on top of the first, enabling another machine-gun to be carried. A further variation was to place two machine-guns in the lower turret, so the IZ was quite heavily armed for a vehicle of its size.

For much of the war the Italian armoured car units could contribute little to the campaigns against Austria-Hungary as most of the

fighting took place in mountainous regions where wheeled vehicles had little chance to operate. A small force of 39 IZ armoured cars did a certain amount of reconnaissance along the Piave during the fighting along that front, and contributed to the limited period of fluid fighting in the aftermath of the Austro-German breakthrough

of 1917. After that there was little enough they could do and some were sent to North Africa for policing duties. By 1918 about 120 cars had been produced, remaining in use for some years thereafter. A few were handed to Albania during the post-war period and long remained the sole equipment for the small armoured element of the new nation.

SPECIFICATION	
Autoblindo Mitragliatrice Lancia Ansaldo IZ **Crew:** 6 **Weight:** 3.8 tons **Powerplant:** one 26/30-kW (35/40-hp) petrol engine	**Dimensions:** length 5.40 m (17 ft 8⅔ in); width 1.824 m (6 ft 0 in); height with single turret 2.40 m (7 ft 10½ in) **Performance:** maximum speed 60 km/h (37 mph); range 300 km (186 miles)

Char d'Assaut Schneider

The **Char d'Assaut Schneider** (or **Schneider CA**) was developed at the behest of Colonel J. E. Estienne, who in 1915 envisaged armoured tractors to tow armoured troop-carrying sledges for surprise assaults on German trenches on the Western Front. Estienne proposed a development of the American Holt agricultural tractor's track and chassis, which was then becoming widely used as an artillery tractor. By going direct to the French commander-in-chief, Estienne obtained support for his proposal, and the Schneider armament manufacturer was contracted as developer.

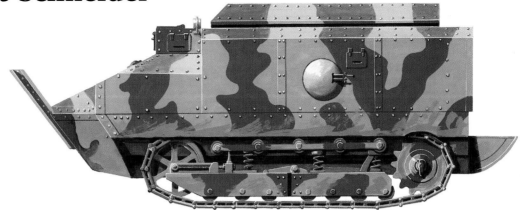

The Char d'Assaut Schneider proved less than effective when first introduced to the field. The short tracks and long body gave dismal obstacle-crossing capability, even with the extra 'nose and tail' ramps fitted. The armour was thin and the vehicle burned easily.

Tardy development

The original proposals called for 200 Schneider CAs by the end of 1916, but progress was so slow that it was the middle of 1917 before useful numbers were ready. The Schneider CA emerged as basically an armoured box mounted over a virtually unaltered Holt tractor suspension and track. The box mounted two machine-guns

and a short 75-mm (2.95-in) gun to one side forward. The engine developed 41 kW (55 hp) and was fed from two petrol tanks situated near the machine-gun mountings. These tanks proved very vulnerable to enemy fire, and many Schneiders fell victim to fires caused by a single armour-piercing bullet. Maximum armour thickness was 11.5 mm (0.45 in), increased to 19.5 mm (0.77 in) on later vehicles. The idea of the armoured personnel-carrying sledge had been dropped, and the

SPECIFICATION	
Char d'Assaut Schneider **Crew:** 7 **Weight:** 14.6 tonnes **Dimensions:** length 6 m (19 ft 8 in); width 2 m (6 ft 6¾ in); height 2.39 m (7 ft 10 in)	**Powerplant:** one Schneider liquid-cooled four-cylinder petrol engine developing 41 kW (55 hp) **Performance:** maximum speed 6 km/h (3¾ mph); range 48 km (30 miles)

Schneiders were used mainly for infantry support, proving less than successful as their cross-country capabilities were very limited. By May 1917 some 300 had been produced, but thereafter the gun version was replaced in production by the stores-carrying **Schneider Char de Ravitaillement**, in which the right-hand gun position was replaced by a door opening into the stores-carrying area. Extra 8-mm (0.31-in)

armour was added to the sides of most examples as the result of experience in action, and the Schneider CA's greatest contribution lay in teaching the French army how to use and maintain armoured vehicles in the field.

The French set up their first armour school at Champlieu in October 1916. They soon learned from actions such as the attack on the Chemin des Dames in April 1917, when 76 out of a total of 132 Schneider CAs taking part were lost, that lack of maintenance and lack of spares could remove a vehicle from the field as thoroughly as enemy action.

The last Schneider CA was delivered in August 1918, but by then attrition and a move towards the Renault FT 17 had reduced the numbers in service to fewer than 100. Most of these were the unarmed supply version but the gun Schneiders had taken part in several 1918 operations, enjoying some success despite their instability and tendency to catch fire.

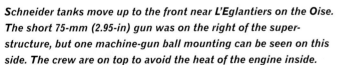

Schneider tanks move up to the front near L'Eglantiers on the Oise. The short 75-mm (2.95-in) gun was on the right of the super-structure, but one machine-gun ball mounting can be seen on this side. The crew are on top to avoid the heat of the engine inside.

Char d'Assaut St Chamond

The fact that the ordering and development of the Schneider CA had by-passed the normal French army supply channels upset some of the normal supply authorities to a marked degree. These authorities therefore decided to proceed with their own tank design. Using one Colonel Rimailho as the designer, the French army thus set about producing its own original design, and by early 1916 the first prototype had been built at the Saint Chamond factory at Homecourt. As a result, the new vehicle became generally known as the **Char d'Assaut St Chamond**. As with the Schneider CA, development and production of this other pioneering vehicle were both slow, so it was not until May 1917 that the first service examples were finally ready for operational service.

Long overhangs

Even for a vehicle of the 'first-try' variety, the **St Chamond CA** had several unusual features. Like the Schneider CA it was based on the chassis, suspension and track of the Holt tractor, but on the St Chamond CA the track was lengthened to provide more track length on the ground. The drive to the track was unusual in that a petrol engine was used to drive an electric transmission system. While this petrol-electric transmission worked, it was also heavy and bulky, which meant the projected design weight was exceeded by over 5 tonnes. This overweight feature was not assisted by the configuration of the hull, which extended both forward and to the rear of the track by a considerable degree. This meant that whenever the vehicle had to traverse rough ground or cross even the shortest trench, it became stuck as the front or rear of the hull dug in. In service this proved a considerable drawback, for the Germans soon learned of the St Chamond CA's poor trench-crossing performance and widened their trenches accordingly. The St Chamond CA mounted a conventional 75-mm (2.95-in) Modèle 1897 field gun in the front of the hull, and it was possible to mount as many as four machine-guns around the hull. The maximum armour thickness was 17 mm (0.67 in).

Inadequate mobility

The poor cross-country performance of the St Chamond CA so severely restricted its use in action as 1917 progressed that the type was gradually replaced by the newer Renault FT 17, and many vehicles were converted to **St Chamond Char de Ravitaillement** supply carrier standard. The type was involved in its last major action as a gun tank in July 1918, when 131 took part in a counter-attack near Reims.

By the end of the war there were only 72 out of the production run of 400 left in service. Although the St Chamond CA had many novel features (the forward-mounted 75-mm gun, the petrol-electric drive and the lengthened track), it was basically an unsound design of poor cross-country capability.

The Char d'Assaut St Chamond's long hull so restricted its use in action that it was often relegated to the supply tank role. It was armed with four machine-guns and a 75-mm (2.95-in) gun, and had an advanced petrol-electric drive.

SPECIFICATION	
Char d'Assaut St Chamond **Crew:** 9 **Weight:** 23 tonnes **Dimensions:** length (with gun) 8.83 m (28 ft 11¾ in); length (hull) 7.91 m (25 ft 11½ in); width 2.67 m (8 ft 9 in); height 2.34 m (7 ft 5⅔ in)	**Powerplant:** one 67-kW (90-hp) Panhard liquid-cooled four-cylinder petrol engine powering a Crochat-Collardeau electric transmission **Performance:** maximum speed 8.5 km/h (5.3 mph); range 59 km (36.7 miles)

Char d'Assaut St Chamond tanks move forward near Moyennville on the Oise in 1917. This picture provides a good indication of the great bulk and shape of these tanks compared with the limited length of track run; note also the limited ground clearance under the hull.

Renault FT 17 Infantry tank

The Renault FT 17 was one of the most successful of the World War I tanks. They were produced in thousands, mainly as infantry support light tanks, but many other uses were found for them. Turret armament was either a machine-gun or a short 37-mm (1.45-in) gun, and a crew of two was carried.

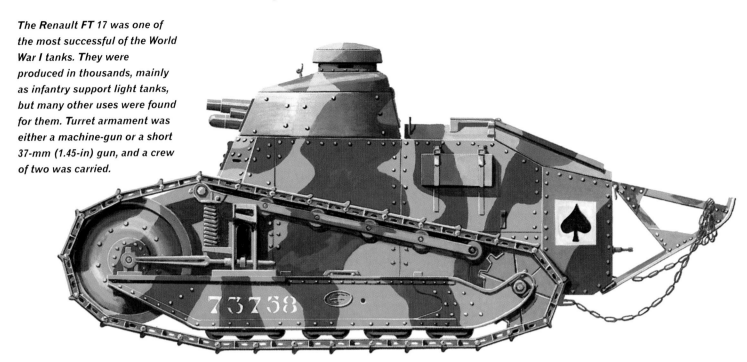

The diminutive **Renault FT 17** was without a doubt one of the most successful of all the World War I tanks. It had its origins in the proposals put forward in 1915 by the far-sighted General Estienne, who saw the need for a light armoured vehicle to support infantry operations directly. It was not until mid-1916 that Renault became involved, and with a potential order for well over 1,000 examples in prospect the Renault company started to produce a design.

Questionable design

By the end of 1916 the design was ready. It emerged as a two-man tank armed with a machine-gun, and did not meet with general approval at the time. The design was considered too cramped and too lightly armed, but an order was pushed through, and it was not long before a further order for 2,500 was placed. By then the

armament had been increased to a 37-mm gun, but many examples were produced with only a single machine-gun.

The FT 17 design was the first of what can now be seen as the classic tank design. It had its armament in a small turret with a 360° traverse, and the thin hull had the tracks on each side. There was no chassis as such, the components being built directly onto the armoured hull. The engine was at the rear, the tracks each had a large forward idler wheel that proved

ideal for obstacle climbing, and to enhance trench-crossing capability a frame 'tail' was often fitted to the rear.

Renault was unable to produce the numbers required so production batches were farmed out to other concerns. Even the

Americans became involved, but as they insisted that their FT 17s would be built to American standards and methods none arrived in France before the Armistice. In France the original cast armoured turret was often replaced on the production lines

---

SPECIFICATION

Renault FT 17
Crew: 2
Weight: 6.485 tonnes
Dimensions: length (with tail) 5 m (16 ft 5 in); width 1.71 m (5 ft 7⅓ in); height 2.13 m (7 ft)

Powerplant: one Renault liquid cooled four-cylinder petrol engine developing 26 kW (35 hp)
Performance: maximum speed 7.7 km/h (4.8 mph); range 35.4 km (22 miles)

The FT 17 was a trim little tank, seen here in its form with a cast rather than riveted turret. The type suffered from several reliability problems, and maintenance was a continual concern.

by an octagonal design using flat armour plates. The 37-mm gun became the virtual norm (**Char-canon FT 17**), although machine-guns could be fitted (**Char-mitrailleuse FT 17**). It was not long before a self-propelled gun version mounting a 75-mm (2.95-in) gun was produced as the **Char-canon Renault BS**, and there was even a special radio version, the **Char Renault TSR**. The maximum armour thickness was 16 mm (0.63 in).

Active service

The first FT 17s were delivered to the French army in March 1917 but it was not until May 1918 that the type was first used in action. By then the French tactics were to use the tanks en masse, but this was not always possible in the face of the constant German attacks under way at that time. At first the FT 17s were used in relatively small numbers, but by July things had settled down to the point where 480 could be concentrated for a counterattack

near Soissons. Here they were successful, and thereafter the type was used to great effect.

Maintenance was a worry, as the FT 17 had been designed with little thought for repairs and long-term spares holdings, so at any one time hundreds were out of action with various faults. But many more were in the line as the sundry manufacturers duly delivered the ordered thousands. Some were passed to American troops. As the war ended there were 1,991 FT 17s fit for combat but another 369

were under repair and another 360 out of use.

After 1918 FT 17s remained in large-scale service and was produced or converted to suit a number of new roles such as mobile bridging, self-propelled artillery, radio versions and others. In 1939 large numbers were still in use, and the Germans took over many after the French collapse of 1940. The Germans retained some for their own use until 1944 when they used many in the Paris fighting.

Autoblindé Peugeot Armoured car

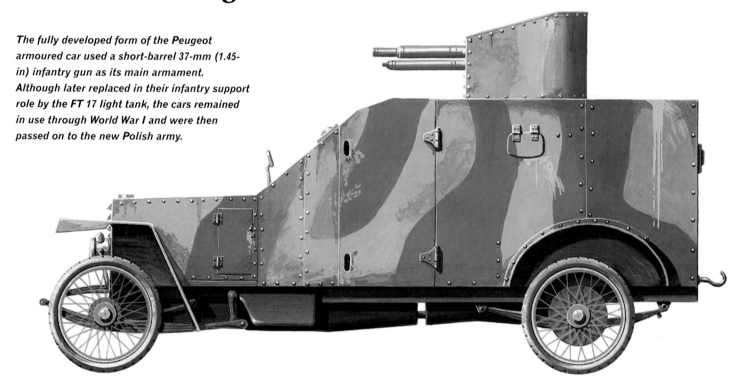

The fully developed form of the Peugeot armoured car used a short-barrel 37-mm (1.45-in) infantry gun as its main armament. Although later replaced in their infantry support role by the FT 17 light tank, the cars remained in use through World War I and were then passed on to the new Polish army.

A French army Peugeot armoured car provides fire support for British infantry during the Battle of the Lys in April 1918. In open country these vehicles were able to provide useful fire support with their gun, but they were often restricted to the available roads.

The first **Peugeot** armoured cars were produced as rather hasty improvisations in 1914, and were typical of their period in that they were based on a commercial model, the 4x2 Peugeot 153. These early conversions used a centrally mounted machine-gun on a pivot in the centre of the open rear body, but once the design had been formalised this armament was increased to a 37-mm (1.45-in) gun. The early slab-sided armour plates (5.5-mm/0.216-in thick) were also revised to provide better all-round protection, but the top was left open.

Heavy armour

By the time the purpose-designed Peugeot armoured cars entered service, the vehicles scarcely resembled the early improvisations. A sloping armour plate now covered the driver's position and the engine was also armoured. The radiator was protected by steel shutters but the wheels

remained as they originally were with their wire spokes, even though the extra weight caused by the armour was partially offset by the use of dual wheels at the rear. Although a machine-gun could be carried on the central pintle, the more usual weapon was a 37-mm gun behind a curved steel shield. This gun was a half-size version of the famous Modèle 1897 field gun, and could fire a useful high explosive shell. This gave the Peugeot armoured car a modest firepower potential that was sometimes used to support infantry attacks. An alternative to the mix of a 37-mm gun and a machine-gun was a pair of machine-guns.

After the end of 1914, there was little enough for these

armoured cars to do on the Western Front. A few were used for patrols to the rear of the front, but they could do little else until the relatively small number that remained in use in 1918 were able to take their part in containing the large-scale German breakthroughs that occurred on some parts of the line. Thereafter a few were used in the relatively fluid warfare that developed. But most of this fighting was carried out by

tanks, particularly the FT 17s, which proved to be of more use over rough country than the Peugeot armoured cars with their narrow wheels.

Post-war service

When World War I ended, the French army still had 28 Peugeot armoured cars in service, but most of these were later handed over to the Polish army, with which they remained in use for some years.

SPECIFICATION	
Autoblindé Peugeot	**Armament:** one 37-mm (1.45-in) gun
Crew: 4 or 5	and one machine-gun, or two
Weight: 5 tons	machine-guns
Powerplant: one 30-kW (40-hp)	**Performance:** maximum speed
Peugeot petrol engine	40 km/h (25 mph); maximum range
Dimensions: length 4.8 m (15 ft 9	140 km (87 miles)
in); width 1.8 m (5 ft 11 in); height	
2.8 m (9 ft 2¼ in)	

Sturmpanzerwagen A7V Tank

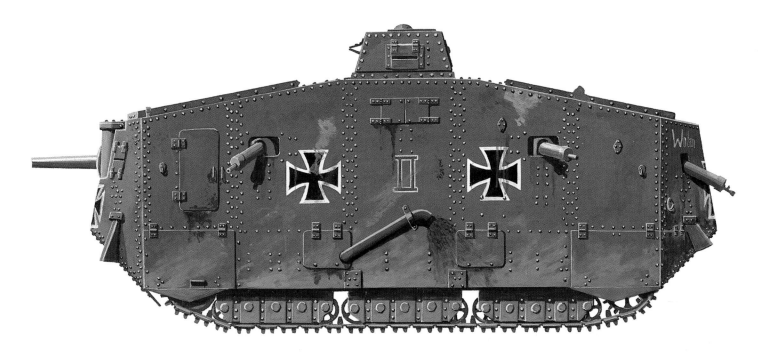

The A7V was a large and bulky vehicle with a crew of 18 and carried six machine-guns. The main armament was a 57-mm (2.24-in) gun in the front hull. The A7V proved to have a poor cross-country performance and its height made it rather unstable, and only about 20 were ever produced. Many of these were pressed into action during 1918.

For a nation that was normally well to the fore in the pursuit of military technology, Germany was surprisingly slow to reach a proper appreciation of the potential possessed by the tank and, despite some early and far-

sighted proposals put forward by various individuals, no official interest was taken in any form of armoured vehicle other than the armoured car. Thus, it was only after the British had first used the tank in the Battle of

Flers-Courcelette in September 1916 that the Germans began to reconsider their position, when they established a committee to undertake the design and production of a German equivalent. Ordered in

November 1916, Germany's first tank was planned to meet a requirement for a 30-tonne Geländespanzer- wagen (all-terrain armoured vehicle).

Like so many other designs produced by a committee under

time constraints, the result of this venture was not a great success. The vehicle became known as the **Sturmpanzerwagen A7V**, the A7V coming from the committee's departmental abbreviation. The design was based on that of the readily available Holt caterpillar track and suspension, but Joseph Vollmer introduced suspension modifications to the original that improved the possible speed. These efforts were largely negated by the installation on the basic chassis of a large armoured box structure that held a crew of no fewer than 18 men. This box had large slab sides with nose and tail arrangements that extended under the body to such an extent that the ground clearance was only about 40 mm (1.57 in). The length of track on the ground was also rather short, and the overall result was a vehicle that was inherently unstable and possessed very

poor cross-country perform-ance. The main armament was a captured 57-mm (2.24-in) Russian gun (mounted at the front) and six machine-guns, each with a crew of two. The one advantage the A7V had over the British tanks was the thickness of its armour, between 10 and 30 mm (0.39 and 1.18 in). By the time production began, the Germans had developed their own armour-piercing ammunition, and the A7V's armour was proof against this new projectile.

Limited production

The first A7V was ready by October 1917, and in December that year 100 were ordered. Production of the A7V involved several firms, all of them already pressed to meet existing production needs, with the result that by the end of the war only about 20 A7Vs had been produced. In March 1918 the first A7Vs went into action.

SPECIFICATION	
Sturmpanzerwagen A7V	**Dimensions:** length 8 m (26 ft 3 in); width 3.06 m (10 ft ½ in); height 3.3 m (10 ft 10 in)
Crew: 18	
Weight: 33 tons	
Powerplant: two Daimler-Benz petrol engines each developing 74.6 kW (100 hp)	**Armament:** one 57-mm (2.24-in) gun, and six machine-guns
	Performance: maximum speed 12.9 km/h (8 mph); range 40 km (25 miles)

When used over good going ground as mobile fire support units they proved successful enough, but over rough ground they proved to be less than successful and some of the first examples soon revealed shortcomings in their special armour plate. The A7V's lack of trench-crossing ability often left the tank behind the infantry it was supposed to support, and all too often when opposed by field artillery firing over open sights the type was easily knocked out.

Three A7Vs took part in the first tank-versus-tank combat on 24 April 1918 at Villers-Bretonneux. Here three Mk IVs (one Male and two Females) encountered three A7Vs. The two Females were soon damaged and had to retire, but the sole Male was able to hit and knock out one of the A7Vs. More such combats took place

before the Armistice, but the A7Vs rarely shone. In fact the Germans favoured the various British tanks they were able to capture, mainly because of the poor cross-country performance of their own machines.

Despite the slow production of the A7V, the Germans produced an unarmoured supply version with an open top, the **Uberlandwagen**, and even went so far as to attempt to produce an **A7V/U** version with the 'all-round' tracks and sponsons of the British tanks. This venture came to nothing, as did the **A7V/U2** and **A7V/U3** projects, the former having smaller sponsons and the latter being a 'female' version armed only with machine-guns. After World War I a few A7V tanks were used in Germany's internal struggles, and a few more examples remained with the newly established Polish army.

Two A7Vs as seen from a sector of the French lines in June 1918. The cloud of smoke came mainly from the twin Daimler-Benz petrol engines, but some was no doubt dust thrown up by the tracks. Some of the machine-guns are visible, but the main 57-mm weapon is obscured by the smoke.

Panzerkraftwagen Ehrhardt 1915/1917 Armoured car

The very first German armoured cars were in fact special large car or truck chassis adapted to carry a skyward-looking artillery piece for use against observation balloons. There were several of these weapons, collectively known as Ballon Abwehr Kanonen (BAK), but although some were used for army trials none was taken into large-scale use. Thus it was left to the Belgians in 1914 to demonstrate to the German army the potential of the armoured car in mobile warfare. Here, German infantry and cavalry were at times distinctly incommoded by the hit-and-run raiding carried out by the Minerva and other converted touring cars fielded by the out-numbered Belgians. Having suffered somewhat at the hands of the Belgians, the Germany army then decided to produce its own equivalent but, in the absence of any practical experience of its own to fall back upon, approached the problem of designing such a weapon in a typically Germanic fashion.

During 1915, the Germans produced prototypes of three different armoured cars. The manufacturers were Ehrhardt, Daimler and Büssing, which all chose to ignore the fact that the Belgian cars were little more than converted touring cars, and went instead for what they thought were more suitable vehicles. All three turned out to have one feature in common, in that they were all vehicles of massive size. The largest of the three was the Büssing, which used a 'double-ended' layout that could at least boast a tactically useful high ground clearance. The other two designs were roughly the same, with the engine (surrounded by armour) at the front and a large box-like body at the rear with a turret or cupolas on its top. Both of

The Panzerkraftwagen Ehrhardt 1915 was one of the first examples of a type of high and flat-sided armoured car design that the Germans were to use until almost World War II for internal policing duties. It weighed nearly 9 tons, had a crew of eight or nine men and an armament of up to three machine-guns.

these other vehicles were tall machines of notably clumsy appearance, and both were also far too heavy for effective fulfilment of the operational tasks demanded of them.

Some indication of this fact is provided by the knowledge that the Daimler and Ehrhardt designs were each reliant on the use of double wheels on each side at the rear, and also flanges on the single wheels at the front of the vehicle, in an effort to reduce the ground pressure and so enhance cross-country mobility to a useful degree. All three cars had a crew of eight or nine men, carried an armament of at least three machine-guns, and possessed a maximum armour thickness of 7 mm (0.28 in).

Internal security role

Along with some improvised conversions, the three prototypes were formed into one unit and sent at first to the Baltic and then to the Western Front. Conditions on both fronts were such that the armoured cars could achieve little, and eventually the vehicles were

deployed on the Russian part of the Eastern Front, where they could at least use their mobility to some effect. It was at this stage that there emerged the need for more cars, and as Büssing and Daimler were already over-extended on war work, Ehrhardt received the contract, being asked to produce a further 20 armoured cars. These were 1.72 tons lighter than the original **Panzerkraftwagen Ehrhardt 1915** and, completed with the designation **Panzerkraftwagen Ehrhardt 1917**, had revised frontal armour. The vehicles were sent to the Eastern Front until the end of the fighting there late in 1917. Thereafter they appear to have been retained within Germany for internal policing duties, a role in which they were so successful that a further 20 were

produced specifically for the purpose in 1919. The Ehrhardt design was in fact considered just what internal policing required, for its height gave it the capacity to tower over crowds and offer police units better control of riots. Vehicles of the Ehrhardt type were in use almost until World War II. Such was the requirement for armoured cars, however, that by 1918 the Germans were forced to employ numbers of captured armoured cars of Rolls-Royce and other makes, and the Ehrhardt armoured cars, clumsy and high though they were, were never around in sufficient numbers. On the Eastern Front the cars were never able to make much of a tactical impression, so the design is now little known and there are very few operational details.

SPECIFICATION	
Panzerkraftwagen Ehrhardt 1915	**Dimensions:** length 5.61 m
Crew: 8 or 9	(18 ft 5 in); width 2 m (6 ft 6½ in)
Weight: 8.86 tons	**Armament:** three machine-guns
Powerplant: one 63.4-kW (85-hp)	**Performance:** maximum speed 59.5
petrol engine	km/h (37 mph); maximum range
	250 km (155 miles)

Light Tank M3

American light tank development can be traced back to the 1920s when several infantry-support light tanks were developed in small numbers. By the early 1930s these designs had evolved into the **Light Tank M2** with a series of designs all using the M2 designation. This series was quite well armed, with a 37-mm (1.46-in) main gun, but by 1940 the type was obsolescent and was used only for training after reaching its apogee with the **M2A4** model.

Thicker armour

The events of 1940 in Europe were followed closely by the US Army, which realised that thicker armour would be required by its light tanks. This involved a better suspension to carry the extra weight. The result was the **Light Tank M3**, based on the M2A4. It was in full-scale production by 1941, and mass production of

the **M3A1** got under way once the US had entered the war. Early versions used riveted construction, but welded turrets and eventually welded hulls were introduced, and there were many detail design changes.

By the time M3 production ceased 5,811 had been built. Basic armament of the M3A1 was one 37-mm gun, a co-axial 7.62-mm (0.3-in) machine-gun, and four additional 0.3-in machine-guns (one on the turret roof for anti-aircraft defence, one in the hull front and two in the sponsons for operation by the driver). Armour thickness ranged from 15 mm (0.59 in) to 43 mm (1.69 in).

Reliability

The Light Tank M3 was used wherever the US Army was involved. It proved to be a reliable vehicle and was liked by

The Light Tank M3A1 was the main combat version of the M2/M3 light tank series in service when the United States entered the war in late 1941. It mounted a 37-mm (1.46-in) main gun, and there was provision for three machine-guns.

its crews. Large numbers of M3s were passed to the America's allies. The largest recipient was the UK, where it was known as the **Stuart**. To the British, the Stuart was large for a light tank, but crews appreciated the agility and reliability of the vehicle. One thing they did not like was that two main types of engine were fitted to different versions: the normal engine was a Continental 7-cylinder radial petrol engine (**Stuart I**). In order to expedite production at a time of high demand the Guiberson T-1020 diesel engine was substituted (**Stuart II**). This sometimes caused supply problems but it

was a burden the Allies learned to survive.

Variations

Major variants were the **M3A1** (**Stuart III** and **Stuart IV** with petrol and diesel engines) fitted with a gyrostabilised gun, powertraverse turret, and the product-improved **M3A3** (**Stuart V**) with a larger driving compartment and thicker armour. The 37-mm gun was retained throughout the production life of the M3. By 1944 it had little combat value, and many M3s and Stuarts serving with reconnaissance units had the turret removed to assist concealment. Extra machine-guns were carried instead. Many of these M3s were employed as command vehicles. The M3 and Stuart tanks were used from the North African campaign onwards and others were passed to the Red Army. The **Light Tank M5** was a development powered by twin Cadillac engines, similar to the M3 series and was recognisable by the rear decking accommodating the twin engines. In British service the M5 was called the **Stuart VI**, the same designation being used for the **M5A1**. The latter had an improved turret with a bulged rear for the radio (as on the M3A3).

SPECIFICATION	
Light Tank M3A1	**Armament:** one 37-mm (1.46-in) main gun; one 7.62-mm (0.3-in) coaxial machine-gun; four 7.62-mm (0.3-in) machine-guns
Crew: 4	
Weight: in action 12.9 tonnes	
Powerplant: one Continental W-970-9A 7-cylinder radial petrol engine developing 186.5 kW (250 hp)	**Performance:** maximum road speed 58 km/h (36 mph); maximum road range 112.6 km (70 miles)
Dimensions: length 4.54 m (14 ft 10¾ in); width 2.24 m (7 ft 4 in); height 2.30 m (7 ft 6½ in)	**Fording:** 0.91 m (3 ft)
	Gradient: 60 per cent
	Vertical obstacle: 0.61 m (2 ft);
	Trench: 1.83 m (6 ft)

The M3 (and the M5) series were used by many Allied armies for reconnaissance. This example is seen negotiating an improvised German roadblock outside Harze in Belgium during the late summer of 1944.

Light Tank M24 Chaffee

By 1942 it was evident that the day of the 37-mm (1.46-in) tank gun had passed, and requests were coming from the field for a light tank with a 75-mm (2.95-in) main gun. Attempts to fit such a gun into the Light Tank M5 were unsuccessful, so a new design was initiated by Cadillac. The first was ready by late 1943 and it carried over several features of the M5, including the twin engines. However, the main change was to the turret and gun.

The new turret mounted the required 75-mm gun, development of which was lengthy. Originally it had been the old 'French 75' field gun altered for use in tanks. Various efforts were made to lighten the gun, to the extent that it could be mounted in B-25 bomber aircraft for anti-shipping use. The result of this was that the gun could be easily adapted as a light tank weapon and in this form was designated T13E1.

Combat team

The new light tank was initially known as the **T24** but when accepted for service it became the **Light Tank M24** and was later given the name **Chaffee**. The Chaffee did not enter full service until late 1944. As a result, it was able to take only a small part in the fighting in Europe during 1945. Perhaps its biggest contribution was not really felt until the war was over, for the M24 was designed to be a single component in what the designers called a 'combat

Armed with a 75-mm (2.95-in) gun, the M24 was introduced into service in late 1944. Post-war, it formed the basis for a new family of armoured vehicles.

team' of armoured vehicles. The basis of this idea was that a common chassis could be used to provide the basis for a whole family of armoured vehicles that included self-propelled artillery, anti-aircraft tanks and so on. In fact this concept did not make the impression that it might have done as the war ended before the combat team concept could be put into full effect, and indeed the M24 did not make its full combat impact until its appearance during the Korean War of the early 1950s.

Agility

The M24 Chaffee was well armed for its size and weight, but the armour (minimum 12 mm /0.47 in and maximum 38 mm/1.5 in) had to be lighter than in heavier tanks. This was important so as to give the vehicle its agility. The M24 had a surprisingly large crew of five

SPECIFICATION	
Light Tank M24	T13E1 gun; two 7.62-mm (0.3-in)
Crew: 5	machine-guns; one 12.7-mm (0.5-
Weight: in action 18.4 tonnes	in) pintle-mounted machine-gun;
Powerplant: two Cadillac Model	one 2-in (51-mm) smoke mortar
44T24 V-8 petrol engines	**Performance:** maximum road speed
developing 82 kW (110 hp) each	56 km/h (35 mph); maximum road
Dimensions: length with gun 5.49 m	range 161 km (100 miles)
(18 ft) and over hull 4.99 m (16 ft	**Fording:** 1.02 m (3 ft 4 in)
4½ in); width 2.95 m (9 ft 8 in);	**Gradient:** 60 per cent
height 2.48 m (8 ft 1½ in)	**Vertical obstacle:** 0.91 m (3 ft)
Armament: one 75-mm (2.95-in)	**Trench:** 2.44 m (8 ft)

men (commander, gunner, loader, radio operator who sometimes acted as an assistant driver, and the driver himself).

Secondary armament

Apart from the main gun there were two 7.62-mm (0.3-in) machine-guns (one co-axial with the main gun and one in the front hull) and a 12.7-mm (0.5-in) gun on the turret mounted on a pintle. In addition to this weaponry, there was a 2-in (51-mm) smoke mortar.

All this was a considerable armament for a vehicle with a tactical responsibility that was limited mainly to reconnaissance missions, but by the time the M24 entered service it had become a luxury that the US could well afford.

Many nations retained on the M24 until after the war. Several of the countries operating the tank went to the trouble of re-engining the vehicles and also updating their fire-control systems.

Medium Tank M3

When the Germans invaded France in May 1940, the consequent tank tactics and doctrines which were being used were closely observed by various US Army agencies. From their observations the Americans learned that the next generation of medium tanks

had to have at least a 75-mm (2.95-in) gun as their main armament. However, this presented the US with problems. This was because their next tank generation, which was already being produced in prototype form, was armed with only a 37-mm (1.46-in). This

gun type was already thought to be obsolete.

Revised design

The US answer was swift and drastic: they simply took their existing design and altered it to accommodate the required 75-mm (2.95-in) gun. The turret

of the new design (the **Medium Tank M2**, destined never to see active service) could not take the larger gun. The solution was to situate the main gun within the tank's hull. Consequently the revised tank design retained the 37-mm gun turret, while the main armament was located in a sponson on the right-hand side of the hull. The 75-mm gun was a revised version of the famous 'French 75' field piece as manufactured in the US. The major modification to this gun was the new ammunition which converted it into what was for the time a powerful tank weapon. The M3 featured a powerful array of secondary armament. This comprised four 7.62-mm (0.3-in) machine-guns (one in the commander's cupola atop the turret, one co-axial with the 37-mm gun, and two within the hull).

Mass production

The new design became the **Medium Tank M3**. The design was rushed into mass production at a factory which had been earlier earmarked for the M2 model. Almost as soon as production had started for the US Army, a British mission arrived in the United States on a purchasing trip. The British needed to obtain tanks to

replace those which the Army had lost in France. The new M3 was high on its shopping list. They requested a few changes to suit their requirements. The most obvious of these modifications was a revised turret rear outline to accommodate radio equipment and the absence of the cupola. This model was produced specifically for the British Army. Once delivered, the British called the M3 the **General Grant I** (or simply **Grant I**). The first of these new tanks went into action at Gazala in May 1942. Their appearance on the battlefield provided the Afrika Korps with a nasty fright as their arrival was entirely unexpected. Their combination of armament and armour proved to be particularly useful.

Popular tank

The Grants were later joined in British Army service by the

The M3 General Lee tank was a hasty design, but it had a powerful 75-mm (2.95-in) gun, which gave Allied tanks a parity with German tanks for the first time.

SPECIFICATION	
Medium Tank M3A2	**Armament:** one 37-mm (1.5-in) main
Crew: 6	gun and four 7.62-mm (0.3-in)
Weight: in action 27.2 tonnes	machine-guns
Powerplant: one Continental R-975-	**Performance:** maximum road speed
EC2 radial petrol engine developing	42 km/h (26 mph); maximum road
253.5 kW (340 hp)	range 193 km (120 miles)
Dimensions: length 5.64 m (18 ft 6	**Fording:** 1.02 m (3 ft 4 in)
in); width 2.72 m (8 ft 11 in); height	**Gradient:** 60 per cent
3.12 m (10 ft 3 in)	**Vertical obstacle:** 0.61 m (2 ft)
	Trench: 1.91 m (6 ft 3 in)

The M3 Grant was the 'British' version of the M3 Lee. The main charge was to the turret profile, which had a rear overhang to house a radio set, and the silhouette was lowered by omitting the machine-gun cupola of the original turret.

unmodified M3 which was then labelled the **General Lee I**. Further improvement led to the **M3A1** (**Lee II**) with welded construction, the up-armoured **M3A3** (**Lee IV**) with two General Motors 6-71 diesels delivering 280 kW (375 hp) and the **M3A4** (**Lee V**) with the Chrysler A-57 multibank engine. This powerplant delivered 276 kW (370 hp). The **M3A5** version was based on the M3A3 but with a riveted hull. By the time production ended in December 1942, the total had reached 6,258 and the M3 was used in virtually every theatre of war in one form or another. Many were passed to the Red Army on a Lend-Lease arrangement.

The M3 turned out to be a reliable and hardwearing vehicle. Despite this, its hull-located main gun was often a cause of tactical difficulties as its traverse was very limited. However, it did provide the punch that Allied 'tankies'

required at that time. Another disadvantage was that the tactical silhouette was too high for comfort, but considering that the basic design was improvised and rushed into production, at a time when there were more questions being asked than answers provided, it turned out to be a remarkable effort.

Many of the suspension and automotive features were later incorporated into other designs and continued to provide excellent service, but perhaps the main lesson to be learned from the M3 was that the latent power of US industry could design and produce such a vehicle from scratch in a short time.

As soon as the M4 entered service the M3s were usually withdrawn and converted to other roles. These new roles included service as armoured recovery vehicles. However, in the Far East they remained in use until 1945 in both Grant and Lee forms.

M4 Sherman Medium tank

While the Medium Tank M3 was being rushed into production, a new design of medium tank with a turret-mounted 75-mm (2.95-in) main gun was being pushed through the drawing board stages. To save time this was to use the same basic hull and suspension as the M3, but the upper hull was revised to accommodate the gun turret. The first example of the new tank was rolled out in September 1941, as the resulting **Medium Tank T6** had proved to

Sherman Crab flail tanks were used by the 79th Armoured Division on D-Day and after, and a small number were passed to the US Army during 1944.

be a very good design. The upper hull was cast, and this not only provided added protection but also speeded production.

Into production

The new weapon was rushed into production as the **Medium Tank M4**, with a 2.96-in (75-mm) main gun and co-axial 0.3-in (7.62-mm) machine-gun, 0.3-in bow gun and 12.7mm (0.5-in) gun for AA defence. This baseline model had minimum and maximum armour

The M4A3 was one of the most developed of all the Sherman variants used until 1945, as it had a 76-mm (3-in) gun and HVSS (horizontal volute spring suspension).

thickness of 15 mm (0.59 in) and 76 mm (3 in), respectively. It proved to be an excellent fighting platform and went on to be one of the war-winning weapons of the Allies, being constructed in thousands. By the time the production lines stopped rolling in 1945 well over 40,000 had been made, and the type was built in a bewildering array of marks, submarks and variants of all kinds. Once in service the M4 series was differently engined;

up-gunned to even more powerful 75-mm, 76-mm (3-in) and 105-mm (4.13-in) main weapons; and developed into numerous 'specials' such as engineer tanks, assault tanks, tank destroyers, flame-throwers, bridging tanks, recovery vehicles, rocket launchers, self-propelled artillery carriages, anti-mine vehicles and so on, which were produced from scratch or improvised in the field. The M4 series became the T-34 of the Western Allies.

British model

The British Army purchased large numbers of M4s or took them over as part of the Lend-Lease Programme. The first of the tanks went into action with the British at El Alamein in October 1942. Thereafter, the M4 was the most numerous tank in British Army service for the remainder of World War II. To the British the M4 was the **General Sherman** (or simply **Sherman**) and they too added their variations to the long list of M4 specials: one of the best known of these was the 1944 **Sherman Firefly**, which had a 17-pdr main gun. This variant was available for service during the Normandy landings, where it proved to be the only British tank capable of countering the German Tiger and Panther.

The main models of this seminally important armoured fighting vehicle were as follows: the **M4** (**Sherman I**), engined with the 263-kW (353-hp) Wright Whirlwind or 298-kW (400-hp) Continental R-975 radials; the **M4A1** (**Sherman II**) with a fully cast rather than cast/welded hull, and alternatively engined with the 336-kW (450-hp) Caterpillar 9-cylinder diesel; the **M4A2** (**Sherman III**) with a welded hull and a 313-kW (420-hp) General Motors 6-71 twin diesel powerplant; the **M4A3** (**Sherman IV**) with a 373-kW (500-hp) Ford GAA III engine and horizontal- rather than vertical-volute suspension; and the **M4A4** (**Sherman V**) with the 317-kW (425-hp)

A US Army M4 provides cover for GIs within an adjacent doorway. Sheer weight of numbers brought the Sherman success during the invasion of Europe.

Chrysler five-bank engine. It is also worth noting that in British service the mark numbers were suffixed whenever the Sherman's main armament was not the standard 75-mm gun,

A indicating a 76-mm gun, **B** a 105-mm howitzer and **C** a 17-pdr anti-tank gun. The suffix **W** in US designations denoted the provision of wet ammunition stowage for reduced fire risk.

It was often left behind in firepower as the German tank guns increased in power and calibre, and the armour thicknesses and arrangement were frequently found wanting.

SPECIFICATION	
Medium Tank M4A3	in); height 3.43 m (11 ft 2¾ in)
Crew: 5	**Performance:** maximum road speed
Weight: in action 32.28 tonnes	47 km/h (29 mph); maximum road
Powerplant: one Ford GAA V-8	range 161 km (100 miles)
petrol engine developing 336 or	**Fording:** 0.91 m (3 ft)
373 kW (450 or 500 hp)	**Gradient:** 60 per cent
Dimensions: length, with gun	**Vertical obstacle:** 0.61 m (2 ft)
7.52 m (24 ft 8 in), over hull 6.27 m	**Trench:** 2.26 m (7 ft 5 in)
(20 ft 7 in); width 2.68 m (8 ft 9½	

Armour protection was also developed during the production run, the M4A2 having a minimum and a maximum of 13 and 105 mm (0.51 and 4.13 in), equivalent figures for the M4A3 and M4A4 being 15 and 100 mm (0.59 and 3.94 in), and 20 and 85 mm (0.80 and 3.35 in).

Strength in numbers

It was the numerical superiority of the M4 that in the end made it a war winner. The M4 had many drawbacks and was far from being the ideal battle tank.

Indeed, many field improvisations had to be used to strengthen the armour. This included the simple expedient of using stacked sandbags. As well as these problems, the tank's silhouette was too high for comfort, and the interior arrangements far from perfect. Another problem frequently encountered was that with so many variants in use, spares were often not available and engine interchangeability was frequently impossible, thus causing logistical troubles.

Above left: By the winter of 1944-45, most US Army M4s had been fitted with 3-in main guns. These examples belonged to the 3rd US Armoured Division, 1st Army.

Left: Several versions of M4, including this USMC M4A3 which was active in the Philippines, were fitted with flame-throwers. Most were mounted in place of the bow machine-gun and utilised the barrel of the old 75-mm M3 gun.

One of the least-known aspects of World War II was the re-arming of the Free French forces from American sources. These M4s were supplied to the Free French in North Africa, and are seen on parade before a training exercise.

M4 Sherman
In action

What the M4 lacked in overall capabilities, it more than compensated for in its very numbers and great reliability. The original model was the M4 (Sherman I), of which 8,389 were delivered with a welded hull and Continental R-975 radial engine. The M4A1 (Sherman II) was built to the extent of 9,677 vehicles with a cast hull and the Continental engine. The M4A2 (Sherman III) was basically the M4 revised with the General Motors 6046 diesel engine, and these 11,283 tanks were joined by 11,424 examples of the M4A3 (Sherman IV) that differed only in its Ford GAA petrol engine. The M4A4 (Sherman V), of which 7,499 were completed, had a longer hull for the Chrysler multi-bank petrol engine that comprised five 6-cylinder car engines on a common crankshaft. The designation M4A5 was reserved for the Canadian Ram cruiser tank based on the M4 hull. The final production model was the M4A6 (Sherman VII), of which only 75 were completed to a standard that differed from that of the M4A4 in its Ordnance RD-1820 diesel engine.

Above: By the time of the Anzio landings in 1944, M4 crews had already learned the hard way that the tank's armour was vulnerable to most German anti-tank weapons. All manner off improvised armour was often added, one example being the use of spare lengths of track draped over the hull as seen here.

Below: A squadron of US Army M4 medium tanks assembles for the relief of the Bastogne garrison in January 1945 during the period that followed the initial German thrusts of the Ardennes campaign. The lack of any tactical camouflage demonstrates Allied air supremacy following the earlier German surprises and attacks.

Above: Seen in the hands of a British unit, these are Sherman DD (Duplex Drive) amphibious tanks photographed shortly before the D-Day landings on 6 June 1944, when this innovation allowed numbers of Shermans to 'swim' ashore from vessels moored off the Normandy beaches. The flotation screen, seen collapsed against the upper hull, was erected before launch into the water to provide buoyancy, and the propellers provided propulsion until the tracks touched the sea bottom and could take over. The DD tanks provided an answer to the problem of making early delivery of tanks on to the assault beaches before it was safe for tank landing craft to arrive, but offered very little margin for error, and many of the tanks foundered. In practice, the DD system was much more suitable for river crossings and DD Shermans were used during the Rhine crossings of 1945. Although other tanks used the DD system, the Sherman was the standard British army tank for the purpose.

SPECIFICATION	
M4A1 Sherman	**M4A2 Sherman**
Crew: 5	**Crew:** 5
Battle weight: 30164 kg (66,500 lb)	**Battle weight:** 31298 kg (69,000 lb)
Powerplant: one Continental R-975 air-cooled radial piston engine	**Powerplant:** twin General Motors 6-71 diesel piston engines
Dimensions: average length 5.9 m (19 ft 4 in); width 2.6 m (8 ft 7 in); height 2.74 m (9 ft)	**Dimensions:** average length 5.9 m (19 ft 4 in); width 2.6 m (8 ft 7 in); height 2.74 m (9 ft)
Armament: one 75-mm (2.95-in) M3 gun; two 7.62-mm (0.3-in) machine-guns; one 12.7-mm (0.5-in) AA machine-gun	**Armament:** one 75-mm (2.95-in) M3 gun; two 7.62-mm (0.3-in) machine-guns; one 12.77-mm (0.5-in) AA machine-gun
Performance: maximum speed 15–18 km/h (24–29 mph); road radius 160–241 km (100–150 miles) depending on engine type	**Performance:** maximum speed 15–18 km/h (24–29 mph); road radius 160–241 km (100–150 miles) depending on engine type
Fording: 0.91 m (3 ft)	**Fording:** 0.91 m (3 ft)
Vertical obstacle: 0.61 m (2 ft)	**Vertical obstacle:** 0.61 m (2 ft)
Trench: 2.3 m (7 ft 5 in)	**Trench:** 2.3 m (7 ft 5 in)

Above left: The T34 Calliope rocket launcher mounted on a converted M4 tank created a formidable close-support weapon. The 60 4.5-in (114-mm) rocket tubes mounted on the turret could be fired independently or in a salvo. The rockets were aimed by traversing the turret and elevating the four banks of tubes by raising the gun barrel.

Left: Seen with an M3 halftrack in the background, this M4 is typical of the US medium tank force that proved so decisive in northwest European operations from the summer of 1944. The M4 may have lacked the outright capabilities of the Germans' Panther battle and Tiger heavy tanks, but were available in far larger numbers and with adequate quantities of fuel.

M26 Pershing US heavy tank

The heavy tank did not have an easy time during World War II as far as the Americans were concerned. Early on they realised the operational need for a heavy tank, but initially concentrated their considerable production potential on the medium tank, the M3 and M4 series in particular. A promising design, the Heavy Tank M6 came to nought as the result of this concentration of effort, but low-priority development facilities were thereafter accorded to the heavy tank. This requirement was further emphasised when the German Panther and Tiger arrived on the battlefield, and the heavy tank was then given a greater degree of priority.

Trial model

The first of the new generation of American heavy tanks was a trial model known as the **Medium Tank T20**. It had a 76-mm (3-in) gun and used a suspension very like that of the M4 medium tank but progressive development led to a newer form of suspension of the torsion-bar type. The gun was also replaced by a new 90-mm

(3.54-in) main weapon in a revised turret, and after a further series of trials models culminating in the **Heavy Tank T26E3** (via the **Medium Tanks T22**, **T23**, **T25** and **T26**), the vehicle was selected for production as the **Heavy Tank M26**. It was given the name **General Pershing** (or simply **Pershing**), but by the time full trials with the new tank had been completed, only a few were ready for action in World War II.

M26s in Europe

It was early 1945 before the first M26s arrived in Europe and of these only a relative handful saw any action there. More were sent to the Pacific theatre where more were used in anger, including during the taking of Okinawa, but by the time they arrived on the scene, there was little a heavy tank could be called upon to perform.

Thus the M26 contributed little to World War II, but its design was the long-term result of the years of combat that had gone before. For perhaps the first time on an American tank, adequate consideration was given to

US Army M26 Pershing heavy tanks roll through occupied Germany in 1945. The first 20 T26E3s arrived in Europe in January 1945 and were issued to the 3rd and 9th Armoured Divisions the following month.

SPECIFICATION	
Heavy Tank M26	in); height 2.77 m (9 ft 1 in)
Crew: 5	**Performance:** maximum road speed
Weight: in action 41.73 tonnes	48 km/h (30 mph); maximum road
Powerplant: one Ford GAF V-8	range 148 km (92 miles)
petrol engine delivering 373 kW	**Fording:** 1.22 m (4 ft)
(500 hp)	**Gradient:** 60 per cent
Dimensions: length with gun 8.79 m	**Vertical obstacle:** 1.17 m (3 ft 10 in)
(28 ft 10 in) and over hull 6.51 m	**Trench:** 2.59 m (8 ft 6 in)
(21 ft 2 in); width 3.51 m (11 ft 6	

armour protection (a minimum of 12 mm/0.47 in and a maximum of 102 mm/ 4.02 in) and firepower. With the 90-mm gun, originally intended for use as an anti-aircraft weapon, the M26

had armament that was the equal of any and the superior of most contemporary tanks. The secondary armament comprised the standard three machine-guns: one 0.5-in (12.7-mm) and two 0.3-in (7.62-mm) weapons.

Design disadvantages

For all that, the M26 still had a few design drawbacks – the turret shape was criticised for its potential to trap shot rather than deflect it, and the retention of the bow machine-gun was even then seen as something of an anachronism (later developments did away with it). In fact the M26 was only the start of a new generation of US tank design. After 1945 the M26 was progressively developed through various models, including the M47, into the highly successful M48 Patton. The M26 saw extensive action in Korea and was for a while one of the main types fielded by the US Army in Europe as part of NATO. The M26 also spawned many variants and hybrids.

1st Army Engineers prepare an M26 to cross the Rhine. Almost on a par with the Tiger in a straight shooting match, the Pershing proved more mobile.

T-40, T-60 and T-70 Light tanks

During the 1920s and 1930s the tankette was a continuing attraction for the military mind and the tank designer, and the USSR was no exception to this trend. By the late 1930s the Red Army had progressed through the stages in which the one-man tankette had been tested and dropped, and was at the usual stage where the tankette had been developed into the two-man light tank. By the time the Germans attacked in 1941 the Red Army had invested fairly heavily in the light tank, and the models in service came from years of development.

One of the main types in 1940 was the **T-40** amphibious light tank. This was the latest in a long line of models that could be traced back to the T-27 of the early 1930s and had progressed through the T-33, the T-34 (not to be confused with the T-34 medium tank), the T-36, the T-37 and finally the T-38. Most of these lacked the amphibious capabilities of the T-40, which was placed in production in about 1940, so that by the time of the invasion of June 1941, only a few (about 230) had been completed. Many of the later T-40 models (with streamlined nose and foldable trim vane) were converted into rocket-launcher carriers and were never used as turreted tanks, whose normal armament was one 12.7-mm (0.5-in) and one 7.62-mm (0.3-in) machine-gun. Armour ranged from 6 to 13 mm (0.25 to 0.5 in) in thickness.

Rapid production

While the amphibious T-40 was being developed, a non-amphibious version, the **T-40S**, was proposed. When Germany invaded, the call was for many more tanks delivered as rapidly as possible, so the simpler T-40S was rushed into production and redesignated the **T-60** light tank. Unfortunately this proved prob-lenmatic in service and carried over the primary bad points of the T-40: it was too lightly armoured and, having only a 20-mm cannon and a co-axial 7.62-mm (0.3-in) machine-gun as armament, was useless against other tanks. Also it was so underpowered that it could not keep up with the heavier T-34 tanks across country. T-60s were kept in production simply because they could be produced quickly from relatively basic factories. They were powered by truck engines, many components being taken from the same source, and the improved **T-60A** appeared in 1942 with slightly thicker frontal armour (35 mm/1.37 in instead of 25 mm/1 in) and solid instead of spoked wheels.

By late 1941 work was underway on the T-60's successor. This was the **T-70**, whose first version used a twin-engined power train that could never have worked successfully in action and which was soon replaced by a revised arrangement. The T-70 was otherwise a considerable improvement over the T-40 and

The T-70 light tank was a useful reconnaissance vehicle, but it had only a 45-mm main gun and was thus of little use in combat against heavier German tanks. In action, the T-70 proved itself to be adequate but wholly unexceptional.

SPECIFICATION

T-40
Crew: 2
Weight: 5.9 tonnes
Powerplant: one 52-kW (70-hp) GAZ-202 petrol engine
Dimensions: length 4.11 m (13 ft 5⅞ in; width 2.33 m (7 ft 7⅝ in); height 1.95 m (6 ft 4¾ in)
Armament: one 12.7-mm (0.5-in) machine-gun, one 7.62-mm (0.3-in) machine-gun
Performance: maximum road speed 44 km/h (27.3 mph); road range 360 km (223.7 miles)
Fording: amphibious
Gradient: 34°
Vertical obstacle: 0.7 m (2 ft 3¾ in)
Trench: 1.85 m (6 ft 1 in)

T-60
Crew: 2
Weight: 6.4 tonnes
Powerplant: one 63-kW (85-hp) GAZ-203 petrol engine
Dimensions: length 4.11 m (13 ft 5⅞ in) width 2.3 m (7 ft 6½ in), height 1.74 m (5 ft 8½ in)
Armament: one 20-mm cannon, one 7.62-mm (0.3-in) machine-gun
Performance: maximum road speed 45 km/h (28 mph); road range 450 km (280 miles)
Gradient: 29°
Vertical obstacle: 0.54 m (1 ft 9⅓ in)
Trench: 1.85 m (6 ft 1 in)

T-70
Crew: 2
Weight: 9.2 tonnes
Powerplant: two GAZ-202 petrol engines delivering 104 kW (140 hp)
Dimensions: length 4.29 m (14 ft 1 in); width 2.32 m (7 ft 7⅓ in); height 2.04 m (6 ft 8⅓ in)
Armament: one 45-mm (1.77-in) gun, one 7.62-mm (0.3-in) machine-gun
Performance: maximum road speed 45 km/h (28 mph); road range 360 km (223.7 miles)
Gradient: 34°
Vertical obstacle: 0.7 m (2 ft 3⅝ in)
Trench: 3.12 m (10 ft 2¾ in)

The 20-mm gun-armed T-60 light tank was not a great success in action, for it was too lightly armed and armoured, and also lacked power and mobility. It was kept in production simply to get some sort of vehicle to the Red Army following the disasters of the 1941 campaigns.

T-60. It had heavier armour (proof against 37-mm/1.46-in anti-tank gun rounds) and the turret mounted a 45-mm (1.77-in) gun and 7.62-mm machine-gun. This was still only of limited use against heavier tanks but was better than a mere machine-gun. The crew remained at two men, the commander acting as gunner and loader in a fashion hardly conducive to effective operation of the tank or tank units.

Production of the T-70 and **T-70A** ended in October 1943, by which time 8,226 had been produced. In service the type proved wholly unremarkable, and the vehicles appear to have been confined to the close support of infantry units and some limited recce tasks. By 1943 the light tank was an anachronism, but the Soviets nonetheless went ahead with a replacement, the **T-80**. Almost as soon as it went into production its lack of value was realised and production was switched to manufacturing components for the SU-76.

T-26 Light infantry tank

In the late 1920s Red Army planners launched a programme to re-equip the USSR's tank arm. In common with many other nations, the USSR decided upon an infantry support tank for its non-cavalry units and, after attempting without success to develop a new design, decided on the mass production of a British commercial model, the Vickers 6-ton Type E light tank. This was named the **T-26**, and the first examples of the British model arrived during 1930, receiving the designation **T-26A-1**.

Soviet production of the T-26 started during 1931. Early models had two turrets mounting machine-guns (two 7.62-mm/0.3-in weapons in the **T-26A-2**, and one 12.7-mm/0.5-in and one 7.62-mm gun in the **T-26A-3**), but some models had a machine-gun in one turret and a gun (27-mm/1.06-in in the **T-26A-4** and 37-mm/1.46-in in the **T-26A-5**) in the other. This arrangement did not survive for long, and later **T-26B** models had a single turret mounting only a gun (37-mm in the **T-26B-1**, although a 45-mm/ 1.85-in weapon was used later).

Soviet developments

The early T-26 tanks were straightforward copies of the British original, and were simple, robust vehicles of largely riveted construction. The first model was the **T-26 Model 1931 (T-26A)**, but this was superseded in production by the **T-26 Model 1933 (T-26B)**, which introduced a number of design improvements. The Model 1933 was the most widely produced of all Soviet tanks before 1941, about 5,500 being built by the time production ceased in 1936. A new model, the **T-26S Model 1937**, was then placed in production. This series was characterised by several changes from the standards of the preceding versions. The T-26S carried the 45-mm main gun fitted to later versions of the Model 1933, but this was installed in a turret of improved design and all-welded construction as introduced on the **T-26B-2**.

The use of welding in place of riveting was introduced as a result of the Red Army's operational experiences in its border clashes with the Japanese army that took place along the Mongolian and Manchurian boundaries in 1934 and 1935. Here combat showed that a T-26 that was hit by hostile fire was likely to have its rivets knocked out to fly around the interior, to the severe detriment of the occupants. Welding was introduced with the later Model 1933 tanks but was standard on the T-26S.

Throughout their lives the T-26 tanks underwent many production and in-service changes, most of them aimed at improving the armament and the protection (minimum and maximum of 6 and 25 mm/0.24 and 1 in of armour respectively). There were also many special versions. Perhaps the most numerous of these were the flame-throwing tanks prefixed by the designation OT. Again there were several of these variants, the earliest being the **OT-26** and the last the **OT-133**. Most of these had the flame-throwing projector in the turret in place of the main gun, but later models retained a gun in addition to the projector. There were also bridge-carrying versions (**ST-26**) and attempts were made to mount 76.2-mm (3-in) guns for increased infantry fire support. The type was also developed as a command vehicle, variants being the **T-26A-4(U)** and **T-26B-2(U)**.

End of the road

Production of the T-26 series ceased in 1941 as the invading German forces overran most of the tank's production facilities. New production centres in the Soviet hinterlands launched the production of later tank designs, but by 1941 well over 12,000 T-26 tanks of all kinds had been made. Consequently they were among the most numerous of the armoured fighting vehicles used by the Red Army in the early stages of the 'Great Patriotic War', and were also used in the 1939–40 campaign in Finland. Some had been earlier used during the Spanish Civil War.

After 1941 huge numbers of T-26 tanks were destroyed or passed into German hands. Many were later converted to artillery tractors or self-propelled gun carriers, usually by the Germans who always had a need for such vehicles.

The T-26 was an unremarkable tank that was unable to withstand the demands of 1941, but it enabled the USSR to establish its own mass production facilities and build up its armour know-how, these factors stood them in good stead after 1941.

One of the many variants of the T-26 light infantry tank was the Model 1931, which had dual turrets, usually mounting two 7.62-mm machine-guns, but sometimes one of these was replaced by a 37-mm short infantry support gun. The later T-26 Model 1933 had a single turret.

SPECIFICATION	
T-26B	**Armament:** one 37-mm (1.46-in) or
Crew: 3	47-mm (1.85-in) gun
Weight: 9.4 tonnes	**Performance:** maximum road speed
Powerplant: one 68-kW (91-hp)	28 km/h (17.4 mph); maximum road
GAZ T-26 8-cylinder petrol engine	range 175 km (109 miles)
Dimensions: length 4.88 m (16 ft);	**Gradient:** 40°
width 3.41 m (11 ft 2¼ in); height	**Vertical obstacle:** 0.79 m (2 ft 7 in)
2.41 m (7 ft 11 in)	**Trench:** 1.9 m (6 ft 2¾ in)

T-28 Medium tank

The Soviet T-28 medium tank was an indigenous design that entered production in Leningrad during 1933. It was greatly influenced by trends revealed in German and British (Vickers) experimental designs in features such as the multi-turret armament layout fashionable at that time. The T-28 had three turrets, that for the main gun being partially flanked by two smaller turrets armed with machine-guns, with the driver's position located between the two auxiliary gun turrets.

The T-28 medium tank was one of the least successful pre-World War II Soviet tank designs. In action in 1940 and 1941 it proved to be cumbersome, inadequately armoured and undergunned. The main gun was a short 76.2-mm (3-in) weapon that was replaced in some cases by a longer gun of the same calibre.

Slab-sided tank

The prototype of the T-28 series had a 45-mm (1.77-in) main gun, but on the T-28 and **T-28A** production models (the latter with thicker front armour) this was replaced by a short-barrel 76.2-mm (3-in) gun, while **T-28B** production models after 1938 had a newer and longer-barrel 76.2-mm gun of improved performance. The secondary armament was three 7.62-mm (0.3-in) machine-guns. Overall the T-28 was large and slab-sided, but Soviet tank design teams were still learning their trade, and experience gained with the T-28 was greatly important.

Construction of the original **T-28 Model 1934** lasted until 1938, when there appeared the improved **T-28B Model 1938** with the new gun, rudimentary gun stabilisation and a number of engine modifications. Manufacture of this version lasted until 1940, when production ceased in favour of later models. Armour thickness of the different versions ranged from a minimum of 20 mm (0.79 in) to a maximum of 80 mm (3.15 in).

Useful experiments

There were several experimental versions of the T-28, including some self-propelled guns and 'specials' such as bridging and assault

engineering tanks. None of these experimental variants proceeded past the prototype stage, but experience with them was of great importance when later variations on production tanks were contemplated. In fact the T-28 was of more value as an educational tank than as a combat tank. Its service life was short, spanning only the years from 1939–41. In 1939 the T-28 was first used in action against the Finns during the 'Winter War'. In that short conflict the T-28 fared badly as its crews found out, in the hardest way possible, that the vehicle's armour was too thin for safety. The tanks that survived the war then underwent a hasty course of modification to add extra armour (up to 80 mm), resulting in the revised designation **T-28E** (Ekanirovki, or screened, i.e. up-armoured). However, the continued indifferent performance of the T-28 in its T-28E form after the German invasion of June 1941 suggests that this crash improvement programme was of doubtful effectiveness. The T-28E was also known as the **T-28M** or **T-28 Model 1940**.

Great vulnerability

Thus in 1941 the surviving T-28 tanks demonstrated themselves to be of only limited combat value. Their large slab sides and stately performance made them notably easy prey for the German anti-tank

artillery arm. The tanks also proved themselves to be vulnerable to mines, and in an effort to obviate this threat during the 'Winter War' of 1939–1940 some T-28 tanks had been modified to carry anti-mine rollers in front of

their hulls' nose sections. These rollers were not a success but, once again, the experience gained with them proved to be of great value later. Thus the T-28 medium tank passed from the scene.

The Soviet T-28 heavy tank weighed 28 tonnes but was termed a medium tank. It had a crew of six and had a short 76.2-mm (3-in) gun as its main armament, plus machine-guns in the two auxiliary turrets mounted in front of the main turret. They were clumsy vehicles with armour that proved to be too thin once in action.

SPECIFICATION	
T-28	**Armament:** one 76.2-mm (3-in), and
Crew: 6	three 7.62-mm (0.3-in) machine-
Weight: 28 tonnes	guns
Powerplant: one M-17 V-12 petrol	**Performance:** maximum road speed
engine developing 373 kW (500	37 km/h (23 mph); maximum road
hp)	range 220 km (136.7 miles)
Dimensions: length 7.44 m (24 ft 4¾	**Gradient:** 43°
in); width 2.81 m (9 ft 2¾ in);	**Vertical obstacle:** 1.04 m (3 ft 5 in)
height 2.82 m (9 ft 3 in)	**Trench:** 2.9 m (9 ft 6 in)

BT-7 Fast tank

When the Red Army tank staff decided to modernise its tank fleet during the late 1920s, it authorised the design bureaux to use whatever sources they liked to obtain the best ideas available. Accordingly, many promising design concepts from all over the world were embraced, and among these were ideas of the US mechanical engineer J. Walter Christie. His advanced suspension designs had little impact in his own country at that time, but the Soviets embraced his concepts willingly and took them over for their own further development. The Christie suspension was integrated into the BT series (*bystrochodya tank*, or 'fast tank').

The first Soviet BTs were copied exactly from a Christie prototype delivered to the Soviet Union in 1930 and designated **BT-1**. The first Soviet model was the **BT-2**, and from 1931 onwards the BT series progressed through a number of design developments and improvements until the **BT-7** was produced in 1935. Like the earlier BT tanks the BT-7 was a fast and agile vehicle intended for Red Army cavalry units, and was powered by a converted aircraft engine.

Suspension

The suspension used the Christie torsion bars that allowed a high degree of flexibility at high speeds. The hull was all-welded

and well-shaped, but the main gun was only a 45-mm (1.77-in) weapon, although this was still larger than that fitted on many contemporary equivalents. The secondary armament was two 7.62-mm (0.3-in) machine-guns, and armour varied from 10 to 22 mm (0.39 to 0.87 in).

The BT-7 proved to be very popular with its users. By the time it entered service (in its original **BT-7-1** form with the cylindrical turret, replaced by a conical turret in the **BT-7-2**) many of the automotive snags that had troubled some of the earlier BT models had been eliminated, and the BT-7 thus proved to be fairly reliable. Also, by the time it appeared there were many BT variants: some were produced as flamethrower tanks, and there was a special **BT-7A** close-support version carrying a short 76.2-mm (3-in) main gun. Other experimental models included amphibious and bridging tanks, and variants with different tracks to improve terrain-crossing capabilities.

The BT-7 did have one major tactical disadvantage in that it was only lightly armoured. On the entire BT series armour protection had been sacrificed for speed and mobility, and once in action during 1939 the BTs, including the BT-7, proved to be unsurprisingly vulnerable to anti-tank weapons such as anti-tank rifles. BT-5s had demonstrated this fact when small numbers

were used during the Spanish Civil War, but even though the BT-7 had some armour increases it was still not enough, as revealed in Finland during 1939 and 1940. As a result the design of a successor to the BT series was undertaken and this led ultimately to the adoption of the T-34. Further variants of the BT-7 included the **BT-7-I(U)** command tank and **BT-7M** (or **BT-8**) improved model with full-width and a well-sloped glacis plate plus a V-2 diesel engine.

Thus the BT-7 played its major part in World War II well before

the Germans invaded the Soviet Union in 1941. Large numbers were still in service in 1941, but they fared badly against the advancing Panzers. Despite their mobility the Soviet tank formations were poorly handled and many tanks, including BT-7s, were lost simply because they broke down as the result of poor maintenance or poor training of their crews. It was an inauspicious beginning for the Red Army, but worse was soon to follow and the large fleet of BT-7s had been virtually eliminated by the end of 1941.

The BT-7 was introduced into service in 1935 and was made in two main versions, both armed with a 45-mm (1.77-in) gun. Although fast and mobile in action, the BT-7 proved to be too lightly armoured, but it led in time to the development of the successful T-34 series.

SPECIFICATION	
BT-7	main gun and two 7.62-mm (0.3-in) machine-guns
Crew: 3	**Performance:** maximum road speed 86 km/h (53.4 mph); maximum road range 250 km (155 miles)
Weight: 14 tonnes	
Powerplant: one 373-kW (500-hp) M-17T V-12 petrol engine	
Dimensions: length 5.66 m (18 ft 7 in); width 2.29 m (7 ft 6 in); height 2.42 m (7 ft 11 in)	**Fording:** 1.22 m (4 ft)
	Gradient: 32°
	Vertical obstacle: 0.76 m (2 ft 6 in)
Armament: one 45-mm (1.77-in)	**Trench:** 1.83 m (6 ft)

T-34 Medium tank

It is difficult to write about the **T-34** medium tank without using too many superlatives, as the T-34 has passed into the realms of legend. It was one of the decisive weapons of World War II, and was produced in such vast numbers and in so many versions that entire books have been written on the subject without exhausting the stories of the vehicle and its exploits.

BT-7 successor

In simple terms the T-34 had its origins in the shortcomings of the BT-7 and its forebears. The first result of the BT series' improvements were the designs known as the **A-20** and **A-30**, produced in 1938 as developments of the **BT-IS**, but passed over in favour of a heavier-gunned tank with increased armour and known as the **T-32**. In the T-32

can be seen most of the features of the later T-34. It had a well-shaped hull with sloped armour, and a cast and sloped turret which mounted a 76.2-mm (3-in) high velocity gun. The strengthened Christie suspension, was carried over from the BT series, but the ability to run on wheels without tracks was abandoned.

Good as the T-32 was, a selection panel requested more

armour and so the T-34 was born. It went into production in 1940 and mass production of the **T-34/76A** soon followed. When Germany attacked the Soviet Union in 1941 the type was already well established, but its appearance came as a nasty shock to the Germans. The T-34's well-sloped and thick armour (minimum of 18 mm/0.71 in and maximum of 60 mm/2.36 in)

The T-34 tank was a very advanced design for its time. This is a late production T-34/76 armed with a 76.2-mm (3-in) main gun, and well provided with sloping armour for added protection. The tank was produced in thousands and proved durable, mobile and highly effective in service.

protected the tank against most German anti-tank weapons and the L/30 76.2-mm gun, soon replaced in service by an even more powerful L/40 gun of the same calibre, was effective against most Panzers. The secondary armament fitted was two 7.62-mm (0.3-in) machine-guns.

From 1941 onwards the T-34 was developed into a long string of models, many of them with few external differences. Production demands resulted in many expediences; the finish of most T-34s being rough to an extreme, but the vehicles were still very effective fighting machines. Despite the disruption of the production lines during 1941, ever-increasing numbers poured off the extemporised lines, and all manner of time-saving production methods (ranging from automatic welding to leaving whole sections of surface unpainted) were used. The second major production model was the **T34/76B** with a rolled-plate turret.

T-34 variants

Successively improved models of the T-34/76 were the **T-34/76C** with a larger turret containing twin roof hatches in place of the original single hatch; the **T-34/76D** with a hexagonal turret and wider mantlet, plus provision for jettisonable exterior fuel tanks. The **T-34/76E** was fitted with a cupola on the turret and was of an all-welded construction. The **T-34/76F** was identical to the T-34/76E apart from its cast rather than welded turret. (It should be noted that the designations are Western, and were designed to provide a means of identification).

In time, the 76.2-mm gun was replaced by an 85-mm (3.34-in) gun using the turret taken from the KV-85 heavy tank. This variant became the **T-34/85**, which remains in service today in some parts of the world. T-34/85s remain in service in Afghanistan, where they have been used by the Taliban militia. They are also used by China which deploys over 500; Croatia, Congo and Mali which deploy 20 each; and Angola and Laos which deploy between 10 and 15 each. Special assault gun versions using the 85-mm gun and later the 100-mm (3.94-in) or 122-mm (4.8-in) artillery pieces were developed and flamethrowing, tractor, engineer and mine-clearing versions also rolled off the production lines.

However, it was as a battle tank that the T-34 has its main claim to fame. High production ensured that the T-34 was available in thousands and the T-34 assumed mastery of the battlefield. This forced the Germans on to the defensive and also took from them both the tactical and the strategic initiative, thus helping win the Soviet war.

The T-34 was manufactured in very large numbers, although production was basic and hulls were sometimes left unpainted. However, such labour-saving measures accelerated the production.

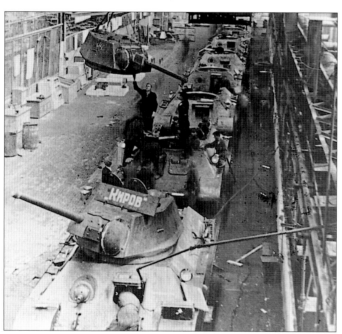

The 85-mm (3.34-in) main armament of the later T-34 is clearly visible on the turret, together with one of the pair of 7.62-mm (0.3-in) machine-guns.

SPECIFICATION	
T-34/76A	machine-guns
Crew: 4	**Powerplant:** one V-2-34 V-12 diesel
Weight: 26 tonnes	developing 373 kW (500 hp)
Dimensions: length 5.92 m (19 ft 5 in); width 3 m (9 ft 10 in); height 2.44 m (8 ft)	**Performance:** road speed 55 km/h (34 mph); range 186 km (115 miles)
Armament: one L/40 76.2-mm (3-in) main gun and two 7.62-mm (0.3-in)	**Gradient:** 40°
	Vertical obstacle: 0.71 m (2 ft 4 in)
	Trench: 2.95 m (9 ft 8 in)

T-34 In action

Soviet T-34/85 tanks are seen before the start of the huge Soviet offensive in East Prussia during the winter of 1944-45. By that time the main production version mounted the 85-mm (3.34-in) gun. The T-34 has a claim to being the finest fighting vehicle of the 20th century, being a generation ahead of any of its contemporaries, and produced in enormous numbers: 11,000 of this more heavily gunned model were produced in 1944 alone.

The T-34 medium tank was crude by the standards of the Germans and the Western Allies, but it was also well armed, heavily protected and mechanically reliable. From the first weeks of its operational service it was clearly seen as a potential war-winner, and as a result was completed in vast numbers: the total for all models was some 39,683 broken down as 115 in 1940, 2,810 in 1941, about 5,000 in 1942, about 10,000 in 1943, 11,758 in 1944, and about 10,000 in 1945. Large numbers remained in important post-war service.

POST-WAR SERVICE: T-34 EXPORTS

After World War II the Soviets distributed T-34 tanks to an increasing number of allies and clients. The tanks were initially of the T-34/76 variant, but the T-34/85 (right) was then delivered as more modern vehicles entered Soviet service. Built up to the mid-1950s, the T-34/85 was armed with the 85-mm (3.34-in) D-5T85 L/51.5 gun later succeeded by the ZIS-S53 L/54.6 weapon. These fired the standard 9.36-kg (20.64-lb) shot at a muzzle velocity of 792 or 800 m (2,599 or 2,625 ft) per second respectively, the latter offering the penetration of 102 mm (4 in) of armour at 1000 m (1,095 yards). The T-34/85 remained in Soviet service until the late 1950s, and with a number of other armies until the late 1960s as a gun tank and later still in a number of special-purpose forms. Among the most important of the non-Soviet T-34 operators were North Korea and both Egypt and Syria, which used their tanks against the American-aided South Koreans and the Israelis respectively, and the T-34/85 also saw service in Angola and Vietnam.

Above: A tank unit crosses the Great Khingan Mountain during the Soviet forces' crossing into north-east China in August 1945. By now an awesome fighting machine, the Red Army was massing on the Manchurian border in preparation for smashing the Japanese army in northern China, Manchuria and Korea.

Below: Tanks and infantry are mutually supporting arms. Most armies have infantrymen somewhere near the tanks, but in World War II no-one had them closer than the Soviets. Trucks were required for tasks such as carrying fuel and food, so Red Army foot soldiers became tank riders, providing protection for their vehicles.

SPECIFICATION	
T-34 medium tank	
T-34/76B	**T-34/85**
Weight: 28250 kg (62,280 lb)	**Weight:** 32000 kg (70,547 lb)
Powerplant: one Model V-2-34 liquid-cooled V-12 diesel engine delivering 373 kW (500 hp)	**Powerplant:** one Model V-2-34 liquid-cooled V-12 diesel engine delivering 373 kW (500 hp)
Dimensions: length 6.58 m (21 ft 7 in); width 3 m (9 ft 10 in); height 2.44 m (8 ft)	**Dimensions:** length 7.5 m (24 ft 7½ in); width 3 m (9 ft 10 in); height 2.39 m (7 ft 10 in)
Armour: hull nose, upper sides and rear 45 mm (1.77 in); hull lower sides and glacis plate 47 mm (1.85 in); hull top and cover plate 20 mm (0.79 in); turret front 65 mm (2.56 in); mantlet 20-46 mm (0.79-1.81 in); turret sides 65 mm (2.56 in); turret rear 47 mm (1.85 in); turret roof front 15 mm (0.59 in); turret roof rear 30 mm (1.18 in)	**Armour:** hull nose, upper sides and rear 45 mm (1.77 in); hull lower sides and glacis plate 47 mm (1.85 in); hull top and cover plate 22 mm (0.87 in); belly 18 mm (0.71 in); mantlet 90 mm (3.54 in); turret sides 75 mm (2.95 in); turret rear 60 mm (2.36 in); turret roof front 18 mm (0.71 in); turret roof rear 22 mm (0.87 in)
Armament: one 76.2-mm (3-in) Model 1940 F-34 L/41.2 rifled gun with 80 rounds, and two 7.62-mm (0.3-in) DT machine-guns (one co-axial and one bow) with 2,394 rounds	**Armament:** one 85-mm (3.35-in) ZIS-S53 L/54.6 rifled gun with 56 rounds, and two 7.62-mm (0.3-in) DT machine-guns (one co-axial and one bow) with 2,394 rounds
Performance: maximum speed 51.5 km/h (32 mph); range 450 km (280 miles)	**Performance:** maximum speed 50 km/h (31.1 mph); range 300 km (24 miles) on internal fuel
Fording: 1.4 m (4 ft 7 in) without preparation	**Fording:** 1.32 m (4 ft 4 in) without preparation
Vertical obstacle: 0.7 m (2 ft 3½ in)	**Vertical obstacle:** 0.73 m (2 ft 4¾ in);
Trench: 2.95 m (9 ft 8 in)	**Trench:** 2.5 m (8 ft 2 in)

INTO ACTION: THE FIRST COMBATS

Their first encounters with the T-34 came as a nasty shock to the Germans during the invasion of the USSR. On 8 July 1941, PzKpfw IIIs of the German 17th Panzer Division saw a single Soviet tank whose silhouette was unfamiliar. As usual, German gunners opened fire on the approaching tank, expecting to destroy it, but instead saw their rounds ricocheting off the tank's turret. Increasingly alarmed, the Germans watched this new tank shrug off the shells from their standard 3.7-cm (1.46-in) anti-tank gun as it advanced on its squat tracks through the German position, crushing the anti-tank gun as it went. The tank, a T-34, then disappeared behind the German positions. In the end, after a 14.5-km (9-mile) excursion behind the German lines, the Soviet tank was stopped only by a shot into its rear from a 10-cm (3.94-in) gun. Again in July 1941, a 3.7-cm anti-tank battery of Panzerjäger Abteilung 42 reported how it had encountered 'a completely unknown type of tank ... We opened fire immediately but the armour was not penetrated until the range was 100 m [110 yards]. Armour-piercing projectiles stick in the armour plating at 200 m [220 yards].' Another gun crew reported: 'Half a dozen anti-tank guns fire at the T-34, which sounds like a drum-roll. But he drives staunchly through our lines like an impregnable

prehistoric monster.' Eventually, only the arrival of the 7.5-cm (2.95-in) Pak 40 anti-tank gun could restore the balance.

The German PzKpfw III tank was unable to take on the T-34. One German crew reported: 'Quite remarkable, Lieutenant Steup's tank made hits on a T-34, once at about 20 m [22 yards] and four times at 50 m [55 yards] with the PzGr. 40 projectile without any noticeable effect...The T-34s came nearer and nearer although they were constantly under fire. The projectiles did not penetrate but sprayed off the side.' A German tank officer from Pz. Abt. 4 reported: 'Time and time again our tanks have been split right open by frontal hits. The commander's cupolas on the PzKpfw III and PzKpfw IV have been completely blown off, proof that the armour is inadequate and the attachments of the cupolas is faulty. It is also proof of the great accuracy and penetration of Russian T-34's 76.2-mm gun...The former pace and offensive spirit [of the Panzer force] will evaporate and be replaced by a feeling of inferiority, since the crews know they can be knocked out by enemy tanks while they are still a great distance away.'

T-35 Heavy tank

The **T-35** was one of the major disappointments for the Soviet tank designers before World War II. It had its origins in design studies that began in 1930, and the first prototype was rolled out in 1932. In appearance and in many other ways the T-35, via the T-28, was greatly influenced by the design of the British Vickers Independent, a tank that was produced as a one-off only and which featured in a notorious espionage court case of the period. The T-28 carried over from the Vickers design one major feature, namely the multi-turret concept.

Although there were changes between the various production batches, the tanks of the main batch (produced between 1935 and 1938) were longer than the originals. This increase in length made the T-35 an unwieldly machine to steer, and its ponderous weight did little to improve matters. The multi-turret approach to tank weaponry also proved to be of limited value.

Multi-turret trouble

Aiming and co-ordinating the fire of the five turrets proved very difficult, and the overall effectiveness of the armament was further limited by the relatively small calibre of the main gun. In fact the main gun and turret were the same as those used on the T-28 medium tank. Armour varied from 10 to 30 mm (0.39 in to 1.18 in).

Production of the T-35 was slow and limited compared with that of other Soviet tank programmes of the time.

Only 61 were produced between 1933 and 1939, and all of these vehicles served with just one tank brigade stationed near Moscow. This was politically useful, for the T-35s featured regularly in the Red Square parades of the time and thus provided a false impression of Soviet tank strengths. The massive vehicles made a great impression as they rumbled past, but the service reality was considerably different.

When they had to go to war in 1941 only a handful actually saw action, for many were retained in Moscow for internal duties and for purely local defence. There appears to be no record of any T-35s going into action around Moscow, but the few used elsewhere to try to halt the German advances did not fare well. They were too lightly armed and their weight made them easy prey for the Panzers.

SPECIFICATION	
T-35	or 45-mm (1.77-in) gun on each of
Crew: 11	two secondary turrets, plus up to
Weight: 45 tonnes	six 7.62-mm (0.3-in) machine-guns
Powerplant: one M-17M V-12 petrol	**Performance:** maximum road speed
engine developing 373 kW (500 hp)	30 km/h (18.6 mph); maximum
Dimensions: length 9.72 m (31 ft 11	road range 150 km (93.2 miles)
in); width 3.2 m (10 ft 6 in); height	**Gradient:** 20°
3.43 m (11 ft 3 in)	**Vertical obstacle:** 1.20 m (4 ft);
Armament: one 76.2-mm (3-in) gun	**Trench:** 3.5 m (11 ft 6 in)
on main turret, one 37-mm (1.45-in)	

The T-35 heavy tank made an impressive showing on parade, but made little impact in action. Control of the five turrets proved very difficult and their bulk and length of hull made these awkward vehicles to manoeuvre.

KV-1 Heavy tank

The KV-1 heavy tank originally mounted a 76.2-mm (3-in) main gun on a chassis that was to be adapted for later models of Soviet heavy tanks. Several versions existed as progressive production changes were introduced to speed manufacture and improve protection for the crew of five.

A KV-1 rolls through Moscow streets to the front in December 1941. The tank had a 76.2-mm main gun and was used by the Red Army for the breakthrough role in which its lack of speed was not a handicap.

By 1938 the Soviets appreciated the need for a T-35 heavy tank successor, and several design bureaux became involved. Many proposed multi-turret designs, but most prototypes had just two turrets. However, one team designed a single-turret heavy tank named after Klimenti Voroshilov, defence commissar at the time. This **KV-1** was far more mobile than the other submissions, and was field-tested during the campaign against Finland in 1940 in a form with a 76.2-mm (3-in) short-barrel gun, three or four 7.62-mm (0.3-in) machine-guns, and armour up to 100 mm (3.94 in) thick.

KV-85
Crew: 5
Weight: 43 tonnes
Powerplant: one V-2K V-12 diesel developing 448 kW (600 hp)
Dimensions: length 6.68 m (21 ft 11 in); width 3.32 m (10 ft 10⅝ in); height 2.71 m (8 ft 10⅝ in)
Armament: one 85-mm (3.34-in)

main gun, and three or four 7.62-mm (0.3-in) machine-guns
Performance: maximum road speed 35 km/h (21.75 mph); maximum road range 150 km (93.2 miles)
Gradient: 36°
Vertical obstacle: 1.2 m (3 ft 11¼ in)
Trench: 2.59 m (8 ft 6 in)

The KV-1 was ordered into production as the **KV-1A** with a 76.2-mm long-barrel gun and the KV-2 with a large slab-sided turret mounting initially a 122-mm (4.8-in) but later a 152-mm (5.98-in) howitzer. The high turret was a ponderous load for the vehicle, though, and the KV-2 (and improved KV-2B) did

not shine in action. With the KV-1 the immediate future for Soviet tank design was established, and the KV-1 was a formidable vehicle that served the Red Army for years. It was often used as an assault (break-through) tank, spearheading many attacks. The KV-1B had an extra 25–35 mm (0.98–1.38 in)

of armour on the hull front and sides. The turret progressed from being a mainly plated affair to a cast component, which on the KV-1C also gave increased protection. Much of the extra armour was simply bolted on.

Gun modifications

For its size, the KV-1 was undergunned, but a scheme to increase the armament to a 107-mm (4.21-in) weapon proceeded no further than trials. Instead the 76.2-mm gun was lengthened and the clumsy 152-mm gun turret was withdrawn. After 1943 the introduction of an

85-mm (3.34-in) gun created the formidable **KV-85**.

The KV-1 did at first have serious automotive problems, but many were eventually eliminated. The numerous increases in armour protection were usually unmatched by increases in engine power, though the KV-1C had an extra 74.6 kW (100 hp). Thus many examples could not reach their expected speed, and on a small number of KV-1S (Skorostnoy, or fast) tanks all appliqué armour was omitted to reduce weight and raise speed. One problem was the commander doubled as gun loader.

KV-2 Heavy tank

The Soviets appreciated that the KV-1 had the makings of an effective heavy tank offering good protection and adequate mobility after the type's automotive problems had been eradicated, but only indifferent firepower. This fact stemmed from the use of the same 76.2-mm (3-in) gun as used in the T-34/76 medium tank: this was an L/30.5 weapon that was soon replaced by an L/41.2 weapon. Further improvements in firepower were considered and trialled, but the Red Army also appreciated the need for a considerably more powerfully armed artillery fire-support variant to aid breakthrough operations. The hull and running gear of the KV-1 were adequate to the task, and to make the **KV-2A** the designers added a large and totally unwieldy turret carrying a 122-mm (4.8-in) M1938 L/22.7 howitzer. The turret was high and slab-sided, and although constructed of thick armour, up to a maximum thickness of 76.2 mm (3 in) on

the front and sides, offered a very tempting target.

Large calibre weapon

The 122-mm weapon had been installed in only a few vehicles before it was superseded by the 152-mm (6-in) M1938 L/24.3 howitzer, the largest-calibre weapon ever installed in a mass-production tank. The 152-mm weapon was provided with 36 rounds of ammunition fired at a muzzle velocity of 508 m (1,667 ft) per second for the AP projectile and 432 m (952 ft)

per second for the HE projectile, which had a maximum range of 12400 m (13,565 yards). The standard defensive armament was two or three 7.62-mm (0.3-in) machine guns (bow,

co-axial and turret rear) with 3,087 rounds. The turret was power-operated through 360°, but one of the KV-2A's most limiting tactical failings was the fact that the turret was virtually

KV-2B
Crew: 6
Weight: 57 tonnes
Powerplant: one V-2K V-12 diesel developing 410 kW (550 hp)
Dimensions: length 6.8 m (22 ft 4 in) overall; width 3.33 m (10 ft 11 in); height 4.18 m (13 ft 8 in)
Armament: one 152-mm (6-in)

M1938 howitzer and two or three 7.62-mm (0.3-in) machine-guns
Performance: maximum speed 26 km/h (16 mph); maximum road range 160 km (100 miles);
Fording: 1.45 m (4 ft 9 in)
Gradient: 34°
Vertical obstacle: 0.9 m (3 ft);
Trench: 2.8 m (9 ft 2 in)

The tall, slab-sided turret of the KV-2 was vulnerable to attack as it presented a large and tempting target. In addition, it was virtually unmovable except when the tank was on level ground.

immovable except when the tank was level. To this was added very poor cross-country mobility: the KV-2 was more than 6 tonnes heavier than the KV-1 but had no more power.

Improved standard

Later production vehicles were completed to the **KV-2B** improved standard based on the chassis of the KV-1B, with the main gun emerging from an asymmetric mantlet on the front of a turret provided with greater protection by the addition of 35 mm (1.38 in) of appliqué armour on its front. A few of the KV-2B vehicles were later adapted as flame-thrower tanks. Battlefield experience revealed that the KV-2 series was of only limited operational use, and most surviving vehicles were soon removed from first-line service.

IS-2 Heavy tank

The IS-2 was introduced into service with the Red Army during 1944 and was the most powerful of all the Soviet heavy tanks. It mounted a long 122-mm (4.8-in) gun in a well-protected cast turret, and carried a crew of four. Ammunition stowage was limited to 28 rounds.

SPECIFICATION	
IS-2	main gun, one 12.7-mm (0.5-in)
Crew: 4	machine-gun, and one 7.62-mm
Weight: 46 tonnes	(0.3-in) machine-gun
Powerplant: one V-2-IS (V-2K) V-12	**Performance:** maximum road speed
diesel developing 447 kW (600 hp)	37 km/h (23 mph); maximum road
Dimensions: length 9.9 m (32 ft 5½	range 240 km (149 miles)
in); width 3.09 m (10 ft 1½ in);	**Gradient:** 36°
height 2.73 m (8 ft 11½ in)	**Vertical obstacle:** 1 m (3 ft 3 in)
Armament: one 122-mm (4.8-in)	**Trench:** 2.49 m (8 ft 2 in)

When the Red Army reached Berlin in 1945, it was IS-2 tanks that led the way; this example is seen near the Reichstag. Note the great length of the 122-mm (4.8-in) gun and the shaping of the turret and glacis plate to deflect armour-piercing projectiles.

The ultimate development of the Soviets' enthusiasm for the heavy tank was the Iosef Stalin (IS, sometimes rendered JS) series, planned from a time early in 1943. Weight no greater than that of the KV was demanded, and as initial plans called for an 85-mm (3.35-in) main gun the designation **IS-85** was allocated.

The first of three prototypes appeared in the autumn of 1943 and, although clearly derived from the KV series in its hull and running gear, was a much more formidable machine with highly sloped armour: the hull armour was welded and varied in thickness from 19 to 120 mm (0.75 to 4.72 in), while the turret was the same cast unit as fitted on the KV-85 with thickness between 30 and 100 mm (1.18 and 3.94 in). The care taken in design was indicated by the fact that the IS-85 emerged with 50 mm (1.98 in) more armour than the KV-85 but weighed some 2000 kg (4,409 lb) less, allowing a slightly higher maximum

speed on a slightly less powerful engine. It is thought likely that the IS-85 saw limited operational service as the **IS-1**.

Weaponry

To provide armament heavier than that of current medium tanks, the **IS-100** was developed with a 100-mm (3.94-in) main gun. A small number of IS-100 tanks was built for evaluation purposes, but the type proceeded no further. The reason behind this was that General F. Petrov, designer of the turret used in the KV-85, T-34/85 and IS-1, proposed an altogether more formidable machine with a new turret of superior ballistic shape and fitted with the 122-mm (4.8-in) D-25 L/43 gun firing a 24.95-kg (55-lb) armour-piercing shot at 780 m (2,559 m) per second.

After development as the **IS-122**, the type was placed in production as the **IS-2**, and the considerably more potent turret/armament combination was also retrofitted to the small number of IS-100s that had been built to create the variant known in the West as the **IS-1B**, the original IS-1 being redesignated **IS-1A** to avoid confusion. The IS-2 was accepted for production in October 1943 after an extremely rapid development programme, and proved excellent in combat.

IS-3 Heavy tank

The IS-3 was the definitive Soviet heavy tank of World War II, with excellent amour protection, and a formidable 122-mm (4.8-in) rifled gun plus three machine-guns. The tank was in service until the late 1970s.

The IS-2 entered combat for the first time during February 1944 at Korsun Shevkenskovsky, and General Zh. Kotin, one of the USSR's most capable tank designers, was present in the battle to gain first-hand information about the IS-2's operational capabilities, both positive and negative. This paved the way for the design and prototype evaluation of several experimental tanks, an evolutionary process which facilitated more advanced thinking about armour layout enhancements. Toward the end of 1944, therefore, the Soviets were in the position to start the introduction of their definitive heavy tank of World War II, the **IS-3**, designed by a team under the supervision of N. Dukhov, that may also be seen as the first of the classic tank designs that formed the core of the Soviet armoured force's equipment in the period after the war.

Increased protection

The IS-3's major improvement over the IS-2 was its protection,

for the Soviets were satisfied that the mobility and firepower of the IS-2 were more than adequate. The better protection may be regarded as a direct evolutionary step in the process that had given birth to the T-34 series, with the armour both increased in thickness and made more capable by effective angling. Thus the hull of the IS-3 was basically that of the IS-2 revised in thicker rolled plate for better ballistic protection, while the totally new cast turret introduced the smooth inverted-saucer or carapace shape that has remained standard with the Soviets and their successors ever since. The hull armour varied from a minimum of 20 mm (0.79 in) on the belly to a maximum of 120 mm (4.72 in) on the front, while the turret was still better protected with minimum and maximum thicknesses of 25 and 230 mm (1 and 9.06 in) respectively.

Yet despite the thickness of the armour, its excellent shaping and disposition meant that the

weight of the IS-3 was no greater than that of German tanks with notably less potent armament: the mass was still only 46500 kg (102,513 lb), a figure somewhat lower than that of the Germans' Tiger with an 88-mm (3.46-in) gun, yet the firepower and protection of the Soviet tank were immeasurably superior to those of the Tiger without any adverse effect on mobility.

Weaponry

The armament of the IS-3 comprised one 122-mm (4.8-in) rifled gun. This was the D-25 (M1943) L/43 rifled weapon, for which 28 rounds of ammunition

were carried. The gun was carried in the front of the turret, which was electrically operated for traverse through 360°, and could be elevated through an arc of 23° (-3° to +20°). The secondary armament comprised three machine-guns in the form of two 7.62-mm (0.3-in) DT weapons (one co-axial and one bow) with 1,000 rounds and one 12.7-mm (0.5-in) DShK weapon with 945 rounds on the turret roof for AA defence.

The IS-3 saw limited service in the last months of World War II, but remained in service with the Red Army into the late 1970s, but latterly only as a reserve weapon.

SPECIFICATION	
IS-3	main gun, one 12.7-mm (0.5-in)
Crew: 4	DShK machine-gun, and two
Weight: 46.5 tonnes	7.62-mm (0.3-in) DT machine-guns
Powerplant: one 387-kW (519-hp)	**Performance:** maximum road speed
V-2-IS V-12 diesel engine	37 km/h (23 mph); maximum road
Dimensions: length 10 m (32 ft	range 210 km (130.5 miles)
10 in) overall and 6.66 m (21 ft	**Gradient:** 70 per cent
10 in) hull; width 3.2 m (10 ft 6 in);	**Fording:** 1.3 m (4 ft 6 in)
height 2.71 m (8 ft 11 in)	**Vertical obstacle:** 1 m (3 ft 3 in)
Armament: one 122-mm (4.8-in) D-25	**Trench:** 2.5 m (8 ft 2 in)

PzKpfw 35(t)/LT vz 35 Light tank

It is a little known fact that Czechoslovakia was a leading exporter of armoured vehicles and artillery prime movers before World War II, with sales made to Austria, Bulgaria, Hungary, Latvia, Peru, Romania, Sweden, Switzerland and Turkey.

In October 1934 the Czech army placed an order for two prototypes of a medium tank called the **S-11-a** (or **T-11**), which were completed in the following year. Army trials started in June 1935 and soon uncovered many faults as a result of the tank's rushed development. Without waiting for these faults to be corrected an order was placed for a first batch of 160 vehicles in October 1935, and the first five were delivered in the following year.

So many faults were found that these vehicles were returned to Skoda for modifications. A further batch of 138 was ordered for the Czech army, which called it the **LT vz 35**, while Romania ordered 126 as the **R-2**. Gradually most of the faults were overcome and the vehicle gained a good reputation.

The Germans took over the remaining vehicles when they occupied Bohemia and Moravia in 1939, giving them the

designation **Panzerkampfwagen 35(t).** A further 219 were built by Skoda for the Wehrmacht.

Such was the shortage of tanks in the German army at the outbreak of war that the 6th Panzer Division was equipped with the PzKpfw 35(t) for the invasion of France in 1940. These continued in service until 1942 when surviving chassis were converted into other roles such as mortar tractors (German designation *Mörserzugmitel*), artillery tractors (German designation *Zugkraftwagen*) or maintenance vehicles with tank battalions.

Construction

The hull of the LT vz 35 was of riveted construction that varied in thickness from 12 mm to a maximum of 35 mm. The bow machine-gunner was seated at the front of the vehicle on the left and operated the 7.92-mm (0.31-in) ZB vz 35 or 37 machine-gun, with the driver to his right. The commander/gunner and loader/radio operator were seated in the two-man turret in the centre of the hull.

Main armament consisted of a 37.2-mm (1.46-in) Skoda vz 34 gun with a 7.92-mm ZB 35 or 37 machine-gun mounted co-axially

Czechoslovakia provided many of the tanks used by the Wehrmacht in the battle for France. The PzKpfw 35(t) equipped the 6th Panzer Division in that campaign and continued in service until 1942.

to the right. Totals of 72 rounds of 37-mm and 1,800 rounds of machine-gun ammunition were carried. The engine and transmission were at the rear, the transmission having one reverse and six forward gears. The suspension on each side consisted of eight small road wheels, with the drive sprocket at the rear, and a front idler. An unusual feature of the tank was

that the transmission and steering were assisted by compressed air to reduce driver fatigue, so enabling the tank to travel long distances at high speed.

Problems were encountered with these systems when the tanks were operated by the Germans on the Eastern Front, because of the very low temperatures encountered.

SPECIFICATION	
LT vz 36	developing 89 kW (120 hp)
Crew: 4	**Performance:** maximum road speed
Weight: 10500 kg (23,148 lb)	40 km/h (25 mph); maximum range
Dimensions: length 4.9 m	193 km (120 miles)
(16 ft 1 in); width 2.159 m	**Fording:** 0.8 m (3 ft 4 in)
(7 ft 1 in); height 2.209 m (7ft 3 in)	**Gradient:** 60 per cent;
Powerplant: one Skoda six-cylinder	**Vertical obstacle:** 0.787 m (2 ft 7 in);
water-cooled petrol engine	**Trench:** 1.981 m (6 ft 6 in)

PzKpfw 38(t)/TNH P-S Light Tank

The rapidly deteriorating international situation in 1937 led the Czech army to issue a requirement for a new light tank. This time the army was determined that the troubles encountered with the LT vz 35, resulting from a lack of testing, would not be repeated. Skoda entered its S-11-a and S-11-b while CKI entered an LT vz 35 with the engine and transmission of the TNH tank, the LT4, the TNH P-S (already in production as a successful export item) as well as a new medium tank called the V-8-H.

Used by two Panzer Divisions in 1940, the PzKpfw 38(t) was in production for the German army until 1942. The basic chassis was later used for a number of self-propelled artillery conversions.

A PzKpfw 38(t) during the invasion of France; the 7th and 8th Panzer Divisions used the tank in this theatre. The commander of the 7th Division became well known later in the war – his name was Rommel.

German service

In a series of extensive trials the **TNH P-S** was found to be the best design and on 1 July 1938 was adopted as the standard light tank of the Czech army under the designation **LT vz 38**. None had entered service at the time of the German occupation in 1939. The vehicle remained in production for the German army between 1939 and 1942, more than 1,400 being built under the designation **Panzerkampfwagen 38(t) Ausf S** to **PzKpfw 38(t) Ausf G** (*Ausführung* is the German word for model or mark). The Germans also exported 69 vehicles to Slovakia, 102 to Hungary, 50 to Romania and 10 to Bulgaria.

During the invasion of France the tank was used by the 7th and 8th Panzer Divisions, the former being commanded with great dash by the ex-commander of Hitler's Army bodyguard, Erwin Rommel. The Panzer 38(t) continued in frontline Wehrmacht service as a light tank until 1942.

The hull and turret of the vehicle were of riveted construction, the top of the superstructure being bolted into position. Minimum armour thickness was 10 mm and maximum thickness 26 mm, although from the Ausf E this was increased to 50 mm.

Armament

The driver was seated at the front of the tank on the right, with the bow machine-gunner operating a 7.92-mm (0.31-in) MG 37(t) machine-gun to his left. The two-man turret in the centre of the hull was armed with a 37.2-mm (1.46-in) Skoda A7 gun, which could fire both armour-piercing and HE rounds. The gun had an elevation of +12° and a depression of -6°. Mounted coaxial with and to the right of the main armament was another 7.92-mm machine-gun. Totals of 90 rounds of 37-mm and 2,550 rounds of machine-gun ammunition were carried.

Powerplant

The engine was at the rear of the hull and coupled to a transmission with one reverse and five forward gears. Suspension on each side consisted of four large rubber-tyred road wheels suspended in pairs on leaf springs with the drive sprocket at the front and idler at the rear, and with two track-return rollers.

Outclassed

While the PzKpfw 38(t) was quickly outclassed as a combat vehicle, it continued to be widely used as a reconnaissance vehicle. In that role the Germans fitted some chassis with the turret of the SdKfz 222 light armoured car, complete with its 20-mm cannon.

The chassis of the light tank also proved suitable as the basis for a large number of specialist vehicles, including the effective **Marder** tank destroyer, which was fitted with a new superstructure armed with a 75-mm anti-tank gun. Other conversions included various self-propelled 15-cm (5.9-in) guns, a 20-mm (0.79-in) self-propelled anti-aircraft gun, several types of weapons carriers and the **Hetzer** tank destroyer. The Hetzer was armed with a 75-mm gun in a fully enclosed fighting compartment with limited traverse, and was considered by many to be one of the best vehicles of its type during World War II. A total of 2,584 were built between 1944 and 1945, and production continued after the war for the Czech army, a further 158 being sold to Switzerland in 1946–7 under the designation **G-13**. These were withdrawn from service in the late 1960s.

SPECIFICATION	
TNH P-S	engine developing 112 kW (150 hp)
Crew: 4	**Performance:** maximum road speed
Weight: 9700 kg (21,385 lb)	42 km/h (26 mph); maximum range
Dimensions: length 4.55 m (14 ft 11	200 km (125 miles)
in); width 2.13 m (7 ft); height 2.31	**Fording:** 0.9 m (3 ft); gradient 60
m (7 ft 7 in)	per cent;
Powerplant: one Praga EPA six-	**Vertical obstacle:** 0.787 m (2 ft 7 in)
cylinder water-cooled inline petrol	**Trench:** 1.879 m (6 ft 2 in)

Panzerkampfwagen I Light tank

In 1933 the German Army Weapons Department issued a requirement for a light armoured vehicle weighing about 5000 kg (11,026 lb) that could be used for training purposes, and five companies subsequently built prototype vehicles. After trials, the Army Weapons Department accepted the Krupp design for further development; the design company being responsible for

the chassis and Daimler-Benz for the superstructure. To conceal the real use of the vehicle, the Army Weapons Department gave the tank the cover name of **Landwirtschäftlicher Schlepper** (industrial tractor). The first batch of 150 vehicles was ordered from Henschel, and production commenced in July 1934 under the designation **PzKpfw I(MG) (SdKfz 101) Ausf**

A. The tanks were powered by a Krupp M 305 petrol engine developing only 42 kW (57 hp).

There were problems with the engine, however, and the next batch had a more powerful

SPECIFICATION	
PzKpfw I Ausf B	developing 75 kW (100 hp)
Crew: 2	**Performance:** maximum road speed
Weight: 6000 kg (13,230 lb)	40 km/h (25mph); maximum road
Dimensions: length 4.42 m (14 ft 6	range 140 km (87 miles)
in); width 2.06 m (6 ft 9 in); height	**Fording:** 0.58 m (1 ft 11 in)
1.72 m (5 ft 8 in)	**Gradient:** 60 per cent
Powerplant: one Maybach NL 38 TR	**Vertical obstacle:** 0.36 m (1 ft 2 in);
six-cylinder petrol engine	trench 1.4 m (4 ft 7 in)

engine, which meant that the hull had to be longer and an additional roadwheel added on each side. This model was a little heavier, but its bigger engine gave it a maximum road speed of 40 km/h (25 mph). This entered service in 1935 under the designation **PzKpfw I(MG) (SdKfz 101) Ausf B**. Most of the vehicles were built by Henschel but Wegmann also became involved in the programme, peak production being achieved in 1935 when over 800 vehicles were completed.

Lack of fire-power

The Panzerkampfwagen I was first used operationally in the Spanish Civil War, and at the start of the invasion of Poland in 1939 no less than 1,445 such vehicles were on strength. It had already been realised, however, that the vehicle was ill-suited for front-line use because of its lack of firepower and armour

protection (7–13 mm), and in the invasion of France in 1940 only 523 were used, although many more were still in service in Germany and Poland.

By the end of 1941 the PzKpfw I had been phased out of front-line service, although the **kleiner Panzerbefehlwagen (SdKfz 265)** command model remained in operational use for a longer period.

Once the light tank was declared obsolete, its chassis underwent conversion to other roles. One of these was the **Munitions-Schlepper,** which was used to carry ammunition and other valuable cargoes. For the anti-tank role the chassis was fitted with captured Czech 47-mm (1.85-in) anti-tank guns on top of the superstructure with limited traverse. These were used in East and North Africa, but became ineffective with the deployment of more heavily armoured Allied tanks.

The PzKpfw I was heavily involved in the Polish campaign after its operational debut in the Spanish Civil War.

Infantry gun

The most extreme conversion entailed the installation of a 15-cm (5.9-in) infantry gun in a new superstructure, but this was found to overload the chassis and less than 40 such conversions were made.

The turret was in the centre

of the vehicle, offset to the right, and for protection the tank was armed with twin 7.92-mm machine-guns, for which a total of 1,525 rounds of ammunition were carried. The driver's seat was positioned to the left of the turret.

Panzerkampfwagen II

Light tank

To bridge the gap until the arrival of the PzKpfw III and PzKpfw IV tanks, a decision was made in 1934 to order an interim model. This became known as the **Panzerkampfwagen II**. Development contracts were awarded to Henschel, Krupp and MAN under the designation **Industrial Tractor 100** or **LaS 100** to conceal its true role.

After evaluation of these prototypes, the MAN model was selected for further development. MAN was responsible for the chassis and Daimler-Benz for the superstructure. Production was eventually undertaken also by Famo, MIAG and Wegmann.

Combat Panzer

The tank formed the backbone of the German armoured divisions during the invasion of France, about 1,000 being in front-line service. The tank was also used in the invasion of the USSR in the following year,

Despite being intended for use as a training vehicle, with little or no combat role, the PzKpfw II was the backbone of the German Panzer arm in the battles for Poland and France.

although by that time it was obsolete, had inadequate armour protection and lacked firepower.

The Panzer II was in fact never intended for combat, being designed primarily as a training machine. The first production **PzKpfw II Ausf A** vehicles were delivered in 1935, and were armed with a 20-mm cannon and 7.92-mm (0.31-in) co-axial machine-gun. Combat weight was 7.2 tonnes.

Tests with the early production models showed that the vehicle was underpowered with its 97-kW (130-hp) engine,

so the **PzKpfw II Ausf B** was introduced with a 104-kW (140-hp) engine and other improvements, notably thicker

SPECIFICATION	
PzKpfw II Ausf F	**Performance:** maximum road speed
Crew: 3	65 km/h (40 mph); maximum road
Weight: 10000 kg (22,046 lb)	range 200 km (125 miles)
Dimensions: length 4.64 m (15 ft	**Fording:** 0.85 m (2 ft 10 in)
3 in); width 2.30 m (7 ft 6½ in);	**Gradient:** 50 per cent; maximum
height 2.02 m (6 ft 7½ in)	**Vertical obstacle:** 0.42 m (1 ft 5 in)
Powerplant: one Maybach 6-cylinder	
petrol developing 104 kW (140 hp)	

A Panzer II (right) and Panzer 38(t) in France in May 1940. Superior tactics and radio communications ensured victory of these light tanks over more heavily armoured foes.

frontal armour. These pushed up its weight to just under 8 tonnes.

More armour

The **PzKpfw II Ausf C** was introduced in 1937, and had even better armour protection. Additionally, the small bogie wheels were replaced by five independently sprung bogies with leaf springs on each side. This remained as the basic suspension for all remaining production vehicles.

In 1938 the **PzKpfw II Ausf D** and **PzKpfw II Ausf E** were introduced, with new torsion-bar suspension which gave them a much increased road speed of 55 km/h (34 mph), although cross-country speed was reduced. The final production model of the series was the **PzKpfw II Ausf F**. This appeared in 1940-41 and had 35 mm (1.4 in) of armour on the front and 20 mm (0.8 in) on the sides. The total weight of the vehicle was now approaching 10 tonnes.

It was felt that the trade-off between reduced speed and greater protection was acceptable. The hull and turret of the PzKpfw II was of welded steel construction. The driver sat at the front. The two-man turret was in the centre, offset to the left, and the engine was at the rear. Armament consisted of a 20-mm cannon (for which 180 rounds were provided) on the left side of the turret, and a 7.92-mm machine-gun with 1,425 rounds on the right of the turret.

The PzKpfw II was also used as the basis for a number of fast reconnaissance tanks called the **Luchs** – this name was subsequently adopted by the new West German Army in the 1970s for its 8x8 reconnaissance vehicle. However, these and similar vehicles were not built in large numbers.

Amphibious

One of the more interesting variants was the special amphibious model developed for the invasion of England in 1940. This model was propelled in the water at a speed of 10 km/h (6 mph) by a propeller run off the main engine. A model with two flame-throwers was also produced as the **Flammpanzer II**; 100 were in service by 1942.

When the basic tank was finally declared obsolete, the chassis was quickly adopted for many other roles. One of the first of these was a highly effective self-propelled anti-tank gun using captured Soviet 76.2-mm (3-in) artillery pieces. It was known as the **Marder I**. This was then followed in production by the **Marder II**, which carried a 75-mm (2.95-in) German anti-tank gun. In all, some 1,200 examples were converted or built from new. The **Wespe**, another effective self-propelled gun using a Panzer II chassis fitted with a 105-mm howitzer, was produced in occupied Poland until 1944.

Panzerkampfwagen III Medium tank

For operations in North Africa the PzKpfw III was fitted with a tropical kit, which included upgraded filters for the engine and wider tracks to make better passage over sand.

In the mid-1930s, evolving German army armoured tactics called for each tank battalion to be equipped with three companies of relatively light medium tanks and one company of heavier and more powerful support tanks. The former eventually became the **Panzerkampfwagen III**

(PzKpfw III) or **SdKfz 141**, while the latter became the Panzerkampfwagen IV, which

was to remain in production throughout World War II.

In 1935 the Weapons Department issued contracts for the construction of prototype vehicles for the lighter concept to Daimler-Benz, Krupp, MAN and Rheinmetall-Borsig. At an early stage it was decided to arm the tank with a 37-mm gun which would fire the same ammunition as that used by the infantry anti-tank gun. The turret

ring was made large enough to facilitate up-gunning of the vehicle to 50 mm (1.97 in) if this should be needed.

Early trials

Following trials with the prototype vehicles the Daimler-Benz model was selected, although the first three production models, the **PzKpfw III Ausf A, PzKpfw III Ausf B** and **PzKpfw III Ausf C**, were built only in

SPECIFICATION	
PzKpfw III Ausf M **Crew:** 5 **Weight:** 22300 kg (49,160 lb) **Dimensions:** length (including armament) 6.41 m (21 ft); length (hull) 5.52 m (18 ft 1½ in); width 2.95 m (9 ft 8 in); height 2.50 m (8 ft 2½ in) **Powerplant:** one Maybach HL 120	TRM 12-cylinder petrol engine developing 224 kW (300 hp) **Performance:** maximum road speed 40 km/h (25 mph); maximum road range 175 km (110 miles) **Fording:** depth 0.80 m (2 ft 8 in); **Gradient:** 60 per cent **Vertical obstacle:** 0.60 m (2 ft); **Trench:** 2.59 m (8 ft 6 in)

small numbers, differing from each other mainly in suspension details. In September 1939 the vehicle was formally adopted for service, and mass production was soon underway.

The PzKpfw III was first used in combat during the invasion of Poland. The next model was the **PzKpfw III Ausf D** with thicker armour and a revised cupola.

In 1939 development began on the 50-mm model, which had an uprated engine and only six road wheels.This entered production in 1940 under the designation **PzKpfw III Ausf F**. The **PzKpfw III Ausf G** followed with similar armament but a more powerful engine. A deep-water wading version was developed and used successfully during the invasion of the USSR in 1941. The **PzKpfw III Ausf H**

introduced wider tracks and a number of important improvements.

Soviet menace

The 50-mm L/42 gun was inadequate to cope with the Soviet T-34 tank so the longer-barrelled KwK 39 L/60 weapon was installed. This had a higher muzzle velocity. Vehicles fitted with this weapon were designated **PzKpfw III Ausf J**. Many vehicles were retrofitted with the 50-mm gun, and by early 1942 the 37-mm version had almost disappeared from front-line service.

Bigger, heavier

The next model was the **PzKpfw III Ausf L**, which had greater armour, pushing its weight up to just over 22

A Panzer III engaged in streetfighting in the USSR in 1941. By this time, the type was completely outclassed by Soviet AFVs such as the T-34 and KV-1.

tonnes. This was almost 50 per cent more than the weight of the original prototype. The **PzKpfw III Ausf M** and **PzKpfw III Ausf N** fielded the 75-mm (3.0-in) L/24 gun which had been

installed in the PzKpfw IV; a total of 64 rounds was carried for this gun. Production of the PzKpfw III ceased in August 1943, though its chassis formed the basis for several assault guns.

Panzerkampfwagen IV
Medium tank

This late-war Panzer IV has added side armour around the turret and sides to protect against anti-tank weapons.

The **Panzerkampfwagen IV** had the distinction of remaining in production throughout World War II, and formed the backbone of German armoured divisions. In 1934 the Army Weapons Department drew up a requirement for a vehicle under the cover name of a 'medium tractor', which was to equip the fourth tank company of each German tank battalion. Rheinmetall-Borsig, MAN and Krupp built prototypes designated VK 2001(Rh), VK 2002(MAN) and VK 2001(K) respectively. Krupp eventually took over total responsibility for the vehicle, which was also known as the **Bataillons Führerwagen** (battalion commander's vehicle). This entered production at the

Krupp-Grusonwerke plant at Magdeburg as the **PzKpfW IV Ausf A**, or **SdKfz 161**.

Upgradable

When the Panzer IV was designed, the relatively light vehicles of the time were not capable of carrying large high velocity guns. In its original form, the Panzer IV was designed to provide support for these lighter tanks. It was armed with a short L/24 howitzer of 75-mm (3-in) calibre – i.e. the length of the barrel was 24 times the calibre.

The Panzer IV had one co-axial

7.92-mm (0.3-in) machine gun in the turret and another in the hull. The driver sat front left, with the radio operator/ hull machine-gunner on his right. The commander sat in the rear centre of the turret, with the gunner on the left of the

howitzer breech and the loader on the right. The rear-mounted engine was coupled to a manual transmission with six forward and one reverse gears. Turret traverse was powered through 360°, though manual controls were provided for emergency

SPECIFICATION	
PzKpfw IV Ausf H	TRM 12-cylinder petrol engine
Crew: 5	developing 300 hp (224 kW)
Weight: 25000 kg (55,115 lb)	**Performance:** maximum road speed
Dimensions: overall length (including	38 km/h (24 mph); maximum road
armament) 7.02 m (23 ft); hull	**Range:** 200 km (125 miles)
length 5.89 m (19 ft 4 in); width	**Fording:** 1.0 m (3 ft 3 in); gradient
3.29 m (10 ft 9½ in); height 2.68 m	60 per cent
(8 ft 9½ in)	**Vertical obstacle:** 0.6 m (2 ft);
Powerplant: one Maybach HL 120	**Trench:** 2.20 m (7 ft 3 in)

use. The normal ammunition load was 122 rounds of 75-mm and 3,000 rounds of machine gun ammunition. Maximum armour thickness was 20-mm on the turret and 14.5-mm on the hull.

Production totals

None of the early variants were built in large numbers: the 35 'A' models were followed by 42 'B' models, 134 'C' models and 229 'D' types. By 1938 the 'E' type had been authorised. Weight increased from 17 to 21 tons as a larger, 320 hp engine was installed and additional armour fitted. After the fall of France the design was changed again, the 'F' type finishing over a ton heavier with wider tracks to reduce ground pressure.

Throughout the PzKpfw IV's long production life, the basic chassis remained little changed, but as the anti-tank threat increased, so more armour and

Mid-war Panzer IVs operate on the Eastern Front in mid-1943. These have been up-gunned with a long high-velocity 75-mm weapon, but lack the extra armour added later.

new weapons were fitted. Other early tanks had to be phased out, as they were incapable of being upgraded, but the Panzer IV was big enough for improvements.

Late-war Panzer IVs were much more powerfully armed and protected than early versions. The **PzKpfw IV Ausf F2** had a maximum hull armour of 60 mm (2.4 in), with

50 mm (2 in) on the turret. Main armament comprised a long barrelled 75-mm (3 in) KwK L/43 gun fitted with a muzzle brake. This could fire HEAT, smoke, armour-piercing and high explosive rounds. The **PzKpfw Ausf H** had an even longer L/48 gun, which was at least as good as the 76.2-mm guns on Soviet T-34s. The final production model was the

PzKpfw IV Ausf J, which appeared in March 1944. Total production of the PzKpfw IV amounted to approximately 9,000 vehicles.

The chassis of the PzKpfw IV was used for a wide variety of specialized vehicles. These included tank destroyers, self-propelled anti-aircraft guns, self-propelled artillery and armoured bridgelayers.

Panzerkampfwagen V Panther

Medium tank

In 1941 the most powerful tank in service with the German army was the PzKpfw IV. This was rarely a match for the new Soviet T–34 tank which appeared in small numbers on the Eastern Front in that year. Work on a successor to the PzKpfw IV had started as far back as 1937, but progress had been slow because of changing needs. In 1941 Henschel and Porsche had each built proto-types of new tanks in the 30/35-tonne class, designated the VK 3001(H) and VK 3001(P) respectively. These were not placed in production, and further development led to the Tiger (VK 4501).

New armament

Late in 1941 a requirement was issued for a new tank with a

The Panther in its late-war form. Skirts have been added to offer some protection to the wheels, and spare track has been used as auxiliary armour. The tank is covered in Zimeritt paste, an anti-magnetic covering protecting against magnetic mines.

long barrelled 75-mm (2.95-in) gun, well-sloped armour for maximum protection within the weight limit of the vehicle, and larger wheels for improved mobility. To meet this requirement Daimler-Benz submitted the VK 3002 (D13) while MAN submitted the VK

3002 (MAN). The former design was a virtual copy of the T-34, but the MAN design was accepted. The first prototypes of the new tank, the **Panzerkampfwagen V Panther** – given the military designation **Sdfkz 171** – were completed in September 1942. The first pro-

duction models left the MAN factory just two months later. At the same time Daimler-Benz started tooling up for production of the Panther, and in 1943 Henschel and Niedersachsen were also brought into the programme together with hundreds of sub-contractors.

It was planned to produce 600 Panthers per month, but Allied bombing meant that the maximum production ever achieved was about 330 vehicles per month. The Panther was rushed into production without proper trials, and numerous faults soon became apparent. Indeed, in the type's early days, more Panthers were lost to mechanical failure than to enemy action. As a result, no matter how much theoretical fighting power it had, crew confidence in the vehicle rapidly dwindled.

The vehicle first saw action on the Eastern Front in July 1943 during the Kursk battles, and from then on it was used on all fronts. Once the mechanical problems had been overcome confidence in the tank soon built up again, and many consider the Panther to be the best all-round German tank of World War II. In the immediate post-war period the French army was equipped with Panthers until more modern tanks were available.

Panther variants

First production models were the **PzKpfw V Ausf A** which were really pre-production vehicles; the **PzKpfw V Ausf B** and **PzKpfw V Ausf C** were never placed in production. Later models were the **PzKpfw V Ausf D**, followed for some reason by another **PzKpfw V Ausf A**. This variant was widely used in Normandy. The final version of the Panther was the **PzKpfw V Ausf G**. Variants of the Panther included the **Jagdpanther** tank destroyer, the **Befehlspanzer Panther** command vehicle, the **Beobachtungspanzer Panther** armoured observation post, and an armoured recovery vehicle. Some were even disguised to resemble the M 10 tank destroyer during the Battle of the Bulge.

Panthers were heavily committed to Normandy, where they were a formidable threat to Allied armour units.

Main armament was a long barrelled 75-mm (2.95-in) gun for which 79 rounds of ammunition were carried. Mounted co-axial with the main armament was a 7.92-mm (0.31-in) MG 34

Grossdeutschland troops advance behind a Panther on the Eastern Front in August 1944. The Panther had the measure of most Soviet tanks.

machine-gun, while a similar weapon was mounted in the hull front and another on the turret roof for anti-aircraft defence. The major problem with the Panzer was that it was expensive and difficult to build. As a result, it would be vastly outnumbered by its opponents. Some 4,800 Panthers were built, as compared to tens of thousands of M4 Shermans and T-34s.

SPECIFICATION	
PzKpfwV Panther Ausf A **Crew:** 4 **Weight:** 45500 kg (100,310 lb) **Dimensions:** overall length (including armament) 8.86 m (29 ft ¾ in); hull length 6.88 m (22 ft 7 in); width 3.43 m (11 ft 3 in); height 3.10 m (10 ft 2 in) **Powerplant:** one Maybach HL 230 P	30 12-cylinder diesel engine developing 700 hp (522 kW) **Performance:** maximum road speed 46 km/h (29 mph); maximum road range 177 km (110 miles) **Fording:** 1.70 m (5 ft 7 in) **Gradient:** 60 per cent **Vertical obstacle:** 0.91 m (3 ft); **Trench:** 1.91 m (6 ft 3 in)

Panzerkampfwagen VI Tiger

Heavy tank

As far back as 1938, the German army had realised that the **PzKpfw IV** tank then being designed would have to be replaced by a more capable vehicle some time in the future. Several companies built prototypes, but none was placed in production. In 1941 an order was placed with Henschel for a 36-ton tank, the VK 3601. The specification called for a maximum speed of 40 km/h (25 mph), good armour protection and a powerful gun.

Bigger designs

A prototype of this tank was built, but further work was stopped as an order was placed in May 1941 for a 45-ton tank called the **VK 4501**. This was to be armed with a modified version of the dreaded 8.8-cm (3.4-in) Flak/anti-tank gun, which had by then become the scourge of European armies. It was required that the prototype be ready for testing on Hitler's next birthday, 20 April 1942. As time was short, Henschel incorporated ideas from the VK 3601 and another abortive project, the VK 3001(H).

The end product was the **VK 4501(H)**, the letter suffix standing for Henschel. Porsche also went ahead with its own design and built the **VK 4501(P)** to meet the same requirement. Both prototypes were completed in time to be demonstrated on Hitler's

This late-war Panzer VI has added side armour around the turret and sides to provide protection against anti-tank weapons.

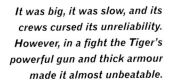

birthday, and the Henschel design was selected for production in August 1942 under the designation **PzKpfw VI Tiger Ausf E, or (SdKfz 181).**

Porsche Tiger

In case trials proved the VK 4501(H) a failure, a batch of 90 VK 4501(P) tanks was ordered. These were subsequently completed as tank destroyers under the designation **Panzerjäger Tiger (P) Ferdinand (SdKfz 184)** – the vehicle was named after its designer, Dr Ferdinand Porsche.

Tiger flaws

For its time, the Tiger was an outstanding design with a powerful gun and good armour, but it was complicated and difficult to produce. One major drawback was its overlapping wheel suspension which became clogged with mud and stones. On the Eastern Front this could be disastrous as during winter nights the mud froze and by the morning the tank had been immobilized, often at the exact time the Soviets would attack. When the vehicle travelled on roads, a 51.5-cm (20.3-in) wide track was fitted. For combat and travel across country a 71.5-cm (28.1-in) wide track was used; this gave a lower ground pressure and so improved traction.

Deadly '88'

The main armament of the Tiger comprised an 8.8-cm (3.46-in) KwK 36 gun, with a 7.92-mm (0.31-in) MG 34 machine-gun coaxial with the main armament, and a similar weapon ball-mounted in the hull front on the right. The tank could carry 84 rounds for the

It was big, it was slow, and its crews cursed its unreliability. However, in a fight the Tiger's powerful gun and thick armour made it almost unbeatable.

main gun and 5,850 rounds for the machine guns. The Tiger was first encountered in Tunisia by the British army and from then on appeared on all of the German fronts. The Tiger was in production from August 1942 to August 1944, a total of 1,350 vehicles being built. There were three main variants. Most production was of the basic gun tank, but a number of **Befehlspanzer Tiger** or Tiger command tanks were built. These had their main armament removed to make more room in the turret for extra communications gear. The Befehlspanzer could also act as a recovery vehicle, being fitted with a winch.

Assault Tiger

The third variant was the heavily-armoured **Sturmtiger**. This had a new superstructure fitted with a huge 38-cm (14.96-in) Type 61 rocket launcher with limited traverse; only 10 were built.

Tigers of the heavy Panzer company of the Das Reich Panzer Regiment were heavily involved in the Kharkov counter-offensive of March 1943.

SPECIFICATION	
PzKpfw VI Tiger Ausf E	P 45 12-cylinder petrol engine
Crew: 5	developing 522 kW (700 hp)
Weight: 55000 kg (121,250 lb)	**Performance:** maximum road speed
Dimensions: length (including	38 km/h (24 mph); maximum road
armament) 8.24 m (27 ft); length	range 100 km (62 miles)
(hull) 6.20 m (20 ft 4 in); width	**Fording:** 1.2 m (3 ft 11 in)
3.73 m (12 ft 3 in); height 2.86 m	**Gradient:** 60 per cent; maximum
(9 ft 3¼ in)	**Vertical obstacle:** 0.79 m (2 ft 7 in);
Powerplant: one Maybach HL 230	**Trench:** 1.8 m (5 ft 11 in)

The Tiger's massive armour and powerful gun made it a very difficult target for the Allied tanks to destroy.

PzKpfw VI Tiger
Heavy Tank

When it first appeared in combat at the end of 1942, the massive Tiger was the most powerful tank in the world. Slow, ponderous and none too reliable, it nevertheless dominated the battlefield. Allied tanks could not match its thick armour and powerful 88-mm gun, and no rivals would appear until the very end of the war.

Tiger PzKpfw VI Ausf E

Cutaway key
1 88-mm KwK 36 L/56 gun
2 7.92-mm (0.31-in) MG 34, co-axial machine-gun fired by gunner's foot
3 7.92-mm (0.31-in) MG 34 machine-gun
4 7.92-mm (0.31-in) MG 34 machine-gun ammunition
5 Smoke generator discharge
6 Escape hatch
7 Commander's seat
8 Commander's traverse handwheel
9 Pistol port
10 Traverse gearbox
11 Commander's shield
12 Gunner's traverse handwheel
13 Gunner's elevating handwheel
14 Gunner's seat
15 MG firing pedal
16 Binocular telescope
17 Feifel air-cleaning system
18 Maybach HL 210 P 45 V-12 water-cooled inline petrol engine

19 Gu G5 radio set
20 88-mm ammunition bins
21 Hydraulic traverse foot control
22 Hydraulic traverse unit
23 Disc-brake drum
24 Steering unit
25 Steering wheel
26 Gearbox
27 Driver's seat
28 Handbrake
29 Accelerator
30 Footbrake
31 Clutch
32 Shock absorber
33 Torsion bar suspension
34 Overlapping bogie-wheels
35 Commander's cupola
36 Fan drive clutch lever
37 Air-intake valve control
38 Petrol primer
39 Petrol tap
40 MG ammunition storage

Suspension

Ride comfort in the Tiger was surprisingly good – the interleaving road wheels helped to spread the massive weight evenly, and the torsion bar suspension gave a smooth ride over rough terrain. However, if an inner road wheel was damaged by a mine, field repairs were a major problem. In winter in the East, mud freezing between the wheels overnight could immobilise the tank.

Tracks

The Tiger needed a track with a width of 72 cm (28½ in) to spread the load. This was too wide for conventional railway flat cars, and so for transport the outer road wheels had to be removed and a narrower 52-cm (20½ in) track fitted. It took considerable effort to refit the outer wheels and wide tracks for combat.

Tigers of the 2nd SS Panzer Division 'Das Reich' move through a Russian wood. The SS heavy tank companies were among the first to be equipped with the Panzer VI. They were particularly effective in combat, combining the tank's fighting power and their own fanatical will to win into a lethal package.

Turret

German tanks introduced the three-man turret layout which became standard on all Main Battle Tanks for four decades after the war. The tank commander sat above and to the left of the gun. He controlled all aspects of the tank, from selecting targets and controlling the gun through map reading and giving instructions to the driver. The gunner sat in front of the commander, while the loader stood to the right of the turret. His main task was to ensure that the gun was kept loaded and ready to fire.

Powerplant

One of the Tiger's main weaknesses was its engine, which required continuous maintenance. The first 250 Tigers were powered by 12-cylinder Maybach HL 210 P 45 engines delivering 485 kW (650 hp), which was not enough for a 55-tonne tank. All tanks manufactured after May 1943 were fitted with the modified 12-cylinder Maybach HL 230 P 45 engine, with power increased to 522 kW (700 hp), but even with the extra power the big panzer was still under powered. The sound of the Tiger engine starting was distinctive even at a distance – it was a sound which the tank's Allied opponents came to fear and respect.

SPECIFICATION	
Panzerkampfwagen VI Tiger I **Manufacturer:** Henschel **Type:** Heavy Tank **Crew:** 5	(13 ft 1 in) **Gradient:** 70° **Vertical obstacle:** 0.80 m (2 ft 7 in) **Trench:** 2.50 m (8 ft 2½ in)
Dimensions **Length (hull):** 6.20 m (20 ft 4 in) **Length (gun forwards):** 8.24 m (27 ft) **Width:** 3.73 m (12 ft 3 in) **Height:** 2.86 m (9 ft 3¼ in) **Track width (travelling):** 0.52 m (20¼ in) **Track width (combat):** 0.72 m (28¼ in)	**Armament** **Main armament:** 1 x 88-mm KwK 36 L/56 rifled cannon **Normal effective range:** 2000 m (6,562 ft) **Maximum range:** 4500 m (14,764 ft) **Muzzle velocity:** 773 m (2,536 ft) per second **Turret traverse:** hydraulic with manual back-up **Traverse rate:** 6° per second **Elevation:** +17°/-6.5°
Combat weight **Early models:** 55000 kg (121,250 lb) **Late models:** 57000 kg (125,661 lb)	**Ammunition** Armour-piercing or High-explosive
Powerplant **Early:** Maybach HL 210 P 45 12-cylinder 485-kW (650-hp) petrol engine **Late:** Maybach HL 230 P 45 12-cylinder 522-kW (700-hp) petrol engine **Transmission:** Hydraulic pre-selector, 8 forward and 4 reverse gears **Steering:** powered hydraulic **Suspension:** Transverse torsion bar	**Secondary armament** **Early:** 2 x 7.92-mm (0.31-in) MG 34 machine-guns **Late:** 3 x 7.92-mm (0.31-in) MG 34/42 machine-guns
Fuel capacity 534 litres (117 Imp gal)	**Ammunition load** 92 rounds of 88-mm; 5,100 rounds of 7.92 mm (0.31 in) (34 x 150-round belts)
Performance **Maximum road speed:** 45.40 km/h (28 mph) **Maximum cross country speed:** 20 km/h (12.5 mph) **Maximum road range:** 195 km (120 miles) **Maximum cross country range:** 110 km (68 miles) **Fording depth without preparation:** 1.60 m (5 ft 3 in) **Fording depth with preparation:** 4 m	**Max armour penetration** 171 mm at 100 m (328 ft); 156 mm at 500 m (1,640 ft); 138 mm at 1000 m (3,281 ft); 123 mm at 1500 m (4,921 ft); 110 mm at 2000 m (6,562 ft)
	Armour thickness **Gun mantlet:** 110 mm **Front hull:** 100 mm **Side and rear hull and turret:** 80 mm **Top/bottom:** 25 mm

Above: Tigers move across the steppe before the Battle of Kursk in 1943, kicking up dust as their turrets nose around looking for Russian tanks.

Below: The crew of a battle-scarred Tiger rests in a pause between the fierce fighting on the Eastern Front. Tigers saw combat in all theatres, becoming a feared opponent to all Allied tank crews.

Armour

The Tiger's great strength was in the protection it offered its crew, and the immense striking power of its gun. The thick, slab-sided armour lacked the good ballistic shape found on contemporary designs like the Panther and the Soviet T-34, but with a thickness which ranged from 25 to 100 mm on the hull and 80 to 100 mm on the turret of the Ausf H, (increased to 110 mm on the Ausf E) it hardly needed to.

Inside the Tiger

Pre-war tanks tended to have two-man turrets. The multiple tasks thus inflicted on the commander and gunner had a bad effect on efficiency. The Tiger, however, followed the standard German practice of having a three-man turret. This enabled each man to concentrate on his most important task. The commander directed the tank and found targets, the gunner located the targets in his sight and engaged them, the loader made sure that the correct ammunition – armour-piercing or high-explosive – was loaded for each specific target. At its best, a well-drilled Tiger crew made the Tiger an even more formidable fighting machine.

Seated in the right front of the Tiger's hull, the radio operator also manned the machine-gun mounted in the front plate of the hull. This was primarily used as an anti-infantry weapon.

Turret and hull front

The gunner's side of the Tiger turret was pierced by two holes for the TZF 9b gun sight. Later tanks were fitted with a shield which could be dropped over the sights, while late-model Tigers had a single sensor hole for the improved TZF 9c gun sight. Other obvious differences between early and late-model Tigers included the two Bosch headlights fitted to the first production tanks as seen here. Late production vehicles carried a single headlight mounted in the centre.

Eighty-Eight

Main armament of the Tiger was the 88-mm KwK 36 L/56, adapted from the anti-tank version of the superb 'eighty-eight' Flak gun. It was the most powerful anti-tank gun then in use by any army, capable of penetrating 123 mm (4.8 in) of armour at 1500 m (4,921 ft). The Tiger's turret housed the gun, which was offset to the right and was mounted on a 1.85-m (6-ft) diameter turret ring. The gun was fired electrically by a switch on the gunner's manual traverse wheel. The Tiger carried 92 rounds of main gun ammunition in stowage bins, lockers in the turret floor and anywhere else that was handy. Armour-piercing rounds usually accounted for half of a Tiger's ammunition load. The other half usually comprised high-explosive rounds for use against enemy soft-skinned vehicles and infantry.

Machine-guns

Self-defence against infantry was provided by two MG 34 7.92-mm (0.31-in) machine-guns, one mounted co-axially with the main gun which was fired by the gunner, and one in a flexible mount in the front of the hull which was fired by the radio operator. Later a third machine-gun was added to the top of the turret for air defence.

Seated next to the radio operator in the left front of the hull, the driver was tasked with driving the heavy vehicle as smoothly as possible, and was often the oldest, most mature member of the crew.

Heat shields
Operational use showed that glowing exhausts could be seen from a long distance away at night. PzAbt 501 was the first unit to fit sheet metal shields around the exhaust stacks in the rear of the hull.

Cupola
Early Tiger cupolas – a mini-turret on the main turret just for the commander – had simple vision slits like this example: later versions had a rotating hatch and were fitted with periscopes with a greater field of view. Even with those improvements, however, visibility was limited and tank commanders preferred to travel standing in the turret hatch.

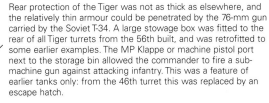

The Commander was the most important member of the crew, directing the vehicle in action and also serving as the primary means of locating targets. Seated at the left rear of the turret, the commander had a rotating cupola equipped with vision blocks, giving limited all-around vision even when the tank was fully 'buttoned up'.

Turret rear
Rear protection of the Tiger was not as thick as elsewhere, and the relatively thin armour could be penetrated by the 76-mm gun carried by the Soviet T-34. A large stowage box was fitted to the rear of all Tiger turrets from the 56th built, and was retrofitted to some earlier examples. The MP Klappe or machine pistol port next to the storage bin allowed the commander to fire a sub-machine gun against attacking infantry. This was a feature of earlier tanks only: from the 46th turret this was replaced by an escape hatch.

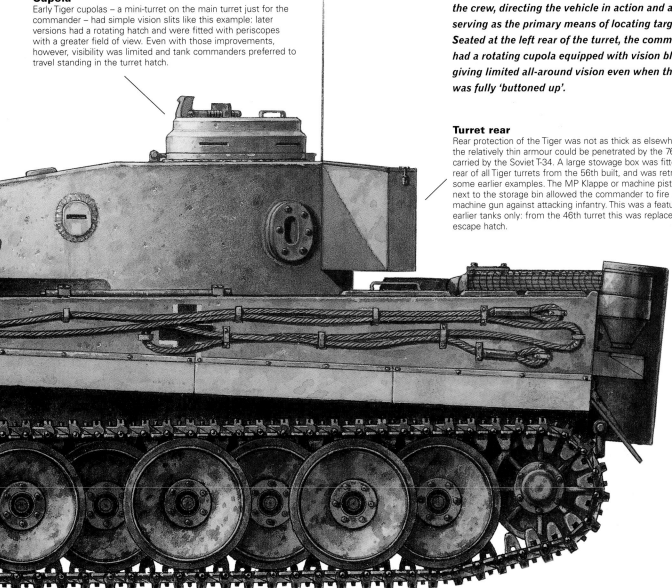

Panzerkampfwagen VI Tiger II 'King Tiger'

Heavy tank

One of the first 50 King Tigers, which were completed with the complex Porsche turret. Utilising thick, highly effective sloped armour and carrying a long-barrelled, high-velocity version of the superb 8.8-cm (3.4-in)tank gun, the Tiger II was safe from most Allied tanks at all but the closest of ranges.

No sooner was the Tiger in production than the decision was taken to develop an even more heavily armed and armoured version. The primary purpose of the new tank was to counter any heavy tank that the Soviets could introduce in the future. Once again Henschel and Porsche were asked to prepare designs. Porsche first designed a tank based on the earlier VK 4501 design, which was armed with a 15-cm (5.9-in) gun. This was rejected in favour of a new design with a higher-velocity version of the classic 8.8-cm (3.46-in) gun, to be fitted in a completely new turret. This was soon cancelled, as its electric transmission used too much copper, which at that time was in short supply. By this time the turrets were already in production.

'Super' Tiger

The **VK 4503(H)** Henschel design was completed in October 1943, somewhat later than anticipated as a decision was taken during the manufacturing process to incorporate components of the projected

Later King Tigers were completed with a simpler Henschel turret without the electric drive which made the Porsche turrets so expensive.

Panther II tank. It was selected for production, and manufacture of the **Panzerkampfwagen VI Tiger II Ausf B (SdKfz 182)** got under way at Kassel in December 1943. It was built alongside the Tiger, the first 50 production vehicles being completed with the Porsche turret.

All subsequent tanks had the Henschel turret, and a total of 485 vehicles was built.

The Tiger II first saw action on the Eastern Front in May 1944 and on the Western Front in Normandy in August of the same year. The Western Allies called the massive new tank the **Royal Tiger**, while the Germans called it the **Königstiger** or **King Tiger.**

Heavy and slow

In many respects the Tiger II was similar in layout to the Panther tank, and was powered by the same engine as later production Panthers. Since the King Tiger was a great deal heavier, it had a lower power-to-weight ratio, and was much slower and less mobile than the PzKpfw V.

The Tiger II had an all-welded hull, with a maximum thickness of 150-mm (5.9-in) in the front of the hull. The driver was seated at the front on the left, with the bow machine gunner/radio operator to his right.

The turret was also of welded construction, with a maximum thickness of 100 mm (3.9 in) at the front, and accommodated the commander and gunner on the left with the loader on the right. The engine was at the hull rear.

'Eighty-Eight'

Main armament comprised a long-barrelled version of the famous 'Eighty-Eight'. This could fire armour-piercing ammunition at a much higher muzzle velocity than the equivalent round fired by the Tiger I.

As was standard on German tanks, a 7.92-mm (0.31-in) MG 34 was mounted co-axially with the main armament, with another mounted in the hull front. Eighty-four rounds of 8.8-cm and 5,850 rounds of 7.92-mm (0.31-in) ammunition were carried.

While its heavy armour was almost impenetrable by the guns carried by most Allied tanks, the Tiger II was not completely reliable. It was extremely large, and its bulk made it difficult to move about the battlefield and it was also very difficult to conceal.

Many were abandoned or destroyed by their crews when they ran out of fuel, since by the end of the war no additional supplies were to hand.

Sole Variant

The Tiger II chassis was also used as the basis for the **Jagdtiger B** tank hunter, which was armed with a 128-mm (5.04-in) gun in a new fixed and thickly-armoured super-structure with limited traverse. By the end of the War, only 48 of these incredibly powerful tank destroyers had been completed.

King Tigers could dominate the battlefield, but they were heavy and lacked mobility. Many used in the Ardennes battles were abandoned for lack of petrol.

SPECIFICATION	
PzKpfw VI Tiger II Ausf B	P 30 12-cylinder petrol engine developing 522 kW (700 hp)
Crew: 5	
Weight: 69700 kg (153,660 lb)	**Performance:** maximum road speed 38 km/h (24 mph); maximum road range 110 km (68 miles)
Dimensions: length (including armament) 10.26 m (33 ft 8 in); length (hull) 7.26 m (23 ft 9¾ in); width 3.75 m (12 ft 3½ in); height 3.09 m (10 ft 1½in)	**Fording:** 1.6 m (5 ft 3 in)
	Gradient: 60 per cent
	Vertical obstacle: 0. 85 m (2 ft 10 in)
Powerplant: one Maybach HL 230	**Trench:** 2.50 m (8 ft 2 in)

Vickers Light Tanks

The Vickers Light Tanks had their origins in a series of tankettes produced by Carden-Loyd during the 1920s. One of these, the **Carden-Loyd Mk VIII**, acted as the prototype for the **Vickers Light Tank Mk I**. Only a few of these innovative vehicles were made, but they provided a great deal of insight into what would be required for later models. The Light Tank Mk I had a two-man crew and a small turret for a single 7.7-mm (0.303-in) machine-gun.

The Mk I led via the **Light Tank Mk IA** (better armour) to the **Light Tank Mk II** (improved turret and modified suspension) which appeared in 1930, and this formed the basis for later versions up to the **Light Tank Mk VI**. All these light tanks used a simple hull with riveted armour, which was 10 to 15 mm (0.39 to 0.59 in) thick. From the **Light Tank Mk V** onwards the turret was enlarged to take two men, making a three-man crew in all, and the same mark also saw the introduction of a 12.7-mm (0.5-in) machine-gun alongside the original 0.303-in weapon. Of course there were other changes: the **Light Tank Mk IV** was the first to use the armour as supporting plates for the chassis, for instance. The series peaked with the **Light Tank Mk VI**, which was agile and fast, and the **Light Tank Mk VIc,** which had a 15-mm (0.59-in) machine-gun in the turret. All manner of changes to items such as engine cooling and vision devices were also introduced on this late mark, and even the machine-gun was changed to the new 7.92-mm (0.312-in) Besa machine-gun.

The tanks were widely used throughout the 1930s and the early war years. Many of the

After suffering heavy losses in France when mistakenly used in close support of the infantry, the Mk VI soldiered on in the Middle East and North Africa.

Mounting a 0.59-in (12.7-mm) and later a 15-mm machine-gun with a 0.312-in (7.92-mm) machine-gun, the Vickers Light Tank was adequate only for armoured scouting.

early marks were used in India and for imperial policing duties, in which they proved ideal, but in action during the early campaigns of World War II they soon revealed themselves as being virtually useless. Their main drawback was their thin armour, which could be penetrated even by small-calibre armour-piercing projectiles, and their lack of a weapon heavier than a machine-gun. In France in 1940 they were often used incorrectly as combat tanks, but in North Africa they remained useful in the desert war.

SPECIFICATION	
Light Tank Mk V	
Crew: 3	**Armament:** (early models) one 12.7-mm (0.5-in) machine-gun, supplemented by one 7.7-mm (0.303-in) machine-gun
Weight: 4,877 kg (10,572 lb)	
Powerplant: one Meadows ESTL 6-cylinder petrol engine developing 66 kW (88 bhp)	**Performance:** maximum speed 51.5 km/h (32 mph); maximum range 201 km (215 miles)
Dimensions: length 3.96 m (13 ft); width 2.08 m (6 ft 10 in); height 2.24 m (7 ft 6 in)	**Gradient:** 60 per cent
	Vertical obstacle: 0.61 m (2 ft)
	Trench: 1.52 m (5 ft)

Light Tank Mk VII Tetrarch

The **Tetrarch** light tank started its life as Vickers' private-venture **Light Tank Mk VII**. The first prototype started its trials in 1938, and these trials demonstrated that the new design, known at that time as the **Purdah**, lacked the attributes that would make it an outstanding weapon. Development of this **A17** continued, though, and the type differed from the earlier light tanks by having four large road wheels on each side. Centrally mounted, the two-man turret was large enough to mount a 2-pdr (40-mm/1.57-in) gun and a 7.92-mm (0.312-in) co-axial machine-gun. The Tetrarch was finally put into production without enthusiasm. By 1941 light tanks were seen as an operational liability so the few that were completed became surplus to all but limited requirements.

However, the fortunes of the Tetrarch changed with the

establishment of the airborne forces, and the lightweight vehicle was accepted as the army's first airborne tank. A new glider, the General Aircraft Hamilcar, was produced as the airborne carrier for the Tetrarch, but it was not until April 1944 that the first trial landings were made. For the tank's new role the turret was revised with a 76.2-mm (3-in) infantry support howitzer to create the **Tetrarch ICS**.

The Tetrarch went into action in the Normandy landings of 6 June 1944 during the second airborne wave. Most of them landed near the River Orne, where their combat life was short. They were next used during the Rhine crossings on 24 March 1945, but only a few were used as their numbers had been supplemented by the American M22 Locust. That marked the limits of the type's airborne operational career, but some were retained

Carried in a Hamilcar glider, the Tetrarch was used by the British airborne forces for the Normandy landings. Outclassed by German tanks, this Tetrarch has a Littlejohn adapter fitted to its 2-pdr gun, increasing muzzle velocity and armour penetration.

SPECIFICATION	
Tetrarch	**Armament:** one 2-pdr (40-mm/1.58in) gun; one 76.2-mm (3-in) howitzer; one 7.92-mm (0.312-in) light machine-gun
Crew: 3	
Weight: 7620 kg (16,800 lb)	
Powerplant: one Meadows 12-cylinder petrol engine delivering 123 kW (165 bhp)	
	Performance: maximum road speed 64 km/h (40 mph); range 224 km (140 miles)
Dimensions: length overall 4.31 m (14 ft 1½ in); length of hull 4.12 m (13 ft 6 in); width 2.31 m (7 ft 7 in); height 2.12 m (6 ft 11½ in)	**Fording:** 0.91 m (3 ft)
	Gradient: 60 per cent
	Vertical obstacle: 0.51 in (1 ft 8 in)
	Trench: 1.53 m (5 ft)

after the war until their Hamilcar gliders were withdrawn from service.

The Tetrarch was used for a few developments in the war. One was the **Light Tank Mk VIII Harry Hopkins** with thicker armour (6–38 mm/ 0.25–1.5 in, as opposed to 4–15 mm/0.15–0.6 in) and another being the **Alecto** light self-propelled 94-mm (3.7-in) howitzer.

Originally a Vickers private venture, the Tetrarch was put into production despite its lack of adequate armour and armament.

Early cruiser tanks

During the early 1930s the British decided to replace the dual-role medium tank with separate single-role cruiser and infantry tanks optimised for the mobile warfare and infantry support roles respectively. The first cruiser tank was the **A9**, otherwise **Cruiser Tank Mk I** designed by Vickers in 1934 as a

simpler and cheaper derivative of the A6 (Medium Tank Mk III). The type entered small-scale production in 1937 as a 12701-kg (28,000-lb) vehicle with a crew of six, armour between 4 and 16 mm (0.16 and 0.63 in) thick, and the armament of one 2-pdr (40-mm/1.57-in) gun and one 7.7-mm (0.303-in) machine-

gun in the power-traversed main turret, and one 7.7-mm (0.303-in) machine-gun in each of two other turrets.

Reduced weaponry

The replacement of the previously standard 3-pdr (47-mm/1.85-in) gun by a 2-pdr weapon was a sensible move,

despite the reduction in main armament calibre thereby involved, as the smaller calibre weapon had a higher muzzle velocity and thus fired its solid projectile with somewhat greater armour penetrating capability than the earlier weapon. Production of the A9 amounted to only 125 vehicles, and the type remained in service up to 1941 in France and North Africa.

At much the same time Vickers undertook design of the 13971-kg (30,800-lb) **A10** as an infantry tank based on the A9 but with the armour thickness increased to a maximum of 30 mm (1.18 in). The A9's subsidiary turrets were not retained in the new type, and in 1940 the Vickers co-axial machine-gun was replaced by a 7.92-mm (0.312-in) Besa, a weapon of the same type sometimes being added in the nose in place of some of the ammunition stowage. By the time the A10 was ready for production it had been reclassified as the **Heavy Cruiser Tank Mk II**. There was also a **Mk IIA** with detail improvements and, as with the A9, an infantry close-support version with a 94-mm (3.7-in) howitzer.

New initiative

There now came a turning point in British tank design with the 1936 decision to develop new cruiser tanks on the basis of the suspension system devised in the US by J. Walter Christie. This led to the **A13** designed by Nuffield. The 14429-kg (31,810-lb) prototype was completed in 1937 and immediately displayed quite

excellent performance as a result of the Christie suspension combined with a high power-to-weight ratio. Only moderate armour was provided, to thicknesses of between 6 and 14 mm (0.24 and 0.55 in) as the tank was intended to rely on performance and agility as the main platforms of its protection, and the armament was also modest. This armament comprised a turret-mounted 2-pdr gun and a 0.303-in Vickers co-axial machine-gun. The reduction in the number of machine-guns had the very useful advantage of allowing a reduction in crew number to a mere four men. Deliveries of this **Cruiser Tank Mk III** began in December 1938 and the production programme was completed in 1939. The Cruiser Tank Mk III was used in France during 1940 and in North Africa during 1941, and proved a failure because of its noticeably inadequate armour.

It was this failing that the **Cruiser Tank Mk IV (A13 Mk II)** was designed to overcome through the thickening of the armour, increasing the protective basis to 20 or 30 mm (0.79 or 1.18 in) in more important areas. Even so, the Mk IV was decidedly under-armoured by contemporary standards. The **Mk IVA** introduced a 0.312-in

The two types of tank produced by pre-war theory: on the left, the fast but very vulnerable Mk IV Cruiser; on the right, the thickly armoured Matilda, which could only make about 13 km/h (8 mph) cross-country.

Besa co-axial machine-gun in place of the original Vickers weapon, and also featured a combined gearchange and steering gearbox. As with the Mk III, range was too limited for effective independent operations, and the angular design of the box-like hull and V-sided turret provided many shot traps.

The **A14** had Horstmann suspension and the **A16** was designed around Christie suspension, but both were unsuccessful and they were cancelled in 1939, the A16 even before the prototype had been completed.

Faster model

The next British cruiser tank was the **A13 Mk III** or **Cruiser Tank Mk V Covenanter**. Intended to provide higher speed for enhanced battlefield capability, the A13 was based on the A13 Mk II with a purpose-designed engine, the thickness of the armour was increased to between 7 and 40 mm (0.28 and 1.575 in), and the turret was a low-silhouette unit carrying the same basic armament as its predecessor. The tank did show distinct potential, and total production amounted to 1,771 units.

Below: Cruiser Mk IVs were armed with the 2-pdr gun, which had weak armour penetration and, worse, no high-explosive round to tackle enemy anti-tank guns and strongpoints.

Below: Cruisers were designed to perform the cavalry roles of reconnaissance and pursuit. These are Mk I A9s, the first Cruiser tanks; they were lightly protected and armed with the feeble 2-pdr. Many were left in France after Dunkirk; survivors served in North Africa until 1941.

SPECIFICATION	
Cruiser Tank Mk V Covenanter	height 2.23 m (7 ft 4 in)
Crew: 4	**Armament:** one 40-mm (1.57-in)
Weight: 18289 kg (40,320 lb)	main gun and one 7.92-mm (0.312-in) Besa co-axial machine-gun
Powerplant: one Meadows DAV petrol engine delivering 224 kW (300 hp)	**Performance:** maximum road speed 50 km/h (31 mph); maximum road range 161 km (100 miles)
Dimensions: length overall 5.79 m (19 ft); width 2.62 m (8 ft 7 in);	

Cruiser Tank Mk VI Crusader

The Crusader III was the first British tank to be armed with an effective gun, the 6-pdr. Its other great strongpoint was its suspension, which was so tough that its theoretical maximum speed could often be exceeded.

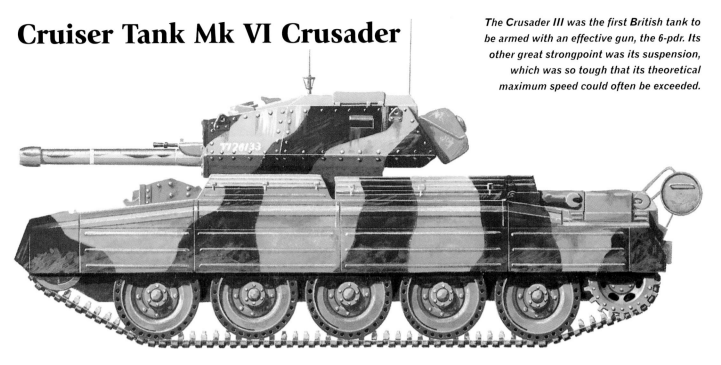

The **Cruiser Tank Mk VI**, or **Crusader**, was a Nuffield design and used the Nuffield Liberty Mk III engine and a Nuffield gearbox. In overall terms the Crusader resembled the Covenanter with differences such as the use of five rather than four road wheels on each side. Known as the **A15**, the prototype had the unusual feature of two auxiliary forward turrets, each with a 7.92-mm (0.31-in) machine-gun, one in front of the driver's hood and the other for a gunner seated in the front hull. The driver's gun and turret were eliminated after early trials, which also highlighted inadequate engine cooling and unreliable gearchange arrangements. These and other problems took a long time to remedy and, indeed, many were still present when the Crusader was withdrawn from service.

Early production

The first production model was the **Crusader I**, which had a 2-pdr (40-mm/1.58-in) gun and armour on a 40-mm (1.58-in) basis. When the Crusader I entered service in 1941 it was already inadequate for combat. The new 6-pdr (57-mm/2.24-in) gun was still in short supply, so only the armour was improved, its thickness being increased to

a 50-mm (1.97-in) basis to produce the **Crusader II**. It was not until the **Crusader III** that the 6-pdr gun was fitted. This turned out to be the main 'combat' version of the Crusader during the North African campaigns before it was replaced by the Sherman. In action the Crusader was fast, but its armour proved to be too thin, and the tanks armed with the 2-pdr gun were no match for their German counterparts. Their reliability problems did little for the Crusaders' chances of survival under desert conditions, but gradually improvements were effected. The **Crusader IICS** was fitted with a 3-in (76.2-mm) howitzer.

Other uses

Once they were no longer in use as combat tanks, Crusaders were used for a variety of special purposes. Some were converted as anti-aircraft tanks mounting either a single 40-mm Bofors gun (**Crusader III AA I**) or twin or triple 20-mm cannon (**Crusader III AA II**). There was a **Crusader ARV** armoured recovery vehicle version without a turret but with an 'A' frame jib, and another turretless version as the **Crusader Dozer** with a dozer blade for combat engineering. Many Crusaders were fitted with an open box

superstructure for use as **Crusader Gun Tractor** high-speed artillery tractors, and these were widely used in Europe in 1944–45 to tow 17-pdr (76.2-mm/3-in) anti-tank guns. More were used for trials ranging from engine tests via mine warfare devices to wading trials that led to 'Duplex Drive' tanks.

The Crusader was one of the classic British tanks of World War II, even taking into account its lack of combat efficiency. Despite its low and aggressive silhouette it was outclassed as a battle tank on many occasions, but saw the war out in several special-purpose variants.

Visible on the upper decking of this Crusader's hull is the small auxiliary turret, armed with a Besa 7.92-mm (0.31-in) machine-gun, that was often removed in the field to provide greater stowage volume in the hull.

SPECIFICATION	
Crusader III	two 7.92-mm (0.31-in) Besa
Crew: 3	machine-guns
Weight: 20067 kg (44,240 lb)	**Performance:** maximum road speed
Powerplant: one Nuffield Liberty	43.4 km/h (27 mph); maximum
Mk III petrol engine developing	cross-country speed 24 km/h (15
254 kW (340 bhp)	mph); range with extra fuel tank
Dimensions: length 5.99 m (19 ft 8	204 km (127 miles)
in); width 2.64 m (8 ft 8 in); height	**Fording:** 0.99 m (3 ft 3 in)
2.24 m (7 ft 4 in)	**Vertical obstacle:** 0.69 m (2 ft 3 in)
Armament: one 6-pdr (57-mm/ 2.24-	**Trench:** 2.59 m (8 ft 6 in)
in) main gun with 65 rds, one or	

Cruiser Tank Mk VIII Cromwell

In the UK the somewhat spurious distinction between the 'cruiser' and the 'infantry' tank persisted almost to the end of World War II, despite the fact that the unfortunate experiences of the early 'cruiser' designs had highlighted the drawbacks of producing a lightly armed and armoured main battle tank, and continued even when a replacement for the Crusader was being sought. The need for thicker armour protection, a larger-calibre gun and considerably more power was finally realised and in 1941, therefore, a new specification was issued. This requirement was answered by two **A27** variants, the A27L with the Liberty engine (this was to become the Centaur) and the **A27M** with the Rolls-Royce Meteor engine that became the **Cruiser Tank Mk VIII Cromwell**.

Ready for conflict

The first Cromwell tanks were completed in January 1943. The first three marks were the **Cromwell I** with one main gun and two Besa machine-guns, the

A Cromwell roars through a village in Normandy, in August 1944. Initially mounting a 6-pdr gun, by D-Day the type was armed with a 75-mm (2.95-in) gun which gave it a reasonable chance against German armour.

Cromwell II with wider tracks and only one machine-gun, and the **Cromwell III**, all of them with the 6-pdr (47-mm/ 2.24-in) gun as their main armament. By 1943 it had been decided that something heavier would be required, and for once things moved quickly, allowing the first 75-mm (2.95-in) **Cromwell IV** tanks to be issued in October 1943. Thereafter the 75-mm gun remained the Cromwell's main

gun until the **Cromwell VIII** tank, which had a 94-mm (3.7-in) gun for the close support role.

Perhaps the main value of the Cromwell to British armoured regiments during 1943 was as a training tank, for at last the troops had a tank that was something of a match for its German counterparts. The Cromwell had thicker armour (8–76 mm/ 0.34–3 in) than any early 'cruiser' tank, and the 75-mm gun, which shared many components with the smaller 6-pdr, at last provided British 'tankies' with an effective weapon. But by the time it was ready for active service, the Cromwell was in the process of being replaced by an American medium tank, the M4 Sherman, for purposes of standardisation and logistic safety. However, the Cromwell did see useful service. Many of the tanks were used by the 7th Armoured Division in the campaigns that followed from the Normandy landings. Here

the excellent performance provided by the Meteor engine made the Cromwell a well-liked vehicle; it was fast and reliable, and the gun proved easy to lay and fire.

Further development

The Cromwell was but a stepping stone to the later Comet tank, which emerged as perhaps the best all-round British tank of World War II. But the Cromwell was an important vehicle. Some were used as mobile artillery observation posts (**Cromwell OP**) with the main gun removed and extra radios installed. Others had their turrets replaced by the various equipment required for the Cromwell to be used as the **Cromwell ARV** armoured recovery vehicle. The Cromwell was also used as the basis for a heavily armoured assault tank that became known as the **A33**, which was ready by May 1944 but never went into production.

Although the majority of British tank units were equipped with the Sherman, the Cromwell was a successful design, doing much to restore the imbalance of quality between British and German armour.

SPECIFICATION	
Cromwell IV	**Armament:** one 75-mm (2.95-in)
Crew: 5	main gun with 64 rds, two 7.92-mm
Weight: 27942 kg (61,600 lb)	(0.31-in) Besa machine-guns
Powerplant: one Rolls-Royce	**Performance:** maximum speed
Meteor V-12 petrol engine	61 km/h (38 mph); road range
developing 425 kW (570 bhp)	278 km (173 miles)
Dimensions: length overall 6.42 m	**Fording:** 1.22 m (4 ft)
(21 ft ¾ in); width 3.05 m (10 ft);	**Vertical obstacle:** 0.91 m (3 ft)
height 2.51 m (8 ft 3 in)	**Trench:** 2.29 m (7 ft 6 in)

Cruiser Tank Mk VIII Centaur

The **Cruiser Tank Mk VIII Centaur** was a contemporary of the Cromwell and derived from the same specification. Whereas the Cromwell was powered by the Rolls-Royce Meteor engine, the Centaur was a Leyland Motors project and was fitted with the Liberty engine. In many other respects the Centaur and the Cromwell were identical and some Centaurs were fitted with Meteor engines at a later stage and then redesignated as Cromwell tanks.

Design problems

Leyland had already produced the **Cruiser Tank Mk VII Cavalier**, which had proved to be a generally unsuccessful design, as a result of poor performance, mechanical unreliability and short engine life. Leyland reused some features of the Cavalier in the Centaur, but unfortunately carried over some of the earlier design's problems, for the Liberty engine lacked the power to provide the Centaur with the same performance as the Cromwell, and was also far less reliable.

Development

The **Centaur I** was produced with the 6-pdr (57-mm/ 2.24-in) gun that was standard for British tanks of the period, and the first examples were ready in June 1942, after which they were used for training purposes. Upgunned with a 75-mm (2.95-in) weapon, the **Centaur III** was produced only in small numbers with armour varying in thickness from 20-76 mm (0.8-3 in). The **Centaur IV** was the main combat version, specially produced with a 94-mm (3.7-in) close-support howitzer for use by the Royal Marines Armoured Support Group during the D-Day landings in Normandy on 6 June 1944. Eighty of the vehicles were issued, and were intended for use only in the initial stages of the amphibious assault. In fact, most of them performed so well on the beaches and the area immediately inland that many were retained for some weeks for the slow and dangerous combat in the bocage country.

Thereafter the Centaur was withdrawn for conversion to other forms. The simplest conversion was as an artillery observation post (**Centaur OP**), while others simply had their turrets removed to become **Centaur Kangaroo** armoured personnel carriers. The usual armoured recovery conversion was the **Centaur ARV**, and the **Centaur Dozer** turretless version carried a dozer blade for the combat engineer role. Two Centaur conversions that did mount guns were the **Centaur III/IV AA I** and **Centaur III/IV AA II** with the same 20-mm anti-aircraft turret as the earlier Crusader AA, but revised with 20-mm Polsten cannon in place of the earlier Oerlikon cannon.

SPECIFICATION	
Centaur III	or two 7.92-mm (0.31-in) Besa
Crew: 5	machine-guns
Weight: 28849 kg (63,600 lb)	**Performance:** maximum road speed
Powerplant: one Nuffield Liberty Mk V V-12 petrol engine developing 295 kW (395 bhp)	43.4 km/h (27 mph); maximum cross-country speed about 25.7 km/h (16 mph); range 265 km (165 miles)
Dimensions: length 6.35 m (20 ft 10 in); width 2.9 m (9 ft 6 in); height 2.49 m (8 ft 2 in)	**Fording:** 0.91 m (3 ft) **Vertical obstacle:** 0.91 m (3 ft)
Armament: (Mk IV) one 94-mm (3.7-in) howitzer with 51 rds, one	**Trench:** 2.29 m (7 ft 6 in)

Cruiser Tank Challenger

The **Cruiser Tank Challenger** was the result of a 1941 request for a tank carrying a gun capable of tackling even the heaviest German tanks, and it was decided to mount the 17-pdr (76.2-mm.3-in) gun on a development of the A27 Cromwell/Centaur chassis. The new gun required a much larger chassis to accommodate the weights involved, and a larger turret ring to cope with the greater recoil forces. The Cromwell chassis was lengthened and another road wheel was added on each side, which permitted the turret ring section to be widened to make feasible the installation of a larger ring. This formed the basis of the **A30**, which was later named Challenger.

Early trials

The first pilot model was ready in March 1942 and performed badly during trials. The extra weight of the high turret was not balanced by the lengthened suspension and the mounting of the heavy gun made the traverse of the turret so slow that the original mechanism had

The Challenger was a stretched Cromwell armed with a 17-pdr gun, armour being reduced to keep weight down. The Sherman Firefly was adopted in its stead.

to be redesigned. The large size of the fixed ammunition meant that only a restricted number of rounds could be carried. Perhaps the biggest problem was that weight considerations demanded a reduction in the armour protection to between 20–102 mm (0.8–4 in).

The first examples were not ready until March 1944, and by then it was too late for the Challenger to have the extensive waterproofing required for the Normandy landings. Another blow was that the M4 Sherman had been adapted to take the 17-pdr, and as the Firefly this conversion assumed many of the responsibilities intended for the Challenger.

Some Challenger tanks did see service from late 1944, but as soon as the war ended most were withdrawn.

SPECIFICATION	
Challenger	3-in) main gun with 42 rds, one co-
Crew: 5	axial 7.62-mm (0.3-in) Browning
Weight: 33022 kg (72,800 lb)	machine-gun
Powerplant: one Rolls-Royce Meteor V-12 petrol engine developing 447 kW (600 bhp)	**Performance:** maximum speed 51.5 km/h (32 mph); range 193 km (120 miles)
Dimensions: length overall 8.15 m (26 ft 8¾ in); width 2.9 m (9 ft 6½ in); height 2.78 m (9 ft 1¼ in)	**Fording:** 1.37 m (4 ft 6 in) after preparation **Vertical obstacle:** 0.91 m (3 ft)
Armament: one 17-pdr (76.2-mm/	**Trench:** 2.59 m (8 ft 6 in)

Cruiser tanks

In action

The cruiser tank was planned as the successor to the medium tank, and as such was deigned to be lighter and cheaper than the infantry tank. The combination of reduced weight and a moderately powerful engine resulted in a tank that was faster and more agile than the infantry tank, and the task of the cruiser tank was therefore determined as longer-range operations to outflank the enemy or exploit any breaches in his line. The fallacy of the concept was brutally exposed in France and North Africa during 1940–42, when the cruisers suffered heavy losses to no good effect.

Above: Fast, but possessing neither the armour nor the firepower of German tanks, the lack of basic balance in the design of the Cruiser Tank Mk VI Crusader had been revealed long before Operation Crusader in 1941. However, the troops in the North African desert had to fight with whatever was available – in this case a Cruiser Mk IV, a type that was fast but also poorly armed and indifferently protected.

In desert operations, natural defensive features are often hard to find. On such occasions, tank units of World War II would cluster into an easily defended laager for the night. The scene, typical of the period of Operation Crusader, includes both of the cruiser tank types that were the mainstays of the 8th Army at time time, namely the Mk IV (left) and Mk VI Crusader (right).

Above: A Cruiser Tank Mk I leads two Cruiser Mk IVs on exercise in August 1940. The Mk IV was an archetypal cruiser tank, thin-skinned and undergunned but capable of high speed. The Christie suspension of the British cruiser tanks proved a great success, allowing high speeds to be reached and maintained in the desert.

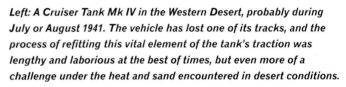

SPECIFICATION

A34 Cruiser Tank Comet
Crew: 5 (comprising commander, gunner, loader/radio operator, driver and hull gunner)
Type: cruiser tank

Dimensions

Length: 7.66 m (25 ft 1½ in) with the gun forward; **Width:** (overall) 3.07 m (10 ft 1 in) and over tracks 3 m (9 ft 10¼ in); **Height:** overall 2.67 m (8 ft 9¼ in)

Combat weight

33225 kg (73,248 lb)

Powerplant

one Rolls-Royce Meteor Mk 3 water-cooled V-12 petrol engine rated at 447.5 kW (600 bhp) at 2,550 rpm
Transmission: Borg & Beck hydraulically operated dry twin-plate clutch and Merritt-Brown Type Z.5 gearbox with five forward and one reverse speeds
Suspension: Christie type with five twin road wheels on each side (hydraulic shock absorbers on the front two and rear two pairs)

Fuel capacity

standard 527.3 litres (116 Imp gal)

Performance

Maximum road speed: 51.5 km/h (32 mph)

Maximum road range: 198 km (123 miles)
Fording: 1.12 m (3 ft 8 in)
Vertical obstacle: 0.91 m (3 ft)
Trench: 2.44 m (8 ft)

Armament

Main armament: one QF 77-mm (3.03-in) main gun with 61 rounds of APCBC and HE ammunition
Secondary armament: two 7.92-mm (0.312-in) Besa machine-guns (one co-axial and one in the bow) with 5,175 rounds of ammunition, one 7.7-mm (0.303-in) Bren machine gun stowed in the rear turret locker with 600 rounds, one 50.8-mm (2-in) bomb thrower on the turret roof with 20 bombs
Smoke dischargers: two on each side of the hull rear

Armour

Welded steel hull: front 76 mm (3 in) vertical; glacis 32 mm (1.26 in) at 32°; nose 63 mm (2.48 in) at 20°; sides and rear 32 mm (1.26 in) vertical; lower sides 29 mm (1.14 in) vertical outer and 14 mm (0.55 in) vertical inner; top 25 mm (0.98 in) horizontal and belly 14 mm (0.55 in) horizontal
Cast/welded steel turret: front and mantlet 101 mm (3.98 in) vertical; sides 63 mm (2.48 in) vertical; rear 57 mm (2.24 in) vertical; top 25 mm (0.98 in) horizontal

Left: A Cruiser Tank Mk IV in the Western Desert, probably during July or August 1941. The vehicle has lost one of its tracks, and the process of refitting this vital element of the tank's traction was lengthy and laborious at the best of times, but even more of a challenge under the heat and sand encountered in desert conditions.

Below: The penalty imposed on a tank crew for its own tactical limitations or the failings of the tank's design is very often lethal. With little cover, the British tanks used in the desert were often hit and then caught fire.

Infantry Tanks Mks I and II Matilda

A requirement for a British Army 'Infantry' tank was first made in 1934 and the immediate result was the **A11 Infantry Tank Mk I**, later nicknamed **Matilda I**. This was a very simple and small tank with a two-man crew but with armour heavy enough to defeat any contemporary anti-tank gun. The small turret mounted a single 12.7- or 7.7-mm (0.5- or 0.303-in) Vickers machine-gun, and the engine was a commercial Ford V-8 unit. An order for 140 was issued in April 1937, but when the type was tried in combat in France in 1940 it revealed shortcomings: it was too slow and underarmed for any form of armoured warfare, and the small numbers that remained after Dunkirk were used only for training.

Improvements

The Matilda I was intended only as an interim type before the **A12 Infantry Tank Mk II** became available. This project began in 1936 and the first examples were completed in 1938. The Mk II, known later as **Matilda II**, was a much larger vehicle than the Matilda I with a four-man crew, a turret mounting a 2-pdr (40-mm/1.575-in) gun, and cast armour (varying in

thickness from 20 to 78 mm/0.8 to 3.1 in) capable of defeating all known anti-tank projectiles. The Matilda II was slow as it was intended for the direct support of infantry units, a role in which speed was not essential. Overall it was a well-proportioned tank and proved to be far more reliable than many of its contemporaries. Despite the light gun it was found to be a good vehicle in combat.

The main combat period for the **Matilda** (the term Matilda II was dropped when the smaller Matilda I was withdrawn in 1940) was the early North African campaign, where the type's armour proved to be effective against all Italian and German anti-tank guns with the exception of the German '88'. The Matilda was one of the armoured mainstays of the British forces until El Alamein, after which its place was taken by better armed and faster designs. However, the importance of the Matilda did not diminish, for it then embarked on a career as a special-purpose tank.

Mine clearance

One of the most important of these special purposes was as a flail tank for mine-clearing.

The Matilda was never fast and was notably undergunned by the standards even of 1940, but had the priceless benefit of offering its crew excellent protection and sound mechanical reliability.

SPECIFICATION	
Matilda II	2.51 m (8 ft 3 in)
Crew: 4	**Performance:** maximum speed
Weight: 26926 kg (59,360 lb)	24 km/h (15 mph); maximum
Powerplant: two Leyland 6-cylinder	cross-country speed 12.9 km/h (8
petrol engines each developing 71	mph); road range 257 km (160
kW (95 bhp) or two AEC diesels	miles)
each developing 65 kW (87 bhp)	**Vertical obstacle:** 0.61 m (2 ft)
Dimensions: length 5.61 m (18 ft 5	**Fording:** 0.91 m (3 ft)
in); width 2.59 m (8 ft 6 in); height	**Trench:** 2.13 m (7 ft)

Starting with the **Matilda Baron** and then the **Matilda Scorpion**, it was used extensively for this role, but Matildas were also used to push AMRA mine-clearing rollers. Another variant was the **Matilda CDL (Canal Defence**

Light), which used a special turret with a powerful light source to create 'artificial moon-light'. Matildas were also fitted with dozer blades as the **Matilda Dozer** for combat engineering, and many were fitted with

The Matilda was the only British tank with enough armour to withstand the efforts of German tank guns in the early years of World War II. After a brief moment of glory at Arras in 1940, it won its real reputation in North Africa with the British 8th Army.

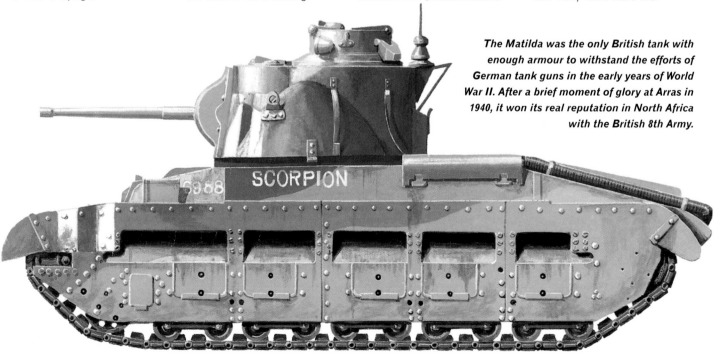

various flame-throwing devices as the **Matilda Frog**. There were many other special and demolition devices used with the Matilda, not all of them under British auspices for the Matilda also became an important Australian tank. In fact Matilda gun tanks were used extensively by the Australian army in New Guinea and elsewhere until the war's end in 1945, and the Australians devised several flamethrowing variants. The Germans also used several captured Matildas to mount anti-tank weapons.

It is doubtful if a complete listing of all the many Matilda variants will ever be made, for numerous 'field modifications' and other unrecorded changes were made to the basic design. However, the Matilda accommodated them all with comparative ease, and many soldiers looked back on this tank

with affection for, despite its slow speed and light armament, it was reliable and steady, and above all it had good armour.

Seen in North Africa as a 'non-runner', this Matilda has its engine covers lifted and its turret traversed right round to the left. The item protruding from the left (in fact the rear) of the turret is the radio antenna in its lowered position.

Infantry Tank Mk III Valentine

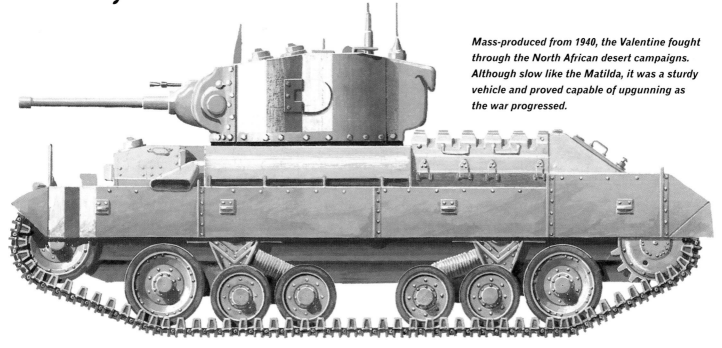

Mass-produced from 1940, the Valentine fought through the North African desert campaigns. Although slow like the Matilda, it was a sturdy vehicle and proved capable of upgunning as the war progressed.

In 1938 Vickers was invited to join in the production programme for the new Matilda II tank, but as the company already had a production line established to produce a heavy 'Cruiser' tank known as the A10, it was invited to produce a new infantry tank based upon the A10. Vickers duly made its

plans and its A10-derived infantry tank was ordered into production in July 1939. Up to that date the army planners had some doubts as to the effectiveness of the Vickers submission, largely as a result of its retention of a small two-man turret which would limit possible armament increases,

but by mid-1939 war was imminent and tanks were urgently required.

Heavy armour

The new Vickers tank, soon known as the **Infantry Tank Mk III Valentine**, drew heavily on experience gained with the A10, but was much more heavily pro-

tected with 8- to 65-mm (0.32- to 2.55-in) armour. As many of the A10's troubles had already been overcome, these solutions were built into the Valentine, which proved to be a relatively trouble-free vehicle. Mass production began rapidly, and the first **Valentine I** examples were ready in late 1940. By 1941 the

Valentine was an established type, and many were used as cruiser tanks to overcome deficiencies.

The Valentine was one of the most important British tanks, but the main reason for this was quantity rather than quality. By early 1944, when production ceased, 8,275 had been made and during one period in 1943 one quarter of all British tank production was of the Valentine series. Valentines were also produced in Canada and by several British concerns other than Vickers.

Multiple variants

There were numerous variants on the Valentine. Gun tanks ran to 11 different marks with the main armament increasing from a 2-pdr (**Valentine I-VII**) via the 6-pdr (**Valentine VIII-X**) to a 75-mm (2.95-in) gun (**Valentine XI**), and there was even a self-propelled gun version mounting a 25-pdr field gun and known as the Bishop. Special-purpose Valentines ran the whole gamut from mobile bridges (**Valentine Bridgelayer**) to **Canal Defence Lights** (**Valentine CDL**) and from observation posts (**Valentine OP**) to mine-clearing devices (**Valentine Scorpion** and **Valentine AMRA**). The number of these variants was legion, many of them 'one-offs' for trials or experimental purposes. Typical were the **Duplex Drive Valentine** vehicles used to test the DD system. Actually these tanks were so successful that the Valentine was at one time the standard DD tank. There were also **Valentine Flame-thrower** tanks, and one attempt was made to produce a special tank-killer with a 6-pdr anti-tank gun behind a shield. This came to nothing but the Valentine chassis was later used

An early model Valentine provides the focus of attention as Malta celebrates King George VI's birthday. The Valentine was one of the more successful pre-war designs, and saw service in many theatres.

as the basis for the Archer, an open-topped vehicle with a 17-pdr gun pointing to the rear. This was used in Europe from 1944 onwards.

The basic Valentine tank was extensively modified throughout its operational career, but it was always reliable and sturdy. The Valentine was one of the British Army's most important tanks at one point. It was used by many Allied armies such as that of New Zealand, and many saw action in Burma. The bulk of the Canadian output was sent to the USSR, where the type appears to have given good service. The Valentine did have its drawbacks, but overall its main contribution was that it was available in quantity at a time when it was most needed, and not many British tank designs could claim the same.

The Valentine was never a great tank, but it was better than many British AFVs of its period and it was also available in useful numbers at a time when it was most needed for service in the North African desert.

SPECIFICATION	
Valentine III/IV	height 2.27 m (7 ft 5½ in)
Crew: 3	**Performance:** maximum speed
Weight: 17690 kg (39,000 lb)	24 km/h (15 mph); maximum
Powerplant: one AEC diesel	cross-country speed 12.9 km/h (8
developing 98 kW (131 bhp) in	mph); road range 145 km (90
Mk III or GMC diesel developing	miles)
103 kW (138 bhp) in Mk IV	**Vertical obstacle:** 0.84 m (2 ft 9 in)
Dimensions: length 5.41 m (17 ft 9	**Fording:** 0.914 m (3 ft)
in); width 2.63 m (8 ft 7½ in);	**Trench:** 2.29 m (7 ft 6 in)

Infantry Tank Mk IV Churchill

The Churchill was essentially designed for a return to trench warfare conditions. As such it was a classic infantry tank, slow but heavily armoured. Introduced in 1943, its chassis was subsequently used for a host of specialist vehicles.

Built in a bewildering array of marks and variants, the **Churchill** was one of the most important British tanks of World War II. In production terms the Churchill came second to the Valentine, but in the scope of applications and variants it came second to none.

The Churchill was born in a specification known as the **A20** which was issued in September 1939 and envisaged a return to the trench fighting of World War I. Hence the A20 tank was a virtual update of the old World War I British 'lozenge' tanks, but experiences with the A20 prototype soon showed that a lighter model would be required. Vauxhall Motors then took over a revised specification known as the **A22** and designed the **Infantry Tank Mk IV**, later named Churchill.

Rushed production

Vauxhall had to work from scratch and yet came up with a well armoured tank with large overall tracks that gave the design an appearance not unlike that of World War I tanks. Unfortunately the early Churchill marks were so rushed into production that about the first 1,000 examples had to be extensively modified before they could even be issued to the troops. But they were produced at a period when invasion seemed imminent and

even unreliable tanks were regarded as better than none. Later marks had these early troubles eliminated.

The armament of the Churchill followed the usual path from 2-pdr (**Churchill I-II**), via 6-pdr (**Churchill III-IV**) eventually to a 75-mm (2.95-in) gun in the **Churchill IV (NA 75)** and **Churchill VI-VII**. There were also **Churchill CS** (close support) variants with 76.2-mm (3-in) and eventually 95-mm (actually 94-mm/3.7-in) howitzers in the **Churchill V** and **Churchill VIII**. The Churchill I also had a hull-mounted 76.2-mm (3-in) howitzer. The turrets also changed from being cast items to being riveted or composite structures, and such refinements as track covers and engine cooling improvements were added successively. In all, there were 11 Churchill marks, the last three of them 'reworks' of earlier marks in order to update early models to Mk VII standard with the 75-mm (2.95-in) gun.

Operational use

In action the heavy armour of the Churchill (16–102 mm/ 0.6–4 in for Mks I–VI and 25–152 mm/1–6 in for Mks VI–VIII) was a major asset despite the fact that the tank's first operational use was in the 1942 Dieppe landings, when many of the Churchills proved

unable even to reach the beach, let alone cross it. However, in Tunisia the type proved it could climb mountains and provide excellent support for armoured as well as infantry units,

though it was often too slow to exploit local advantages.

It was as a special purpose tank that the Churchill excelled. Many of these special variants became established as

SPECIFICATION	
Churchill VII	Besa machine-guns
Crew: 5	**Performance:** maximum speed
Weight: 40642 kg (89,600 lb)	20 km/h (12.5 mph); maximum
Powerplant: one 261-kW (350-bhp)	cross-country speed about
Bedford twin-six petrol engine	12.8 km/h (8 mph); range 145 km
Dimensions: length 7.44 m (24 ft 5	(90 miles)
in); width 2.44 m (8 ft); height 3.45	**Fording:** 1.02 m (3 ft 4 in)
m (11 ft 4 in)	**Vertical obstacle:** 0.76 m (2 ft 6 in)
Armament: one 75-mm (2.95-in)	**Trench:** 3.05 m (10 ft)
gun, and two 7.92-mm (0.31-in)	

Churchills (left-hand column) move up to the front line in Normandy past a column of US M4 Sherman medium tanks early in August 1944. Note how the crews have attached large sections of track to the front hull and the turret side as additional armour.

important vehicles in their own right, and included in this number (some of which are discussed elsewhere) were the **Churchill AVRE** (**Armoured Vehicle Royal Engineers**), **Churchill Crocodile** flamethrower tank and various **Churchill Bridgelayer** and **Churchill ARK** vehicles. There were also the numerous Churchill mine-warfare variants from the **Churchill Plough** variants to the **Churchill Snake** with Bangalore torpedoes.

The Churchill lent itself to modification, and was able to carry a wide assortment of odd equipments such as wall demolition charges (**Churchill Light Carrot**, **Churchill Onion** and **Churchill Goat**) mine-clearing wheels (**Churchill AVRE/CIRD**), carpet-laying devices for use on boggy ground (**Churchill AVRE Carpetlayer**), armoured recovery vehicles (**Churchill ARV**), and so on. The Churchill

Right: The Churchill VII introduced an all-cast turret armed with a 75-mm gun, a high-velocity weapon characterised by a single-baffle muzzle brake to help reduce the recoil forces transmitted to the turret.

Below right: Cumbersome and slow on its own tracks, the Churchill was generally moved to its operational area on some type of special transporter whenever possible. This also reduced the wear on the tanks' engine, transmission, suspension and tracks.

may have looked archaic compared to its contemporaries, but it gave excellent service and many were still around in the mid 1950s in various guises, the last Churchill AVRE not being retired until 1965.

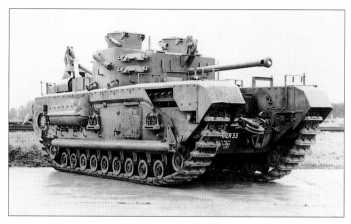

Cruiser Tank Sentinel AC Australian tank

In 1939 Australia's armed forces had virtually no modern tanks and the country had almost none of the heavy engineering capacity to produce them. The Australian government realised that it was unlikely to receive large amounts of heavy war materiel from overseas, and thus planned to produce its

own. The army issued a specification for the **AC1** (**Australian Cruiser 1**) with a 2-pdr (40-mm/1.57-in) gun and two 7.7-mm (0.303-in) machine-guns, and using as many components of the American M3 tank as possible. The powerplant was to be three Cadillac car engines joined

together, and extensive use was to be made of cast armour. A more advanced second model, the **AC2**, was mooted but not produced. The AC1 had armour ranging from 25 to 65 mm (1 to 2.55 in) in thickness.

Sound design

The first AC1 tanks were ready by January 1942, and were soon named **Sentinel**. The whole project up to the hardware stage had taken only 22 months. Only a few AC1 tanks were produced as by 1942 it had been realised that the 2-pdr gun was too small, and that the hurried design still had teething problems that had to be

modified out of it. Overall, however, the Sentinel turned out to be a remarkably sound design capable of considerable stretch and modification.

This was just as well, for the **Sentinel AC3** mounted a 25-pdr (87.6-mm/3.45-in) gun to overcome the shortcomings of the 2-pdr. The 25-pdr was chosen as it was already in local production as a field gun, but it was realised that this gun would have only limited effect against armour and the prototype of a **Sentinel AC4** with a 17-pdr (76.2-mm/3-in) anti-tank gun was built. This was during mid-1943, and by then there was no longer the chance that Japan might

In spite of the speed with which it was produced, the Sentinel AC1 was a remarkably innovative design featuring an all-cast hull and a heavy armament. This is the AC4, which mounted a 17-pdr gun.

SPECIFICATION	
Sentinel AC1	2.56 m (8 ft 4¾ in)
Crew: 5	**Armament:** one 2-pdr (40-mm/ 1.57-in) gun and two 0.303-in (7.7-mm) machine-guns
Weight: 28450 kg (62,720 lb)	
Powerplant: three Cadillac petrol engines combined to develop 246 kW (330 bhp)	
	Performance: maximum speed 48.2 km/h (30 mph); range 322 km (200 miles)
Dimensions: length 6.33 m (20 ft 9 in); width 2.77 m (9 ft 1 in); height	**Trench:** 2.44 m (8 ft)

invade Australia. M3 and M4 tanks were pouring off the US production lines in such numbers that there would be more than enough to meet demand. Thus Sentinel production came to an abrupt halt in July 1943 in order to allow the diversion of industrial potential to other priorities.

The Sentinel series was remarkable not only from the industrial side but also from the design viewpoint. The use of an all-cast hull was advanced, and the acceptance of heavy guns like the 25-pdr and the 17-pdr was also ahead of contemporary thought. Even so, the Sentinel tanks were used only for the training of Australian armoured units.

The outbreak of war found Australia with no modern tank force and little industrial infrastructure. The Sentinel AC1 was a home-grown tank developed in a very short time to provide part of the equipment needed to fight off the anticipated Japanese invasion.

Cruiser Tank Ram Canadian tank

When Canada entered World War II in 1939 it did not have any tank units, and the first Canadian tank training and familiarisation units had to be equipped with old World War I tanks from American sources. It was not long before the Canadian railway industry was asked by the UK if it could manufacture and supply Valentine infantry tanks, and this proved to be a major task. These Valentines were 'infantry' tanks, however, and the new Canadian tank units would need 'cruisers' for armoured combat. At that time there was little prospect of obtaining tanks from the UK, and the US was not involved in the war, so the only solution was tanks of Canadian design and manufacture.

Production decisions

Thought was first given to manufacture of the American M3 (then entering production for a British order) but, later known as the Grant/Lee, this had the drawback of a sponson-mounted main gun, whereas a turret-mounted gun was much more efficient. Thus the Canadians decided to combine the main mechanical, hull and transmission components of the M3 with a new turret mounting a 75-mm (2.95-in) gun. As there was no prospect of a 75-mm (2.95-in) gun at the time, the

readily available 2-pdr (40-mm/1.57-in) weapon was chosen for installation, with a larger-calibre gun to be introduced later: this was the 6-pdr (57-mm/2.24-in) weapon.

Building such a tank from scratch was a major achievement for Canada, and the prototype was rolled out in June 1941 as the **Cruiser Tank Ram Mk I**. This was a remarkably workmanlike design making much use of cast armour. It was not long before the initial 2-pdr gun was replaced by a 6-pdr in the **Ram Mk II**, and production got under way by the end of 1941. The secondary armament was two 7.62-mm (0.3-in) machine-guns (one co-axial and one hull-mounted). The thickness of the armour ranged from 25 to 89 mm (1 to 3.5 in).

Combat role

All the output went to the new Canadian armoured regiments, many of which were sent to the UK. However, the Ram was never to see action as a gun tank: by mid 1943 large numbers of M4 Shermans were pouring off US production lines and as this tank already had a 75-mm (2.95-in) gun it was decided to standardise on the M4 for all Canadian units. Thus

Canada had no armoured forces in 1939 but decided to build its own tank to equip the expanding Canadian army. The Ram tank utilised the chassis of the American M3, but mounted its main armament in the turret rather than in a sponson as on the original US vehicle.

the Ram was used only for training, and as they were withdrawn many had their turrets removed to produce the **Ram Kangaroo**, a simple yet efficient armoured personnel carrier widely used in the European campaign after June 1944. Some Rams had their guns removed and were used as artillery observation posts (**Ram Command/OP Tank**), while others were more extensively modified to become

armoured recovery vehicles. Some were used for various experimental and trial purposes, such as the mounting of a 94-mm (3.7-in) anti-aircraft gun on top of the hull.

The Ram's greatest contribution to World War II was ultimately as the **Sexton** self-propelled gun with the original tank being adapted to take a 25-pdr artillery piece in a simple open superstructure on top of the hull.

SPECIFICATION	
Ram Mk II **Crew:** 5 **Weight:** 29484 kg (65,000 lb) **Powerplant:** one 298-kW (400-bhp) Continental R-975 radial petrol engine **Dimensions:** length 5.79 m (19 ft); width 2.9 m (9 ft 6 in); height 2.67 m (8 ft 9 in)	**Armament:** one 6-pdr (57-mm/ 2.24-in) gun, and two 7.62-mm (0.3-in) machine-guns **Performance:** maximum speed 40.2 km/h (25 mph); range 232 km (144 miles) **Gradient:** 60 per cent **Vertical obstacle:** 0.61 m (2 ft) **Trench:** 2.26 m (7 ft 5 in)

Fiat L.6/40 Light tank

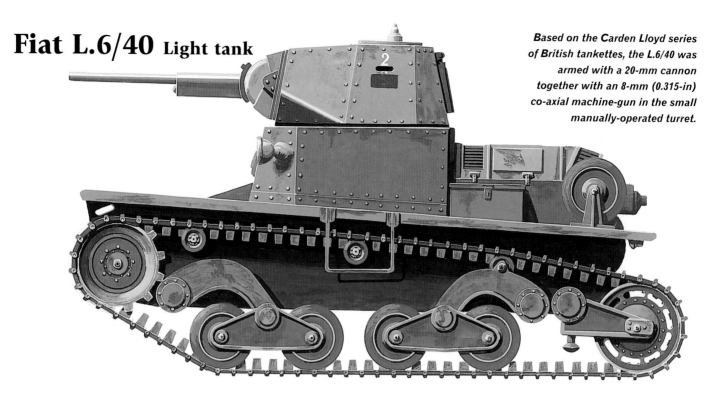

Based on the Carden Lloyd series of British tankettes, the L.6/40 was armed with a 20-mm cannon together with an 8-mm (0.315-in) co-axial machine-gun in the small manually-operated turret.

In the 1930s Fiat Ansaldo built an export tank based on the chassis of the L.3 tankette, itself a development of the British Carden Lloyd Mark VI tankette. The first prototype was armed with twin machine-guns in the turret and a 37-mm (1.46-in) gun in a sponson. This was followed by models with a turret-mounted 37-mm gun and a co-axial machine-gun, and another with twin turret-mounted 8-mm (0.315-in) machine-guns. The production version, designated **Carro Armato L.6/40**, was built from 1939 and armed with a 20-mm Breda Modello 35 cannon with an 8-mm Breda Modello 38 co-axial machine-

gun. Totals of 296 rounds of 20-mm and 1,560 rounds of 8-mm ammunition were carried. At the time of its introduction the L.6/40 was roughly equivalent to the German PzKpfw II, and was used by reconnaissance units and cavalry divisions. A total of 283 vehicles was built, and in addition to being used in Italy itself the type was also used in North Africa and on the Russian front. The L.6/40 continued in service with the militia in post-war Italy, finally being phased out in the early 1950s.

Construction

The hull of the L.6/40 was of

all-riveted construction varying in thickness from 6 mm (0.24 in) to 30 mm (1.26 in). The driver was seated at the front right, the turret was in the centre, and the engine at the rear. The turret was manually operated and could be traversed through 360°; its weapons could be elevated from -12° to +20°. The commander also acted as gunner and loader, and could enter the vehicle via the hatch in the turret roof or via a door in the right side of the hull. The suspension on each side consisted of two bogies each with two road wheels, with the drive sprocket at the front and idler at the rear; there were three track-return rollers.

There was also a flamethrower version of the L.6/40 in which the 20-mm cannon was replaced by a flamethrower for which 200 litres (44 Imp gal) of flame liquid were carried. The

command model had additional communications equipment and an open-topped turret.

Some of the L.6/40s were completed as Semovente L.40 da 47/32 self-propelled anti-tank guns (see tank destroyers entry), which were essentially the L.6/40 with the turret removed and a 47-mm (1.85-in) anti-tank gun mounted in the hull front to the left of the driver. This had an elevation from -12° to +20°, with a total traverse of 27°; 70 rounds of ammunition were carried. In addition to conversions from L.6/40 standard, about 300 vehicles were built as such, and the type saw service in Italy, North Africa and the USSR from 1941. A command version was also built on the same chassis and this had its armament replaced by an 8-mm Breda machine-gun, which was made to look like the larger-calibre gun to make detection of the vehicle more difficult.

A knocked-out L.6/40 light tank is inspected by Australians in the desert. In spite of being unsuitable for front-line service, the L.6/40 saw action in North Africa and the USSR as well as in Italy.

SPECIFICATION	
Carro Armato L.6/40	four-cylinder petrol engine
Crew: 2	developing 52 kW (70 hp)
Weight: 6800 kg (14,991 lb)	**Performance:** maximum road speed
Dimensions: length 3.78 m (12 ft 5 in); width 1.92 m (6 ft 4 in); height 2.03 m (6 ft 8 in)	42 km/h (26 mph); maximum range 200 km (124 miles)
Armament: one Modello 35 20-mm cannon, and one co-axial 8-mm (0.315-in) Modello 38 machine-gun	**Fording:** 0.8 m (2 ft 8 in)
	Gradient: 60 per cent
	Vertical obstacle: 0.7 m (2 ft 4 in)
Powerplant: one SPA 18D	**Trench:** 1.7 m (5 ft 7 in)

Fiat M.11/39 and M.13/40 Medium tanks

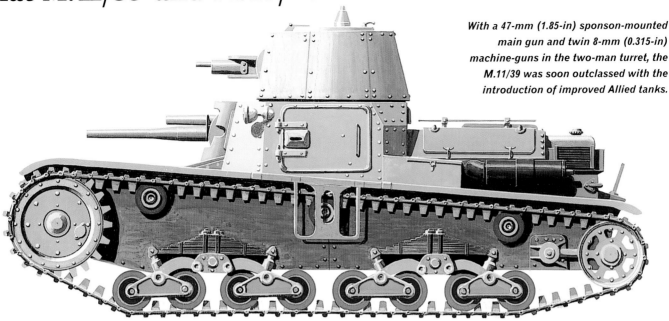

With a 47-mm (1.85-in) sponson-mounted main gun and twin 8-mm (0.315-in) machine-guns in the two-man turret, the M.11/39 was soon outclassed with the introduction of improved Allied tanks.

In 1937 the prototype of the **Carro Armato M.11/39** tank was built, with the suspension system of the L.3 tankette but with six road wheels on each side. In layout this was similar to the American M3 Lee tank, but with a 37-mm (1.46-in) rather than 75-mm (2.95-in) gun in the right sponson, driver on the left, and in the centre of the hull a one-man turret armed with twin 8-mm (0.315-in) machine-guns. Further development resulted in a model with eight road wheels and this basic chassis was used for all subsequent Italian medium tanks. Only 100 M.11/39s were built as the design was already considered obsolete, and in 1940 70 of these tanks were sent to North Africa, where many were captured or destroyed during the first battles with the British.

Further development resulted in the **M.13/40**, which had a similar chassis but a redesigned hull of riveted construction varying in thickness from 6 mm (0.24 in) to 42 mm (1.65 in). The driver was seated at the front of the hull on the left with the machine-gunner to his right; the latter operated the two 8-mm Modello 38 machine-guns as well as the radios. The two-man turret was in the centre of the hull, with the commander/

gunner on the right and the loader on the left, and with a two-piece hatch cover in the turret roof. Main armament comprised a 47-mm (1.85-in) L/32 gun with an elevation of +20° and a depression of -10°; turret traverse was 360°. An 8-mm Modello 38 machine-gun was mounted co-axial with the main armament, and a similar weapon was mounted on the turret roof for anti-aircraft defence. Totals of 104 rounds of 47-mm and 3,048 rounds of 8-mm ammunition were carried. The engine was at the rear of the hull, its power being transmitted to the gearbox at the front of the hull via a propeller shaft. Suspension on each side consisted of four double-wheel articulated bogies mounted on two assemblies each carried on semi-elliptic leaf springs, with the idler at the rear; there were three track-return rollers.

The M.13/40 was built by Ansaldo-Fossati at the rate of about 60 to 70 vehicles per month, a total of 779 being produced. The tank was widely used in North Africa by the Italian army, but was cramped, proved to be very unreliable in service and was prone to catching fire when hit by anti-tank projectiles.

Captured vehicles

Many such vehicles were captured by the British Army after being abandoned by their crews and subsequently issued to the British 6th Royal Tank Regiment (RTR) and the Australian 6th Cavalry Regiment early in 1941 when tanks were in short supply to the Allies.

The **Semovente Comando M.40** command vehicle was the M.13/40 tank with its turret removed and fitted with additional communications equipment for use in the command role. Further development of the M.13/40 resulted in the M.14/41 and the M.15/42.

M.13/40 tanks in the desert, 1941. These are of the Semovente Comando version, without turrets and with additional radio gear. Many were abandoned by the Italians and taken over by the British.

SPECIFICATION	
Carro Armato M.13/40	cylinder diesel engine developing 93 kW (125 hp)
Crew: 4	**Performance:** maximum road speed 32 km/h (20 mph); maximum range 200 km (125 miles)
Weight: 14000 kg (30,865 lb)	
Dimensions: length 4.92 m (16 ft 2 in); width 2.2 m (7 ft 3 in); height 2.38 m (7 ft 10 in)	**Fording:** 1 m (3 ft 3 in)
Armament: one 47-mm (1.85-in) L/32 main gun, and four 8-mm (0.315-in) Modello 38 machine-guns	**Gradient:** 70 per cent
	Vertical obstacle: 0.8 m (2 ft 8 in)
Powerplant: one SPA TM40 eight-	**Trench:** 2.1 m (6 ft 11 in)

Fiat M.15/42 Medium tank

The **Carro Armato M.14/41** was essentially the M.13/40 fitted with a more powerful diesel engine, which was equipped with air filters designed to cope with the harsh conditions of the desert. Production amounted to just over 1,100 of these vehicles, which had a similar specification to the M.13/40 except for an increase in speed to 33 km/h (20 mph) and in weight to 14.5 tonnes. Further development resulted in the **Carro Armato M.15/42**, which entered service in early 1943. A total of 82 of these were built, most being issued to the Ariete Division which took part in the Italian attempt to deny Rome to the Germans in September 1943. Some of these vehicles were captured by the Germans and then used against the Allies.

The M.15/42 was slightly longer than the M.14/41 and distinguishable from it by the lack of a crew access door in the left side of the hull. It was driven by a more powerful engine, which made it slightly faster, and had improved armour protection and other more minor modifications as a result of operator comments.

The hull of the M.15/42 was of all-riveted construction that varied in thickness from 14 mm (0.55 in) to 42 mm (1.65 in), with a maximum of 45 mm (1.77 in) on the turret front. The driver was seated at the front of the hull on the left, with the bow machine-gunner to his right, the latter operating the twin 8-mm 0.315-in) Breda Modello 38 machine-guns as well as the radios. The turret was in the centre of the hull and carried a 47-mm (1.85-in) L/40 gun with an elevation of +20° and a depression of -10°; turret

A squadron of M.14/41 tanks in Cyrenaica in 1942. More than 1,100 of these tanks, in effect tropicalised M.13/40s, were produced.

traverse, which was electric, was 360°. An 8-mm Modello 38 machine-gun was mounted co-axial with the main armament, and a similar weapon was mounted on the turret roof for anti-aircraft defence. Totals of 111 rounds of 47-mm and 2,640 rounds of 8-mm ammunition were carried. The suspension on each side consisted of four double-wheel articulated bogies mounted in two assemblies each carried on semi-elliptical springs, with the drive sprocket at the front and the idler at the rear; there were three track-return rollers. The engine was located at the rear and was coupled to a manual gearbox with eight forward and two reverse gears.

By the time the M.15/42 had been introduced into service it was already obsolete, and design of another tank had been under way for several years. In 1942 the first prototypes of the **Carro Armato P.40** heavy tank were built. This was a major advance on the earlier Italian tanks and used a similar type of suspension to the M.15/42. The layout was also similar with the driver at the front, turret in the centre and engine at the rear. Armour protection was much improved and the hull and turret sides sloped to give maximum possible protection within the weight limit of 26 tonnes. The P.40 was powered by a V-12 petrol engine that developed 420 hp (313 kW) to give it a maximum road speed of 40 km/h (25 mph). The main armament comprised a 75-mm (2.95-in) L/34 gun with an 8-mm Modello 38 co-axial machine-gun, and totals of 75 rounds of 75-mm and 600 rounds of machine-gun ammunition were carried. The P.40 was produced by Fiat in northern Italy, but none of these tanks entered service with the Italian army and most were subsequently taken over by the German army, which ensured continued production for itself. Some reports state that over 50 vehicles were built specifically for German use.

SPECIFICATION	
Carro Armato M.15/42	eight-cylinder petrol engine
Crew: 4	developing 143 kW (192 hp)
Weight: 15500 kg (34,800 lb)	**Performance:** maximum road speed
Dimensions: length 5.04 m (16 ft 7	40 km/h (25 mph); maximum range
in); width 2.23 m (7 ft 4 in); height	220 km (136 miles)
2.39 m (7 ft 11 in)	**Fording:** 1 m (3 ft 3 in)
Armament: one 47-mm (1.85-in) L/40	**Gradient:** 60 per cent
main gun, and four 8-mm (0.315-in)	**Vertical obstacle:** 0.8 m (2 ft 8 in)
Modello 38 machine-guns	**Trench:** 2.1 m (6 ft 11 in)
Powerplant: one SPA 15 TB M42	

Another M.14/41, abandoned after the 1st Battle of El Alamein. The M.15/42 looked similar but had no side hatch. Only 82 were built.

Japanese Light tanks

Japan's first light tank was the four-man **Light Tank Type 89 Experimental Tank No. 2**. The 9800-kg (21,605-lb) Type 89's turret was mounted over the front of the hull and carried a 37-mm or, according to some sources, 57-mm (2.24-in) gun and a rearward-firing 6.5-mm (0.256-in) machine-gun, a second machine-gun of the same type being located in the bow. The prototype appeared in 1929, but it soon became clear that the vehicle was better suited to the medium tank role.

First production

First into production was the **Light Tank Type 95**. An improved version was the **Light Tank Type 98 (KE-NI)**, which entered service in 1942. By this time the day of the light tank was over except for Japanese operations in China, to which the Type 98 was admirably suited. The **Light Tank Type 2 (KE-TO)** was essentially similar but for its 37-mm gun, secondary armament limited to one 7.7-mm (0.303-in) machine-gun, and armour varying in thickness between 6 and 16 mm (0.24 and 0.63 in). Only a few were built from 1944. Closer to the Type 95 were the **Light Tanks Type 3 (KE-RI)** and **Type 4 (KE-NU)**, both based on the Type 95 hull but the Type 3 having the standard turret reworked to accommodate a 57-mm gun, and the Type 4 being fitted with the complete turret/gun assembly of the Medium Tank Type 97. The Type 3 weighed 7400 kg (16,314 lb) and proved impractical because of its extremely cramped turret, and the Type 4 was too unwieldy at a weight of 8400 kg (18,519 lb).

Only for evaluation

The **Light Tank Type 5 (KE-HO)** was designed in 1942 and evaluated in prototype form with first-class results, but was not considered for production until too late. It was a four-man machine turning the scales at 10000 kg (22,046 lb) with armour from 8 to 20 mm (0.315 to 0.79 in). The tank was armed with one 47-mm gun and just one 7.7-mm machine-gun.

One of the first Japanese tanks to enter production was the Type 89. This was derived from the thinking behind a British type, the Vickers Mk C, of which the Japanese had imported a single example in 1927.

SPECIFICATION	
Light Tank Type 98 KE-NI **Crew:** 3 **Weight:** 7300 kg (16,093 lb) **Dimensions:** length overall 4.10 m (13 ft 5 in); width 2.12 m (6 ft 11 in); height 1.80 m (5 ft 11 in)	**Powerplant:** one air-cooled 6-cylinder diesel engine developing 112 kW (150 hp) **Performance:** maximum road speed 50 km/h (31 mph)

The Light Tank Type 95 was one of the best tanks developed by Japan before World War II. Though most of the rolled plate armour was riveted and bolted, some of the plates were welded.

Type 95 Light tank

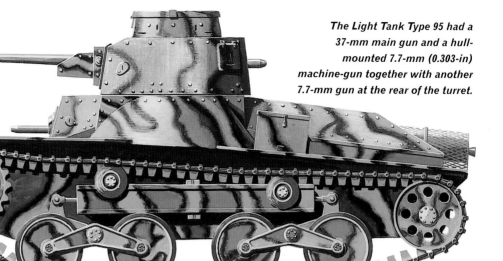

The Light Tank Type 95 had a 37-mm main gun and a hull-mounted 7.7-mm (0.303-in) machine-gun together with another 7.7-mm gun at the rear of the turret.

The **Light Tank Type 95** was developed to meet the requirements of the Imperial Japanese army in the early 1930s, the first two prototypes being completed in 1934 by Mitsubishi Heavy Industries. These were tested in China and Japan, and the type was then standardised, the company calling the vehicle the **HA-GO** while the army called it the **KE-GO**. Over 1,100 were built before production was completed in 1943, although some sources have stated that production continued until 1945.

Construction details

The hull and turret of the Type 95 were of riveted construction and varied in thickness between minimum and maximum figures of 6 and 14 mm (0.25 and 0.55 in) respectively. The driver was seated at the front of the vehicle on the right-hand with the bow machine-gunner to his left. The latter operated the 6.5-mm (0.255-in) Type 91 weapon (with a traverse of 35° left and right), which was later replaced by a 7.7-mm (0.303-in) Type 97 machine-gun. The turret

was in the centre of the hull, offset slightly to the left, and carried the vehicle's primary armament of one 37-mm (1.46-in) Type 94 tank gun firing armour-piercing and HE ammunition. This gun was later replaced by a Type 98 weapon of a similar calibre but with a higher muzzle velocity. There was no co-axial machine-gun, but another machine-gun was mounted in the turret rear on the right-hand side. The ammunition totals were 2,970 rounds for the two machine-guns, and 119 rounds for the main armament. A major drawback of this tank, as it was for many tanks of the period, was the fact that

SPECIFICATION	
Type 95	engine developing 89.5 kW (120 hp)
Crew: 4	**Performance:** maximum road speed
Weight: 7400 kg (16,314 lb)	45 km/h (28 mph); maximum range
Dimensions: length 4.38 m (14 ft 4	250 km (156 miles)
in); width 2.057 m (6 ft 9 in); height	**Fording:** 1.0 m (3 ft 3 in)
2.184 m (7 ft 2 in)	**Gradient:** 60 per cent
Powerplant: one Mitsubishi NVD	**Vertical obstacle:** 0.812 m (2 ft 8 in);
6120 air-cooled six-cylinder diesel	**Trench:** 2.0 m (6 ft 7 in)

the tank commander also had to aim, load and fire the main armament in addition to carrying out his primary role of commanding the tank.

The Mitsubishi air-cooled six-cylinder diesel engine was mounted in a compartment at the rear of the hull, and was coupled to a manual transmission with one reverse and four forward gears. In the absence of any air-conditioning system the walls of the crew compartment were lined with asbestos padding, which also gave some protection to the crew during cross-country movement.

In 1943 a few Type 95 light tanks were modified to carry a 57-mm gun under the name

KE-RI, but the variant was not useful as the turret was too cramped. The **KE-NU** was another Type 95 subvariant with the turret of the Type 97 CHI-HA medium tank. The Type 95 was succeeded in production by the **Type 98 KE-NI** light tank, but only about 200 of these were built before production was completed in 1943. The **Type 2 KA-MI** amphibious tank used automotive components of the Type 95 light tank, and was widely used in the early Pacific campaigns.

When used in the early World War II campaigns, the Type 95 proved useful, but after it had been confronted by American tanks and anti-tank guns, it was wholly outclassed.

Below right: Type 95 tanks cross paddy fields while on exercise. The Type 95 suffered in its anti-infantry role, as the Japanese army did not come up against any armour of consequence until meeting the US Army and US Marine Corps in 1943.

Below: A Type 95 at speed, probably in Manchuria. Japan's conquests were aided considerably by the fact that none of its opponents possessed any significant amount of armour, or even any useful anti-tank capability.

Type 97 Medium tank

In the mid-1930s a requirement was issued for a new medium tank to replace the Type 89B medium tank, which by then was rapidly becoming obsolete. As the Engineering Department and the General Staff could not agree on the better design, two prototypes were built. Mitsubishi built the design of the Engineering Department while Osaka Arsenal built the design of the General Staff. There was little to choose between the two designs, although the Mitsubishi tank was heavier and driven by a more powerful engine. The Mitsubishi prototype was standardised as the **Medium Tank Type 97** (**CHI-HA**), of which 3,000 were built before production was completed during World War II.

The hull and turret were of riveted construction that varied in thickness from 8 mm (0.315 in) to 25 mm (0.98 in). The driver was seated at the front on the right, with the 7.7-mm (0.303-in) Type 97 machine-gunner to his left. The two-man turret was in the centre of the hull, offset to the right, and could be traversed manually through 360°. The main armament consisted of a 57-mm (2.24-in) Type 97 gun with an elevation of +11° and depression of -9°, and another 7.7-mm machine-gun was located in the turret rear. Totals of 120 rounds of 57-mm (80 high-explosive and 40 of armour-piercing) and 2,350 rounds of 7.7-mm ammunition were carried.

Simple propulsion

The air-cooled 12-cylinder diesel was mounted at the rear of the hull and transmitted its power via a propeller shaft to the gearbox in the nose of the tank; the gearbox had four forward and one reverse gears. Steering was of the clutch and brake type, and the suspension on each side consisted of six dual rubber-tyred road wheels, with

the drive sprocket at the front and idler at the rear; there were three track-return rollers. The four central road wheels were paired and mounted on bell-cranks resisted by armoured compression springs, while each end bogie was independently bell crank-mounted to the hull in a similar manner.

Service introduction

When first introduced into service, the Type 97 was quite an advanced design apart from its main armament, which had a low muzzle velocity. A feature of most Japanese tanks of this period was that they were powered by diesel rather than petrol engines, which gave them a much increased operational range as well as reducing the ever-present risk of fire, the dread of any tank crew.

In 1942 the **Medium Tank Type 97 (SHINHOTO CHI-HA)** appeared, with a new turret armed with a 47-mm Type 97 gun that fired ammunition with

Probably the best Japanese armoured vehicle to see any great amount of service, the Type 97 was a fairly advanced design that was handicapped by an inadequate gun.

a higher muzzle velocity and so improved penetration characteristics. This weapon used the same ammunition as Japanese anti-tank guns and therefore helped ammunition commonality.

The chassis of the Type 97 was also used as the basis for a number of other vehicles including a flail-equipped mine-clearing tank, self-propelled guns (including the 150-mm/5.9-in **Type 38 HO-RO**), self-propelled anti-aircraft guns

(including 20-mm and 75-mm/2.95-in), an engineer tank, a recovery vehicle and an armoured bridgelayer. Most of these were built in such small numbers that they played little part in actual operations. The Type 97 was replaced in production by the **Type 1 CHI-HE** medium tank, followed by the **Type 3 CHI-NU**, of which only 60 were built by the end of the war. The last Japanese medium tanks were the Type 4 and 5 (neither saw combat).

Japanese light and medium tanks were adequate for operations in Asia and the Pacific until they met the better protected and more powerfully armed tanks deployed by the Allies from 1942 onward.

SPECIFICATION	
Type 97	developing 127 kW (170 hp)
Crew: 4	**Performance:** maximum road speed
Weight: 15000 kg (33,069 lb)	38 km/h (24 mph); maximum range
Dimensions: length 5.516 m (18 ft 1	210 km (130 miles)
in); width 2.33 m (7 ft 8 in); height	**Fording:** 1.0 m (3 ft 3 in)
2.23 m (7 ft 4 in)	**Gradient:** 57 per cent
Powerplant: one Mitsubishi air-	**Vertical obstacle:** 0.812 m (2 ft 6 in);
cooled 12-cylinder diesel engine	**Trench:** 2.514 m (8 ft 3 in)

Hotchkiss H-35, H-38 & H-39

French light tanks

During the early 1930s the French army, in common with the armies of many other European countries, decided that the worsening political situation in the continent made it sensible to embark on a programme to re-equip its ageing tank parks with modern equipment. At that time the French army followed the current practice of dividing tank functions into faster-moving 'cavalry' and slower-moving 'infantry' elements, and one of the tanks intended for cavalry use was a design known as the **Char Léger Hotchkiss H-35**.

Origins

The origins of this tank can be found in 1933 with a requirement for a light infantry tank to partner the SOMUA S-35. The

Hotchkiss prototype of 1934 was then rejected by the infantry in favour of the Renault R-35, but was then accepted by the cavalry as the **Char de Cavalerie 35H** before finally being

Fitted with the 37-mm (1.46-in) SA 33 L/33 gun, the H-39 had a respectable performance by the standards of the 1930s. Its only major disadvantage was that the commander had to work the gun.

accepted by the infantry as the Char H-35. The type thereby became one of the most important French tanks.

The H-35 was a small vehicle with a crew of two, and it was

lightly armed with only a 37-mm (1.46-in) short-barrel gun and a 7.5-mm (0.295-in) machine-gun. The armour was also light, ranging in thickness from 12 to 34 mm (0.47 to 1.34 in). The tank was also underpowered by a Hotchkiss petrol engine delivering only 55.9 kW (75 hp) in a vehicle turning the scales at 11400 kg (25,132 lb) for a maximum speed of just 28 km/h (17.4 mph). After 400 had been produced from 1936 onward, the basic model was supplemented by the **H-38** and then the **H-39**. The H-38 had thickened armour, up to a maximum of 40 mm (1.57 in), and an engine delivering 89.5 kW (120 hp) for a speed increased to 36 km/h (22.4 mph) despite an increase in weight to 12000 kg (26,455 lb). The H-39 was a further development of the H-38 with armour up to 45 mm (1.77 in) thick and, in place of the earlier variants' 37-mm SA 18 L/21 gun, a longer SA 33 L/33 weapon firing exactly the same round with a muzzle velocity of 701 m (2,300 ft) rather than 388 m (1,273 ft) per second for greater armour penetration. The production total for the H-38 and H-39 eventually reached some 890 units. It is worth noting that in general French tank production was slow, being severely

The H-35, seen here on parade, equipped many French mechanised cavalry units. Although armed with the ineffectual 37-mm (1.46-in) SA 18 L/21 gun, the type could still have performed effectively in the reconnaissance role but was instead used to bolster the infantry.

limited by a lack of mass production facilities, and was also beset constantly by labour troubles, even after the outbreak of World War II.

Detail differences

The H-38 and H-39 thus differed from the H-35 in their thicker armour, more powerful engine and, in the H-39, more capable gun, and were visually distinguishable from the first model by their raised rear decking, which was almost flat compared with the pronounced slope of that on the H-35. Despite the improved performance of the SA 33 gun over the SA 18, the French were soon to learn that even the better gun was virtually useless against the more capable of the German armour, most notably the PzKpfw III medium and PzKpfw IV battle tanks.

Wrong tactics

The H-35, H-38 and H-39 were all used in action in France after the German invasion of May 1940, and in general gave a moderately good account of themselves despite their indifferent armament. However, the tanks suffered from dismal tactical use. Instead of being used *en masse* in the German fashion, the French tanks were scattered along the line in penny packets for infantry support rather than being grouped as an effective anti-armour force. On occasion they were able to surprise the Germans, but only in purely local actions, so many were either destroyed or captured by the advancing Germans. Always short of matériel, the Germans took many Hotchkiss tanks into their own service as the **PzKpfw 35-H 734(f)** and **PzKpfw 39-H**

735(f), and these were used for some years by second-line and occupation units. At a later date many of the tanks had their turrets removed and replaced by German anti-tank guns for use as mobile tank destroyers, the turret being used in the 'Atlantic Wall' coastal defences.

Not all the French tanks fell into German hands. Many were located in the French Middle East possessions and some were either taken over by the Free French or were used in action by the Vichy French during the campaign in Syria in 1941. Perhaps the Hotchkiss tanks with the most unusual travel tales were those taken to the USSR in 1941 by the Germans when they were so short of tanks that even the captured French vehicles were found useful.

By 1945 there were few H-35 and H-39 tanks left anywhere: the Middle East examples survived in small numbers, and some were used to form part of the Israeli army tank arm to a time as late as 1956.

SPECIFICATION	
Hotchkiss H-35	**Powerplant:** one 89.5-kW (120-hp) Hotchkiss 6-cylinder petrol engine
Crew: 2	**Performance:** maximum road speed 36 km/h (22.3 mph); maximum road range 120 km (74.5 miles)
Weight: 12100 kg (26,675 lb)	
Dimensions: length 4.22 m (13 ft 10 in); width 1.95 m (6 ft 4¾ in); height 2.15 m (7 ft ½ in)	**Fording:** 0.85 m (2 ft 10 in)
	Vertical obstacle: 0.5 m (1 ft 8 in)
Armament: one 37-mm (1.46-in) main gun, and one 7.5-mm (0.295-in) machine-gun	**Trench:** 1.8 m (5 ft 11 in)

Renault R-35 French light tank

The **Renault R-35** light tank had its origins in a design known originally as the **ZM**, produced late in 1934 in answer to a French army request for a new infantry support tank to supplement and eventually replace the ageing Renault FT 17 which dated back to World War I. Trials of the new tank started in early 1935, and in that same year the design was ordered into production before its evaluation had been completed as Germany appeared to be in a mood for conflict. Before production got under way, the French army decided to increase the armour basis of the new **Char Léger Renault R-35** from 30 to 40 mm (1.18 to 1.575 in).

In service

The R-35 never entirely replaced the FT 17 in service, but by 1940 over 1,600 and possibly as many as 1,900 had been built, and the type was the most numerous French infantry tank in use. Its overall appearance was not

A two-man infantry support tank in the 'Great War' tradition, the R-35 was built in the erroneous belief that tank warfare had changed little in the years since 1918.

unlike that of the FT 17, for it was a small tank with a crew of only two. The design made much use of cast armour, and the suspension followed the Renault practice of the day, being of the horizontal coil-spring 'scissors' type used on the company's cavalry tank designs.

The driver's position was forward, while the commander

in the cast turret had to act as his own loader and gunner firing the 37-mm (1.46-in) L/21 gun (later replaced by a longer L/33 weapon of the same calibre) and the co-axial 7.5-mm (0.295-in) machine-gun: the ammunition totals were 100 37-mm and 2,400 7.5-mm rounds. This turret was poorly equipped with vision devices, and its internal disposition was such that the

commander had to spend much of his time in action standing on the hull floor. With the vehicle out of action, the rear of the turret opened as a flap on which the commander could sit.

Limited use

For its day the R-35 was a sound enough vehicle, and was typical of contemporary French design. The **AMX R 40** version appeared in 1940 with revised suspension, and a few of this variant were produced before the Germans invaded in May 1940. The R-35 soon proved to be no match for the German Panzers. For a start it was usually allocated in small numbers in direct support of infantry formations, and could thus be picked off piecemeal by the massed German tanks. Its gun proved virtually ineffective against even the lightest German tanks, though in return its 40-mm (1.575-in) armour was fairly effective against most of the German anti-tank guns. Thus the R-35 was able to contribute little to the campaign, and many were destroyed or abandoned by their crews in the disasters that overtook the French army as the Germans swept through France.

Large numbers of R-35s fell into German hands virtually intact. These were put to use by garrison units in France with the designation **PzKpfw 35-R(f)**, many later passing to driver and

The R-35 reflected obsolescent tactical thinking in its conception, and therefore provided an inadequate battlefield tank. The commander is seated on the opened back of the turret.

other tank training schools. With the invasion of the USSR many R-35 tanks were stripped of their turrets for service as artillery tractors or **Munitionpanzer 35-R(f)** ammunition carriers. At a later date many of the R-35 tanks still in France had their turrets removed so that their hulls could be converted as the basis of several types of self-propelled artillery or an anti-tank gun known as the **4.7-cm Pak(t) auf GW 35-R(f)**. The turrets were emplaced in concrete along the 'Atlantic Wall' coastal defences.

Therefore, the R-35 passed into history, and despite its numbers its combat record was such that it proved to be of more use to the Germans.

The cast turret of the R-35 was hand operated for traverse through 360°, and the 37-mm (1.46-in) gun could be elevated in an arc between -18° and +18°. The armour was generally adequate.

SPECIFICATION	
Renault R-35	**Powerplant:** one 61-kW (82-bhp)
Crew: 2	Renault 4-cylinder petrol engine
Weight: 10000 kg (22,046 lb)	**Performance:** maximum road speed
Dimensions: length 4.2 m (13 ft	20 km/h (12.4 mph); range 140 km
9¼ in); width 1.85 m (6 ft ¾ in);	(87 miles)
height 2.37 m (7 ft 9¼ in)	**Fording:** 0.8 m (2 ft 7 in)
Armament: one 37-mm (1.46-in)	**Vertical obstacle:** 0.5 m (1 ft 7¾ in)
main gun, and one 7.5-mm (0.295-	**Trench:** 1.6 m (5 ft 3 in)
in) machine-gun	

SOMUA S-35 Medium tank

When the re-equipment of the French cavalry arm with tanks started during the mid-1930s, among the several concerns that became involved was a Schneider subsidiary known as SOMUA (Société d'Outillage Mécanique et d'Usinage d'Artillerie). In 1935 this revealed a tank prototype that attracted immediate attention, and its very advanced design was soon recognised by the award of a production order. One of the best armoured fighting vehicles of its day, the **SOMUA S-35** was more formally known as the **Auto-Mitrailleuse de Combat (AMC) modèle 1935 SOMUA**.

Despite the weakness of having the commander operate the main armament, the S-35 was a robust tank.

Countless facets

The S-35 had many features that were later to become commonplace. The hull and turret were both cast components at a time when most vehicles were based on structures of riveted steel plate. The cast armour was not only well shaped for extra protection, but also much thicker than the norms of the time: the minimum was 20 mm (0.79 in) and the maximum 55 mm (2.16 in). For all that, the tank still had good power for lively battlefield performance, and a good operational radius of action was ensured by large internal fuel tanks. Radio was standard at a time when hand signals between tanks were still common. The S-35 was also armed with a capable main gun: the 47-mm (1.85-in) SA 35 was one of the most powerful weapons of the day and a gun that could still be regarded as a useful weapon in 1944. The secondary armament was a single 7.5-mm (0.295-in) co-axial machine-gun.

Labour problems

The S-35 was ordered into production but, as in nearly all other sectors of the French defence industry before 1939, this production was slow and beset by labour and other troubles. Only about 400 S-35 tanks had been produced by the time the Germans invaded in May 1940, and only about 250 of these were in front-line service. In action the S-35 gave a good account of itself though revealing a serious design defect when under fire: the upper and lower hull halves were joined by a ring of bolts along a horizontal join, and if an anti-tank projectile hit this join line the two halves split

SPECIFICATION	
SOMUA S-35	35 main gun, and one 7.5-mm
Crew: 3	(0.295-in) co-axial machine-gun
Weight: 19500 kg (42,989 lb)	**Performance:** maximum road speed
Dimensions: length 5.38 m (17 ft 7¾ in); width 2.12 m (6 ft 11½ in); height 2.62 m (8 ft 7 in)	40 km/h (24.85 mph); maximum road range 230 km (143 miles)
Powerplant: one SOMUA V-8	**Fording:** 1 m (3 ft 3 in)
Armament: one 47-mm (1.85-in) SA	**Vertical obstacle:** 0.76 m (2 ft 6 in)
	Trench: 2.13 m (7 ft)

In 1940 many S-35 tanks were damaged and abandoned, such as the vehicle seen here, but were often good enough for the Germans to use against the Allies four years later.

apart with obvious dire results. But at the time this mattered less than the way in which the tanks had to be handled: the S-35 had a crew of three (driver, commander and radio operator), and it was the location of the commander alone in the small turret that caused the problems, for this unfortunate had not only to keep an eye on the local tactical scene, but also to assimilate orders from the radio while loading and firing the gun. The tasks were far too much for one man, so the S-35's potential was very rarely attained.

As with other French tanks of the day, the S-35s were split into small groups scattered along the French line, and were grouped on only a few occasions for worthwhile counterstrokes against the Panzer columns. After the occupation of France the Germans took over as many S-35 tanks as they could find for issue to occupation and training units under the designation **PzKpfw 35-S 739(f)**. Some were handed over to the Italian army, but many were still based in France when the Allies invaded in 1944 and the S-35 tank was once more in action, this time in German hands.

Any S-35s taken by the Allies were passed over to the Free French, who in their turn used them in the reduction of the beleaguered German garrisons locked up in Atlantic sea-port strongholds.

Well protected and manoeuvrable, the SOMUA S-35 was undoubtedly the best Allied tank in 1940. It had a radio and its 47-mm (1.85-in) gun could fire both armour-piercing shot and HE shell, an obvious requirement which had escaped British designers.

Char B1 Heavy tank

The 400 or so Char B1 tanks possessed by the French army in 1940 were potentially a devastating strike force.

The series of tanks known as the **Char B** had a definite look of the 'Great War' era about them, and this is not surprising for their development can be traced back as far as 1921 and the immediate aftermath of World War I. What was demanded at that time was a tank with a 75-mm (2.95-in) gun set in a hull-mounted embrasure, but it was not until about 1930 that the result of this request was finally built. This was the Char B heavy tank with a weight of about 25 tonnes, and prolonged development led in 1935 to the emergence of the full production version, the **Char B1**.

Advanced design

The Char B1 was a powerful tank for the period as it had a turret-mounted 47-mm (1.85-in) gun with 50 rounds of ammunition and a 75-mm (2.95-in) gun with 74 rounds of ammunition set in the front of the hull; the secondary armament was two 7.5-mm (0.295-in) machine-guns with 5,100 rounds of ammunition. The limited traverse of the hull gun was partially offset by a complex steering system that allowed the vehicle to be aligned rapidly on to the correct target sector. Although its archaic appearance belied the fact, the Char B was full of very advanced design features that ranged from self-sealing fuel tanks to grouped lubrication for the many bearings; an electric starter was also provided and attention was given to internal fire protection.

The crew of four men was scattered about the interior in a way that made internal communication difficult, however, and this led to many operational problems. The crew of the Char B1 had to be a highly trained group of specialists to make the best of the tank's potential as a fighting vehicle, and in 1940 these teams were few and far between.

The final production variant was the **Char B1-bis**, which had thicker armour (minimum of 14 mm/0.55 in and maximum of 65 mm/ 2.56 in) by comparison with the Char B1's figures (14 and 40 mm/0.55 and 1.57 in), a revised turret design and a more powerful engine. Later production models had an even more powerful engine of aircraft origins and still more fuel capacity.

Slow manufacture

Production of the Char B1-bis started in 1937, and by 1940 there were about 400 Char B tanks of all types in service. By then the Char B1 and Char B1-bis were the most numerous and powerful of all the French heavy tanks, and the basic type was the main battle tank of the few dedicated armoured formations of the French army.

The Germans had a great respect for the Char B1, for the 75-mm gun was quite capable of knocking out even the PzKpfw IV battle tank, but the Germans were considerably assisted during the fighting of May and June 1940 by several

The tanks of the Char B series were well armoured and possessed good performance, but the whole of the vehicle's mass had to be manoeuvred in order to train the hull-mounted main gun on its target.

The Char B1 could cope easily with any German tank in existence, but abysmal tactical handling rendered the type useless as the weapon that might have checked Germany's advances.

factors. One of these was that the Char B1 was a complex vehicle and required a great deal of careful maintenance: many simply broke down *en route* to battle and were left for the Germans to take over undamaged. Another drawback for the French was that, as was the case with other tank units, those operating the Char B1 were frequently broken up into small local-defence groups instead of being grouped to provide a cohesive mass that could meet the advance of Germany's fast-moving armoured divisions.

German service

The Germans took over the Char B1-bis as the **PzKpfw B1-bis 740(f)** and used it for a variety of purposes. Some of the vehicles were passed intact to occupation units such as those in the Channel Islands, while others were converted for driver training or were altered to become self-propelled artillery carriages. Some were fitted with flamethrowers as the **PzKpfw Flamm(f)**. In 1944 a few were still around to pass again into French army use.

SPECIFICATION	
Char B1-bis	machine-guns
Crew: 4	**Powerplant:** one 229-kW (307-hp)
Weight: 31500 kg (69,444 lb)	Renault 6-cylinder petrol engine
Dimensions: length 6.37 m (20 ft 10¾ in); width 2.5 m (8 ft 2½ in); height 2.79 m (9 ft 1¾ in)	**Performance:** maximum road speed 28 km/h (17.4 mph); maximum road range 180 km (112 miles)
Armament: one 75-mm (2.95-in) hull gun, one 47-mm (1.85-in) turret gun, and two 7.5-mm (0.295-in)	**Vertical obstacle:** 0.93 m (3 ft 1 in) **Trench:** 2.74 m (9 ft)

Panhard 178 French armoured car

The **Automitrailleuse Panhard et Levassor Type 178** armoured car was first produced in 1935, and was developed from a design known as the TOE-M-32, which was intended for use in the French North African colonies and mounted a short 37-mm turret gun. Panhard used this design as a basis for a new French army require-ment but gave the new vehicle a 4x4 drive configuration and moved the engine to the rear of the vehicle. The result was the Panhard 178 and the armament varied from a single 25-mm cannon on some vehicles to two 7.5-mm (0.30-in) machine-guns on others, while some command vehicles had extra radios but no armament. The Panhard 178 was known also as the **Panhard Model 1935**.

The Panhard 178 was put into production for the French infantry and cavalry formation reconnaissance groups. Production was slow, but by 1940 there were appreciable numbers available for the fighting which followed the German invasion in May.

Into service

Many of the Panhard 178s were in widely scattered units and were unable to take much part in the fighting that ensued, so many were seized intact by the victorious Germans. The Germans liked the sound design of the Panhard 178 and decided to adopt it for their own service as the **Panzerspähwagen P 204(f)**, some of them being rearmed with 37-mm anti-tank guns and/or German machine-guns. Some of these were retained for garrison use in France, but others were later sent to the USSR, where the type was used for behind-the-lines patrol duties against Soviet partisans. Some were even converted for railway use, having their conventional wheels changed to railway wheels, and many of these 'railway' conversions were fitted with extra radios and prominent frame aerials.

Perhaps the most unusual use of the Panhard 178s took place in 1941 and 1942, when 45 vehicles, hidden from German forces by French cavalry units following the defeat of 1940, were prepared by Resistance personnel for possible use against the enemy. These vehicles had no turrets, but were manufactured under the nose of the Germans and fitted with 25-mm or 47-mm guns and/or machine-guns. The armoured cars were then secretly distributed throughout centres of resist-ance mainly in unoccupied France, where many were subsequently taken over by the German forces when they took over the unoccupied areas of France in November 1942.

Further production

After the Liberation, the Panhard 178 was once more put into production during August 1944 at the Renault factory outside Paris. These new vehicles had a larger turret with a 47-mm gun, and were later known as the **Panhard 178B**. The new vehicles were issued to the new French cavalry units and were used for many years after 1945. Some saw action in Indo-China, and it was not until 1960 that the last of them was taken out of service.

SPECIFICATION	
Panhard 178	78 kW (105 bhp)
Crew: 4	**Performance:** maximum road speed
Weight: (in action) 8.5 tonnes	72 km/h (45 mph); road range 300
Dimensions: length overall 4.79 m	km (186 miles)
(15 ft 8½ in); width 2 m (6 ft 7¼ in);	**Fording:** 0.6 m (1 ft 11½ in)
height 2.31 m (7 ft 7 in)	**Gradient:** 40°
Powerplant: one 6.3-litre water-	**Vertical obstacle:** 0.3 m (11¾ in)
cooled petrol engine developing	**Trench:** 0.6 m (1 ft 11½ in)

Two Automitrailleuse Panhard et Levassor Type 178s are seen here in German service following the fall of France in 1940. The Germans found these vehicles good enough to take into their own service, and many were used for anti-partisan operations in the USSR.

leichter Panzerspähwagen SdKfz 222 Light armoured car

When the Nazis came to power in Germany, the army was given a virtually free hand in selecting new equipment for the expanding German armed forces, and among the equipment requested was a new series of light armoured cars to be built on a standard chassis.

New design

The requirements laid down by the army were so demanding that commercial models could not be adapted to meet them, so an entirely new design was produced and in 1935 this was used as the basis for the **leichter Panzerspäh-wagen SdKfz 221** 4x4, a light three-man vehicle with a small turret mounting a single 7.92-mm (0.31-in) machine-gun. From this evolved the **SdKfz 222** armoured car with a slightly larger armoured turret with an open top and the potential to mount a slightly heavier armament. The first SdKfz 222 appeared in 1938 and thereafter was adopted as the standard German army armoured car for use by the new divisional reconnaissance units.

The SdKfz 222 was initially referred to as a Waffenwagen, or weapons vehicle, as it mounted a 20-mm KwK 30 cannon, a version of the standard antiaircraft cannon adapted for use in armoured vehicles. Later the 20-mm KwK 38 was also used. Mounted

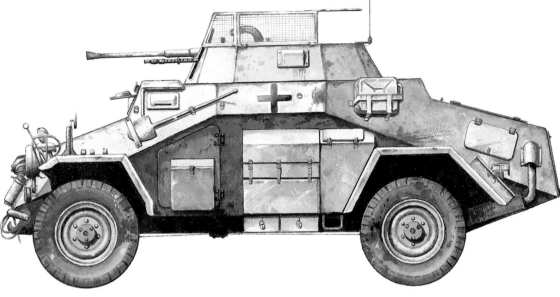

A leichter Panzerspähwagen SdKfz 222 is seen here in the type's usual form, armed with a 20-mm cannon and MG 34 machine-gun. The wire mesh anti-grenade screen roof is in position. Note the tool and fuel can stowage and the number of stowage boxes on the exterior, the result of a rather cramped interior.

alongside this cannon was a 7.92-mm MG 34 machine-gun, and this combination left little room inside the turret for the commander/ gunner and the radio operator, who were further restricted in action by the use of a wire screen over the top of the open turret to prevent hand grenades from being lobbed into the vehicle. The driver was situated centrally in the front of the hull, and the superstructure was made up from well-sloped armoured plates to provide extra protection. During the war the thickness of the front hull plates was increased from 14.5 mm (0.57 in) to 30 mm (1.2 in) and the 20-mm cannon mounting was adapted to

provide more elevation for use against enemy aircraft.

Once in widespread service the SdKfz 222 proved to be a reliable and popular little vehicle. It served well in France during 1940, often racing far ahead of the following Panzer columns, and in North Africa the type proved itself to be a very useful reconnaissance vehicle, although somewhat restricted in its operational range by the amount of fuel that could be carried in the internal tanks. This restriction proved to be a problem during the invasion of the Soviet Union after 1941, to the extent that the SdKfz 222 was replaced by the SdKfz 250/9 halftrack mounting the same turret and used for the same role. In the west the SdKfz 222 continued in service until the very end of the war, and in the Soviet Union the type

was used for conducting patrol duties in rear areas.

The SdKfz 221 and SdKfz 222 were not the only armoured cars of their line. There was also the **SdKfz 223**, which could be recognised by a large frame aerial over the rear of its hull; as the vehicle was used as a command and communications centre it carried only a single machine-gun. The **SdKfz 260** was a long-range radio vehicle used at higher command levels only, and the **SdKfz 261** was similar. The **SdKfz 247** was a personnel and stores carrier.

The SdKfz 222 was exported in some numbers to China before 1939, and once there, was adapted to take a wide range of armament that ranged from heavy machine-guns to light anti-tank guns. Numbers of SdKfz 221s were also sent to China.

On the left is an SdKfz 223 light communications vehicle with its large and distinctive frame aerial; on the right is an SdKfz 250/3 halftrack, a type of vehicle that proved more suited to service in the USSR.

SPECIFICATION	
SdKfz 222	developing 60 kW (81 hp)
Crew: 3	**Performance:** maximum road speed
Weight: (in action) 4.8 tonnes	80 km/h (50 mph); maximum cross
Dimensions: length overall 4.80 m	country speed 40 km/h (25 mph);
(14 ft 8½ in); width 1.95 m (6 ft	road radius of action 300 km (187
4¾ in); height 2 m (6 ft 6¾ in) with	miles); cross-country radius of
grenade screen	action 180 km (110 miles)
Powerplant: one Horch/Auto-Union	**Gradient:** 20°
V8-108 water-cooled petrol engine	**Fording:** 0.6 m (1 ft 11½ in)

schwerer Panzerspähwagen SdKfz 231

Heavy armoured car

The SdKfz 231 was really too heavy for the lorry chassis on which it was based. Nevertheless, where the going was good, it proved an effective fighting vehicle.

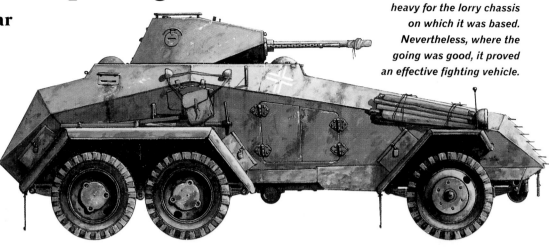

The **schwerer Panzerspähwagen SdKfz 231** 6x4 heavy armoured car had its origins at the Kazan test centre established in the Soviet Union during the 1920s. At the centre the German automobile industry developed an 8x8 armoured car chassis that proved to be too expensive for further development, so a 6x4 chassis was tried instead. This model used a truck chassis as its basis, and originally this was a Daimler-Benz product, but later Büssing-NAG and Magirus chassis and engines were employed. These chassis were fitted with suitable armoured hulls and turrets, and modifications were made to allow steering from either end of the hull.

Trial phase

Early trials demonstrated the need for stronger front axles and revised radiators, and the resulting vehicle was issued to German army units during 1932. Production continued until 1935, by which time about 1,000 had been produced.

The 6x4 armoured cars were not a great success, but they were produced at a time when the German army lacked experience in the use of armoured vehicles, and were thus invaluable as training and preparation equipments. Using lorry chassis carrying armoured hulls that were really too heavy for their supporting structures, the six-wheeled armoured cars were underpowered and had only limited cross country capabilities. But when used on roads they were as good as anything else available. After 1940 they gradually faded from front-line use and were relegated mainly to training second-line roles.

Early examples of the six-wheeled heavy armoured cars had provision for only one 7.92-mm (0.31-in) MG 34 machine-gun in the turret, but the version used mainly by the heavy platoons of the German army motorised units was the SdKfz 231. This had a turret mounting a 20-mm cannon, originally the KwK 30 but later the KwK 38 with a higher rate of fire. Mounted co-axially with this cannon was a 7.92-mm MG 34, and there was provision for an AA machine-gun on the turret roof.

SPECIFICATION	
SdKfz 231	between 45 and 60 kW (60 and 80 bhp)
Crew: 4	**Performance:** maximum road speed
Weight: (in action) 5.7 tonnes	65 km/h (40 mph); maximum road
Dimensions: length overall 5.57 m	range 250 km (150 miles);
(18 ft 6¾ in); width 1.82 m (5 ft	maximum cross-country range
11½ in); height 2.25 m (7 ft 4½ in)	200 km (125 miles)
Powerplant: one Daimler-Benz,	**Gradient:** 20°
Büssing-NAG or Magirus water-	**Fording:** 0.6 m (24 in)
cooled petrol engine developing	

Tactical vehicle

The SdKfz 231 was used as a tactical vehicle (undertaking a combat role in direct fire support of motorised infantry units mounted on trucks or later on halftracks), but at times was also used in support of light reconnaissance units for Panzer formations. Another vehicle that was very similar to the SdKfz 231 was the **SdKfz 232**. This was essentially an SdKfz 231 fitted with a long-range radio set that required the fitting of a large and prominent frame aerial above the turret and over the hull rear, the turret acting as a support for the forward part of the aerial. Another similar vehicle was the **SdKfz 263**, which also had a large frame aerial (it was used as a command vehicle), though on this the turret was fixed and had a single machine-gun.

Schwerer Panzerspähwagen SdKfz 232s seen during a pre-war parade in Berlin. These vehicles were equipped with a large and cumbersome radio antenna mounted over the turret, which remained static while the turret rotated.

schwerer Panzerspähwagen SdKfz 231 (8-Rad)

Heavy reconnaissance car

The wide-ranging war in North Africa provided German reconnaissance units with the ideal terrain to test the abilities of their armoured cars. The Achtrad ranged ahead of the armoured columns of the Afrika Korps, seeking out the information which would allow Rommel, the Desert Fox, to make his tactical decisions.

Almost as soon as the first six-wheeled armoured cars were issued to the expanding German army during the mid-1930s, the German staff planners realised that they were not the vehicles that would be required in the long term as they were under-powered and lacked cross-country mobility.

They requested an eight-wheeled armoured car with an engine to match, and decided to develop a Büssing-NAG 8x8

chassis for use as an armoured car. Development began in full during 1935 and the first production examples were issued to the army in 1937.

This 8 x 8 heavy armoured car was the **schwerer Panzerspähwagen SdKfz 231**, and to avoid confusion with the six-wheeled armoured cars with the same designation, the new series was always suffixed **(8-Rad)**. The troops knew the type as the **Achtrad**.

SPECIFICATION	
SdKfz 231(8-Rad)	**Performance:** max. road speed 85
Crew: 4	km/h (53 mph); max. cross-country
Weight: (in action) 8.3 tonnes	speed 30 km/h (19 mph); road
Dimensions: length overall 5.85 m (19	radius of action 270 km (170
ft 2 in); width 2.20 m (7 ft 2½ in);	miles); cross-country radius of
height 2.34 m (7 ft 8 in)	action 150 km (95 miles)
Powerplant: one Büssing-NAG L8V-	**Fording:** 1 m (3 ft 3½ in)
Gs water-cooled petrol e ngine	**Gradient:** 30 per cent
developing 112 kW (150 hp)	**Vertical obstacle:** 0.5 m (1 ft 7¾ in);
	trench 1.25 m (4 ft 3 in)

When the new eight-wheelers appeared in service they were among the most advanced cross-country vehicles yet produced,

but their high road-speeds and mobility had been purchased at an equally high price in chassis complexity. The vehicles were highly complicated, expensive and very slow to produce.

The chassis had all-wheel drive and steering, and fully independent suspension – the vehicle was even able to travel across the thick mud of the Eastern Front. If the vehicle had one major fault other than its complexity, it was that it had rather a high profile and was difficult to hide in combat.

Early war production

The SdKfz 231 series remained in production until 1942, when it was phased out in favour of the improved SdKfz 234 series. By then 1,235 had been produced, and the type remained in

This early example of an SdKfz 231(8-Rad) is armed with a 20-mm cannon and shows the distinctive spaced armoured stowage bin mounted on the front hull. The size and bulk of this vehicle in relation to the armament carried is obvious; its internal complexity is less so.

widespread use throughout the war on all fronts. The type was particularly prominent in the North African campaigns.

The SdKfz 231 (8-Rad) had a turret with a 20-mm KwK 30 or KwK 38 cannon with a co-axial 7.92-mm (0.31-in) MG 34 machine-gun. The **SdKfz 232(8-Rad)** was the radio version with a prominent frame aerial, and the **SdKfz 263(8-Rad)** was a command version with a fixed superstructure in place of the rotating turret, and featuring a large frame aerial for the long-range radio equipment carried.

Fire support

The **SdKfz 233** had no direct six-wheeler equivalent, for it mounted a short 75-mm (2.95-in) tank gun (*Stummelkanone*) as used on early PzKpfw IV tanks.

This gun was mounted in an open compartment formed by the removal of the normal turret and there was only a limited traverse. This vehicle had a crew of only three men, and was used to provide armoured reconnaissance units with improved offensive power and to give them fire support.

The first SdKfz 233 was issued during late 1942 and proved to be highly effective, but there were times when the gun's limited traverse and lack of armour-piercing performance proved to be a liability. However, when pitted against the usual run-of-the-mill reconnaissance vehicles it was likely to encounter, the SdKfz 233 was very effective and often provided covering fire for other *Achtrads*.

An SdKfz 231 Achtrad crew mounts up. The distinctive tank berets, which covered a leather protective helmet, indicate that this photograph was taken prewar or in Poland, since they had mostly fallen out of use by 1940.

SdKfz 234(8-Rad)
Heavy reconnaissance car

In 1940 German army planners issued a requirement for a new 8 x 8 armoured car series to be based on the SdKfz 231(8-Rad) series, but having a monocoque hull (one in which the basic hull structure was made up of the plates themselves rather than a framework on which the body was fixed) and an engine more suited to operations in hot climates.

The resultant vehicle was built by Büssing-NAG with other firms under its control, and the basic hull and chassis was known as the **ARK**. It was delivered in July 1941, but the original engine installation proved troublesome and was replaced by another. A different engine installation was intended for vehicles used in North Africa, but with the end of that campaign early in 1943, the project proceeded slowly and it was not until 1944 that the first 'tropical' version was delivered.

New variants

The new series of vehicles was designated **schwerer**

A captured SdKfz 234/1 has its third axle welded into place for the camera. This damaged example has the turret with its 20-mm cannon traversed to the rear, and the anti-grenade mesh screen can be seen over the open turret top. Note the stowage bins, one with the cover missing.

Panzerspähwagen SdKfz 234 and was much lower and more streamlined than the earlier SdKfz 231(8-Rad) series. The vehicles had thicker armour, increased internal fuel capacity and a more powerful engine bestowing a better all-round performance. It is now generally acknowledged that the variants of the SdKfz 234 series were probably the best all-round vehicles in their class used during World War II. Most of the mechanical attributes of

the SdKfz 231(8-Rad) vehicles were carried over, and there were four basic versions of the SdKfz 234. By the end of the war about 2,300 had been produced after the type had entered full production during 1943.

Designations

In designation order, the first version was the **SdKfz 234/1**, a commander's vehicle with a 20-mm KwK 30 or KwK 38 cannon in a small open-topped

turret along with a co-axial 7.92-mm (0.31-in) MG 42 machine-gun. Normally, the turret was covered by a wire screen to prevent the ingress of hand grenades.

The most famous of the range was the **SdKfz 234/2 Puma**, a superb armoured car with a turret enclosing a 50-mm (1.96-in) KwK 39/1 gun. The turret had originally been intended for the Leopard light tank, which was cancelled, and when reworked for the Puma the result was powerful enough for the vehicle to counter the increasing use of light and other tanks in Soviet army reconnaissance units. The turret had an excellent ballistic shape and also mounted a co-axial MG42.

So good was the vehicle that by 1945, when German industry was being drastically reorganised to maintain war production outputs, the Puma was the only reconnaissance vehicle to be kept in production (along with a Skoda light tank).

Tank-killer

There were times when the 50-mm gun of the Puma was unable to cope with enemy tanks, and so the **SdKfz 234/3**

Right: A wrecked SdKfz 234/1 Puma. Well able to take care of itself against other armoured cars and light tanks, the Puma was still vunerable to heavier tanks.

Below: Probably the best balanced armoured car of World War II in terms of speed, firepower and protection, the Puma was complex and expensive to manufacture. Even so, it remained in production until 1945.

was produced to replace the earlier SdKfz 233. It, too, mounted the short 75-mm (2.95-in) tank gun of the SdKfz 233, and was placed in production at the direct order of Hitler, who by 1944 was concerning himself directly with such matters as fighting vehicle armament. The last variant of the SdKfz 234 series was another placed in production as the result of a direct order from Hitler. The **SdKfz 234/4** mounted a 75-mm PaK 40 anti-tank gun in an open

compartment in place of the turret. Only a few trial models were produced, but by the time they appeared things were

becoming so desperate that they were rushed into operational use, and some were captured by the Allies.

SPECIFICATION	
SdKfz 234/2 Puma	**Performance:** maximum road speed
Crew: 4	85 km/h (53 mph); maximum
Weight: (in action) 11.74 tonnes	cross-country speed 30 km/h
Dimensions: length (gun forward)	(19 mph); road radius of action
6.80 m (22 ft 3⅔ in); length (hull)	1000 km (625 miles); cross-country
6.00 m (19 ft 8¼ in); width 2.33 m	radius of action 550 km (350 miles)
(7 ft 6½ in): height 2.38 m	**Fording:** 1.2 m (3 ft 10¾ in)
(7 ft 9½ in)	**Gradient:** 30 per cent
Powerplant: one Tatra Model 103	**Vertical obstacle:** 0.5 m (1 ft 7¾ in);
air-cooled diesel engine developing	**Trench:** 1.35 m (4 ft 5 in)
157 kW (210 hp)	

Reconnaissance aircraft such as the versatile Fieseler Fi 156 Storch STOL type provided invaluable service in the open spaces of the desert, and co-operated with other reconnaissance forces.

German reconnaissance battalion In action

Above: A squadron of leichter Panzerspähwagen SdKfz 221s put on a show of force in Prague on 23 March 1939. They heralded a Nazi occupation which was to endure until 8 March 1945.

Below: A handful of American M8 Greyhound 6x6 armoured cars, with 37-mm guns, were taken in 1944 and used by German special forces during the Ardennes offensive. The Germans made extensive use of captured vehicles and by 1942 had over 1,500 different types in service.

The sPzSpw(8 Rad) heavy armoured cars of the SdKfz 234 series were built in four variants, of which only the first two can really be classified genuinely as reconnaissance vehicles. The SdKfz 234/1 was armed with a 2-cm cannon in a hexagonal open-topped turret, but the definitive SdKfz 234/2 introduced a fully enclosed turret armed with a 5-cm (1.97-mm) high-velocity gun offering good anti-armour capabilities.

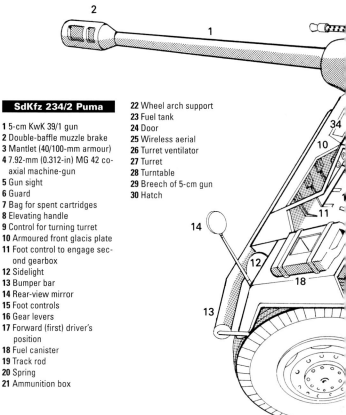

SdKfz 234/2 Puma

1 5-cm KwK 39/1 gun
2 Double-baffle muzzle brake
3 Mantlet (40/100-mm armour)
4 7.92-mm (0.312-in) MG 42 co-axial machine-gun
5 Gun sight
6 Guard
7 Bag for spent cartridges
8 Elevating handle
9 Control for turning turret
10 Armoured front glacis plate
11 Foot control to engage second gearbox
12 Sidelight
13 Bumper bar
14 Rear-view mirror
15 Foot controls
16 Gear levers
17 Forward (first) driver's position
18 Fuel canister
19 Track rod
20 Spring
21 Ammunition box
22 Wheel arch support
23 Fuel tank
24 Door
25 Wireless aerial
26 Turret ventilator
27 Turret
28 Turntable
29 Breech of 5-cm gun
30 Hatch

Above: A Luftwaffe field division recce unit in the Anzio/ Netturno area in early 1944. The vehicles are SdKfz 231 (8-Rad) armed with 2-cm cannon and carrying aircraft look-outs.

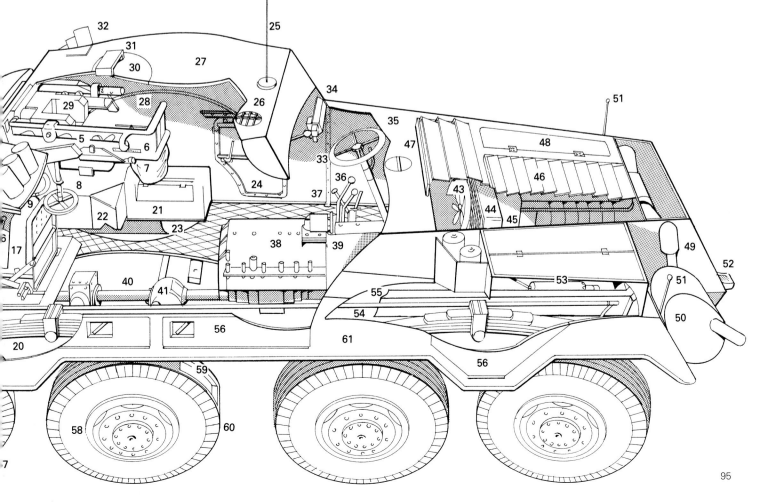

Above: The SdKfz 234/4 mounted a 7.5-cm (2.95-in) L/24 short tank gun at the front of an open superstructure. The vehicle was produced to provide a measure of fire-support for armoured car units from 1944 onward, and thus possessed little or no reconnaissance capability.

Left: The SdKfz 222 was a 4x4 light reconnaissance vehicle offering adequate cross-country performance, modest speed and an armament centred on a 2-cm cannon or 2.8-cm anti-tank gun.

31 Handle
32 Smoke canister ejectors
33 Hull frame
34 Visor
35 Second driver's position
36 Gear-change
37 Hand brake
38 Three-speed main gear-box
39 Two-speed secondary gearbox
40 Final drive
41 Differential
42 Reduction box
43 Fan (two)
44 Radiator
45 Tatra 103 diesel engine
46 Engine vents
47 Radiator vents
48 Engine access hatch
49 Exhaust
50 Silencer
51 Sensors to enable drivers to judge ends of car
52 Towbar
53 Hydraulic brake cylinder
54 Steering rod to four wheels
55 Main frame of chassis
56 Storage bins
57 Four-wheel drive
58 Pressed steel wheels
59 Self-sealing coating to inner tubes
60 Low-pressure cord-rein-
forced cross-country tyres
61 Mudguards

Autoblinda 40 & 41 Armoured cars

The **Autoblinda 40** and **Autoblinda 41** armoured cars had their origins in a requirement for a high-performance car for use by the Italian colonial police in the new Italian colonies in Africa. The Italian cavalry branch had a requirement for a new armoured car at about the same time, so the two projects were merged to produce a new vehicle design that appeared in 1939. This new design had the engine at the rear and a turret (mounting a machine-gun) towards the front. There was another machine-gun in the hull rear and the vehicle could be driven from either the normal front position or another position in the hull rear. From this design evolved the Autoblinda 40, of which production began by the middle of 1940.

Cannon armament

When the original production order was placed it was specified that a small number

This Autoblinda 41, one of the most numerous Italian armoured cars, carried one 20-mm cannon and one co-axial machine-gun in the turret, and one machine-gun at the rear of the fighting compartment.

of Autoblinda 40s would be produced with a 20-mm cannon in place of the two 8-mm (0.315-in) machine-guns in the turret. This was achieved by using the turret of the L 6/40 light tank in place of the original turret. With the appearance of this version known as the Autoblinda 41, it was realised that this vehicle/weapon combination was far more effective than the machine-gun

An Autoblinda 41 in North Africa in 1941 where both variants were used extensively by reconnaissance units. In German hands, the armoured cars were known as the Panzerspähwagen AB 40 and 41.

SPECIFICATION	
Autoblinda 41	**Performance:** maximum road speed
Crew: 4	78 km/h (49 mph); maximum
Weight: 7.5 tonnes	cross-country speed 38 km/h
Dimensions: length (overall) 5.2 m	(24 mph); maximum road range
(17 ft 1½ in); width 1.92 (6 ft	400 km (248 miles)
4¼ in); height 2.48 m (7 ft 11½ in)	**Fording:** 0.7 m (28 in)
Powerplant: one SAP Abm 1 water-	**Gradient:** 40 per cent
cooled 16-cylinder petrol engine	**Vertical obstacle:** 0.3 m (12 in)
developing 60 kW (80 bhp)	

version, and thereafter production centred on the Autoblinda 41. Relatively few 40s were produced, and many of these were later converted to the Autoblinda 41 configuration. For its time the Autoblinda 41 was an advanced design and possessed good performance marred only by recurrent steering troubles that were never entirely eliminated. The main armament was a converted 20-mm Breda Modello 35 anti-aircraft cannon, and this weapon was mounted co-axially with an 8-mm Breda Modello 38 air-cooled machine-gun, which was a type specially designed for use in armoured vehicles. Another of these machine-guns was mounted at the hull rear. One vehicle in four had provision for an anti-aircraft machine-gun mounting on top of the turret. Special sand or normal road tyres could be fitted and there was a kit available to convert the vehicle for use on railway tracks. This kit included

railway wheels and extra lighting and signalling devices, along with a searchlight to be mounted on the turret. Autoblinda 41s fitted with these kits were used a lot for anti-partisan patrols in the Balkans.

The Autoblinda 40 and Autoblinda 41 were widely used by Italian reconnaissance units in the Western Desert and Tunisia. At the end of September 1942 there were 298 Autoblinda 41s in use, and more were employed by the colonial police. Some development work was carried out on the basic design, which later led to the mounting of a 47-mm (1.85-in) gun in the turret to create the **Autoblinda 43**, while an open-hulled variant had a German 50-mm (1.97-in) tank gun. However, neither of these vehicles was placed in production. There was also an open-hulled variant that was produced in small numbers as a command vehicle.

Marmon Herrington armoured cars

Despite the fact that the vehicle construction industry in South Africa had never before produced any armoured vehicles, in 1938 the government of the day ordered the development of two types of armoured car. Work on these was slow until the outbreak of war in 1939 when, after a quick survey of possible alternatives, the experimental vehicles were ordered into production. Orders soon swelled to 1,000 and, despite the fact that no facilities existed for the large-scale production of such vehicles, within only a few months the first examples were appearing.

The South Africans produced their armoured cars by importing Ford truck chassis from Canada, four-wheel drive transmissions from Marmon Herrington in the US, and the armament from the United Kingdom. Local assembly and production were undertaken in vehicle assembly plants and railway workshops, and the armour plate was produced at South African steel mills. The first vehicles were known under the designation **South African Reconnaissance Vehicle Mk I**, and these had a long wheelbase and a 4x2 drive configuration. The **South African Reconnaissance Vehicle Mk II** had a shorter wheelbase and a full 4x4 drive. After early experience with the Mk I vehicles against the Italians in East Africa, the South Africans thereafter confined the vehicles mainly to training purposes, but the Mk IIs went on to better things.

The Mk II, known to the British as the **Armoured Car, Marmon Herrington, Mk II**, was a fairly simple but effective conversion of the original truck chassis to take the new 4x4 transmission and a well-shaped armoured hull. The early versions had a turret on the roof mounting a Vickers 7.7mm

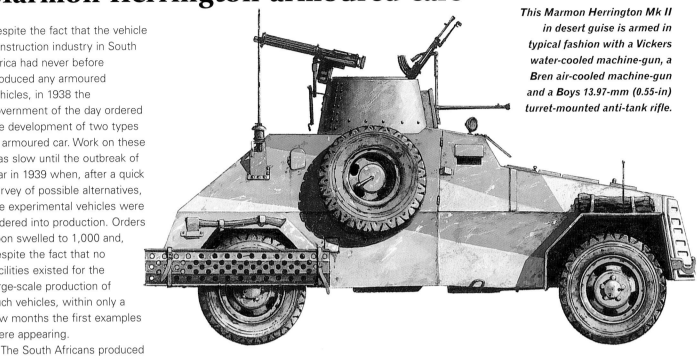

This Marmon Herrington Mk II in desert guise is armed in typical fashion with a Vickers water-cooled machine-gun, a Bren air-cooled machine-gun and a Boys 13.97-mm (0.55-in) turret-mounted anti-tank rifle.

(0.303-in) machine-gun, another light machine-gun being located in the hull front, but once this combination had been tried in action it was changed to a Boys 13.97-mm (0.55-in) anti-tank rifle mounted alongside a 0.303-in machine-gun in the turret. The vehicle had a crew of four housed in the roomy hull, and the engine was a Ford V-8.

When they were first produced and issued to South African and British units in North Africa, the Marmon Herringtons were the only armoured cars available in any numbers, and thus they formed the main equipment of reconnaissance units operating during the early Western Desert campaigns. They proved to be surprisingly effective vehicles, but their 12-mm (0.47-in) armour was often too thin to be of much use, and the armament was really too light. The troops in the field made their own changes to the armament and all manner of weapons sprouted from the turrets or from the open hulls once the turrets had been removed. One of the more common weapon fits was a captured Italian 20-mm Breda cannon, but Italian and German 37-mm (1.45-in) and 45-mm (1.77-in) tank or anti-tank guns

were also used. One vehicle mounted a British 2-pdr (40-mm/1.57-in) tank gun, and this became the preferred armament for later marks. The **Armoured Car, Marmon Herrington Mk III** was basically

similar to the Mk II though based on slightly shorter chassis, and lacked the double rear doors of the Mk II.

The Mk IIs had a hard time during the desert campaigns, but they kept going and were

This official photograph shows a Marmon Herrington Mk II armoured car in its original form with a Vickers 0.303-in (7.7-mm) machine-gun in the turret and another in a side-mounted mantlet. This latter weapon position was soon discarded and extra weapon positions were provided around the open turret.

SPECIFICATION	
Marmon Herrington Mk IV	**Powerplant:** one 63-kW (85 hp) Ford
Crew: 4	V-8 petrol engine
Weight: 6.4 tonnes	**Performance:** maximum speed 80.5
Dimensions: length 4.57 m (15 ft)	km/h (50 mph); maximum range
without gun; height 2.13 m (7 ft);	322 km (200 miles)
width 1.83 m (6 ft)	

well-liked and sturdy vehicles. Local modifications were many and varied, and ranged from command and repair vehicles to versions with as many as four Bren guns in a turret. Gradually they were supplemented and eventually replaced by more formal armoured car designs such as the Humber. Later

marks of Marmon Herrington served in other theatres, some even falling into Japanese hands in the Far East, and the number of formal versions was later extended to eight, including the **Mk IV** inspired by the German eight-wheeler armoured cars, but after the Mk IV most remained as

prototype vehicles only. The **Armoured Car, Marmon Herrington Mk IV** was a markedly different vehicle, being a monocoque design with rear engine. Weighing 6.4 tons, the Mk IV was armed with a 2-pdr gun and co-axial 7.62-mm (0.3-in) Browning machine-gun. A variant of this was the

Mk IVF which used Canadian Ford rather than Marmon Herrington automotive components. For a nation with limited production and development potential the Marmon Herrington armoured cars were an outstanding South African military and industrial achievement.

BA-10 Armoured car

The first **BA-10** six-wheeled armoured car appeared in 1932. It was produced at the Gorki automobile plant, and was the logical outcome of a series of six-wheeled armoured cars that could be traced back to World War I, even though the configuration had been in abeyance for some years. The BA-10 was built on the chassis of the GAZ-AAA six-wheeled civilian truck, although the suspension was modified to assume the loads involved, and some reinforcements were made to the chassis members. The layout of the BA-10 was orthodox, with the engine under an armoured cover at the front and the turret mounted at the rear over the twin rear axles. There were several variations in the armament carried, but the main armament was either a 37-mm (1.46-in) tank gun or a 12.7-mm (0.5-in) DShK heavy machine-gun. Later versions mounted a 45-mm (1.77-in) main gun.

All-terrain equipment

Like other Soviet armoured fighting vehicles, the BA-10 was a functional and hefty item of equipment. It had several typically Soviet design sub-features such as the ability to wear tracks or chains on the rear wheels to assist traction in mud and snow, and the spare wheels were located so that they could turn when obstacles under the chassis were encountered, and thus take some of the load. There was a

The Soviet BA-10 armoured car looked as though it belonged to a previous era, but despite its weight and bulk it proved to be well suited to the distances and terrain of the USSR. The large turret mounted a 37-mm (1.46-in) or 45-mm (1.77-in) main gun.

crew of four, one of whom attended to the 7.62-mm (0.3-in) machine-gun fitted into a mounting on the front superstructure to the right of the driver.

Later versions of the BA-10 are sometimes known as the **BA-32**, and to confuse matters further one of these latter variants is sometimes known as the **BA-10M**. This first appeared in 1937 and used the turret of the T-26B light tank with its 45-mm gun. This was not the only tank turret so used, others known to have been fitted were the turret of the experimental T-30 light tank and that of the BT-3 tank. One odd variation of the BA-10 that appeared in 1932 was the **BAZ** amphibious vehicle, which used the basic BA-10 hull allied to a flotation body derived from

contemporary German experimental vehicles. Only a few were produced.

When the Germans invaded the USSR in 1941, the BA-10 and its later derivatives were in service in some numbers with the Red Army, the number 1,200 often being quoted. However, the events of 1941–42 decimated the numbers of BA-10s, and large quantities fell into the hands of the Germans, who found these Soviet types to be serviceable vehicles, although they considered them not really

modern or mobile enough for use with their Panzer units, and kept them for use with anti-partisan units both in the USSR and in the Balkans. The Germans knew the BA-10 as the **Panzerspähwagen BAF 203(r)**; some of their reports mention the vehicle as a Ford product.

After 1942 the Soviets started to phase out the use of heavy armoured cars such as the BA-10. Those that remained were often relegated to the armoured personnel carrier role, having their turrets removed.

SPECIFICATION	
BA-10M	
Crew: 4	**Powerplant:** one GAZ-M-1 water-cooled 4-cylinder petrol engine developing 63 kW (86 hp)
Dimensions: length 4.7 m (15 ft 5 in); width 2.09 m (6 ft 10½ in); height 2.42 m (7 ft 11¼ in)	**Performance:** maximum speed 87 km/h (54 mph); maximum range 320 km (199 miles)

AEC armoured cars

The first AEC (Associated Engineering Company Ltd of Southall, London) armoured car was virtually a wheeled tank. The resultant vehicle was large by contemporary standards and equipped with armour nearly as thick as that used on contemporary 'cruiser' tanks. The chassis was based on the Matador artillery tractor. By the time this had been revised for the armoured car role many changes had been introduced, including an engine set at a slight front-to-rear angle to enable the overall height of the vehicle to be lowered.

The AEC vehicles, used to provide fire-support for armoured car regiments until the end of the war, had a conventional layout with the engine located at the rear.

Initial order

The first example was demonstrated in early 1941 and an order was placed in June of that year. The **Armoured Car, AEC Mk I** mounted a 2-pdr (40-mm/1.57-in) gun and co-axial 7.92-mm (0.31-in) Besa machine-gun in the same turret that was used on the Valentine tank, but only 120 vehicles were produced before calls came for something more powerful for use in North Africa. The result was a revision that introduced a new three-man turret mounting a 6-pdr (57-mm/2.24-in) gun, but this was not powerful enough, and the **Armoured Car, AEC Mk II** was replaced in production by the **Armoured Car, AEC Mk III** with the same turret mounting a British-developed version of the American M3 75-mm (2.95-in) tank gun. This made the AEC Mk III a very powerful armoured car.

Restricted vision

The AEC armoured vehicles had a full 4x4 drive configuration, but it was possible to alter this to a 4x2 form. The degree of protection for the crew was such that the driver had no direct vision devices, and as a result, had to rely on periscopes. However, with the hatch open, the driver's seat could be raised to allow him to see. The vehicle had a slab-sided appearance,

mainly as a result of the large lockers between the front and rear mudguards. Revisions, therefore, had to be made to the front hull on the AEC Mk II to improve obstacle crossing and armour protection.

Production of all the AEC armoured car marks ceased after 629 had been built. The vehicles were used in North Africa, Tunisia and Italy. Some Mk IIIs were used by regiments in north west Europe until the end of the war.

SPECIFICATION	
Armoured Car, AEC Mk I	**Powerplant:** one AEC 6-cylinder
Crew: 3	diesel engine developing 78 kW
Weight: (in action) 11 tonnes	(105 bhp)
Dimensions: length overall 5.18 m	**Performance:** maximum speed
(17 ft); width 2.7 m (8 ft 10½ in);	58 km/h (36 mph); maximum range
height 2.55 m (8 ft 4½ in)	402 km (250 miles)

SPECIFICATION	
Armoured Car, AEC Mk II and Mk III	**Powerplant:** one AEC 6-cylinder
Crew: 4	diesel engine developing 116 kW
Weight: (in action) 12.7 tonnes	(155 bhp)
Dimensions: length overall (Mk II)	**Performance:** maximum speed
5.18 m (17 ft) or (Mk III) 5.61 m	66 km/h (41 mph); maximum range
(18 ft 5 in); width 2.7 m (8 ft	402 km (250 miles)
10½ in); height 2.69 m (8 ft 10 in)	

This AEC Mk I, recognisable by the ex-Valentine infantry tank turret and 2-pdr gun, was one of the first to arrive in North Africa.

Daimler armoured cars

When the BSA Scout Car was undergoing its initial trials, it was decided to use the basic design as the foundation for a new vehicle to be called the **Tank, Light, Wheeled**. Daimler took over the development of the project, and the result was a vehicle that resembled the diminutive Scout Car but was nearly twice as heavy and had a two-man turret. Development started in August 1939 and the first prototypes were running by the end of the year. However, the extra weight of the turret and armour overloaded the transmission. It was some time before these problems were fixed, but in April 1941, the first production examples appeared. By then the vehicle was known as the **Armoured Car, Daimler Mk I**.

The Daimler Armoured Car was basically a Scout Car enlarged to accommodate a turret mounting a 2-pdr (40-mm/1.57-in) gun. The turret also mounted a co-axial 7.92-mm (0.31-in) Besa machine-gun. The four-wheel

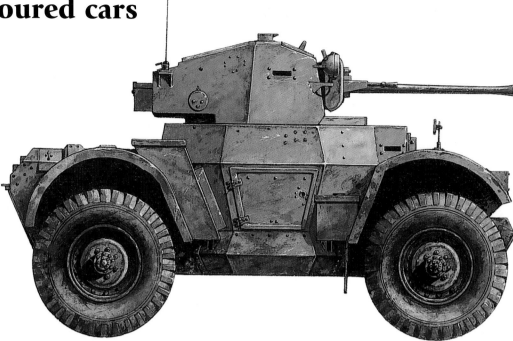

The Daimler armoured car was one of the best of all the British armoured cars, and the one that became the standard equipment for many reconnaissance regiments. Armed with a 2-pdr gun, it had limited combat capability but proved to be an excellent and reliable reconnaissance vehicle in all theatres.

drive used double-coil springs on each wheel, although the early idea of using four-wheel steering was discarded as being too complex. One advanced feature was the use of Girling hydraulic disc brakes. A fluid flywheel was used in place of the more usual clutch arrangement. A duplicate steering wheel and simple controls were provided for use by the commander in an emergancy to drive to the rear.

New guns

The Daimler underwent surprisingly few changes once in service. An **Armoured Car, Daimler Mk II** version was later introduced with a new gun mounting, a slightly revised radiator arrangement and an escape hatch through the engine compartment for the driver. There was also an experimental **Armoured Car, Daimler Mk I CS**, which had a 76.2-mm (3-in) howitzer in place of the 2-pdr (40-mm) gun to provide close support fire. Another alteration was a small number of operational Mk Is, which were fitted with the Littlejohn Adaptor, a squeeze-bore muzzle attachment that enabled the 2-pdr gun to fire small projectiles that could penetrate thicker armour.

Performance

When the first Daimler Armoured Cars arrived in North Africa during 1941–42, they soon gained a reputation for good all-round performance and reliability. By the end of the war, some were employed as scout or command vehicles with their turrets removed, but turreted vehicles continued to serve for many years after 1945. The total production was 2,694.

A Daimler Mk I armoured car engaging enemy targets while a patrol of infantry stands by ready to go into action.

SPECIFICATION	
Armoured Car, Daimler Mk I	**Powerplant:** one Daimler 6-cylinder petrol engine developing 71 kW (95 bhp)
Crew: 3	
Weight: (in action) 7.5 tonnes	
Dimensions: length 3.96 m (13 ft); width 2.44 m (8 ft); height 2.24 m (7 ft 4 in)	**Performance:** maximum speed 80.5 km/h (50 mph); maximum range 330 km (205 miles)

Daimler scout cars

During the late 1930s the British Army was converting to mechanised traction and forming its first armoured divisions. These new formations required a small 4x4 scout car for liaison and reconnaissance duties. BSA Cycles Ltd, Morris Commercial Cars Ltd and Alvis Ltd all produced prototype designs. The BSA submission won. The War Office ordered a total of 172 examples as the **Car, Scout, Mk I** and more orders followed later.

By the time the order was placed the project had been taken over by Daimler, and the designation **Car, Scout, Daimler Mk I** was applied to the vehicle. The War Office also called for more all-round protection, as the original vehicle only provided the two-man crew with frontal armour.

Extra armour

The extra armour and a folding roof added enough weight to require an improved suspension and more powerful engine. Once these changes had been incorporated in the **Daimler Mk IA**, the Daimler Scout Car

remained virtually unaltered throughout its long service life. It was a simple design with a full 4x4 drive configuration and front-axle steering from the **Daimler Mk II** onwards. The only armament carried was a single 7.7-mm (0.303-in) Bren Gun firing through a hatch in the front superstructure, although other arrangements such as anti-aircraft mountings were sometimes provided.

The Daimler Scout Car proved itself to be a very tough and reliable vehicle. It had the unusual distinction of being one of the few World War II vehicles in service when the war started and still remaining in production as the war ended. As well as being a reconnaissance platform, it was used by artillery units as a mobile observation post and by the Royal Engineers for locating mine fields and bridging positions. Many staff officers used them as run-arounds and liaison vehicles, and they were often added to motorised infantry units for reconnaissance and liaison purposes.

The Daimler Scout Car was in production as World War II began and was still in production when it ended. Although only lightly armed it was quiet and highly mobile, and proved to be one of the best of all the reconnaissance vehicles in use by any side throughout the war.

Below: These Daimler Scout cars are ready for the Tunis Victory Parade of May 1943. Behind them is a Daimler armoured car and a Humber Mk II; the aircraft is a French Caudron Goeland captured from the Luftwaffe. These vehicles were used on the occasion as escorts for some of the VIPs arriving for the parade.

SPECIFICATION	
Car, Scout, Daimler Mk I	**Powerplant:** one Daimler 6-cylinder
Crew: 2	petrol engine developing 41 kW
Weight: (in action) 3 tonnes	(55 bhp)
Dimensions: length 3.23 m (10 ft 5	**Performance:** maximum speed 88.5
in); width 1.72 m (5 ft 7½ in); height	km/h (55 mph); maximum range
1.50 m (4 ft 11 in)	322 km (200 miles)

Humber armoured cars

The Humber armoured cars were numerically the most important types produced in the UK and production eventually reached 5,400. The type had its origins in a pre-war Guy armoured car known as the **Tank, Light, Wheeled Mk I**, of which Guy produced 101 examples. By October 1940, it was realised that Guy's production facilities would be fully occupied producing light tanks and production was switched to the Rootes Group and Karrier Motors Ltd of Luton. The Guy design was rejigged for installation on a Karrier KT 4 artillery tractor chassis, Guy continuing to supply the armoured hulls and turrets. Although the new model was virtually identical to the original Guy design it was re-named the **Armoured Car, Humber Mk I**.

The Humber Mk I had a relatively short wheelbase, but it was never manoeuvrable and used a welded hull. The turret mounted two Besa machine-guns, a heavy 15-mm (0.59-in) and a lighter 7.92-mm (0.31-in) weapon. The first production batch ran to 500 vehicles before the **Armoured Car, Humber Mk II** introduced some improvements to the front hull, which had a pronounced slope. The **Armoured Car, Humber Mk III** had a larger turret that allowed a crew of four to be carried, while the **Armoured Car, Humber Mk IV** reverted to a crew of three as the turret housed an American 37-mm (1.45-in) gun. An odd feature of this vehicle

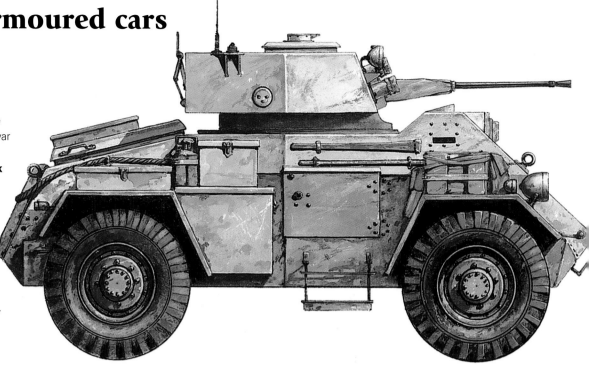

was that the driver was provided with a lever which raised a hatch in the rear bulkhead for use as rear vision in an emergency.

North Africa

The first Humber armoured cars were used operationally in North Africa from late 1941 onwards, while the Humber Mk IV did not see service until the early stages of the Italian campaign. Thereafter all four marks were used wherever British and Allied troops fought in Europe. A version was produced in Canada with some changes to suit Canadian production methods. This was known as the **Armoured Car, General Motors Mk I, Fox I**, and the main change was that the main armament was a 12.7-mm (0.5-in) Browning heavy machine-gun plus a

The Humber Armoured Car Mk II was one of the few armoured vehicles to use the 15-mm (0.59-in) Besa heavy machine-gun as its main armament. Originally known as a wheeled tank, these vehicles gave sterling service in many theatres throughout the war.

7.62-mm (0.3-in) Browning medium machine-gun. There was also an extensive conversion of the Humber Mk III as a special radio carrier known as a Rear Link vehicle. This had a fixed turret with a dummy gun. Another radio-carrying version was used as a mobile artillery observation post, and numbers of Canadian Foxes were converted for this role. A later addition to many Humber

armoured cars was a special anti-aircraft mounting using Vickers 'K' machine-guns that could be fired from within the turret. A final variant, known as the **Armoured Car, Humber, AA, Mk I**, had four 7.92-mm (0.31-in) Besa machine-guns installed in a special turret. These were introduced in 1943, but were later withdrawn during 1944 as there was no longer any need for them.

SPECIFICATION	
Humber Mks I to IV	
Crew: 3 (4 in Mk III)	**Powerplant:** one Rootes 6-cylinder water-cooled petrol engine developing 67 kW (90 bhp)
Weight: (in action) 6.85 tonnes (Mk I) or 7.1 tonnes (Mks II to IV)	
Dimensions: length 4.57 m (15 ft); width 2.18 m (7 ft 2 in); height 2.34 m (7 ft 10 in)	**Performance:** maximum speed 72 km/h (45 mph); maximum range 402 km (250 miles)

Light Armored Car M8

Armoured cars have long been a feature of the American armoured fighting vehicle scene, and in 1940 and 1941 the US Army was able to observe operational trends in Europe and so develop a new armoured car with a good

performance, a 37-mm (1.46-in) gun, 6x6 drive, a low silhouette and light weight. In typical American fashion, design submissions were requested from four manufacturers. One of the manufacturers, Ford, produced a design known as

the **T22**, and this was later judged to be the best of all submissions and was ordered into production as the **Light Armored Car M8**.

Superior performance

The M8 subsequently became

the most important of all the American armoured cars and by the time production was terminated in April 1945 no fewer than 11,667 had been produced. It was a superb fighting vehicle with an excellent cross-country performance, and an indication of its sound design can be seen in the fact that many were still in use with several armies until the mid 1970s.

It was a low vehicle with a full 6x6 drive configuration, with the axles arranged as one forward and two to the rear. The wheels were normally well covered by mud-guards, but these were sometimes removed in action. The crew of four had ample room inside the vehicle, and the main 37-mm (1.46-in) gun was mounted in a circular open tur-ret. A 7.62-mm (0.3-in) Browning machine-gun was mounted co-axially, and there was a pintle for a 12.7-mm (0.5-in) Browning heavy machine-gun (for anti-air-craft use) on the turret rear.

A close cousin of the M8 was the **Armored Utility Car M20**, in which the turret was removed and the fighting compartment cut away to allow the interior to be used as a personnel or supplies carrier. A machine-gun could be mounted on a ring mount over the open area. In many ways the M20 became as important as the M8 for it proved an invaluable run-about for many purposes, from an observation post to an ammuni-tion carrier for tank units.

Popular vehicle

The US Army employed the M8 and M20 widely from the time

The American Light Armored Car M8 was considered too light in armour by the British, but was otherwise widely used. The main gun was a 37-mm (1.46-in) gun with a 7.62-mm (0.3-in) machine-gun mounted co-axially. A common addition was a 12.7-mm (0.5-in) Browning machine-gun mounted on the turret.

the first production examples left the production lines in March 1943. By November of that year over 1,000 had been delivered, and during 1943 the type was issued to British and Commonwealth formations. The British knew the M8 as the **Greyhound** but it proved to be too thinly armoured to suit British thinking, the thin belly armour proving too vulnerable to anti-tank mines. Operationally this shortcoming was overcome by lining the interior floor areas with sandbags. These drawbacks were more than overcome by the fact that the M8 was

available in large numbers and that it was able to cross almost any terrain. The 37-mm main gun was well able to tackle almost any enemy reconnais-sance vehicle the M8 was likely to encounter, and the vehicle's crew could defend the M8 against infantry with the two machine-guns. The M8 could be kept going under all

circumstances, but its main attribute was that it nearly always seemed to be available when it was wanted.

The M8 can still be found in service in Central and South America, most partially updated with diesel power packs and automatic transmission. A few are anti-tank missile carriers.

A typical M3 advances through a wrecked village in early 1945. Judging by the all-opened up state of the vehicle hatches, the crew do not seem to anticipate trouble.

An M8 armoured car seen during a routine reconnaissance situation during the Normandy fighting of 1944. The crew have stopped to observe some enemy movement or positions, and two men are observing through binoculars to obtain as comprehensive an assessment as possible.

SPECIFICATION	
Light Armored Car M8	82 kW (110 hp)
Crew: 4	**Performance:** maximum road speed
Weight: (in action) 7.94 tonnes	89 km/h (55 mph); maximum range
Dimensions: length 5 m (16 ft 5 in);	563 km (350 miles)
width 2.54 m (8 ft 4 in); height	**Fording:** 0.61 m (2 ft)
2.25 m (7 ft 4½ in)	**Gradient:** 60 per cent
Powerplant: one Hercules JXD	**Vertical obstacle:** 0.3 m (1 ft)
6-cylinder petrol engine developing	

M8 in operation

Scouting with the Greyhound

The M8 had a commendably low silhouette in comparison with the World War II German armoured cars. The reasonably well sloped front hull was proof against light cannon fire.

Colombia was one of the few countries operating the M8 into the 1980s to modernise its vehicles. NAPCO Industries in the US supplied new Detroit diesel engines and Allison automatic transmissions, and the company also sold the Colombian army a conversion kit that enabled the M8 armoured car to be fitted with the well-respected TOW long-range anti-tank missile. The kit included the launcher system, training simulators for the crew and necessary spares. The TOW system was mounted above the turret and could be rapidly dismounted for use in the ground role. One missile was carried on the launcher itself, one on the turret and three more reloads could be carried in the vehicle, fixed to a sliding rack in the driver's compartment. Thus equipped, this was an unusual example of an armoured vehicle carrying missiles, each one of which cost more than the vehicle!

Colombian M8s

The Colombians replaced the M8's 37-mm gun with a remotely fired M2 Browning 0.5-in machine-gun, which used

FIGHTING SCOUT: M8 FIREPOWER

Above: An M8 in action during the Allied advance to the German border in 1944. The 37-mm gun could deal with most enemy reconnaissance vehicles that the M8 was likely to encounter.

A well-laden M8, with the Browning 0.5-in heavy machine-gun fitted to the turret roof, rolls down the Champs-Elysées. The co-axial 0.3-in machine-gun can be seen to the immediate right of the 37-mm main gun in the front of the turret. The 37-mm M6 weapon fired a 0.86-kg (1.90-lb) projectile at 885 m (2,904 ft) per second, and could penetrate 48 mm (1.89 in) of armour at 800 m (870 yards).

the original elevating mechanism and sight. Since ammunition for the 37-mm gun was equally obsolete, machine-guns were the main armament of most of the M8s that remained operational in Africa. Armies credited with operating M8s into the late 1980s included Benin, Cameroon, Congo, Madagascar, Niger, Senegal, Togo and Upper Volta. Larger forces still using the M8 at this time ranged from Brazil to Turkey, Colombia and Mexico.

Utility variant

A close relative of the M8 was the Armored Utility Car M20, in which the turret was removed and the fighting compartment cut away to allow the interior to be used as a personnel or supplies carrier. A machine-gun could be attached on a ring mount over the open area. In many ways the M20 became as important as the M8, for it proved to be an invaluable 'run-about' for a number of purposes, ranging from an observation or command post to an ammunition carrier.

The US Army employed the M8 and M20 widely from the time the first production examples left the production lines in March 1943. By November of that year over 1,000 had been delivered, and during 1943 the type was issued to British and Commonwealth formations. The British knew the M8 as the Greyhound, but it proved to be too thinly armoured to suit British thinking, the thin belly armour proving too vulnerable to anti-tank mines. Operationally this shortcoming was overcome by lining the interior floor areas with sandbags.

The 37-mm main gun was well able to tackle almost any enemy reconnaissance vehicle the M8 encountered, and the vehicle's crew could defend the M8 against infantry with the two machine-guns. The M8's main attribute was that it nearly always seemed to be available.

The M8 armoured car was adopted by the US Army on the eve of its involvement in World War II. Here, US M8s advance along a road in Tunisia after the Allied landings in North Africa. As internal space was limited, the crew of the M8 had to strap their kit to any convenient location on the hull or turret.

Scout Car M3 White

The US Army employed scout cars for reconnaissance and general battlefield liaison duties as far back as 1917. In the 1930s a new 4x4 model was required, with the entrant from the White Motor Company emerging as the final choice.

The main production model was the **Scout Car M3A1** which appeared in 1939 and was manufactured in quantity for the US Army. The M3A1 was lightly armoured (up to a maximum of 12.7 mm/0.50 in) and the top was left open, other than canvas weather protection, to provide a good field of view but this exposed the occupants, up to six in the rear, to overhead fire. Underside protection was also limited,

exposing the occupants to the effects of land mines.

While the 82-kW (110-hp) or 89.5-kW (120-hp) petrol engine provided a good road speed, the cross-country performance was eventually judged as below requirements, even after a front-mounted obstacle crossing roller was added. In addition the original road range (410 km/255 miles) was regarded as too short, although measures were taken to increase this. The M3 half track series, developed from the Scout Car by adding half tracks at the rear and enlarging the rear area, therefore assumed many of the Scout Car's intended tasks in US service.

The Scout Car M3A1, which first appeared in 1939, was produced for the US Army. It was lightly armoured and had a good road speed performance.

Varied weapon fits

A total of 20,918 Scout Cars were produced, many handed out as 'Lend-Lease' on a generous scale to Allied armed forces, including the USSR where a post-war copy, the BTR-40, was produced in quantity.

The usual armament, if carried, was limited to one or two machine-guns and the crew's personal weapons, although some other weapon fits were proposed. Attempts to convert the vehicle into a light tank destroyer with a 37-mm

(1.46-in) anti-tank gun came to nothing. Some Scout Cars were employed as light weapon tractors, while others served as light front-line supply carriers, forward area ambulances, or communication and command vehicles. After 1945 surviving Scout Cars were distributed worldwide where their employment extended to police and other internal security forces. They may still be encountered in Central and South America although many have now been provided with diesel engines.

SPECIFICATION	
M3A1 Scout Car	**Performance:** maximum speed
Crew: up to 8	90 km/h (56 mph); maximum range
Weight: (in action) 5.92 tonnes	410 km (255 miles)
Dimensions: length 5.63 m (18 ft	**Fording:** 0.71 m (2 ft 4 in)
5 in); width 2.03 m (6 ft 8 in);	**Gradient:** 60 per cent
height 1.99 m (6 ft 5 in)	**Vertical obstacle:** 0.31 m (1 ft)
Powerplant: one 89.5-kW (120-hp)	
Hercules JXD petrol engine	

Light Armored Car T17E1 Staghound

Although the **Staghound** armoured car was an American product, it was not used by the American forces, all output going to the British Army and other Allied and Commonwealth forces. The design had its origins in a US Army requirement for a heavy armoured car, the **T17E1**. The British Tank Mission asked for an initial batch of 300, more

orders followed and by the end of 1942 the first examples were coming off the production lines to be issued to British and Commonwealth units as the **Staghound Mk I**.

Sturdy vehicle

It emerged as a large and well-armoured vehicle with a turret mounting a 37-mm (1.46-in) gun and a co-axial 7.62-mm (0.3-in)

A Staghound AA armoured car with twin 0.5-in (12.7-mm) machine-guns intended specifically for the defence of armoured units against low-flying aircraft.

Browning machine-gun. The type first went into action in Italy in 1943 and was then issued to Canadian, New Zealand, Indian and Belgian units. The Staghound had several unusual features such as a fully automatic hydraulic transmission, two engines mounted side-by-side at the rear, and the crew were

The T17E1 Staghound was a reliable and sturdy vehicle with a 37-mm (1.46-in) main gun and was unusual in being powered by two petrol engines.

provided with periscopes. The turret was hydraulically traversed, with additional armament provided by two more 7.62-mm (0.3-in) Browning machine-guns, one pintle-mounted for anti-aircraft use and the other in the hull front.

Once in service several variations appeared. One was the fitting of a 76.2-mm (3-in) close-support howitzer in place of the 37-mm (1.46-in) gun. The **Staghound Mk III** accommodated a Crusader tank turret mounting a 75-mm (2.95-in) gun.

American version

A production variant developed in the US was the **Staghound AA** (**T17E2**) with a power-operated turret mounting two 12.7-mm (0.5-in) Browning machine guns for anti-aircraft use. There were numerous other conversions and local variations of the Staghound, ranging from mine-clearing experimental models pushing heavy rollers to the **Staghound Command**. The Staghound was a sturdy and well-liked armoured car that gave excellent service.

SPECIFICATION	
Staghound Mk I	**Performance:** maximum speed
Crew: 5	89 km/h (55 mph); maximum range
Weight: (in action) 13.92 tonnes	724 km (450 miles)
Dimensions: length 5.49 m (18 ft);	**Fording:** 0.8 m (2 ft 8 in)
width 2.69 m (8 ft 10 in); height	**Gradient:** 57 per cent
2.36 m (7 ft 9 in)	**Vertical obstacle:** 0.53 m (1 ft 9 in)
Powerplant: two 72-kW (97-hp)	
GMC 270 6-cylinder petrol engines	

World War II recce
Looking for trouble

In warfare there are three main categories of reconnaissance: strategic or operational; tactical, and battle reconnaissance.

A Daimler armoured car opens up with the first shots of the Battle of Tripoli. Although more used to operating on reconnaissance missions, this vehicle is engaging enemy targets, while accompanying infantry prepare to fight.

Operational or strategic reconnaissance deals mainly with the larger aspects of warfare, such as the disposition of armies rather than divisions, and the likely major supply routes (railways, etc). This is conducted by radio interceptions at high command levels, aerial reconnaissance on a large scale, and economic appreciations. It is not an intelligence level with which armoured car units have everyday involvement. However, the two lower levels of battlefield and tactical reconnaissance frequently involve armoured units.

On the battlefield

Battlefield reconnaissance deals with the reconnaissance of definite objectives within the immediate operational area. Here again, armoured car and other reconnaissance units can become involved. Battlefield reconnaissance concerns several separate aspects, such as pure terrain reconnaissance down to special patrols and battlefield patrols to probe enemy strengths.

Tactical reconnaissance is the most important part of the armoured car units' tasks. It

Keeping watch downstream for the enemy. A German armoured car commander fixes his gaze through his binoculars. Meanwhile, his gunner sits at the ready with his 20-mm cannon.

involves scouting ahead of one's own forces to determine the path of an advance by probing the enemy strengths and weaknesses and gathering information on defensive belts and mobility-blocking measures. This information gives the main body time to prepare for difficulties. One old maxim says that: 'time spent in reconnaissance is rarely wasted'.

Rommel short-circuited the reconnaissance report bottle-

neck as information flowed up the chain of command, by riding forward with reconnaissance units.

During World War II all units up to divisional level had at least one battalion or equivalent-sized unit that dealt entirely with reconnaissance. The British even began a formation known as the Reconnaissance Corps to deal with this subject. The German Panzer division had an integral reconnaissance battalion as did

the Soviet mechanised and armoured divisions.

Generally speaking, the British and Commonwealth forces tended to keep their mobile reconnaissance low key. Armoured and scout car units

FINDING THE BATTLE: AMERICAN ARRANGEMENTS

The American reconnaissance arrangements were similar to those of the British and Germans. Throughout World War II, the Americans preferred M8 light armoured cars (above) or M20 utility vehicles for the reconnais-sance role, operating with their armoured and tank destroyer battalions. However, American and German reconnaissance vehicles tended to be armed with noticeably heavier weapons than their British counterparts.

were intended to be used in as stealthy and concealed a manner as possible. They were not intended to be used as direct combat troops. They had sufficient strength that if they did encounter opposition, they could fight their way out to a limited degree.

Light armament

Another aspect was the relative lightness of the British armament carried on scout and armoured cars. At the beginning of the war most British armoured cars were limited to machine-guns, while American

equivalents were armed with at least a 37-mm cannon.

The Germans later upgunned their armoured cars to 50-mm (0.97-in) and even short 75-mm (2.95-in) tank guns. The British tended to stick to their 2-pdr gun with a 40-mm (1.575-in) calibre. Only relatively few vehicles were equipped with 6-pdr (57-mm/2.244-in) guns, 76.2-mm (3-in) howitzers or 75-mm (2.95-in) guns.

Soviet methodology

The Soviets started their 'Great Patriotic War' with some armoured cars, but they

accorded the armoured car a low production and develop-ment priority. After 1942 the Red Army reconnaissance units used whatever they had to hand, which tended to mean the T-34 tank. Some units were issued with light tanks such as the T-60, and a few units used

the BA-64 armoured car for reconnaissance, but most units had to rely on the T-34. Ranging ahead of the massed Red Army tank units, small units of T-34s could carry out their reconnaissance functions while maintaining a considerable potential with their 76-mm (3-in) main guns and thick armour.

Scouting

It was not unusual during World War II for small units of armoured or scout cars to be attached to tank companies for local scouting. The unit commander would often ride forward in a scout vehicle. The Germans were frequently forced by equipment shortages to use any vehicle available. This could include captured Soviet vehicles or even completely unarmoured and unarmed light vehicles.

However, there was often the problem of reconnaissance units moving too far ahead of the formations. The typical interval between the forward recce troops and the main body of the formation was supposed to be one day's march, typically 25 km (15 miles), although this was not always observed.

*Above: Light tanks such as this **German Panzerkampfwagen II** were used for reconnaissance. The use of light tanks by the **Germans** was the exception rather than the norm. The **Soviets**, however, made use of **T-34** tanks in the reconnaissance role when their production facilities for armoured cars became overrun during the Axis advance following the commencement of **Operation Barbarossa**.*

*Left: Another grim day on the eastern front. The **German** army used its **Puma** armoured cars for reconnaissance missions. The vehicle pictured is seen behind two normal road cars, which coincidentally were also used for reconnaissance missions when equipment shortages became critical.*

Demolition charges

The demolition charges used by the British 'funnies' of World War II were mainly carried by Churchill AVREs, for the emplacing of these powerful charges was one of the tasks for which the AVRE was created. The charges themselves were special obstacle-demolishing packs of high explosive that had to be placed against the target, which could be anything from a sea or anti-tank wall to a blockhouse.

Various charges

Sometimes the charges were large single chunks of explosive, and in others they were small charges set in a pattern and held in a steel frame. One thing all the various charges did have in common was odd and even bizarre names. One of the more straightforward of these charge devices was the **Bangalore Torpedo**. These pipe charges were intended for clearing mines and barbed wire entan-

glements, but could be used for other purposes.

Jones Onion

On the AVRE they were held in front-mounted frames, also used for the **Jones Onion**. The Jones Onion first appeared in 1942 and was the codename

The Jones Onion, seen here carried by a Churchill tank, was a demolition device carried on a steel frame that could be placed against an obstacle such as an anti-tank wall. The frame was then released to allow the tank to retire to safety and detonate the charge.

given to a frame on to which various charges could be attached. The frame was carried on two arms, one on each side of the AVRE, and held upright as the target was approached. Once in position the frame was released by pulling on a cable, and two legs on the bottom of the frame were so arranged that the frame always fell against the target obstacle. The charges could then be fired electrically by a trailing cable after the AVRE had reversed away.

Another device that appeared in 1942 was the **Carrot**. This was a much simpler device than the large Onion and consisted of a charge held in front of the AVRE on a simple steel arm. The idea was that the AVRE simply

An alternative view of the Jones Onion charge-carrying frame being lifted into position on its Churchill AVRE carrier. No charges have yet been installed.

moved up to the target and the charge was then ignited. The charges involved ranged in weight from 12 lb (5.44 kg) up to 25 lb (11.34 kg), the smaller charge rejoicing in the name of **Light Carrot**. The Carrot was used extensively for trials but was abandoned during late 1943 and not used in action. The Goat was used in action, and may be considered as a development of the **Onion** although it was much larger and involved the use of a frame 3.2 m (10 ft 6 in) wide and 1.98 m (6 ft 6 in) long. On to this frame could be arranged up to 816 kg (1,800 lb) of explosives, and the whole device was carried on the AVRE by side arms.

Goat variants

The Goat was so arranged that it could be pushed against the structure to be demolished and the frame would automatically release in a vertical position. The AVRE would then reverse, leaving the charges in position to be fired either electrically or by means of a pull igniter. A close cousin of the Goat was the **Elevatable Goat**. This was intended for use against high obstacles such as anti-tank walls, and when fitted on the AVRE was carried on the nose of the hull rather like an assault bridge.

Linked charges

The 'bridge' was in fact a frame on which linked charges were slung. The frame was placed against the wall to be demolished and then released from the AVRE. Once in position, another release cable allowed the linked charges to fall away from the frame. The top section of the frame was above the top of the wall, and this allowed the charges to fall onto each side of the wall, which could then be destroyed once the AVRE had moved away. Although some of these devices were used in action, they were somewhat clumsy contraptions that relied upon the carrier getting very close to the target and becoming exposed to retaliatory fire. Any wrong emplacement resulted in less than optimum results.

Spigot mortar

The obstacle demolition solution for the AVRE turned out to be the **'Flying Dustbin'**, a spigot mortar that fired a 290-mm (11.4-in) demolition charge with reasonable accuracy from a safer stand-off position.

In combat, the demolition charges laid by the AVREs amply fulfilled the expectations of the engineers who designed them. In 1944–45, the Western Allied armies broke through the strongest defences ever created, from the Normandy defences to the Siegfried line of fortifications that shielded the German border. These concrete and steel emplace- ments, surrounded by mines and barbed wire, were a tougher proposition than anything tackled by either the Germans themselves, when they were on the offensive, or the Russian armies closing in from the East. The use of specially converted armoured vehicles to lay demolition charges paved the way for today's AEVs (Armoured Engineer Vehicles) used by most major armies.

Churchill AVRE

Combat engineer vehicle

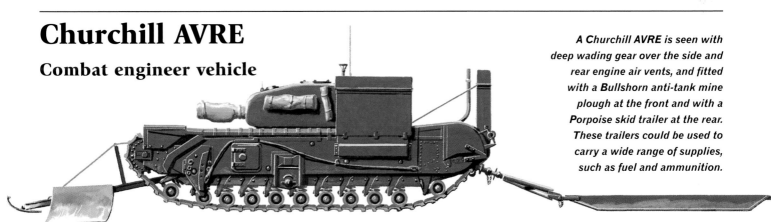

A Churchill AVRE is seen with deep wading gear over the side and rear engine air vents, and fitted with a Bullshorn anti-tank mine plough at the front and with a Porpoise skid trailer at the rear. These trailers could be used to carry a wide range of supplies, such as fuel and ammunition.

One of the lessons learned during the Dieppe raid of 1942 was that the Canadian engi- neers were unable to proceed with their obstacle demolitions and general beach-clearing because of a complete lack of cover against enemy fire. In the period after the raid, a Canadian engineer officer put forward the idea of using a tank converted to the combat engineer role so that it could carry engineers to the point at which they had to operate, and be capable of carrying a heavy demolition weapon. This would enable the combat engineers to operate from under armoured cover and would also enable them to oper- ate in close co-operation with armoured formations.

'Flying Dustbin'

The idea was accepted, and after some deliberation the Churchill tank was selected as the basic vehicle for conversion. The task consisted mainly of completely stripping out the tank's interior and removing the main armament, the interior then being completely rearranged to provide stowage for the various items combat engineers have to use, such as demolition explosives, special tools and mines. The main turret was retained but in place of the normal gun a special device known as a Petard was fitted. This was a spigot mortar that fired a 290-mm (11.4-in) demoli- tion charge known to the troops from its general shape as the 'Flying Dustbin'. The Petard pro- jectile weighed 40 lb (18.14 kg) and could be fired to a range of

73 m (80 yards) to demolish structures such as pillboxes, bunkers and buildings. The

The Churchill AVRE Mk II featured a fixed turret mounting a dummy gun. It could carry a front-mounted dismountable jib crane or a rear jib with a greater lift capacity. There was also a powerful front- mounted winch that could be used in conjunction with the jibs, and an earth anchor was mounted at the rear to stabilise the vehicle in winching mode.

*A **Churchill** **AVRE** special-purpose armoured vehicle climbs a ramp-type bridge toward the crest of an obstacle. Held at the front of the **AVRE** is a large fascine, which was a bundle of wooden stakes, about 3.66–4.26 m (12–14 ft) long and bound into a bundle some 2.44 m (8 ft) in diameter, used to fill gaps.*

Petard could be reloaded from within the vehicle.

Chuchill version

The Churchill version was known as the **Churchill AVRE (Armoured Vehicle Royal Engineers)** and quickly became standard equipment for armoured engineers attached to formations such as the 79th Armoured Division and the assault brigades, RE. As well as providing protection, the AVRE was soon tasked to carry many types of special equipment.

Mk III and IV

The Churchill versions used for the AVRE were the **Mks III** and **IV**. Many of the conversions were effected with kits, some by industry and some by REME workshops. The conversions included brackets and other attachment points around the hull to which specialised equipment items could be fixed. A hook at the rear was used to tow a special AVRE sledge for carrying combat stores.

New gun

The AVREs were first used on a large scale during the Normandy landings of June 1944, where they excelled themselves to such an extent that AVRE vehicles are still in service. The Churchill AVRE remained in service until the mid-1950s, and even later with some units. They were used to lay fascines, place mats across soft ground, demolish strongpoints with their Petard mortars, bring forward combat engineering stores, place heavy demolition charges and generally make themselves useful. Perhaps the most important long term function of the Churchill AVRE was to emphasise that specialised combat engineer tanks were an essential adjunct to armoured formation operations. One important post-war Churchill AVRE development was the replacement of the 'Flying Dustbin' spigot mortar by a specially developed 165-mm (6.5-in) demolition gun firing a 60-lb (27.2-kg) projectile with a HESH payload that could shatter even the strongest concrete obstacle. This gun was not only more accurate than the 'Flying Dustbin' but it could be breech loaded from within the protection of an AVRE turret. During the early 1950s about 13 Churchill AVREs were provided with the new gun. They served until 1962, when the last of them was replaced by the updated Centurion AVRE, still using the 165-mm demolition gun.

SPECIFICATION	
Churchill AVRE	2.79 m (9 ft 2 in)
Crew: 6	**Performance:** maximum road speed
Weight: 38 tons	24.9 km/h (15.5 mph); maximum
Powerplant: one Bedford Twin-Six	road range 193 km (120 miles)
liquid-cooled petrol engine	**Fording:** 1.02 m (3 ft 4 in)
developing 261 kW (350 hp)	**Vertical obstacle:** 0.76 m (2 ft 6 in)
Dimensions: length 7.67 m (25 ft 2	**Trench:** 3.05 m (10 ft)
in); width 3.25 m (10 ft 8 in); height	

*Having dropped its fascine, a **Churchill** **AVRE** teeters on the forward edge of an obstacle before nosing down onto the fascine and, if all goes well, moving forward away from the obstacle that had to be crossed. This was a training exercise.*

Mine-clearing rollers

The mine-clearing roller was one of the very first anti-mine devices used with tanks, and in theory rollers are among the simplest to use. They consist of a set of heavy rollers pushed ahead of the tank, their weight and pressure alone being sufficient to destroy the mines by setting them off in front of the tank. Translating this theory into practice should also have been simple, but was not. The main problem was the weight and bulk of the rollers that had to be used: in order to make the rollers heavy enough they had also to be large, and this made them very difficult loads to handle using the average tank of the period. In fact some of them were so large and awkward to push that it sometimes took two tanks (the carrier tank plus another behind it to provide extra 'push') to move them forward. This two-tank arrangement was often necessary when rollers had to be pushed over soft or rough ground.

Early experimentation

The British were probably the first to develop anti-mine rollers, and experimented with them in the years before World War II

The Lulu roller device did not detonate mines by pressure, as the front rollers were only light wooden containers carrying electrical sensor devices to denote the presence of buried metal objects such as mines. Although it worked in practice, the Lulu was considered too fragile for operational use.

fitted to vehicles such as the Covenanter. They knew their first models as the **Fowler Roller** or the **Anti-Mine Roller Attachment** (**AMRA**). From these were developed the **Anti-Mine Reconnaissance Castor Roller** (**AMRCR**) system that was fitted to Churchills and

British Shermans. These rollers used leaf springs to keep the rollers in contact with the ground, but they were so cumbersome that they were not used operationally. A more successful design appeared in 1943 as the **Canadian Indestruc-tible Roller Device**

(**CIRD**). This used two heavy armoured rollers mounted on side arms, and was so arranged that if a roller detonated a mine the resulting blast lifted the roller, and a lever came into contact with the ground. The subsequent movement of the tank then operated the lever so that the roller returned to the ground for further use. CIRD was fitted to both Churchills and Shermans, but the system was not used in action.

The Americans also became involved with mine rollers and produced three main models. The first version was the **Mine Exploder T1** and was intended for use with M3 Lee tanks, but not many were made as these tanks had passed from front-line service by the time the rollers had been developed. From this evolved the **Mine Exploder T1E1** or **Earthworm**, but again this was devised for use by one vehicle only, in this case the M32 Tank Recovery Vehicle. For use with the M4 Sherman there came the **Mine Exploder T1E3**

An M4 Sherman medium tank with one of the prototypes of the Mine Exploder T1E3 (later the Mine Exploder M1), generally known as the 'Aunt Jemima'. The size and bulk of this device are clearly shown.

(later the **Mine Exploder M1**), generally known as the '**Aunt Jemima**'. This used two very large sets of roller discs mounted on side arms in front of the carrier, and the system was used in action despite its great bulk and awkwardness. It proved to be successful enough, and was developed into an even heavier **M1A1**.

US developments

The Americans developed a whole string of other types of mine roller, few of which got past the experimental stage. Perhaps the oddest of them was the **Mine Exploder T10** on which the rollers became the road wheels for an M4 tank body, complete with gun turret. Two rollers were mounted

forward and another set of roller discs was at the rear with the tank body slung between them. This device got no further than trials, and neither did the series of vehicles known as the **Mine Resistant Vehicle T15**. This was an M4 tank fitted with extra body and belly armour and intended to set off mines by simply driving over them, relying on its extra protection for survival. None of these vehicles was ready for use by the time the war ended, and work on the type then ceased.

Mine rollers are still employed, especially by former Warsaw Pact armed forces, but other mine-clearing methods such as ploughs or flails are now more favoured. Apart from their awkwardness, mine rollers

Rollers were an apparently obvious solution to a minefield, but it proved exceedingly difficult to detonate enough mines by the rollers' weight alone. Solutions included rollers so heavy that it took several vehicles to move them, and various plough and roller combinations.

can be easily overcome by special land mine fuses that do not react to the first pressure so may detonate under the carrier

tank. In addition, no matter how solid they may appear rollers have only a finite life before replacement.

Mine-clearing flails

This Sherman Crab has its flail drum and chains in the lowered position ready to start. The Crab was the standard British mine-clearing vehicle; not only were its flails efficient, but they were so arranged that the carrier tank could retain its 75-mm (2.95-in) gun.

The notion of using chain flails to detonate mines in the path of a tank came from a South African engineer, Major A. S. J.

du Toit. The idea was that a horizontally mounted drum carried on arms in front of a tank would be rotated under power

and, as it turned, would beat the ground in front with chains weighted at their ends: this beating would provide enough pressure to set off any mines under the flails. Early trials proved the effectiveness of the idea, and the first sets of mine flails were fitted to Matilda tanks in North Africa in 1942.

Soft sand was one of the specialist tanks' most feared terrain, and its hazards are clearly shown by this bogged-down Sherman Crab. Note the deep wading gear fitted to the engine intakes at the rear.

First models

These first flails had the name **Scorpion**, and on the **Matilda Scorpion** the flail drum was powered by an auxiliary engine mounted on the right-hand side of the tank. These Scorpions were used during the El Alamein battle in October 1942 and also during some later North African actions. They proved to be so effective that a more specialised version, known as the **Matilda Baron**, was developed. On the Baron the turret was removed and the flail drum was powered by two auxiliary engines, one on

each side. However, the Scorpion concept offered more long-term promise as it could be fitted to several types of tank to produce, for example, the **Grant Scorpion** and the **Valentine Scorpion**. However, before that could happen a great deal of further development work had to be carried out, for the early flails had demonstrated some unwelcome traits. Among these were uneven beating patterns that left unbeaten patches, and flail chains that either became tangled and useless or simply beat themselves to pieces. Another problem became apparent on uneven ground, where the flails were unable to beat into sudden dips.

The development work carried out in the UK resulted in a device known as the **Crab** which was usually fitted to Sherman tanks to produce the **Sherman Crab**. The Crab had 43 chains mounted on a drum powered by a take-off from the main engine and had such features as side-mounted wire cutting discs to hack through barbed wire entanglements, screens to shield the front of the tank from flying dust and debris and, later in the Crab's development, a device to follow ground contours and enable the

The Sherman Crab was the most widely used mine flail tank of World War II. Although the Crab was fitted to other tank types, the Sherman was the preferred carrier. The odd-looking device at the hull rear is a station keeping marker to guide other flail tanks.

flail drum to rise and fall accordingly. Crabs were used by the 79th Armoured Division and later a number were handed over to the US Army for use in the combat zones of North West Europe The main advantages of the Crab system were that it was very effective in its own right, and also permitted the carrier to retain its turret and gun, enabling it to be used as a gun tank.

Needless to say there were many other experimental models of mine flails. One was the **Lobster**, a device that came chronologically before the Crab but was not accepted for service. The **Pram Scorpion** was an off-shoot of the Scorpion with the drum drive coming from gears on the front sprockets of the carrier tank. Again, it was passed over in favour of the Crab.

The US did not spend much development time on mine flails. Instead they concentrated on anti-mine rollers and when they did require flails, as they did when they encountered the large defensive mine belts along the German borders in the winter of 1944–45, they used numbers of British Crabs which they redesignated the **Mine Exploder T4**.

The Matilda Scorpion prototype shown here was an early attempt to produce a mine flail tank. The main flail drum was driven by two 22.4-kW (30-hp) Bedford auxiliary engines, one mounted each side of the hull, and the device was later fitted to Valentine and Grant tanks as well as the Matilda.

ARK Bridging tanks

The **ARK** bridging tanks were only one type of armoured bridging vehicles used by the Allies during World War II. The British Army had been interested for a long time in producing bridging tanks, manufacturing its first such equipment during the latter stages of World War I. In the years just before World War II, the British Army carried out a great deal more experimental work, and one of its main achievements was a scissors-type bridge carried and laid by a Covenanter tank. During the early war years this work had to be put aside for more pressing things until the 1942 Dieppe landing emphasised the need for armoured bridging vehicles, not only to cross wet or dry gaps, but to enable other vehicles to cross beach obstacles such as sea walls.

Churchill conversions

It was the 79th Armoured Division that produced the first ARK (**Armoured Ramp Carrier**) late in 1943. This **ARK Mk I** was

Two Churchill ARK Mk IIs are used to allow other vehicles to cross a deep ravine. The first ARK was driven into the ravine and the second ARK was then driven onto it, after which the ramps were lowered to form a bridge. The ravine was formed by the River Senio in Italy, April 1945.

a Churchill tank conversion with the turret removed and a blanking plate (with an access hatch in the centre) welded over the turret aperture. Over the tracks were placed two timbered trackways carried on a new superstructure, and in front, in line with the trackways, were two ramps, each 1.05 m (3 ft 5½ in) long. At the rear were two more ramps, each 1.72 m (5 ft 8 in) long. In use the ARK Mk I

was driven up to an obstacle such as a sea wall. The front and rear ramps were then lowered from their travelling positions and other vehicles could then use the ARK to cross the obstacle. The ARK could also be driven into a wet or dry obstacle to act as a bridge.

The ARK Mk I was soon supplemented by the **ARK Mk II**. Again this used a Churchill tank as the basis, and the same

superstructure/ramp layout was used. However, the ARK Mk II used much longer ramps (3.8 m/12 ft 6 in) at each end, and the right-hand set of trackways and ramps was half the width of the other (0.61 m/2 ft) as opposed to 1.21 m (4 ft). This allowed a much wider range of vehicles to use the ARK. In use the ramps were set up front and rear and held in the travelling

A Churchill ARK Mk I is shown with its approach ramp raised. These vehicles were supposed to be driven up against anti-tank walls as far as possible, to enable other vehicles to be driven up and over the roadway carried above their tracks.

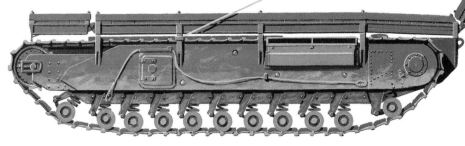

position by cables and chains connected to front and rear king-posts. When the ARK came to a gap it drove into it and then released the cables to allow the ramps to drop. Other vehicles could then cross the ARK bridge.

The British 8th Army in Italy produced its own ARK Mk IIs, but made them much simpler by omitting the trackways over the Churchill tank, the tank tracks and the top of the body being used as the roadway instead. This version was known as the **ARK Mk II (Italian Pattern)**.

There were numerous variations on the basic ARK design. One was a raised ramp system carried on a Churchill and known as the Churchill Great Eastern, but this project was discontinued. Some Sherman tanks were converted in Italy to what was roughly the equivalent of the ARK Mk II, but the numbers involved were not large.

Churchill Woodlark

Another system, known as the **Churchill Woodlark**, was

A Churchill gun tank is seen alongside a Churchill ARK near Le Havre in 1944. Note the sections of tank track applied to the sides of each vehicle in order to provide additional armour protection.

generally similar to the ARK Mk II but went into action with the ramps closed down; they were meant to be opened up into position by the use of rockets on the end of each ramp, and more rockets were used to soften the shock of the ramps hitting the ground. The type did not pass the trials stage. No data can be

provided regarding these Churchill conversions but a Churchill ARK Mk II had a crew of four men and weighed 38.5 tons. Most conversions were made using Churchill Mks III and IV. The ARK 'drive over' concept was eventually replaced in service by front-mounted assault bridges that could be

lowered across an obstacle. The original concept meant that once in place an ARK had to remain there to be used. An assault bridge allowed the carrier to deploy its bridge and then move off to follow the formation so that it could be used in other purposes.

Fascine and mat-laying devices

The fascine is an item of combat engineering equipment that dates back to ancient times, and for armoured warfare the type was resurrected during World War I to be dropped by tanks taking part in the Battle of Cambrai. At that time fascines were used traditionally, being dropped into trenches to allow other tanks to cross, and they were used for the same purpose during World War II. The advantage of the fascine for the combat engineer is that they can be made on the spot when they are required. The usual method was to cut brushwood and tie it into large bundles 3.35 m (11 ft) or more long. The bundles were tied into rolls between 1.83 m (6 ft) and 2.44 m (8 ft) in diameter and pulled onto wooden or steel cradles on the front of the tank.

*This **Churchill AVRE** is equipped for amphibious assault, with deep-wading engine intakes at the side and rear, and is fitted with the **Carpet-Layer Type C** which laid a hessian carpet to allow following vehicles to cross areas of sand or other soft terrain.*

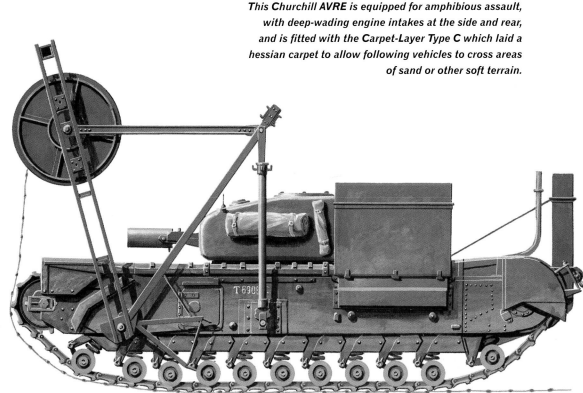

This post-war Churchill AVRE has an early Centurion-style turret equipped with smoke dischargers. The cargo remains much as it would have looked in 1944 – or 1917 for that matter – and the restrictions the fascine placed on the driver's field of vision are obvious.

They were then held in place by cables that could be released from within the carrier tank. The main disadvantage was that the fascines usually restricted the driver's vision so that a crew member had to position himself to give driving instructions. Attempts were made to use periscopes to overcome this drawback but in the end the solution was found by redesigning the form of fascine cradle.

Assault roadway

A type of fascine could also be used to make an assault roadway over soft or rough ground. This was formed by rolling up lengths of chespaling joined together by wire, rather like a length of fencing. A Churchill AVRE would carry this roll into position, where one end of the roll could be placed under the front tracks. As the AVRE moved forward it unrolled the mat and rolled over it to allow other vehicles to use the rough roadway so formed. Rolls of up to 30.5 m (100 ft) could be laid using this method, and more durable roadways could be produced by using a similar arrangement involving logs tied together (**Log Carpet**).

These chespaling or log roadways were intended for heavy use, but for assault purposes hessian mats were also employed. These mats were carried in front of a Churchill AVRE on bobbins held by side arms or, on one model, above a **Churchill AVRE Carpetlayer** turret. There were two main types: the **Bobbin Carpet** unrolled a hessian mat reinforced by chespaling at intervals that was wide enough to cover the full width of a tank; the other was wide enough to cover only a track width. Both were intended to cover wire obstacles, therefore allowing troops or wheeled vehicles to cross. The first of them was used during the Dieppe raid of 1942. On all types the bobbin could be dropped when empty or in an emergency.

Sherman Crib

Most of these fascine- or mat-laying devices were carried on Churchill AVREs, but Shermans were also used. In fact a special fascine carrier, known as the **Crib**, was developed for the Sherman. This was a frame that could be tilted forward to drop a fascine or a log mat. Some 'war weary' Shermans even had their turrets removed to allow them to be used as full-time fascine carriers.

It should be stressed that the mat-laying devices were meant only for short-term use. Prolonged use by heavy or tracked vehicles soon broke them up or simply tore them to pieces, so they were used only for assault purposes or during amphibious landings. It was not until well after World War II that flexible metal roadways were developed to replace the earlier devices.

A Churchill AVRE operates a Carpet-Layer Type C, used to lay a continuous hessian mat over rough or soft ground to enable other wheeled or tracked vehicles to follow. These devices were used to cross the sand on some of the Normandy beaches during the D-Day invasion on 6 June 1944.

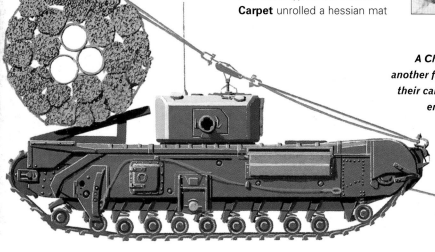

A Churchill AVRE carries a brushwood fascine at the front and tows another fascine on an AVRE skid trailer. The fascines were released from their carrier frame by a quick release device, and once in position could enable most tanks or tracked vehicles to cross with relative ease.

ARV Armoured recovery vehicles

This Cromwell ARV is seen in the final throes of being prepared for the heavy lifting task. Its A-frame jib is erected over the front of the hull, with its head braced against downward loads by two substantial wire strops.

To the front-line soldier every tank is a valuable asset, so any damaged or disabled tank that can be got back into action is a useful item. As a result, the recovery from the battlefield of damaged or broken-down tanks is a very important aspect of armoured warfare. Very often these recovery operations have to be undertaken under enemy fire, however, so it makes sense to provide the recovery crews with their own armoured vehicles and even more sense to provide these vehicles with mechanical handling devices, winches and other special recovery tools. Thus World War II saw the first large-scale use of

recovery vehicles, and on the Allied side there were many different types of varying capabilities.

Enter the ARV

Virtually all types of **ARV** (**Armoured Recovery Vehicle**) were conversions of existing tanks, usually models that were obsolescent and could therefore be spared for the role. Nearly every type of Allied tank was used for the ARV role at some time or another, but the main types involved on the British

side were the Crusader, Covenanter, Centaur, Cavalier, Cromwell, Ram and inevitably the Churchill. Most of the early ARV conversions to the so-called **ARV Mk I** standard involved the removal of the turret (along with the main

A Cromwell ARV is caught by the camera as it tows a captured German PzKpfw IV tank out of the way of other vehicles. The Cromwell ARV was a turretless conversion of an early mark of Cromwell tank that could be fitted with a jib crane and other recovery gear.

armament) and its replacement by an open compartment for the crew. Winches were installed and various forms of jib crane or sheerlegs were added. Many types also had the assistance of an earth spade to provide the winch with better purchase and thus extra pull. The British also made extensive use of turret-less Shermans for the ARV role.

The **ARV Mk II** conversion, which was effected on Churchill III and IV, and also on the Sherman V, resulted in a similar overall capability but with a number of operational improvements. The most obvious improvement was the adoption of a fixed turret (complete with a dummy gun) in place of the ARV Mk I's open compartment. This fixed turret accommodated the 60-ton winch's operator, who therefore had both a higher field of vision

and a good measure of protec-tion. The ARV Mk II also had the 3.5-ton jib crane relocated to the back of the hull, which also featured an earth anchor, to free the forward position for the carriage of a 6-ton jib crane.

The American ARVs were generally more complex vehicles. They too were based on existing tank chassis, but the conversions were often carried out in factories rather than the base workshops of the other Allied armies (including the British) and thus more detail design care could be lavished upon the final product. A typical American product was the **Tank Recovery Vehicle M32**. On this the turret was fixed and a smoke-firing 81-mm (3.2-in) mortar was fitted. In the volume normally reserved for the fight-ing compartment was placed a powerful 27216-kg (60,000-lb)

capacity winch, and an A-frame jib was mounted on the forward hull. Extra stowage points for special equipment were added all over the hull. Several sub-variants of the M32 were produced. The M3 medium tank series was also used to produce the **Tank Recovery Vehicle M31** with a jib crane over the rear of the hull. The British also made their own conversion of the M3 Grant by removing armaments and installing a powerful winch in the main compartment.

The American ARVs were produced in large numbers, so

SPECIFICATION	
Churchill ARV Mk II	**Powerplant:** one Bedford Twin-Six liquid-cooled petrol engine developing 261 kW (350 hp)
Crew: 5 or 6	
Weight: 40 tons	**Performance:** maximum road speed 24.9 km/h (15.5 mph); maximum road range 193 km (120 miles)
Dimensions: length 8.28 m (27 ft 2 in); width 3.35 m (11 ft); height 3.02 m (9 ft 11 in)	
	Armament: one or two 0.303-in (7.7-mm) machine-guns

large in fact that some of the M32 vehicles could be made available for conversion to an allied but somewhat different role, namely that of the artillery tractor. However, there was one factor that both British and US ARVs had in common, and that was that none of them could match the power of the German **Bergepanther** armoured recovery vehicle based on the Panther battle tank. The Bergepanther was unassailed in its position as the most powerful ARV of the World War II period as far as operational models were concerned. Even so, the Allied ARVs were adequate for the workaday task of recovering armoured fighting vehicles without undue difficulty, for they did not have to cope with seeking to recover the altogether larger and heavier Tiger heavy tanks and Panther battle tanks used by the German army.

Beach ARV

Included in the planning for the D-Day invasion of North-West Europe was the provision of vehicles able to recover 'drowned' or otherwise disabled armour and vehicles from positions both above and below the high water mark on the invasion beaches. For this work the REME Experimental Beach Recovery Section created for trials purposes in 1943 **BARV (Beach Armoured Recovery Vehicle)** prototypes based on the Churchill and Sherman tanks.

These early BARVs were ordinary Sherman and Churchill tanks with the gun turrets replaced by a fixed rectangular structure and the engine air inlets and exhaust revised with tall metal cowls. The hulls were

A Tank Recovery Vehicle M32 rolls through a village in north-west Europe, in 1945. Based on the M4 tank hull, these vehicles were used from 1943 onwards and used a fixed superstructure in place of the M4 turret. A large winch was fitted along with other special recovery gear and tools.

also waterproofed so that the vehicles could wade in water up to a depth of some 2.1 m (7 ft). The BARV crews were trained to use shallow diving apparatus so that they could operate under the water level to attach tow ropes to vehicles awaiting recovery.

The **Churchill BARV** was abandoned at the prototype stage since the hull with its side entry doors needed more waterproofing attention than the Sherman, and the Churchill needed three cowls to the Sherman's one. Further development of the BARV was therefore based on the Sherman in the forms first of the Ford petrol-engined model and later of the diesel-engined Sherman III. A multi-sided superstructure was created to allow the tank to operate in water up to 3.05 m (10 ft) deep according to weather conditions. Other additions included towing equipment, and a pair of wooden railway sleepers was attached to the BARV's front to reduce the chances of damage when vehicles were being pushed or landing craft were being nudged

off the beach. A trackway was added round the top of the hull for the crew, and hanging ropes (as on lifeboats) were attached to the sides.

As with other ARVs, 'production' conversions to **Sherman BARV** standard were performed under REME supervision at two Ministry of Supply workshops. The vehicles were very successful in helping to keep the D-Day beaches clear and one BARV even caused the Germans a measure of worry as being an Allied 'secret weapon' as the crew of the landing craft carrying this Sherman BARV made a mistake and brought their craft in to the beach at a stage far earlier than had been planned.

It is worth noting that the REME was also responsible for the creation and production of an armoured amphibian tractor based on the Caterpillar D8. This too was generally successful, operating in much the same way as the BARV on the Normandy beaches, though it was a more limited type, lacking the Sherman BARV's submersible capability.

Above: A Churchill ARV Mk I has its front jib erected and twin 0.303-in (7.7-mm) Bren machine-guns mounted in the hull. This vehicle had a crew of three and carried special tools and welding equipment for the recovery role. The vehicle was basically a turretless Churchill Mk IV.

Below: A Sherman ARV Mk I tows a Sherman gun tank during the campaign in Normandy during June/July 1944. This ARV was a British conversion of a Sherman tank with the turret removed, and a front-mounted jib crane and other equipment added.

The 'Funnies'
Allied engineer vehicles

An opposed landing on the French coast presented a host of engineering problems for the Allies, ranging from how to land tanks on a beach, how to pass safely through minefields, and how to breach the huge sea walls. The British developed the 'Funnies', a unique series of armoured vehicles designed to overcome all these obstacles.

Above: Flame has been an engineer tool as far back as there have been engineers, but the development of modern high-pressure flamethrowers turned fire into an awesomely destructive weapon. The jet of fire was ignited as it left the barrel, and could envelop a target in flame at ranges of more than 100 m (109 yards).

To the rest of the British Army the 79th Armoured Division were the 'Funnies', a name prompted by the odd appearance of their combat vehicles, and a name that stuck.

Prior to the D-Day landings, the men of the 79th Armoured Division were hard at work formulating tactics and methods in an area of warfare where they had no previous experience. Everything they did had to be worked out from scratch, but they conquered the problems and their successes made them proud of their nickname. The vehicles designed by the 79th

were intended to hit the beaches in sequence. This meant that the Duplex Drive (DD) Shermans had to swim ashore from the landing craft and arrive at the same time as the combat engineers' AVREs.

Fire support

Once ashore, the DD Shermans dropped their wading screens and were ready to use their main 75-mm (2.95-in) guns to provide fire support for the AVREs. The DD tank gunners had been trained to the point where their gunnery was up to firing at the German gun

emplacements and hitting them within their first few shots.

In some places, the AVREs had to go into action as soon as they landed just to clear the obstacles forward of where the Shermans could make their first shot. In places the AVREs often used the Petard spigot mortars to knock out defence

The Churchill was selected for the armoured engineer role because it had large side doors which enabled Sappers to dismount easily to place charges. It was equipped with a large turret-mounted, short-range spigot mortar which fired a heavy demolition charge.

emplacements, but these bombs, although large and powerful, were not very accurate. It usually took a direct hit to destroy the enemy gun, hence the need for the supporting gun tanks.

Mine clearance

On the beach the gun tanks usually took up a position to provide covering fire as the AVREs and Crab flail tanks started their tasks. The Crabs would usually move first as every beach and its immediate hinterland was liberally covered by minefields laid by the Germans in the years before the invasion. The Crabs usually operated in troops of four or five and had the task of clearing paths through the minefields on every battalion front, each battalion requiring at least two clear paths.

The Crabs moved forward slowly to enable their flails to detonate every mine encountered. As the tanks moved, their flails kicked up debris and dust which attracted the enemy's attentions. They also churned up the ground, requiring them to be followed by AVREs with mat-laying devices to allow wheeled vehicles to cross the broken terrain.

The Crabs usually worked two or three abreast. Every minefield they crossed was covered by some form of defence-work or obstacle, so covering fire had to be provided from the gun tanks at all times. On some beaches extra covering fire was provided by naval vessels offshore, fire orders and corrections being provided by Royal Artillery forward observation officers in gun tanks landed in the wave just behind the assault engineers.

Demolition charges

In a typical scenario, the Crabs would flail right up to the anti-tank wall and one would then flail a path to one side of the point where the obstacle was to be cleared. The Crabs then moved out of the way for the AVREs to move in. An AVRE

ARMOURED ENGINEER VEHICLES

Engineers have played a vital part in military operations for more than 2,000 years. They have built bridges, crossed obstacles, prepared defences and demolished enemy defences. The advent of modern mobile warfare in the 20th century presented engineers with new challenges: they had to keep up with fast-moving armoured troops, and they had to survive on the modern battlefield. The British solution was the AVRE, or Armoured Vehicle Royal Engineers. Based on a tank chassis – in this instance, the Churchill infantry tank – the AVRE could be equipped with equipment for bridge-laying, vehicle recovery, ditch crossing (using fascines as seen here), laying or firing demolition charges, or bulldozer blades for earth moving.

This odd-looking device was known as the Bullshorn; it was a mine plough device developed by the 79th Armoured Division to clear anti-tank mines from the path of the carrier tank. Seen here in the travelling position, the Bullshorn was used operationally during the Normandy landings and after, but only in small numbers.

would approach the obstacle, equipped with one of the various forms of explosive frame, such as the Jones Onion, which carried a heavy demolition charge.

The frame would be set against the obstacle and the AVRE would retire to the cleared area nearby. The charge would be detonated with a fearful roar, and more Crabs and AVREs would move forward. If all was well the charge would have blown a hole right through the obstacle, but this was not always possible, so AVREs with various forms of assault bridging would then be used.

The beach in front of the obstacle could get rather

crowded during this obstacle-busting stage. The Sherman Crabs, by the very nature of their task, were likely to become casualties, so two spare Crabs were usually held in reserve. They could always be called upon to use their guns for fire support or to provide local defence for the reserve AVREs that were also maintained to the rear of any action. Once the obstacle breach had been made, everyone would move forward with care as the main German defensive area was behind the beach. It would be covered with systems of bunkers, gun emplacements and tank traps. The gun tanks once more provided the initial fire support

as the AVREs and Crabs moved forward. By this time they would also have infantry support from recently landed troops.

AVREs with fascines could be used to cross the tank ditches and more assault bridging could be used to cross water obstacles.

Flamethrowers

German bunkers could be difficult to destroy by gunfire or Petard bombs. Some were built very low to the ground and their

weapon embrasures were difficult even to spot, let alone to hit. One solution was the Crocodile tank. These were Churchill tanks with a flamethrower mounted in place of the hull machine-gun. The flame projector could spray a jet of fire up to 110 m (120 yards) although more usually this was 73 m (80 yards).

The Crocodiles' flame projectors used a fuel pressure systemwhich was prone to leaks. The 79th Armoured Division's procedures enabled the Crocodiles to 'come up to steam' just when they were needed. However, some local commanders wanted to keep Crocodiles on hand at all times for use at short notice, hence the machines often broke down.

The projectile fired by the Petard spigot mortar carried by the Churchill AVRE had a diameter of 290 mm (11.4 in) and weighed 18.1 kg (40 lb). It was known to the troops as the 'Flying Dustbin', and it could be fired to a range of about 73 m (80 yards).

Munitionpanzer IV Ausf F Karl ammunition carrier

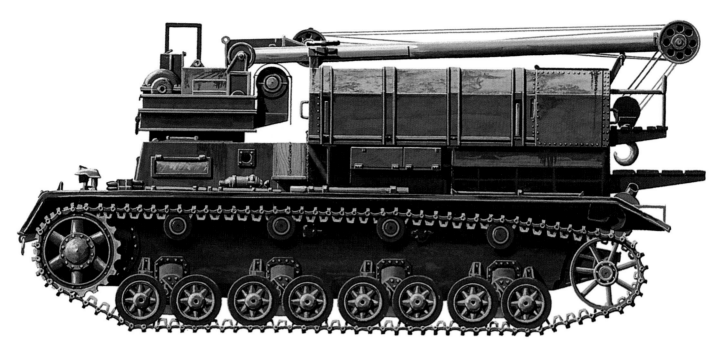

When the design teams that produced the massive Karl siege howitzer were drawing up their plans they at first overlooked one item: the massive short-barrelled howitzers they were producing were mounted on large tracked chassis to provide some measure of mobility (even though this mobility was strictly limited by the sizes and weights involved), but they forgot the matter of ammunition supply. This oversight was soon realised and plans were made to provide special ammunition carriers that could move to wherever the Karls might be emplaced, and these carriers had to be tracked as well. They also had to be large, for the Karls fired a huge concrete-busting projectile that

Munitionpanzer IV Ausf F carried shells for the Karl self-propelled mortar on a platform over the hull. The shells were lifted on to the Karl loading tray by a front-mounted jib crane, seen here folded over the shell platform.

weighed no less than 2170 kg (4,784 lb) and with a diameter of 60 cm (23.62 in). Later versions of the weapon had a 54-cm (21.26-in) calibre and fired a projectile weighing 1250 kg (2,756 lb).

Construction

The vehicle selected as the basis of the ammunition carrier for the Karls was the PzKpfw IV Ausf F. The type was not produced as a conversion, but was built from new using the basic tank hull, suspension and other components but with the usual turret replaced by a platform that covered the entire top of the hull. At the front of the platform was a crane with a capacity of 3000 kg (6,614 lb), offset to the left and with the swivelling jib

normally stowed facing to the rear. The main platform was used as a carrying area for the projectiles, with space for two or three shells. Small metal side walls were fitted, but these were often removed in the field.

Much of the movement of the Karl equipments had to be carried out on railways, and the train that carried the Karl components also had a couple of flat-cars to carry the standard complement of two **Munitionpanzer** (or **Munitionschlepper**) ammunition carriers. Close to the intended

Below: The Munitionpanzer IV Ausf F is shown in its travelling configuration with the jib folded and with the shell lifting grab stowed on the front of the hull. Each of these ammunition carriers could carry three 60-cm (23.62-in) projectiles for the Karl siege howitzer.

Right: The unarmed Munitionpanzer IV Ausf F was used to carry the heavy projectiles for the 60-cm Karl self-propelled mortar, and is seen here with its lifting jib raised ready for use. The jib could be traversed through 360 degrees.

SPECIFICATION	
Munitionpanzer IV Ausf F	**Dimensions:** length 5.41 m (17 ft 9 in); width 2.88 m (9 ft 5½ in)
Crew: 4	
Weight: 25 tonnes	**Performance:** maximum road speed 39.9 km/h (24.8 mph); maximum road range 209 km (130 miles)
Powerplant: one Maybach HL 120 TRM liquid-cooled petrol engine developing 223.7 kW (300 hp)	

firing position the Karls were assembled and moved off to the exact firing position. Projectiles for the weapons were taken from the train box-cars either by overhead gantry or the crane mounted on the carriers. The carriers then moved to the firing position and unloaded their projectiles by parking next to the Karl's breech and lifting the ammunition directly to the breech loading tray with its crane. Special ammunition handling grabs were used on the crane itself. Once their load had been fired, the carriers trundled off for more.

Not all Karl moves were made by rail. There was an arrangement whereby a Karl could be broken down into relatively small loads for road traction, but it was a long and arduous process to assemble the weapon on site. When this occurred the carriers were towed on wheeled trailers towed by large halftracks. Also included in each Karl 'train' were two trucks,

The acute nature of the weightlifting task allocated to the Munitionpanzer IV Ausf F is attested by the fact that the tank chassis used as the basis of the shell carrier was the PzKpfw IV battle tank.

two light staff cars and at least one 12-tonne halftrack to carry the Karl's crew. The Karl howitzers were among the most specialised of all German artillery weapons. They were designed as fortification smashers, and during World War II were not much in demand. However, they and their ammunition carriers did see use during the siege of Sevastopol, and in 1944 saw more action during the Battle of Warsaw against the unfortunate Polish.

SdKfz 265 kleiner Panzerbefehlswagen
Armoured command vehicle

Once the German army had accepted the concept of the Panzer division with its large tank component, it also appreciated that the large mass of tanks would entail consider-

able command and control problems. Tank formation commanders would have to move forward with the tanks and maintain contact with them at all times, and at first it

Kleiner Panzerbefehlswagen was a command version of the PzKpfw I light tank. It had a crew of three, and the fixed superstructure contained two radios, a map table and extra electrical equipment. The vehicles were widely used, as they allowed commanders to keep up with the armoured formations they were supervising.

seemed that the best way of doing this was to have the commanders travelling in tanks. However, it was also appreciated that commanders would have to have available to them all manner of special equipment and extra personnel to transmit orders and generally assist the commander in his task. Thus some form of dedicated command tank was needed.

In typically thorough style, the German designers came up with an answer as early as 1938. They decided to convert the PzKpfw I training tank for the command role, and the result was the **SdKfz 265 kleiner Panzerbefehlswagen** (small armoured command vehicle). The command vehicle was a relatively straightforward conversion of the basic tank in which the rotating tank turret was replaced by a box-like superstructure to provide extra internal space. The crew was increased from the two of the tank to three, in the form of the driver, the commander and a signaller/general assistant. The extra internal space was taken up with items such as a small table on which the commander

could work, map display boards, stowage for more maps and other paperwork, and two radios – one for communicating with the tanks and the other to provide a link to higher command levels. These radios required the provision of extra dynamo capacity to power them and keep their associated batteries fully charged. For armament, a single 7.92-mm (0.312-in) MG 34 machine-gun was mounted in the front plate.

Three variants

There were three variants of this command vehicle, one of them with a small rotating turret set onto the superstructure. This feature was soon discontinued as it took up too much of the limited internal space and was found to be unnecessary. The other two variants differed only in detail. In all of them the small size of the vehicle inflicted space limitations, and with two men attempting to work within the close confines of the body things could get very cramped.

However, the concept worked very well and about 200 such conversions from PzKpfw I tank standard were made. The first of them saw action during the

Polish campaign of 1939 and more were used in France during May and June 1940. Later these command vehicles equipped the Afrika Korps. One of these North African campaign examples was captured by the British Army and taken back to the UK where it was closely examined by tank experts who produced a large report on the vehicle's capabilities and structure.

Despite its relative success in the command role, the diminutive PzKpfw I tank conversion was really too small and cramped for efficiency, and in time the type was replaced by conversions of larger tanks.

Just how cramped the PzKpfw I command tank was can be gauged from this photograph of the basic model PzKpfw I. About 200 conversions were made but they proved too small for the task, and they were replaced by modified versions of later tanks.

The PzKpfw I was intended mainly as a training tank for the creation of the crews who would operate the larger and more capable tanks that followed the PzKpfw into service, but formed the basis of a useful though small and therefore interim light command tank vital to German successes in 1939 and 1940.

SPECIFICATION	
kleiner Panzerbefehlswagen I	**Dimensions:** length 4.45 m (14 ft 7 in); width 2.08 m (6 ft 10 in); height 1.72 m (5 ft 7¾ in)
Crew: 3	
Weight: 5.8 tonnes	**Armament:** one 7.92-mm (0.312-in) MG 34 machine-gun
Powerplant: one Maybach NL 38 TR liquid-cooled petrol engine developing 74.6 kW (100 hp)	**Performance:** maximum road speed 40 km/h (25 mph); maximum road range 290 km (180 miles)

Panzerjäger I Tank destroyer

When the first PzKpfw I (Panzerkampfwagen I) light tanks were produced in 1934, it was intended that they would be used only as training vehicles. In the event they had to be used as combat tanks during the early years of World War II for the simple reason that larger and heavier tanks were not yet available in sufficient numbers. However, the PzKpfw I had a crew of a mere two men, carried only a machine-gun armament and was poorly protected. By no stretch of the imagination was it a viable battle tank and most were phased out of operational service in 1941 but retained for the original training role. This left a number of spare tank chassis with no operational role, so the opportunity was taken to convert these vehicles into the first German self-propelled anti-tank guns.

It had already been decided that some form of mobile anti-tank gun would be a great asset to the anti-tank units, which otherwise had to use towed guns. Thus the first example of this requirement was met by mounting a 3.7-cm (1.46-in) Pak 35/36 onto a turret-

This SdKfz 101 Panzerjäger I was the first example captured by the Allies in North Africa, and was then subjected to a great deal of technical scrutiny. It mounted an ex-Czechoslovak 4.7-cm (1.85-in) anti-tank gun in an open mounting that provided only a frontal shield for crew protection.

less PzKpfw I. While this conversion showed promise, it was not adopted because even by mid-1940 it was appreciated that the 3.7-cm gun lacked the power to deal with future armour. Thus a Czech 4.7-cm (1.85-in) anti-tank gun was mounted instead, and this combination was adopted for service as the **Panzerjäger I für 4.7-cm Pak(t)**.

The Czechoslovakian gun was a powerful, hard-hitting weapon that was well capable of penetrating most armour it was likely to encounter during the early 1940s, and Alkett AG produced a total of 132 conversions. The result was very much a first attempt, for all that was required was the removal of the tank turret, plating over the front of the turret ring and arranging a small working platform over the engine covers. The gun itself was mounted behind a lightly armoured shield that was left

This photograph of a Panzerjäger I reveals the extemporised nature of this early German conversion, made in an attempt to prolong the service life of the PzKpfw I light tank. The gun was powerful enough but the mounting provided virtually no protection.

open at the top and rear.

The crew consisted of the driver, still seated in his original PzKpfw I position, and two soldiers serving the gun. A total of 74 rounds could be carried as standard, although more could be added to this figure. The chassis mainly used for the conversion was that of the PzKpfw I Ausf B. Similar conversions mounting either the German 3.7-cm or Czechoslovakian 4.7-cm gun were created on all manner of captured tracked, half-tracked and even wheeled chassis. The majority of these conversions were carried out at unit level rather than being officially sanctioned, usually in order to provide extra local mobility for towed guns.

Vulnerable target

The Panzerjäger I served in North Africa and during the early

stages of the campaigns in the USSR. It proved to possess sufficient firepower to defeat opposing tanks, but its overall lack of protection for the crew made the type a very vulnerable target. As soon as better equipment became available the type was withdrawn from front-line use and assigned to theatres where it could be used for policing rather than for combat duties. Among the locations so honoured were the Balkans, where the vehicles were used on anti-partisan operations. Units operating on the Eastern Front after about the end of 1942 frequently removed the guns and used the chassis for supply carrying, and some units replaced their Czech guns with captured French 4.7-cm guns. Few Panzerjäger Is remained in service after mid-1944.

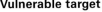

SPECIFICATION	
Panzerjäger I	6 cylinder petrol engine
Crew: 3	**Performance:** maximum road speed
Weight: 6000 kg (13,228 lb)	40 km/h (24.9 mph); maximum
Dimensions: length (overall) 4.14 m	road range 140 km (87 miles)
(13 ft 7 in); width 2.01 m (6 ft 7¼	**Fording:** 0.6 m (2 ft)
in); height 2.1 m (6 ft 10¾ in)	**Gradient:** 57 per cent
Powerplant: one 74.6-kW (100-hp)	**Vertical obstacle:** 0.37 m (14½ in)
Maybach NL 38 liquid-cooled	**Trench:** 1.4 m (4 ft 7¼ in)

Marder II Tank destroyer

This Marder II profile shows the rather high mounting of the 7.5-cm (2.95-in) Pak 40/2, a special version of the standard German anti-tank gun of the period late in World War II.

As with the PzKpfw I, when it entered service in 1935 the PzKpfw II was meant to be used only as a training and development tank. In the event it had to be used as a combat tank from 1939 to 1942 simply because there were not enough combat tanks to replace the type, which acquitted itself well enough despite the fact that its main armament was limited to a 20-mm cannon. By 1941 the PzKpfw II was overdue for replacement as its armament was able to penetrate only soft-skinned targets and the small turret ring could not accommodate a heavier weapon. The production line for the chassis was still in operation, however, and at the time this seemed to be too valuable to waste so the opportunity was taken to convert the PzKpfw II to a Panzerjäger.

The prototype of this new Panzerjäger was fitted with a 5-cm (1.97-in) anti-tank gun, but the full production version was fitted with the special Pak 40/2 version of the 7.5-cm (2.95-in) Pak 40 anti-tank gun. This powerful gun was the German army's standard anti-tank weapon, and the incorporation of greater mobility added considerably to the gun's anti-armour potential. The gun was

placed behind a 10-mm (0.39-in) thick armoured shield that sloped to the rear to provide the gun crew with adequate protection. To balance the weight of the gun, the engine was moved to the rear of the hull and the engine covers were used as a working platform to serve the gun. The vehicle was known as the **Marder II** (Marder meaning marten), although other and more cumbersome designations (such as **7.5-cm Pak 40/2 auf Slf II** and **SdKfz 131**) were used in official documents.

Widespread service

The Marder II remained in production until 1944 and became one of the most widely used of all the many German self-propelled gun conversions. In production terms it was manufactured in greater numbers than any other weapon of its type – 1,217 were made. The Marder II was certainly a useful and efficient weapon in combat, for it was relatively small, had a good cross-country performance, and possessed a gun able to knock out virtually any Allied tank other than super-heavy Soviet tanks such as the IS-2. Racks for 37 rounds of main armament ammunition were provided over the engine covers, and there was also

space for stowing 600 rounds for the machine-gun; this was usually a 7.92-mm (0.312-in) MG 34 or MG 42 weapon.

Most Marder II production was sent to the Eastern Front, but the Marder II was found wherever German troops were in action. By 1944 the type was out of production and the crew was often reduced by one man to conserve

manpower, but development did not cease. During the latter stages of the war some Marder IIs were equipped with infra-red (IR) searchlights to provide a night engagement capability, and some of these were used in action on the Eastern Front during the last stages of the war. By then such novel equipment could have but little impact.

SPECIFICATION	
Marder II	**Performance:** maximum road speed
Crew: 3 or 4	40 km/h (24.8 mph); maximum
Weight: 11000 kg (24,251 lb)	road range 190 km (118 miles)
Dimensions: length 6.36 m (20 ft	**Fording:** 0.9 m (2 ft 11 in)
10¾ in); width 2.28 m (7 ft 5¾ in);	**Gradient:** 57 per cent
height 2.2 m (7 ft 2½ in)	**Vertical obstacle:** 0.42 m (1 ft 4½ in)
Powerplant: one 104.4-kW (140-hp)	**Trench:** 1.8 m (5 ft 11 in)
Maybach HL 62 liquid-cooled	
6-cylinder petrol engine	

The SdKfz 131 Marder II mounted a 7.5-cm (2.95-in) Pak 40/2, and was one of the more important of the Panzerjäger conversions. Based on the PzKpfw II Ausf A, C or F, 1,217 were produced for service on all fronts. There was a crew of four including the driver.

Marder III Tank destroyer

There were two self-propelled guns known as the Marder III, both using the same chassis derived from that of the Skoda TNHP-S tank. This tank was originally produced by Skoda at Pilsen for the Czechoslovakian army, but with the seizure of the rump of the Czechoslovak state by Germany in 1939, Skoda continued production under the designation PzKpfw 38(t) for the German army. The Germans introduced so many production and in-service changes to the original Skoda design that by 1941 the PzKpfw 38(t) could be regarded as a German tank, but the original turret was too small to carry weapons powerful enough to defeat Allied armour after 1941. The chassis was kept in production for other purposes.

By 1941 the appearance of more modern Allied tanks meant the German army lacked a tank powerfully enough armed to knock out types such as the Soviet T-34, so hasty improvisations were made to remedy this problem. One was the installation of a captured Soviet field gun, the 76.2-mm (3-in) Model 1936, on the chassis of the PzKpfw 38(t). The gun was a dual-purpose weapon with anti-tank capability, and in addition the Germans also adapted many as dedicated anti-tank guns.

Potent capability

On the PzKpfw 38(t) the gun was mounted behind a fixed shield and the conversion went into production in early 1942 as the **Marder III**, otherwise the **Panzerjäger 38(t) für 7.62-cm Pak 36(r)**. Some 344 of these conversions were made for deployment on the Eastern Front, North Africa and elsewhere. However, this type was regarded only as a stopgap until sufficient numbers of the German 7.5-cm (2.95-in) Pak 40 became available during 1942. Production of the Soviet-

This Marder III was captured in North Africa in April 1943 and mounted its 7.5-cm (2.95-in) Pak 40/3 in a central position. It was a very simple conversion of a Czechoslovakian tank chassis but proved effective.

gunned Marder III was then replaced by that of the German-gunned version. The gun/chassis combination was still the Marder III, but had the designation **Panzerjäger 38(t) Ausf H für 7.5-cm Pak 40/3**, otherwise **SdKfz 138**, using a slightly different gun shield and mounting from the earlier model.

Pak 40-armed Marder IIIs were rushed into action during the last stages of the Tunisian campaign. Up to 1943 the various German self-propelled guns using the Skoda chassis used the PzKpfw 38(t) tank as a basis. Early conversions (including the original Marder III) were nose-heavy, which limited mobility and so German engineers relocated the engine to the front of the chassis and moved the combat platform to the rear. Marder III production then changed once more to the new **Panzerjäger 38(t) Ausf M für 7.5-cm Pak 40/3** with the gun and its protection at the rear. This provided a vehicle of better balance, and the new chassis

was used to mount a variety of other weapons. The late Marder III was manufactured by BMM

of Prague. Production ended in May 1944, after 799 vehicles were made.

The later Marder IIIs had the main gun position moved to the rear of the chassis and the engine to the front. This provided a better balanced and more useful vehicle, and nearly 800 were produced, still using the basic components of the PzKpfw 38(t) tank.

SPECIFICATION	
Panzerjäger 38(t) Ausf M	
Crew: 4	**Performance:** maximum road speed
Weight: 11000 kg (24,251 lb)	42 km/h (26 mph); maximum road
Dimensions: length (overall) 4.65 m	range 140 km (87 miles)
(15 ft 3 in); width 2.35 m (7 ft 8½	**Fording:** 0.9 m (2 ft 11 in)
in); height 2.48 m (8 ft 1½ in)	**Gradient:** 57 per cent
Powerplant: one 112-kW (150-hp)	**Vertical obstacle:** 0.84 m (2 ft 9 in)
Praga AC liquid-cooled petrol engine	**Trench:** 1.3 m (4 ft 3 in)

Hetzer Light tank destroyer

This Jagdpanzer 38(t) Hetzer has a roof-mounted machine-gun for local defence. The small stand-off armour side plates are fitted over the upper part of the tracks to provide more side-on protection. Well over 1,500 of these vehicles were produced.

Tank-destroyer conversions of existing tank chassis to produce weapons such as the Marder III were moderately successful. In overall terms, though, the results were high, clumsy, lacked finesse and showed every sign of the haste in which they had been produced. In contrast, the various Sturmgeschütz close-support artillery vehicles showed that they too could be used as tank destroyers. Thus in 1943 it was decided to produce a light tank destroyer along assault gun lines, the chassis of the PzKpfw 38(t) being taken as the basis.

Small but potent

The result was one of the best of all German tank destroyers: the **Jagdpanzer 38(t) für 7.5-cm Pak 39**, or **Hetzer** (baiter, as in bull-baiting), otherwise the **SdKfz 138/2**. The Hetzer used the basic engine, suspension and running gear of the PzKpfw 38(t) allied to an armoured hull that sloped inward to provide extra protection for the crew of four. The armament was a modified 7.5-cm (2.95-in) tank gun and a

The low height of the Hetzer can be clearly appreciated. Note the well-shaped 'Saukopf' (pig's head) gun mantlet that provided extra head-on protection and the lack of a muzzle brake, usually fitted to other German vehicles of this type.

roof-mounted machine-gun. Production began in Prague at the end of 1943. In action the Hetzer proved to be a very successful gun/chassis combination. It was small and low, yet well protected and with a good cross-country perform-ance. The gun could knock out all but the heaviest Allied tanks, yet the Hetzer itself was difficult

to knock out. In combat it was so small as to be virtually invisible to

enemy gunners. Calls for more and more came from the front

SPECIFICATION	
Hetzer	**Performance:** maximum road speed 39 km/h (24 mph); road maximum range 250 km (155 miles)
Crew: 4	
Weight: 14500 kg (31,967 lb)	
Dimensions: length (overall) 6.2 m (20 ft 4 in); width 2.5 m (8 ft 2½ in); height 2.1 m (6 ft 11 in)	**Fording:** 0.9 m (2 ft 11 in)
	Gradient: 75 per cent
	Vertical obstacle: 0.65 m (2 ft 1½ in)
Powerplant: one 112-119 kW (150-160 hp) Praga AC/2800 petrol engine	**Trench:** 1.3 m (4 ft 3 in)

line, to the extent that by late 1944 all available PzKpfw 38(t) production was diverted to the Hetzer programme. Manufacture continued until the factories were overrun in May 1944, by which time 1,577 had been built.

Normal variants

Several versions of the Hetzer were produced. One was the

Flammpanzer 38(t) flamethrower, and another the **Bergepanzer 38(t)** light recovery version. The Hetzer story did not cease in 1945, moreover, for the type was soon restored to production for the Czechoslovakian army and exports to Switzerland in 1947–52. The Swiss continued to use the type into the 1970s.

Wartime Hetzers were used

for a series of trials and various weapon mountings, including guns with no recoil mechanism connected directly to the front hull armour for successful evaluation of the concept. One trial model was an assault howitzer mounting a 15-cm (5.91-in) infantry howitzer, and there were several similar projects. None reached the production stage, for the

assembly lines concentrated on the basic Hetzer.

The Hetzer was regarded as one of the best of all the Panzerjäger. It was a small but powerful vehicle that was much more economical to produce and use than many of the larger vehicles. It could knock out nearly every tank it was likely to encounter yet it was little higher than a standing man.

Jagdpanzer IV Tank destroyer

The Jagdpanzer IV (SdKfz 162) was a Panzerjäger version of the PzKpfw IV tank and housed its 7.5-cm (2.95-in) main gun in a superstructure formed from well-sloped armoured plates. This is an early example with the gun still retaining the muzzle brake, an item later omitted.

Combat experience gained during the 1942 campaigns showed the German staff that its Sturmgeschütz close-support artillery vehicles would have to be upgunned if they were to remain viable as tank-destroyers. The future standard weapon selected was the long version of the 7.5-cm (2.95-in) tank gun fitted to the Panther tank.

L/70 gun

This gun was an L/70 weapon, whereas the tank and anti-tank versions of the Pak 40 family were L/48 weapons, and the accommodation of this gun would entail considerable modification of vehicles such as the Sturmgeschütz III. These modifications would take time, so it was decided to adapt the larger PzKpfw IV tank chassis to act as a 'fail safe' model. Design work was soon under way on

this new model, which emerged in 1943 as the **Jagdpanzer IV Ausf F für 7.5-cm Pak 39** or **Panzerjäger 39**, otherwise the **SdKfz 162**. However, by the time the first examples were ready, the long 7.5-cm guns

were earmarked for use on Panther tanks and consequently

the first examples had to be content with model L/48 guns.

This early production Jagdpanzer IV has the muzzle brake still fitted. Later versions used a much longer 7.5-cm (2.95-in) main gun, but this longer gun rather overloaded the chassis, and later versions also used side armour plates. This Panzerjäger was later considered to be one of the best of its type.

The first Jagdpanzer IVs appeared in October 1943 as the well-tried suspension and propulsion layout of the PzKpfw IV allied to a new armoured carapace with well-sloped sides. The resultant silhouette was much lower than the hull/turret combination of the tank, and mounted the gun in a well-protected mantlet on the front hull. The result was well-liked by the Panzerjäger crews, who appreciated the low silhouette and the well-protected hull, so the Jagdpanzer IV was soon in great demand. The gun was powerful enough to tackle virtually any Allied tank, and in action the Jagdpanzer IV was soon knocking up appreciable 'kill' totals, especially on the Eastern Front, to which most were sent. The secondary armament of two 7.92-mm (0.312-in) MG 34 or MG 42 machine-guns also proved highly effective.

Many Panzer commanders considered that the Jagdpanzer IV was good enough in its

original form to require no upgunning, but Hitler insisted that the change to the long gun had to be made. Thus during 1944 there appeared some **Jagdpanzer IV mit 7.5-cm StuK 42** equipments with the longer L/70 gun. However, the changeover on the production line took time, too much time for Hitler, who insisted that the switch to the new gun had to be made even if it meant diverting all PzKpfw IV tank production to that end.

Interim model

Thus a third Jagdpanzer IV appeared, this time a hasty conversion of a basic PzKpfw IV hull to take a form of Jagdpanzer IV sloping carapace and again mounting the 70-calibre gun. This conversion was known as the **Panzer IV/70 Zwischenlösung** (interim) and was in production by late 1944. Not many were produced as by then many of the main PzKpfw IV production centres,

SPECIFICATION

Jagdpanzer IV mit 7.5-cm Stuk 42
Crew: 4
Weight: 25800 kg (56,879 lb)
Dimensions: length (overall) 8.58 m (28 ft 2 in); width 2.93 m (9 ft 7½ in); height (overall) 1.96 m (6 ft 5 in)
Powerplant: one 198-kW (265-hp) Maybach HL 120 petrol engine

Performance: maximum road speed 35 km/h (22 mph); maximum road range 214 km (133 miles)
Fording: 1.2 m (3 ft 11 in)
Gradient: 57 per cent
Vertical obstacle: 0.6 m (23½ in)
Trench: 2.3 m (7 ft 6½ in)

along with the industrial transport infrastructure, were in ruins as a result of Allied bombing.

In service the Jagdpanzer IV vehicles with the L/70 gun proved to be powerful tank killers, but the extra weight of the long gun made the vehicles nose-heavy to the extent that the front road wheels had to be ringed with steel instead of rubber to cope with the extra weight. The gun weight also unbalanced and reduced the overall performance of the vehicle, especially across rough terrain. By late 1944 and early 1945 such drawbacks simply had to be overlooked, for the Allies were at the gates of

the Reich and anything that could be put into the field was used.

The Jagdpanzer IV proved to be a sound Panzerjäger that enabled the Germans to utilise existing production capacity and maintain the PzKpfw IV line in being when it would otherwise have been phased out. In service the Jagdpanzer IV was a popular vehicle and a powerful tank-killer. It was a good example of how a sound basic armoured vehicle design, that of the PzKpfw IV tank, could be adapted to assume a combat role that had not even been imagined when the tank design was first mooted in the early 1930s.

Nashorn Tank destroyer

In the middle of World War II the German army adopted a large number of hurried improvisations in order to get useful numbers of Panzerjäger into the field, and some of these improvisations fared better than others. One of these hasty measures was the adoption of the special weapon-carrier vehicle that had originally been produced to carry the large 15-cm (5.91-in) sFH 18 field howitzer. It was known as the Geschützwagen III/IV as it was based on the chassis of the PzKpfw IV but used some of the drive components of the PzKpfw III.

Design modifications

Despite the great demand for the artillery version of this

weapon carrier it was decided to adapt it to carry the large 8.8-cm (3.46-in) Pak 43 anti-tank gun as the **8.8-cm Pak 43/1 auf GW III/IV,** or **SdKfz 164.** The first of these new Panzerjäger were issued during 1943, and the type went under

The SdKfz 164 Hornisse was the first Panzerjäger to mount the famous 8.8-cm Pak 43/1, and used the same chassis as the Hummel self-propelled artillery vehicle.

two names: the official name was **Nashorn** (rhinoceros) but **Hornisse** (hornet) was also widely applied in service.

The Nashorn was very much one of the interim Panzerjäger designs, for although the gun was mounted behind armour at

the front and sides this armour was relatively thin, and the top and rear were open. The gun mounting itself was rather high, so the Nashorn had definite combat deficiencies, not the least of which was the problem of battlefield concealment of the vehicle's height and bulk. As the chassis had been intended as an artillery carrier, the bulk problem was originally of little significance, but for a tank destroyer it was of considerable importance, making the stalking of tank targets very difficult. Thus the Nashorn was often used as a 'stand-off' weapon that was able to use the considerable power and long-range accuracy of its main gun to pick off targets at ranges of 2000 m

(2,185 yards) and more; most of the other Panzerjäger types fought at much closer combat ranges.

The Nashorn carried a crew of five, with only the driver under complete armour protection. The rest of the crew was carried in the open fighting compartment with only a canvas cover to protect it from the elements. Most of the 40 rounds carried were located in lockers along the sides of the open compart-ment. The gunner was

equipped not only with the usual direct-vision sighting devices but also with artillery dial sights for the occasions when the Pak 43 could be used as a long-range artillery weapon. During the later stages of production the Pak 43 gun was replaced by the similar 8.8-cm Pak 43/41, a weapon introduced to speed production of the Pak 43; although it was manufactured differently from the original it was identical as far as ballistics were concerned. The Nashorn also carried a machine-gun for local defence and the crew was supposed to be issued with at least two sub-machine guns for self-defence.

Powerful weapon

Most of the Nashorn production was centred at the Deutsche Eisenwerke at Teplitz-Schönau and Duisburg, and 473 had been made by the end of production in 1944. In combat the powerful gun made the Nashorn a potent vehicle/ weapon combination, but it was really too high and bulky for the Panzerjäger role and only a shortage of anything better at the time maintained the type in production.

The type was eventually succeeded in service by the Jagdpanther model.

SPECIFICATION	
Nashorn	petrol engine
Crew: 5	**Performance:** maximum road speed
Weight: 24400 kg (53,793 lb)	40 km/h (25 mph); maximum road
Dimensions: length (overall) 8.44 m	range 210 km (131 miles)
(27 ft 8 in) and (hull) 5.8 m (19 ft);	**Fording:** 0.8 m (2 ft 7½ in)
width 2.86 m (9 ft 4½ in); height	**Gradient:** 57 per cent
2.65 m (8 ft 8 in)	**Vertical obstacle:** 0.6 m (1 ft 11½ in)
Powerplant: one 197.5-kW (265-hp)	**Trench:** 2.3 m (7 ft 6½ in)
Maybach HL 120 liquid-cooled	

On this captured example of a rather battered Nashorn, the soldier provides an indication of the weight and size of the powerful 8.8 cm (3.46 in) Pak 43/1 anti-tank gun. The rear decking and side armour appear to have been removed.

Jagdpanther Tank destroyer

This Jagdpanther, straight off the production line, has its tool and other stowage intact. The superstructure is coated with Zimmerit, a substance intended to prevent magnetic charges being applied; the overlapping road wheels added extra side protection against incoming projectiles.

When the **Jagdpanther** was first produced in February 1944, it marked a definite shift away from a period when Panzerjäger were hasty conversions or improvisations to the point where the tank destroyer became a purpose-built combat vehicle. The Jagdpanther was first mooted in early 1943 at a time when tank destroyers were required in ever-increasing quantities. By taking the best readily available tank chassis as the basis for the new vehicle, it was hoped that production totals would finally meet demand. The Panther chassis was thus used virtually unaltered as the basis for the new vehicle and an 8.8-cm (3.46-in) Pak 43 anti-tank gun was mounted on a well-sloped armoured superstructure, with a 7.92-mm (0.31-in) MG34 or MG42 machine-gun for local defence.

The prototype, then known as the **Panzerjäger Panther**, was demonstrated to Hitler in October 1943. He decreed that the name should be changed to Jagdpanther and then took a personal interest in further developments, providing the programme with his own personal priority rating.

Fearsome reputation

The Jagdpanther was one of those vehicles where superlatives could be justifiably lavished, for it was a superb combat vehicle and destined to

be one of the most famous of all World War II armoured fighting vehicles. It was fast, well protected and it mounted a potent gun. Not content with all that, it had about it a definite aura that distinguished it from its contemporaries. So well balanced was the design that it would not be too out of place in any tank park today, 60 years after it first appeared.

The Jagdpanther could knock out virtually any enemy tank it was likely to encounter, including the heavy Soviet IS-2s (although for them a side shot was required for a certain kill). For an indication of its power, the 7.3-kg (16.1-lb) armour-piercing projectile could penetrate 226 mm (8.9 in) of sloped steel armour at a range of 457 m (500 yards) and it could knock out or severely damage most Allied tanks at 1,000 m (1,093 yards). At times, single Jagdpanthers or small groups of them could hold up Allied armoured advances for considerable periods. Fortunately for the Allies, production of the Jagdpanther never reached anywhere near the planned rate of 150 per month. By the time the production facilities were overrun during April 1945, only 382 had been completed and not all those had been delivered

– a fact for which Allied tank crews must have been very grateful. The main cause of these low and slow production totals was the disruption and damage caused by Allied bomber raids on the two main centres of production, the MIAG plant at Braunschweig and the Brandenburg Eisenwerk Kirchmöser at Brandenburg, and the German transport infrastructure. These disruptions led to several variations of Jagdpanther. Some early models had large bolted-on gun mantlets while others had much smaller mantlet collars. Late-production versions used guns built with the barrels in two parts to ease barrel changing when the bores became worn, and the stowage of tools and other equipment on the outside also varied considerably.

Weaponry

The Jagdpanther had a crew of five and there was space inside

the well-sloped and heavily-armoured superstructure for 60 rounds of ammunition. When the war ended, plans had been made to produce a new version mounting a 12.8-cm (5.04-in) anti-tank gun, though in the event only a wooden mock-up had been built. But even with the usual 8.8-cm gun the Jagdpanther was truly a formidable tank destroyer that was much feared and respected by Allied tank crews. Few other armoured fighting vehicles of World War II achieved its unique combination of power, lethality, mobility and protection. If the war had continued as the Germans planned (and the factories had been producing at the planned rate) the prospect of Panzer divisions equipped with a combination of Tiger II and Panther tanks – along with ever-growing numbers of Jadgpanthers – was enough to make any Allied tank commander shiver.

SPECIFICATION	
Jagdpanther	**Armament:** one 8.8-cm (3.46-in) Pak
Crew: 5	43 main gun, one 7.92-mm (0.31-in)
Weight: 46000 kg (101,411 lb)	MG34 or MG42 machine-gun
Powerplant: one Maybach HL 230	**Performance:** maximum road speed
petrol engine developing	55 km/h (34.2 mph); road range
447.4–522 kW (600–700 hp)	160 km (99 miles)
Dimensions: length overall 9.9 m	**Gradient:** 70 per cent
(32 ft 6 in) and hull 6.87 m (22 ft	**Vertical obstacle:** 0.9 m (35 in)
6½ in); width 3.27 m (10 ft 9 in);	**Trench:** 1.9 m (6 ft 3 in)
height 2.7 m (8 ft 11 in)	**Fording:** 1.7 m (5 ft 7 in)

Panzerjäger Tiger (P) Elefant Tank destroyer

The Panzerjäger Tiger (P) Elefant used a complex twin-engine power pack driving an electric transmission that did not work very effectively in service. The vehicle was heavy, slow and ponderous, making it more of a heavy assault gun than a Panzerjäger. Most were used in Russia but a few ended up in Italy in 1944.

When the tank that was to become the Tiger was still in its planning stage, two concerns, Henschel and Porsche, competed for the production contract. The Porsche entry was at one time the more favoured as the design employed a petrol-electric drive with electric motors propelling the vehicle. However, this approach proved to be technically over-complicated so the Henschel entry became the PzKpfw VI Tiger.

Early development

By the time the Henschel design was in production, Porsche drives and the hulls to put in them were also ready for

production. It was decided to produce the Porsche design as a heavy tank-destroyer mounting the 8.8-cm (3.46-in) Pak 43/2 anti-tank gun. The gun was installed in a large armoured superstructure with limited traverse, and 90 examples were produced to become the **Panzerjäger Tiger (P)**, later known as either **Ferdinand** or **Elefant**. The (P) denoted Porsche. The Elefants were produced at the Nibelungwerke in a great rush during early 1943, the urgency being occasioned by the fact that Hitler demanded

them to be ready for the opening of the main campaign of 1943 against the Kursk salient on the Eastern Front. Production delays and training the Panzertruppen to use their new charges delayed the start of the offensive until 5 July 1943.

Inauspicious start

By the time the tanks were ready for battle, the Red Army was prepared for them. The defences of the Kursk salient were formidable and the delays had enabled the Red Army to add to their effectiveness. When the Germans finally attacked, their efforts were of little avail. For the Elefants the Kursk battles were a dreadful baptism of fire. The Elefants were organised in two battalions (*Abteilungen*) of Panzerregiment 654, and even before going into action their troubles began. The Elefants had been rushed into service before their many

technical bugs had been eliminated, and many broke down as soon as they started to move forward. Those that did make it to the Soviet lines were soon in trouble, for although the vehicles were fitted with the most powerful anti-tank guns then available, they lacked any form of secondary armament for self-defence. Soviet infantry tank-killer squads swarmed all over them and placed charges that either blew off their tracks or otherwise disabled them. The Elefant crews had no way of defending themselves. Those that could either withdrew or abandoned their vehicles.

Some Elefants did survive Kursk and were later fitted with machine-guns to defend themselves, but the Elefant never recovered from its inauspicious debut. The few left were withdrawn to other fronts such as Italy but their unreliability rendered them useless.

The Elefant was one of the failures of the German Panzerjäger designers, for despite its main 8.8-cm (3.46-in) gun it was too cumbersome. More importantly, the first examples lacked any kind of self-defence armament. It was also too complicated and was generally unreliable.

SPECIFICATION	
Elefant	height 2.9 m (9 ft 10 in)
Crew: 6	**Armament:** one 8.8-cm (3.46-in) Pak 43/2 main gun
Weight: 65000 kg (143,300 lb)	
Powerplant: two Maybach HL 120 TRM V-12 petrol engines, each developing 395.2 kW (530 hp) and driving a Porsche/Siemens-Schuckert petrol-electric drive	**Performance:** maximum road speed 20.1 km/h (12.5 mph); road range 153 km (95 miles)
	Gradient: 40 per cent
	Vertical obstacle: 0.8 m (31.5 in)
Dimensions: length overall 8.1 m (26 ft 8 in); width 3.4 m (11 ft 1 in);	**Trench:** 2.65 m (8 ft 8 in)
	Fording: 1 m (3 ft 3 in)

Jagdtiger Tank destroyer

By 1943 it was an established German policy that when any new tank design became available, a fixed-superstructure version mounting a limited-traverse gun would be produced. Thus when the massive Tiger II appeared, a corresponding Panzerjäger was developed. A mock-up of this super-heavy tank destroyer appeared in October 1943, with production commencing during 1944 under the designation **Panzerjäger Tiger Ausf B**, or **Jagdtiger**.

Heavy armour

With the Jagdtiger the Germans produced the most powerful armoured vehicle of World War II. It had an official weight of 70,000 kg (154,324 lb) but by the time combat equipment, ammunition and the crew of six had been added the weight rose to around 76,000 kg (167,551 lb). The main armament was originally a 12.8-cm (5.04-in) Pak 44 anti-tank gun, later changed to the similar Pak 80. At one time a shortage of these guns meant

Two types of suspension were used on the Jagdtiger. This example has the Henschel suspension; the other type used larger road wheels from Porsche. Based on the Tiger II tank chassis, only about 70 were produced, and it was the heaviest armoured fighting vehicle (AFV) to see service during World War II.

that the smaller 8.8-cm (3.46-in) Pak 43/3 had to be used. The 12.8-cm guns were the most powerful anti-tank weapons used by any side during World War II, although the bulk of the ammunition meant each Jagdtiger could carry only 38 or 40 rounds. The defensive armament was two 7.92-mm (0.31-in) machine-guns. Armour thickness was 250 mm (9.84 in) on the superstructure front.

The Jagdtiger was a massive, powerful vehicle as far as weaponry and protection were concerned, but in mobility terms it had to be regarded as extremely ponderous. It was driven by the same engine used in the Jagdpanther, but this

engine had to drive the much greater weight of the Jagdtiger. This considerably increased the fuel consumption and reduced range across country. The

SPECIFICATION	
Jagdtiger	Pak 44 or Pak 80 main gun, two
Crew: 6	7.92-mm (0.31-in) machine-guns
Weight: 76000 kg (167,551 lb)	**Performance:** maximum speed 34.6
Powerplant: one Maybach HL 230	km/h (21.5 mph); road range 170
petrol engine developing	km (105 miles)
447.4–522 kW (600–700 hp)	**Gradient:** 70 per cent
Dimensions: length overall 10.65 m	**Vertical obstacle:** 0.85 m (33½ in)
(34 ft 11½ in); width 3.63 m (11 ft	**Trench:** 3 m (9 ft 10 in)
11 in); height 2.95 m (9 ft 8 in)	**Fording:** 1.65 m (5 ft 5 in)
Armament: one 12.8-cm (5.04-in)	

Jagdtiger had a speed of only 14.5 km/h (9 mph), often less, and the maximum possible cross-country range was 120 km (74.5 miles).

The Jagdtiger production centre was the Nibelungwerk at St Valentin where total production ran to only 70 vehicles. By the time the war ended two types of Jagdtiger could be encountered, one with Henschel suspension. Later versions had an extra road axle and Porsche suspension. In both forms the Jagdtigers were ponderous and underpowered, reducing them to little more than mobile weapon platforms.

The massive Jagdtiger with its 12.8-cm (5.04-in) gun was a powerful weapon, but it was underpowered and too heavy to be anything other than a purely defensive weapon. Not many were made before the war ended, but the 250-mm (9.84-in) frontal armour made it a difficult vehicle to knock out.

A Sturmgeschütz IIIF with a short 75-mm (2.95-in) gun and armoured skirts resists the Allied landings at Salerno. The StuG was based on the chassis of the Panzer III. The driver's station was unaltered from that of the tank, but behind him was now a very cramped compartment, which made fighting with hatches down an extremely arduous experience.

German tank destroyers

In action

Germany made great use of tracked tank destroyers throughout World War II. The earliest such vehicles were Panzerjäger (literally 'tank hunter') types, which were little more than older chassis adapted to carry a standard anti-tank gun mounting. These types paved the way for the Jagdpanzer (hunter tank) based on the hull of a more advanced tank built up with a well-protected barbette in whose front was fitted a larger-calibre anti-tank gun. These varied from the 7.5-cm (2.95-in) Pak 39, via the 8.8-cm (3.46-in) Pak 43, to the 12.8-cm (5.04-in) Pak 44 carried only by Tiger heavy tank adaptations.

A battery of four Hummels stands ready for action on a Russian steppe in 1942. The Hummel, or 'bumblebee', was the first of a series of hybrids, combining components from the PzKfpw III and IV. The close grouping of the guns and the relative lack of camouflage suggests that the Luftwaffe still had air superiority at this time.

MARDER III: IMPROVISED HUNTER

The SdKfz 139 Marder III (an early example is illustrated below) was typical of the improvised Panzerjäger that were still very efficient fighting vehicles. Based on a Czech light tank chassis – itself adopted by the Germans as the PzKpfw 38(t) – the Marder III carried a powerful 7.5-cm (2.95-in) Pak 40/3 gun. Although largely replaced by purpose-designed Panzerjäger by the end of the war, the Marder III gave good service to the Panzer and Panzer Grenadier divisions that capitalised on its mobility.

Above: The Jagdpanzer IV, known commonly as 'Guderian's duck', was designed as a replacement for the Sturmgeschutz III. It possessed thick, well-sloped armour and an extremely low profile. The first units to receive the vehicle were the Hermann Goering Division in Italy and the 12th SS Panzer 'Hitler Jugend' Division in Normandy.

Right: Based on the hull and propulsion arrangements of the Panther battle tank, what began life as the 8.8-cm Pak 43/3 auf Panzerjäger Panther was renamed as the Jagdpanther at Hitler's suggestion in February 1944. The basic lines of the hull were continued upward and inward to create a large superstructure containing the fighting compartment with its exceptional 8.8-cm (3.46-in) anti-tank gun.

Below: Allied soldiers examine a knocked-out Jagdpanther. This is an early version lacking the later bolt-on mantlet around the gun barrel. Note the size of the spent propellant case in front of the vehicle and the distinctive appearance given to this excellent tank destroyer by its well-sloped superstructure.

Semovente L.40 da 47/32 Light tank destroyer

The Italian Semovente L.3 da 47/32 was an early attempt to mount an anti-tank gun on a light tank chassis, and was much used for trials and various gunnery tests. It lacked adequate protection and was later replaced by better designs.

During World War II Italy was not noted for dramatic innovations in armoured vehicle design. In one field, however, Italy was abreast of tactical thinking as it became interested in the tank destroyer concept during the late 1930s. At that time Italy produced an intriguing design known as the **Semovente L.3 da 47/32** mounting a 47-mm (1.85-in) anti-tank gun with a barrel 32 calibres long (hence 47/32). The L.3 had the gun on an open mounting at the front of a small and low chassis based on that of the L.3 tankette; a two-man crew was carried. This early project did not get far for there was virtually no protection for the crew.

When Italy entered the war in 1940 it soon realised that their much-vaunted tank arm was seriously undergunned and lacked protection. This was particularly true of lighter tanks, in which the Italian treasury had invested to a considerable degree, especially the L.6 series that generally lacked protection and were armed only with a short 37-mm (1.46-in) gun of limited anti-armour capability. The main combat version, the L.6/40, soon proved to be of little combat value against the British armour in North Africa and was obviously ripe for the usual limited-traverse anti-tank

gun treatment. It was not long in coming when Fiat-SPA and Ansaldo combined to use the chassis for the basis of a tank destroyer.

Small tank destroyer

The gun used for the new vehicle was a licensed version of a powerful Austrian weapon, the Böhler 47-mm dual-role anti-tank/infantry support gun, one of the hardest-hitting of all anti-armour weapons in its day. On the new **Semovente L.40 da 47/32** the gun was mounted in a simple box-like superstructure built directly onto the light tank chassis, and while this arrangement worked well enough, the slab sides of the superstructure lacked the added protection that sloping sides would have provided. However it was better than nothing and went straight into service in 1942. About 280 were produced, and in action the type proved to be capable of dealing with the lighter British and other armour on the battlefields of North Africa. Ammunition stowage was 70 rounds.

When the Italians surrendered to the Allies in 1943 the Germans seized as much Italian equipment as they could. The Semovente L.40 da 47/32 was among this booty, and was quickly impressed as part of the equipment of German units

fighting in Italy. However, the terrain of many of the Italian battlefields in 1944–45 was such that armour could seldom be used, and the Semovente L.40s often had their anti-tank armament removed for service as mobile command posts, with an armament of one 8-mm (0.315-in) machine-gun.

The Semovente L.40 da 47/32 was a simple conversion that had little impact on enemy armour, but demonstrated that the Italians had absorbed the tank destroyer concept at an early stage of the war and used it as well as their limited production basis allowed.

The Semovente L.40 da 47/32 was used in some numbers by the Italian and later the German armies, and was a conversion of the L.6/40 light tank to take the powerful Italian 47-mm (1.85-in) anti-tank gun. Its box-like superstructure was later widely used to act as a mobile command post or ammunition carrier.

SPECIFICATION	
Semovente L.40 da 47/32	(5 ft 4 in)
Crew: 2	**Performance:** maximum road speed
Weight: 6500 kg (14,330 lb)	42.3 km/h (26.3 mph); road range
Powerplant: one SPA 18D 4-cylinder	200 km (124 miles)
petrol engine developing 50.7 kW	**Gradient:** 84 per cent
(68 hp)	**Vertical obstacle:** 0.8 m (31½ in)
Dimensions: length 4 m (13 ft 1½ in)	**Trench:** 1.7 m (5 ft 7 in)
and hull 3.78 m (12 ft 5 in); width	**Fording:** 0.8 m (31½ in)
1.92 m (6 ft 3½ in); height 1.63 m	

Semovente M.41M da 90/53 Heavy tank destroyer

The Semovente M.41M da 90/53 was the most powerful Italian tank destroyer, and combined the 90-mm (3.54-in) anti-aircraft gun with the chassis of the M.14/41 or M.15/42 tank.

Italy used the M.13 tank chassis for several self-propelled guns, but most of them were built along the lines of the German Sturmgeschütz types and were intended for use as close-support assault artillery. At times they could be used against tanks with some degree of success, but that was not their primary function and the Italians produced only one really heavy type of tank destroyer. This was the **Semovente M.41M da 90/53**, which used the chassis of the M.14/41 or later the M/15/42 tank.

The Semovente M.41M da 90/53 carried a powerful anti-armour weapon in the form of the cannone da 90/53 anti-aircraft gun, a long and very powerful weapon with performance very similar to that of the famous German 8.8-cm (3.46-in) Flak series. The gun's primary characteristics were denoted by the 90/53 designation, for it was a 90-mm (3.54-in) gun with a barrel 53 calibres long. To

accommodate the gun mounting at the rear, the engine was moved to the front of the chassis.

In action two men sat on the gun mounting behind the only protection, a gun shield. No ammunition was carried on the vehicle, but 26 were carried in a special conversion of the L.6 light tank that had a box-like superstructure very similar to that of the Semovente L.40 da 47/32, and another 40 rounds were carried in a trailer towed by the ammunition carrier. In action the long rounds were loaded into the gun breech by ammunition numbers standing on the ground behind the Semovente M.41.

German impetus

After noting the power of the German 8.8-cm Flak series the Italians were quick to get their Semovente M.41M into production. The first examples came off the Fiat, SPA and Ansaldo lines during 1941, but in the end only 48 were produced.

The main reason for this small total was the lack of production potential within Italian industry and the ever-pressing requirements for the cannone da 90/53 in its original role as an anti-aircraft gun.

In the field the M.41M proved to be a powerful weapon, especially across the flat wastes of the North African deserts, but once that campaign ended, so did the gun's career with the Italian army. Soon after the fall of Sicily and the invasion of the Italian mainland the Italians surrendered. The Germans had been expecting such a move and

promptly took control of as much Italian *matériel* as they could, and among the loot were several Semovente M.41Ms. The Germans soon had control of the gun's ammunition production facilities and thus the weapon ended in the German army's inventory, and was still in full service in northern Italy when the war ended. By then there was little call for their tank-killing capabilities, for much of the Italian campaign took place over mountainous country where few tanks could move, so the Semovente M.41M were used mainly as long-range artillery.

A Semovente M.41M da 90/53 is examined by American troops after being knocked out in Sicily during 1943. To serve the gun, the crew had to stand behind the breech and only the driver had all-round armour. These guns were first used in North Africa in late 1943 and were much respected.

SPECIFICATION	
Semovente M.41M da 90/53	2.15 m (7 ft)
Crew: (on gun) 2	**Performance:** maximum road speed
Weight: 17000 kg (37,479 lb)	35.5 km/h (22 mph); road range
Powerplant: one SPA 15-TM-41	200 km (124 miles)
8 cylinder petrol engine developing	**Vertical obstacle:** 0.9 m (35.4 in)
108.1 kW (145 hp)	**Trench:** 2.1 m (6 ft 11 in)
Dimensions: length 5.21 m (17 ft 1	**Fording:** 1 m (3 ft 3 in)
in); width 2.2 m (7 ft 2½ in); height	

Archer Tank destroyer

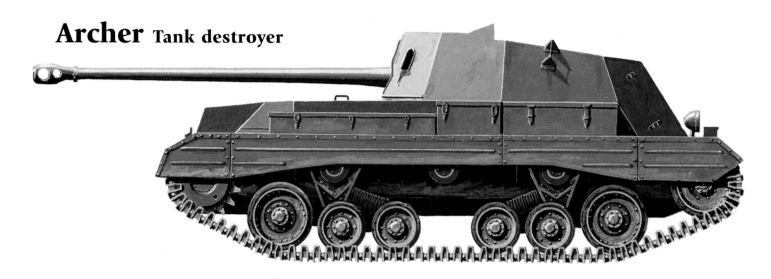

The British Archer was a conversion of the Valentine infantry tank to mount a 17-pdr (76.2-mm/3-in) anti-tank gun that fired over the rear of the hull. The first of the weapons were used in action late in 1944, and proved to be very useful weapons with a low silhouette. They were used by the Royal Artillery.

Although the British Army tended to lag behind the Germans in upgunning its tanks as World War II progressed, an early decision by British planners to make a quantum leap in anti-tank gun calibre, from 57 mm (2.244 in) in the 6-pdr to 76.2 mm (3 in), was bold as it was made at a time when the 6-pdr was only just getting into production.

Long and heavy

It was realised that the new 3-in gun, soon to be known as the 17-pdr, would be a very large and heavy weapon on its towed carriage, so it was decided to find some means of making it mobile. Ideally the 17-pdr was to be used as a tank gun, but the tanks large enough to carry such

a large weapon were still a long way off (indeed had not even left the drawing boards) so a short-term alternative had to be found.

After in-production chassis such as the Crusader tank had been considered, it was decided to mount the 17-pdr on the Valentine infantry tank chassis. The Valentine was in production and could be rapidly adapted for its new gun-carrying role by adding a sloping superstructure, open at the top, on the forward part of the hull. To ensure the gun/chassis combination would not be nose-heavy and unwieldy, it was decided to

place the gun in a limited-traverse-mounting facing over the rear of the chassis. This vehicle was obviously meant to be a tank destroyer and it was placed in production in late 1943.

Supreme ambusher

It was March 1943 before the first **Self-Propelled 17-pdr Valentine** rolled off the production lines. The troops looked at the new vehicle with some trepidation, for the idea of having a gun that faced only to the rear was against established practice. Drivers were also less than enchanted, for they were positioned at the centre front of the fighting compartment and the gun breech was directly behind their heads: on firing, the breech block came to within a short distance of the back of the driver's head. The rest of the crew was made up of the gun layer, the commander and the loader. Protective fire was supplied by one 7.7-mm (0.303-in) Bren gun.

It was October 1944 before the first of these Valentine/17-pdr combinations reached the fighting in Europe. By then the type had become known as the **Archer**, and in action the Archer's tank-killing capabilities were soon revealed. The rear-facing gun was soon seen to be a virtue. The Archer was soon in use as an ambush weapon where its low silhouette made it easy to conceal in a hide. As enemy tanks approached a few shots could be fired to kill a tank, and then the Archer was facing the right way to make a quick getaway before enemy retaliation arrived. The Archers were used by the anti-tank companies of the Royal Artillery, and they were definitely preferred to the weight and bulk of the towed 17-pdr guns used by the same companies.

The end of the war brought a halt in Archer production at a point where 655 of the original order for 800 had been produced. The Archers then equipped British anti-tank units.

Although the rear-facing main gun of the Archer could have been a tactical liability, crews used the layout to advantage by placing their Archers in ambush positions and then driving away after the action with the gun barrel still pointing to the rear.

SPECIFICATION	
Archer	2.25 m (7 ft 4½ in)
Crew: 4	**Performance:** maximum road speed
Weight: 16257 kg (35,840 lb)	32.2 km/h (20 mph); road range
Powerplant: one General Motors 6-71 6-cylinder diesel developing 143.2 kW (192 hp)	225 km (140 miles)
	Gradient: 32°
Dimensions: length overall 6.68 m (21 ft 11 in) and hull 5.54 m (18 ft 6 in); width 2.76 m (9 ft); height	**Vertical obstacle:** 0.84 m (33 in)
	Trench: 2.36 m (7 ft 9 in)
	Fording: 0.91 m (3 ft)

M10 3-in gun motor carriage

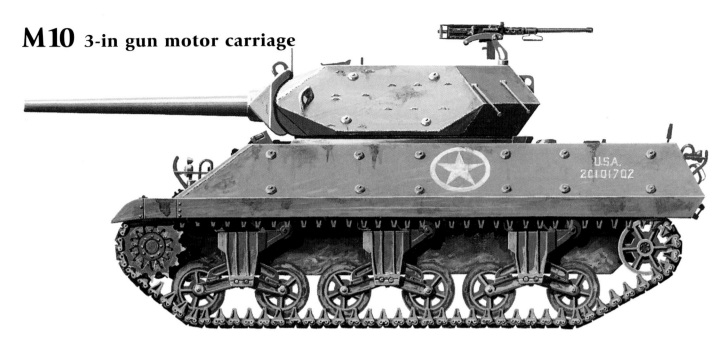

During the late 1930s and early 1940s the US Army formulated a novel tactical doctrine in which fast-moving armoured formations were to be countered by a new tank destroyer force comprising towed and self-propelled high-velocity anti-tank guns. This tank destroyer force was to be used en masse and armed with powerful guns. One of the first operational results of this doctrine was the **Gun Motor Carriage M10** self-propelled mounting armed with a 76.2-mm (3-in) M7 gun, a development of an anti-aircraft weapon. The secondary armament was one 12.7-mm (0.5-in) Browning MG.

Sherman chassis

The M10 used the chassis of the M4A2 medium tank allied to a thinly armoured upper hull and an open-topped turret. The relatively thin armour of the hull was improved by the use of sloping armour plates to increase protection, and sloped armour was also used on the

turret. The M10 had a turret with 360° traverse, for although the M10 was intended for use as a tank destroyer it was seen by the US Army as a gun carrier and a close-combat vehicle, hence the relatively thin armour.

Production commenced during September 1942, and such was the capability of American industry, 4,993 had been manufactured by the end of production in December 1942.

The bulk of this total went to US Army's 106 active tank destroyer battalions. As World War II continued, their number gradually decreased as it became clear that the best counter to a tank was another tank. But the tank destroyer force remained in being until the war ended, most of the battalions being used in Europe.

Assault gun service

By the end of the war many of the M10s were being used more as assault guns than as tank destroyers, by then distributed among the more

The American M10 was designed to be the main weapon of the Tank Destroyer Command's mobile units, and mounted a 3-in (76.2-mm) gun in an open-topped turret. The armour protection was relatively thin, as the weight of better armour was sacrificed for all-round performance and speed in action.

conventional armoured formations. The M10 was the primary equipment of these battalions and was used not only by the US Army but, via Lend-Lease, by the British (who knew the M10 as the **Wolverine**) and later by the French and Italians. The M10 was a large and bulky vehicle and, as time went on, the gun lost much of its anti-armour effectiveness against tanks.

When the war ended the British had re-gunned many of their M10s with 17-pdr guns and re-named the type **Achilles**. The M10 was joined by the **M10A1**, the same vehicle as before but using the chassis of the M4A3 medium tank with its different engine installation and some other changes. By 1945 turretless examples of both were used as artillery tractors.

Late in World War II the M10 (left) was supplemented by the M36 (right) which used a 90-mm (3.54-in) gun, though still in an open-topped turret. The M36 was designed as early as 1942 but took a long time to get into production, and it was late 1944 before the first of the type reached units fighting in Europe. By then they were used mainly as assault guns.

SPECIFICATION	
M10	cylinder diesel engines
Crew: 5	**Performance:** maximum road speed
Weight: 29937 kg (66,000 lb)	51 km/h (32 mph); maximum road
Dimensions: length (overall) 6.83 m	range 322 km (200 miles)
(22 ft 5 in); width 3.05 m (10 ft);	**Fording:** 0.91 m (3 ft)
height 2.57 m (8 ft 5 in)	**Gradient:** 25 per cent
Powerplant: two 276.5-kW (375-hp)	**Vertical obstacle:** 0.46 m (1 ft 6 in)
General Motors liquid-cooled 6-	**Trench:** 2.26 m (7 ft 5 in)

M18 Hellcat 3-in gun motor carriage

Whereas the M10 was produced for the tank destroyer battalions by converting an existing tank chassis (the M4A2), the **Gun Motor Carriage M18** was designed from the outset for the tank destroyer role. Development as the **Gun Motor Carriage T70** began during 1942, and the first examples were ready during 1943.

In service the M18 proved to be one of the best and most successful examples of the American tank destroyer concept. It was much smaller and more compact than the M10, making it difficult to spot, and weighed only about half as much, but it carried a more powerful gun and was much faster. Indeed, the M18 was the fastest tracked vehicle used in action during World War II.

The gun was the 76.2-mm (3-in) M1A1 or M1A2, the latter having a muzzle brake. The M1A1 gun was a development of the gun used in the M10, but had a better all round performance and it was mounted in an open-topped turret. The gun could penetrate 100 mm (3.94 in) of armour at 915 m (1,000 yards).

In appearance the M18 resembled a tank, and it did indeed have a 360° traverse

The M18 Hellcat had the distinction of being the fastest of all AFVs used during World War II. Armed with a long 3-in (76-mm) gun, it was an ideal tank-hunting vehicle, but as with other vehicles of its type it generally lacked armour and was fitted with an open-topped turret.

turret, but its armour protection was much less than would be expected in a tank, to a maximum of 12.7 mm (0.5 in). In addition, the top of the turret was left open (apart from canvas weather protection), exposing the turret occupants to the effects of overhead fire. The M18 Hellcat therefore had to rely on its agility, low silhouette and striking power to survive in combat.

Power to weight ratio

The engine was positioned at the rear of the hull and was an air-cooled radial petrol engine with aviation origins and the rating to give the M18 a good power/weight ratio and thus excellent acceleration and agility. Internal stowage was such that as well

as carrying the crew of five men there was space for 45 3-in rounds and a 12.7-mm (0.5-in) heavy machine-gun for local and anti-aircraft defence. The rear of the turret was provided with a bustle acting as a stowage box for extra equipment and the crew's personal kit.

In service with tank destroyer battalions, the M18 was given the name **Hellcat**. Despite its success in action the M18 was gradually switched from the tank destroyer battalions as the enthusiasm for the exclusive tank destroyer concept dwindled, and by 1945 many M18s had been reassigned to conventional armoured formations within the US Army. By then they were being used more and more as assault guns or conventional self-propelled artillery.

Numerous variants

The production run of the M18 lasted from July 1943 to October 1944, when it was obvious that

SPECIFICATION	
M18	**Performance:** maximum road speed
Crew: 5	88.5 km/h (55 mph); road range
Weight: 17036 kg (37,557 lb)	169 km (105 miles)
Dimensions: length (overall) 6.65 m	**Fording:** 1.22 m (4 ft)
(21 ft 10 in) and (hull) 5.44 m (17 ft	**Gradient:** 60 per cent
10 in); width 2.87 m (9 ft 5 in);	**Vertical obstacle:** 0.91 m (3 ft)
height 2.58 m (8 ft 5½ in);	**Trench:** 1.88 m (6 ft 2 in)
Powerplant: one 253.5-kW (340-hp)	
Continental R-975 C1 radial engine	

the war was not going to last much longer. Between those dates 2,507 M18s were produced, some being completed without turrets to the **M39** standard for use as high-speed troop or supply carriers. They were also used as heavy artillery tractors, a mobile command and communications post, and as a front-line utility carrier. There was also a **Flame Tank T65** based on the M18 with a much revised upper hull mounting a flame gun in front. The **Howitzer Motor Carriage T88** was an attempt to mount a 105-mm (4.13-in) howitzer on the basic M18, and there were also attempts to mount a 90-mm (3.54-in) gun and turret on the chassis. None of these versions got past the experimental stage – a fate shared by many other trial versions of the basic M18. Numbers of M18s were distributed on Lend-Lease terms to various Allied nations before 1945.

The M18 Hellcat went out of production in October 1944 after 2,507 had been built. The M18 was the only vehicle specifically designed for the US Army's tank destroyer role, and was a most successful combat vehicle capable of tackling all but the very heaviest German tanks.

M36 90-mm gun motor carriage

The 90-mm (3.54-in) **Gun Motor Carriage M36**, originally the **T71** during its development period, can be regarded as an enhanced M10 tank destroyer, the main change coming with the larger-calibre gun, namely the 90-mm M3. This was a powerful high-velocity weapon that became a maid-of-all work for the US Army as it had close anti-aircraft, towed anti-tank and tank gun variants. Before type classification in June 1944, M10A1 chassis were used for development of the new type. Production was not entirely carried out from new as 2,324 examples were converted (in the US and Canada) to the up-gunned state using existing M10A1 hulls as the basis, although an undefined number of pilot vehicles were also manufactured by the Chevrolet Division of General Motors. A further 187 examples of the **M36B1** variant were built based on the M4A3 tank hull. A further variant was the **M36B2** based on the M10;

237 examples of this model were produced.

Larger turret

Apart from the gun (with or without a muzzle brake), the engine was brought up to M10A1 standard by installing a Ford GAA V-8 petrol engine, and a larger turret with a revised outline was introduced, though this remained open-topped. Some modifications were introduced to cater for the stowage of the heavier 90-mm ammunition, the number of rounds carried being reduced to 47 from the M10's figure of 54. One detail was the addition of an auxiliary generator in the engine compartment to save fuel, conserve main engine life and provide power for routine services when the vehicle was in a stand-by state for extended periods. Despite all the changes, the M36 emerged as slightly lighter than the M10, although overall performance remained much the same.

SPECIFICATION	
M36	
Crew: 5	**Performance:** maximum road speed 48 km/h (30 mph); maximum range 241 km (150 miles)
Weight: 28554 kg (62,950 lb)	**Fording:** 0.91 m (3 ft)
Dimensions: length 6.15 m (20 ft 2 in); width 3.05 m (10 ft); height 2.72 m (8 ft 11 in)	**Gradient:** 60 per cent
Powerplant: one Ford GAA V-8 engine developing 335 kW (450 hp)	**Vertical obstacle:** 0.61 m (2 ft)
	Trench: 2.29 m (7 ft 6 in)

Potent but flawed

The M36 inherited many of the M10's shortcomings in that the armoured protection remained as before and the overall height made the vehicle conspicuous and bulky. Even so, the gun and vehicle combination created a successful and potent tank destroyer. The gun possessed the power to knock out any German tank – including the Tiger II – that was likely to be encountered. The gun's armour penetrating projectiles were able to defeat 76 mm (3 in) of armour at a range of 4300 m (4,700 yards), assuming that a target could be detected at that extreme range. As tank targets diminished during 1945, the M36 became a specialist bunker-buster and was gradually integrated into armoured divisions rather than operating within the context of specialised tank destroyer battalions.

After 1945 the M36 was handed out in substantial numbers to several nations friendly to the US cause. They served on for many years, the last of them emerging (to the surprise of many) during the early stages of the Balkan troubles of the late 1990s, when the type appeared in both Bosnian and Serbian hands. That appearance marked the M36 as the last of the US tank destroyers of World War II to remain in combat service.

The 90-mm Gun Motor Carriage M36 was a highly successful and potent tank destroyer, able to knock out any tank it encountered. Based on the M10A1 hull, it had a larger turret to accommodate the 90-mm gun.

The tank destroyer
Countering tanks

Tank will kill tank, and that is just how it is. In their quest to defeat the Panzers and T-34s of World War II, however, all of the major combatants experimented with the design and construction of tank destroyers.

Tank destroyers were a product of expediency and combat doctrine. Specifically designed 'tank killers' were soon supplemented by obsolescent vehicles modified to carry massive anti-tank guns.

The concept of the tank destroyer emerges from two basic philosophies: an armed vehicle produced as a tank killer; and the use of existing tanks or other armoured vehicles to carry weapons larger and more powerful than those for which they had been designed.

The concept of specialised anti-armour vehicles was a result of US thinking during the late 1930s and early 1940s. The Americans argued that fast-moving Panzer columns could be stopped only by the use of massed, self-propelled, high-velocity guns of large calibre. At that time some armies considered that tanks would not meet tanks in combat, but it emerged that the tank was the ideal platform to counter other tanks. It had good mobility, powerful main armament, and protection for the crew.

Right: The SdKfz 138 variant of the Marder III was typical of the improvised Panzerjäger produced by the Germans, and was a very efficient fighting vehicle. Based on a Czechoslovak tank chassis, the SdKfz carried the 7.5-cm (2.95-in) Pak 40/3 gun.

Below: This SdKfz 184 Elefant, captured in Italy, bears a warning of booby traps. The photograph shows the size of the fighting compartment for the 8.8-cm (3.46-in) Pak 43/2 gun and five of the six-man crew, but this made the vehicle bulky, difficult to hide and easy to hit.

The US Army tank destroyers lacked this balance. They had powerful main guns, but lacked protection for the crew. With the exception of the remarkable M18 Hellcat, they had little mobility by comparison with conventional tanks. By 1944 the US Army had realised this fact. Tank destroyers were diverted to more conventional armoured formations, by which they were used as assault guns or self-propelled artillery.

Undergunned

Many of the tanks that were in use when World War II began were soon found to be under-gunned: a situation common to

Below: The American M10 was used by several of the Allied armies including that of the Free French, seen here on exercises in North Africa. The M10 was based on the widely used M4 chassis, but was relatively lightly armoured and had an open-topped turret mounting the main 76.2-mm (3-in) high-velocity gun.

Right: Based on the readily available PzKpfw IV chassis, the SdKfz 162 Jadgpanzer IV combined the powerful 7.5-cm (2.95-in) Pak 39 L/48 gun with a low, well-armoured superstructure and good overall performance. Well-sloped armour added to the overall protection afforded to the crew of four. Later versions of this excellent equipment mounted the 7.5-cm Pak 42 L/70 gun firing its projectile at somewhat greater velocity.

Left: The SdKfz 184 Ferdinand (or Elefant) was first used in action at Kursk in 1943. It proved a failure as it carried no secondary armament and was thus vulnerable to Soviet tank-killer squads attacking from the sides or rear. Although it was meant to be a Panzerjäger it was often used as an assault gun.

Below: Conversions from PzKpfw II Ausf D standard, with Luchs (lynx) suspensions and captured Soviet 76.2-mm (3-in) field guns revised for German anti-tank ammunition, were used mainly on the Eastern Front, but some also appeared in France during 1944.

nearly all tank designs of the period as it had been considered that there would be little call for tank guns with calibres larger than 40 mm (1.57 in). Opposing tanks would be relatively lightly armoured and really heavy guns would not be needed. Relatively small tanks were produced with small turrets and turret rings. However, new tanks had thicker armour applied to their hulls.

The only way to get through this was the use of heavier projectiles.

Many of the early World War II tanks were effectively obsolete within a few months of taking the field. Some form of vehicle to mount larger guns had to be found.

The answer was to convert these tanks to accommodate new superstructures in which

Below: This rather awkward-looking conversion was based on a French Hotchkiss H-39 tank chassis to carry a 7.5-cm (2.95-in) Pak 40 gun. The type was created early in 1944 as part of the attempt to provide more weapons for the defences of northern France, and about 24 such anti-tank conversions were produced.

larger-calibre guns could be fitted in mountings offering only limited traverse. Usually this meant removal of the old turret and building onto the chassis a boxlike superstructure, usually with sloped sides to improve projectile deflection, with a new gun mounted on the front plate. There were many of these conversions during the period 1940–43, usually by the German army to produce what it called a Panzerjäger (tank hunter).

The Panzerjäger

The Panzerjäger is not a tank. One of the main attributes of the tank was and indeed still is its combination of firepower, mobility and protection, but the Panzer-jäger often lacked at least two of these attributes. Most of the Panzerjäger were only indifferently armoured and, generally being underpowered, suffered from poor mobility.

The early generation of conversions was replaced by

Left: This is an SdKfz 132 conversion of the PzKpfw II with a captured Soviet 76.2-mm (3-in) gun. Using a new large-wheeled suspension, the conversion was sometimes known as the Marder II. The ex-Soviet guns were fitted with Pak 40 muzzle brakes.

full production examples. For Germany this was a deliberate policy to boost the number of armoured vehicles in the field. German armoured vehicle designers appreciated that a limited-traverse mounting on a tracked chassis could be produced in less time at less cost than a turreted tank on the same chassis. The price that had to be paid was that the limited-traverse main armament suffered from severe tactical disadvantages. In mobile armoured warfare targets can appear from any point of the compass. If a target appeared to the side of a Panzerjäger the entire vehicle had to be turned towards it. This often took too long, and once the Panzerjäger had been turned the target had either gone or had fired.

However, tank destroyers often had a lower silhouette than tanks. They were usually used as ambush weapons that could lie in wait for targets, fire, then move out.

After World War II the tank destroyer concept died. There remain in service only a few tank destroyers, some of which use missiles. It has been accepted that the best counter to the tank is another tank.

Volkswagen Kübel

Light personnel carrier

The Volkswagen Kübel was not at first successful in the desert, so a Tropenfest (tropical) version was developed. Changes were numerous, including the use of sand tyres, and the altered models came to be known as the 'Deutsches Kamel' or 'German camel'.

One of the most famous military cars of World War II was the **Volkswagen Kübel** (bucket), the German equivalent of the American Jeep. The origins of the vehicle can be discovered in the instructions issued in 1933 by Adolf Hitler, newly arrived in office as chancellor of the German state, to a pair of car designers (Dr Ferdinand Porsche of Auto-Union and Werlin of Mercedes-Benz) to create and ensure the speedy development of a reliable and affordable 'people's car' (Volkswagen). The basic Volkswagen was offered for approval in January of the following year. Between 1935 and 1938 there appeared a number of prototype vehicles as well as two 30-vehicle series of pre-production cars, as the design was finalised with a 0.998-litre air-cooled engine. It was planned that the new car would enter production as soon as its purpose-built factory had been completed. Production at the Wolfsburg factory began in March 1940, by which time over 250,000 people had each paid 1,000 Reichsmarks in advance for their cars.

Cross-country vehicle

In 1936 there appeared the first design for a Volkswagen cross-country vehicle, this being known as the **Typ 62**. When the decision was reached in 1938, after Germany's seizure of much of Czechoslovakia, that the only new light personnel carrier to be employed by the German armed forces would be the Volkswagen, serving as the standard light passenger car for all arms, design changes were requested, resulting in the **Typ 82**. The first examples of the Type 82 were delivered to the army for evaluation, which was not complimentary as it was the consensus in army circles that a water-cooled engine was required and that only a 4x4 vehicle could provide adequate cross-country mobility for any tactical vehicle. Even so, a number of vehicles were allocated to Panzer units during

The ubiquitous Kübel (bucket) served wherever the German armed forces were found, and was highly popular for its reliability. Unlike certain other German equipments of the period, the design of the Kübel stressed ease of manufacture and light weight.

SPECIFICATION	
Volkswagen Type 82 Kübel **Dimensions:** length 3.73 m (12 ft 3 in); width 1.6 m (5 ft 3 in); height 1.35 m (4 ft 5 in); wheelbase 2.39 m (7 ft 10 in) **Weight:** net 635 kg (1,400 lb) **Powerplant:** one Volkswagen Typ 1 4-cylinder HIAR 0.998-litre petrol engine delivering 17.9 kW (24 bhp)	or, from March 1943, one Volkswagen 4-cylinder 1.131-litre petrol engine developing 18.6 kW (25 bhp) **Transmission:** limited-slip differential giving four forward and one reverse gears, with overdrive on fourth gear **Tyres:** 5.25 × 16

Men of the Waffen SS are seen with their Kübel vehicles in the USSR, probably during late spring of 1942 or 1943. Unlike many of Germany's heavier vehicle, the Kübel could cope with such conditions.

the invasion of Poland in September 1939, and proved very successful as they offered cross-country capability at least as good as that offered by other light transport vehicles.

Production from 1940

Production began before the Wolfsburg factory was complete, civilian production having been postponed until military requirements had been satisfied, and body panels had at first to be delivered from a factory in Berlin. In overall terms the vehicle was designed for lightness and ease of manufacture. Built as cheaply as possible, it comprised components of simple design. Generally, the layout was very similar to that of the Jeep. The suspension, of the transverse torsion-bar type, combined with a self-locking differential to give remarkable cross-country performance. After initial problems, the 0.998-litre Volkswagen Typ 1 four-cylinder HIAR air-cooled engine soon became wholly reliable, and in its original form was rated at 17.9 kW (24 hp). The engine was later enlarged to a capacity of 1.131 litres for 18.6 kW (25 hp), and this engine was used in all vehicles completed after March 1943. With its excellent automotive qualities and simple maintenance requirements, the Typ 82 fully met the high demands of military use, especially in the deserts of North Africa and the open country of the western and southern USSR: in the latter the Typ 82 was one of the few vehicles that could move over the *rasputitsa* (mud) of the spring and autumn without becoming bogged down, and even when it did become stuck it was so light that two men could generally extract it.

Simple structure

The military version had a touring body of sheet metal with a folding top. Four doors were provided, and weather protection was afforded by a folding canvas hood and side screens. The body panels were mostly of 18-gauge stampings. Tubular struts were used as the basic structural members of the body. The engine cylinders were of 'H' form and laid flat at the bottom of the car. The chassis consisted of a central welded-steel tube bifurcating at the rear to support the engine and transmission, and the steel floor on each side of the central member supported the body. The front axle consisted of steel tube which housed the two torsion bars of the suspension. At each side of the differential were universal joints providing centres about which the two rear driving axles could articulate, and the rear wheels were stabilised laterally from the differential housing. The auxiliary gearboxes in each rear wheel brought the two half-shafts higher and so gave a greater ground clearance. There was independent suspension on all four wheels, and double-action hydraulic shock absorbers controlled the movement of the rear springing. The steering gear and connectors were of conventional type. The brakes were cable-operated and of the mechanical type with double lever action on the brake shoes. Transmission was through a single-plate clutch gearbox. An overdrive was incorporated in fourth gear.

A Volkswagen Kübel in desert configuration is pictured in Tunis during April 1943, the weapons of its occupants including a 7.92-mm (0.312-in) MG 34 general-purpose machine-gun.

The 40-litre (8.8-Imp gal) fuel tank was located below the instrument panel, facing the front right-hand seat.

Enclosed body

The basic vehicle was also developed with an enclosed body, and this variant was designated as the **Typ 92** and, in common with all vehicles delivered from March 1943, this had the larger engine. When manufacture of the Type 82 ended in mid-1944, some 55,000 such vehicles had been completed. This figure provides an interesting contrast with the Jeep, of which more than 600,000 were manufactured between 1941 and the end of World War II in 1945.

To accommodate the various bodies required, an order was issued on 2 August 1940 demanding the widening of the chassis by between 6 and 8 cm (2.36 and 3.15 in) in what became the **Typ 86**. The normal Kübel was not very successful in the desert and so the *Tropenfest* (tropical) version was developed with numerous changes including larger sand tyres. Kübel vehicles used in Africa were often referred to as *'Deutsches Kamel'* ('German camel'). There were numerous special-role Kübel vehicles, many of used by the Wehrmacht.

Above: A Kübel is put through its paces with five men aboard. The driver is purportedly Dr. Ferdinand Porsche, the co-designer of the vehicle and also a key figure in the development of some of Germany's most important tanks.

Below: A Kübel undergoes maintenance in North Africa. In this theatre the vehicle was not very successful in its first form, but was subsequently developed in a tropicalised form.

Kraftfahrzeug 2 (Stöwer 40) Personnel carrier

During 1934 the Germans made the first attempts to create standardised (*Einheit*) vehicles for the Wehrmacht. The intention was to create a substantial motorised element within the army, combining mechanised infantry with armoured fighting vehicles. However, the rearmament programme was far from complete at the end of the 1930s and the ideal of a standard series of vehicles was never fully achieved. The use of captured foreign vehicles became essential but spares were often unattainable.

The new army motorization programme placed great emphasis upon the design of vehicles from not only technical but also operational considerations. A new system of Kfz (*Kraftfahrzeug*, or motor vehicle) numbers was introduced whereby numbers were allotted to vehicles (irrespective of make or model) to denote their tactical or military function. With few exceptions, for the vehicles covered here these Kfz numbers were broken down into the following classes: 1 to 10 covered 1.Pkw (*leichter*

Personenkraftwagen, or light personnel carrier); 11 to 20 covered m.Pkw (*mittlerer Personenkraftwagen*, or medium personnel carrier); and 21 to 30 covered s.Pkw (*schwerer Personenkraftwagen*, or heavy personnel carrier).

The 1.Pkw was a standard vehicle irrespective of its models or manufacturers, with the exception of the engine, which was always that of the manufacturer and commercially available. The engine was made by Stöwer, BMW and Hanomag from 1936 onwards. The Stöwer model (**Kraftfahrzeug 2**) used AW2 and R18OW water-cooled

A Luftwaffe Kfz 2 in the desert. The Ju 87 Stukas are returning from a mission, as evidenced by their bombless condition. Although the German military pursued a standardisation programme for their vehicles, the resulting equipment was often complex, and mass-produced civilian models were also adopted.

4-cylinder OHV petrol engines with dry-sump lubrication. The chassis was of normal type with a frame of rectangular section, side- and crossmembers, and

bracing to support the engine, transmission and body. The chassis was used for the 4-seater light car (**Kfz 1**) and a variety of other military vehicles.

SPECIFICATION	
Kfz 2 (Stöwer 40) **Dimensions:** length 3.58 m (11 ft 9 in); width 1.57 m (5 ft 2 in); height 1.78 m (5 ft 10 in); wheelbase 2.24 m (7 ft 4 in) **Weight:** net 1815 kg (4,001 lb)	**Powerplant:** one Stöwer AW2 or R180W 4-cylinder OHV petrol engine developing 37.3 kW (50 bhp) **Transmission:** five forward and one reverse gears **Tyres:** 5.50 x 18 (metric)

Built from 1936, the Kfz 2 was a standard (Einheit, or 'E' vehicle) body design based on mechanical components supplied by several different manufacturers. The Stöwer 40 was a 4x4 design, and, as illustrated here, often formed the basis for radio cars.

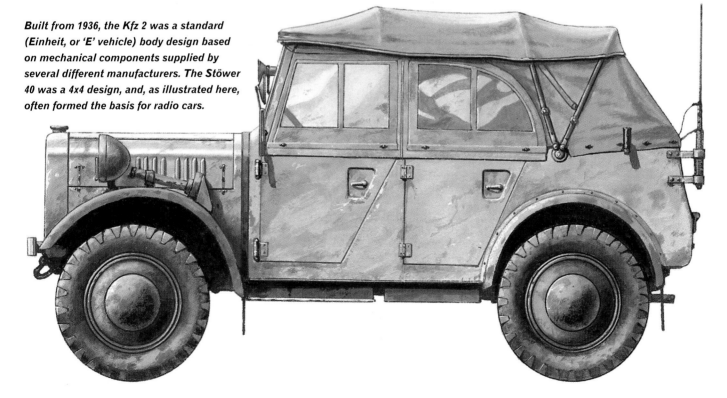

Kraftfahrzeug 11 (Auto-Union/Horch 830) Personnel carrier

Before the introduction of the standard (*Einheit*) vehicles, the German army made extensive use of commercial cars as a means of rapidly motorising the various arms and services. The **Auto-Union/Horch Typ 830** was one of the many commercial passenger car chassis fitted with various military bodies between the late 1920s and early 1930s. V-8 petrol power-plants with a capacity of 3, 3.2 and 3.5 litres were installed. Since only the rear wheels of the cars were driven, larger

tyres and different rear axle ratios helped to increase the types' cross-country performance.

Widespread service

The vehicles saw action in most theatres of war, the majority of them fitted with open superstructures and used as prime movers for light infantry guns, as well as radio communications vehicles. The signal troops also used a variety of enclosed van-type bodies. The **Kfz 11** was a closed-bodied

communications or radio vehicle based on this chassis which incorporated two seats and a boot. The closed body of the vehicle was often made of wood. Later production models were fitted with sheet-metal doors and removable side

windows. Eventually production was discontinued in favour of the medium standard cross-country personnel carrier that was built from 1937 onwards by Horch and, after 1940, by the Opel concern.

SPECIFICATION	
Kfz 11 (Auto-Union/Horch Type 830) **Dimensions:** length 4.8 m (15 ft 9 in); width 1.8 m (5 ft 11 in); height 1.85 m (6 ft 1 in); wheelbase 3.2 m (10 ft 6 in) **Weight:** net 990 kg (2,183 lb)	**Powerplant:** one Horch V-8 2.98-litre petrol engine developing 52.2 kW (70 bhp) **Transmission:** ZF Aphon with four forward and one reverse gears **Tyres:** 6.0 x 18 (metric)

The Horch Typ 830 was one of many commercial designs fitted with military bodies during the 1930s. Originally used as a troop carrier and radio car, the vehicle saw action in most theatres.

Kraftfahrzeug 15 (Mercedes-Benz 340) Personnel carrier

The **Kfz 15 mittlerer geländegängiger Personenkraftwagen** (**m.gl.Pkw**, or medium cross-country personnel carrier) was used as a communications (*Fernsprech*) or radio (*Funk*) car. It had an open 4-seater body and a boot, and it was fitted with a towing hook. The vehicle was powered by a V-8 engine. Commercial chassis used for this role comprised in 1933–8 the Horch 830 and 830B1, in 1937–9 the Wanderer W23S, and in 1938–40 the **Mercedes-Benz 340**.

The Mercedes-Benz 340, a larger version of the 320, was powered by a 3.5-litre engine and had a very long

wheelbase, which tended to impair its cross-country performance.

Einheit successor

In common with the Kraftfahrzeug 11 described in the previous entry, production of this vehicle was discontinued in favour of the medium standard (*Einheit*) cross-country personnel carrier. This latter vehicle differed basically from

The fall of Tobruk in June 1942 was a shock to the British, and soon the town square was filled with a motley collection of Afrika Korps vehicles, including this Mercedes-Benz 340 configured as an ambulance.

SPECIFICATION	
Kfz 15 (Mercedes-Benz 340) **Dimensions:** length 4.44 m (14 ft 7 in); width 1.68 m (5 ft 6 in); height 1.73 m (5 ft 8 in); wheelbase 3.12 m (10 ft 3 in) **Weight:** net 2405 kg (5,302 lb)	**Powerplant:** one Mercedes-Benz 6cylinder petrol engine developing 67.1 kW (90 bhp) **Transmission:** four forward and one reverse gears **Tyres:** 6.5 x 20 (metric)

the light model (described under Kfz 2, or Stöwer 40) in that the rear wheels were not steerable. As before, however, all-wheel-drive was used. The chassis was a conventional type used for staff cars, radio vehicles and other specialized types. Depending upon the manufacturer, the engine had a swept volume of between 2.9 and 3.5 litres. Horch engines were standard for most models, the few exceptions being equipped with an Opel type.

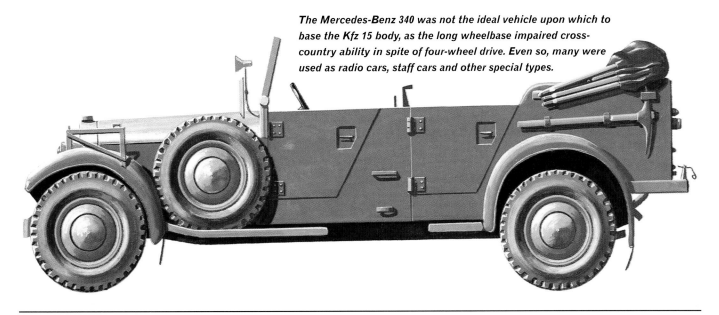

The Mercedes-Benz 340 was not the ideal vehicle upon which to base the Kfz 15 body, as the long wheelbase impaired cross-country ability in spite of four-wheel drive. Even so, many were used as radio cars, staff cars and other special types.

Daimler-Benz G 5 Personnel carrier

During 1925–6 the first proposals were considered for the development of specialised vehicles for the Reichswehr (predecessor of the Wehrmacht). Among others, a requirement was laid down for a fully cross-country personnel carrier. This was to have six seats and use a six-wheeled chassis with more than one driven axle. The development of such a vehicle was taken up by the firms of Horch-Werk AG of Zwickau, Daimler-Benz AG of Stuttgart and Selve Automobilwerk AG of Hamelin, each of them supplying several models for trial purposes. The first Daimler-Benz model, designated **Daimler-Benz G 1**, several of which were produced between 1926 and 1928, was powered by a 37.3-kW (50-hp) M03 6-cylinder engine. This had the drive taken to the four rear wheels. The unladen weight was 1200 kg (2,645 lb), and the payload was 1000 kg (2,205 lb). Daimler-Benz alone continued development of the three-axled personnel carrier. Between 1933 and 1934 Daimler-Benz produced a small number of its **G 4** model. This was a vehicle widely known for its use by Adolf Hitler,

although it was never suited to military usage. It had a poor cross-country performance and was too large, too heavy and too expensive. Between 1933 and 1934 only 57 were built and these were almost exclusively employed by high officials of the Nazi party and the general staff. One was modified as a special communications vehicle for use by Hitler during his field trips.

Private venture model

With the development of the *Einheit* series of personnel

carriers, Daimler-Benz, which appears to have been neglected in the share-out of production contracts for these vehicles, prepared a model of its own as a private venture. The **Daimler-Benz G 5** was orientated to the production model by

Auto-Union AG. Between 1937 and 1941 a total of 378 of these vehicles were built, although only a few were actually adopted by the army. The vehicle had four-wheel drive and steering. A few were fitted with elaborate superstructures for desert travel.

SPECIFICATION	
Daimler-Benz G 5	**Powerplant:** one Mercedes-Benz 6-cylinder petrol engine developing 67 kW (90 hp)
Dimensions: length 4.52 m (14 ft 10 in); width 1.7 m (5 ft 7 in); height 1.8 m (5 ft 11 in); wheelbase 2.79 m (9 ft 2 in)	
Weight: net 1630 kg (3,593 lb)	**Transmission:** five forward and one reverse gears
	Tyres: 5.50 X 18 (metric)

A powerful vehicle, with four-wheel drive and four-wheel steering, the Daimler-Benz G 5 was designed as a private venture to meet the Wehrmacht Einheit specification.

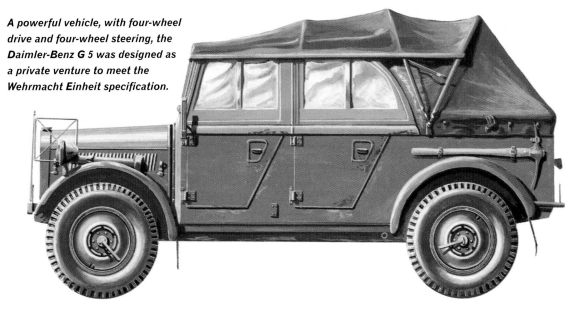

GAZ-67 Light utility car

The **GAZ-67**, in which the first part of the designation stood for Gorky Avtomobil Zavod (Gorky Car Factory) was first manufactured in the USSR during 1943 as a rugged and reliable cross-country vehicle for the movement of personnel and light equipment. In its basic design and constructional features the GAZ-67 was obviously influenced very strongly by an American vehicle, the Bantam Jeep, of which the USSR received some 20,000 examples during World War II under the terms of the Lend-Lease programme. This American legacy was nowhere more apparent than in the arrangement of the body and headlamps, which were very similar to those of the Bantam.

The vehicle was powered by the Soviet Ford (GAZ) Model A water-cooled four-cylinder side-valve engine, and the wheels, suspension and other automotive components were similar to those developed for other GAZ cars, but a new feature was the four-wheel

drive arrangement. The suspension was based on the use of quarter-elliptic springs. The fuel tank was located below the dashboard.

Accommodation

The vehicle was fitted out as standard with four seats, and was capable of a maximum speed of up to 90 km/h (56

The GAZ-67B was used in Korea, where this vehicle was captured, after seeing large-scale service in World War II. The type was replaced by the GAZ-69.

First built in 1943 at Gorky, the GAZ-67 was influenced by the early Jeep, of which 20,000 had been sent to the USSR.

mph), but by comparison with the US Jeep it was characterised by very poor acceleration. The **GAZ-67B** differed from the original GAZ-67 primarily in its adoption of a wheelbase lengthened to 1.85m (6ft ¾ in) by comparison with the GAZ-67's

figure of 1.27 m (4 ft 2 in). This model saw extensive service in Korea and Indo-China. Production ceased in 1953, the role being taken over by the GAZ-69A. This type of light vehicle was the workhorse transport of the Soviet airborne divisions.

SPECIFICATION	
GAZ-67B **Dimensions:** length 3.34 m (10 ft 11⅛ in); width 1.68 m (5 ft 6 in); height 1.7 m (5 ft 7 in); wheelbase 1.85 m (6 ft ¾ in) **Weight:** 1220 kg (2,690 lb)	**Powerplant:** one GAZ-A 4-cylinder 3.28-litre petrol engine developing 40.3 kW (54 bhp) **Transmission:** four forward and one reverse gears **Tyres:** 6.50 x 16 or 7.00 x 16 metric

Car, Heavy Utility, 4x2, Ford C 11 ADF Heavy utility car

The **Car, Heavy Utility, 4x2, Ford C 11 ADF** was a commercial Canadian vehicle, based on the 1942 Ford Fordor Station Wagon, adopted for military use with minimal changes. Canadian Ford produced this type of vehicle mainly for service with the British Army, although examples were also used by the Canadian army. The type was much used in the Western Desert and Italian campaigns.

The military version had right-hand drive when delivered to the UK, heavy-duty tyres, black-out equipment, simplified and strengthened bumpers, internal rifle racks, a map container, a first aid and medical kit, radio-interference suppression, fire-extinguishers, entrenching tools and other standard fittings, the last including a removable roof rack. In addition to the driver's position, the all-steel body had

seating for five passengers accommodated as two in front and three on the single bench-type rear seat. The vehicle was entered and left

via four doors. In addition there was a full-width rear door split horizontally and hinged top and bottom so that the lower portion formed a tailboard.

SPECIFICATION	
Car, Heavy Utility, 4x2, Ford C 11 ADF **Dimensions:** length 4.93 m (16 ft 2 in); width 2.01 m (6 ft 7 in); height 1.83 m (6 ft); wheelbase 2.9 m (9 ft 6 in) **Weight:** 1814 kg (4,000 lb)	**Powerplant:** one Ford Mercury V-8 3.91-litre petrol engine developing 70.8 kW (95 bhp) **Transmission:** three forward and one reverse gears **Tyres:** 9.00 x 13 for C 11 ADF, and 6.00 x 13 for C 11 A5

A similar vehicle, seating seven passengers and designated **Ford C 11 A 5**, was also used, this having lighter tyres and axles and making use of the luggage space for the additional two seats.

Another Ford heavy utility car was essentially the same as the C 11 ADF but based on the 1941 production chassis. Weighing 91 kg (200 lb) more than its predecessors, this variant had a slightly different estate car body and front radiator grill. Some of these vehicles were completed to a modified standard with roof hatches and external racks for the carriage of fuel and water cans.

The C 11 was developed from a commercial station wagon, and in its right-hand drive variant was used extensively by the British in North Africa and Italy. This example carries the flag of a lieutenant general.

Autovettura Fiat 508 C.M. Light utility car

Most light vehicles used by the Italian armed forces in World War II were of Fiat design and manufacture. In common with Germany, Italy had designed and produced several pseudo-military vehicles during the 1930s. A classic example of these Italian types was the **Autovettura Fiat 508 C.M.**, which was of the type generally known to the Italians as a colonial vehicle. Such types were specially designed for use over rough terrain such as that encountered in Italy's African empire, which included Libya along the Mediterranean coast, Eritrea and Italian Somaliland on the Red Sea and Indian Ocean

SPECIFICATION	
Autovettura Fiat 508 C.M.	**Powerplant:** one Fiat 108C
Dimensions: length 3.35 m (11 ft); width 1.37 m (4 ft 6 in); height 1.57 m (5 ft 2 in); wheelbase 2.26 m (7 ft 5 in)	4-cylinder petrol engine developing 23.9 kW (32 bhp)
	Transmission: four forward and one reverse gears
Weight: 1065 kg (2,348 lb)	**Tyres:** 5.00 x 18 metric

coasts of the Horn of Africa, and from 1936 the conquered nation of Abyssinia. Motor transport, civil as well as

The Fiat 508 was developed from pre-war designs for use in Africa. In common with many other Italian vehicles, it required little militarisation.

military, in these regions demanded great strength and reliability. One of the vehicles that provided a capability of just this type was the Autovettura Fiat 508 C.M., which was also known as the **Fiat 1100 Torpedo Militare**.

This was the most prolific Italian military vehicle of the period before Italy's June 1940 entry into World War II. Just before the war the Italian army's supervisory body for vehicles, the Ispettorata della Motorizzazione (Inspectorate of Motorisation) had requested development of a light,

Based on the 'Balilla' civil model, the 508 C.M. was in production from 1939–45 as a vehicle with reasonable cross-country performance.

simple and robust vehicle capable of achieving high speeds on roads and also offering reasonable performance across country, together with low production costs. To meet this need Fiat developed the **Torpedo 508**, derived from a similar civil model but differing in its greater ground clearance, reduced gearbox ratios, and special body.

The vehicle was built in substantial numbers and in various versions between 1939 and 1945, one of which was the

Modello 1100 Col. special colonial model adapted to avoid ingress of sand and sinking in soft terrain.

Type 95 Scout Car (Kurogane Black Medal) Utility car

The **Type 95 Scout Car** was a lightweight reconnaissance vehicle developed in light of Imperial Japanese army operations along Japan's Manchurian border with the USSR, where frontier clashes and more serious combat had revealed the urgent need for light scouting vehicles with a 4x4 drive arrangement for good cross-country mobility. The result was design of the Type 95, of which some 4,800 examples were then manufactured by Kurogane with variations in bodywork.

This was about the only indigenously designed vehicle of

its type used by the Imperial Japanese army, most of the service's other vehicles being either of direct American origin or alternatively patterned on American designs. The air-cooled engine was ideal for operations in Manchuria and northern China, where there was often a lack of unpolluted water and the temperature was often very cold. Initial difficulties were experienced with the four-wheel drive and front universal joints, but these were eventually overcome. Special tyres, with heavy rubber treads, were provided for negotiating exceptionally difficult terrain.

SPECIFICATION	
Type 95 Scout Car **Dimensions:** length 3.38 m (11 ft 1 in); width 1.52 m (5 ft); height 1.68 m (5 ft 6 in); wheelbase 3.84 m (12 ft 7 in) **Weight:** 1100 kg (2,425 lb)	**Powerplant:** one 2-cylinder 4-stroke V-1-A-F petrol engine developing 24.6 kW (33 bhp) **Transmission:** selective sliding type giving three forward and one reverse gears **Tyres:** 18 x 6

Two-cylinder engine

Power was supplied by a 1399-cc (85.37-cu in) two-cylinder four-stroke, V-1-A-F engine, operating on petrol and developing a maximum power of 24.6 kW (33 bhp). The engine had a compression ratio of 5:1 and a removable cylinder head. Ignition was provided by a high-tension magneto with a 12-volt generator for charging the battery; a 12-volt electric starter motor was used. Oil

pressure was maintained by a gear-pressure feed pump, and a conventional fuel pump was used. There was a main fuel tank for 35 litres (7.7 Imp gal) and an auxiliary fuel tank of 4-litre (0.88-Imp gal) capacity. Fuel consumption was stated to be 4 litres (0.88 Imp gal) per hour. A dry single-plate clutch was used. The foot brakes were mechanical contracting with an emergency mechanical expanding type.

The Type 95 Scout Car was one of the few unarmoured Japanese army vehicles not based on a US model. The 'Black Medal' was made in convertible, closed cab and truck versions.

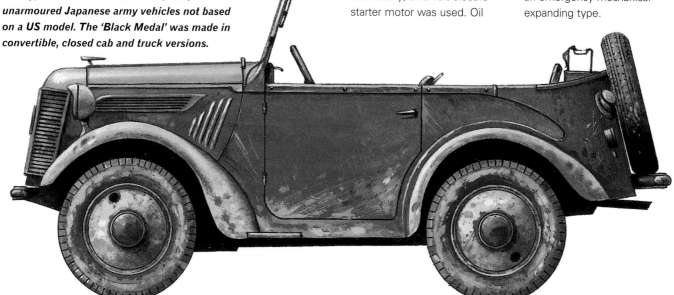

British light utility cars

In the early years of World War II the British Army used a variety of light 4x2 utility vehicles, most of which were based on pre-war commercial designs. Officially designated 'Car, Light Utility', they were affectionately known to servicemen and women as 'Tillies'. They were responsible for a great variety of work, carrying cargo and personnel on bases and airfields throughout the world.

British-built vehicles included the **Austin 8HP Series AP**, a militarised tourer with a four-cylinder 15.7-kW (23.5-bhp) engine. This vehicle had vertical instead of horizontal bonnet louvres, a folding windscreen and luggage space at the back of the seats.

The **Austin 10 HP Series G/YG** was powered by a four-cylinder 22-kW (29.5-bhp) engine and was derived from the 10 HP commercial saloon and produced in large numbers in World War II for British and Allied forces.

The **Morris 10 HP Series M** was based on the 1939 civilian 10 HP saloon. This vehicle had a four-cylinder 27.7-kW (37.2-bhp)

The Austin 10 HP utility car was produced both as a saloon and as utility truck with a cargo area covered by a canvas canopy.

engine driving the rear wheels. Late production models had a wire mesh radiator grille and one-piece canvas canopy.

The **Standard 12 HP Series UV** was a militarised Standard Flying Twelve car chassis with a rigid front axle. The early production types were supplied to the RAF and had independent front suspension with transversal leaf springs and a civilian-style radiator grille. The vehicle was powered by a 32.8-kW (44-bhp) engine.

The most numerous utility vehicle in British service in World War II was the **Hillman 10 HP**. Derived from the civilian Hillman Minx it appeared in six marks all differing in detail. These vehicles were two-seaters with a pick-up type body integral with the open back cab. A canvas canopy was carried on four hoops and cov-

SPECIFICATIONS

Car, Light Utility, 4x2, Austin	
Dimensions: length 3.96 m (13 ft); width 1.52 m (5 ft); height 1.93 m (6 ft 4 in) **Weight:** net 1514 kg (3,330 lb) **Powerplant:** one Austin Type G3-222AB liquid-cooled 4-cylinder	1.237-litre petrol engine delivering 22 kW (29.5 bhp) **Transmission:** four forward and one reverse gears **Tyres:** 6.00 x 16

ered a cargo area that could also be fitted with folding seats. A **Convertible Van** and **Ladder Van** were produced for the RAF between 1941 and 1942. The Hillman 10 HP was powered by a four-cylinder 22.4-kW (30-bhp) engine.

While strictly not a utility vehicle, a **Car, 4-seater, 4x2** based on the Humber Super Snipe saloon was produced in large numbers. The militarised version that entered service in December 1939 had larger tyres and mudguards, the hard top version had a roof luggage rail.

Two **Staff Saloon Mk 2** versions of the Humber Snipe named 'Old Faithful' and the 'Victory Car' became famous as the personal transport of Field Marshal Montgomery.

Humber also produced the six- to seven-seater, six-cylinder 63.4-kW (85-bhp) **Humber Pullman** that had the distinction of being used not only by all the British armed services but also the US Army. Some were fitted with armour protection.

A 1943 Morris 10 HP utility truck. More than 8,000 such vehicles were built under five War Department contracts.

Humber 8-cwt Lorry Utility and command truck

The early production version of the Humber 8-cwt Lorry was based on the chassis of the pre-war Humber Snipe saloon, and could be identified by the louvres in the sides of the bonnet. These were later omitted, as shown here.

In 1939 the British Army was in the process of intensive mechanisation, and several classes of load capacity had been defined for 'B' vehicles. The second class was the 8-cwt truck which fulfilled such roles as the GS (General Service) and FFW (Fitted For Wireless). Such 8-cwt trucks, with both 4x2 and 4x4 wheel arrangements, were produced in considerable numbers from a period just before the war, but were eventually phased out of production in order to rationalise output and reduce the number of types in service.

The vehicles had detachable well-type bodies with seating for three men and canvas tilts, though the wireless version had seating for only two. Folding

The Humber FFW (Fitted For Wireless) was an 8-cwt 4x2 truck with seating for two wireless operators in the body. The body was detachable for use on the ground as a wireless station or as a command centre. The GS used the same body without radio equipment.

legs were fitted which enabled the body to be placed on the ground for use as a mobile command centre or wireless station. The early **Humber 8-cwt Lorry** vehicles employed the chassis of the original 1939 Humber Snipe saloon with louvres in the bonnet sides. The **Lorry, 8-cwt, 4x4, FFW** incorporated the No. 11 wireless set, a

map table and other fittings necessary for command operations. The wireless

batteries could be recharged from a generator and then driven off the vehicle's main engine.

SPECIFICATION

Lorry, 8 cwt, 4x2, FFW, Humber
Dimensions: length 4.44 m (14 ft 7 in); width 1.96 m (6 ft 5 in); height 1.89 m (6 ft 2½ in); wheelbase 2.84 m (9 ft 4 in)
Weight: net 1769 kg (3,900 lb)

Powerplant: one Humber 6-cylinder petrol engine delivering 63.4 kW (85 bhp)
Transmission: four forward and one reverse gears
Tyres: 9.00 x 13

Car, Heavy Utility, 4x4 (FWD), Humber Staff car

Derived from a 4x4 estate car, the Humber Heavy Utility Car was the basic staff and command car in British service, and remained so for some years after 1945. It was the only British vehicle of its type.

Together with the Ford 4x2 Heavy Utility, the **Humber Heavy Utility Car** was the basic staff and command car of the British Army during World War II at all levels of command. Nicknamed the **'Box'**, this was the only four-wheel drive utility car of British design to be manufactured in World War II, and entered production during May 1941, continuing for the duration of the war for service with the army, Royal Air Force and Royal Navy. Employed on a very wide scale in most of the theatres in which British forces were involved, this useful staff car remained in service until the late 1950s.

Steel construction

The cab and body were integral and of all-steel construction, and later models were fitted with a sliding roof. The body was configured as a six-seater with four individual seats and, at the rear, two tip-up occasional seats which could be folded away to leave the rear of the body clear for stowage: there was also a folding map table behind the front seats. There were two hinged doors on each side with a full-width double door arrangement at the rear. The

Fitted with a folding map table, the Humber Heavy Utility Car, otherwise known as the 'Box', was used mainly as a staff car. Some were given folding canvas tops for operations in North Africa. Staff officers occasionally had forward sliding roofs fitted.

front mudguards, radiator grill and bonnet were identical to those of the Humber 8-cwt 4x4 chassis. In the Western Desert this vehicle was sometimes

modified by replacement of the roof by a canvas folding tilt offering the possibility of a better movement of air and therefore a less stifling environment for

those who had to work in the vehicle. Some of the cars, especially those used by higher-ranking officers, were also fitted with a sliding roof.

SPECIFICATION	
Car, Heavy Utility, 4x4 (FWD), Humber **Dimensions:** length 4.29 m (14 ft 1 in); width 1.88 m (6 ft 2 in); height 1.96 m (6 ft 5 in); wheelbase 2.84 m (9 ft 3¾ in) **Weight:** net 2413 kg (5,320 lb)	**Powerplant:** one Humber 6-cylinder 1-L-W-F 4.08-litre petrol engine delivering 63.4 kW (85 bhp) **Transmission:** four forward and one reverse gear with auxiliary two-speed **Tyres:** 9.25 x 16

Dodge T207 series Multi-role ½-ton light trucks

US Army ½-ton trucks were provided by a number of manufacturers including Dodge, Chevrolet, Diamond T, Ford, Marmon-Herrington and GMC. The ½-ton 4x4 vehicle was originally developed by the Marmon-Herrington Company of Indianapolis in July 1936. During the early stages of World War II most of the ½-ton 4x2 vehicles were slightly modified civilian models and were retained for the home front.

With the development of the war, standard tactical chassis began to be adopted to supersede these earlier models.

Mass production

As regards the **Truck, ½-ton 4x4**, Chrysler's Dodge Division began mass production during 1939. The **Truck, ½-ton, 4x4, Weapons Carrier, Dodge T207-WC3** was introduced in 1941, and replaced all previous models then in use. It became one of the basic transportation mainstays for all arms and services of the US armed forces. The vehicle was ruggedly reliable, and was of the open-topped type with dismountable bows and a canvas tilt. As with most other Dodge trucks, a spare wheel was carried on the offside of the vehicle.

Recce derivatives

The **WC6** and **WC7** were reconnaissance versions, the latter being equipped with a winch. The **WC8** had a radio body, whilst the **WC9** was an ambulance.

The WC6 was a ½-ton command and reconnaissance vehicle of the same family as the T207. A sloping bonnet distinguished the 1941 pattern vehicles from the heavier models that appeared in 1942.

SPECIFICATION	
Truck, ½-ton, 4x4, Weapons Carrier, Dodge T207-WC3	**Powerplant:** one Dodge liquid-cooled 6-cylinder petrol engine developing 63.4 kW (85 bhp)
Dimensions: length 4.6 m (15 ft 1 in); width 1.93 m (6 ft 4 in); height 2.24 m (7 ft 4 in); wheelbase 2.95 m (9 ft 8 in)	**Transmission:** four forward and one reverse gears
Weight: net 2014 kg (4,440 lb)	**Tyres:** 7.50 x 16

Dodge T215 series Multi-role ½-ton light trucks

In the ½-ton range of trucks, Dodge was the sole producer to US Army contracts. The first contract for 14,000 ½-ton 4x4 trucks was placed with Dodge in mid-1940. The basic chassis was a slight modification of the normal commercial vehicle to incorporate a new transfer gearbox and forward transmission to cater for the four-wheel drive requirement. The chassis was then employed for numerous roles including command, command reconnaissance, radio, weapons carrier and **Truck, ½-ton, Ambulance, 4x4, Dodge T215-WC27**. The trucks had the option of a fixed bodywork or open cab. The ambulance version had the former and the command, command reconnaissance, radio and weapons carrier versions had the latter.

The Dodge T215-WC42 was the panel radio version of the ½-ton T215. Command and reconnaissance, weapons carrier, emergency repair and telephone installation variants were also built on the chassis.

Enhanced version

These earlier US military pattern 4x4 trucks were superseded in 1942 by a range of wider and more robust body types (¾-ton) with a lower silhouette and shorter wheelbase, also built by Dodge. By this time 82,000 ½-ton trucks had been built. These left-hand drive vehicles were manufactured by the Dodge Brothers Corporation Division of the Chrysler Corporation of America and

also, in a modified form, in Canada. The **International M-1-4** range was similar in layout but produced solely for the US Marine Corps and US Navy. A great number of these Dodge ½-ton truck series were supplied to the UK and the USSR under the Lend-Lease programme.

SPECIFICATION	
Truck, ½-ton, Ambulance, 4x4, Dodge T215-WC27	**Powerplant:** one Dodge T215 liquid-cooled 6-cylinder petrol engine developing 68.6 kW (92 bhp)
Dimensions: length 4.67 m (15 ft 4 in); width 1.93 m (6 ft 4 in); height 2.13 m (7 ft); wheelbase 2.95 m (9 ft 8 in)	**Transmission:** four forward and one reverse gears
Weight: net 2046 kg (4,510 lb)	**Tyres:** 7.50 x 16

Dodge trucks were adapted to serve as ambulances, as the WC27 variant, with sheet steel bodies accommodating up to four stretcher cases. Early versions had enclosed cabs as shown, but later reverted to the open cab of the weapon carrier version.

Dodge T214 series Multi-role ¾-ton light trucks

Introduced during 1942, the **Dodge ¾-ton 4x4** range of light trucks superseded the original ½-ton 4x4 range. Both Ford and Dodge, previously the main suppliers of ½-ton 4x4 vehicles, each produced prototypes for US Army evaluation: these were slightly wider and lower than their predecessors, had larger wheels and tyres, and possessed stronger suspensions. The Dodge version was selected and officially introduced during June 1942 when production started into full swing.

Multiple variants

As with the ½-ton vehicles there were several special body types. The **Dodge T214** series comprised the **WC51** weapons carrier, **WC52** weapons carrier

with winch, **WC53** general-purpose and field command vehicle, **WC54** ambulance, **WC55 37-mm Gun Motor**

A ¾-ton Dodge T214-WC56 command and reconnaissance car with its canvas top taken down. In 1941 the Dodge division of Chrysler became the large-scale producer of such 4x4 vehicles for the US armed forces.

Carriage M6, **WC56** command reconnaissance vehicle, **WC57** command reconnaissance with winch, **WC58** radio vehicle, **WC59** light maintenance and installation vehicle, **WC60** emergency repair vehicle, **WC61** telephone maintenance and installation vehicle, and **WC64** ambulance. Generally, the vehicles in this series were referred to as **'Beeps'** (a contraction of 'Big Jeeps'). The

WC51 weapons carrier was used principally to transport personnel, weapons, tools and other equipment. It had an open body with a canvas tilt and canvas side-screens. The WC53 was fitted with a 'safari' type body with rear side doors, a map table, special seats and internal lighting. The WC56 command reconnaissance was the most common variant, and was used for reconnaissance

and liaison, and as a staff car. It was fitted with map-boards and had a detachable canvas top and side-screens.

SPECIFICATION	
Truck, ¾-ton, 4x4, Command Reconnaissance, Dodge T214-WC56 **Dimensions:** length 4.24 m (13 ft 11 in); width 1.99 m (6 ft 6½ in); height 2.07 m (6 ft 9½ in); wheelbase 2.49 m (8 ft 2 in) **Weight:** net 2449 kg (5,400 lb)	**Powerplant:** one Dodge T214 liquid-cooled 6-cylinder petrol engine developing 68.6 kW (92 bhp) **Transmission:** four forward and one reverse gears **Tyres:** 9.00 x 16

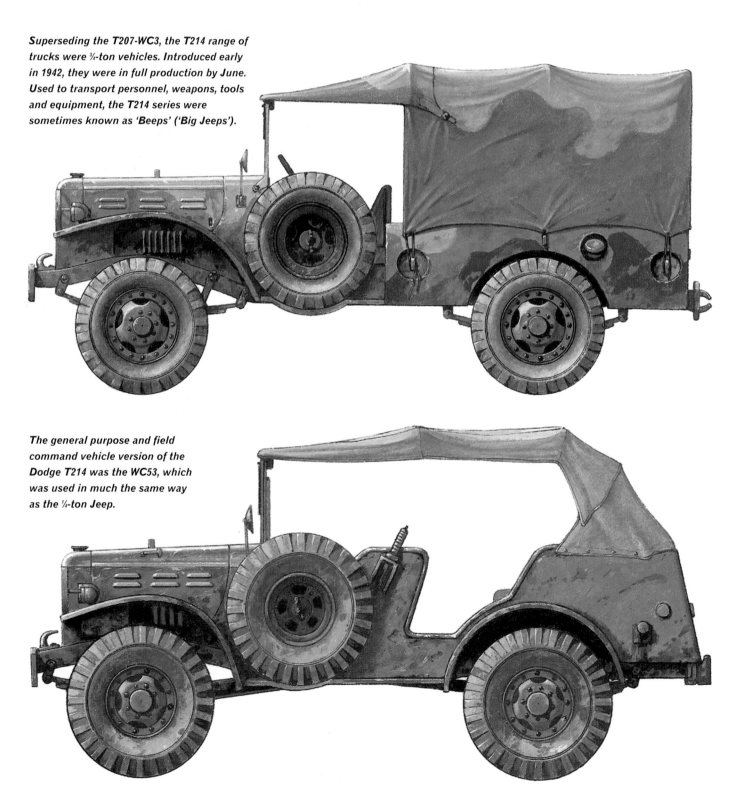

Superseding the T207-WC3, the T214 range of trucks were ¾-ton vehicles. Introduced early in 1942, they were in full production by June. Used to transport personnel, weapons, tools and equipment, the T214 series were sometimes known as 'Beeps' ('Big Jeeps').

The general purpose and field command vehicle version of the Dodge T214 was the WC53, which was used in much the same way as the ¼-ton Jeep.

Truck, ¼-ton, Utility, 4x4, Jeep Light multi-purpose vehicle

During the second half of the 1930s several experimental US military multi-purpose vehicles were called 'Jeep', after the Popeye cartoon character, particularly the 2½-ton Dodge Command Reconnaissance Car, while the original ¼-ton vehicle (which eventually became the **Jeep**) was referred to as **'Peep'**. From 1942 onwards, however, the name Jeep was adopted for the ¼-ton 4x4, regardless of make or type.

The Jeep was developed to meet a long-standing military requirement for a light four-wheel drive general purpose vehicle and reconnaissance car. In the US Army the Jeep fell into an additional load category, ¼-ton, which had not been allowed for when the original five basic classes of military vehicle were defined. The original designation '**Command Reconnaissance**' was later changed to '**Utility**'. In June 1940 the US Army drafted a specification for a 'go-anywhere' field car which was submitted to 135 manufacturing centres for tender. Initially, only two of these responded: the American Bantam Car Company and Willys-Overland. Prototypes were delivered for test by both companies in late 1940, by which time Ford also had been drawn into the development programme.

Bantam prototype

The original Bantam prototype, using components from the company's small pre-war runabout car, was completed within 50 days. Representatives of the US Ordnance Technical Committee studied the product, and an order was placed for 70 pre-production vehicles, eight of which were to have four-wheel steering. Built to US Army specifications, these cars were purely military vehicles. Only 3.35 m (11 ft) long and 0.91 m (3 ft) high, they were powered

by a 33.6-kW (45-hp) 4-cylinder Continental engine and weighed 907 kg (2,000 lb), about half as heavy again as the original maximum weight. After successful tests of Bantam vehicles the US Army was ready to buy Jeeps in quantity. In March 1941 Bantam received a contract for 1,500 production vehicles of the improved **Model 40**, but the Army was reluctant to place the entire order with Bantam. As Willys and Ford had shown interest in producing such a vehicle, and were building pilot models, the Quartermaster Corps (QMC) made similar awards to Willys and Ford. In July 1940 Willys received an order to produce 70 examples of the preproduction vehicle, then referred to as the **'Quad'**. The first completed vehicle was delivered to the

Above: By the time of the Allied invasion of Europe, Jeeps were being put to a wide variety of purposes, many of which could not have been anticipated by the designers of a simple utility vehicle. It was used in combat, and the addition of the potent Browning M2HB 0.5-in (12.7-mm) machine-gun made the Jeep an opponent to be feared.

Above right: Australian and native New Guinea troops confer prior to a reconnaissance at Hollandia, northern new Guinea, in April 1944. General MacArthur had just landed during the latest stage of the south-west Pacific campaign.

Right: Emphasising the vehicle's utility, a Jeep provides an innovative power source for a rotary saw at a 5th Army field hospital in Italy during 1944.

Army in November 1940. Willys redesigned the Quad to reduce weight, resulting in the **Model MA**, and 1,500 were built from November 1940. Ford delivered its version, referred to then as the **'Pygmy'**, in November 1940, and received a contract in December for 1,500 vehicles of improved type (designated **GP**). Rigorous tests of Bantam, Willys and Ford Jeeps revealed structural weaknesses in all three and led to many design changes. The Willys model was selected as the most suitable and was designated **Model MB**. When the QMC was authorised to procure 16,000 vehicles, it called for bids on an 'all-or-nothing' basis. Although Willys submitted the lowest bid, the QMC preferred Ford, and recommended that it be given the contract. When the Office of Production management refused to go along with this recommendation, the contract went to Willys in July 1941.

Willys proved unable to keep pace with fast-moving requirements and another producer was added. Ford thus received contracts to produce the Willys vehicle according to Willys blueprints, and for the rest of the war both firms turned out thousands of Jeeps

with interchangable parts. Between them Willys and Ford built a total of 639,245 (Willys delivered 277,896). The Ford production model was designated **GPW**.

Production

The Jeep was assembled at 26 foreign plants and by 1950 had evolved into the **Model MC** which became **Truck, Utility, ¼-ton, 4x4, M38**. More than 60,000 of these were produced by the end of 1952, and the

type was used extensively during the Korean War. In April 1953, Willys-Overland was taken over and became the Kaiser Jeep Corporation. The CJ series of Jeeps was then developed, evolving into the **CJ-3B** (**Truck, Utility, ¼-ton, 4x4 M606**), the **CJ-5** (**Truck, Utility ¼-ton, 4X4, M38A1**), **CJ-6** (**Truck, Ambulance, ¼-ton, 4X4, M170**) and the **Truck, Utility, ¼-ton, 4X4, M151** (**Mutt**). The latter, designed by Ford, was a complete redesign incorporating the

latest modern engineering techniques.

In service the Jeep was intended for reconnaissance and liaison duties, but it was soon found to be invaluable for other work. In 1943 Nuffield Mechanization & Aero Ltd in the UK produced a special airborne version called the **Para Jeep** with only two seats. Willys produced the **'Stripped Jeep'**, commonly known as the **Gipsy Rose Lee**, for airborne purposes. The British developed a special airborne trailer (designated Trailer, 10 cwt, 2-wheel, Lightweight, GS Type) to increase the capability of transporting heavy weapons and equipment in airborne units. The combination could carry eight men.

The Jeep was used by all arms for OP, Provost, wireless, recovery and cargo-carrying roles. Both the US and British armies used armed reconnaissance versions, and of particular interest were the special heavily-armed vehicles used by

A US Jeep speeds ashore onto New Guinea to take part in the Hollandia operation. Alongside, a large landing craft is beaching, and its packed complement of troops wait to take part in the assault on the Japanese fortified base.

the SAS (Special Air Service) and LRDG (Long-Range Desert Group). These vehicles were stripped to allow for the attachment of special equipment, armament, fuel and water-cans. Both LRDG and SAS vehicles usually carried a combination of Browning and Vickers K guns. The fuel tanks were enlarged to allow for increased range (the fuel capacity was about 136 litres/30 Imp gal).

Specialist variants

The British Army converted some Jeeps to **Royal Signals Line-Laying Vehicles**: usually the cable was reeled off at the rear from a single cable drum, and four replacement reels were often attached over the bumper at the front. The Jeep could also mount a recoilless rifle or multiple rocket-launcher. A tandem hitch made it possible to use two of these vehicles for emergency towing of a heavy

Light utilities accompanied the airborne troops into Normandy in 1944. Here an airborne unit in training unloads a Jeep from an RAF Horsa glider, probably during April or May of 1944.

artillery piece. Wading equipment was developed, consisting of a flexible 'breathing' tube from the engine supported by the windscreen, and an exhaust extension at the rear. This enabled the vehicle to wade up to a depth of 1.83 m (6 ft), adequate for driving ashore from amphibious landing craft. Jeeps were also used extensively as front-line ambulances. Two-, three- and four-litter conversions were carried out in the US, UK, Canada and Australia. From late 1943, Jeeps assembled in the UK could support a tubular frame capable of carrying three stretchers (one alongside the driver and two above). The four-litter version had a high canvas

tilt and carried the stretchers in two layers.

The **Amphibious Jeep** was designated **GPA** (**General Purpose Amphibious**) and based on the standard Jeep chassis with a boat-like body. Water propulsion was by a pro-

peller driven by a power take-off from the transmission, and the GPA was more than 544 kg (1,200 lb) heavier than the land version. Mass-production by Ford began in September 1942, and in service the vehicle was known as **'Amphib'** or **'Seep'**.

SPECIFICATION	
Truck, Utility, ¼-ton, 4x4, Jeep **Dimensions:** length 3.33 m (11 ft ¼ in); width 1.57 m (5 ft 2 in); height 1.14 m (3 ft 9 in) to top of hood **Weight:** net 1247 kg (2,750 lb) **Powerplant:** one Willys 441 or 442 'Go Devil' 4-cylinder petrol engine developing 44.7 kW (60 bhp)	**Transmission:** Warner Gear T-84-J three-speed synchromesh giving six forward and two reverse gears **Tyres:** 6.0 x 16 six-ply (mud and snow)

In 1943 the Canadian army developed the Tracked Jeep, intended as a light armoured carrier for airborne units. Five pilot models were built by Willys with the engine mounted tranversely at the rear.

German motorcycles and sidecar combinations

Zündapp KS-750 and BMW R-12/R-71/R-75

Between 1940 and 44, some 18,635 examples of the **Zündapp KS-750** motorcycle and sidecar combination were built at the factory of the Zündapp Werke GmbH in Nürnberg. Interestingly, a further 450 examples were also built after the end of World War II. The motorcycle was based on a pressed steel frame, and employed the same sidecar that was also fitted to the BMW R-75 with a 3x2 drive.

The all-up weight of the motorcycle was 420 kg (925 lb), this figure increasing to 670 kg (1,477 lb) when the sidecar was added. The maximum road speed was 92 km/h (57 mph) with the sidecar added, and road range was 330 km (205 miles). The motorcycle was powered by a 751-cc (45.83-cu in) two-cylinder four-stroke petrol engine, and by modern standards this seems comparatively underpowered as it developed just 19.4 kW (26 bhp) at 4,000 rpm. Its single crawler gear allowed it to cross fairly rugged and uneven terrain with some confidence.

Motorcycle reconnaissance troops in their full-length rubberised coats and with their helmets remain an enduring image of the era of the 'Blitzkrieg'.

The sidecar combination had a crew of two or three men, and mounted a 7.92-mm (0.312-in) MG 34 or MG 42 machine-gun on a bar on the sidecar. Other military equipment included a rear carry rack, leather panniers, masked lighting, a high-level exhaust, and a spare wheel. The motorcycle had a ground clearance of 160 mm (6.2 in).

In the last two years of World War I, BMW (Bayerische Motoren Werke, or Bavarian Motor Works) had manufactured aero engines, but as a result of the Treaty of Versailles in 1917, the company was obliged to switch development to non-military products: these included motorcycles designed by the talented Max Fritz.

The **BMW R-12**, produced from 1935 up to 1941 as a solo machine and the motorised

component of a sidecar combination, was constructed on the basis of a rigid pressed steel frame. It had a left-foot kick start, mechanical brakes, a horizontally opposed two-cylinder engine delivering 13.4 kW (18 bhp) rather than the 14.9 kW (20 bhp) of the purely civil version to the rear wheel via a

four-speed hand-change gearbox and cardan shaft. The telescopic front fork had helical springs and hydraulic damping.

The R-12 weighed 188 kg (414 lb) while a later derivative, the **R-71** that entered service in 1938, weighed 187 kg (412 lb). The R-12 had a 14-litre (3.08-Imp gal) fuel tank, a maximum

Below right: A convoy of motorcycles and sidecars belonging to the Waffen SS Division 'Das Reich' are seen in the Soviet Union during the summer of 1941.

Below: A BMW motorcycle sidecar combination struggles through the mud on the Eastern Front. Extra equipment was added for Operation Barbarossa.

Italian troops help the crew of an R-75 motorcycle sidecar combination get their machine to the top of a steep incline.

speed of 100 km/h (62 mph) and ground clearance of 120 mm (4.7 in). The R-71 also had a 14-litre fuel tank, but its max speed was 125 km/h (78 mph) and it had a slightly better clearance figure of 130 mm (5.1 in).

Production

Some 2,000 examples of the R-71 were made, and both BMW motorcycle types were used for solo and sidecar despatch duties, escort, convoy control and personnel transport. The motorcycles were popular with the German armed forces for their astonishing pulling power and relatively generous load-carrying capability.

The ability of motorcycle combinations like the KS-750 and R-75 to tow weapons such as the 3.7-cm (1.46-in) Pak 35/36 anti-tank gun made these motorcycles ideal for airborne forces. For transport the motorcycles were packed into a

metal frame, suspended under the fuselage, between the wheels, of transports like the Ju 52/3m and dropped by parachute. As the calibre and weight of anti-tank weapons increased, however, the ability of motorcycle combinations to tow them diminished.

Special design

The **BMW R-75 mit Seitenwagen** was a special military-design motorcycle sidecar combination of which 16,510 were built at the Bayerische Motoren Werke in 1940–44. It had a crew of two or three men, and carried additional equipment such as panniers for the crew's kit and ammunition, and a spare wheel on the sidecar. A 7.92-mm (0.312-in) MG 34 or MG 42 trainable machine-gun could be mounted over the front of the sidecar to give the R-75 combination useful

Below: With seven men onboard, this sidecar combination seen in Tunisia in March 1943 was decidedly overloaded. With only two men and a machine-gun, however, the sidecar combination provided a useful light capability for reconnaissance.

In skilled hands the BMW motorcycles and the equivalent Zündapp type, were effective vehicles. However, if thorough training was not provided they could be hazardous to rider and crew.

This BMW R-35 motorcycle is operating in the despatch-carrying role, its rider wearing the typical rubberised coat and carrying his rifle slung over his back.

firepower. The R-75 was used for reconnaissance, front-line liaison, and the transport of middle-ranking officers to front-line units.

Crew fatigue

Such motorcycle sidecar outfits looked impressive, but after a day's operations the men could be very tired as the motorcycle had a helically sprung saddle rather than proper rear suspension.

The motorcycle was built on a tubular duplex cradle frame, and its engine drove the rear and sidecar wheels via a four-speed and reverse gearbox, cardan shaft and cross shaft. The R-75 had a lockable differential and hydraulic brakes on the driven wheels, a mechanical brake on the front wheel, and a 'maintenance free' telescopic front fork. The R-75 was not the first motorcycle with telescopic front forks, but it was the first series-built type to adopt hydraulic damping. The motorcycle was powered by a

746-cc (45.52-cu in) two-cylinder four-stroke petrol engine developing 19.4 kW (26 hp) at 4,400 rpm, which by today's standards represents only a modest volume/power ratio.

The all-up weight was 420 kg (926 lb) rising to 670 kg (1,477 lb) with the sidecar. The maximum road speed was 92 km/h (57 mph) with the sidecar, and the road range was 340 km (211 miles) that could be boosted to 800 km (497 miles) by the use of additional fuel cans strapped to the sidecar. Low ratio gears on the BMW allowed it to travel almost anywhere, and the R-75 was only rendered obsolescent by the advent of lightweight 4x4 vehicles. BMW and Zündapp types were among the most complex military motorcycles ever

Most German sidecars could mount a single general-purpose machine-gun: this soldier carries a sub-machine gun for local defence.

produced. In combination with their cost, this was one of the reasons that production ended before 1945. In the extreme cold of the Eastern Front the exhausts of the BMW and Zündapp types were modified with a heat exchanger that provided a flow of warm air over

the rider's feet and hands and also into the sidecar.

One of the original concepts for the R-75 was the towing of light guns for airborne forces. It was found, though, that the tow bar weight lifted the front wheel off the ground. The R-75 did work with a two-wheel trailer.

Allied motorcycles British and American designs

The two most prolific manufacturers of military motorcycles in World War II were the US and UK. Some 47,599 examples of the **Ariel W/NG** were built by the British company Ariel Motors between 1940 and 1944. This was a standard production model fitted with a rear carrier rack or pillion pad, canvas panniers, additional tool box, longer prop and stand that hinged down below the saddle and masked lighting. The top speed was 110 km/h (68 mph).

In 1940 BSA Cycles modified its **BSA B30** standard production model for the military role with many of the same fittings as the Ariel motorcycle. Its top speed was 120 km/h (75 mph).

As airborne forces grew, the Excelsior Motor Co. Ltd developed the collapsible **Welbike Mk II** in 1942. Some 3,840 of these were made. The Welbike weighed just 32 kg (70 lb) unladen and could be collapsed and fitted into a parachute container.

The **James ML** was another motorcycle developed for airborne forces. Some 6,040 were built between 1942 and 1944, and the type earned the affectionate nickname 'Clockwork Mouse'. The ML weighed 72.2 kg (157 lb) unladen and had a maximum speed of 65 km/h (40 mph). It had a rear carrier rack and folding handlebars.

Matchless Motor Cycles Ltd took a commercial model and produced 63,000 examples of the **Matchless G3L** between 1941 and 1945. The G3L could reach 110 km/h (68 mph) and weighed 149 kg (328 lb).

Norton Motors made two motorcycles for the British Army, the **Norton Big Four** and the **Norton 16H**. The powerful Big Four, of which 4,737 were supplied, was used with a sidecar for despatch, personnel and ammunition carrier duties. It weighed 308 kg (679 lb) and had

a top speed of 90 km/h (50 mph). It could be fitted with a Bren gun with spare ammunition carried in the rear of the sidecar.

Norton and Enfield

The Norton 16H was used for despatch, military police, reconnaissance, convoy control and escort duties and during the war Norton supplied 100,000 to

the army. It had a respectable top speed of 110 km/h (68 mph) and weighed 176 kg (388 kg).

During World War II the Enfield Cycle Company produced three motorcycles for the army: the **Royal Enfield WD/C** appeared in 1940, the

WD/CO in 1942 and the **WD/RE** in 1942. The WD/C was a standard model modified for military use. It weighed 160 kg (353 lb) and had a top speed of 88 km/h (55 mph). The WD/CO superseded the WD/C and between 1942 and 1944 some

*A posed photograph taken during a **US reconnaissance training exercise in England, perhaps during February 1943. **Note** the rider's Thompson M1928A1 sub-machine gun.*

These British Army despatch riders, seen undergoing training prior to service in France after D-Day, are riding Ariel motorcycles.

British motorcycle troops patrol a country road within the area controlled by Northern Command. As World War II progressed, there was less demand for the use of motorcycle troops in front-line tasks.

model, the **3SW**, was used by the WRNS. The 3HW weighed 161 kg (355 lb) and reached 115 km/h (71 mph).

Finally, Veloce produced the **Velocette MAF** in 1942 from its civilian MAC. The motorcycle was used by the RAF, which used most of the 5,000 built for solo despatch and liaison. It weighed 154 kg (340 lb) and reached 110 km/h (68 mph).

American production

In the US the Cushman Motorworks company built the **Cushman 53 Autoglide** in 1944 for airborne forces, supplying a total of 4,734. It weighed 116 kg (255 lb) and had a top speed of 64 km/h (40 mph).

Harley-Davidson produced three types for the US Army in the form of the **Harley-Davidson WLA** and **ELA** in 1939 and the **XA** in 1942. Over 89,000 examples of the WLA were built, more than 60,000 going to the US armed forces

and the remainder to British and Commonwealth forces, which continued to use them after the war. It had leather panniers and a bucket for a Thompson sub-machine gun. The type weighed 242 kg (535 lb) and had a top speed of 96 km/h (60 mph). The heavier ELA was sometimes fitted with a sidecar and many were sent as Lend-Lease aid to the UK. It weighed 386 kg (850 lb) and had a top speed of 88 km/h (55 mph). The XA was produced for the US Army and more than 1,000 were built before the project was dropped. Weighing 238 kg (525 lb), it reached 96 km/h (60 mph).

Indian and Simplex

The Indian Motorcycle Company built the **Indian 340**, **640-A** and **640-B** in 1939, and the **841** in 1942. The 841 was developed for the US armed forces but after 1,000 had been built the US government cancelled the project. The type weighed

29,037 machines were built: the type weighed 154 kg (340 lb) and had a top speed of 110 km/h (68 mph). The WD/RE was a production model modified for airborne troops and known as the 'Flying Flea'. Weighing only 62.1 kg (137 lb),

it could be handled easily on drop zones and had a top speed of 65 km/h (40 mph).

The **Triumph 3HW** was a standard Tiger modified for service use. It was used mainly by the Royal Navy for despatch and liaison duties. A side-valve

Men of a Royal Marine Commando of the 4th Special Service Brigade make their way inland from St Aubin-sur-Mer after D-Day, 6 June 1944. Their miscellany of transport items includes a motorcycle.

*An **RAF** despatch rider on an **Ariel** motorcycle is seen on a road out of the Normandy beaches in June 1944. Such links were vital when telephone lines had been brought down.*

256 kg (564 lb) and had a top speed of 96 km/h (60 mph). The 340 was a modified commercial motorcycle originally destined for the French army. It was used by US and British forces, weighed 383 kg (845 lb) and had a top speed of 88 km/h (55 mph). At least 18,600 examples of the 640-A were built, this type weighing 209 kg (460 lb) and

attaining 88 km/h (55 mph). Finally the 640-B, derived from a standard type, weighed 245 kg (540 lb) and reached 96 km/h (60 mph).

Some 654 examples of the **Simplex Servi-Cycle** were produced by Simplex for the use of American airborne troops. This type weighed only 74.8 kg (165 lb) and had a top speed of 48 km/h (30 mph).

*The crew of a **Humber Mk II** light reconnaissance car mounting a Boys 13.97-mm (0.55-in) anti-tank gun and 7.7-mm (0.303-in) Bren machine-gun ask the way from a **BSA**-riding courier.*

British Army motorcyclists patrol the South Downs of England for signs of any German airborne landing. Motorcycle reconnaissance offered moderately good cross-country mobility and fast response times.

PzKpfw III (Tauchfähig) Amphibious medium tank

In preparation for the *Seelöwe* (sea lion) invasion of the UK planned by the Germans in 1940, armoured vehicles were modified for amphibious and even submerged operation down to a depth of 15 m (50 ft).

Between September and October 1940 three units from Panzerregiment Nr 2 were formed as Panzer-abteilungen A, B and C. Their PzKpfw III and PzKpfw IV tanks were made submersible, and trials were conducted at Putlos in northern Germany.

All existing openings in the vehicles were sealed and the air intake for the engine was eliminated. The turret ring was sealed with a rubber ring and rubber covers were fitted over the main armament, gun mounts and commander's cupola. All the covers had detonation cord embedded within them so that

The planned invasion of the UK led to a demand for tanks able to move on the seabed, although such submersibles were used only on the Eastern Front.

when the tank surfaced the covers could be blown off to leave the tank ready for action once more.

Air supply

While the tank was driving underwater fresh air was supplied through a 20-cm (8-in) diameter flexible hose 18 m (59 ft) long and reinforced with wire mesh. The upper end of this hose was buoyed to remain on the surface. For submerged communications a radio antenna was also attached to the buoy.

The exhausts were equipped with one-way valves to keep water out, the engine was cooled by seawater during

submerged operations, and a bilge pump expelled seepage.

Amphibious trials

Navigation under water was aided by a directional gyro, but co-ordinates for underwater travel were generally provided via radio link from the landing craft from which the tanks had been offloaded onto the seabed via ramps on the craft's sides. General Georg-Hans Reinhardt, who supervised the trials, ordered that the tanks should be painted in camouflage that resembled seawater.

Trials of this **PzKpfw III (Tauchfähig)** were conducted under the super- vision of Kapitän zur See (Ing) Paul Zieb, who took every precaution to ensure the safety of the tank crews. He wrote: 'In order to maintain visual contact with the tank at all times two 7-m (23-ft) depth gauges were mounted on the tank, painted red for port and green for starboard. Two shallow-draught floating cranes were anchored nearby; onboard both were doctors and medical

personnel with resuscitation equipment in case water or exhaust gases penetrated the tanks. The crane ships were supported by two diving vessels, two tugs and two motorboats, kept at the ready. Radio transmitters were installed on both crane ships.'

Accidents happened during the trials and there was at least one death from the effects of unvented exhaust fumes. On 20 July a submersible tank drove into a trench and became stuck. An amphibious tractor attempted to recover it, but it was stuck solid and so the crew flooded the tank and escaped using their life saving apparatus. Two days later a tank stalled on a rock and had to be lifted out. These incidents showed the problem of avoiding obstacles under water. Production continued to April 1941, most of the tanks being allocated to a battalion of Panzerregiment Nr 18 of the 18th Panzer Division. Eighty were used in Barbarossa to cross the Bug river in June 1941.

A PzKpfw III (Tauchfähig), or U-Panzer, of the 18th Panzer Division's 18th Panzerregiment. This photo was reportedly taken at the crossing of the River Bug at Patulin in June 1941 during Operation Barbarossa.

Land-Wasser-Schlepper Amphibious tractor

In 1936 the German army's general staff called upon Rheinmetall Borsig AG to develop a special amphibious tractor. The idea was that the tractor could tow behind it a special trailer that could also float, capable of carrying vehicles or other cargo up to a weight of about 18000 kg

(39,683 lb). Afloat the tractor would act as a tug for the floating trailer, but once ashore the tractor would have to pull the trailer to a point where it could be safely unloaded.

Land-water tractor

Rheinmetall undertook the project and produced the

Land-Wasser-Schlepper (land-water tractor) or **LWS**. The LWS was very basically a motor tug fitted with tracks, and was a large and awkward-looking machine that nevertheless turned out to be a remarkably workmanlike vehicle. The LWS had a flat bottom on each side of which were two long sets of

tracks. On each side four sets of road wheels were suspended in pairs from leaf springs. The LWS had a pronounced bow and on top was a cabin for the crew of three men and space for a fur- ther 20. What appeared to be a small funnel was in fact an air intake for the engine. At the rear, or stern, two large

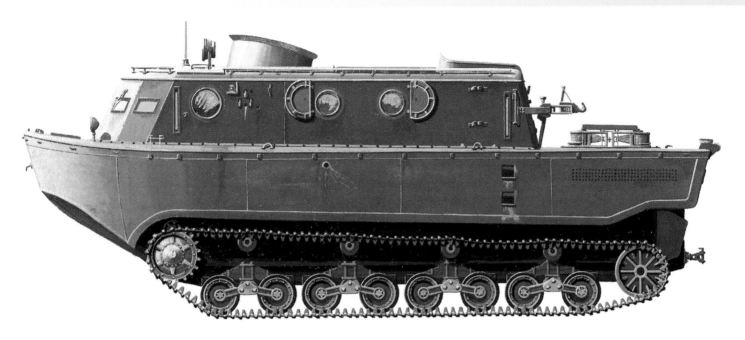

The German LWS was built to carry a payload of up to 20 men in addition to its crew of three, and could also tow a floating trailer carrying a vehicle or some form of weapon.

propellers were placed for water propulsion. To complete the nautical appearance of the LWS the sides of the crew cabin had portholes.

By contrast, the floating trailer was a large slab-sided affair that, on land, moved on wheels located on one forward and two rear axles. At the rear a ramp could be hinged down for loading, a typical load being an SdKfz 9 18-tonne halftrack, whose crew transferred to the LWS for the water journey.

The LWS and trailer concept was conducted through a series of trials with no great sense of

urgency until the aftermath of May and June 1940 brought the prospect of *Seelöwe*, the operation to invade the UK, to the forefront of German thinking. The LWS and trailer could no doubt have been used for such an operation, but the combination was really intended for the calmer waters of rivers and lakes. Even, so the LWS was pushed with a greater sense of urgency for a while, but the project never really got off the ground and by 1941 it had been abandoned.One point that counted against the LWS was that it was unarmoured,

and it was felt that armour would be needed for any operations likely to be undertaken. It was also felt that the floating trailer was a bit cumbersome, so a new idea was taken up. The overall layout of the LWS was retained, but this time the trackwork and suspension of a PzKpfw IV tank were used to carry a lightly armoured floating chassis. It was proposed that two of these vehicles, known as

Panzerfähre or **PzF**, should be employed with a large pontoon between them to carry a tank or other load. Thus the PzF would have been the core of a ferry rather than a tractor, but the whole project was abandoned during 1942 after two prototypes had been built and tested. In 1945 an example of the LWS was captured in Germany and brought to the UK for a technical evaluation by the British.

SPECIFICATION	
LWS	**Dimensions:** length 8.6 m (28 ft 2½ in); width 3.16 m (10 ft 4½ in); height 3.13 m (10 ft 3⅓ in)
Crew: 3 + 20	
Weight: 13000 kg (28,660 lb)	
Powerplant: one Maybach HL 120 TRM patrol engine delivering 197.6 kW (265 hp)	**Performance:** maximum road speed 40 km/h (25 mph); maximum water speed unloaded 12.5 km/h (7.8 mph); road range 240 km (149 miles)

Schwimmwagen Light amphibious vehicle

The term **Schwimmwagen** for the amphibious version of the military Volkswagen was not strictly correct, for this term means merely 'amphibious vehicle', and the correct designation was **Schwimm-fähiger Gelandeng Typ 166**. Nevertheless the term Schwimmwagen was altogether more frequent. The vehicle was developed during 1940 for airborne troops, and was supposed to combine good cross-country performance with an amphibious capability. The

vehicle was designed to make as much use as possible of components from the Kübelwagen, which was the military version of the Volkswagen. In the end most of the vehicles, of which 14,625 were completed, were used on the Eastern Front.

Multiple capabilities

The Schwimmwagen was used to supplement the various types of motorcycle and sidecar combinations used by reconnaissance and other units.

SPECIFICATION	
Schwimmfähiger Gelandeng Typ 166	**Dimensions:** length 3.825 m (12 ft 6⅔ in); width 1.48 m (4 ft 10½ in); height 1.615 m (5 ft 3⅗ in)
Crew: 1 + 3	
Weights: unloaded 903.5 kg (1,992 lb); payload 434.5 kg (958 lb)	
Powerplant: one VW 1.33-litre petrol engine delivering 18.6 kW (25 hp)	**Performance:** maximum road speed 80 km/h (50 mph); maximum water speed 11 km/h (7 mph); range 400-450 km (250-280 miles)

It was a small, sturdy vehicle with a rather bulky body to provide flotation, and with a propeller at the rear for water propulsion. It could seat four men at a squeeze, especially if they carried all their

equipment, for internal space was rather limited.

The German army asked for more of these vehicles during the early years of the war, for the Schwimmwagen was a useful, if small, machine. The

Above: A snarl-up of German motor transport with a Schwimmwagen evident at the front. It has been estimated that the average life of this very useful and capable vehicle was only two weeks after reaching the front. There were also small numbers of the Type 128, a longer-wheelbase model built in 1940-41.

production line was at the Volkswagen plant at Wolfsburg, and it was often disrupted by Allied bombing raids before the line was closed during 1944, mainly as a result of shortages of raw materials.

Apart from its reconnaissance role, the Schwimmwagen was often used by commanders in all types of formation, for they found the type very useful for visiting scattered units, especially over the wide expanses of the Eastern Front. The vehicle was powered by a 1.33-litre petrol engine that was slightly more powerful than that of the Kübelwagen and provided the Schwimmwagen with better all-round performance. To make sure that as little as possible of the cross-country power was wasted, special all-terrain tyres were fitted.

The propeller used to drive the vehicle in the water was located on a swinging arm at the rear. Before the vehicle entered the water this arm had to be lowered to align the screw with the drive chain, and once propeller drive had been selected the rest of the transmission was isolated. Water steering was effected via the front wheels.

Despite its usefulness in water, the Schwimmwagen was just at home in the desert wastes of North Africa. Rommel requested more of the type, but most vehicles went to the Eastern Front, where the air-cooled engine and more numerous water obstacles meant it could be used to better effect. Many of the Eastern Front models were fitted with a special tank containing a higher-volatility fuel for enhanced starting capability under winter conditions.

Above right: Waffen-SS soldiers from one of the SS Balkan units prepare to board their Schwimmwagen during operations against partisans. During such operations the amphibious qualities of this vehicle could often be used to good advantage, as water obstacles were no problem.

Right: British troops maintain a captured German Schwimmwagen that has been pressed into Allied use as a runabout. They are working on the propeller unit that was lowered as the vehicle moved into the water. Note the overall rotund appearance of the design, produced by the use of flotation chambers.

T-37 and T-38

Light amphibious tanks

In 1931 the USSR purchased from Vickers Carden-Loyd of the UK a number of light tankettes. Among the purchases was a small number of Carden-Loyd A4E11 amphibious tanks, and these so impressed the Soviets that they decided to undertake licensed local production in order to meet a Red Army requirement for light scouting tanks. However, it was not long before the Soviet design teams realised that the Carden-Loyd A4E11 did not meet all their requirements, and so they set about developing their own light amphibious tank based on the British design. This resulted in the **T-33**, which was subjected to some rigorous trials before it was deemed unsatisfactory. Further design resulted in the **T-37** light amphibious tank.

Test programme

By the time the T-37 was produced there was little left of the original British design other than the concept. The T-37 had a GAZ AA engine and the suspension was an improved version of that used on the French AMR light tank. Once again the first T-37s were subjected to a thorough testing programme, and as a result changes were introduced to the full production models, which first came off the lines late in 1933 and early in 1934. The production T-37 was a small vehicle with a two-man crew, the commander in a turret offset to the right and the driver seated in the hull to the immediate left. Most of the buoyancy came from two pontoons on each side of the

The tiny T-37 light amphibious tank was produced in several versions, but all were very lightly armoured and had only a two-man crew. They were in production from 1935 onward, but few survived after the end of 1941 as they were too frail to stand up to prolonged combat.

upper hull above the tracks, and at the rear there was the usual single propeller and a rudder. The T-37 was meant to be amphibious on inland water-ways only. As it was designed as a light scouting or reconnaissance vehicle, the T-37 had only light armament, com-prising a single 7.62-mm (0.3-in) air-cooled machine-gun.

Production of the T-37 continued until 1936, and during the production run several variants occurred. One was known as the **T-37TU** and had a prominent radio frame aerial around the upper hull; this was used only by commanders needing to maintain contact

with rear command levels, while orders were transmitted to other tanks by signal flags. On some vehicles the usual riveted turret was replaced by a cast item. As was to be expected of so small and light a tank, armour was very thin, the maximum being only 9 mm (0.354 in) thick and the norm only 3 mm (0.118 in). This armour could not withstand even light anti-armour projectiles, but the T-37s were to be used as scouting vehicles only and were not intended for employment in a stand-up armoured fight. Nevertheless they were so used during the desperate days of 1941–42 when the Soviet army had at

times virtually nothing with which to stem the advance of the German forces. By the end of 1942 the last of the T-37s had passed from use, though a few hulls were retained for use as light tractors.

Improved model

Almost as soon as the first T-37s were rolling off the production lines a redesign was under way. A team based in Moscow virtually took apart the T-37 design and did whatever it could to modernise it, for it was realised by 1934 that the T-37 design approach was already out of date. The result was known as the **T-38**, and although

The T-38 (left) could easily be distinguished from the T-37: the turret was now mounted on the left-hand side, and the driver's position moved to the right. It remained utterly inadequate as a combat vehicle.

it looked very different the T-37 was little advanced over the original.

The T-38 was of the same general concept as the T-37 and the two-man crew was retained, but the turret position was switched to the left and the driver's position was also switched. The T-38 was wider than the T-37 and had better floating characteristics. Carried over from the T-37 was the armament of a single 7.62-mm DT machine-gun and the power train of the GAZ AA truck.

The first T-38 was built in 1936 and full production commenced in the following year. Manufacture continued until 1939, by which time about 1,300 had been completed. Some changes were introduced during production, the first of which was the **T-38-M1**, an attempt to introduce a new transmission system that in the end proved too complicated for mass production. The **T-38-M2**

used the power train and engine of the new GAZ-M1 truck. One field modification was the changing of the machine-gun for a 20-mm ShVAK cannon.

When the T-38 went into action alongside the T-37 during the 1939-40 campaign in Finland, the weaknesses of the design became apparent. The tank was too lightly protected, for even machine-gun rounds could pierce the thin armour and knock out the vehicle. Despite attempts by their crews to keep out of the way and simply observe enemy positions, the T-37s and T-38s were shown to be too vulnerable on the battlefield; but they were not immediately withdrawn, for the simple reason that there was nothing to replace them at that time. T-38s were still in use until 1942, to the detriment of their crews, who suffered heavy casualties as army commanders attempted to use them as light support tanks.

In an attempt to continue the use of the existing T-38 production facilities an effort was made to develop the T-38 by adding extra armour, but this offered few advantages over the original and the project was terminated.

The T-38 did take part in some interesting experiments involving radio control. T-26 light tanks packed with

explosives were to be directed towards bridges or other demolition targets and then exploded by radio command from a T-38. The T-38 was equipped with special radios for the purpose and was designated **NII-20**. There are references to this demolition method being used during the Finnish campaign, but its success is not recorded.

SPECIFICATION	
T-37	
Crew: 2	1.82 m (5 ft 11¾ in)
Weight: 3200 kg (7,055 lb)	**Performance:** maximum road speed 56.3 km/h (35 mph); maximum road range 185 km (115 miles)
Powerplant: one GAZ AA petrol engine developing 29.8 kW (40 hp)	
Dimensions: length 3.75 m (12 ft 3⅝ in); width 2.1 m (6 ft 10¾ in); height	**Armament:** one 7.62-mm (0.3-in) DT machine-gun

SPECIFICATION	
T-38	
Crew: 2	height 1.63 m (5 ft 4¼ in)
Weight: 3300 kg (7,275 lb)	**Performance:** maximum road speed 40 km/h (24.9 mph); maximum road range 170 km (105.6 miles)
Powerplant: one GAZ AA or GAZ M1 petrol engine developing 29.8 kW (40 hp)	
Dimensions: length 3.78 m (12 ft 4¾ in); width 3.33 m (10 ft 11 in);	**Armament:** one 7.62-mm (0.3-in) DT machine-gun or one 20-mm ShVAK cannon

Type 2 Ka-Mi Light amphibious tank

The Type 2 Ka-Mi amphibious light tank was the most commonly used of the Japanese 'swimming' tanks. It had pontoon floats fore and aft to give most of the swimming buoyancy, and the bulky hull also had large buoyancy chambers to provide still more waterborne flotation.

The Japanese army produced an amphibious halftrack in 1930, but this lacked adequate power for full cross-country mobility. The idea of an amphibious armoured vehicle was not entirely lost, however, and work continued through the 1930s in an attempt to create an amphibious vehicle for the Japanese navy. One of these

projects was to add kapok-filled floats to a Type 95 Kyu-Go light tank, the combination being propelled by two outboard motors. The idea was to produce a tank landing or river-crossing system only but, though the floats worked, the combination was very difficult to steer and the project was eventually abandoned.

The idea of making the Type 95 into an amphibious light tank did not disappear. It was decided to redesign the hull and use steel pontoons fore and aft to provide buoyancy. The wheels, track, suspension, engine and other Type 95 components were retained, but the hull became a larger and bulkier shape. Slabs of armour

plate were used on the hull, which had inbuilt buoyancy chambers, and a redesigned turret carried a 37-mm anti-tank gun with a co-axial 7.7-mm (0.303-in) machine-gun. Special-to-role extras included a bilge pump, and drain holes were inserted into the road wheels. In the water the two steel pontoons were held in place by clamps, but were discarded on shore. Steering was effected by rudders on the rear pontoon, controlled by cables from a steering wheel in the turret. As there was very little freeboard, a trunk arrangement was usually erected around the engine intake grills on the hull top.

Into production

The result was the **Amphibious Tank Type 2 Ka-Mi**, which went into production in 1942. Compared with land-based light tanks it had several innovations, not the least of which was radio and a telephone intercom

system for all crew members. Compared with land-based tanks, the Type 2 also had an increase in crew numbers: the Type 95 Kyu-Go had a crew of only three, but the Type 2 had five, mainly as a result of the increased hull volume. One of this increased crew was a mechanic who looked after the engine and the power transfer from the road wheels to the two propellers providing water propulsion.

The Type 2 was successful, and was used in combat on several occasions by the Japanese navy. However, it

SPECIFICATION	
Type 2 Ka-Mi	in) or, without pontoons, 4.83 m
Crew: 5	(15 ft 10 in); width 2.79 m (9 ft
Weight: 11301 or 9571 kg	1¾ in); height 2.34 m (7 ft 8 in)
(24,914 or 21,100 lb) with or	**Performance:** maximum land speed
without pontoons	37 km/h (23 mph); maximum road
Powerplant: one 6-cylinder diesel	range 200 km (124 miles)
developing 82 kW (110 hp)	**Armament:** one 37-mm and two 7.7-
Dimensions: length 7.42 m (24 ft 4	mm (0.303-in) guns

suffered the fate of most Japanese armour, being used in dribs and drabs to provide purely local infantry support. By 1944 the type was generally used as a land-based pillbox in island defences, which was a waste of their amphibious potential. Its other problem was

that there were never enough of them. Japanese industry could never produce enough to meet demands, and as every vehicle was virtually hand-built production was always slow. But despite this, the Type 2 was still one of the best designs of its period.

Terrapin Light amphibious load carrier

Designed by Thornycroft, the unarmed **Terrapin** was manufactured by Morris Commercial. About 500 were built, most being used by the 79th Armoured Division and first going into action during the autumn of 1944, when they were used to supplement DUKWs during operations to open up the water approaches to Antwerp.

Simple design

The Terrapin was a straightforward amphibious design but it had some odd features, some of which were not to its advantage. One concerned its two Ford V-8 petrol engines, each driving the four wheels on each side and, in the water, one of the two propellers. The snag with this arrangement turned out to be that if one of the engines stalled the other engine kept driving, causing the vehicle to go into a rapid turn. The engines were mounted almost centrally to spread wheel loadings, but this had the effect of dividing the cargo compartment into two halves. Thus although the Terrapin could carry more than the DUKW, it could not carry large loads such as guns or vehicles.

The overall performance of the Terrapin was not all that good. It was rather slow on land and in the water, and it was in the water

that this performance really mattered. When fully loaded the Terrapin had only a limited freeboard, and could be all too easily swamped in rough water. The top of the vehicle was completely open, but raised moulding boards around the holds kept out the worst of the water. The driver was located roughly in the centre of the vehicle and his view to the front and rear was therefore rather limited. The Terrapin was also a rather uncomfortable vehicle in bad weather: seated in the open, the driver and crew had to rough it. An awning could be raised over the front compartment to serve as a spray shield, but this

SPECIFICATION	
Terrapin Mk 1	**Dimensions:** length 7.01 m (23 ft);
Crew: 1 + at least 2	width 2.67 m (8 ft 9 in); height
Weights: unloaded 6909 kg (15,232	2.92 m (9 ft 7 in)
lb); loaded 12015 kg (26,488 lb)	**Performance:** maximum land speed
Powerplant: two Ford V-8 petrol	24 km/h (15 mph); maximum water
engines each developing 63.4 kW	speed 8 km/h (5 mph)
(85 bhp)	

further restricted the driver's forward field of vision.

Even so, the Terrapin gave good service. Before it was used operationally some of the drawbacks had been realised, and Thorny croft was asked to produce a new design. This emerged as the **Terrapin Mk 2**, the basic model then becoming the **Terrapin Mk 1**. This had a large one-section hold, better

all-round performance and the driver positioned well forward under cover. The hull shape was modified to improve seaworthiness. But the Terrapin Mk 2 arrived on the scene too late: the war ended before it could be placed in production and the large numbers of DUKWs to hand meant there was no point in developing it further.

The Terrapin was powered by two Ford V-8 petrol engines and was driven in the water by two propellers at the rear. There were two cargo holds and the driver sat in the vehicle's centre.

DD Sherman Amphibious tank

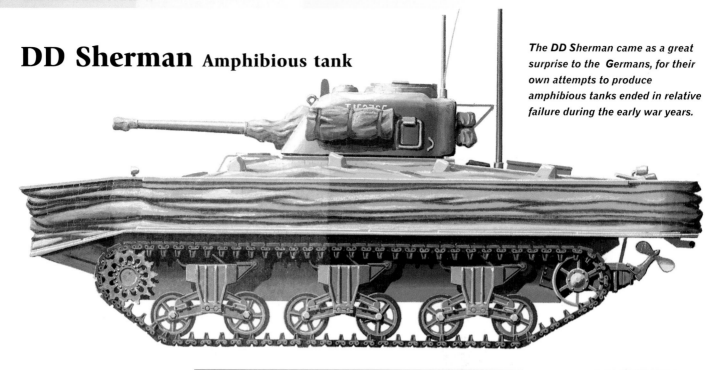

The DD Sherman came as a great surprise to the Germans, for their own attempts to produce amphibious tanks ended in relative failure during the early war years.

The **DD Sherman** was a British development that was initiated during 1941. An engineer named Nicholas Straussler turned his attention to producing a method by which an ordinary tank could float in water during amphibious operations. Early experiments involved the Tetrarch light tank (Valentines were also used at a later date) but in the end it was decided to standardise the eventual results on the Sherman tank, then available in some numbers. To provide a cover of secrecy, these floating tanks were named **Duplex Drive** (DD) **Shermans**.

Flotation equipment

The first DD Shermans were ready in 1943 and were converted by the addition of a collapsible fabric screen and 36 rubber air tubes or pillars. This screen/tube assembly was attached to a boat-shaped platform welded around the hull of the tank. The idea was that the pillars were inflated from two air cylinders carried on the tank, and as the inflation process continued the pillars raised the screen to a point above the level of the Sherman's turret. The screen was then locked into position using struts. All these operations could be carried out by the tank's crew, and the whole process could be undertaken in 15 minutes aboard

a tank landing craft. Once ready, the tank could be driven off the landing craft ramp into the water, where the tank would then float with the turret at water level, about 0.914-m (3-ft) freeboard being provided by the screen.

Propulsion in water

Drive in the water was provided by two small screw propellers at the rear of the tank. These were driven via a gearbox from the track drive, and steering was accomplished by swivelling the propellers. Extra steering could be carried out by the tank commander using a simple

Above: The twin propellers of this DD Sherman can be clearly seen under the wading screen, which is in the collapsed position.

Below: Only Sherman medium tanks were used operationally with DD equipment from D-Day onwards until the crossing of the Elbe in 1945.

rudder and tiller arrangement positioned behind the turret.

Forward progress in the water was slow, depending on the sea state, and the sea state also severely affected the ability of the DD tanks to float as intended. Anything over sea state 5 was considered too risky, but at times this limitation was disregarded, often with dire results. Once the DD Sherman was in about 1.5 m (5 ft) of water the screen could then be collapsed. It was here that the main advantage of the DD

Sherman became apparent, for it was able to retain its main gun for immediate use after landing. The bow machine-gun could not be fitted to the DD Shermans but the main gun was often used to support 79th Armoured Division operations directly after landing on the beaches, especially during the D-Day landings of 6 June 1944.

Rhine and Normandy

During the Normandy landings the DD Shermans came as a nasty surprise for the German

defenders as their own experiments with amphibious tanks had proved generally unsuccessful and had been terminated some years earlier. The sight of DD Shermans clambering up the beaches was too much for some defenders who promptly made themselves scarce. In other

locations the DD Shermans provided invaluable immediate fire support for units already in action on the beaches and in the immediate hinterland. DD Shermans were also used towards the end of the war at the Rhine crossings and during some north Italian operations.

Below left: The DD Sherman in the foreground is in the process of lowering its wading screen just after a river crossing. The wading screens were supported on columns of air contained in rubber tubes, and the soldier in the foreground is assisting their collapse.

Below: DD Shermans are seen after crossing the River Elbe in the late stages of the war in Europe in 1945. The wading screens could remain attached to their parent tanks after use, as they did not hinder the tank's fighting efficiency.

DUKW Amphibious truck

This DUKW has its canvas tilt raised over the load-carrying area and the driver's screen is in the raised position.

The amphibious truck that became universally known as the **'Duck'** first appeared in 1942, and was a version of the standard GMC 6x6 truck fitted with a boat-like hull to provide buoyancy. It derived its name from the GMC model designation system: D showed that it was a 1942 model, U that

it was amphibious, K indicated that it was an all-wheel-drive model, and W denoted twin rear axles. From this came **DUKW**, and this was soon shortened to 'Duck'.

Duck production

The Duck was produced in large numbers. By the time the war

ended 21,147 had been built, and the type was used not only by the US Army but also by the British Army and many other Allied armed forces. Being based on a widely-used truck chassis it was a fairly simple amphibious vehicle to maintain and drive, and its performance was such that it could be driven

over most types of country. In the water the Duck was moved by a single propeller at the rear driven from the main engine, and steering was carried out using a rudder behind the propeller; extra steering control could be achieved by using the front wheels. The driver was seated in front of the main cargo compartment, which was quite spacious and could just about carry loads such as light artillery weapons – it was even possible to fire some weapons such as the 25-pdr field guns during the 'run in' to a beach. The driver was seated behind a folding windscreen and a canvas cover could be erected over the cargo area. For driving over soft areas such as sand beaches the six wheels used a central tyre pressure-control system.

The Duck was meant for carrying supplies from ships over beaches, but it was used for many other purposes. One advantage was that it did not always have to unload its supplies directly on the beach: on many occasions it was able to drive its load well forward to where the freight was needed and then return. Many were used as troop transports and the number of special-purpose versions were legion. Some were fitted with special weapons, such as the 4.5-in (114-mm) rocket-firing version used in the Pacific and known as the **Scorpion**. Mention has been made of field guns firing from the cargo area, and some Ducks were armed with heavy

A US Third Army 'Duck' moves up the bank of the Danube near Donaustauf, Germany in May 1945. DUKWs were used extensively during nearly all Allied amphibious operations from 1943 onwards.

machine-guns for self-defence or anti-aircraft use. A tow hook was fitted at the rear and some vehicles also had a winch.

Many Ducks were sent to the USSR, and the type so impressed the Soviet army that the USSR produced its own copy, known as the BAV-485. This differed from the original by having a small loading ramp at the rear of the cargo area. Many of these BAV-485s were used by the Warsaw Pact nations, and the DUKW gave long service after the war to several Western

SPECIFICATION	
DUKW	**Dimensions:** length 9.75 m (32 ft);
Crew: 1 + 1	width 2.51 m (8 ft 3 in); height
Weights: unloaded 6750 kg (14,880	2.69 in (8 ft 10 in)
lb); loaded 9097 kg (20,055 lb);	**Performance:** maximum land speed
payload 2347 kg (5,175 lb)	80 km/h (50 mph); maximum water
Powerplant: one GMC Model 270	speed 9.7 km/h (6 mph)
engine developing 68.2 kW	**Armament:** see text
(91.5 bhp)	

armed forces. For example, the British Army did not pension off its Ducks until the end of the 1970s.

The Duck has been described as one of the war-winners for the Allies and certainly gave good service wherever it was

used. It had some limitations in that the load-carrying capacity was rather light and performance in rough water left something to be desired, but the Duck was a good sturdy vehicle that was well-liked by all who used it.

Below left: A DUKW with its trim vane lowered acting as a personnel carrier during the D-Day landings. The rope fenders were to prevent the vehicle banging into a ship's side during the loading operation.

Below: The main use of the DUKW was as a stores carrier loading supplies from ships standing offshore. They could also carry overland to supply dumps. This DUKW is seen during a training operation in the period immediately before D-Day in 1944.

LVT2, 3 and 4 Amphibious tractors

Developed from a Roebling civil design for use in the Florida swamps, the LVT1 (Landing Vehicle Tracked model 1) was meant solely as a supply vehicle. The Pacific War was to prove the need for a more capable amphibious assault vehicle, which emerged as the **LVT2** with a better all-round shape to improve water performance, though it was still a high and bulky vehicle. Another improvement was a new suspension, and the track grousers were improved by the use of aluminium W-shaped shoes bolted onto the track and thus easily changed when worn or damaged. A logistic enhancement was use of the engine, final drive and transmission of the M3 light tank. At first the steering system gave considerable trouble, but training and experience found a cure.

The engine was mounted at the rear, which restricted the size of the cargo compartment. This was relatively easily designed out of the overall layout by moving the engine forward and mounting a ramp at the rear to ease loading and unloading. Thus the LVT2 became the **LVT4**, which was otherwise generally similar. The LVT4 was produced in larger numbers than any other LVT: 8,348 from five production lines in contrast with 2,963 LVT2s from six lines. There were some design differences between the LVT2 and LVT4: for instance, the driver's controls were rearranged on the LVT4, but the main improvement was that all manner of loads could be

The LVT4 differed from the LVT2 in having its ramp at the rear, facilitating larger loads such as a Jeep or light artillery. It was armed with pintle-mounted machine-guns on the cargo bay's sides and front.

The LVT(A)1 was armed with the turret and 37-mm gun of the M3 light tank to provide some measure of local fire support in the initial stages of an amphibious landing.

carried on the LVT4, ranging from a Jeep to a complete 105-mm (4.13-in) howitzer.

Most LVT2s and LVT4s were armed with 0.5- and 0.3-in (12.7- and 7.62-mm) machine-guns on rails or pintles, but there were two versions of the LVT2 that had heavier weapons. The **LVT(A)1** had the M3 light tank turret mounting a 37-mm (1.46-in) gun for use in the fire-support role in amphibious operations. The gun proved to be too light for the role, so there appeared the **LVT(A)4** with the turret of the M8 Howitzer Motor Carriage carrying a 75-mm (2.95-in) howitzer. On both of these gun vehicles the turrets were

mounted toward the rear of the cargo area, which was covered by armoured plate.

The LVT2 and LVT4 were the main load carriers of the early Pacific operations, the LVT first seeing service on Guadalcanal. The types also saw limited European service in 1944–45,

and were used by the US Army and US Navy as well as the US Marine Corps.

The **LVT3**, otherwise the **Bushmaster**, was an entirely new design with a pair of Cadillac engines in side sponsons. This allowed an increase in size of the cargo-

SPECIFICATIONS	
LVT2	**LVT3**
Crew: 2 + 7	**Crew:** 3
Weights: 11000 kg (24,250 lb) unloaded; 13721 kg (30,250 lb) loaded	**Weights:** 12065 kg (26,600 lb) unloaded; 17509 kg (38,600 lb) loaded
Dimensions: length 7.975 m (21 ft 6 in); width 3.25 m (10 ft 8 in); height 2.5 m (8 ft 2½ in)	**Dimensions:** 7.95 m (26 ft 1 in); width 3.25 m (10 ft 8 in); height 3.023 m (9 ft 11 in)
Powerplant: one Continental W-970-9A petrol engine delivering 186.5 kW (250 hp)	**Powerplant:** two Cadillac petrol engines delivering a total of 164 kW (220 hp)
Performance: maximum land speed 32 km/h (20 mph); maximum water speed 12 km/h (7. 5 mph); maximum road range 241 km (150 miles); maximum water range 161 km (100 miles)	**Performance:** maximum road speed 27.3 km/h (17 mph); maximum water speed 9.7 km/h (6 mph); maximum road range 241 km (150 miles); maximum water range 120.7 km (75 miles)
Armament: one 0.5-in (12 7-mm) and one 0.3-in (7.62-mm) machine-guns	**Armament:** one 0.5-in (12.7-mm) and two 0.3-in (7.62-mm) machine-guns

carrying area and enabled a loading ramp to be installed at the rear. The track was entirely new, being rubber-bushed, and the width was reduced without affecting water speed.

Late-war arrival

The first LVT3 appeared during 1945. and production totalled 2,692. It went on to be the 'standard' post-war vehicle of its type.

The LVT3's driver and co-driver were located in a cab forward of the cargo area with the gunner's firing step behind them. By the time the LVT3 arrived on the scene the standard armament was one 0.5-in and two 0.3-in machine-guns. Along each side of the cargo area were the sponsons containing the engines,

LVTs lumber ashore in a training exercise, the right-hand vehicle with shielded weapons that could be flamethrowers. In any real assault the LVTs landed side-by-side.

hydramatic transmissions, bilge pumps and fume-removal blowers. The rear ramp was operated by a hand-powered winch and had heavy rubber seals along its sides.

Like the LVT2 and LVT4, the LVT3 was armoured, but extra protection could be added by means of an armoured cab for and add-on panels of armour that could also be used on the

LVT2. Perhaps the most reassuring item of equipment carried was a wooden box packed with rags, waste material and tapered wooden plugs to stop any leaks.

M29C Weasel Amphibious cargo carrier

In 1943 an Allied invasion of German-held Norway was suggested, and it was appreciated that some form of snow-crossing cargo carrier would be required. After a series of trials a tracked vehicle known as the **T15 Weasel** was selected for service and this was later developed into the **T24**, still named Weasel but now capable of traversing not only snow but mud, swamp and rough terrain. In time the T24 was standardised as the **M29 Cargo Carrier** and from this evolved the **M29C** amphibious light cargo carrier. The name Weasel was once more carried over, even though the official name **Ark** was promulgated.

The M29C was a simple conversion of the land-use M29. The flexible rubber tracks were revised to provide waterborne propulsion, flotation chambers were created at the front and rear, and twin rudder units were added to create a waterborne steering facility.

The land M29 had already demonstrated its abilities to cross just about any type of terrain, including snow and

The M29C was an amphibious cargo carrier with a limited but nonetheless useful payload, and could also be used to carry small numbers of personnel.

rough stony ground, and the M29C retained this capability in full. In water the M29C was somewhat slow, and it was incapable of operating in anything other than inland waterway conditions, so its utility in surf or rough water was very limited. But when employed correctly the M29C soon proved to be a valuable vehicle. Its uses were legion, especially during the many island-hopping campaigns of the Pacific theatre. Once ashore the M29C was used to cross terrain that no other vehicle could attempt, and the type carried

men and supplies, and even towed artillery using its rear-mounted towing pintle. Rice paddies were no obstacle, and the M29C was equally at home crossing sand dunes.

The M29C and the land-based M29 Weasels were used as ambulances on many occasions. Another use was for crossing minefields as the Weasel's ground pressure was very low, often too low to set off anti-tank mines. A technique was even

evolved whereby a Weasel could be controlled remotely using hand-tugged cords, but this technique had its limitations. The Weasel was also very reliable: it rarely broke down, and its track life was later found to be far longer than had been anticipated.

Multi-role capability

The M29C was extensively used by signal units, for its ability to cross water and land impassable to other vehicles made it a very valuable wirelaying vehicle, but it was as a supply or personnel carrier that the type was most useful. Although unarmoured, the M29C was often used to carry armed troops and supplies across water obstacles and land them in front of an enemy positions.

By the end of World War II about 8,000 examples of the M29C had been produced, and orders for a further 10,000 were then cancelled. But the M29C concept had been well established by that time, and since 1945 many follow-on designs have appeared.

M29Cs were used by several of the Allied armies. The British

Army made use of a number during 1944–45 and for a few years after that.

Some European armies used them for some years after World War II. It is possible that limited numbers may still be around and if so, they will be in civilian

hands, hard at work over swampy terrain.

US personnel take a somewhat bumpy ride over swampy terrain in an M29C. Evident are the rear rudders, lowered into the water when needed.

SPECIFICATION	
M29C Weasel	**Powerplant:** one Studebaker Model
Crew: 1 + 3	6170 liquid-cooled petrol engine
Weights: 2195 kg (4,840 lb)	delivering 55.9 kW (75 bhp)
unloaded; 2740 kg (6,040 lb) loaded	**Performance:** maximum road speed
with a 390-kg (860-lb) maximum	58.6 km/h (36.4 mph); maximum
payload	water speed about 6.4 km/h (4
Dimensions: length 4.794 m (15 ft	mph); maximum land range 282
8¾ in); width 1.7 m (5 ft 7 in);	km (175 miles)
height 1.797 m (5 ft 10¾ in)	

Ford GPA Amphibious Jeep

The **Truck, ¼-ton, 4x4 Amphibian** – more commonly known as the **Amphijeep** or **GPA** from **General Purpose Amphibian** – was based on the chassis of the hugely successful Jeep. The hull was designed by Sparkman & Stephens Co. and the prototype was built by Marmon-Herrington, who designed the mechanical linkages – a challenging task within the confined space of the Amphijeep. The first contract for the GPA was placed in April 1942. Ford took over production and between 1942 and June1943 some 12,778 had been built. The bodywork was sheet steel treated against corrosion and all nuts and bolts were cadmium plated. It was longer than a Jeep and with its boat-like hull it looked rather like a miniature version of the DUKW. The vehicle was heavier than a Jeep and consequently had a more robust leaf-spring suspension. The turning circle on land and in the water was almost identical at just over 10.98 m (36 ft). The engine could either drive the rear wheels or all four wheels, via a three-speed gearbox and a two-speed transfer box. The electrical system was two six-

volt batteries screened and waterproofed. The engine was cooled by a water radiator and by forced air circulation. Air was drawn in through a large intake on the front deck of the hull and out through grilles level with the front seats. There was a power take-off for the propeller that gave a maximum speed in water of 8.5 km/h (5.2 mph). The freeboard was 0.43 m (1 ft 5 in) with the breakwater erected. In water the GPA was steered by the normal steering wheel which turned the front wheels and operated the rudder at the rear by means of a cable and pulleys. The equipment in the GPA included an anchor and capstan which was driven from the engine by a clutch and belt. The GPA was used by the US Army in World War II and was supplied under Lend Lease to the British and Soviet armies. In Soviet service it was popular, allowing the crossing of vast rivers on the Eastern Front that would have been a serious obstacle for more conventionally

The Amphijeep could carry five personnel, the rear seat having a lifebuoy cushion, or 360 kg (794 lb) of cargo. Note the breakwater at the front of the hull.

SPECIFICATION	
Ford GPA	**Powerplant:** one four-cylinder side-
Crew: 1 + 3	valve petrol engine delivering 44.7
Weights: 1656 kg (3650 lb)	kW (60 bhp) at 3600 rpm
unloaded; 2018 kg (4450 lb) with	**Performance:** maximum road speed
maximum load	95 km/h (59 mph); maximum water
Dimensions: length 4.623 m (15 ft 2	speed about 8.5 km/h (5.2 mph)
in); width 1.626 m (5 ft 4 in)	

equipped forces. After the war the design was copied in the USSR as the **MAV** that used the

components of the GAZ-60 a 4x4 that owed much to the Jeep.

SdKfz 2 kleines Kettenrad Light halftrack

The **SdKfz 2 kleines Kettenrad** (SdKfz standing for *Sonderkraftwagen* or special vehicle, and *kleines Kettenrad* meaning small wheel-track or halftrack) was developed initially for use by the new German army and Luftwaffe airborne and paratroop units, and was supposed to be a very light type of artillery tractor. It was originally intended as a towing vehicle for the specialised 3.7-cm (1.46-in) Pak 35/36 anti-tank gun developed for the airborne role, and also for light recoilless guns.

The first Kettenrads entered service in 1941. The initial Kettenrad service model was the **NSU-101**, a small but complex vehicle that could carry three men. The relatively long tracks took up much of the length of the vehicle on each side, and the engine was located under and behind the driver. Two men could sit at the rear, facing backwards, and the equipment to be towed was connected by a hitch at the rear. Apart from light artillery pieces

the vehicle could also tow a specially-designed light trailer that could carry ammunition or fuel.

By the time the Kettenrad entered service its main intended use had passed with the mauling of the Luftwaffe airborne forces on Crete. Thereafter the German airborne formations fought as ground troops, and the need for their light artillery tractors was no longer pressing. Accordingly the Kettenrad was used mainly as a

The diminutive SdKfz kleines Kettenrad was originally intended for use as a light artillery tractor by airborne units, but after Crete these vehicles were more often used as light forward area supply vehicles for use over difficult terrain. Three men could be carried. Two cable-laying SfKfz 2 derivatives were also manufactured.

supply vehicle for troops operating in areas where other supply vehicles could not move without difficulty. While the Kettenrads could carry out supply missions over seemingly impassable tracts of mud or sand they could not carry very much, and their towing capacity was limited to 450 kg (992 lb).

Enlarged model

At one point it was proposed that a larger version to be

British soldiers try out a captured SdKfz 2 kleines Kettenrad. The driver sat in a well between the two tracks, with the engine located just behind him.

known as the **HK102** would be produced. This would have a larger 2-litre (122-cu in) engine – the original version had a 1.5-litre (91.55-cu in) engine – that could power a larger vehicle capable of carrying five men or a correspondingly larger payload of supplies. It reached the design stage but got no further, since by 1944 it was finally appreciated that the Kettenrads were an expensive luxury that the German armed forces could no longer afford and the type went out of production. Kettenrads were in use until 1945, and there were specialised types for high speed cable-laying.

SPECIFICATION	
SdKfz 2	**Dimensions:** length 2.74 m (9 ft);
Crew: 3	width 1 m (3 ft 3½ in); height
Weights: 1200 kg (2,646 lb)	1.01 m (3 ft 3¾ in)
Powerplant: one Opel Olympia 38	**Performance:** maximum road speed
petrol engine developing 26.8 kW	80 km/h (49.7 mph)
(36 hp)	

SdKfz 10 leichter Zugkraftwagen 1t Light artillery tractor

From the mass and weight of the 18-tonne SdKfz 9 the numerical sequence changed back to the lightest of the artillery tractors, the **SdKfz 10 leichter Zugkraftwagen 1t**. This light tractor had its origins in a 1932 army requirement, and the development work was carried out by Demag of Wetter-Ruhr.

The first prototype was completed during 1934 and in 1937 the production model (the **D 7**) emerged. This remained in production until 1944 with its basic form virtually unchanged, and later attempts to replace this model never got very far since the original was deemed more than adequate for its

role. The task was to tow light infantry and other weapons, and to carry the weapon detachment of up to eight men. These weapons included the 3.7-cm (1.46-in) Pak 35/36 anti-tank gun, the 7.5-cm (2.95-in) leIG 18 infantry support gun, and the larger 15-cm (5.9-in) sIG 33 infantry gun. Other weapons

towed included light anti-aircraft guns and later in the war the 5-cm (1.97-in) Pak 38 and 7.5-cm Pak 40 anti-tank guns. The basic vehicle was also used as the basis for the armoured SdKfz 250 series. All in all the SdKfz 10 was a very popular vehicle that remained in demand by all arms throughout the war. Production was carried out at two main centres, one of which was the Sauerwerke in Vienna, but by 1943 production concentrated at the other main centre, the Mechanische Werke at Cottbus. In German terms the production totals were large (over 17,000).

Production versions

By far the most numerous of this production total was the basic tractor but as usual this vehicle was used for other things. The first variants were produced as a reflection on the expected nature of the coming war for three variants, the **SdKfz 10/1**, **SdKfz 10/2** and **SdKfz 10/3**, were all produced as chemical warfare vehicles. Very few of these special vehicles appear to have been produced. It was different with **SdKfz 10/4** and **SdKfz 10/5**, for these two vehicles were produced to mount single-barrel 2-cm light anti-aircraft guns: the SdKfz 10/4 carried the Flak 30 and the SdKfz 10/5 the faster-firing Flak 38 from 1939 onwards. These two vehicles were so arranged that their sides and rear could fold down to form a working platform for the gun crew, and many examples that operated in direct support of ground formations were fitted with extra armour over the driver's position. As was usual at the time, there were unofficial modifications to the SdKfz 10 series to carry local 'field fit' weapons. A not uncommon weapon so fitted was the 3.7-cm Pak 35/36 anti-tank gun, which was usually mounted to fire forward.

Below: SdKfz 10 tractors are used in their intended role to tow Pak 38 anti-tank guns. The vehicles have their canvas covers stowed, and the gun crew's kit and equipment is stowed at the vehicle rear.

SPECIFICATION	
SdKfz 10	**Dimensions:** length 4.74 m (15 ft 6⅔ in); width 1.83 m (6 ft); height 1.62 m (5 ft 3¾ in)
Crew: 8	
Weight: 4900 kg (10,803 lb)	
Powerplant: one Maybach HL 38 or 42 6-cylinder petrol engine developing 74.6 kW (100 hp)	**Performance:** maximum road speed 65 km/h (40.4 mph); range 150 km (93 miles)

SdKfz 11 leichter Zugkraftwagen 3t Medium artillery tractor

The basic **SdKfz 11 leichter Zugkraftwagen 3t** was intended for use primarily as an artillery tractor, and once in service it became a standard tractor with 10.5-cm (4.13-in) leFH 18 field howitzer batteries, and was later used to tow 7.5-cm (2.95-in) Pak 40 anti-tank guns. The SdKfz 11 was so successful with leFH 18 batteries that the larger SdKfz 6 which was also meant to tow these howitzers was phased out of production in favour of the lighter (and less expensive) tractor. SdKfz 11 tractors were also used by the Luftwaffe to tow light flak weapons such as the 3.7-cm (1.46-in) Flak 36 and 37, but it was by Nebelwerfer batteries that the SdKfz 11 was mainly used. The SdKfz 11s used with these batteries not only towed various multi-barrel

The SdKfz 11 was used primarily as a tractor for medium field artillery such as the 10.5-cm howitzer and Pak 40 anti-tank gun.

launchers but also carried spare rockets, launcher frames for statically-emplaced launchers and the crews to carry out the fire missions. Since Nebelwerfer units retained smoke-laying skills, some SdKfz 11s (**SdKfz 11/1** and **SdKfz 11/4** models) were fitted with smoke-

SPECIFICATION	
SdKfz 11	**Dimensions:** length 5.48 m (17 ft 11¾ in); width 1.82 m (5 ft 11¾ in); height 1.62 m (5 ft 3¾ in)
Crew: 9	
Weight: 7100 kg (15,653 lb)	
Powerplant: one Maybach NL 38 6-cylinder petrol developing 74.6 kW (100 hp)	**Performance:** maximum road speed 53 km/h (33 mph); range 122 km (76 miles)

generating equipment but this could usually be removed for the rocket-firing duties.

Chemical warfare

Two variants, the **SdKfz 11/2** and **SdKfz 11/3**, were produced for the chemical warfare decontamination role. These vehicles could carry more equipment than the SdKfz 10 equivalents, and were intended for use with larger equipments such as tanks.

An Afrika Korps SdKfz 11 tows an leFH 18 howitzer soon after the arrival of the Korps in North Africa in 1941 – hence the pith helmets (soon discarded).

SdKfz 6

mittlerer Zugkraftwagen 5t

The SdKfz numbers allotted to the artillery halftracks used by the new German army during the early 1930s did not follow a logical sequence, and the **SdKfz 6 mittlerer Zugkraftwagen 5t** was a medium tractor. Development of this vehicle commenced during 1934, the early work being carried out by Bussing-NAG in Berlin. There were two main purposes envisaged – one was for the SdKfz 6 to act as the main tractor vehicle for the 10.5-cm (4.13-in) leFH 18 batteries, and the other was for the engineer units, where the tractor would be able to tow heavy combat engineer equipment on trailers. In both cases the vehicle could carry up to 11 men, and more at a squeeze.

Interim vehicle

Production of the SdKfz 6 vehicles was carried out by Bussing-NAG and Daimler-Benz, but the numbers involved came to no more than about 737. The main reason for this was that the SdKfz 6 was rather an interim vehicle that fell between two stools: lighter vehicles could be used to tow the artillery pieces, and it was really too light for some of the heavier engineer equipment. It was also rather costly to produce, so by 1941 a decision was made to phase the vehicle from production and replace it with the far less expensive sWS. Even so, it was late 1942 before production finished and the vehicles already produced continued in use right until the war ended, sometimes pulling artillery pieces far heavier than those for which the type had been designed.

The Czech-built Praga SdKfz 6s featured longer track bogies than the Bussing-NAG models. They were powered by a Maybach HL54 TUKRM engine.

Two versions of engine were produced for the SdKfz 6, the first developing 67 kW (90 hp) and the later version 75 kW (100 hp). Surprisingly enough, the SdKfz 6 was modified only slightly during its service career. Most were produced as standard tractors with seating for the artillery detachment that could be covered by a canvas tilt, but there were also three weapon-carrier variants. The first was the **7.5-cm Slf L/40.8** and never really got past the prototype stage; it was an attempt to produce a mobile 7.5-cm gun for use with cavalry units, and at least three prototypes were produced between 1934 and 1935. The type was never placed in production, but at least one was captured during the fighting in North Africa.

Gun-chassis

Then there was the model known as the 'Diana' or **7.62-cm Pak 36(r) auf Panzerjäger S1f Zugkraftwagen 5t**, an attempt to mount captured Soviet

First produced in 1937, the SdKfz 6 AA variant mounted a 3.7-cm (1.45-in) Flak 36 on an open platform. This AFV had a crew of four.

76.2-mm guns in a high armoured superstructure built onto the rear of an SdKfz 6. This superstructure was open and the gun was placed on the vehicle complete with its wheels and attenuated trails. The gun was the Soviet Model 1936 which was used as a dual anti-tank/field gun. Only nine 'Dianas' were produced and again one was captured in North

Africa by the Allies. The third SdKfz 6 weapon carrier was the **SdKfz 6/2**, which mounted a 3.7-cm Flak 36 anti-aircraft gun on an open platform behind the driver's position; the sides folded down to act as a working platform for the gun crew. The first of these variants was produced during 1937 and most of them went to the Luftwaffe.

SPECIFICATION	
SdKfz 6	
Dimensions: length 6.01 m (19 ft 8½ in); width 2.20 m (7 ft 2½ in); height 2.48 m (8 ft 1½ in)	**Powerplant:** one Maybach NL38 6-cylinder petrol engine developing 67 kW (90 hp)
Crew: 11	**Performance:** maximum road speed 50 km/h (31 mph)
Weights: 8700 kg (19,180 lb)	**Armament:** see text

SdKfz 7 mittlerer Zugkraftwagen 8t

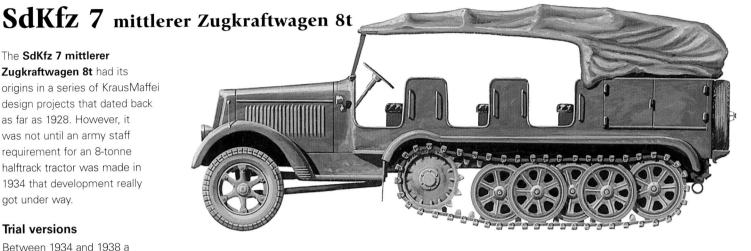

The **SdKfz 7 mittlerer Zugkraftwagen 8t** had its origins in a series of KrausMaffei design projects that dated back as far as 1928. However, it was not until an army staff requirement for an 8-tonne halftrack tractor was made in 1934 that development really got under way.

Trial versions

Between 1934 and 1938 a number of trial versions was produced until the final version appeared in 1938 as the SdKfz 7 mittlerer Zugkraftwagen. This vehicle was used as a tractor for many artillery weapons including the 8.8-cm multi-purpose gun, the 15-cm sFH 18 and the 10.5-cm K 18.

In its tractor form the SdKfz 7 could carry up to 12 men and their kit, and there was still space left for ammunition and/or other supplies. The gun detachment sat on open bench seats behind the driver, and could be covered by a canvas tilt to keep out some of the weather. The vehicle could tow weights up to 8000 kg (17,637 lb), and most vehicles were fitted with a winch that could pull up to 3450 kg (7,606 lb). The SdKfz 7 proved to be a most

This SdKfz has its canvas tilt deployed to provide weather protection for the crew. It was usually stowed to allow all-round vision against air attack.

useful vehicle and was widely admired. A captured example was copied in the United Kingdom by Bedford Motors with a view to manufacture for Allied use, and the Italians produced a near copy known as the **Breda 61**. But the Germans carried on churning out as many as they could. By the end of 1942 there were 3,262 in service. Not all of these were tractors, for the load-carrying capacity of the SdKfz 7 was such that it also made an ideal weapon platform.

The first of these weapon carriers was the **SdKfz 7/1**, which mounted a 2-cm (0.78-in) Flakvierling 38 four-gun anti-aircraft mounting on the open

SPECIFICATION	
SdKfz 7	**Powerplant:** one Maybach HL62 6-
Dimensions: length 6.85 m (20 ft	cylinder petrol engine developing
3 in); width 2.40 m (7 ft 10½ in);	104 kW (140 hp)
height 2.62 m (8 ft 7 in)	**Performance:** maximum road speed
Crew: 12	50 km/h (31 mph)
Weights: 11550 kg (25,463 lb)	**Armament:** see text

rear. On many of these vehicles the driver's position and the engine cover were provided with armoured protection. The SdKfz 7/1 was used extensively for the protection of columns in the field and the four cannon proved deadly to many Allied low-level fliers. This was not the only anti-aircraft version, for the **SdKfz 7/2** mounted a single 3.7-cm Flak 36 anti-aircraft gun. An attempt was made to mount a

5-cm Flak 41 on a SdKfz 7, but since neither the gun nor the conversion was very successful no further work was carried out once trials had been completed. Some SdKfz 7s were also converted to mount single-barrel 2-cm cannon for anti-aircraft use.

V-2 controller

Perhaps the oddest use for the SdKfz 7 was when existing vehicles were converted to accommodate armoured super-structures for use as observation and command posts for V-2 rocket batteries during 1944. The V-2 rockets were prone to explode on their launch stands as they were being fired so the armour protected the launch crews. How many of these **Fuerleitpanzer auf Zugkraftwagen 8t** conversions were made is uncertain.

Production of the SdKfz 7 series ceased in 1944, but by then numbers had been built by Krauss-Maffei in Munich, the Sauserwerke in Vienna and the Borgward works at Bremen. In the post-war years many were appropriated for Allied use, and the Czech army used numbers for some years.

A 2cm Flakvierling 38 SdKfz 7/1 anti-aircraft halftrack. When firing, the sides of the vehicle were folded down to provide a working platform around the gun.

SdKfz 8

mittlerer Zugkraftwagen 8t

The SdKfz designation followed no logical sequence and the **SdKfz 8 schwerer Zugkraftwagen 12t** was actually the first of the German halftracks to be developed and produced. It consequently established many of the features and design details that were later to be used on other German halftrack designs. The line of development that led to the SdKfz 8 can be traced back to World War I, when Daimler-Benz was involved in some early halftrack design work. One result of this was an advanced vehicle known as the Marienwagen. After 1919 Daimler-Benz continued its development work, bringing out a series of vehicles, one of which attracted the attention of the Red Army (in 1931 there was even talk of a Soviet production order). This appears never to have come about, for instead the German army ordered a model known as the **Daimler-Benz DB S 7**. Later versions followed the general

layout of this 1931 vehicle, but gradually more powerful engines were fitted until the series reached the **Daimler-Benz DB 10**.

Artillery tractor

The SdKfz 8 was designed as an artillery tractor and an artillery tractor it remained throughout its service life. There was only one variation, a 1940 conversion of what was probably only one vehicle to mount an 8.8-cm Flak 18. This was used in action in France in May 1940, and thereafter no mention of this offshoot can be found.

The SdKfz 8 remained in production until 1944. Originally it was produced to tow two modernised ex-World War I artillery pieces, the 15-cm K 16 and the 21-cm lange Mörser, a stubby howitzer. As more modern equipment came into use the SdKfz 8 switched to towing weapons such as the heavy 8.8-cm Flak 41 and the even larger 17-cm K 18 long-range gun. The SdKfz 8 was also

A group of British soldiers takes advantage of a ride on a captured SdKfz 8 somewhere in North Africa. This was the basic artillery tractor version of the series.

SPECIFICATION	
SdKfz 8	**Powerplant:** one Maybach HL85 12-cylinder petrol engine developing 138 kW (185 hp)
Dimensions: length 7.35 m (24 ft 1¼ in); width 2.50 m (8 ft 2¼ in); height 2.81 m (9 ft 2¾ in)	**Performance:** maximum road speed 51 km/h (32 mph)
Crew: 13	**Armament:** see text
Weight: 15000 kg (33,069 lb)	

used by the Luftwaffe to tow the ponderous 10.5-cm Flak 38 and 39 anti-aircraft guns. At times these tractors were called upon to tow tank-carrying semi-trailers or other forms of heavy trailer, but usually the German artillery batteries retained their vehicles jealously.

By late 1942 there were 1,615 SdKfz 8s in service. Production was concentrated at two main centres, the Daimler-Benz works at Berlin-Marienfelde and the Kruppwerke at Mülhausen. At one time some production work was also carried out at the Skodawerke in Pilsen, and in the years after the war the new Czech army used a large number of SdKfz 8s, some of them lasting until the 1960s.

One variation of the SdKfz 8 was a vehicle known as the **HK 1601**. This differed from the normal SdKfz 8 in many ways and was an attempt to combine the features of the large 18t halftracks and the SdKfz 8. The prototype appeared in late 1941 and after three more had been built it was decided to produce a batch of another 30. These were apparently built and used on the Eastern Front. They had a cargo-type body to carry the crew of 13. Production of the SdKfz 8 ceased during 1944.

The 12-tonne SdKfz 8 was the first halftrack to enter service with the Wehrmacht. It is seen here on parade, towing modernised 15-cm K 16s.

SdKfz 9 schwerer Zugkraftwagen 18t Heavy halftrack

This example of an SdKfz 9 is a heavy artillery tractor and could carry nine men. Others were fitted with cranes and jibs for the recovery role.

By far the largest of all the World War II halftracks was the **SdKfz 9 schwerer Zugkraftwagen 18t**, a vehicle that had its origins in a requirement made during 1936 for a heavy recovery vehicle to support the Panzer formations and tow disabled tanks. The development contract was awarded to the Famo Fahrzeugwerke und Motorwerke AG at Breslau, which became the sole producer. The first example appeared in 1936: this was the **FM gr 1**, and later came two other models, the **FM gr 2** and **FM gr 3** which used larger and more powerful engines.

In the end both tractor and recovery versions of the SdKfz 9 were produced. The tractor version was the basic SdKfz 9, which was used to tow the German army's heaviest artillery weapons and some heavy engineer equipment including bridging (for which there was a tractor unit towing bridge units on special trailers and carrying

15 men). Among the heavy artillery towed by the SdKfz 9 was the 24-cm (9.45-in) K 3 (so large it had to be towed in five loads), the Krupp 21-cm (8.27-in) K 38, and the various Skoda heavy howitzers and guns. The Luftwaffe used a small number of tractors to tow the mobile versions of the super-heavy 12.8-cm (5.04-in) Flak 40. An anti-aircraft gun was used on the only weapon-carrier version of the SdKfz 9 which appeared in 1943. This variant carried an 8.8-cm (3.46-in) Flak 37, and the vehicle had an armoured cab. The sides of the rear firing platform could be folded down to act as a working platform for the gun crew, and there were small outrigger arms to stabilise the vehicle in action. Only one conversion was made.

The recovery versions appeared in two forms, the **SdKfz 9/1** and **SdKfz 9/2**. The SdKfz 9/1 had a crane (*Drehkran*) with a 6000-kg (13,228-lb) lifting capacity, but this was insufficient for some

lifting tasks and the SdKfz 9/2 was produced with a 10000-kg (22,046-lb) crane. Outrigger legs were fitted on the latter, and an extra jib was provided to suspend a counter-weight when really heavy loads were to be lifted. These vehicles were massive equipments, and although they were capable of dealing with tanks up to the size of the PzKpfw IV they could not handle the heavier Panthers and Tigers. Since the SdKfz 9 was the only recovery vehicle in use when these 'heavies' entered service, a way had to be found and the type was used in sections of three vehicles, at least two being needed to recover Tigers from some situations. In order to provide them with more

traction some were fitted with a large earth spade at the rear, but even so two vehicles still had to be used to drag a Tiger out of a ditch, and sometimes three to tow one in a disabled state. The only answer to that was to develop a heavy tracked recovery vehicle, which duly appeared as the Bergepanther.

Production of the SdKfz 9 ceased during 1944, by which time the last versions were powered by the same Maybach engines as those fitted to PzKpfw IV tanks. They were massive vehicles that were certainly very impressive to look at, but one has to bear in mind that the basic tractor version cost 60,000 Reichsmarks and a Panther cost 117,100.

SPECIFICATION	
SdKfz 9	**Dimensions:** length 8.25 m (27 ft ¾ in); width 1.6 m (8 ft 6 in); height 2.76 m (9 ft ¾ in)
Crew: 9	
Weight: 18000 kg (39,683 lb)	
Powerplant: one Maybach HL V-12 petrol engine developing 186.4 kW (250 hp)	**Performance:** maximum road speed 50 km/h (31 mph)

schwerer Wehrmachtsschlepper Medium infantry halftrack

By the end of 1941 front-line experience in several theatres had revealed to the German army that its fleet of halftrack carriers was in need of some revision. At the bottom end of the range the 1-tonne and

3-tonne cargo and supply/artillery tractors were well capable of carrying on as they were already performing, but it was clear that the medium to heavy range was proving more problematical. It was

decided at this stage that the 5-tonne range would be discontinued but that the 8-tonne range would be retained as it was required for heavy artillery towing and other purposes. Thus an interim

between the 3-tonne and 8-tonne vehicles was sought. This had to be a relatively low-cost solution to the army's needs as by the end of 1941 the German war machine was being stretched, not just in capacity

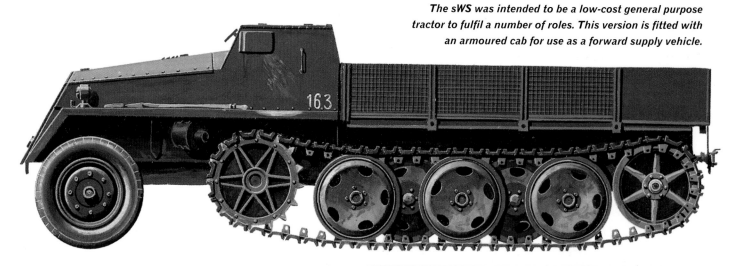

The sWS was intended to be a low-cost general purpose tractor to fulfil a number of roles. This version is fitted with an armoured cab for use as a forward supply vehicle.

but also in the range of equipment now needed.

The design accepted was a Büssing-NAG offering, and eventually became known as the **schwerer Wehrmachtsschlepper (sWS**, or army heavy tractor). This was schemed not so much for the Panzer or artillery formations but for infantry units, for which it would act as a general personnel carrier and supply vehicle. Accordingly it was virtually a halftrack truck with virtually no armour in its cargo-carrying form and an open cab with a soft top for the driver and one passenger. In order to keep cost as low as possible, the tracks were not of the costly rubber-capped type used by front-line vehicles, but single dry-pin all-steel tracks.

Slow production

The sWS went into production at the Büssing-NAG plant in Berlin and also at the Ringhofer-Tatra plant in Czechoslovakia, but production was very slow. The sWS did not have a very high production priority and from time to time Bomber Command weighed in to disrupt things to an extent that in place of the expected 150 vehicles per month, from the start of production in December 1943 to the end of September 1944 only 381 had been delivered. These production shortfalls led to the hastily created Maultier improvisation, but sWS production limped on almost until the end of the war

and some survived to serve the new Czechoslovak army for a number of years after the end of World War II.

sWS variants

The small numbers produced did not prevent the sWS from being adapted into the usual special purpose variants. The basic truck model could be converted as a rudimentary front-line ambulance carrying stretchers under a canvas awning mounted on a frame. A special front-line supply version was fitted with an armoured cab and engine cover, and a similar arrangement was used for a projected version that would have carried a 3.7-cm (1.46-in) Flak 43 anti-aircraft gun on a flatbed area at the rear; only a few of these **3.7-cm Flak 43 auf sWS** versions were

produced. Another variant proposed but built only in small numbers was an armoured version with a hull over the rear. On the roof of this hull was placed a 10-barrel launcher for 15-cm (5.9-in) artillery rockets: 10 rockets were carried in the launcher tubes and additional examples were inside the hull.

This **15-cm Panzerwerfer 42 (Zehuling) auf sWS** version

had a crew of five, but it is doubtful if many of the equipments actually reached front-line service.

Although only a small number were actually produced by comparison with the totals for other German halftracks, the sWS proved efficient enough in service, and was proportionately far more cost-effective than some other models.

SPECIFICATION	
sWS	**Powerplant:** one Maybach HL 42
Crew: 2	liquid-cooled 6-cylinder petrol
Weight: about 13500 kg (29,762 lb)	engine developing 74.6 kW (100 hp)
Dimensions: length 6.68 m (21 ft 11 in); width 2.5 m (8 ft 2½ in); height 2.83 m (9 ft 3½ in)	**Performance:** maximum road speed 27 km/h (16.8 mph)

Production of the Wehrmachtsschlepper began in 1943 but lagged behind demand, leading to the introduction of the Maultier. This sWs is seen in an unarmoured flat-bed configuration.

SdKfz 5 Maultier Halftrack vehicle

The Maultier was a makeshift conversion of an Opel truck into a halftrack truck able to serve as a supply vehicle in forward areas as a supplement to the sWS.

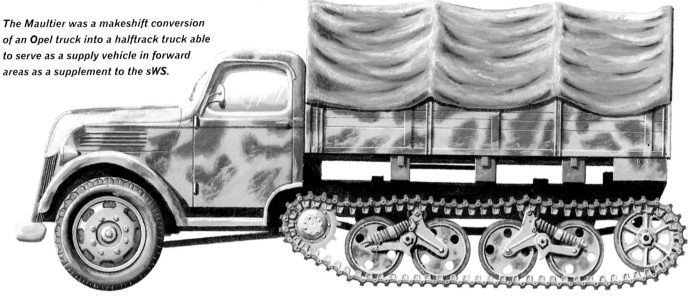

The first winter of World War II in the USSR (1941–42) demonstrated to the German army that most of its wheeled transport was completely incapable of dealing with the dreadful muddy conditions produced during the freeze-thaw weather that marked the beginning and end of the Soviet winter. During these conditions it was only halftracks that could make any headway. However, to divert the precious halftracks from their operational purposes to undertake mundane supply functions was obviously uneconomic, so it was decided to produce low-cost halftrack trucks. This was done quite simply by taking Opel and Daimler-Benz trucks from the production lines and removing their rear axles. In their place went new driveshafts connected to tracked assemblies made from PzKpfw II running wheels and tracks. In itself this was a considerable economic advantage since the PzKpfw II was then going out of production and existing capacity could be retained, making the truck conversion an even more cost-effective venture.

Mule by name

The new **SdKfz 5** halftrack trucks were given the name **Maultier** (mule) regardless of the provenance of the chassis. Among the

chassis types were KHD and Ford, the latter from Ford's pre-war licensee at Asnieres in France, but in the end the most numerous conversions were those based on Opel Typ S/SSM trucks, of both the 2x4 and 4x4 varieties, and in service these were generally a success although they tended to lack the overall mobility and durability of the 'proper' halftrack vehicles. Not surprisingly, their use was confined to the Eastern Front, and the vehicles were used mainly for routine supply purposes. The *Wehrmachts-Einheitskofferaufbau*, as the box-like body of these vehicles was called, could be adapted for a large number of tasks (more than 100 different versions are known) ranging from delousing installations to radio stations. A change made in 1944 as a reflection of Germany's worsening military and industrial situation was the replacement of the standard metal cab by the so-called *Wehrmachts-Einheitfahrerhaus* cab, which was made from wood and pressed cardboard. Not content with a good thing, the Germans as ever were forced to employ the Maultier for yet another purpose. The German Nebelwerfer (rocket) batteries had become an established part of the army artillery system by late 1942, and it was decided

that the Panzer formations should have their own dedicated rocket units. At that time most Nebelwerfer units used towed launchers, so in order to keep up with the armoured forces a self-propelled version was required. The halftrack was the obvious choice as a starting point, but as none could be allocated the Maultier was pressed into use.

Rocket launcher

The basic truck was provided with a fully armoured cab, engine cover and hull. On the hull roof a 10-barrel launcher known as the 15-cm Panzerwerfer 42 was placed. This launcher had 270 degrees of traverse and 80 degrees of elevation, and it fired its 10 rockets in a rippled salvo. The army ordered 3,000 of these conversions with the understanding that production would eventually switch to the sWS when production totals of the latter allowed: they never did permit the changeover, and only a small batch of prototypes was made on sWS chassis.

Service entry

The first of these Maultier rocket-launcher conversions was effected and entered service during 1943 with a crew of three. The rockets were carried in the launcher, with reload rockets in compartments along each side of the lower hull. A 7.92-mm (0.312-in) machine-gun was usually carried as a means of providing a local-defence capability. Some of these armoured Maultier vehicles were produced without the launcher, it should be noted, and these were used to carry additional supplies of rockets for the launcher-fitted vehicles. Some of these carrier vehicles were used by units other than the Nebelwerfer batteries as front-line ammunition supply vehicles, although they were somewhat vulnerable as their armour was proof only against small arms projectiles and shell splinters. This resulted from their conception as vehicles for use behind the very front line, and the need to conserve steel armour for other vehicles.

SPECIFICATION	
Maultier (rocket launcher)	**Powerplant:** one 3.6-litre liquid-cooled 6-cylinder petrol engine
Crew: 3	
Weight: 7100 kg (15,653 lb)	
Dimensions: length 6 m (19 ft 8¼ in); width 2.2 m (7 ft 2½ in); height 2.5 m (8 ft 6 in)	**Performance:** maximum road speed 38 km/h (30 mph)

SdKfz 250 leichter Schützenpanzerwagen

In the 1930s the German army chose to develop two halftracks, both to fulfill reconnaissance requirements and to provide mobility for infantry. Two models were adopted, the 3-tonne SdKfz 251 and the 1-tonne **SdKfz 250 leichter Schützenpanzerwagen**.

Armoured hull

The SdKfz 250 was first produced by Demag AG of Wetter in the Ruhr, although later on other concerns were also involved in manufacture. The vehicle was based on the chassis of the SdKfz 10 leichter Zugkraftwagen 1-tonne vehicle, but featured an armoured hull

wedded to an open top to accommodate the crew of five men plus the driver. The first examples were produced during 1939. The SdKfz 250 first went into action during the May 1940 campaign in France. Compared with its larger counterpart, the SdKfz 251, the SdKfz 250 half-track was built and used on a much smaller scale.

Because of its small size, stowage arrangements in the SdKfz 250 were very compact. The original superstructure was complicated in shape, being bowed outward in the middle. Considerable modifications were made in 1943; the number of panels used in construction

was reduced by half; integral side-stowage panels were built in; front and rear plates were reduced to single pieces; vision flaps were replaced by slits and a larger rear door was fitted. Armour thickness ranged from 6 to 14.5 mm (0.24 to 0.57 in).

Weapon carrier

The main run of SdKfz 250 vehicles commenced with the **SdKfz 250/1**, which had a crew of six men and carried two machine-guns. There followed a number of models equipped for either radio (**SdKfz 250/3**) or telephone (**SdKfz 250/2**) communications, and a variety of weapon-carrying variants. These were armed with all manner of weapons from an 8.1-cm (3-in) mortar (**SdKfz**

250/7) to a 2-cm (0.79-in) anti-aircraft cannon (**SdKfz 250/9**). Perhaps the oddest of these weapon carriers was the **SdKfz 250/8**, which appeared to be rather overloaded with a short 7.5-cm (2.96-in) tank gun (from the early versions of the PzKpfw IV tank) allied with a co-axial/ranging 7.92-mm (0.31-in) MG34 or MG42 machine-gun. There were two variants that were allocated their own special designation numbers. One was the **SdKfz 252** which was supposed to be a special ammunition carrier towing a trailer; the reshaped and fully enclosed interior was meant to carry ammunition for Sturmgeschütz (assault gun) batteries. Only a few were made before it was realised that

Fast, reliable and robust, the SdKfz 250 was very popular and remained in production until the end of the war. The SdKfz 250/3 depicted is the command and communication model, as used by Erwin Rommel.

SPECIFICATION	
SdKfz 250	**Dimensions:** length 4.56 m (14 ft 11½ in); width 2.10 m (6 ft 10¾ in); height 1.98 m (6 ft 6 in)
Crew: 6	
Weight: 5380 kg (11,861 lb)	
Powerplant: one Maybach HL 42 6-cylinder petrol engine developing 75 kW (100 hp)	**Performance:** maximum road speed 59.5 km/h (37 mph); road range 299 km (186 miles); gradient 24°; fording 0.75 m (29½ in)
	Armament: see text

The SdKfz 250/10 was armed with a 3.7-cm (1.45-in) PaK 35/36 anti-tank gun. This was just one of a total of 13 official variants of this light armoured carrier.

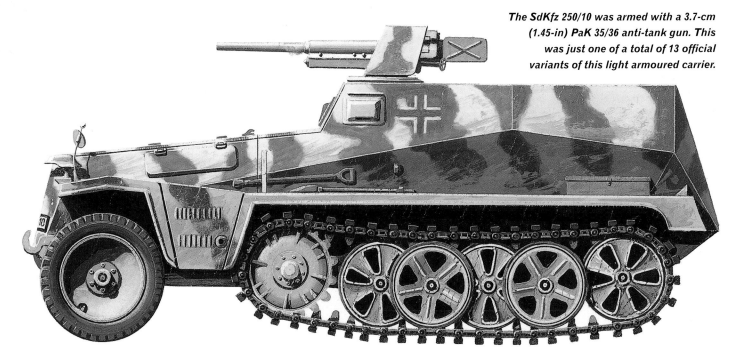

decided to replace wheeled armoured cars such as the SdKfz 222 as far as the resources allowed.

There were also light anti-tank models armed with either a 37-mm (1.45-in) anti-tank gun (**SdKfz 250/10**) or a special 'taper-bore' 2.8-cm (1-in) heavy anti-tank rifle (**SdKfz 250/11**).

Long run

Robust, capable and also flexible, the SdKfz 250 series was popular with the Wehrmacht. Although expensive to build, it remained in production right up until the end of the war.

the ordinary SdKfz 250 could carry out the role just as well and the SdKfz 252 was thus replaced by the **SdKfz 250/6** which could carry 70 7.5-cm (3-in) rounds. The other special version was the **SdKfz 253**,

which acted as an observation post for the Sturmgeschütz batteries and was given a special comprehensive radio 'fit'.

Other SdKfz 250 variants included the **SdKfz 250/9**, a special turreted version for the

reconnaissance role. By 1942 the armoured car had proved unsuitable to the extremes of the Russian campaign. Halftracks had a better survival and maintenance record than wheeled vehicles and it was

SdKfz 251 mittlerer Schützenpanzerwagen

The **SdKfz 251 mittlerer Schützenpanzerwagen** series of halftracks had its origins in the same staff requirement as the SdKfz 250, but whereas the SdKfz 250 was a light 1-tonne vehicle, the SdKfz 251 was classed as a medium (mittlerer) 3-tonne vehicle. The SdKfz 251 was a product of the Hanomag concern, based at Hanover, but the hull and superstructure were produced by Büssing-NAG. The basis of the SdKfz 251 was the SdKfz 11 leichter Zugkraftwagen 3-tonne artillery tractor halftrack, and the first production examples were issued to the 1st Panzer Division early in 1939.

There were four basic production models, each a further simplification of its predecessor, so reducing production time and costs.

Infantry carrier

The SdKfz 251 was primarily an armoured personnel carrier capable of carrying up to 12 men (a complete infantry section), and it was this **SdKfz 251/1** version that was produced in the

greatest numbers. Armed with at least two machine-guns plus the carried crew weapons, the SdKfz 251/1 was a very useful fighting platform capable of keeping up with the fast-moving Panzer formations.

There were no fewer than 22 special-purpose variants on the basic design, not counting the usual local and unofficial modifications. They ranged from weapon carriers to ambulances.

In between came observation vehicles, command and communications versions (both radio and telephone), versions carrying searchlights or anti-aircraft weapons and even tank-killers mounting long 7.5-cm (2.95-in) anti-tank guns. Perhaps the most powerful of the weapon carriers was a version of the basic SdKfz 251/1 known as the 'Stuka zum Fuss' (dive-bomber on foot, or infantry Stuka). This

The Germans intended that all motorised troops be equipped with the SdKfz 251, but as in many other areas production fell short of requirements.

was the personnel carrier with a tubular steel frame slung over the hull that carried three rocket launcher frames on each side of the vehicle; 28-cm (11-in) or 32-cm (12.6-in) rockets were mounted on these side frames while still in their carrying crates. They were fired at short ranges against fixed or area targets. They were powerful weapons, especially for street fighting, but other SdKfz 251 versions, such as the **SdKfz 251/9** armed with a short 7.5-cm tank gun, were far more accurate. There was even a flamethrower version (the **SdKfz 251/16**) and a late-war low-level anti-aircraft defence expedient, the **SdKfz 251/21**, mounting three 1.5-cm (0.59-in) or 2-cm (0.70-in) aircraft guns on a single mounting.

Gun-carriage

More fire power against the ever-growing number of enemy tanks led to the 1944 conversion of the **SdKfz 251/22**. Hitler ordered maximum self-propelled anti- tank fire power and the PaK 40 75-mm (3-in) gun was simply fitted into the fighting compartment of the halftrack with its wheels and trails removed. This was the last official version of the SdKfz 251. There were however numerous other prototypes carrying varying armament such as 88-mm PaK guns, Flavierling quad 20-mm mounts and a variety of old turrets and odd weapons.

Of particular interest was the **SdKfz 251/20 Uhu**. Developed in 1944, when special night attack units were formed, it carried an infra-red searchlight and worked in co-operation with tank units.

The SdKfz 251/7 was produced for use by army engineers. It carried specialist equipment such as a light assault bridge slung along the top of the hull.

Some 14,500 units of the SdKfz 251 in all its forms, were built up until 1944. It is arguably the most recognisable of all AFVs in service with the panzer formations. It was deployed on all fronts, usually in close co-operation with tanks. Although the early versions displayed some unfortunate reliability problems, the type settled down to become a rugged and dependable vehicle in whatever kind of role it was deployed in.

A Skoda-built model of the SdKfz 251 re-emerged after World War II. Designated the OT-810, it remained as one of the standard troop carriers of the Czechoslovakian Army well into the 1970s.

The SdKfz 251/16 Flammpanzerwagen was introduced in 1943. It stowed two 700-litre (185-Imp gal) flame-fuel tanks and two 14-mm (0.5-in) projectors, one on each side of the hull.

The SdKfz 251 served as an armoured personnel carrier for infantry accompanying the newly formed panzer divisions during World War II. It could carry up to 12 soldiers, and was armed with two MG 34 machine-guns.

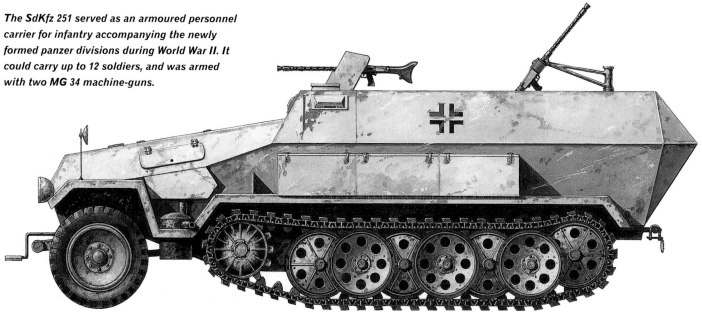

Unic Kégresse P 107 French halftrack

Some confusion still remains as to the actual manufacturer of the French halftrack, or *autochenille*, known as the **P 107**. Some references state it was produced by the Unic concern while others refer to this vehicle as the Citroën-Kégresse P 107. The truth is that both companies produced the P 107, Citroën having what may now be described as the design parentage. Citroën employed Kégresse for some years after the engineer's return from Russia to France, and accordingly Citroën produced a long line of halftrack designs using the Kégresse rubber-based track under the Citroën-Kégresse label. The P 107 was but one of these designs, and the first of this type appeared during the late 1930s. The P 107 went on to be among the more numerous of the many French halftracks.

P 107 variants

The P 107 was produced in two forms. One was an artillery tractor for light field pieces and anti-tank guns. This version had a soft top covering the space for the crew of five to seven men, and lockers at the rear for ammunition and other supplies. The second version, produced in smaller numbers, was an engineer tractor. This had an open cargo body behind the cab and was used to tow trailers carrying combat engineer equipment such as bridging pontoons. By 1939 both types were in French army service in some numbers. Both were sound and reliable vehicles and the demand for them was such that both Unic and Citroën had production lines devoted to them, hence the confusion in name.

The events of May 1940 caused a change of ownership for the P 107s. Large numbers of both types of vehicle fell into German hands and they had another change of name, this time to **leichter Zugkraftwagen U 304(f)**. Always short of half-tracks, the German army took the

type into immediate service and the French halftracks that had once towed French anti-tank guns were used to tow German weapons such as the 3 7-cm (1.46-in) Pak 35/36 anti-tank gun and later the hybrid 7.5-cm (2.95-in) Pak 97/38. But not content with this use the Germans decided to go one better. Deciding that the vehicle fell into the same category as the SdKfz 250 series, the Germans converted the P 107s as substitute **leichter Schützenpanzerwagen**. The French vehicles were stripped of their superstructures and fitted with armoured hulls almost exactly like those of the SdKfz 250 series. The one 'French' feature the Germans did not

This Citroën-Kégresse five-seater was one of many French light halftracks that were used during the 1920s to develop the Kégresse rubber-based track. Many of these light halftracks were still in use in 1939, mainly as staff cars.

Above: Citroën-Kégresse halftracks used as artillery tractors for a battery of '75' field guns. Halftracks were also used by French forces in North Africa.

change was the forward-mounted roller under the nose of the vehicle. This was used to assist the vehicle in and out of

rivers and similar obstacles and proved so useful it was not removed. Most of these conversions were used in France.

This heavily-armed Citroën-Kégresse-Hinsten M 28 is typical of the innovative halftracks developed in France prior to the German invasion of 1940.

Soviet halftracks YaSP, Zis-33/42, VM, BM, VZ and GAZ-60

For various reasons the Soviet Union did not make great use of halftracks during World War II other than employing American halftracks supplied to them under Lend-Lease. One of the main reasons for this was the relative cost in expense and production facilities that the halftrack demanded, and as the Soviet Union already had a large and productive fully-tracked tractor industry geared to the requirements of the various agricultural Five-Year Plans, tracked tractors were frequently used for artillery when halftracks might otherwise have been considered.

This suggests that the Soviets were not interested in the half-track concept, but they were. They recognised the strength of their mobility and handling advantages, and in 1931 considered the purchase of 12-tonne halftracks from Germany. At that time their interest was such that two indigenous designs were placed into limited production. These were the **YaSP** and the **Zis-33** trucks converted to the halftrack configuration, and later also used as artillery tractors. The YaSP was produced at Yaroslavl and was a Ya G-5 Komits truck fitted at the rear with a halftrack suspension (derived from the

The Soviets made extensive use of US M3 halftracks supplied under Lend-Lease, modifying them for their own use. Here two M3s of the Red Army are seen fitted with 76-mm (3-in) guns as improvised tank destroyers, an arrangement with which the US Army also experimented.

track system of the T-26 light tank) allied to a new drive shaft from the main engine at the front. The Zis-33 was a somewhat simpler vehicle that retained the main rear drive wheel allied to a halftrack suspension, and was built using the existing Zis-5 truck.

The relative success of these two design ventures engendered more during 1936. Most of these did not get very far. One was the **VM Pikap**, a version of the Zis-6 light truck. In 1937 more models appeared, most of them intended for the artillery tractor role. They included a 1¼-ton model (the **Vezdekhods Model B**), a 1½-ton model (the **BM**) and a 2-ton

model (the **VZ**). As far as can be determined only the latter two models actually got to the production stage, and again they were halftrack conversions of existing trucks.

By the time 1941 came around the Soviet armed forces had few halftracks in service compared with the number of wheeled or fully-tracked vehicles. Many of what they did have were soon lost during the German advances of 1941, and all captured German halftracks were pressed into Soviet use.

Captured vehicles

The Red Army soldiers soon learned how useful these were, and from 1942 onwards there

was a deliberate programme to make use of even damaged German halftracks. Hulks were salvaged from battlefields and stripped of all useful items, especially the running wheel, tracks and drive components. These were taken to the GAZ plant in the Urals where they were allied with GAZ-63 trucks to form **GAZ-60** troop carriers. The GAZ-60 used all manner of German components, the most favoured being those from the SdKfz 251 series of vehicles. Few of these wartime expedient vehicles survived the war. One other known Soviet halftrack produced during 1942 was known as the **Zis-42**, a 2½-ton semitracked weapons carrier.

One of the most successful Soviet pre-war halftracks, the Zis-33 was built on a truck chassis. This vehicle is seen with a propaganda unit broadcasting news of Red Army victories in the south to German positions in the north.

Bren Gun Carrier British tracked carrier

Widely known as the **Bren Gun Carrier**, the **Carden-Loyd Universal Carrier** was evolved in 1939 from a series of vehicles derived from the Carden-Loyd tankettes and reconnaissance vehicles developed through the 1930s. There were numerous marks, only one of which was designed to carry the Bren gun, which was the infantry section's standard automatic weapon. The vehicle was conceived as an ammunition carrier for the 18-pdr field gun, and as such to move ammunition across areas that were under fire and thus impassable by anything other than an armoured vehicle.

The chassis was also used as the carrier for infantry support weapons, such as 2- and 3-in (51-and 76-mm) mortars, in its **Mortar Carrier** form, and was also employed to tow anti-tank guns. As a carrier the vehicle was frequently overloaded with troops and equipment, but its suspension and engine proved rugged and reliable.

Some crews rigged a canvas cover over a frame for foul-weather protection. The carrier was a popular vehicle that could move through mud and snow even when laden.

Bren Gun Carriers of the Rifle Brigade pursue the retreating Axis armies through the North African desert in December 1942 after El Alamein.

Among the different versions of the Universal Carrier built during World War II were the **AOP Carrier** armoured observation post for the Royal Artillery, and the **Wasp** flamethrower designed by R. P. Fraser of Lagonda and tested in July 1942. These were issued on a scale of six per infantry battalion, and saw action in North-West Europe and Italy from August 1944 onwards.

Wheeled steering

The driving controls were like those of a truck, which removed the need for specialised training as was the case with tank crews. Steering was effected by movement of a wheel: small movements bowed the track and sharper movements brought the steering brakes into play.

About 35,000 Universal Carriers were built in the UK during World War II by manufacturers such as Aveling-Barford, Ford, Sentinel, Thornycroft and Wolseley. Some 5,600 were built in Australia, 520 in New Zealand, and over 29,000 in Canada. In the US 14,000 were built as the **T16**.

Captured carriers were converted by the Germans as the **3.7-cm Pak auf Fahrgestell (Bren)** mounting a 37-mm (1.46-in) anti-tank gun.

A Bren Gun Carrier in service with the Red Army. Interestingly, the pedestal-mounted machine-gun remains a Bren gun rather than a Soviet weapon.

A Bren Gun Carrier in service on the British Home Front during March 1941 is used to assist in the demolition of bomb-damaged housing.

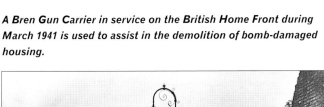

SPECIFICATION	
Bren Gun Carrier	in); width 2.1 m (6 ft 11 in); height
Crew: 4 to 5	1.6 m (5 ft 3 in)
Weight: 4318 kg (9,519 lb)	**Performance:** maximum speed
Powerplant: one Ford 8-cylinder	51 km/h (32 mph); maximum range
water-cooled inline petrol engine	256 km (160 miles)
developing 63.3 kW (85 bhp) at	**Armament:** one 0.303-in (7.7-mm)
2,800 rpm	Bren light machine-gun, or one
Dimensions: length 3.75 m (12 ft 4	0.5-in (12.7-mm) Boys anti-tank rifle

M2 & M3 US halftracks Multi-purpose vehicles

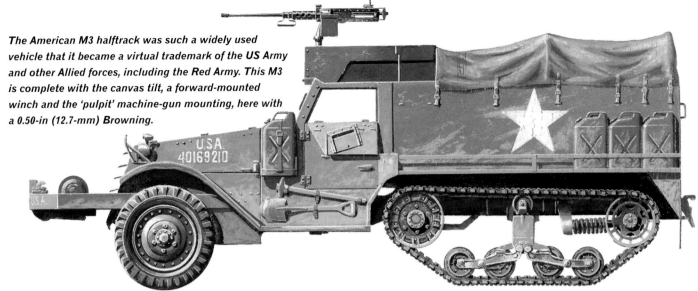

The American M3 halftrack was such a widely used vehicle that it became a virtual trademark of the US Army and other Allied forces, including the Red Army. This M3 is complete with the canvas tilt, a forward-mounted winch and the 'pulpit' machine-gun mounting, here with a 0.50-in (12.7-mm) Browning.

The halftrack was first used by the British in World War I as an artillery tractor. However, the UK eventually abandoned the halftrack in favour of four-wheel-drive, six-wheeled vehicles. The American halftrack's development history started during the 1920s, when some Citröen Kegresse P17 halftracks were purchased, and subsequent trials led to a long series of development models. In 1931, the **T14** prototype was produced in partnership with the Army Ordnance Depot and several private companies. The T14 saw the hull of the White Scout Car M2 allied with a Kegresse half-track suspension – the 'classic' American halftrack was born. Designated **Half-Track Car M2**, this was the example that entered production in early 1941, with the first examples reaching the troops in May of that year.

Production

After 1941, the halftracks rolled off the assembly lines in their thousands. Four US companies manufactured the vehicles, producing around 41,000 between 1940 and 1944. It would be easy to say that most of them were personnel carriers, but also included in the totals were mortar carriers, multiple gun motor carriages, gun motor carriages, trucks and a vast array of experimental types. All

M9A1 gun tractors of the First Battalion of the French Armoured Division were extensively involved in the liberation of Paris in 1944 operational vehicles.

manner of weapons were hung upon the basic halftrack chassis at one time or another but among those that were used in action were 57-mm anti-tank guns, 75-mm field guns and even 105-mm howitzers. Anti-aircraft versions carried varying multiples of 0.5-in (12.7-mm) machine-guns, 20-mm cannon and 40-mm Bofors guns. Combat engineer equipment was another

An early shot of the M2 halftrack, taken when the US Army was still using World War I helmets and equipment. This vehicle still has the original centre-mounted machine gun mount for a 0.3-in (7.62-mm) Browning machine-gun, and lacks the side racks for anti-tank mines that were often fitted to operational vehicles.

widely carried load (each model had racks for anti-tank mines).

However, it was the personnel carriers that were the most widely used, and in several versions. The early M2 was supplemented by the later **Half-Track Personnel Carrier M3**

Variants of the M3 carried all manner of weapons. Based on the M3A1, the M15A1 was an anti-aircraft vehicle, mounting a 37-mm M1A2 AA gun and two coaxially mounted 0.5-in machine-guns, with an M5 sighting system. However, the M16 variant, carrying four M2 'fifties', was more common.

which could also be used as a communications vehicle, an artillery tow vehicle and as an armoured ambulance. The even later halftrack **Half-Track Personnel Carrier M5** differed in production methods and there was also a **Half-Track Car M9**. Seating varied between models from 10 to 13, and there were various dispositions of machine-gun mountings. The usual arrangement was a 0.5-in Browning at the front on a large ring mounting and a 0.3-in (7.62-mm) Browning on a pintle at the rear. To this could be added the weapons of the carried troops, and the picture of halftracks firing away as they went into action is complete. It now seems impossible to visualise troops operating in Europe in 1944 and 1945 without halftracks somewhere in the picture, for the Americans issued halftracks of all kinds to their Allies, including the British who started to use American halftracks even before the fighting in North Africa ended. It should not be forgotten that during World War II one of the halftrack-user nations was the Soviet Union, for large numbers were shipped there from 1942 onwards.

Extended service

After the war the halftrack story did not end. The US Army

deployed halftracks during the war in Korea and several were also used by the Israeli Defence Force as a mechanised troop carriers and combat engineer and recovery vehicles.

However, apart from these exceptions the halftrack did not survive the end of World War II as it was not considered to be as reliable as wheeled vehicles, and lacked the cross-country mobility of the tank. The functions of the halftrack were eventually taken over by wheels and tracks.

Above: M3 series halftracks had no floor armour, making the passengers extremely vulnerable to mines laid on roads. The poor armour protection of the M3 led to troops who had to ride in them calling them 'Purple Heart Boxes'. Note the front-mounted anti-ditching roller for cross-country operations.

Below: The M3 halftrack was developed as a support carrier for the US Army's motorised units, but it proved so versatile that it became one of the workhorses of the US Army, often functioning in extreme conditions in a variety of roles.

SPECIFICATION	
M3	**Performance:** maximum road speed
Crew: 13	64.4 km/h (40 mph), range 282 km
Weight: 9,299 kg (20,500 lb)	(175 miles)
Powerplant: one White 160AX	**Gradient:** 31°
6-cylinder petrol engine developing	**Fording:** 0.81 m (32 in)
110 kW (147 hp)	**Armament:** one 0.5-in (12.7-mm)
Dimensions: length 6.18 m (20 ft 3½	machine-gun and one 0.3-in
in), width 2.22 m (7 ft 3½ in);	(7.62-mm) machine-gun
height 2.6 m (7 ft 5 in)	

M5 and M9 series Halftrack vehicles

The French had developed half-track vehicles in the 1920s, notably the Somua MCG and Unic P 107, and these were used to support French operations in the deserts of North Africa, and in 1931 the US Army bought a Citroën-Kègresse P 107 vehicle from France. The German SdKfz 251 was also a significant influence on US thinking, however, since it was the world's first mass-production halftrack armoured personnel carrier (APC) to enter service, being manufactured to the extent of some 16,000 examples by the end of World War II.

Cross-country

The M2 and M3 halftracks were the truck and APC models developed in the 1930s by the

Passing battle damage strewn by the side of a dusty desert road, US Army halftracks advance with embarked troops and equipment-filled trailers.

US. The attraction of the halftrack was its combination of conventional front-wheel steering (removing the need for special driver training) with the transmission of tractive power to the ground by rear tracks (providing much enhanced cross-country performance).

Below: A US Army halftrack converted into a motor carriage by the installation of a medium-calibre gun in the troop compartment disembarks from a landing craft during Operation Overlord in June 1944.

The US Department of War initially standardised two basic types of halftrack as the 1937 Truck, Half-Track, M2 intended to tow a 105-mm (4.13-in) howitzer and carry the crew and ammunition, and the 1938 Scout Car M3. These were combined in 1939 to create the Car, HalfTrack, M2 that was designed to carry a 10-man infantry squad. Later in the same year an armoured development appeared as the 13-man Carrier, Personnel, Half-Track, M3 with a longer, protected body. The M3A1 was distinguished by a ring mount for the 0.5-in (12.7-mm) Browning M2 machine-gun used in the AA and local-defence role. Some 41,170 halftracks were built during the war by the Autocar, Diamond T and White companies later joined by

International Harvester. Like the SdKfz 251, the US half-track had been conceived as a fast reconnaissance vehicle offering good cross-country performance as well as protection against small arms fire and shell fragments, but it became a very versatile vehicle generally used as a utility vehicle along the lines of a smaller British machine, the Universal Carrier. However, unlike this fully tracked vehicle, widely known as the Bren Gun Carrier, the M2 and M3 were large enough to be modified for a wider variety of roles.

As well as the M2 and M3, generally used in the gun tractor and APC roles respectively, the US half-track series was built in dozens of specialist versions, including tank destroyers, self-propelled howitzers and

Left: Driving into Europe after the Allies' D-Day invasion, the M2 and M9 played a vital role in the towing of artillery and carriage of anti-tank weapons.

SPECIFICATION	
Carrier, Half-track, M3	**Performance:** maximum road speed
Crew: 13	72 km/h (45 mph); maximum range
Weight: 9477 kg (20,893 lb)	322 km (200 miles)
Dimensions: length 6.34 m (20 ft 9½ in); width 2.22 m (7 ft 3½ in); height 2.26 m (7 ft 5 in)	**Fording:** 0.82 m (2 ft 8 in)
	Vertical obstacle: 0.3 m (1 ft)
Powerplant: one White Model 160AX 6-cylinder petrol engine developing 110 kW (147 hp)	**Armament:** one 0.5-in (12.7-mm) and two 0.3-in (7.62-mm) machine guns
	Armour: 13 mm (0.512 in)

Above: Driving through typically dusty hot-climate conditions, these M3 halftracks have their troops' kit fastened on to the rear of the vehicles.

Left: This M2 has a trio of bows over the rear compartment to allow a tarpaulin cover to be fitted, a practice typical of a host of field modifications.

right around the tracks. Special 'overall chains' were also developed to convert 6x6 trucks into extemporised 'halftracks'. Some 4,296 of these vehicles were supplied to the UK from 1943, and the USSR received 421 M5 and 413 M9 halftracks, and the Red Army was an enthusiastic operator of the M17.

Common body

Work began in April 1943 to rationalise halftrack design and produce a 'universal' vehicle with common body features for either the gun tractor/mortar carrier role or the personnel carrier role. This led to the M3A2 and **M5A2** types. Standardisation of these revised designs took place in October 1943. By now US Army interest in the halftrack was beginning to wane, and the manufacture of this type of vehicle was tailed off from mid-1944, though halftracks remained in service with the US Army until the end of World War II.

The series enjoyed an extended life with the Israeli army as the **Zahal**, which has been used as a conventional APC and also to mount 120-mm (4.72-in) mortars, anti-tank guns, and French-supplied SS.11 wire-guided anti-tank missiles. The Zahal featured prominently in the 1967 'Six-Day War'.

Given that so many of these US vehicles were transferred to the USSR in World War II, it is believed that several of the halftrack models served in the Soviet forces during the later 1940s and with the Warsaw Pact countries in the 1950s.

anti-aircraft gun platforms. For example, the T19 developed at the Aberdeen Proving Ground in 1941 mounted a 105-mm howitzer and, though it was not a success, it has the distinction of having been the first SP gun adopted by the US Army. However, the Carriage, Motor, Multiple Gun, M13 and M16 (M14 and M17 when based on the M5 chassis) with a mount carrying two or four 0.5-in

Browning machine guns respectively proved very effective in the AA role.

The **M5** and **M9** were externally identical to the M3 and M2 respectively except that they were built by the International Harvester Company and powered by their own 7.39≠litre Model RED 450B 'Red Diamond' engine, rather than the otherwise standard 6.32-litre White Model 160AX

engine, driving either the rear axle or both axles by means of a gearbox (four forward and one reverse gears) and two-speed transfer box. The types were fitted with semi-elliptical leaf springs on the front wheels and vertical volute springs on the rear tracks. The body was of homogeneous plate instead of the face-hardened plate used in the M2 and M3 series. Detail differences included flat-section mudguards, a welded hull, rounded rear corners and a banjo-type front axle. To improve cross-country performance, US Army halftracks could be fitted with special track chains, simply versions of ordinary single-tyre snow chains long enough to fit

Below: Big vehicles in little Europe as cobbled streets shudder to the sound of this US M3 halftrack under the gaze of local residents.

Below right: All of the halftracks could be adapted to carry a range of weaponry. A Browning machine-gun can be clearly seen on the 'pulpit' mount of this vehicle.

The Cold War

After 1945, most armies were equipped with tanks and fighting vehicles built or designed during the war. These were much larger and more powerfully armed than the tanks of 1939, but they still fell into the three main categories of light, medium and heavy tank. Light tanks and armoured cars still had a valuable role on the battlefield, primarily for reconnaissance and escort duties.

Heavy tanks, on the other hand, remained painfully slow. Medium tanks became the all purpose weapons of future armoured warfare. Large enough to carry the same guns as the heavy tanks, but with the mobility of much lighter vehicles, they became known as Main Battle Tanks. They were joined on the battlefield by a new breed of armoured vehicle, the Armoured Personnel Carrier. Built in both tracked and wheeled versions, these enabled the infantry to keep up with armour and protected them from small arms fire and shell splinters.

Left: A large proportion of Soviet armoured strength in the 1950s and 1960s was provided by the T-54 and T-55 series of MBTs. Some estimates of the T-54/55's sixteen-year production run places the total built at well over 100,000 vehicles, making it far and away the most widely produced and used tank in history.

T-10 Heavy tank

During the later stages of World War II the USSR developed the IS series of excellently protected heavy tanks armed with a very potent 122-mm (4.8-in) gun firing separate-loading ammunition. After the war this basic type saw service in the Middle East with Egypt, and some captured by Israel in the Six-Day War of 1967 were then used for static defence on the Suez Canal against their former operators.

Prototypes

In the immediate post-war period the USSR continued its development of heavy tanks, and prototype vehicles included the IS-5 to **IS-9**. The last was accepted for service as the **T-10**, an improved model being the **T-10A**, with two-axis gun stabilisation. The following **T-10B** version introduced in 1957 had improved sighting and gun stabilisation. It is believed that at least 2,500 tanks of all

A T-10 heavy tank showing the 12.7-mm DShKM anti-aircraft machine-gun on the commander's cupola. Developed from 1948, the first prototypes of the T-10 (initially IS-10) appeared in 1955. Although manufacture ended in 1966, the last examples of the T-10 were not retired from the reserve until 1996.

models were built before production was completed in the late 1950s. The T-10 was never exported. The main role of the T-10 was the provision of long-range fire support for the T-54/55 tanks armed with a 100-mm (3.94-in) gun, and also perhaps to act as the spearhead of any armoured thrust through areas with a high degree of anti-tank defences, where the T-10's heavy armour protection would have proved useful.

The T-10's hull was of rolled steel armour varying in thickness between 20 and 230 mm (0.79 to 9.06 in). The turret

The T-10M heavy tank had the original 12.7-mm machine-guns replaced by 14.5-mm KPVs, and had a multi-baffle muzzle brake for the 122-mm gun, infra-red night vision equipment for the commander, gunner and driver, and an overpressure system.

was a cast unit varying in thickness between 25 and 250 mm (1 and 9.84 in), the latter figure applying specifically to the mantlet. The driver was seated at the front of the hull with the other three crew members in the turret: the commander and gunner on the left, and the loader on the right. The powerplant was located at the rear of the hull.

Main armament

Comprising a D-25TA 122-mm gun with a double-baffle muzzle brake and a bore evacuator, the main armament fired separate-loading ammunition of the APC-T, HEAT and HE fragmentation types: the APC-T type was the primary anti-tank round, and was capable of penetrating 185 mm (7.28 in) of armour at 1000 m (1,095 yards). Separate-loading ammunition had to be used as otherwise the complete round would have been too heavy and difficult for handling in the cramped confines of the turret, and 30 122-mm rounds were carried. A 12.7-mm (0.5-in)

DShKM machine-gun was mounted co-axial with the main armament, and a similar weapon was mounted on the loader's cupola for anti-aircraft defence.

Alterations

The later **T-10M** was characterised by the following recognisable alterations: the 12.7-mm DShKM machine-guns were replaced by weapons of the more powerful 14.5-mm (0.57-in) KPV series also used in a number of other Soviet AFVs including the BRDM-2 4x4 wheeled reconnaissance vehicle and the BTR-60PB 8x8 wheeled armoured personnel carrier; the new M-62-T2 122-mm gun was fitted with a multi-baffle muzzle brake in place of the double-baffle muzzle brake; the main armament was stabilised in both the horizontal and vertical planes; IR night vision and an overpressure NBC system were installed; and finally a large sheet-metal stowage box was often mounted externally at the turret rear.

SPECIFICATION	
T-10	**Powerplant:** one V-12 diesel developing 522 kW (700 hp)
Crew: 4	**Performance:** maximum road speed 42 km/h (26 mph); maximum road range 250 km (155 miles)
Weight: 50 tonnes	
Dimensions: length (including gun) 9.88 m (32 ft 4¾ in); length (hull) 7.04 m (23 ft 1 in); width 3.57 m (11 ft 8½ in); height 2.25 m (7 ft 4½ in)	**Gradient:** 62 per cent
	Vertical obstacle: 0.9 m (2 ft 11½ in)
	Trench: 3 m (9 ft 10 in)
Armament: one 122-mm (4.8-in) main gun, and two 12.7-mm (0.5-in) DShKM machine-guns	

T-54 Main battle tank

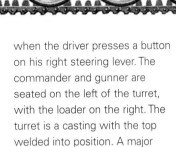

The T-54 tank was developed in the late 1940s and was probably produced in greater numbers than any other Soviet tank in the postwar period. It has seen combat in countless campaigns since World War II, especially in the Middle East, where it has been used by the Arab states against Israel.

In 1946 prototypes of the new **T-54** design were completed, and this type entered production several years later. The T-54 and its variants were built in larger numbers than any other Soviet and/or Russian tank to appear after World War II, and by the time production of the improved T-55 was completed in 1980–81 it is estimated that production amounted to well over 50,000 vehicles, of which large numbers are still in service. The series

was also built in Czechoslovakia and Poland for the home and export markets, while the Chinese produced an almost identical Type 59 version.

The T-54 has an all-welded hull divided into forward driving, central fighting and rear power-plant compartments. The driver is seated at the front of the hull, and an unusual feature of the T-54 is its 7.62-mm (0.3-in) machine-gun fixed in the centre of the glacis plate to fire forward

when the driver presses a button on his right steering lever. The commander and gunner are seated on the left of the turret, with the loader on the right. The turret is a casting with the top welded into position. A major

weakness of the T-54 has been its engine and transmission, which have proved unreliable.

D-10 main gun

The main armament is a 100-mm (3.94-in) D-10 rifled gun, and a

*A **C**hinese T-54 with turret traversed to the rear, and the loader manning the 12.7-mm DShKM anti-aircraft machine-gun. The tank can also lay its own smoke screen by injecting diesel fuel into the exhaust outlet.*

SPECIFICATION	
T-54	(0.5-in) machine-gun
Crew: 4	**Powerplant:** V-12 diesel developing
Weight: 36 tonnes	388 kW (520 hp)
Dimensions: length (with gun	**Performance:** maximum road speed
forward) 9 m (29 ft 6½ in); length	48 km/h (30 mph); maximum range
(hull) 6.45 m (21 ft 2 in); width	400 km (249 miles)
3.27 m (10 ft 8¾ in); height (turret	**Fording:** 1.4 m (4 ft 7 in)
roof) 2.4 m (7 ft 10½ in)	**Gradient:** 60 per cent
Armament: one 100-mm (3.94-in) D-	**Vertical obstacle:** 0.8 m (2 ft 7½ in)
10 main gun, two 7.62-mm (0.3-in)	**Trench:** 2.7 m (8 ft 10¼ in)
machine-guns, and one 12.7-mm	

well-trained crew can fire about four rounds per minute: 34 rounds are carried, and the ammunition types are AP-T, APC-T, HE, HE-FRAG, HEAT-FS and HVAPDS-T. The last was introduced some time after the T-54 entered production and will penetrate well over 200 mm (7.9 in) of armour at 1000 m (1,095 yards). One of the T-54's major drawbacks is that the main gun can be depressed to only -5°, which makes the adoption of a hull-down firing position almost impossible. The secondary armament is a 7.62-mm (0.3-in) SGMT co-axial machine-gun, a

similar weapon in the bow, and a 12.7-mm (0.5-in) DShKM anti-aircraft machine-gun on the loader's hatch. The tank does not have smoke dischargers as it can lay its own smoke screen by injecting diesel fuel into the exhaust on the left side of the hull just above the track.

The later **T-54A** added stabilisation of the 100-mm gun in the vertical plane. The **T-54B** was the first production model to incorporate IR night vision equipment and two-axis stabilisation for the main gun. The **T-54C** was not fitted with the AA machine-gun although

such a weapon was later retrofitted. There has been a very large number of T-54 series variants, these including a flamethrower tank, armoured recovery vehicles (including Soviet, Polish and Czech versions), bridgelayers (built by Czechoslovakia, East Germany and the USSR), dozer tanks, a combat engineer vehicle fitted with a hydraulic crane and front-mounted dozer blade, and mineclearing vehicles fitted with rollers, ploughs and rocket-assisted devices, to name but a few. In recent years surviving tanks have been taken in hand

for a number of upgrade programmes including the installation of improved fire-control systems, including an externally mounted laser rangefinder.

The T-54 has seen extensive combat in the Middle East, North Africa, Angola and the Far East. On a one-for-one basis Western tanks of the same period, such as the British Centurion and American M48, have proved more than a match for the T-54, especially during the fighting between Israel and its Arab neighbours, Egypt and Syria.

T-55 Main battle tank

The T-54 inevitably underwent a number of improvements including an NBC system and a deep-wading snorkel. Later examples introduced what became the standard turret without a bulged rear, and the right-hand cupola had a 12.7-mm (0.5-in) machine-gun. Most of the tanks were later improved to T-54(M) standard with IR driving equipment. The T-54A introduced improved main armament in the form of the D-10TG gun with a bore evacuator, stabilisation in the vertical plane and powered elevation; when retrofitted with IR driving lights it is designated as the T-54A(M). In 1957 the Soviets introduced the T-54B and, apart from being the first model produced with IR night-vision devices as standard, it has the D-10T2S main gun with two-axis stabilisation. Variously described as the T-54C or T-54X, the next model is identical with the T-54B except that the gunner's cupola is replaced by a plain forward-opening hatch.

Revised T-54

These collective modifications

Production of the T-55 at the Omsk plant is believed to have continued until 1980–81, long after production of the far more capable T-62 had ceased. With the downsizing of East European armies in the wake of post-Cold War treaties, large numbers of T-55s have been exported in recent years.

resulted in a basically similar tank with the revised designation **T-55**, which was introduced in the late 1950s with standard features such as no loader's cupola with its 12.7-mm AA machine-gun, no turret dome ventilator, a 432-kW (580-hp) V-55 diesel engine with 960 rather than 812 litres (211 rather than 179 Imp gal) of internal fuel for a range of 500 rather than 400 km (311 rather than 249 miles), and 37 rounds of ammunition for the D-10T2S gun. The 12.7-mm has been re-installed on some tanks which are then designated **T-55(M)**. Seen for the first time in 1963, the **T-55A** is the final production version, and is similar

to the T-55 apart from having a 7.62-mm (0.3-in) PKT co-axial machine-gun in place of the original SGMT, no nose machine-gun to allow an increase in main ammunition stowage to 43 rounds, and a number of detail improvements such as an

anti-radiation lining. When fitted with the AA machine-gun this model is the **T-55A(M)**. The T-55 is still in widespread service in a number of upgraded forms, and is also the basis of numerous special-purpose variants.

SPECIFICATION	
T-55	**Performance:** maximum road speed
Crew: 4	50 km/h (31 mph); maximum road
Weight: 36 tonnes	range 500 km (311 miles) on
Dimensions: length (with gun	internal fuel and 600 km
forward) 9 m (29 ft 6 in); length	(373 miles) with external fuel
(hull) 6.45 m (21 ft 2 in); width	**Fording:** 1.4 m (4 ft 7 in) without
3.27 m (10 ft 8 in); height (to turret	preparation and 4.55 m (14 ft 11 in)
top) 2.4 m (7 ft 10 in)	with snorkel
Armament: one 100-mm (3.94-in) D-	**Gradient:** 58 per cent
10T2S main gun, one 7.62-mm	**Vertical obstacle:** 0.8 m (2 ft 6 in)
(0.3-in) co-axial machine-gun	**Trench:** 2.7 m (8 ft 10 in)
Powerplant: one V-55 V-12 diesel	
developing 432 kW (580 hp)	

T-54/55 in operation

The poor man's main battle tank

The T-54/55 series of main battle tanks has seen more combat than any other post-war tank. They rumbled into Prague in 1968 to extinguish Czech hopes of freedom, and they crashed through the gates of the Presidential Palace in Saigon in 1975.

The T-54/55 series has fought in most major African and Asian wars since the 1960s, and is still operated in large numbers by Soviet-supplied forces around the world. Although the first production T-54 tanks were manufactured in the USSR as long ago as 1947 (the new type was first identified by Western sources in 1949), various manufacturers have since offered conversions to modernise these veteran fighting vehicles.

The T-54/55 series includes a bewildering number of different models. The original T-54 production tank was soon altered, and many modifications introduced by subsequent versions were applied retrospectively. Therefore it can be difficult to identify the various models.

Early model T-54s were very basic, World War II-style medium tanks, with a very powerful armament for their time. The low turret offered a small silhouette to the enemy

*Festooned with soldiers as a proxy personnel carrier, a **T-55** of the Soviet Naval Infantry rumbles up a beach during exercises in the Baltic. Carrying troops in this manner was a tactic widely employed by the Soviets in World War II.*

(the T-54/55 is around 1 m/3.28 ft lower than the M60), but only by cramming the commander, gunner and loader into an incredibly small space. The gunner and commander are together on the left of the gun while the loader sits to its right.

D-10T main gun

The T-54/55's main armament was originally the D-10T 100-mm (3.9-in) rifled gun, a mighty piece for its time but long since rendered inadequate for modern warfare. The basic AP ammunition types for the

D-10T lack the penetration to destroy the latest generation of armour except at very close range, and the HEAT round is equally ineffective by modern standards. Against M48s, Leopard 1s and other lightly protected AFVs the gun would be effective, but the time needed to reload the weapon would cost the T-54/55 dearly in action against most modern tanks with a competent crew.

The engines on Soviet-built T-54/55s were often so badly made that they self-destructed. Oil lines were easily blocked by a mass of loose metal filings and the engine could overheat and catch fire. Made of magnesium alloy, the engine burnt well and the whole tank could easily be destroyed by a direct hit. Some Warsaw Pact armies thus took the precaution

of rebuilding the engines in the T-54/55 tanks they had bought, or, better still, manufactured the engines themselves.

The T-54 was succeeded by the T-54A and T-54B, these adding marginal improvements. The main gun received a bore-evacuator, power elevation and vertical stabilisation (T-54A variant). Other changes included infra-red night-vision equipment (T-54B), deep-fording equipment, automatic fire-extinguishers and an air filter. In addition, early production T-54s and later models had numerous detail differences, with some having a wider mantlet and turret undercut at the rear.

Introduced in 1958, the T-55 has a more powerful engine offering increased range, improved transmission, a revised turret and nine more

East German T-54 training tanks in operation. Like many Warsaw Pact forces, the East German army continued to rely on the T-54/55 rather than convert entirely to the T-62. By 1989 the first-line units were equipped with T-72s, but T-54/55s still equipped second-line and training formations.

The Israeli army captured large numbers of T-54/55s in 1967 when the Egyptian advance into the Sinai desert was defeated. Many T-54/55s had broken down and had been abandoned after the Israelis overran Arab positions. Israel pressed these captured vehicles into service during the 1973 Yom Kippur War. That conflict netted another large haul of T-54/55s which were also modified for use against their former owners. Israel extensively improved the tanks by replacing the obsolete 100-mm gun with the L7 105-mm weapon widely used within NATO, a modern fire-control system, new night-vision aids and US-supplied machine-guns. Air conditioning was also installed, a vital feature for desert operations. The Israeli T-55 tank pictured is armed with the 105-mm rifled gun and has modifications for desert warfare.

rounds of ammunition. In the early 1960s production switched to the T-55A, featuring an anti-radiation lining and NBC protection system. Many modifications were retrofitted to earlier tanks, some of the more significant improvements being a laser rangefinder, AT-10 'Stabber' ATGM gun-launcher and an active protection system.

Despite various improvements, the basic T-54/55 remains a crude and simple combat vehicle, although offering excellent long-range capability. At the beginning of the 21st century the T-54/55 remains in widespread service. One possible reason for this is that its intended replacement, the T-62, failed to live up to

One of the more unusual T-55 variants offered by Western companies for export was this T-55 chassis fitted with Marksman twin 35-mm anti-aircraft guns and radar.

expectation: it was estimated that the T-62 cost about three times the price of a T-54/55 but it did not provide good value. Its armour protection is very similar, and its weight and battlefield mobility are also little different. The most significant change on the T-62 was the adoption of a 115-mm (4.53-in) smoothbore gun which, although capable of destroying tanks at longer ranges, probably did not offer a wide enough margin to satisfy its critics. For these reasons the USSR continued to build T-55s until 1981.

China copied the T-54/55, producing one of the least well regarded tanks since 1945. Designated the T-59, it incorporated few of the improvements added to the T-54/55 in Warsaw Pact service. The gun of the T-59 is not stabilised, so firing on the move

is simply wasting ammunition; the choice of ammunition is more limited, and this is as badly manufactured as the rest of the tank.

In recent years Israel has offered modernised T-54/55s for export. These tanks bear little relation to the poorly made and badly maintained specimens acquired from the Arab forces during their years of conflict with Israel. Powered by American General Motors engines with completely new transmissions, these Israeli upgrades have a comprehensively revised driver's

station with a steering wheel instead of sticks and an improved suspension system.

Royal Ordnance also developed a T-54/55 upgrade kit which replaced the 100-mm gun with a British 105-mm (4.13-in) weapon. This was aimed at countries that needed to modernise their tank fleets at low cost. The T54/55 remains one of the world's most numerous tanks. Some of the users include many former Soviet and Warsaw Pact nations. However, the T-54/55's stronghold remains in the Middle East and Africa.

An Iraqi T-55 booby-trapped by its crew before coalition forces overran the position during Desert Storm in 1991. At the beginning of the war over half of Iraq's 5,500 tanks were T-55s or Chinese-built T-59s.

Conqueror Heavy tank

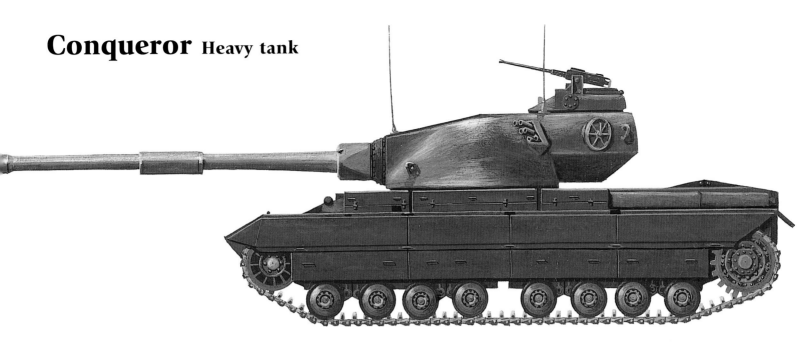

This Conqueror heavy tank clearly shows its 120-mm gun that fired separate loading ammunition, and the commander's cupola, which was fitted with a rangefinder and a 7.62-mm (0.3-in) anti-aircraft machine-gun.

In 1944 authorisation was given to commence the **A45** heavy tank project as the replacement for the A43 Black Prince, which itself was based on the Churchill infantry support tank. The **A45** was intended to work with the A41 Centurion tank and shared a number of common components.

Universal tank family

In 1946 however, it was decided to develop a whole new range of armoured vehicles including the **FV200 Universal Tank** family, and in addition to the **FV201** basic gun tank, a number of specialised vehicles were proposed, including an AVRE, mine-clearing vehicle of the flail type, bridgelayer, ARV, assault personnel carrier, and a number of specialised vehicles for the Royal Artillery. The FV200 series was based on the A45 but had a longer hull, and the first prototype was completed in 1948. It was soon realised that many of the proposed variants were not feasible: the bridgelayer, for example, would be too large for the Royal Navy's standard tank landing craft. A decision was therefore taken to continue development of the Centurion as a gun tank and as the basis for a complete family of specialised vehicles. The Centurion family became

the most successful British tank of the immediate post-war period.

There was, however, a requirement for a heavy gun tank, the **FV214**, and the FV201 was used as the basis for this vehicle. To provide some experience with a tank of this size, a chassis was fitted with the complete turret of the Centurion Mk 3 tank and called the **FV221 Medium Gun Tank Caernarvon**.

Just under 200 **FV214 Conqueror** tanks were built between 1955 and 1958, the majority of these being deployed to the British Army of the Rhine, where they were issued to some of the armoured regiments on the basis of a troop of three vehicles per regiment, or one Conqueror per Centurion squadron. The only advantage of the Conqueror over the Centurion with the 20-pounder gun, was the former's much thicker armour protection and the longer range of its main armament.

Its major disadvantages were that it was too large, too heavy and was difficult to maintain. The Conquerors were all withdrawn in the mid-1960s with the arrival of the Centurion

with the 105-mm gun, and most ended up on ranges as hard targets, although one or two have been preserved.

In all there were over 30 projected models on the FV200 chassis, but the only model to see service apart from the Conqueror tank was the **FV219 ARV Mk 1**. One of the more interesting projects was the **FV215b** heavy self-propelled anti-tank gun which had the engine moved forward to enable a limited-traverse turret (armed with a 180-mm gun) to be mounted at the rear.

Conventional layout

The layout of the Conqueror was conventional, with the driver at the front on the right and ammunition to his left; turret and fighting compartment in the centre, and engine and transmission at the rear. The commander was provided with his own cupola in the

centre of the turret at the rear, with the gunner forward to the right and loader to the left.

Main armament comprised a 120-mm rifled gun with an elevation of +15° and a depression of -7° in a turret capable of traversing through 360°. A weapon stabilisation system was installed, this being similar to that of the Centurion. A total of 35 rounds of APDS or HESH ammunition was carried, this being of the separate loading type. An unusual feature of the Conqueror was the cartridge case election system: this ejected the spent brass cartridge case out through a trap door on the right side of the turret. A 0.3-in (7.62-mm) machine-gun was mounted co-axially with the main armament, and a similar machine-gun was mounted on the commander's cupola for anti-aircraft defence.

SPECIFICATION	
Conqueror **Crew:** 4 **Weight:** 65 tonnes **Dimensions:** length (gun forwards) 11.58 m (38 ft); length (hull) 7.72 m (25 ft 4 in); width 3.99 m (13 ft 1 in); height 3.35 m (11 ft)	**Powerplant:** one 12-cylinder petrol engine developing 604 kW (810 bhp) **Performance:** maximum road speed 34 km/h (21.3 mph); maximum road range 155 km (95 miles) **Gradient:** 60 per cent **Vertical obstacle:** 0.91 m (36 m) **Trench:** 3.35 m (11 ft)

Vickers MBT

Vickers' Elswick facility built many of the 4,423 Centurion MBTs manufactured by 1961, but the company realised that for some operators the Centurion's successor, the Chieftain, would be too heavy and too expensive. At about that time, the Indian army issued a requirement for a new MBT, and in 1961 a Vickers proposal was accepted.

This was based on the company's private venture design which had become known as the **Vickers Main Battle Tank**. This used the proven 105-mm L7 series gun as well as some of the components from the Chieftain MBT, which was then about to enter production at both Royal Ordnance Factory in Leeds and Vickers' Elswick facility. This included the 0.5-in (12.7-mm) ranging machine-gun, Leyland L60 engine, TN12 transmission, brakes and steering.

Indian production

The first two prototypes were completed in 1963 and by the following year a production line had been established at the Avandi Company, Madras, India. Renamed **Vijayanta** (Victorious), the first tank was completed in 1965 from components supplied by Vickers. Over 2,200 Vijayantas were produced.

In 1968, Kuwait ordered 70 **Vickers MBT Mk 1** tanks which were delivered between 1970 and 1972. Vickers continued development of the tank with its own funds, the first stage being the replacement of the L60 engine with a Detroit Diesel 537-kW (720-bhp) engine, followed by a new all-cast turret with a welded bustle which could be fitted with different types of fire-control system.

African orders

In 1977 Kenya ordered 38 **Vickers MBT Mk 3** MBTs plus three **Vickers ARV** armoured recovery vehicles; these were delivered by 1980, and a second order was placed in 1978 for a further 38 MBTs plus four ARVs, all these being delivered by late 1982.

In 1981 Nigeria ordered 36 MBTs plus five ARVs and six **Vickers VAB** bridge-layers. In 1990, Vickers received another order from Nigeria; completing deliveries in 1991. These tanks were built at Vickers Defence Systems Armstrong Works, which opened in late 1982. The famous Elswick works, which produced armoured fighting vehicles and artillery pieces for some 100 prestigious years, has since been closed down and demolished.

This Vickers MBT Mk 3 belongs to the Kenyan army, which took delivery of 76 tanks, plus seven armoured recovery vehicles between 1979 and 1982. The Mk 3 is powered by the Detroit Diesel engine.

Mk 3 turret

The Mk 3 is also armed with the 105-mm gun mounted in a turret which can be traversed through 360° and provides the gun with an elevation of +20° and depression of -10°. The gun can fire the full range of ammunition including armour piercing discarding sabot shells, along with traditional high-explosive rounds. A 0.3-in (7.62-mm) machine-gun is mounted co-axially with the main armament and a similar weapon is mounted on the commander's cupola. The latter can be aimed and fired from within the turret and can be elevated to +90°. A bank of six electrically-operated smoke dischargers is mounted on each side of the turret.

The Nigerian tanks are fitted with the Marconi Radar SFCS-600 (Simplified Fire Control System) which gives a high probability of a first-round hit. This system was fitted to some of the Indian MBT Mk 1s. The commander has a Pilkington PE Condor day/night sight enabling him to lay and fire the main gun.

As usual a whole range of optional equipment can be fitted

to the Vickers MBT Mk 3 according to requirements. This includes a computerised fire-control system, laser-range finder, Nuclear-Biological-Chemical protection, deep wading/flotation system, fire extinguishing system, and explosive-reactive armour.

The **Vickers Armoured Bridgelaying Vehicle** (**VABV**) is fitted with a bridge 44 ft (13.41 m) long, which is launched hydraulically over the front of the vehicle. The **Vickers Armoured Repair and Recovery Vehicle** (**ARRV**) is provided with a front mounted dozer/stabilising blade and a winch with a maximum capacity of 25 tonnes, which can be increased to 65 tonnes if required. Some vehicles have a hydraulic crane to enable them to change powerpacks (engine and transmission) in the field.

Vickers Shipbuilding and Engineering Ltd also produced a self-propelled gun variant. The MBT Mk 3 can be fitted with a with a 155-mm howitzer which fires HE rounds to a range of 24000 m (26,250 yards), or 30000 m (32,800 yards) with a rocket-assisted projectile (RAP).

Vickers MBT Mk 1 with its turret traversed to the right and firing its 105-mm L7 rifled gun during a demonstration at the Royal Armoured Corps gunnery range at Lulworth. The Mk 1 is in service with Kuwait and India, the Indian vehicles having been upgraded with the Detroit Diesel engine and new armour.

SPECIFICATION	
Vickers MBT	width 3.17 m (10 ft 4¾ in); height
Crew: 4	(overall) 3.10 m (10 ft 2 in)
Weight: 38.7 tonnes	**Performance:** maximum road speed
Engine: 12-cylinder Detroit Diesel	31 mph (50 km/h); range 600 km
diesel developing 537 kW (720	(375 miles)
bhp)	**Gradient:** 60 per cent
Dimensions: length (with gun	**Vertical obstacle:** 0.91 m (3 ft)
forward) 9.79 m (32 ft 1¾ in);	**Trench:** 2.44 m (8 ft)
length (hull) 7.56 m (24 ft 9¾ in);	

Centurion MBT

The **Centurion** was developed during World War II as a cruiser tank under the designation **A41**, the first prototypes armed with a 17-pounder, (76.2-mm/3-in) gun being completed early in 1945. The A41 was subsequently renamed Centurion and entered production shortly after the end of the war. By the time production was completed in 1962, some 4,423 examples had been completed at the Royal Ordnance Factories at Leeds and Woolwich (early vehicles only), Leyland Motors at Leyland and Vickers at Elswick.

Upgunned Centurions

The **Centurion Mk 1** and **Mk 2** were armed with the wartime 17-pdr gun, while the **Mk 3** carried a new 20-pounder (83.4-mm/ (3.28-in) weapon. A total of 13 basic marks of Centurion was fielded, some having up to three sub-variants. For example, the **Centurion Mk 10** was a **Mk 8** with more armour and a 105-mm L7 gun, the **Centurion Mk 10/2** was a Mk 10 with a ranging machine-gun.

All through its British army life the Centurion had the standard Rolls-Royce Meteor petrol engine, which was a development of the Merlin aero engine. The Centurion was replaced as a gun tank in the British army by the Chieftain, but the last Centurions, used as observation post vehicles by the Royal Artillery, were not phased out of service until the 1980s.

Exported vehicles

Many countries placed orders for the Centurion, including Denmark, Israel, Jordan, the Netherlands, Somalia, South Africa, Sweden and Switzerland. Many of these countries rebuilt the vehicle to extend its life well into the 1990s. For example, Israel replaced the petrol engine with a Teledyne Continental AVDS-1790-2A diesel coupled to an Allison CD-850-6 automatic transmission, giving the tank a maximum speed of 43 km/h (27 mph) and a cruising range twice that of the **Mk 5** hull on which the conversion was based. The Israeli Centurions, which when rebuilt were redesignated **Upgraded Centurion**, all had the 105-mm gun and carried additional ammunition.

Specialised variants

There have been many specialised versions, including a variety of self-propelled artillery variously carrying the 25-pounder, 5-in (127-mm) and 180-mm guns, and a 120-mm tank destroyer.

The last variants in service with the British army included the **Centurion Mk 2 ARV** (Armoured Recovery Vehicle) fitted with large spades at the hull rear and a winch with a capacity of 31 tonnes. The **Centurion/AVRE** (Assault Vehicle Royal Engineers) was fitted with a turret-mounted 165-mm demolition gun for the destruction of battlefield fortifications, and a dozer blade at the front of the hull. It could also carry a fascine (large bundle of wood) which were dropped into anti-tank ditches to enable following vehicles to cross, as well as tow a trailer carrying the ROF Giant Viper mine-clearance equipment.

The **Centurion BARV** (Beach Armoured Recovery Vehicle) served into the 1990s. The BARV was successfully used during the British landings in the Falklands. Other versions include the **Centurion AVLB** (Armoured Vehicle-launched Bridge) and target tanks, while the Israelis fitted a number of the vehicles with special dozer blades and roller-type mine-clearing equipment.

The reason why the Centurion battle tank has been such a successful design is that it has been able to accept more armour, larger guns, gun-stabilisation systems, advanced fire-control systems and laser rangefinders.

The Centurion, one of the most successful battle tanks in history, saw combat with the British Army in Korea, with the Australian army in Vietnam, with the Indian army against Pakistan and with the armies of Israel, Egypt and Jordan.

SPECIFICATION	
Centurion	3.39 m (11 ft 1½ in); height (without
Crew: 4	AA MG) 3.01 m (9 ft 10½ in)
Weight: 51.82 tonnes	**Performance:** maximum speed on
Engine: one Rolls-Royce Meteor Mk	the road 34.6 km/h (21.5 mph);
II V-12 petrol developing 485 kW	range 190 km (118 miles)
(650 bhp)	**Gradient:** 60 per cent
Dimensions: length (with guns	**Vertical obstacle:** 0.91 m (3 ft)
forward) 9.85 m (32 ft 4 in); length	**Trench:** 3.35 m (11 ft)
(hull) 7.82 m (25 ft 8 in); width	

Australian Centurions saw extensive combat in Vietnam, fighting a number of epic battles in the defence of firebases. Their 20-pdr main guns were lethal against the unprotected Viet Cong, especially when firing 'Beehive' anti-personnel rounds.

The Centurion saw intermittent active service in South West Africa. The South African Defence Forces operated a number of Centurions which they updated to take locally-produced 105-mm guns and new engines and transmissions. These modified vehicles are known as Olifants (elephants) and on occasion provided support for the deep penetration operations against SWAPO guerrillas in Angola. Late in 1996, South Africa maintained 224 Olifants, together with associated ARVs.

Centurion
In action

The Centurion tank arrived just too late to take part in any major operation before the end of World War II in Europe. A few did take part in some minor infantry support operations, allowing some valuable tactical evaluation experience to be gained. The Centurion had to wait over five years before going into real action. The Centurion first saw combat in Korea. On 14 November 1950, three squadrons of the King's Royal Irish Hussars landed their Centurion Mk 3s at Pusan as part of the United Nations response to the invasion of South Korea by North Korea. Since then the Centurion has seen its share of action, especially in the Middle East. It has always proved itself to be a sound and sturdy vehicle capable of taking all manner of punishment, not only from the enemy but from long hard use over difficult terrain. Despite its age, it is likely that the Centurion will remain in service for some years to come.

Above: This is a Centurion Mk 5 armoured bridgelayer of the British Army in travelling order. When required, the bridge could be swung forwards through 180° and laid in position.

The Centurion AVRE (Assault Vehicle Royal Engineers) was a specialised type fitted with a front-mounted dozer blade and a 165-mm (6.5-in) demolition gun for the destruction of pillboxes and field fortifications at short ranges.

Above: *Unlike the tanks of other armies, which have a highly regimented appearance, the armoured fighting vehicles of the Israeli army reflect to a greater extent the experience of their crews and the practical demands of operations in regions that are generally hot and dusty. Thus the exterior of this Centurion tank is littered with personal kit (some of it wrapped in plastic sheeting) and additional stowage boxes, and other tanks have been seen with extemporised efforts to improve the protection by the addition of sandbags and the like, and also additional machine-guns for local defence purposes in the urban operations that are the Israeli army's other main type of tactical fighting: this Centurion carries an additional 12.7-mm machine-gun over the main gun. The vehicle seen here in Beirut in summer 1982 is of the Sho't type created by the Israeli Ordnance Corps with a diesel-engined powerplant including an automatic transmission rather than the original type of British transmission with a triple dry-plate clutch and a gearbox with five forward and two reverse speeds. Also evident on the left-hand side of the tank's rear are a number of towing wires, the use of which allows the tank to pull other vehicles out of soft sand or mud, or itself to be towed in the event that it itself becomes bogged down or suffers a mechanical failure. The gun has a bore evacuator but appears not to have any thermal protection. Note the red air recognition flag on the turret rear.*

SPECIFICATION	
Olifant Mk 1A	**Sho't**
Crew: 4	**Crew:** 4
Weight: 56000 kg (123,457 lb)	**Weight:** 53500 kg (117,945 lb)
Dimensions: length 8.29 m (27 ft 2½ in); width 3.39 m (11 ft 1½ in); height 2.94 m (9 ft 7 in)	**Dimensions:** length (gun forwards) 7.55 m or 7.84 m (24 ft 9½ in or 25 ft 8½ in) depending on model; width 3.38 m (11 ft); height 2.94 m (9 ft 7 in)
Armament: one 105-mm (4.13-in) L7 main gun, one 7.62-mm (0.3-in) co-axial machine-gun, and one 7.62-mm anti-aircraft machine-gun; eight 81-mm (3.2-in) smoke grenade launchers	**Armament:** one 105-mm (4.13-in) L7 series main gun, one 7.62-mm (0.3-in) co-axial machine-gun, and two 7.62-mm anti-aircraft machine-guns
Powerplant: one V-12 diesel delivering 559 kW (750 hp)	**Powerplant:** one 559-kW (750-hp) AVDS-1790-2AC air-cooled diesel
Performance: maximum road speed 45 km/h (28 mph); maximum road range 500 km (311 miles)	**Performance:** maximum road speed 50 km/h (31 mph); maximum road range 500 km (311 miles)

Left: *The Centurion went to war with the Australian contingent that added its weight to the US and South Vietnamese forces fighting the North Vietnamese. The 1st Armoured Regiment, Royal Australian Armoured Corps, and various squadrons from this regiment served in Vietnam at different times. In Vietnam there was little enough in the line of armoured warfare to perform and their activities were largely confined to local support and escort operations, with their main guns being fired only infrequently. Centurions of the Royal Australian Armoured Corps armed with 20-pdr guns are seen in South Vietnam in the 1960s (left). In the background is a Centurion Mk 2 ARV, while overhead is a UH-1 Iroquois of the RAAF.*

M47 Medium tank

The M26 Pershing and the M46 were the standard US medium tanks when the Korean War broke out in 1950. The new T42 medium tank was being developed but was not yet ready for production, so the requirement for an interim medium tank for early production was met by the combination of a modified M26 chassis and the T42's turret, armed with a new 90-mm (3.54-in) gun. This created the **M47** tank, also known as the **Patton 1**, whose manufacture started almost immediately at the Detroit Tank Arsenal and the American Locomotive Company. Even so, the M47 did not see combat in Korea.

The hull and the turret of the M47 were of all-cast

construction, with the driver and bow machine gunner in the front of the hull, the commander, gunner and loader in the 360° traverse turret, and the engine and transmission in the rear of the hull. The main armament was a 90-mm rifled gun (elevation +19°/-5°). One 0.3-in (7.62-mm) co-axial machine-gun was mounted to the left of the main gun, and there was a similar weapon in the bow, although this was soon removed to make more volume for additional fuel and main-gun ammunition. A 0.5-in (12.7-mm) M2 heavy machine-gun was on the commander's cupola.

The M47 was one of the earlier members of a family of armoured vehicles stretching from the M26 Pershing tank through to the M60. Essentially a modified M26 chassis fitted with the turret developed for the T42 tank, the M47 was too late to see service in Korea. After more than 8,500 examples had been built, the M47 was replaced by the M48.

Variants

The M47 was replaced after only a few years by the M48, so there were few variants of the basic type. The **M102** was an engineer model with the 90-mm gun replaced by a short-barrel 105-mm (4.13-in) howitzer, a dozer blade at the front of the hull and jibs at front and rear. The **T66** flamethrower variant was developed but did not enter service.

In the 1950s the M47 was issued to many NATO countries under the Military Assistance Program (MAP), but at the beginning of the 21st century the type remained in service

only with Portugal. Other recipients were Austria, Brazil, Iran, Jordan, Pakistan, Saudi Arabia, South Korea, Taiwan and Yugoslavia. Several countries, including Austria, France, Italy and Spain, at various times remanufactured their M47s to more modern standards: in Italy, for example, OTO Melara rebuilt an M47 with a new engine and transmission and replaced the 90-mm gun with the British 105-mm L7 gun, but the type was not adopted. The Spanish army revised some of its M47s with a diesel engine, modified transmission and numerous other improvements.

SPECIFICATION	
Crew: 5 **Weight:** 46.17 tonnes **Dimensions:** length (gun forward) 8.51 m (28 ft 1 in); hull length 6.36 m (20 ft 10 in); width 3.51 m (10 ft 6 in); height 3.35 m (11 ft) including AA machine-gun **Armament:** one 90-mm (3.54-in) M36 rifled gun with 71 rounds, one 0.3-in (7.62-mm) M1919A4E1 co-axial machine-gun, one 0.3-in M1919A4E1 bow machine-gun, and	one 0.5-in (12.7-mm) M2 machine-gun on the commander's cupola **Powerplant:** one Continental AV-1790-5B air-cooled 12-cylinder petrol engine developing 604 kW (810 hp) at 2,800 rpm **Performance:** maximum road speed 48 km/h (30 mph); maximum road range 130 km (80 miles) **Gradient:** 60 per cent **Vertical obstacle:** 0.91 m (3 ft) **Trench:** 2.59 m (8 ft 6 in)

M48 Medium tank

Design of a medium tank to supplant the interim M47 began in the early 1950s under the designation **T48**, and this was ordered into production even before the first prototypes had been completed. The first **M48** production vehicles were completed at the Chrysler-run Delaware Tank Plant in July 1952, when the widow of General George Patton christened the type **Patton**. With such a short development period, which was justified by the international situation at that time, there were many problems with the early tanks, including poor reliability and a very short operating range of

Israel's M48s have 105-mm (3.94-in) guns, diesel engines and low-profile commander's cupolas. Many have been retrofitted with the same explosive reactive armour (ERA) fitted to the IDF's M60 tanks.

only 113 km (70 miles). The M48 was followed by the **M48A1**, **M48A2** and finally the **M48A3**. The last had many modifications to overcome the earlier vehicles' problems, and was powered by a AVDS-1790-2A diesel which increased the operational range

of the tank to some 463 km (288 miles).

Production of the M48 series continued until 1959, by which time over 11,700 had been built. The M48 was succeeded in production by the M60, itself an M48 development. The M48 is

still used by many countries including Greece, Iran, Israel, Jordan, Lebanon, Morocco, Pakistan, Portugal, South Korea, Spain, Taiwan, Thailand, Tunisia, Turkey and Vietnam.

The M48, M48A1, M48A2 and M48A3 are all armed with a

90-mm (4.13-in) M68 gun, with a 0.3-in (7.62-mm) co-axial machine-gun and a 0.5-in (12.7-mm) machine-gun on the commander's cupola. To extend the type's operational life, the **M48A5** was developed in the mid-1970s. This is an earlier-model M48 rebuilt and fitted with a 105-mm M68 gun, a 7.62-mm (0.3-in) M60D machine-gun on the turret roof, a new powerpack and many other detailed modifications. From 1975 the Anniston Army Depot converted well over 2,000 older tanks to the M48A5 configuration.

The US also supplied kits to allow other operators to convert their earlier M48s to M48A5 standard. For the West German army the German company

Wegmann also upgraded some 650 M48A2 tanks to **M48A2GA2** with the British 105-mm L7A3 gun, new ammunition racks, new commander's cupola, passive night vision equipment, smoke dischargers and modifications to the fire-control system.

The automotive components of the M48 were also used in the M88 ARV and the M53 and M55 self-propelled artillery weapons. Variants of the M48 include the **M67**, **M67A1** and **M67A2** flamethrower tanks (now out of service) and the M48 AVLB with a scissors bridge launched over the front of the vehicle.

The M48 saw combat in South Vietnam, with the Pakistani army against India, and

An M48 advances during street-fighting in Saigon in May 1968. The M48 was intended for long-range engagements, and in Vietnam a gunner often had to be carried on the rear deck for close-in protection.

also with the Israeli army against Jordan, Egypt and Syria. It has now proved to be a reliable tank and, fitted with the 105-mm L7A3 or M68 gun,

could destroy most tanks likely to be encountered up to the 1990s, especially when it is firing modern ammunition.

M48 in operation Pattons on patrol

The **M48** main battle tank has seen action all over the world, from the Middle East to Asia. It was the most powerful armoured vehicle used in the Vietnam War by the US forces.

Named **Patton** after the most famous US tank commander of World War II, the M48 was designed hurriedly and rushed into production in 1953, after the Korean War, a conflict which had exposed the US Army's alarming shortage of modern tanks. Despite the type's hasty origins, however, modernisation

kits have since prolonged the M48's career into the early part of the 21st century.

Early M48s were plagued by problems stemming from the tank's rushed introduction to service. Although a sound vehicle with reasonable armour protection and a relatively powerful armament, it suffered initially from an embarrassingly short range (just 113 km/70 miles). Furthermore, it still used the complicated stereoscopic rangefinder that had defeated so many tank crews on the M47.

SPECIFICATION
M48A5 Patton

Crew: 4
Weight: 48987 kg (107,996 lb)
Dimensions: length (gun forward) 9.29 m (30 ft 6 in); length (hull) 6.4 m (21 ft); width 3.62 m (11 ft 11 in); height 3.25 m (10 ft 1 in)
Powerplant: one Continental AVDS-1790-2D water-cooled diesel developing 559 kW (750 hp)
Armour: hull front 120 mm (4.7 in); hull sides, front 76 mm (2.9 in) and rear 51 mm (2 in); hull rear 44 mm (1.7 in); hull floor 63 mm (2.48 in);

turret front 110 mm (4.3 in); turret sides 76 mm; turret rear 50 mm (1.9 in)
Armament: one 105-mm (4.13-in) M68 rifled gun, one 0.5-in (12.7-mm) M2HB machine-gun, and one 7.62-mm (0.3-in) co-axial machine-gun
Performance: maximum road speed 48 km/h (30 mph); road range 499 km (310 miles)
Fording: 1.2 m (3 ft 10 in)
Vertical obstacle: 0.91 m (36 in)
Trench: 2.59 m (8 ft 6 in)

The West German armoured divisions were equipped with M48s until enough Leopard tanks were available for first-line units.

The rangefinder allowed the 90-mm (3.54-in) main gun to fire accurately to over 1500 m (1,640 yards), but it was anything but soldier-proof. Several successive variants which improved the design were produced. The **M48A2** had a fuel-injected engine, which more than doubled its range. However, only with the **M48A3** did the US Army finally get what it needed. Diesel-powered and with a coincidence rangefinder, the M48A3 was the version taken to Vietnam by 1st Battalion, 69th Armored Regiment, in 1966.

Inside the M48

The layout of the M48 is entirely conventional. The driver sits in the centre of the hull front. The commander and gunner sit in the turret to the right of the main armament, and on the other side of the gun sits the loader.

US Marines advance through a clearing near Cam Lo in 1967. An M48 lends its weight to the defence of the landing zone as a CH-46 helicopter arrives to evacuate the wounded.

The M48 was the first American tank to abandon the fifth crewman, who used to man a hull machine-gun and act as a spare driver or radio operator. Most M48s had an infra-red/white light searchlight mounted above the 90-mm gun. This is of limited use today, but 2/34th Armored used their lights to spring violent night ambushes on Viet Cong supply vessels navigating the Saigon river.

The main armament of the M48A3 is the M41 gun. This has a distinctive blast deflector on the end of the barrel. With a maximum effective range of 2500 m (2,735 yards), this fires armour-piercing rounds, smoke, canister and HEAT (high-explosive anti-tank) projectiles. The last are effective at penetrating the armour of tanks, but AP (armour-piercing) rounds are more accurate. The driver is surrounded by ammunition: 19 rounds are stored on his left and 11 on his right. Eight more are on the turret floor, and a further 16 around the turret ring. Israeli combat experience has revealed that storing such large amounts of ammunition in the turret is a recipe for a catastrophic secondary explosion should the tank suffer a penetrative hit on the turret.

Senior American officers in Vietnam opposed the deployment of the M48 in the country. They believed that the terrain was unsuitable. Argument were raised that armoured units should stick to M113 APCs and light tanks like the M41.

But, where the tank was used in Vietnam, it proved surprisingly effective. Its armour enabled the M48 to survive repeated hits from anti-tank weapons. The concussion and blast damage from such a hit could be traumatic for the crew, however.

With the exception of one night-time conflict at Ben Het, American M48s fought their battles against communist infantry, though the 90-mm HE shell was far from ideal in the battles at point-blank range in

Left: An M48 noses through thick bush country in Vietnam. Infantry support was essential to prevent the enemy firing RPGs into the thin side armour.

Below: A US Marine Corps M48 participates in one of the frequent amphibious landings conducted in South Vietnam during operations against Viet Cong guerrillas and the North Vietnamese army.

which the US armoured forces usually found themselves.

The crews' favourite anti-personnel ammunition was the canister round, which converted the 90-mm gun into a giant shotgun. These shells contained 1,280 shot or between 5,000 and 10,000 flechettes (steel darts). These 'beehive' rounds were devastatingly effective. On one occasion, when the beehives ran out, a troop from 5th Cavalry fired HE shells with delayed fuses in front of their ambushers. The shells ricocheted before detonating, producing an effective airburst.

Mines were the main source of armour casualties during the Vietnam War. Several M48s were fitted with mine-rollers, but they were slow, ineffective in soft ground and often wrecked when they detonated a mine.

The M48 was supplied to many US allies and played a crucial role in the Israeli victory in the 1967 Six-Day War. Together with British Centurions, M48s spearheaded the Israeli campaign that routed the Egyptian army in Sinai. In engagements with Soviet-supplied T-54/55 MBTs the Israeli M48s performed well: they were far more reliable than the Arab armour, and their 90-mm HEAT rounds easily penetrated the T-54's armour. The M60 was, originally, no more than an M48 with a 105-mm (4.13-in) gun and new turret possessing a better ballistic profile. As they acquired M60s, the Israelis improved their M48s to M60 standard by fitting their version of the M68 105-mm gun and installing a Continental V-12 diesel engine.

The US Army upgraded its M48 fleet in much the same way. The resulting **M48A5** was the ultimate M48 in American service. It took five years from 1975 to modernise the 1,600 or so M48s still in American service. These tanks served with the National Guard until replaced by M60s as regular armoured units received the M1 Abrams. The M48 was the mainstay of the post-war West German army until the Bundeswehr received enough of its own Leopard tanks. However, the M48s soldiered on. An upgrade programme resulted in 650 being rebuilt to M48A5 standard during the late 1970s. Improvements included the a 105-mm L7 gun passive night vision equipment, and a new commander's cupola.

Soldiering on

The M48 continues to serve in many armies, several German and American companies have offered modernisation kits. Greece modernised its force of about 600 M48s to M48A3 standard. Spain, Pakistan and Turkey all had large fleets of M48A5s. The M48 remained South Korea's MBT into the 2000s. Other M48 operators include Iran, Israel, Jordan, Lebanon, Morocco, Portugal, Taiwan and Thailand.

M103 Heavy tank

With the advent of the Cold War, US design work commenced on three new tanks, the T41 light tank which was standardised as the M41, the T42 medium which resulted in the M47, and the **T43**. Trials with prototypes of the last revealed numerous deficiencies, and further trials with modified vehicles designated **T43E1** showed that over 100 additional modifications were required, but the vehicle was eventually standardised as the **Tank, Combat, Full Tracked, 120-mm, M103**.

A total of 200 vehicles was built by Chrysler at the Detroit Tank Plant between 1952 and 1954 for deployment with the 7th Army in Europe, where it was found that the tank's weight and small range of action made it difficult to employ.

There were also constant reliability problems, and the M103s were phased out of service with the US Army in the 1960s. A number was supplied to the US Marine Corps, and in the 1960s 153 vehicles were fitted with a type of new engine, which increased operational range from 130 to 480 km (80 to 300 miles); these were designated **M103A2**. They have since been phased out of service with the US Marine Corps, and none was supplied to any foreign countries under the MAP (Military Assistance Program). The role of the M103 was to provide direct assault and long-range anti-tank support to the M47 and later the M48 (a similar role to that of the British Conqueror).

Enlarged M48

In many respects, the M103 tank was virtually a scaled-up M48, with the driver at the front, turret and fighting compartment in the centre, and the engine and transmission at the rear. The commander's cupola, which was provided with an externally mounted 0.5-in (12.7-mm) M2HB machine-gun for anti-aircraft defence, was in the centre of the turret at the rear, while the gunner and one of the loaders were seated forward on the right with the second loader on the left. The torsion-bar suspension consisted of seven dual rubber-tyred road wheels (with the drive sprocket at the rear and idler at the front) and six track-return rollers.

Main armament comprised a 120-mm (4.72-in) rifled gun with an elevation of +15° and a depression of -8°, turret traverse being 360°. Ammunition was of the separate-loading type and a total of 38 rounds (38 projectiles and the same number of charges) was carried. The

A prototype M103A1E1 is seen with its turret traversed to the rear and the gun travel lock open. The size and weight of the M103 made operations difficult.

following types of ammunition could be fired: AP-T, HE, HE-T, WP, WP-T and TP-T. A 0.30-in (7.62-mm) machine-gun was mounted co-axial with the main armament. Standard equipment in the tank included heaters, deep-fording equipment, infantry telephone and a reassuring fire extinguishing system.

SPECIFICATION	
M103	in (12.7-mm) M2 AA machine-gun
Crew: 5	**Powerplant:** one Continental AV-1790-5B or 7C V-12 petrol engine developing 810 hp (604 kW)
Weight: 56.7 tonnes	
Dimensions: length (gun forwards) 11.32 m (37ft 1½ in); length (hull) 6.98 m (22 ft 11 in); width 3.76 m (12 ft 4 in); height 2.88 m (9 ft 5½ in)	**Performance:** maximum road speed 34 km/h (21 mph); maximum road range 130 km (80 miles)
Armament: one 120-mm (4.72-in) rifled gun, one co-axial 0.3-in (7.62-mm) machine-gun and one 0.5-	**Gradient:** 60 per cent
	Vertical obstacle: 0.91 m (36 in)
	Trench: 2.29 m (7 ft 6 in)

TAM Medium tank

For many years the M4 Sherman tank was the backbone of Argentine armoured units. By the early 1970s this type was becoming increasingly difficult to maintain and, as most of the tanks available at that time weighed 40 tonnes or more and were therefore too heavy to pass safely over many of Argentina's bridges, it was decided to have a new tank designed specifically to the Argentine army's requirements. The task was contracted to a West German company, Thyssen Henschel (now Rheinmetall Landsysteme), then building the Marder mechanized infantry combat vehicle for the West German army.

The first prototype of the **TAM** (**Tanque Argentine Mediano**) was completed in 1976, a further two vehicles being completed in the following year. The type was accepted for Argentine service, and a factory was established near Buenos Aires. By the beginning of the 21st century not all of the 512

vehicles of the family required by the Argentine army had been delivered, and none of the completed vehicles was deployed to the Falklands during the conflict that took place in 1982. To work with the TAM, the **VCTP** infantry fighting vehicle was developed by Thyssen Henschel, and up to 250 of these have been built in Argentina.

Marder derivative

The hull of the TAM is based on that of the Marder MICV. The driver is seated at the front on the left-hand side with the powerpack (engine and transmission) to his right. The glacis plate is well sloped to give the best possible protection within the weight limits of the vehicle. However, the armour does not compare well to that fitted to more advanced and heavier MBTs. The three-man turret is an electro-hydraulically operated unit of all-welded construction carried over the rear of the vehicle, with the commander and gunner on the right and the

The TAM tank was designed by the West German company of Thyssen Henschel for the Argentine army, and is based on the chassis of the Marder MICV. Useful numbers of this limited medium tank have been built in Argentina.

loader on the left. The main armament comprises a 105-mm (4.13-in) gun fitted with two-axis stabilisation and an extractor to remove fumes when the gun is fired: the main gun has a total elevation arc of 25° (-7° to +18°). A 7.62-mm (0.3-in) machine-gun is co-axial with the main gun, and a similar weapon can be mounted on the turret roof for anti-aircraft defence. Four dischargers for smoke/fragmentation grenades can be fitted each side of the turret. Totals of 50 rounds of 105-mm and 6,000 rounds of 7.62-mm ammunition are carried, and there is an NBC system.

The primary variants of the TAM and VCTP in service with or developed for the Argentine army are the **VCA 155**, **VCRT** and **VCLC**. The in-service VCA 155 is a self-propelled artillery equipment that combines the hull of the TAM with the turret and 155-mm (6.1-in) gun/

howitzer developed by Otobreda in Italy for the Palmaria system. The VCRT is an armoured recovery vehicle based on the VCTP with a new superstructure and specialised equipment developed by MaK (now Rheinmetall Landsysteme): the specialised equipment included a rear-mounted dozer blade, a front-mounted 30-tonne winch, and a 22-tonne crane jib on the right-hand side of the superstructure. The in-service VCLC is a multiple-launch rocket system using the chassis of the TAM with the turret replaced by two 18-round launchers of the Israeli LAR 160 system.

Unbuilt family

Using the chassis of the TAM medium tank, Thyssen Henschel developed, as a private venture, a complete family of fighting vehicles, although as yet none of these has been placed in full production.

SPECIFICATION	
TAM	top) 2.42 m (7 ft 11¼ in)
Crew: 4	**Performance:** maximum road speed
Weight: 30.5 tonnes (loaded)	75 km/h (46.6 mph); maximum
Powerplant: one MTU 6-cylinder	range 550 km (342 miles)
diesel developing 537 kW (720 hp)	**Fording:** 1.4 m (4 ft 7 in)
Dimensions: length (with gun	**Gradient:** 65 per cent
forward) 8.23 m (27 ft); length	**Vertical obstacle:** 1 m (3 ft 3¼ in);
(hull) 6.77 m (22 ft 2½ in); width	**Trench:** 2.5 m (8 ft 2½ in)
3.25 m (10 ft 8 in); height (turret	

Type 59 Main battle tank

Following its victory in the Chinese civil war in 1949, the Communist Chinese army was revised on a more permanent basis, but much of its equipment was obsolete or in urgent need of repair, including a number of American and Japanese tanks of World War II vintage. The USSR supplied large numbers of armoured vehicles including T-34/85 tanks, SU-100 100-mm (3.94-in) tank destroyers, and BTR-40 and

BTR-152 armoured personnel carriers. In the early 1950s there followed a quantity of T-54 MBTs, and production of the type was subsequently undertaken in China under the designation **Type 59**.

The first production models were very austere and were not fitted with night-vision equipment or a stabilisation system for the 100-mm Type 59 gun. Later vehicles were fitted with a full range of IR night-vision

equipment for the commander, gunner and driver, as well as a stabilisation system. The 7.62-mm (0.3-in) bow-mounted and co-axial machine-guns are

designated Type 59T, while the Soviet-designed 12.7-mm (0.5-in) DShKM machine-gun on the loader's cupola is designated Type 54 by China.

SPECIFICATION	
Type 59	ft 9 in); height 2.59 m (8 ft 6 in)
Crew: 4	**Performance:** maximum road speed
Weight: 36 tonnes	50 km/h (31 mph); maximum range
Powerplant: one V-12 diesel	400 km (249 miles)
developing 388 kW (520 hp)	**Fording:** 1.4 m (4 ft 7 in)
Dimensions: length (with gun	**Gradient:** 60 per cent
forward) 9 m (29 ft 6 in); length (hull)	**Vertical obstacle:** 0.79 m (2 ft 7 in)
6.17 m (20 ft 3 in); width 3.27 m (10	**Trench:** 2.68 m (8 ft 9½ in)

MEL, a British company, provided 30 sets of passive night-vision equipment for the Type 59, including the driver's periscope and the commander's and gunner's sights. Later, a number of Type 59 tanks were observed with a laser rangefinder mounted externally above the gun mantlet. This is in a very exposed position, however, and is vulnerable to small arms fire and shell splinters.

Variants are the **Type 59-I** with a simplified fire-control system and laser range-finder, **Type 59-II** with a 432-kW (580-hp) diesel engine and a 105-mm (4.13-in) rifled gun with two-axis stabilization, and **Type 59 ARV**.

The Type 59 was exported in some numbers, and is known still to be in service with Albania, Bangladesh, Cambodia, Congo, Iran, Iraq, North Korea, Pakistan, Sudan, Tanzania, Vietnam, Zambia and Zimbabwe.

The Type 59 was replaced in production by the **Type 69-I** main battle tank, which was first seen in public in September 1982. This tank is almost

The Chinese-built Type 59 is essentially a Soviet T-54. Later production Type 59s have IR night vision equipment and an externally-mounted (and thus vulnerable) laser rangefinder.

identical in appearance to the Type 59 but has a new 100-mm gun with a fume extractor near its muzzle: early tanks featured both smooth-bore and rifled weapons, but the latter was standardised. Other changes were an improved fire-control with a laser rangefinder, IR night-vision equipment, a complete NBC system, and a semi-automatic fire-extinguishing system. The **Type 69-II** has an improved fire-control system, smoke grenade launchers on the turret, and an automatic fire-extinguishing system.

In-service variants of the Type 69 include the **Type 69-II MBT**

Command (two models), **Type 80** self-propelled anti-aircraft mounting with two 57-mm (2.24-in) guns, **Type 84 ALVB**, Type 84 armoured mineclearing system, and **Type 653 ARV**. Export sales have been made to Bangladesh, Iran, Iraq, Myanmar, Pakistan and Thailand.

AMX-30 Main battle tank

When the French army was fully re-formed after the end of World War II, its initial tank fleet comprised American-supplied M4 Sherman tanks and a few examples of the French-designed ARL-44. These were replaced from the mid-1950s by another American type, the M47 battle tank, which was supplied to France in large numbers under the Mutual Defense Aid Program (MDAP). Then in 1956 France, West

Germany and Italy drew up a requirement for a new MBT that was to be lighter and more powerfully armed than the M47 currently being used by the armies of all three countries. France and West Germany each built prototypes of MBTs to meet this specification, the French contender being the **AMX-30** and the West German vehicle the Leopard (later the Leopard 1). It was expected that one of these tank types would

be adopted by both countries, but in the end each nation adopted its own tank.

The AMX-30 was designed by the Atelier de Construction d'Issy-les-Moulineaux (AMX), creator of most of France's heavier armoured fighting vehicles since the end of World War II. The first prototypes were

completed in 1960, the first production tanks were completed by the Atelier de Construction de Roanne in 1966, and production ended in 1993 after the completion of well over 2,000 AMX-30 series vehicles, many of them for export to countries that now include Abu Dhabi (United Arab

A French army AMX-30 showing the 105-mm CH-105-F1 main gun whose primary anti-tank round is the OCC (HEAT) type, which has a muzzle velocity of 1000 m (3,280 ft) per second and will penetrate 400 mm (15¾ in) of armour at an incidence of 0°. At a later date an APFSDS (Obus Fleche) was introduced into French army service but not exported.

The AMX-30 series of main battle tanks has a good power/weight ratio by contemporary standards, and therefore possesses good acceleration and cross-country mobility.

Emirates), Bosnia, Chile, Croatia, Cyprus, Greece, Iraq, Kuwait, Nigeria, Qatar, Saudi Arabia, Spain (where the type was built under licence) and Venezuela.

The AMX-30 is the lightest of the first-generation NATO tanks, and has a welded hull of rolled steel plate, while the three-man turret is of cast construction. The main armament consists of a 105-mm (4.13-in) rifled gun, and there are a 20-mm co-axial cannon and a 7.62-mm (0.3-in) machine-gun on the commander's cupola. The co-axial weapon is unusual in that it

can be elevated independently of the main armament to +40°, enabling it to be used against low-flying aircraft and helicopters. Ammunition totals are 47 105-mm (19 in the turret and the remaining 28 in the hull), 1,050 20-mm and 2,050 7.62-mm rounds. The types of ammunition fired by the 105-mm gun include HEAT, HE, Smoke and Illuminating, with a modern APFSDS round introduced later in the tank's career. This last has a muzzle velocity of 1525 m (5,005 ft) per second, and will penetrate 150 mm

(5.91 in) of armour at an angle of 60° at a range of 5000 m (5,470 yards).

For desert operations there is the **AMX-30S** used by Qatar and Saudi Arabia, and the definitive production model for the French army is the **AMX-30 B2**, which introduced a number of improvements including an integrated fire-control system incorporating a laser rangefinder and a low-light TV system, and an upgraded automotive system including a new transmission.

The basic AMX-30 chassis has given birth to a family of related vehicles. The **AMX-30D** armoured recovery vehicle has a dozer/ stabiliser blade mounted at the front of the hull, two winches and a hydraulic crane on the right side of the hull for changing engines and other components in the field. The AMX-30 bridgelayer has a bridge to fill gaps of up to 20 m (65 ft 7 in). The chassis was also used to carry the launcher for the Pluton surface-to-surface tactical nuclear missile. The **AMX-30**

EBG and **AMX-30 B DT** or, on the chassis of the AMX-30 B2, **AMX-30 B2 DT** are respectively the combat engineer tractor and mine-clearing tank used by the French army. The chassis is also used for the French version of the Euromissile Roland SAM system and the Shahine SAM system, the latter developed by Thomson-CSF to meet the requirements of the Saudi Arabian army. A twin 30-mm self-propelled anti-aircraft gun system, the **AMX-30-S 401 A**, was developed for Saudi Arabia, this providing close-in protection for Shahine batteries. The **GCT** is essentially a modified AMX-30 chassis with a new turret carrying a 155-mm (6.1-m) howitzer whose automatic loading system enables the GCT's howitzer to fire eight rounds per minute until its ammunition supply is exhausted. The GCT serves with the French army, and in the Middle East was ordered by Iraq, Kuwait and Saudi Arabia.

AMX-30 of the French army showing its cross-country mobility. This is one of the few Western MBTs that is not fitted with a two-axis stabilisation system for the main armament, and cannot therefore fire with any accuracy while on the move.

SPECIFICATION	
AMX 30 B2	ft 2 in); height (overall) 2.86 m (9 ft 4 in)
Crew: 4	
Weight: 36 tonnes	**Performance:** maximum road speed 65 km/h (40 mph); maximum range 600 km (373 miles)
Powerplant: one Hispano-Suiza 12-cylinder diesel developing 537 kW (720 hp)	
Dimensions: length (gun forward) 9.48 m (31 ft 1 in); length (hull) 6.59 m (21 ft 7 in); width 3.1 m (10	**Gradient:** 60 per cent
	Vertical obstacle: 0.93 m (3 ft ½ in)
	Trench: 2.9 m (9 ft 6 in)

AMX-32 Main battle tank

The **AMX-32** was designed by the Atelier de Construction d'Issy-les-Moulineaux as a possible export to countries whose armies required more firepower and better armour protection than available on the AMX-30. The first prototype, armed with the same 105-mm (4.13-in) gun as the AMX-30, was revealed in 1979, while the second prototype, revealed in 1981, had a new 120-mm (4.72-in) gun as well as improved protection. However, no orders were received.

Layout

In layout the AMX-32 was similar to the AMX-30, with the driver at the front, three men in the central turret, and the engine and transmission at the rear. The main armament comprised a 120-mm smooth-bore gun developed by the Etablissement d'Etudes et de Fabrications d'Armement de Bourges with a vertical sliding breech block. The barrel was fitted with a thermal sleeve and fume-extraction system.

Ammunition

The two types of ammunition fired were APFSDS and multi-purpose with muzzle velocities of 1630 and 1050 m (5,350 and 3,445 ft) per second respectively. The gun also fired the range of ammunition developed for the German-designed

Leopard 2. A total of 38 rounds of 120-mm ammunition was carried as 17 rounds in the turret, with the other 21 rounds in the hull. Mounted co-axially to the left of the main gun was a 20-mm M693 cannon with independent elevation to +40°; 480 rounds were carried for this weapon. A 7.62-mm (0.3-in) machine-gun was mounted on the commander's cupola, and attached to each side of the forward part of the turret was a bank of three smoke dischargers.

One of the most significant differences between the AMX-32 and the AMX-30 was the later tank's integrated COTAC fire-control system developed from the system fitted to the AMX-10RC 6x6 amphibious reconnaissance vehicle. The COTAC system allowed the AMX-32 to engage moving as well as stationary targets under day and/or night conditions with a 90 per cent first-round hit probability. To the left of the 20-mm cannon was a low-light-level TV camera transmitting its imagery to screens at the commander's and gunner's positions. The commander had a roof-mounted sight with x2 and x8 day magnification and x1 night magnification, and the separate gunner's sight had x10 magnification and also incorporated a modern laser rangefinder.

Compared to the AMX-30, the AMX-32 had a redesigned turret and hull front, with improved armour protection. The fire control system included a laser rangefinder and a roof-mounted stabilised sight.

The AMX-32 had the same Hispano-Suiza HS 110 engine as the AMX-30, with the option of a supercharged model developing 597 kW (800 hp). Its greater weight meant that the AMX-32 had an inferior power/weight ratio than the AMX-30, with a slightly adverse effect on mobility. The suspension was a modified version of that fitted to the AMX-30, but side skirts were added to give a measure of

protection against attack from HEAT projectiles. The AMX-32 was fitted with an NBC system and a snorkel, the latter allowing the vehicle to ford to a depth of 4 m (13 ft 1 in). Optional equipment included a different transmission, fire extinguishing system, air conditioning system, different tracks and a system to inject diesel fuel into the exhaust to create smoke.

SPECIFICATION	
AMX-32	(0.3-in) machine-gun
Crew: 4	**Powerplant:** Hispano-Suiza 110
Weight: 40 tonnes	12-cylinder multi-fuel engine
Dimensions: length (with 120-mm	developing 720 hp (537 kW)
gun forward) 9.85 m (32 ft 3¾ in);	**Performance:** maximum road speed
length (hull) 6.59 m (21 ft 7½ in);	65 km/h (40.4 mph); maximum
width 3.24 m (10 ft 7½ in); height	range 530 km (329 miles)
(overall) 2.96 m (9 ft 8½ in)	**Gradient:** 60 per cent
Armament: one 120-mm (4.72-in)	**Vertical obstacle:** 0.9 m (2 ft 11½ in)
smoothbore gun, one co-axial 20-	**Trench:** 2.9 m (9 ft 6¼ in)
mm cannon and one 7.62-mm	

OF-40 Main battle tank

The standard Italian army tank in the 1950s was the American-supplied M47. The country did take part in the formulation of the requirement leading to the production of the French AMX-30 and West German Leopard 1 MBTs, but decided instead to take the American M60A1, of which 300 (including 200 made under licence) were bought. In 1970, Italy ordered 200 Leopard 1

tanks from West Germany, and at the same time OTO Melara (now Otobreda) obtained a licence for Italian production. By 1982 some 720 had been completed for the Italian army and a further 160 of the ARV, AVLB and AEV specialised versions were completed by the mid-1980s.

Export problems

Under the terms of its licence

OTO Melara could not export the tank, so the company designed the **OF-40**: the letters in the prefix stand for OTO Melara and Fiat (prime contractor and automotive contractor respectively), and the numerical part indicates an empty weight of 40 tonnes. The first prototype was completed in 1980, and the only production contract was placed by Dubai, which received its

first vehicles in 1981.

Construction

The hull and turret of the OF-40 are of welded steel construction and divided into a driver's compartment at the front, a fighting compartment in the centre, and the engine and transmission at the rear. The main armament is an OTO Melara 105-mm (4.13-in) rifled gun. When the gun recoils the falling-wedge breech block opens automatically and ejects the empty cartridge case into a bag under the breech. A total of 61 rounds of ammunition is carried, 42 to the left of the driver and the remainder in the turret. A 7.62-mm (0.3-in) machine-gun is mounted co-axially with the main armament, and a similar weapon is mounted on the turret roof for AA defence. Four smoke/fragmentation grenade launchers are mounted on each side of the turret.

Fire-control system

The OF-40 has an OG14LR fire-control system which includes a computer and a laser rangefinder. A fully stabilised fire-control system can also be fitted, enabling the OF-40 to engage enemy tanks when moving at speed across country. The commander has a roof-mounted stabilised sight, which is used for both surveillance and target acquisition. Standard equipment includes night-vision equipment and an NBC pack mounted to the driver's left.

An OF-40 of the Dubai army, which received 36 such vehicles and three OF-40 ARVs. The OF-40 MBT uses automotive components of the Leopard 1 and is armed with a 105-mm gun and two 7.62-mm machine-guns.

The **OF-40 Mk 2** introduced the more capable OG14L2A fire-control system, and Dubai ordered 18 of these tanks to supplement its 18 OF-40 vehicles upgraded to Mk 2 standard, and the only other in-service variant is the **OF-40 ARV** armoured recovery vehicle, of which Dubai has three.

SPECIFICATION	
OF-40	7.62-mm AA machine-gun
Crew: 4	**Powerplant:** 10-cylinder diesel
Weight: 43 tonnes	developing 830 hp (619 kW)
Dimensions: length (with gun	**Performance:** maximum road speed
forward) 9.22 m (30 ft 3 in); length	60 km/h (37.3 mph); maximum
(hull) 6.89 m (22 ft 7¼ in); width	range (road) 600 km (373 miles)
3.51 m (11 ft 6¼ in); height (turret	**Fording:** 1.2 m (3 ft 11¼ in)
top) 2.45 m (8 ft ½ in)	**Gradient:** 60 per cent
Armament: one 105-mm (4.13-in)	**Vertical obstacle:** 1.15 m (3 ft 9¼ in)
rifled gun, one co-axial 7.62-mm	**Trench:** 3 m (9 ft 10 in)
(0.3-in) machine-gun and one	

Merkava Mks 1 and 2 Main battle tanks

After the Six-Day War of 1967 Israel became concerned that it might not be able to obtain AFVs from its traditional suppliers (France, the UK and the US), and also that many of the tanks did not meet Israel's unique requirements. Israel therefore started to develop its own **Merkava** (chariot) tank. This was announced in 1977. The first production vehicles were completed in 1979, and it has been estimated that by 2001 more than 1,000 vehicles had been built. The Merkava was used for the first time against Syrian armoured units in southern Lebanon in 1982.

Unique layout

The layout of the Merkava is unique in that the whole of the front of the vehicle is occupied by the 671-kW (900-hp) AVDS-1790-6A diesel engine, transmission, cooling system and fuel tanks. The driver is seated just forward and to the left of the turret. The turret, of cast and welded construction, is situated well to the rear of the hull with the commander and gunner on the right and the loader on the left. The turret is well sloped to give the greatest possible degree of armour protection, and its small cross section makes it a very difficult target. At the rear of the hull is a compartment able to carry additional ammunition or (supposedly) four litters or 10 infantrymen if the standard ammunition load is reduced. A hatch is provided in the hull rear

The Merkava offers a very high level of protection for the crew and vital systems. Potent firepower includes a 60-mm mortar whose availability allows more economical use of the main gun, a very capable fire-control system but only moderate mobility.

to allow for the rapid exit of the tank crew or infantrymen.

Standard equipment includes a full range of night-vision

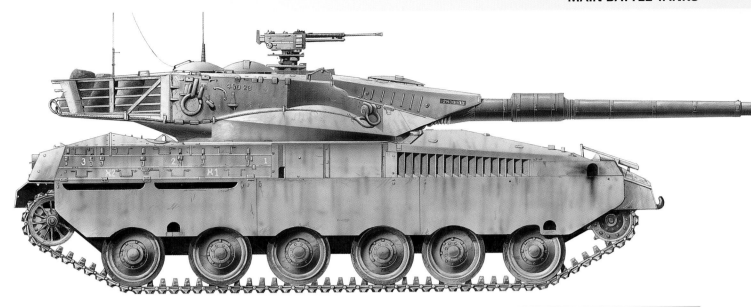

The Israeli army's Merkava Mk 1 is armed with the same 105-mm M68 gun as fitted to the M48A5 and M60 series of MBT. The Merkava was first used in combat in the 1982 invasion of the Lebanon, when it engaged and defeated Syrian T-72s. It can carry infantrymen, additional ammunition or a number of stretcher patients in the hull rear.

systems, an NBC system and an automatic fire detection/extinguishing system.

Armament

The main armament is the proven 105-mm (4.13-in) rifled tank gun, which can fire a wide range of ammunition (62 rounds). The 105-mm gun has an elevation arc of 28.5° (-8.5° to +20°), turret traverse and gun elevation/depression are electro-hydraulic with manual back-up. A two-axis stabilisation system is fitted, enabling the gun to be aimed accurately and fired while the vehicle is moving across country. The Elbit Matador

SPECIFICATION	
Merkava Mk 1 **Crew:** 4 **Combat weight:** 60 tonnes **Dimensions:** length with gun forward 8.63 m (28 ft 3½ in); width 3.7 m (12 ft 1½ in); height 2.75 m (9 ft) to commander's cupola **Armament:** one 105-mm (4.13-in) rifled gun, one 7.62-mm (0.3-in) co-axial machine-gun, two 7.62-mm AA machine-guns and one 60-mm (2.36-in) mortar	**Powerplant:** one General Dynamics Land Systems AVDS-1790-6A V-12 diesel developing 671 kW (900 hp) **Performance:** maximum road speed 46 km/h (28.6 mph); range 400 km (248.6 miles) **Fording:** 2 m (6 ft 7 in) with preparation **Gradient:** 70 per cent **Vertical obstacle:** 0.95 m (3 ft 1 in) **Trench:** 3 m (9 ft 10 in)

fire-control system includes a targeting computer.

Performance

Compared with other recent MBTs the **Merkava Mk 1** has a very low speed and poor power/weight ratio, but it was

Although no production figures have been released, it has been estimated that by 2002, total Merkava production had reached over 1,000 vehicles, including the latest Mk 4 version.

designed for a tactical scenario different from that prevalent in Central Europe. It should also be remembered that Israel has had more experience than any other country of successful armoured warfare since World War II. In designing the Merkava, the Israelis placed great emphasis on crew survivability: with a national population of around only four million, every trained crew man is a very valuable person who must be given the maximum possible protection.

Further development yielded the **Merkava Mk 2** variant of 1982. This has improved armour on the front and sides of the turret, a revised 60-mm (2.36-in) mortar (which is mounted in the turret roof rather than externally), the more capable Matador Mk 2 fire-control system, spring-attached skirt armour and a more advanced Israeli-developed transmission system. The Merkava Mk 2 increases the range of the tank by 25 per cent compared to the original vehicle, but with only a minor increase in fuel capacity.

Leopard 1 Main battle tank

When the West German army was re-formed in the mid-1950s it was equipped with American M47 and M48 tanks, both armed with a 90-mm (3.54-in) gun. A decision was soon taken that the former would be replaced by a tank armed with a 105-mm (4.13-in) gun, and Gruppen A and B design teams were selected to build prototypes for comparative trials. At the same time France built prototypes of the AMX-30 to replace its American-supplied M47s. It had been expected that one of the West German MBTs or alternatively the French AMX-30 would become the common MBT of both armies, but in the end each country went its own way. Development of the Gruppe A design resulted in its standardisation as the **Leopard 1**. The first production

The impressive capability of the Leopard 1 is attested to by the fact that tanks of this family were delivered to 13 armies around the world, and are still operational in the first years of the 21st century.

By the standards of its design period, the Leopard 1 was a capable MBT offering a high level of agility and firepower (the latter through the use of an excellent 105-mm rifled gun) together with modest protection based on welded steel armour.

tanks were completed by Krauss-Maffei of Munich in September 1965 and production of the MBT continued until 1979.

Extensive production

Some 2,437 MBTs were built for West Germany in four basic models designated **Leopard 1A1** (with additional armour the **Leopard 1A1A1**), **Leopard 1A2**, **Leopard 1A3** (with a new welded turret) and **Leopard 1A4** (with a new welded turret and new fire-control system). The tank was also adopted by Australia (90 vehicles), Belgium (334), Canada (114), Denmark (120), Italy (920 including 720 built in Italy by OTO Melara), Netherlands (468) and Norway (78). Production was resumed by Krauss Maffei and Krupp MaK in 1982 to meet Greek and Turkish orders (106 and 77 tanks respectively).

Proven British gun

The Leopard 1 is armed with the British L7 series rifled tank gun, which can fire a variety of ammunition including APDS, APFSDS, HEAT, HESH and Smoke, a total of 60 rounds being carried. A 7.62-mm

Evident in the Leopard 1 are the lessons the Germans learned in World War II. Thus the West German army's first MBT of post-war German design provided an attractive blend of firepower, protection and mobility.

(0.3-in) machine-gun is mounted co-axially with the main armament, a similar weapon is mounted on the turret roof for use in the anti-aircraft role, and four triple smoke dischargers are mounted on each side of the turret. A gun stabilisation system is fitted, enabling the main armament to be laid and fired while the tank is moving across country. Leopard 1s have an NBC system and a full set of night-vision equipment for the commander, gunner and loader. When originally introduced, the night vision equipment was of the first-generation IR type but this has been replaced by second-generation passive gear.

Optional equipment

A wide range of optional equipment has also been developed for the Leopard 1, including a snorkel which enables the tank to ford deep rivers and streams to a maximum depth of 4 m (13 ft 1½ in). A hydraulic blade can be mounted at the front of the hull; this is operated by the driver to clear or prepare battlefield obstacles. Most German and Dutch Leopards have appliqué armour fitted to their turrets to give increased armour protection against missiles and HEAT projectiles.

Family of variants

The basic Leopard 1 chassis has been the basis for a complete family of vehicles which have been designed for full support of the MBT on the battlefield. All of the specialised versions, with the exception of the Gepard, have been designed and built by MaK of Kiel, which also manufactured a few Leopard 1 MBTs.

SPECIFICATION	
Leopard 1	(0.3-in) MG3 machine-guns
Crew: 4	**Powerplant:** one MTU 10-cylinder
Weight: 40 tonnes	diesel developing 619 kW (830 hp)
Dimensions: length (with gun forward) 9.54 m (31 ft 4 in); length (hull) 7.09 m (23 ft 3 in); width 3.25 m (10 ft 8 in); height (overall) 2.61 m (8 ft 7 in)	**Performance:** maximum road speed 65 km/h (40.4 mph); maximum range 600 km (373 miles)
	Fording: 60 per cent
	Vertical obstacle: 1.15 m (3 ft 9¼ in)
Armament: one 105-mm (4.13-in) L7A3 rifled gun, and two 7.62-mm	**Trench:** 3 m (9 ft 10 in)

Type 74 Main battle tank

The **Type 74** main battle tank was designed by Mitsubishi to meet the requirements of the Japanese Ground Self-Defence Force. The first **STB** prototype was completed in 1969, and the first production vehicles followed in 1975. Production continued into the mid-1980s and amounted to 873 tanks.

The main armament is the British 105-mm (4.13-in) L7A1 gun, stabilised in two axes and provided with 55 rounds; there are also a 7.62-mm (0.3-in) co-axial machine-gun (4,500 rounds), a 12.7-mm (0.5-in) machine-gun (660 rounds) on the roof for anti-aircraft defence, and three smoke-dischargers on each side of the turret. The fire-control system includes a ballistic computer and a laser rangefinder to enable the exact range to the target to be determined, so increasing the possibility of a first-round hit. Some models have an IR/white-

The Type 74 MBT entered service in 1976. An unusual feature of the vehicle is its hydro-pneumatic suspension, allowing the driver to adjust the height of the suspension to suit the type of terrain being crossed, and also to improve the gun's elevation arc.

light searchlight mounted to the left of the main armament, and the driver also has IR night vision equipment.

Unusual suspension

The Type 74's most unusual feature is its hydro-pneumatic suspension, which enables the driver quickly to adjust the height of the vehicle to suit the type of ground being crossed or to meet different tactical situations. The ground clearance can be varied from 0.2 to 0.65 m (7.9 to 25.6 in), and the driver can tilt the tank laterally or longitudinally. The 105-mm gun has an elevation arc of 16° (-6.5°

to +9.5°), but use of the suspension increases this to +15° and -12.5°. This is a very useful feature when the tank is firing from behind a crest or from a position on a reverse slope.

Specialised variants

As a result of Japan's ban on weapon exports, only the Japanese army uses the tank. The only variants of the Type 74 are the **Type 78** armoured recovery vehicle and the **Type 87** self-propelled anti-aircraft mounting. The Type 78 has a hydraulically operated dozer/anchor blade at the front of the hull, a winch, and a

hydraulic crane on the right side of the hull. The Type 87 is basically the hull of the Type 74 with a new turret carrying a two-man crew, paired surveillance and tracking radars, a fire-control system

including a laser rangefinder, and the potent armament of two 35-mm Oerlikon Contraves Type KDA cannon. A total of 45 Type 87s had been delivered by the end of 1999.

SPECIFICATION	
Type 74	12.7-mm (0.5-in) machine-gun
Crew: 4	**Powerplant:** one Mitsubishi diesel
Weight: 38 tonnes (loaded)	developing 560 kW (750 hp)
Dimensions: length (with gun	**Performance:** maximum road speed
forward) 9.41 m (30 ft 10½ in);	53 km/h (33 mph); maximum range
length (hull) 6.7 m (21 ft 11¾ in);	300 km (186 miles)
width 3.18 m (10 ft 5¼ in); height	**Fording:** 1 m (3 ft 3¼ in)
(overall) 2.67 m (8 ft 9 in)	**Gradient:** 60 per cent
Armament: one 105-mm (4.13-in)	**Vertical obstacle:** 1 m (3 ft 3¼ in)
L7A1 rifled gun, one 7.62-mm	**Trench:** 2.7 m (8 ft 10¼ in)
(0.3-in) machine-gun, and one	

Pz 61 and Pz 68 Main battle tanks

The Federal Construction Works at Thun, which had already designed and built prototypes of the NK I 75-mm (3-in) self-propelled anti-tank gun and the NK II 75-mm assault gun, completed the **KW 30** prototype of a Swiss-designed MBT in 1958 with the armament of one 90-mm (3.54-in) gun; a second prototype was completed in 1959. Between 1960 and 1961 10 pre-production tanks were built under the designation **Pz 58**: these were armed with the British 20-pdr (83.4-mm/3.28-in) gun as then installed in the Centurion. In 1961 an order was placed for 150 production vehicles armed with another British gun, the 105-mm (4.13-in) L7. These **Pz 61** tanks were delivered to the Swiss army in 1965–1966 as a partial replacement for Centurion tanks.

Enter the Pz 68

The Pz 61 was followed by the **Pz 68**, which featured a 7.5-mm (0.295-in) co-axial machine-gun in place of the 20-mm cannon, a gun-stabilisation system, and wider tracks with increased ground-contact length. A total of 170 Pz 68 tanks was built between 1971 and 1974, and there followed 50 examples of the **Pz 68 Mk 2** delivered in 1977, 110 of the **Pz 68 Mk 3** delivered in 1978-79 with a larger turret, and finally 60 of the **Pz 68 Mk 4** delivered in 1981–82 to an improved Mk 3 standard.

No radical features

The layout of the Pz 68 is conventional, with the driver at the front, turret in the centre, and engine and transmission at the rear. The turret is of cast steel

SPECIFICATION	
Pz 68	(0.295-in) machine-guns
Crew: 4	**Powerplant:** one MTU 8-cylinder
Weight: 39.7 tonnes	diesel developing 492 kW (660 hp)
Dimensions: length (with gun	**Performance:** maximum road speed
forward) 9.49 m (31 ft 1½ in);	55 km/h (34 mph); maximum road
length (hull) 6.98 m (22 ft 11 in);	range 350 km (217 miles)
width 3.14 m (10 ft 3½ in); height	**Fording:** 1.1 m (3 ft 7¼ in)
(including AA MG) 2.88 m (9 ft	**Gradient:** 60 per cent
5½ in)	**Vertical obstacle:** 1 m (3 ft 3¼ in)
Armament: one 105-mm (4.13-in)	**Trench:** 2.6 m (8 ft 6¼ in)
rifled gun, and two 7.5-mm	

with the commander and gunner on the right and the loader on the left; the loader fires the 7.5-mm anti-aircraft machine-gun, allowing the tank commander to carry out his proper command function. The main armament is a 105-mm gun with an elevation arc of 31° (-10° to +21°). There are also three smoke dischargers on each side of the turret, and as a retrofit two Bofors Lyran launchers on the turret roof to provide target illumination at night.

Several other vehicles have been developed on the basis of the Pz 68's chassis. These include the **Entpannung spanzer 68** armoured recovery vehicle, the **Brückenpanzer 68**

Pz 68 MBT of the Swiss army showing the thermal sleeve fitted to the 105-mm L7 gun. Switzerland is now making the German Leopard 2 under licence.

armoured bridgelayer, and the **Panzerzielfahrzeug** target tank. Prototypes of an anti-aircraft tank (armed with two 35-mm cannon) and a 155-mm (6.1-in) self-propelled gun were built but neither of these types was placed in production. The ARV is fitted with a dozer/anchor blade at the front of the hull, an A-frame that can lift 15 tonnes, and a hydraulic winch with a capacity of 25 tonnes, which can be increased to 75 tonnes with the aid of snatch blocks.

Service problems

The Pz 61 and Pz 68 have not been among the more successful of post-war designs, and in 1979 a report stated that there were some 50 faults with the Pz 68: some of these were quite serious, including short track life, the gun not staying on the target, and cracking fuel tanks.

Strv 103 (S-tank) Main battle tank

After World War II light tanks formed the bulk of Sweden's armoured strength. To meet the country's immediate requirement for more capable tanks 300 Centurions were purchased from the UK. Development of the KRV heavy tank armed with a 150-mm (5.91-in) smooth bore gun began. At the same time Sven Berge of the Swedish army was developing a new AFV concept in that the gun was fixed to the chassis and not mounted in a turret, traverse being secured by turning the tank on its vertical axis and elevation/ depression by lowering or raising the front or rear of the vehicle. Test rigs proved the basic concept, and in 1958 Bofors was awarded a contract for two prototypes, completed in 1961. So certain was the Swedish army that the concept was sound that it had placed a 1960 order for a further 10 pre-production examples of the **Stridsvagn 103**, or **S-tank**. The first production vehicles were completed in 1966 and manufacture continued until 1971, by which time 300 had been built.

Automatic loader

The main armament of the S-tank was the British 105-mm (4.13-in) L7 weapon with an automatic loader supplying ammunition from a 50-round magazine in the hull rear. The ammunition mix depended on the tactical

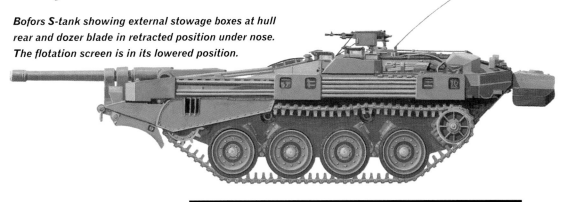

Bofors S-tank showing external stowage boxes at hull rear and dozer blade in retracted position under nose. The flotation screen is in its lowered position.

situation, but typically comprised 25 APDS (Armour-Piercing Discarding Sabot), 20 HE and five smoke fired at a maximum 15 rounds per minute. A 7.62-mm (0.3-in) machine-gun was mounted on the commander's cupola, and another two 7.62-mm machine-guns were fixed on the left side of the hull to fire forward; 7.62-mm ammunition amounted to 2,750 rounds. On the roof were two Lyran launchers for illumination of targets.

The engine and transmission were at the front of the vehicle, and the powerpack consisted of a 179-kW (240-bhp) Rolls-Royce K60 multi-fuel engine and a 365-kW (490-shp) Boeing 553 gas turbine. In normal use the tank was powered by the diesel, the turbine being engaged when the vehicle was in combat or moving across country demanding a higher power/ weight ratio. The driver was seated on the left of the hull and

SPECIFICATION	
Stridsvagn 103	**Powerplant:** one diesel engine
Crew: 3	developing 119 kW (240 hp) and
Weight: 39 tonnes	one Boeing 553 gas turbine
Dimensions: length (with gun) 8.99	developing 366 kW (490 shp)
m (29 ft 6 in); length (hull) 7.04 m	**Performance:** maximum road speed
(23 ft 1 in); width 3.63 m (10 ft 8¼	50 km/h (31 mph); maximum range
in); height (overall) 2.5 m (8 ft 2½	390 km (242 miles)
in)	**Fording:** 1.5 m (4 ft 11 in)
Armament: one 105-mm (4.13-in)	**Gradient:** 60 per cent
main gun, two co-axial 7.62-mm	**Vertical obstacle:** 0.9 m (2 ft 11½ in)
(0.3-in) machine-guns, and one	**Trench:** 2.3 m (7 ft 6½ in)
7.62-mm AA machine-gun	

had a combined periscope and binocular sight with x1, x6, x10 and x18 magnifications, the right eyepiece having a sighting graticule. The radio operator was seated to the rear of the driver and faced the rear. The commander was on the right, and his optical equipment included a combined periscope and stabilised optical sight almost identical to that of the driver and enabling him to aim and fire the gun. In a typical engagement the commander acquired the target, then used the handlebars on the tiller columns to lay the armament onto the target. The type of ammunition was then

selected and loaded, the gun was fired, and the empty cartridge case was ejected through the rear of the hull.

Suspension system

The suspension was of the hydro-pneumatic type and gave the armament/hull an elevation arc between -10° and +12°. The main drawback of the S-tank was that it could not fire on the move, but Sweden was content to accept this as its armed forces were optimised for defensive rather than offensive operations.

Mounted under the nose was a dozer blade to prepare defensive positions. Around the top of the hull was a flotation screen (standard on the **Strv 102B** and retrofitted on the initial **Strv 103A**) that could be erected in 20 minutes, and the tank was propelled in the water by its tracks at a speed of 6 km/h (3.7 mph). In the late 1980s the Strv 103 fleet was updated to **Strv 103C** standard with a 216-kW (290-hp) Detroit Diesel 6V-71T diesel units, an automatic transmission, and a laser rangefinder. The last S-tanks were retired from Swedish service in 2001.

In order to elevate the S-tank's main gun the front of the hull could be raised. Without a turret the S-tank had a notably low silhouette.

Chieftain Main battle tank

The **Chieftain** was designed to succeed the Centurion. The first prototype appeared in 1959, and another six followed in 1961–62. The Chieftain was accepted for service in May 1963 and two production lines were laid down. Until the introduction of the Leopard 2 into West German service in 1980, the Chieftain was arguably the best armed and armoured tank in the world. About 900 Chieftain MBTs were built for the British Army, Kuwait ordered 165 **Chieftain Mk 5/2K** vehicles, and Oman took delivery of 12 ex-British tanks in 1981 before adding 15 purpose-built **Qayd al Ardh** tanks. The largest export order was placed by Iran, which ordered about 707 tanks, ARVs and bridgelayers, and later 187 examples of the **Improved Chieftain**. In 1974 Iran ordered 125 **Shir 1** and 1,225 Shir 2 MBTs, the latter a new design, but this order was cancelled by the new fundamentalist regime that took power in 1979. The Shir 1 became the **Khalid**, of which Jordan took 274. In the 1980s Iraq captured about 100 Iranian tanks, and passed most of these to Jordan.

The Chieftain's layout is conventional, with the driver at the front, turret in the centre (with the commander and gunner on the right and the loader on the left), and the engine and transmission at the rear. To reduce overall height, the driver sits in a reclined position, lying almost horizontal when driving with the hatch closed. The turret is of cast steel with a well-sloped front. The commander has a cupola that can be traversed through 360°, and mounted externally on this is a 0.3-in (7.62-mm) machine-gun which can be aimed and fired from within the turret.

Devastating gun

The Chieftain's main armament is the 120-mm (4.72-in) L11A5

A British Chieftain MBT with 120-mm L11A5 rifled tank gun, which has a thermal sleeve to reduce distortion, and is also used by Iran, Iraq, Jordan Kuwait and Oman.

rifled gun, which fires separate-loading ammunition with the bagged charges in special water-filled containers below the turret ring to reduce the risk of an explosion. The projectile types include APDS-T (Armour-Piercing Discarding Sabot-Tracer), APFSDS-T (Armour-Piercing Fin-Stabilised Discarding Sabot-Tracer), HESH (HE Squash Head) and smoke. The tanks in British service were retrofitted with the Improved Fire Control System (IFCS) which, used in conjunction with a laser rangefinder, enabled the successful engagement of targets at ranges of well over 2010 m (2,200 yards). Co-axial with the 120-mm gun is a 7.62-mm (0.3-in) machine-gun, and on each side of the turret is a bank of six electrically operated smoke dischargers.

Ammunition totals are 64 120-mm and 6,000 7.62-mm rounds. The NBC pack is mounted on the turret bustle, and a fire detection and extinguishing system is installed in the engine compartment. Night-vision equipment is the IR type with an IR/white light searchlight. It has a range of 1000 m (1,100 yards) in the IR mode and 1500 m (1,640 yards)

SPECIFICATION	
Chieftain Mk 5 **Crew:** 4 **Weight:** 55 tonnes **Dimensions:** length (with gun forward) 10.795 m (35 ft 5 in); length (hull) 7.518 m (24 ft 8 in); width 3.5 m (11 ft 8½ in); height (overall) 2.895 m (9 ft 6 in) **Armament:** one 120-mm (4.72-in) main gun, one co-axial 0.3-in (7.62-mm) machine-gun, and one cupola-mounted 0.3-in machine-gun	**Powerplant:** one Leyland 6-cylinder multi-fuel engine developing 560 kW (750 bhp) **Performance:** maximum road speed 48 km/h (30 mph); maximum road range 400 to 500 km (250 to 310 miles) **Fording:** 1.07 m (3 ft 6 in) **Gradient:** 60 per cent **Vertical obstacle:** 0.91 m (3 ft) **Trench:** 3.15 m (10 ft 4 in)

in the white light mode.

Special variants

The primary operational variants of the Chieftain, now out of British service, were the **Chieftain Mk 2** with a 485-kW (650-bhp) engine, improved **Chieftain Mk 3**, **Chieftain Mk 5** with an uprated engine, **Chieftain Mks 6**, **7** and **8** revisions of older marks with an improved engine and ranging machine-gun, and **Chieftain**

Mks 9, **10**, **11** and **12** revisions of intermediate marks with the IFCS and, in the last two, the Stillbrew passive armour package and the Thermal Observation and Gunnery Sight providing a night and adverse-weather capability. Chieftain variants for other roles are the **Chieftain Armoured Vehicle Royal Engineer**, **Chieftain Armoured Repair and Recovery Vehicle**, **Chieftain Armoured Recovery Vehicle**, and **Chieftain Armoured Vehicle-Launched Bridge**.

Until the introduction of the West German Leopard 2 with its 120-mm (4.72-in) gun, the British Chieftain with its 120-mm rifled gun was the most well armoured and powerful tank in NATO's inventory of main battle tanks.

Challenger 1 Main battle tank

In 1974 Iran ordered 125 Shir 1 and 1,225 **Shir 2** MBTs from Royal Ordnance Factory, Leeds. The Shir 1 was essentially a late-production Chieftain, already entering service with Iran, while the Shir 2 was a new design with the same powerpack, armament and fire-control system as the Shir 1 in combination with a hull and turret of Chobham armour which would provide a high degree of protection against weapons such as HEAT warheads. It also had hydrogas suspension which gave an excellent ride across rough country as well as being easy to maintain and repair in the field.

The British were to have replaced the Chieftain with a British/West German design, but this fell by the wayside in March 1977 and the UK went ahead on its own with a new project designated MBT-80. With the fall of the Shah of Iran in 1979, the massive Iranian order was cancelled before deliveries could start, although by that time the Shir 1 was already in production. In 1980

Packing a powerful punch with its L11A5 rifled gun, the Challenger 1 was able to fire a wide array of ammunition, which proved especially useful during Operation Desert Storm in 1991.

the Ministry of Defence announced that the MBT-80 project had been cancelled as it was becoming too expensive and its in-service date was slipping. Instead an order was placed for 237 (later 319) examples of the **Challenger**, which became the **Challenger 1** after the advent of the Challenger 2. The Challenger is basically the Shir 2 with modifications to suit it for a European rather than Middle Eastern climate. The first production Challengers were handed over to the British Army in March 1983, and equipped five regiments in Germany.

120-mm main gun

The production vehicles were fitted with the standard 120-mm (4.72-in) L11A5 rifled gun (64 rounds), but plans for its replacement in later vehicles by a new high-technology gun developed by the Royal Armament Research and Development Establishment (RARDE) at Fort Halstead were cancelled. Carried by the Challenger 2, this L30A1 weapon is of electro-slag refined steel with a new split breech design and chromed barrel, firing its projectiles with a very high muzzle velocity to provide increased penetration over current projectiles.

The first Challengers were accepted by the British Army in March 1983. This retained the Chieftain's 120-mm gun but introduced a new powerpack and advanced Chobham armour for enhanced protection.

SPECIFICATION	
Challenger 1 **Crew:** 4 **Weight:** 58 tonnes **Dimensions:** length (with gun forward) 11.55 m (37 ft 10¾ in); width 3.52 m (11 ft 6½ in); height (overall) 2.975 m (9 ft 9 in) **Armament:** one 120-mm (4.72-in) main gun, one co-axial 0.3-in (7.62-mm) machine-gun, and one 0.3-in AA machine-gun	**Powerplant:** one Perkins Condor V-12 diesel developing 895 kW (1,200 bhp) **Performance:** maximum road speed 56 km/h (35 mph); maximum range about 400 km (250 miles) **Fording:** 1.07 m (3 ft 6 in) **Gradient:** 60 per cent **Vertical obstacle:** 0.91 m (3 ft) **Trench:** 3.15 m (10 ft 4 in)

Variant family

In most other respects the Challenger 1 is akin to late-variant Chieftain tanks, and the type was operated in four variants as the basic **Challenger**

Mk 1 without the Thermal Observation and Gunnery Sight, the **Challenger Mk 2** with the TOGS, the **Challenger Mk 3** with a safer interior, and the definitive **Challenger Mk 4** model. Conversions included the **Challenger 1 Control** brigade commander's tank, **Challenger 1 Command** squadron commander's tank, **Challenger Training Tank** with a fixed superstructure, and **Challenger Armoured Repair and Recovery Vehicle**.

The last Challenger 1 tanks were retired from first-line British service late in 2000. A refurbishment programme is bringing some 288 of the tanks up to 'as new' condition for sale to Jordan, which received its first vehicles in 1999. In Jordan the Challenger 1 is known as the **Al Hussein**.

Challenger 1
In action

In the Gulf War of 1991 the tank showed itself to be a type that bridged the capability gap between the now-ageing Chieftain and its proposed successor, which emerged as the Challenger 2.

Though its origins could be found not so much in an operational requirement as in the British government's desire to keep alive an indigenous capacity for the design and manufacture of main battle tanks armed with powerful guns and protected by advanced armour, the Challenger 1 proved itself a capable tank and saw considerable action in the Gulf War of 1991.

Gunnery equipment
The gunner had a Tank Laser Sight with magnifications of x1 and x10. The laser rangefinder could be used up to 10000 m (10,935 yards). The fire-control system was based on a more modern computer than that installed in the Chieftain's fire-control system, and this FCS had greater capacity for 'stretch'.

Despite its origins in the Shir 2 developed for Iran, the Challenger 1 was optimised for operations under temperate European conditions, but nonetheless performed well in the heat and dust of desert conditions in the Arabian peninsula.

Powerpack
The whole powerpack weighs nearly 5.5 tonnes but was designed for quick replacement in the field. The contemporary British Army armoured repair vehicle, the FV434, could not cope with the weight, so a new vehicle based on the Chieftain chassis had to be introduced as the Chieftain Armoured Repair and Recovery Vehicle.

Rolls-Royce (Perkins) Condor 12V-1200 engine
Based upon proven conventional components, this is an excellent engine with low specific fuel consumption. It uses high-efficiency turbochargers and can develop 895 kW (1,200 bhp) at 2,300 revolutions per minute. The same engine is fitted to the Khalid tank, essentially a development of the late-production Chieftain main battle tank sold to Jordan.

120-mm L11A5 rifled gun
The Challenger 1's main armament was fitted with a thermal sleeve, fume extractor and muzzle reference system. The L30 high-pressure tank gun was introduced on the follow-on Challenger 2 tank.

Gunner
BAOR Challenger 1s were fitted with the TOGS (Thermal Observation and Gunnery Sight) in an armoured barbette on the right of the turret. This provided separate outputs for the commander and gunner.

Single pin track
The Challenger 1's track was not interchangeable with that of the Chieftain. It was of the single-pin type with removable rubber pads, and thought was given to its replacement by a new track offering less rolling resistance and also a longer life.

Chobham armour
The classified Chobham armour was named after the Ministry of Defence establishment at which it was developed. It was particularly effective against chemical-energy attack, so infantry anti-tank rockets and anti-tank guided missiles presented much less of a threat to the Challenger 1 than they did to its predecessor, the conventionally armoured Chieftain.

The Challenger 1 on manoeuvres in West Germany. The Challenger 1, which entered service in March 1983 was finally withdrawn from British Army service late in 2000, leaving Jordan as the only operator, with vehicles renamed Al Hussein. British Army Challenger 1 units included the Royal Tank Regiment (which received its first vehicles in late 1984) and the Royal Hussars (equipped by May 1985).

SPECIFICATION

Challenger 1 Mk 4
Type: main battle tank
Crew: four (commander, driver, gunner and loader)

Dimensions
Length: 11.56 m (37 ft 11 in) with the gun forward and hull length 8.327 m (26 ft 3 in); **width:** overall 3.518 m (11 ft 7 in) and over tracks 3.42 m (11 ft 3 in); **height:** 2.5 m (8 ft 3 in) to turret roof and 2.95 m (9 ft 8 in) to top of commander's sight

Combat weight
62000 kg (136,684 lb)

Powerplant
One Rolls-Royce (Perkins) Condor V-12 1200 water-cooled 12-cylinder diesel engine delivering 895 kW (1,200 bhp) at 2,300 rpm and one 27.6-kW (37-bhp) Coventry Climax H30 or (later vehicles) Perkins Type 4108 diesel auxiliary engine
Transmission: David Brown TN37 including Borg-Warner torque converter with lock-up clutch giving four forward and three reverse gears
Suspension: Hydro-pneumatic with six road wheels, two track-return rollers, rear drive sprocket and front idler on each side

Fuel capacity
Usable 1592 litres (350 Imp gal)

Performance
Maximum road speed: 36 km/h (22.4 mph)
Maximum road range: 450 km (289 miles)
Maximum cross-country range: 250 km (155 miles)
Fording: 1.07 m (3 ft 6 in)
Gradient: 58 per cent
Vertical obstacle: 0.91 m (3 ft)
Trench: 2.8 m (9 ft 2 in)

Armament
One 120-mm (4.72-in) L11A5 rifled gun with 64 rounds; the turret had electrical traverse through 360° and the main gun could be elevated electrically through an arc of 30° (-10° to +20°); the main gun had two-axis stabilisation and was controlled with the aid of an Improved Fire-Control System on the basis of a number of sensors including the commander's and/or gunner's sights, the latter including a laser rangefinder

Secondary armament
One 0.3-in (7.62-mm) L8A2 co-axial machine-gun and one 0.3-in L37A2 AA machine-gun with a total of 4,000 rounds

Smoke dischargers
Two quintuple dischargers for 66-mm (2.6-in) smoke grenades on the sides of the turret front

Commander's machine-gun
The commander's cupola had a 0.3-in (7.62-mm) L37A2 machine-gun provided optimistically for anti-aircraft defence. The 0.3-in L8A2 co-axial weapon was of much greater value since it could be fired from within the vehicle to provide local defence.

Commander
The commander had a modified No. 15 cupola fitted with either a day sight or image intensifier sight for night combat. Nine periscopes provided the commander with all-round fields of vision.

Loader
The loader's task was to load the Challenger 1's 64 rounds of 120-mm (4.72-in) ammunition: generally 20 'fin' and 44 HESH and Smoke rounds. The ammunition was of the separate-loading type. Each charge storage position contained either one charge for a DS type round or two charges for HESH and Smoke rounds.

Driver
The driver could swing his single-piece hatch forward so he could drive with his head out. He had a wide-angle periscope for day driving, and this could be replaced by a Pilkington passive night sight for driving in conditions of darkness. In an emergency the driver could escape to the rear through the fighting compartment.

M60, M60A1 and M60A2 Main battle tanks

In 1956 the US Army decided to develop an improved version of its M48 tank to incorporate a new engine and a larger-calibre main gun. The former was the Continental AVDS-1790-P diesel unit, and the latter the British 105-mm (4.13-in) L7A1 barrel fitted with an American-designed breech. The L7A1 was subsequently licence-made in the US with the designation M68 and fitted to all production examples of the **M60** series of main battle tanks, with the exception of the M60A2. It proved so successful that it was also fitted to the initial variant of the M1 Abrams, the M60's successor and like the earlier type a product of Detroit Arsenal Tank Plant, at that time operated by the Chrysler Corporation but later taken over by the General Dynamics Corporation.

It is worth noting that late-production M48 tanks were rebuilt with the same engine and gun as the M60, making it difficult to tell to two types apart despite the fact that the welded hull of the M60 had

less of a 'boat' shape than that of the M48.

The M60 was developed via three **XM60** prototypes, which were converted from M48 standard in 1958, and the tank was standardised for service in March 1959. The M60 baseline model entered service with the US Army in 1960 with basically the same turret as the M48. This turret provided the standard 360°

powered traverse, and the gun could be elevated through an arc of 29° between -9° and +20°. Within the tank stowage was provided for 57 rounds of 105-mm ammunition, this ultimately being of the APFDS, APDS, HESH, HEAT and Smoke types.

The M60A2 was intended to be the main production version, but problems with its complex gun/missile armament meant that is was replaced by the M60A3 with a more conventional 105-mm main gun.

Improved model

The M60 was soon succeeded in production by the **M60A1**, which introduced a number of modifications including a redesigned turret with a more pointed front offering somewhat greater ballistic protection. During the course of M60A1

A pair of US Army M60A1 tanks participate in a platoon live-fire exercise in Germany in August 1978. Many M60A1s were brought up to M60A3 standard through the addition of thermal night vision equipment.

production, the RISE (Reliability Improved Selected Equipment) package was added to the type, this including a more reliable version of the AVDS-1790 engine, a passive night-vision system, and a smaller searchlight.

Next, during the course of 1964, came the **M60A2** that differed from the M60A1 primarily in its new turret, which was armed with a new and promising weapon system based on a 6-in (152-mm) gun. This could fire the MGM-51 Shillelagh anti-tank missile with semi-automatic command to line-of-sight guidance (which also armed the M551 Sheridan), as well as a range of ammunition types with combustible cartridge cases. A total of 526 M60A2 tanks was

built, but there were considerable problems with the weapon system and the type was introduced to service in 1972, seeing only a short time in first-line use before being withdrawn so that the chassis could become the basis of conversions to the specialised variants listed below.

The two main specialist variants are the **M60 AVLB** and the M728 Combat Engineer Vehicle (CEV). The M60 AVLB has a scissors bridge on top of the hull, and this is launched over the vehicle front to span gaps up to 60 ft (18.29 m) wide. The M728 CEV (discussed in detail elsewhere) has a hull and turret similar to those of the M60A1, but with a 165-mm (6.5-in) low-pressure gun firing a HESH round.

Above: US Army M60 series battle tanks are seen on exercise under typical weather conditions in West Germany. Note the dozer blade of the central example.

Below: The large commander's cupola carries a 0.5-in M85 machine-gun for local and anti-aircraft defence. This weapon is traversed with the cupola, but has independent elevation between -15° and +60°. The weapon is provided with 900 rounds of ammunition.

SPECIFICATION	
M60A1	Continental AVDS-1790-2A
Crew: 4	liquid-cooled 12-cylinder
Weight: 52617 kg (115,999 lb)	turbocharged diesel engine
Dimensions: length with gun	**Performance:** maximum road speed
forward 9.44 m (30 ft 11½ in);	48.3 km/h (30 mph); maximum
length of hull 6.95 m (22 ft 9½ in);	road range 500 km (311 miles)
width 3.63 m (11 ft 11 in); height	**Fording:** 1.22 m (4 ft)
3.27 m (10 ft 8¼ in)	**Vertical obstacle:** 0.91 m (3 ft)
Powerplant: one 560-kW (750-bhp)	**Trench:** 2.59 m (8 ft 6 in)

T-62 Main battle tank

The **T-62** is a development of the T-54/55 series with a slightly longer hull to accommodate a turret armed with a 115-mm (4.53-in) smooth-bore gun. Production began in 1962 and continued to 1975, ending after the completion of some 20,000 tanks. The type was also made in Czechoslovakia, mainly for the export market, and in North Korea. The T-62 was more expensive to produce than the earlier T-54 and T-55 series, and for this reason the T-55 remained in production for some years after the more modern T-62 had been phased out of production.

The U-5TS main gun is fitted with a bore evacuator and is stabilised in elevation and traverse. An unusual feature of the T-62 is that it has an integral shell case ejection system, which is activated by the recoil of the gun. This system ejects the spent case through a trapdoor in the turret rear, but reduces the rate of fire to about four rounds per minute as the gun has to elevate to +3.5° for the ejection cycle to be carried out.

Three rounds

Three main types of ammunition are fired by the U-5TS (otherwise 2A20) gun, namely HE-FRAG-FS (High Explosive Fragmentation Fin-Stabilised) with a muzzle velocity of 750 m (2,460 ft) per second, HEAT-FS (High Explosive Anti-Tank Fin-Stabilised) with a muzzle velocity of 900 m (2,955 ft) per second and capable of

penetrating over 430 mm (16.9 in) of armour, and APFSDS (Armour-Piercing Fin-Stabilised Discarding-Sabot) with a muzzle velocity of 1680 m (5,510 ft) per second, a very flat trajectory and the ability to penetrate 330 mm (13 in) of armour at a range of 1000 m (1,095 yards). Some 40 rounds of 115-mm ammunition are carried, of which four are ready rounds in the turret; of the 36 other rounds, 16 are to the right of the driver and 20 in the rear of the fighting compartment. A 7.62-mm (0.3-in) PKT

Above: These T-62 are seen in the service of the Afghan 'Northern Alliance'. The upper and lower angled parts of the nose are of well-sloped 102-mm (4-in) armour, while the front of the turret is 242 mm (9.53 in) thick.

machine-gun is mounted co-axial with the main armament, and 2,500 rounds are carried for this weapon.

Modern equipment

Standard equipment on all T-62 tanks includes IR night vision equipment for the commander, gunner and driver; an unditching beam carried at the rear of the hull; a turret ventilation system to remove fumes when the gun is fired; a nuclear collective protection system; and provision for fuel to be injected into the

Above: Seen above the rear of the hull of this T-62, embarked on a MAZ heavy-duty road transporter, are the side-by-side pair of jettisonable drum tanks whose fuel contents can add considerably to the tank's range.

Below: The T-62's U-5TS main gun has an elevation arc of 22° (-6° to +16°). The angle to which the gun can be depressed is slightly more than that of the T-54 and T-55 series, offering a slight improvement in the later tank's ability to adopt a hull-down firing position.

SPECIFICATION	
T-62	12.7-mm (0.5-in) DShKM AA machine-gun
Crew: 4	
Weight: 40 tonnes	**Powerplant:** one V-12 diesel developing 433 kW (580 hp)
Dimensions: length (with gun forward) 9.34 m (30 ft 7½ in); length (hull) 6.63 m (21 ft 9 in); width 3.3 m (10 ft 10 in); height 2.4 m (7 ft 10¼ in)	**Performance:** maximum road speed 50 km (31 mph); maximum road range 650 km (404 miles)
	Gradient: 60 per cent
	Vertical obstacle: 0.8 m (2 ft 7½ in)
Armament: one 115-mm (4.53-in) main gun, one 7.62-mm (0.3-in) PKT machine-gun, (T-62M) one	**Trench:** 2.85 m (9 ft 4¼ in)

diesel engine's exhaust to provide a smoke screen. The vehicle carries 675 litres (148.5 Imp gal) of fuel internally, with a further 285 litres (63 Imp gal) externally on the running boards, and this gives the T-62 a road range of 450 km (280 miles). A further two 200-litre (44-Imp gal) fuel drums can be fitted on the hull rear, increasing the road range to some 650 km (404 miles). All T-62s can ford rivers to a depth of 5.5 m (18 ft ½ in) with the aid of a snorkel erected over the loader's hatch. A centralised fire-extinguisher system is provided for the engine and fighting compartments, and this can be operated automatically or manually.

Variants

The extent of the T-62's production meant that several variants were produced. Bearing the standard T-62 designation are the **Model 1962** of 1962 with detail enhancements, the

Model 1972 with a 12.7-mm (0.5-in) DShKM AA machine-gun over the loader's position, and the **Model 1975** with a laser rangefinder over the main gun. The **T-72D** has the Drozd anti-tank missile defence system, passive armour protection and the V-55U engine, while the **T-72D-1** differs in its V-46-5M

engine, while the **T-62M** and **T-62M-1** are equivalent to the T-62D and T-62D-1 but with the Sheksna (AT-12 'Swinger') system that fires a laser beam-riding anti-tank missile from the main gun, the **T-62M1** and **T-62M1-1** are upgrades without the passive armour and Sheksna system, the **T-62M1-2**

and **T-62M1-2-1** are upgrades without the Sheksna system and with passive armour protection only for the belly and turret, and the **T-62MV** and **T-62MV-1** are upgrades with the Sheksna system and explosive reactive armour. Another major variant is the **T-62K** command tank.

Soviet T-62 tanks advance through an artillery barrage during training exercises. This tank was first used operationally in the Middle East.

T-64
Main battle tank

The T-64 has a similar layout to the T-72 but is armed with the 2A26 125-mm (4.92-in) smoothbore main gun with a vertical feed rather than the 2A46 model (which is also used by the T-80) and horizontal feed. This T-64 is fitted with Kontakt explosive reactive armour (ERA).

In the 1960s the Soviets built prototypes of a new MBT which, in the absence of any information about its real designation, became known in the West as the **M-1970**. This vehicle had a new suspension consisting of six small dual road wheels with the drive sprocket at the rear, idler at the front and four track-return rollers supporting the inside of the track only. All previous MBTs designed in the USSR since

World War II, namely the T-54, T-55 and T-62, had been characterised by larger road wheels with no return rollers. The turret of the M-1970 was similar to that of the T-62 and was armed with the same 115-mm (4.53-in) smoothbore gun.

Enter the T-64

Further development of the M-1970 resulted in the **T-64** MBT, which was placed in production at one tank plant in the USSR.

The first production vehicles were completed with the 115-mm D-68 (otherwise 2A21) smoothbore gun with two-axis stabilisation and an automatic loader for 30 rounds, with another 10 rounds carried for partial reloading. So far the T-64 has not been exported to any countries outside the USSR, and of course the nations into which the USSR split during the emergence of the CIS, whereas the later T-72 has been exported

on a wide scale, both within the Warsaw Pact and overseas. Some reports have stated that the T-64 was so poor a design and so plagued with mechanical troubles that it was in production only to 1969, although in that time as many as 8,000 were built. Another theory is that the T-64 had advanced armour (including pockets of ceramic) for its time, and was therefore reserved for Soviet units.

The layout of the T-64 is similar to that of the T-72, with the driver's compartment at the front, turret in the centre and powerplant at the rear. The driver is seated in the centre with a well-shaped glacis plate (probably of laminate armour) to his front. A V-type splashboard on the glacis plate stops water rushing up when the vehicle is fording a deep stream. When driving in the head-out position, the driver can quickly erect a cover over his position to protect himself against rain and snow. The turret is similar in design to that of the T-72, but is thought not to incorporate advanced armour, and carries the gunner and commander on the left and right.

Armament change

The first definitive variant to reach units, after some 600 examples of the T-64, was the **T-64A**. This differs from its predecessor mainly in its armament, which is centred on the 125-mm (4.92-in) 2A26M2 smoothbore gun, fitted with a thermal sleeve, and again fully stabilised and supplied with ammunition by a modified

automatic loader. Other elements of the armament include a 7.62-mm (0.3-in) PKT co-axial machine-gun with 1,250 rounds, and a 12.7-mm (0.5-in) NSVT anti-aircraft machine-gun on the commander's cupola with 300 rounds, with provision for this weapon to be operated from within the closed-down turret. A more advanced fire-control system was also incorporated, as was a bank of smoke grenade launchers on each side of the turret, and other changes included increased turret protection, a new fire detection and suppression system, a multi-fuel diesel engine, a dozer blade under the nose, and fittings for a mine-clearing system. The T-64 series has an NBC system, a full range of night vision equipment and, like most other Soviet MBTs, provision for a snorkel to provide deep-wading capability. The only known variant of the T-64A is the **T-64AK** command vehicle, which carries an additional radio set and, in place of the AA machine-gun, a telescopic mast 10 m (32 ft 10 in) tall. When raised over the turret, this mast

The T-64 has been seen in service only with the USSR and its successors, never having been offered for export as a result of its advanced features.

is held in position by stays pegged to the ground, a fact that prevents the tank from moving off quickly.

The next T-64 variant to appear was the **T-64B**, created as a major reworking of the T-64A with new hull and turret armour less bulky that the first-generation laminate armour used in the earlier variants. Other changes included provision for the gun to fire the Kobra (AT-8 'Songster') anti-tank missile (a radio command-guided weapon of which six are carried in the automatic loader in addition to 36 conventional rounds of ammunition), a new fire-control system including a laser rangefinder, a napalm resistant defence system, provision for the attachment of explosive reactive armour to create the **T-64BV** variant, a system to fire smoke grenades,

quick-disconnect units for the gun's barrel and breech, side skirts to protect the running gear against the effects of HEAT warheads, and greater travel in the suspension. Other T-64B variants include the **T-64BK** command tank, **T-64BM** with the 745-kW (999-hp) 6TD six-cylinder diesel engine, **T-64B1** without Kobra missile capability, **T-64B1K** command tank version of the T-64B1, **T-64BV1K** command tank with explosive reactive armour, and **T-64R** rebuild of the T-64 to virtual T-64B standard. Ukraine is planning to upgrade some of its older T-64B and T-64B1 tanks to a virtual T-80UD/T-80 standard under the designation **T-64U**, and CIS armies also operate the **BREM-64** armoured recovery version of the T-64 with a dozer/anchor blade, winch and crane.

SPECIFICATION	
T-64B	**Powerplant:** one 5DTF water-cooled 5-cylinder diesel engine developing 522 kW (700 hp)
Crew: 3	
Weight: 39.5 tonnes	**Performance:** maximum road speed 75 km/h (47 mph); maximum road range 550 km (342 miles)
Dimensions: length (with gun forward) 9.9 m (32 ft 6 in); length (hull) 7.4 m (24 ft 3 in); width (with skirts) 4.64 m (15 ft 3 in); height 2.2 m (7 ft 3 in)	
	Fording: 1.8 m (5 ft 11 in) without preparation
Armament: one 125-mm (4.92-in) smoothbore gun, one 7.62-mm (0.3-in) PKT co-axial machine-gun, and one 7.62-mm (0.3-in) NSVT machine-gun	**Gradient:** 60 per cent
	Vertical obstacle: 0.8 m (2 ft 7 in)
	Trench: 2.28 m (7 ft 6 in)

Magach Israeli M48 and M60 MBT upgrades

Two US tanks bear the name **Magach** in Israeli service, these being updated versions of the M48 and M60 main battle tanks. During the early 1960s a batch of M48s was sent to Israel where they were upgraded, principally by the provision of a 105-mm (4.13-in) main gun and diesel-engined powerpack, to near M60 standard. More M48s followed from the US after 1965. Further M48s captured from Jordan were added to the Israeli inventory following the Six-Day War of 1967, followed by deliveries of M60s from the US after 1973.

All these vehicles were gradually upgraded in many ways by the Israeli Ordnance Corps Workshops at Tel a Shomer, near Tel Aviv. These upgrades included a revised cupola for the commander, and a liberal application of Blazer passive reactive armour add-on blocks to defeat shaped-charge projectiles. Other innovations included extra external fuel tanks at the rear to improve the operational range, and the provision of machine-guns and locally produced smoke-dischargers on the turret roof. Some revision of internal ammunition stowage was also introduced. All these improvements were gradually phased in over a period of years and following operational experience.

The upgrading programmes eventually resulted in the **Magach 7** and the **Magach 7 Gimel**, both identifiable by their revised turret outlines created

The appearance of the original M60 is radically altered under the Magach 7 alterations. Note the additional armour and the stowage at the rear of the turret.

by the installation of modular appliqué armour and large blocks of reactive armour. There is also a **Magach 7D** with an improved hull and turret armour package. The later models also have additional turret armour providing a pronounced frontal wedge outline, and improved flat armoured plates over the hull glacis.

On later models the original 559-kW (750-hp) powerpack was replaced by a 677-kW (908-hp) General Dynamics (originally Continental) diesel coupled to a new transmission system. The gun, still of 105-mm calibre, was improved by the introduction of more effective ammunition and revised fire-control systems with

night-vision capabilities. The original tracks were replaced by those fitted to the Merkava, reducing maintenance demands and saving weight by about 1700 kg (3,748 lb). The **Sabra**, an export model of the latest Magach is armed with a 120-mm (4.72-in) gun. Some of

the older Magach series vehicles based on the M48 were withdrawn as the locally designed Merkava became available, only to be totally rebuilt as a heavy armoured personnel carrier known as the **Nagmachon**.

SPECIFICATION	
Magach 7	hatches), and one IMI CL-3030
Crew: 4	instant smoke discharger on each
Combat weight: 54 tons	side of the turret
Dimensions: not available	**Powerplant:** one General Dynamics
Armour: steel plus flat blocks of	AVDS-1790-5A air-cooled 12-
Blazer armour containing a	cylinder diesel developing 677 kW
sandwich of metal and explosives	(908 hp)
Armament: one 105-mm (4.13-in)	**Performance:** not available
M68 (L7) series rifled gun, one	**Fording:** 1.22 m (4 ft) without
7.62-mm (0.3-in) co-axial machine-	preparation
gun, two 7.62-mm (0.3-in) local	**Gradient:** 60 per cent
defence and AA machine-guns (on	**Vertical obstacle:** 0.91 m (3 ft)
the commander's and loader's	**Trench:** 2.59 m (8 ft 6 in)

Sho't Israeli Centurion MBT

Beginning in 1958, the young state of Israel started to purchase Centurion tanks from the UK. Over the years more were purchased from the Netherlands, as numbers became surplus to Dutch requirements, until about 1,000 to 1,100 examples of the

Centurion, known locally as the **Sho't**, were in Israeli service.

Upgraded firepower

Over the years these vehicles underwent a series of upgrades of much the same magnitude as the Magach. The original

20-pounder gun was replaced by a locally licence-produced 105-mm (4.13-in) weapon, and from 1967 onwards, following numerous troubles with the original engine installation under local conditions, the petrol engine was replaced by an American diesel

powerpack developing 559 kW (750 hp) and coupled to a fully automatic transmission. Both automotive measures considerably reduced the driver's workload and greatly improved the operational range, as well as reducing a potential fire hazard.

Numerous changes had to be made to the cooling system to accommodate the new engine, resulting in a raised engine deck. The brakes and other similar details were also either modified or were replaced entirely. Another modification was the introduction of the same commander's cupola as fitted to the Magach. Over the years, more effective 105-mm ammunition was gradually introduced, along with new computer fire-control systems.

Following all these upgrades and modifications the Sho't still managed to look similar to the original Centurion and remained as dependable, even under harsh local conditions – once the engine change had been introduced. The Sho't also proved to be remarkably rugged in combat, acquitting itself well during the 1967 Six-Day War and the 1973 Yom Kippur War, despite its low top speed in comparison with other Israeli tanks. Following the hasty introduction of front hull appliqué armour during the 1967 war, further frontal and turret protection was provided along with extra machine-guns on the turret roof, later reduced to a single 12.7-mm (0.5-in) Browning machine-gun. As the type became available, Blazer passive reactive armour blocks were added to the hull front and turret.

Sho't conversions

As the Merkava MBT gradually entered service in the 1980s, the older Sho't tanks were either withdrawn or passed to reserve units. The last of these vehicles were withdrawn as battle tanks

Despite its slow speed by modern standards, the rugged Sho't acquitted itself well during the 1967 and 1973 Arab-Israeli wars and in Lebanon.

in 2002. By then some of the vehicles were well over 40 years old, but many hulls and chassis have been reworked into heavy armoured personnel carriers such as the **Nagmash'ot**, or as combat engineer vehicles such as the **Nakpodon** and **Puma**. All these reworked vehicles are turretless; the armoured personnel carriers are heavily armed with machine-guns.

SPECIFICATION	
Sho't	machine-guns (commander's and
Crew: 4	loader's hatches) with 7,500 rounds
Combat weight: 53.5 tonnes	**Powerplant:** one General Dynamics
Dimensions: length (with gun	AVDS-1790-2AC air-cooled 12-
forward) 7.55 or 7.84 m (24 ft 9¼ in	cylinder diesel developing 559 kW
or 25 ft 8½ in) depending on	(750 hp)
model; width 3.38 m (11 ft 1 in);	**Performance:** maximum road speed
height (overall) 2.94 m (9 ft 7¾ in)	50 km/h (37 mph); range 500 km
Armour: steel plus Blazer reactive	(311 miles)
armour	**Fording:** 1.45 m (4 ft 9 in)
Armament: one 105-mm (4.13-in) L7	**Gradient:** 60 per cent
series rifled gun with 72 rounds,	**Vertical obstacle:** 0.91 m (3 ft)
one 7.62-mm (0.3-in) co-axial	**Trench:** 3.35 m (11 ft)
machine-gun, and two 7.62-mm	
(0.3-in) local defence and AA	

Olifant South African Centurion MBT

South Africa obtained a number of Centurion tanks from the UK during the late 1950s, although about half of the initial batch received were later sold to Switzerland as they were considered surplus to requirement. By the mid-1970s, however, it had been decided to increase the size of the local tank fleet and so further Centurions were obtained from Jordan and India. By 1976 it had been decided to upgrade the South African Centurions to a new standard known locally as **Olifant** (elephant).

For the **Olifant 1**, the original Meteor petrol engine was replaced by a turbo-charged V-12 diesel unit developing 559 kW (750 hp). This powerpack was coupled to an automatic transmission. The **Olifant 1A** entered production in 1983, this variant being automotively similar to the initial Olifant 1. The main change in armament terms was the replacement of the original 20-pounder main gun with a locally produced copy of the British 105-mm (4.13-in) L7 weapon, although this new gun still retained the original 20-pounder breech mechanism.

New suspension

A complete rebuild then resulted in the **Olifant 1B**. This model had the old bogie-type

Above: The Olifant Mk 1B represents the definitive version of the Centurion tank in South African service. The gun of the Mk 1B is fitted with a thermal sleeve for sustained accuracy.

Right: In October 2003, Alvis OMC was awarded a contract to upgrade existing Olifant Mk 1B tanks with an uprated powerpack, improved gun control equipment and a new target detection/engagement system.

SPECIFICATION

Olifant Mk 1B
Crew: 4
Combat weight: 58 tonnes
Dimensions: length (with gun forward) 8.61 m (28 ft 3 in); width 3.42 m (11 ft 2½ in); height (overall) 3.55 m (11 ft 7¾ in)
Armour: steel
Armament: one 105-mm (4.13-in) L7 series rifled gun with 68 rounds, one 7.62-mm (0.3-in) co-axial machine-gun and one 7.62-mm (0.3-in) local defence and AA machine-gun with 5,000 rounds, and two quadruple 81-mm (3.2-in) smoke grenade launchers
Powerplant: one liquid-cooled V-12 diesel engine developing 708 kW (950 hp)
Performance: maximum road speed 58 km/h (36 mph); range 500 km (311 miles)
Fording: 1.5 m (4 ft 11 in)
Gradient: 60 per cent
Vertical obstacle: 0.98 m (3 ft 3 in)
Trench: 3.45 m (11 ft 4 in)

suspension entirely replaced by a new torsion-bar system housed within double floor plates. The powerpack was uprated by the introduction of a 708-kW (950-hp) engine coupled to a suitable automatic transmission, while the fuel tanks were also revised accordingly. All these features added greatly to the Olifant's operational range and the quality of the cross-country ride for the crew of four. To assist the crew in their operations and improve their external vision, numerous internal stowage and optical device

revisions were introduced on the Olifant. Gunnery performance was considerably enhanced by the installation of a new fire-control system incorporating a laser rangefinder and offering night-vision capability. The combat weight of the Olifant 1A model was approximately 56000 kg (123,457 lb). The Olifant saw action during the 'bush' wars of the 1980s and during the Angolan struggles.

Specialist versions
Gradually all existing Olifant gun tanks were brought up to the

definitive Olifant 1B standard. Numerous add-on options were developed, such as a front-mounted dozer blade or a bush-basher bar to force a path through dense undergrowth. Mine ploughs or rollers can also be installed. Also developed from the Centurion was a turretless armoured recovery vehicle (ARV) variant, while at one time mention was made of a bridgelayer version.

At one stage it had been intended to retrofit an **Olifant 2** turret with a fully state-of-the-art

fire-control system controlling either a new locally developed GT8 105-mm or a 120-mm (4.72-in) gun, both of which would have been installed within wedge-shaped protection. The current, more modest, upgrade programme to extend the operational life of the Olifant MBT is to be undertaken by Alvis OMC in South Africa, with the first upgraded tanks to be delivered in May 2004. The upgrade will introduce an uprated powerpack and thermal-imaging capability.

Pictured with side armour panels removed to reveal the original bogie-type suspension configuration, the Olifant Mk 1A was the first model to introduce the 105-mm (4.13-in) L7 gun.

Steyr SPz 4K 7FA Armoured personnel carrier

Between 1961 and 1969 Saurer, which was taken over by Steyr Daimler-Puch in 1970, built 450 fully tracked APCs for the Austrian army, the final production model being the **Schützenpanzer 4K 4FA** with a more powerful engine. In addition to the usual specialised versions, the Austrian army procured two basic models of the 4K 4FA as the **SPz G2** fitted with an Oerlikon-Bührle one-man turret armed with a 20-mm cannon, and the **SPz G1** fitted with a 12.7-mm (0.5-in) M2HB machine-gun.

Improvements

In 1976 Steyr-Daimler-Puch completed the prototype of the **4K 7FA** APC with much improved protection as well as the more powerful engine and transmission of the SK 105 tank destroyer, a type armed with a 105-mm (4.13-in) gun and already in production for the Austrian army and, subsequently, for a number of other countries.

The first production examples of the 4K 7FA were completed in 1977, and orders were secured from countries such as Austria, Bolivia, Cyprus, Greece (where the vehicle was manufactured under licence as the **Leonidas**) and Nigeria.

The all-welded steel hull of the **4K 7FA G127** basic model provides protection against projectiles of up to 20-mm calibre over the frontal arc, and

The Steyr-Daimler-Puch 4K 7FA-KSPz infantry fighting vehicle is a further development of the basic 4K 7FA which is used by Austria, Greece (manufactured under licence) and Nigeria. It shares many components with the SK 105 tank destroyer armed with a 105-mm (4.13-in) gun in a turret.

accommodates the driver at the front left with the engine to his right, and the troop compartment at the rear. The gunner is seated to the rear of the driver, and his cupola is provided with a two-part hatch cover that in the vertical position provides protection to his sides, the 12.7-mm machine-gun being fitted with a shield for frontal protection. On the rear of the gunner's cupola are four smoke dischargers.

The eight troops enter and leave the vehicle through twin doors in the hull rear, and sit in two rows of four down the middle of the vehicle facing outward. Over the troop compartment is a two-piece hatch cover that opens to each side,

and around the roof can be mounted up to four 7.62-mm (0.3-in) machine-guns; to fire these weapons the troops have to expose their heads and shoulders above the roof. Standard equipment includes heating and ventilating systems, and passive night vision equipment can be installed.

The chassis is the basis for a family of vehicles. The **4K 7FA-KSPz** MICV has ball mounts for

two rifles in each side of the hull. The **4K 7FA FSCV 90** prototype for a fire-support model has a turret with the 90-mm (3.54-in) Cockerill Mk III gun. The **4K 7FA MICV 30/1** prototype has a turret with the 30-mm RARDEN cannon. There are also **4K 7A-Fü** command, **4K 7FA-San** ambulance, **4K 7FA AMC 81** 81-mm (3.2-in) mortar carrier and, not in production, two AA variants.

SPECIFICATION	
SPz 4K 7FA	
Crew: 2 + 8	**Performance:** maximum road speed
Weight: 14800 kg (32,628 lb)	63.6 km/h (41 mph); maximum
Dimensions: length 5.87 m (19 ft	road range 520 km (323 miles)
3 in); width 2.5 m (8 ft 2 in); height	**Fording:** 1 m (3 ft 3 in)
(without MG) 1.69 m (5 ft 7 in)	**Gradient:** 75 per cent
Powerplant: one 238-kW (320-hp)	**Vertical obstacle:** 0.8 m (2 ft 7 in)
Steyr liquid-cooled 6-cylinder diesel	**Trench:** 2.1 m (6 ft 11 in)

Chinese APCs YW 531, YW 534 and Type 77 series

Manufactured by a number of Chinese state factories but marketed by NORINCO (China North Industries Corporation) are a number of current tracked APC families. The oldest of these, dating from the late 1960s, is the **YW 531** 12.6-tonne amphibious vehicle with a two-man crew and accommodation for 13 infantry.

The organic armament comprises one 12.7-mm (0.5-in) Type 54 machine-gun, and the 238.5-kW (320-hp) diesel provides a maximum road speed of 66 km/h (41 mph). Variants include three upgraded APCs as well as command post, ambulance, two rocket launcher, two mortar carrier, anti-tank and 122-mm (4.8-in)

self-propelled howitzer vehicles. The YW 531 series is in large-scale Chinese service and has also been exported to eight other countries.

Also in Chinese service but exported on a smaller scale is the **Type 85**, developed as the **YW 531 H**, a 13.6-tonne amphibious APC with 2+13 accommodation and an organic

armament of one 12.7-mm Type 54 machine-gun. Family variants include the **YW 309** 3+8 ICV which has a 73-mm (2.87-in) low-pressure gun mounted in the turret of a **WZ 501** copy of the Soviet BMP-1; **WZ 702** and Type 85 command posts, **WZ 751** ambulance, **HJ-62C** scout, and Type 85 subvariants for the 120- and 82-mm (4.72-and 3.2-

SPECIFICATION

Type 90
Crew: 2 + 13
Weight: 14500 kg (31,966 lb)
Dimensions: length 6.74 m (22 ft 1½ in); width 3.15 m (10 ft 4 in); height (overall) 2.38 m (7 ft 9½ in)
Powerplant: one 238.5-kW (320-hp) KHD BF8L413F liquid-cooled 8-cylinder diesel

Performance: maximum road speed 67 km/h (41.5 mph); maximum road range 500 km (311 miles)
Fording: amphibious
Gradient: 60 per cent
Vertical obstacle: 0.7 m (2 ft 3½ in)
Trench: 2.2 m (7 ft 2½ in)

in) mortar carrier, ARV, maintenance engineering, and artillery command post roles. The chassis is also used as the basis for a 122-mm self-propelled howitzer.

APC successor

The **YW 534** APC is used only by China, and is thought to be the successor to the YW 531. It is a 14.3-tonne amphibious type providing 2+13 accommodation, and has the 12.7-mm Type 54 machine-gun as its organic armament. Variants include the **YW 307** IFV with a one-man

turret carrying a 25-mm cannon and 7.62-mm (0.3-in) co-axial machine gun, and an anti-tank model with a retractable four-tube launcher for Red Arrow 8 missiles.

The **Type 77** is very similar to the Soviet BTR-50PK, and is thought to be in service only with China. The variants include carriers for the HJ-2J ('Guideline') SAM and HY-2 ('Seersucker') AShM, and recovery vehicle.

The latest models are the 3+8 13.3-tonne **WZ 501** IFV and **YW 535** APC, the latter serving

The Type 70 is the rocket-launcher variant of the YW 531 APC with a traversing and elevating launcher for 19 130-mm (5.12-in) rockets, and is allocated to armoured and mechanised divisions, with a truck-mounted version allocated to infantry divisions.

as the **Type 90**. Both have been developed in several variants for a number of roles, and the

organic armament is one 73-mm gun and one 12.7-mm machine-gun respectively.

AMX VCI Infantry combat vehicle

To meet a French army requirement for an infantry combat vehicle, Hotchkiss, which is no longer involved in the design, development or production of vehicles, built a number of prototypes in the

early 1950s, but these were all rejected. It was then decided to build an IFV based on the chassis of the AMX-13 light tank, which was already in large-scale production for both the French and other armies.

Following trials with prototype vehicles, the **AMX VCI** (**Véhicule de Combat d'Infanterie**) was adopted by the French army, first production vehicles being completed at the Atelier de Construction Roanne

(ARE) in 1967. Some 3,400 vehicles of the series were built for the domestic and export markets. Once the ARE started to turn out the AMX-30 MBT, production of the AMX-13 light tank family, including the VCI, was transferred to Creusot-Loire at Chalon-sur-Saône.

AMX VCI infantry fighting vehicle of the French army fitted with a cupola-mounted machine-gun. The troop compartment at the rear of the hull is provided with firing ports. In the French army the type has now been replaced by the AMX-10P amphibious MICV.

Machine-gun turret

In many respects the VCI was an advance on other Western vehicles of its period as not only was it fitted with a machine-gun turret for the generation of suppressive fire, but the infantry could also use their rifles from within the vehicle. The major drawback of the VCI was its lack of amphibious capability, and when originally deployed it was not fitted with an NBC system or night vision equipment. The VCI is no longer in service with the French army, having been replaced by the amphibious AMX-10P, or with the armies of Belgium and Morocco, but is still operational with the forces of Argentina, Cyprus, Ecuador,

Indonesia, Lebanon, Mexico, Qatar, Sudan, UAE and Venezuela.

The AMX VCI is of all-welded steel construction, with the driver at the front left, engine to his right, commander and gunner in the centre and the troop compartment at the rear. The last has rear doors and hatches in the sides, the latter with four firing ports each. The torsion-bar suspension consists of five single road wheels, with the drive sprocket at the front and idler at the rear; there are four track-return rollers.

In addition to the basic VCI, there were also the **VTT/TB** unarmed ambulance, **VTT/PC** command post, **VTT/Cargo** cargo, combat engineer, anti-tank (with ENTAC wire-guided missiles), **VTT/RATAC** ground radar (this system has since been transferred to the 4x4 VAB), **VTT/LT** artillery fire-control, **VTT/PM** mortar carrier (two subvariants with an 81- or 120-mm/3.2- or 4.72-in weapon) and **VTT/VCA** support vehicle, the last carrying the remainder of the gun crew and additional ammunition for

the 155-mm (6.1-in) Mk F3 self-propelled gun.

From 1987 the manufacturer offered the **AMX-13 VTT Version 1987** as a conversion package for the VCI and all other members of the AMX-13 light tank family with a number

of automotive improvements, as well as the Detroit Diesel 6V-53T engine developing 208 kW (280 hp) for improved operational range, slightly higher speed and reduced fire risk.

SPECIFICATION	
AMX VCI	petrol engine
Crew: 3 + 10	**Performance:** maximum road speed
Weight: 15000 kg (33,069 lb)	60 km/h (37 mph); maximum range
Dimensions: length 5.7 m (18 ft	350 km (218 miles)
8 in); width 2.67 m (8 ft 9 in);	**Fording:** 1 m (3 ft 3 in)
height (overall) 2.41 m (7 ft 11 in)	**Gradient:** 60 per cent
Powerplant: one 186-kW (250-hp)	**Vertical obstacle:** 0.65 m (2 ft 2 in)
SOFAM liquid-cooled 8-cylinder	**Trench:** 1.6 m (5 ft 3 in)

VCC-1 Camillino Armoured IFV

OTO Melara of La Spezia, well known as a manufacturer of naval weapons and now called Otobreda, has been engaged in the design and production of armoured vehicles since the 1960s, and has built several thousand M113 tracked APCs for the Italian army under licence from FMC of the US.

While the M113 is an excellent vehicle, it suffers from two major drawbacks, namely its unprotected

12.7-mm (0.5-in) machine-gun mounting and its lack of provision for the infantry to fire their weapons from within the vehicle. The Automotive Technical Service of the Italian army subsequently modified the M113, and after trials this was adopted by the Italian army with the designation **VCC-1**, or more commonly the **Camillino**, and well over 1,000 of these were delivered to the Italian army up to 1983. In the same year the

manufacturer started delivery to Saudi Arabia of 200 vehicles fitted with the Emerson Improved TOW launcher as fitted to the American-built M901 Improved TOW Vehicle.

The forward part of the VCC-1, which has seen active service in Somalia, is identical to that of the M113, with the driver at the front on the left-hand side and the engine to his right. The rest of the vehicle is new, the commander being seated to the rear of the driver and provided with a cupola and periscopes. The 12.7-mm M2HB machine-gun is to the right of the driver in a cupola that can be traversed through 360°, lateral and rear armour protection being provided.

Troop compartment

The troop compartment is at the rear, and in each side of the upper hull, which is angled inward on each side, are two firing ports each surmounted by a vision block. There is another firing port in the power-operated rear ramp.

In the centre of the hull at the rear is a machine-gunner controlling an externally mounted 7.62-mm (0.3-in) machine-gun. To make more room in the troop compartment the fuel tank has been removed and the diesel fuel is now carried in two panniers externally at the hull rear, one on each side of the ramp.

The VCC-1 is amphibious, being propelled in water by its tracks at a speed of 5 km/h (3.1 mph). Before entering water a trim vane is erected at the front of the hull and the two electric bilge pumps are activated.

The basic version is the **VCC-1 Mk 1** described above; the **VCC-1 Mk 2** (not in Italian service) has a remotely controlled 12.7-mm machine-gun, and the **VCC-1 Mk 3** prototype has a 20-mm cannon in a mounting above the roof. The **VCC-2** variant is basically the Italian-built M113 with applique armour on the front and sides.

SPECIFICATION	
VCC-1 Camillino	water-cooled diesel
Crew: 2 + 7	**Performance:** maximum road speed
Weight: 11600 kg (25,573 lb)	64.4 km/h (40 mph); maximum
Dimensions: length 5.04 m (16 ft	road range 550 km (342 miles)
9 in); width 2.69 m (8 ft 10 in);	**Fording:** amphibious
height (to hull top) 1.83 m (6 ft)	**Gradient:** 60 per cent
Powerplant: one 160-kW (215-hp)	**Vertical obstacle:** 0.61 m (2 ft)
GMC Model 6V-53 6-cylinder	**Trench:** 1.68 m (5 ft 6 in)

The Otobreda VCC-1 Mk 3 is a development with a 20-mm cannon on the roof. The VCC-1 is a further development of the M113, which has been built under licence by the company.

Type 73 Armoured personnel carrier

When the Japanese Ground Self-Defence Force was formed in the 1950s, its first armoured personnel carriers were half-tracks supplied by the United States. The first Japanese-designed vehicle to enter service was the **Type SU 60** APC which was produced by Mitsubishi Heavy Industries and the Komatsu Manufacturing Corporation, final deliveries being made in the early 1970s. The Type SU 60 is not amphibious, has a four-man crew and can carry six fully equipped troops. Over 400 of these entered service, and variants include an NBC detection vehicle, 81- and 107-mm (3.19- and 4.2-in) mortar carriers and a dozer.

The **Type 73** then supplemented and largely replaced the Type SU 60, but production was at a very low rate, sometimes as low as six per year, and by the end of the manufacturing programme only 340 such vehicles had apparently been completed.

The Type 73 has a hull of all-welded aluminium armour with the commander, driver and bow machine-gunner at the front. The location of a 7.62-mm (0.3-in) machine-gun in the bow is unique and this weapon can be traversed 30° left, right, up and down; a similar weapon is installed in the earlier Type SU 60 APC.

The engine is toward the front on the left, with troop compartment at the rear. Entry

The Japanese Type 73 APC and the earlier Type SU 60 APC are the only vehicles of their type with a bow-mounted 7.62-mm (0.3-in) machine-gun.

to the latter is via two doors rather than a power-operated ramp as in the M113 APC and M2 Bradley IFV. One of the nine infantry-men normally mans the roof-mounted 12.7-mm (0.5-in) machine-gun, which is on the right side of the vehicle and can be aimed and fired from within the vehicle. The cupola can be traversed through 360° and the weapon elevated between -10° and +60°. The nine infantrymen are seated on benches down each side of the troop compartment facing each other; the benches can be folded up to allow stores and other equipment to be carried.

Indifferent equipment

On each side of the troop compartment are two T-type firing ports, although these have a limited value compared with the firing ports/vision blocks fitted to vehicles such as the German Marder. Another

unusual feature of the Type 73 is the installation, on the very rear of the hull roof on each side, of a bank of three electrically operated smoke dischargers. In action these would be fired when the vehicle came under attack, allowing the vehicle to pull back to the rear.

The Type 73 has night-vision equipment and an NBC system, but is only amphibious after lengthy preparation. This preparation includes flotation aids alongside the hull and attached to the road wheels, a trim vane mounted at the front of the hull, and boxes fitted around the air inlet, air outlet

and exhaust pipes on the roof of the vehicle. If the last were not fitted, any surge of water over the roof would go in the engine.

Unlike many other APCs, there is only one known variant of the Type 73, namely the **Type 75** self-propelled ground-wind measuring unit that is used with the 130-mm (5.12-in) multiple rocket-launcher and uses some components of the Type 73.

The Type 73 is already obsolete as it lacks both armour protection and firepower, but has not been wholly replaced by the Mitsubishi Type 89 infantry combat vehicle, armed with a 25-mm chain gun.

SPECIFICATION	
Type 73	Mitsubishi air-cooled diesel
Crew: 3 + 9	**Performance:** maximum road speed
Weight: 13300 kg (29,321 lb)	70 km/h (45 mph); maximum range
Dimensions: length 5.8 m (19 ft	300 km (186 miles)
1 in); width 2.8 m (9 ft 1 in); height	**Fording:** amphibious
(with MG) 2.2 m (7 ft 3 in) and	**Gradient:** 60 per cent
(hull) 1.7 m (5 ft 7 in)	**Vertical obstacle:** 0.7 m (2 ft 4 in)
Powerplant: one 224-kW (300-hp)	**Trench:** 2 m (6 ft 7 in)

Pbv 302 Armoured personnel carrier

Although the Swedish army deployed tanks well before World War II, it was not until the post-war period that it fielded its first fully tracked armoured personnel carriers. These were called the **Pbv 301** and were essentially the older Strv m/41 light tank stripped down to the basic chassis and rebuilt to

armoured personnel carrier standard. The type was armed with a 20-mm cannon and could carry eight fully equipped infantrymen as well as the two-man crew. The conversion work was carried out by Hägglund & Söner in 1962-63.

Even before work had started the Swedish army realised that

this would only be a interim solution as the basic chassis was so old. Design work on the new **Pbv 302** armoured personnel carrier started in 1961 and progress was so quick that the first prototypes were completed in the following year. After the usual trials the company was awarded a full-scale production

contract and production was undertaken from 1966 to 1971.

The Pbv 302 was not sold abroad, although it was offered to several countries. The main reason for this is that the export of defence equipment is subject to such strict controls that Sweden can deal with only a very few countries.

Advanced concept

In some respects the Pbv 302 is very similar in layout to the American M113, although the Swedish vehicle has some noticeable features that, when the vehicle was introduced, put it some way ahead of its competitors. The hull is of all-welded steel armour with the driver in the centre at the front, the gunner to the left rear and the commander to the right rear. The main armament comprises one 20-mm Hispano cannon mounted in a turret with a traverse of 360° and elevation from -10° to +60°. The cannon can fire either high-explosive (in belts of 135 rounds) or armour-piercing (in 10 round magazines) ammunition. The same turret has also been fitted to a number of other vehicles including the M113s of the Swiss army and EE-11 6x6 vehicles of Gabon.

The troop compartment is at the rear of the hull, with the 10 infantrymen seated five along each side facing inward. No firing ports are provided, although hatches over the troop compartment allow the troops to fire their weapons from

The Pbv 302 APC is only used by the Swedish army, and is fitted with a turret-mounted 20-mm cannon. Before entering water the bilge pumps are switched on and the trim vane erected at the front.

within the vehicle. The infantry enter and leave the vehicle via two doors in the hull rear. The Pbv 302 is fully amphibious, being propelled in the water by its tracks.

Basic uses

The basic vehicle can also be used as an ambulance or a cargo carrier, while more specialised versions include the **Stripbv 3021** armoured command vehicle, **Epbv 3022** armoured observation post vehicle, and **Bplpbv 3023**

fire direction post vehicle. A prototype of the **Pbv 302 Mk 2** APC was built by Hägglund as a private venture. This had a separate cupola at the rear for the squad commander, a Lyran

flare system and other minor modifications. The company also proposed that the vehicle be developed as a mechanised infantry fighting vehicle with a turreted 25-mm cannon.

SPECIFICATION	
Pbv 302	developing 209 kW (280 hp)
Crew: 2 + 10	**Performance:** maximum road speed
Weight: 13500 kg (29,762 lb)	maximum road speed 66 km/h (41
Dimensions: length 5.35 m (17 ft 7	mph); maximum road range 300
in); width 2.86 m (9 ft 5 in); height	km (186 miles)
(turret top) 2.5 m (8 ft 2 in) and	**Fording:** amphibious
(hull top) 1.9 m (6 ft 3 in)	**Gradient:** 60 per cent
Powerplant: one Volvo-Penta Model	**Vertical obstacle:** 0.61 m (2 ft)
THD 100B 6-cylinder inline diesel	**Trench:** 1.8 m (5 ft 11 in)

MOWAG Tornado Mechanised infantry combat vehicle

The MOWAG company has been engaged in the design and development of tracked and wheeled vehicles since just after World War II, and in the early 1960s its was awarded a contract by the then West German government for the construction of prototypes of a mechanised infantry combat vehicle (MICV) that became the Marder.

Private venture

In the 1970s the company developed as a private venture the very similar **Tornado** MICV whose definitive version, called the **Improved Tornado**, was announced in 1980. At this time the Swiss army's standard APC was the American M113, though many of these had been fitted

with a Swedish turret carrying one 20-mm cannon. The Swiss decision of 1983 to order the Leopard 2 MBT suggested an obvious need for a complementary MICV, but after great delay Switzerland opted for the CV 9030CH from Sweden.

The hull of the Improved Tornado was of all-welded steel construction and probably offered better protection against armour-piercing projectiles than most vehicles on the market at that time, as its sides and front were very well sloped for the maximum possible protection. The driver was at the front of the vehicle on the left, with the commander to his rear and the powerpack to his right.

In the centre of the hull could be mounted a wide range of

The Tornado MICV was developed by MOWAG of Switzerland as a private venture. This Tornado had a 25-mm turret-mounted cannon and two remotely controlled machine-guns at the rear.

armament installations depending on the mission requirement. One of the most powerful installations was the Swiss power-operated Oerlikon-Bührle Type GDD-AOE two-man turret, which had an externally mounted 35-mm KDE cannon

fed from two ready-use magazines each holding 50 rounds. One could hold armour-piercing rounds to engage other vehicles, while the other could hold high-explosive rounds for use against softer target such as trucks. Mounted co-axially with the 35-mm cannon was a 7.62-mm (0.3-in) machine-gun with 500 rounds of ammunition to tackle soft targets.

The infantrymen were seated in the troop compartment at the hull rear, and entered and left via a power-operated ramp. On each side of the troop compartment were spherical firing ports that allowed some of the troops to fire their weapons from within the vehicle. If required, two remotely controlled 7.62-mm (0.3-in) machine-guns could be fitted (one on each side) at the rear on the troop compartment roof. These were almost identical to those fitted to the Marder. Each mount could be traversed through 230° and the guns could be elevated from -15° to +60°.

As with most vehicles of its type, the Improved Tornado was fitted with an NBC system and night-vision equipment. The

SPECIFICATION	
MOWAG Tornado	Detroit Diesel Model 8V-71T diesel
Crew: 3 + 7	**Performance:** maximum road speed
Weight: 22300 kg (49,162 lb)	66 km/h (41 mph); maximum road
Dimensions: length 6.7 m (22 ft);	range 400 km (249 miles)
width 3.15 m (10 ft 4 in); height	**Fording:** 1.3 m (4 ft 3½ in)
(hull top) 1.75 m (5 ft 8⅓ in) and	**Gradient:** 60 per cent
(turret top) 2.86 m (9 ft 4¾ in)	**Vertical obstacle:** 0.85 m (2 ft 9½ in)
Powerplant: one 290-kW (390-hp)	**Trench:** 2.2 m (7 ft 2⅓ in)

design of the chassis was such that it could have been adopted for a wide range of other roles such as command vehicle, missile carrier, recovery vehicle, mortar carrier and so on, but none of these even reached the prototype stage.

M-80 Mechanised infantry combat vehicle

The first armoured personnel carrier designed and built in Yugoslavia to enter service was the M-60P, which was designed to transport men across the battlefield where they would dismount and fight on foot.

Realising the obvious shortcomings of this vehicle, Yugoslavia then started design work on a mechanised infantry combat vehicle which appeared in 1975 as the **M-980**, changed to **M-80** in 1991. The short development period was made possible by the use of a number of proven components from other sources. For example, the engine came from Renault of France, the road wheels are similar to those of the Soviet PT-76 amphibious light tank, and the 'Sagger' anti-tank missile is fitted to a wide number of Soviet vehicles including MICVs, APCs and tank destroyers.

In many respects the design of the M-80 is very similar to that of the Soviet BMP-1. The driver is seated at the front of the vehicle on the left, with the vehicle commander to his rear and the engine to his right. The one-man turret is in the centre of the vehicle and armed with a 20-mm cannon with elevation between -5° and +75°; mounted co-axially is a 7.62-mm (0.3-in) machine-gun. The high elevation of these weapons enables them to be used against low-flying aircraft. Mounted externally on the right rear of the turret are two locally-built 'Sagger' wire-guided anti-tank missiles. The compartment for the embarked troops is located at the vehicle's rear, and entry to this compart-ment is via two doors in the hull rear. Above the troop compartment are roof hatches and firing ports (with periscopes

SPECIFICATION	
M-80	(overall) 2.5 m (8 ft 2 in)
Crew: 2 + 8	**Performance:** maximum road speed
Weight: 13000 kg (28,660 lb)	60 km/h (37 mph); maximum range
Powerplant: one HS 115-2 V-8 diesel	500 km (310 miles)
developing 194 kW (260 hp)	**Fording:** amphibious
Dimensions: length 6.4 m (21 ft);	**Vertical obstacle:** 0.8 m (2 ft 8 in)
width 2.59 m (8 ft 6 in); height	**Trench:** 2.2 m (7 ft 3 in)

above) allowing weapons to be fired from within the vehicle.

Fully amphibious

The M-80 is amphibious, being propelled in the water by its tracks; before the vehicle enters the water a trim vane is erected at the front of the hull and the bilge pumps are switched on. The M-80 is also fitted with a fire-extinguishing system, an NBC pack and a smoke laying system.

The **M-80PB** variant is an anti-tank vehicle fitted with two 82-mm (3.23-in) recoilless rifles on a rotating mount on top of the hull. In some respects the M-80 is an improvement over the Soviet BMP-1 as it has two rather than one 'Sagger' missile in the ready-to-launch position, and its 20-mm cannon is probably more suited to the role of the vehicle than the 73-mm (2.87-in) gun of the BMP-1. It is of note that in the BMP-2 the Soviets switched from the 73-mm weapon to a smaller-calibre 30-mm (1.18-in) gun, and most Western vehicles of this type are armed with weapons in the 20- to 30-mm (0.78-in–1.18-in) range rather than heavy weapons such as the 73-mm (2.87-in) gun of the BMP-1.

In 1980 there appeared the improved **BVP M-80A** with weight increased by one tonne due to a more powerful engine being installed; the width and height were also increased. Further BVP development yielded the **M-80AK** IFV with a 30- rather than 20-mm cannon, **M-80A KC** company comman-der's vehicle, **M-80A KB** battalion commander's vehicle, **M-80A LT** anti-tank vehicle with six 'Saggers', **M-80A Sn** ambulance, and **M-80 VK** command post.

Production completed, the M-80 and M-80A series is now operated by Bosnia, Croatia, Macedonia and Slovenia and Yugoslavia.

M-80 MICVs prior to the break-up of Yugoslavia, showing the twin launchers for AT-3 'Sagger' ATGWs located above the turret roof. The engine is as used in the French AMX-10P armoured infantry carrier.

BMD Airborne combat vehicle

From the end of World War II, the Soviet Union placed great emphasis on its airborne forces. For many years it maintained at least seven airborne divisions at full strength. At the start of the Cold War the only armoured vehicles these divisions used were the 57-mm (2.24-in) ASU-57 or the 85-mm (3.35-in) ASU-85 self-propelled anti-tank guns.

To give these units increased firepower and mobility once they were landed behind enemy lines the **BMD** airborne combat vehicle was designed, entering service in 1969. Each Soviet airborne rifle division had 330 of these vehicles in various configurations, although it is unlikely that all seven divisions operated their full complement of vehicles, primarily because the USSR did not have the capability to lift more than one airborne rifle division at any one time.

Unusual layout

The BMD was used to spearhead the invasion of Afghanistan in 1979. It has also been used in Chechnya, and has been exported in very small numbers to India and Iraq.

The layout of the vehicle is unusual, the driver being seated at the front of the hull in the centre with the commander to his left and the bow machine-gunner to his right. The latter operates the two single 7.62-mm (0.3-in) machine-guns mounted internally at the front of the hull, one on each side. The turret, which is identical to that fitted to the BMP-1, is in the centre of the hull and is armed with a 73-mm (2.87-in) gun, a 7.62-mm co-axial machine-gun and a launcher rail for the 9M14 Malyutka (AT-3 'Sagger') ATGW mounted above the main gun. To the rear of the turret is a small compartment with seats for the gunner, the grenade-launcher and his assistant; the only means of entry to this compartment is via the concertina-type roof hatch.

The independent suspension of the BMD consists of five road wheels, with drive sprocket at the rear and idler at the front; there are four track-return rollers. An unusual feature of this suspension is that a hydraulic system is incorporated that allows the ground clearance of the vehicle to be altered from 100 mm to 450 mm (4 in to 18

The BMD airborne combat vehicle was used primarily by the Soviet Air Assault Divisions and saw extensive service in Afghanistan. Its turret is similar to that fitted to the BMP-1 MICV, carrying a low-pressure 73-mm (2.87-in) gun and a Malyutka or a Konkurs anti-tank guided missile mounted above the gun or on the roof.

in), a factor of some importance for airborne operations.

The BMD is fitted with an NBC system and a full range of night-vision equipment. It is also fully amphibious, the only preparation required being the erection of the trim vane at the front of the hull and the engagement of the bilge pump.

The command version of the BMD is called the **BMD-U (command)**, and this has a longer chassis with six road wheels on each side and no turret. There is also an 82-mm (3.23-in) mortar version that has seen action in Afghanistan.

The original BMD was

replaced in production by the **BMD-2**, in which the original turret has been replaced by a one-man turret mounting a 2A42 30-mm (1.18-in) gun and a 9M113 Konkurs (AT-5 'Spandrel') ATGW. Production started in 1989 and was completed at the end of the 1990s.

Current model

The latest **BMD-3** is in low-rate production at the Volgograd tractor plant. The BMD-3 has the same turret as the previous version, but the chassis is new with much better amphibious capability.

SPECIFICATION	
BMD	0.45 m (17 in)
Crew: 3 plus 4 troops	**Performance:** maximum road speed
Weight: 7500 kg (16,530 lb)	70 km/h (43 mph); maximum water
Powerplant: one 240-hp (179-kW)	speed 10 km/h (6.2 mph);
5D-20 liquid-cooled V-6 diesel	maximum range 320 km
Dimensions: length 5.40 m	(200 miles)
(17 ft 9 in); width 2.63 m (8 ft 8 in);	**Fording:** amphibious
height 1.62 m to 1.97 m	**Gradient:** 60 per cent
(5 ft 4 in to 6 ft 6 in); track width	**Vertical obstacle:** 0.80 m (2 ft 8 in);
230 mm (9 in); ground clearance	**Trench:** 1.60 m (5 ft 3 in)

BMD in operation

Airborne assault vehicle

During the Cold War, the Soviet Airborne Forces (Vozdushov Desantniye Voyska, or VDV) were transformed into powerful mechanised units, capable of seizing heavily defended targets and attacking well-armed forces deep behind enemy lines.

Unlike British paratroopers, who drop with minimum arms and equipment and rely on speed and aggression to win the day, Soviet airborne forces had a complete series of specialised vehicles that matched all but the strongest allied forces in firepower and manoeuvrability.

The BMD-1 airborne amphibious infantry combat vehicle entered service in 1969 and at a stroke turned the VDV from light to mechanised infantry. Because of outward similarities, it is often mistaken for the BMP, but it has a totally new hull design and suspension, is far lighter, and is considerably more cramped inside.

The BMD-1 can be carried in the hull of the Il-76 or An-12 that, between them, accounted for the majority of Soviet military air transport. With its pneumatic suspension system folded up, the BMD-1 can be dropped from the air.

Airborne deployment

The vehicle is pulled from the rear of the aircraft with the aid of a drogue chute. Then the main canopy deploys, and four probe poles unfold beneath the

*A **BMD-1** in Afghanistan where Soviet airborne forces spearheaded the initial invasion in December 1979 and later formed the cutting edge of the Soviet war effort against the Mujahideen. This **BMD-1** appears to have lost its 'Sagger' launching rail.*

pallet. As soon as one of the poles makes contact with the ground, a retro-rocket system fires, considerably slowing the final stages of descent. The crew drop immediately after their vehicle and, during night drops, are guided to it by a radio 'bleeper'. They detach the pallet restraints and are operational within minutes.

The BMD-1's main armament is the same 2A28 73-mm (2.87-in) low-pressure smooth-bore gun as that mounted on the BMP-1. The low turret is also similar to that of the BMP-1. Loaded mechanically from a 40-round magazine, the gun fires fin-stabilised, rocket-propelled HEAT and HE-FRAG rounds at up to eight rounds per minute. Although ineffective against modern tank armour, the HEAT round will penetrate the much thinner skins of infantry combat vehicles. Its maximum range is 1300 m (1,422 yards), but it is badly affected by wind and is therefore only accurate to 800 m (875 yards).

The BMD-1 is itself very lightly protected: there is no more than 25 mm (0.98 in) of armour in the frontal arc of the turret and 15 mm (0.59 in) in

the hull. The thin frontal armour is just enough to keep out small-arms fire, but nothing larger, making it easy prey for the 25-mm Chain Gun mounted on the US Bradley fighting vehicle.

BMD-1 performance

A rear-mounted Type 5D-20 V-6 liquid-cooled diesel engine that develops 179 kW (240 hp) powers the BMD-1. It has a maximum road speed of 80 km/h (49 mph) and through water, aided by two waterjets mounted in the rear, can reach 10 km/h (6.2 mph). The driver is seated centrally, immediately in front of the small one-man turret. The driver observes through three periscopes positioned in front of his hatch, with IR periscopes available for night driving. Either the squad commander or gunner, seated to the left and right of the driver, can fire the section RPK MG. The commander can also access the gyro-compass.

*This **BMD-KSh** command vehicle in Afghanistan has its antenna raised. Note the sixth road wheel and lack of turret. There is another version carrying the **AGS**-17 Plamya 30-mm grenade launcher.*

The main armament is unstabilised and, despite the help of a co-axial 7.62-mm (0.3-in) PKT machine-gun supplied with 2,000 rounds of ammunition, it is very inaccurate when fired on the move. The automatic loader and 40 rounds of ready-to-use 73-mm ammunition take up much of the remaining space inside, leaving room for normally only three passengers. Four 9M14 (AT-3 'Sagger') missiles are carried and can be fired from a rail above the gun barrel. The gunner relies on the familiar Soviet stadiametric rangefinder, in which graticules coincide with different ranges assuming a target height of 2.7 m/8 ft 10 in (average NATO tank height). The gunner keeps the controls for the 'Sagger' missile under his seat, pulling them out when the vehicle stops to fire a missile.

Disadvantages

Despite its excellent reputation, the BMD-1 does have a number of drawbacks. The 'Sagger' demands an unbroken line of sight between firer and target, and cannot be reloaded by the crew unless they break the vehicle's NBC seal.

The troop compartment itself is small, able to accommodate

BMD-1 ON PARADE: SOVIET AIRBORNE ARMOUR

On parade in Moscow in November 1980, this BMD-1 carries an AT-3 'Sagger' anti-tank guided missile on the launch rail above the 73-mm smoothbore gun. Three missile re-loads are stowed within the hull. The small size of the vehicle compared to the crew is readily apparent; the BMD is even more cramped than the BMP.

Fire support

Until 1985, Soviet airborne troops relied on the D-30 122-mm (4.8-in) towed field howitzer for artillery support, and on the ASU-85 for limited anti-tank protection. Whereas the D-30 was powerful enough to engage the majority of rear-echelon enemy artillery, it was too cumbersome to be towed by anything smaller than a BMD-2. The ASU-85, self-propelled, fast and manoeuvrable though it was, was far too small to engage modern MBTs.

The problem was partly resolved in 1985 by the introduction of the 2S9 assault artillery vehicle: a 120-mm (4.72-in) breech-loading mortar, mounted in a large turret on a BMD-2 chassis.

A small stub charge boosts the projectile out of the barrel, when a rocket motor cuts in to accelerate the round to cruise speed. It is not as accurate as the ground forces' 122-mm 2S1 howitzer, but the 9-tonne 2S9 is light enough to be air-dropped. Its high elevation lets it attack downhill targets (which was very important in Afghanistan), while in direct-fire its HEAT round will penetrate all but the latest generation of tanks.

only three men in relative comfort, although more can be carried if needed. The only means of access is via a concertina-type hatch in the roof.

The fuel tanks are poorly constructed and have a marked tendency to break away from their mountings, while the additional tanks in the rear are vulnerable to incendiary fire. Finally, the transmission is too fragile to withstand heavy drops, with the result that the shift lever can disengage at critical moments, leaving the vehicle helplessly stuck in gear.

Variations on the BMD

The most important, if least known, of the BMD-1 family is the BTR-D air assault transporter variant. First seen during the 1979 invasion of Afghanistan, this vehicle is 60 cm (23.6 in) longer than the original, has an extra road wheel and return roller, and a built-up superstructure but no turret.

Two basic variants exist, of which the multi-purpose armoured transporter version is the more common. Used for route control in larger drops and as a prime-mover whenever support weapons such as the ZU-23 or Vasilek mortar are deployed, the transporter can also carry up to nine fully-equipped troops. Each soldier

has a firing port, two capable of taking automatic weapons in the bow, two in the front hatches, two each side and one in the rear. The other variant, known as the BMD-KSh, is a command vehicle equipped with a folding 'clothes line' antenna around the superstructure, a single commander's hatch and no firing ports.

There were important changes in armament in the later BMDs. For the BMD-2 version, the 73-mm smoothbore gun was replaced by a far more accurate 30-mm autocannon in a one-man turret (also mounted on the BMP-2), while the 9M111 (AT-4 'Spigot') was mounted in place of the 'Sagger'. 'Spigot' has a range of 2000 m (2,187 yards) and can be taken from the vehicle and used on the ground. However, it can only be fired from the vehicle if a crewman opens one of the rear hatches and leans forwards. In this position, he is unprotected and would break the NBC

First observed in public in May 1985, the 2S9 Anona fire-support vehicle carries an enlarged turret mounting a long-barrelled 120-mm mortar. This replaced the ageing ASU-85 assault/anti-tank gun. The breech-loading mortar can carry a HEAT round for anti-tank action.

seal if the system were operating.

Introduced in 1990, the latest BMD-3 version features the turret of the BMP-2 and is somewhat heavier than its predecessors. The BMD-3 can be air-dropped together with its complement of seven personnel, who are protected by an all-welded hull. The two-man turret is armed with a 30-mm 2A42 cannon, while both types can carry the longer-range 9M113 (AT-5 'Spandrel') missile in place of the 9M111 anti-tank weapon.

BMP-1 Mechanised infantry fighting vehicle

The **BMP-1** was developed as the replacement for the BTR-50 armoured personnel carrier and caused a major stir throughout Western armies when it rolled through Red Square for the first time in 1967. Previous armoured personnel carriers simply transported the infantry to a point near the scene of action, where it dismounted to attack the objective on foot. The BMP-1 not only has firing ports that allow all of the embarked troops to fire their weapons from within the vehicle in relative safety, but also a 73-mm cannon and a wire-guided anti-tank missile.

Fighting vehicles

Since the introduction of the BMP-1 several countries have also developed mechanised infantry combat vehicles: the West German Marder (20 mm cannon), the French AMX-10P (20-mm cannon), the British Warrior (30-mm cannon) and the US M2 Bradley (25-mm cannon) are all good examples. The Marder has been fitted with an externally mounted MILAN ATGW, but although this is more accurate than the 9M14 Malyutka ('Sagger') fitted to the BMP-1 it has a shorter range. The M2 has a twin launcher for the TOW ATGW, which has a longer range than the Malyutka and is much more accurate.

The layout of the BMP-1 is unusual, with the driver at the front left, the commander to his rear and the engine on the right. The turret is in the centre of the hull and the infantry

Finland operates both the original BMP-1 and the improved BMP-2. First used in combat by Arab forces in 1973, the BMP-1 later saw action with the Soviets in Afghanistan, with Iraq in various Middle East conflicts and with Libyan forces fighting in Chad and Angola.

compartment at the rear. The eight infantrymen are seated four down each side, back to back, and enter the vehicle via twin doors in the hull rear. Over the top of the troop compartment are roof hatches. The main drawback of this arrangement is that the troop commander is out of immediate contact with the men he must command in battle.

The 73-mm gun is fed from a magazine that holds 40 rounds of HEAT (high explosive anti-tank) or HE-FRAG (high explosive fragmentation) ammunition, and there is a 7.62-mm (0.3-in) co-axial machine-gun. Turret traverse is electric, with manual controls for emergency use. The main drawbacks of the 73-mm low-pressure gun is its low muzzle velocity and its lack of accuracy in high winds. To fire

and achieve a first-round hit the BMP-1 must first halt.

The Malyutka ATGW is mounted on a launcher rail over the 73-mm gun and controlled (via a joystick) by the gunner. The missile has a maximum range of 3000 m (3,280 yards), but takes 27 seconds to reach this range. The BMP-1 is fitted with a full range of first-generation infra-red night-vision equipment for the commander, gunner and driver, as well as a NBC system. It is fully amphibious with little

preparation, being propelled in the water purely by the motion of its tracks.

'Small Fred'

In addition to the basic BMP-1 there were also command versions of the vehicle, a radar carrier fitted with two-man turret armed with a 7.62-mm machine-gun and fitted with a 'Small Fred' mortar/artillery-location radar on turret rear, a reconnaissance vehicle that has a new two-man turret and a mine clearing variant.

SPECIFICATION	
BMP-1	**Performance:** maximum road speed
Crew: 3 plus 8 troops	80 km/h (50 mph); maximum range
Weight: 13500 kg (29,762 lb)	500 km (311 miles)
Powerplant: one 6-cylinder diesel	**Fording:** amphibious
developing 300 hp (224 kW)	**Gradient:** 60 per cent
Dimensions: length 6.74 m (22 ft 1	**Vertical obstacle:** 0.80 m (2 ft 8 in);
in); width 2.94 m (9 ft 8 in); height	**Trench:** 2.20 m (7 ft 3 in)
(overall) 2.15 m (7 ft 1 in)	

BMP-2 Mechanised infantry combat vehicle

The **BMP-2** mechanised infantry fighting vehicle is a further development of the BMP-1 and was first observed in public during a parade held in Red Square, Moscow, late in 1982, although it entered service with the Soviet army several years before that. Since then it has

been exported to more than 18 armies around the world, and is in service with most of the former Soviet states.

The basic chassis of the BMP-2 is very similar to that of the original BMP-1, but has a new turret and different crew positions. On the BMP-1 the

commander was seated behind the driver and therefore had poor observation to the right side of the vehicle. In the BMP-2 the commander now sits in the much enlarged turret alongside the gunner, and has an excellent position for all-round battlefield observation.

The original BMP-1's 73-mm (2.87-in) weapon suffers from a number of drawbacks and, while powerful, is very inaccurate in high winds. The first-generation 9M14 Malyutka ('Sagger') missile needed a well-trained gunner to ensure a first-round hit.

Effective armament

These major disadvantages have been overcome in the BMP-2, as the armament now comprises a 30-mm rapid-fire automatic cannon, which can be elevated to +74°, so enabling it to be used against low-flying aircraft and helicopters. The gunner can select either single shots or one of two rates of automatic fire (200/300 or 500 rounds per minute) and 600 rounds of HE-T (High Explosive – Tracer) and AP-T (Armour-Piercing – Tracer) are carried. A 7.62-mm (0.3-in) PKT machine-gun is mounted co-axial with the main armament.

Mounted on the turret roof is a 9M111 Fagot (AT-4 'Spigot') anti-tank guided weapon, which has a maximum range of 2000 m (2,187 yards) and is fitted with a HEAT warhead. Based on plans stolen from Euromissile, the 'Spigot' is much easier to use. All the operator has to do to ensure a hit is to keep the crosswires of his sight on the target. On the earlier 'Sagger' he had to operate a small joystick.

In addition to being able to inject diesel fuel into the exhaust to lay its own smoke-

The BMP-2 is an updated version of the BMP mechanised infantry combat vehicle, and substitutes a 30-mm cannon for the 73-mm smooth bore gun of the first model. It also carries 9M111 Fagot (AT-4 'Spigot') ATGMs in place of outdated the 9M14 Malyutka (AT-3 'Sagger').

screen, the BMP-2 has three electrically-operated smoke-dischargers mounted on each side of the turret towards the rear. More recent BMP-2s have appliqué armour on their turret sides.

Seven fully equipped infantrymen are carried, compared with eight in the earlier vehicle: one man is seated to the rear of the commander and the other six in the troop compartment at the rear facing outwards, each being provided with a firing port with an observation periscope above.

Like the BMP-1, the BMP-2 is fully amphibious, being propelled in the water by its tracks. Before entering the water a trim vane is erected at the front and the bilge pumps are switched on.

Nearly 30,000 BMPs have been built, mainly at the Kurgan Machine Construction plant in the Urals. Production has now been switched to the improved **BMP-3**.

SPECIFICATION	
BMP-2	2.06 m (6 ft 9 in)
Crew: 3 plus 7 troops	**Performance:** maximum road speed
Weight: loaded 14600 kg (32,187 lb)	60 km/h (37.3 mph); range 500 km
Powerplant: believed to be one Type	(311 miles)
5D20 turbocharged 6 cylinder	**Fording:** amphibious
water-cooled diesel developing 350	**Vertical obstacle:** 0.7 m (2 ft 3 in);
hp (261 kW)	**Trench:** 2.0 m (6 ft 7 in)
Dimensions: length 6.71 m (22 ft);	**Gradient:** 60 per cent; side slope 30
width 3.09 m (10 ft 17 in); height	per cent

Like most Soviet AFVs, the BMP-2 was first seen by Western observers at one of the major military parades which took place in Moscow in May and October. At the time of its disclosure in 1982 it had already been in service with the Red Army for several years. Since then the vehicle has been produced under licence in India and in the Czech Republic. The chassis of the BMP-2 is almost identical to the earlier BMP-1, but offers increased armour protection. The driver sits at the front of the vehicle on the left side, and is provided with a hatch and three periscopes. Active/passive night vision equipment can also be fitted.

BTR-50P Armoured personnel carrier

In the mid-1950s the **BTR-50P** was the first fully tracked armoured personnel carrier to enter service with the Soviet army, and is essentially the chassis of the PT-76 amphibious light tank with its turret removed and a superstructure added to the forward part. The commander and driver are seated under armour protection at the front of the vehicle, while the 10 fully equipped infantrymen are seated in the troop compartment on bench seats that run across the width of the vehicle.

The main drawbacks of this model are the lack of an NBC system and overhead armour protection for the infantry carried. The main armament is a 7.62-mm (0.3-in) machine-gun on a pintle mount at the front of the crew compartment. On the rear engine decking ramps are

provided so that a 57-mm (2.24-in) or 85-mm (3.35-in) anti-tank gun can be carried and, if required, fired from the vehicle.

The next major model was the **BTR-50PK**, which has a fully enclosed troop compartment and is fitted with an NBC system. The armament comprises a roof-mounted 7.62-mm machine-gun without protection for the gunner. An improved version of the BTR-50PK was built in Czechoslovakia as the **OT-62**, this being distinguished from the Soviet vehicle by its lack of chamfer between the side and top of the hull. Whereas most western APCs are propelled in the water by their tracks, the BTR-50P is driven by waterjets.

Command versions

There are two command versions, the **BTR-50PU**

The BTR-50 armoured personnel carriers are now obsolete, but survive in limited numbers for their ready availability, simplicity, and basic reliability.

Model 1 and **BTR-50PU Model 2**. Both have a fully enclosed crew compartment, the former having one projecting bay and the latter two. The vehicles have additional communications equipment and can be recognised by their radio aerials, external stowage and a generator. The basic vehicle has been out of production for some time, and in many Soviet units the type was replaced by the BMP-1 MICV. Two later versions are the **MTK** mineclearing vehicle and the **MTP** technical

support vehicle. The former is fitted with a rear-deck launcher that fires explosive tubes across the minefield, and the latter has a higher roof with chamfered sides and supports the BMP in the forward battlefield area.

The BTR-50P and its variants are still used by many countries. The type was used in Vietnam by the North Vietnamese army and in the Middle East campaigns by Syria and Egypt, the latter using the BTR-50P in its crossing the Suez Canal during the 1973 Yom Kippur War.

The BTR-50PK has overhead protection for the troop compartment, whereas the original BTR-50P has an open-top troop compartment, which leaves the 10 seated infantrymen very vulnerable to the effects of shells and mortar bombs. This Egyptian example is seen leaving an LCU during Operation Bright Star in 1985.

SPECIFICATION	
BTR-50PK	179 kW (240 hp)
Crew: 2 + 10	**Performance:** maximum road speed
Weight: 14200 kg (31,305 lb)	44 km/h (27 mph); maximum range
Dimensions: length 7.08 m (23 ft);	400 km (273 miles)
width 3.14 m (10 ft 4 in); height	**Fording:** amphibious
(without armament) 1.97 m (6 ft	**Gradient:** 70 per cent
6 in)	**Vertical obstacle:** 1.1 m (3 ft 7 in)
Powerplant: one Model V-6 water-	**Trench:** 2.8 m (9 ft 2 in)
cooled 6-cylinder diesel developing	

MT-LB Multi-purpose tracked vehicle

In the period immediately after World War II the Soviets introduced the AT-P armoured tracked artillery tractor, which tow anti-tank guns and how-itzers up to 122 mm (4.8 in) in calibre. This was then replaced by the **MT-LB** multi-purpose

armoured vehicle, which is used for many roles in addition to towing anti-tank guns such as the 100-mm (3.94-in) T-12.

Crew compartment

The crew compartment is at the front, with the engine to the

rear of this on the left and the troop compartment at the rear. The 11 infantrymen are seated on canvas seats down each side of the troop compartment that can be folded up to allow cargo to be carried. The infantry can quickly leave the vehicle through

two large doors in the hull rear, and two hatches are provided over the top of their compartment. Mounted at the front of the hull on the right side is a manually operated turret armed with a 7.62-mm (0.3-in) machine-gun. The road wheels are similar to those of the PT-76 amphibious light tank and the BTR-50 series of armoured personnel carriers. The torsion-bar suspension consists on each side of six road wheels, with the drive sprocket at the front and idler at the rear. The MT-LB is normally fitted with 350-mm (13.8-in) wide tracks, but when operating on snow-covered ground these can be replaced by the much wider 565-mm (22.25-in) wide tracks, which give a lower ground pressure and therefore better mobility.

Amphibious

The MT-LB is fully amphibious, being propelled in the water by its tracks at a speed of between 5 and 6 km/h (3 to 4 mph), and has IR night vision equipment and an NBC system.

In some areas of the former USSR, where the terrain is swampy or normally covered by snow, the MT-LB is used in place of the BMP mechanised infantry combat vehicle.

As usual, the MT-LB chassis has been used for a number of specialised applications including the MT-LBU command vehicle, the ADZM engineer

vehicle with hydraulic dozer blade, the MT-LB with 'Big Fred' battlefield surveillance radar on the roof at the rear, the RKhM chemical reconaissance vehicle, and the MTL-LB repair vehicle. The last is used for repair and recovery operations in the forward area and fitted (at the front) with an A-frame, plus a winch and a full range of tools and other specialised equipment. The chassis is also used as the basis for the SA-13 'Gopher' surface-to-air missile system that has four missiles in the ready-to-launch position. Automotive components of

The MT-LB multi-purpose armoured vehicle is a member of a family of vehicles that all share the same basic automotive components. This example is seen in Swedish service, one of 800 purchased from East German stocks.

the MT-LB, including the engine and transmission, are also used in the 122-mm (4.8-in) 2S1 self-propelled howitzer,

which entered service in the 1970s and is widely used by the former USSR as well as being exported to other countries.

SPECIFICATION	
MT-LB	**Performance:** maximum road speed
Crew: 2 + 11	61.5 km/h (38 mph); maximum
Weight: 11900 kg (26,235 lb)	range 500 km (311 miles)
Dimensions: length 6.454 m (21 ft 2	**Fording:** amphibious
in); width 2.85 m (9 ft 4 in); height	**Gradient:** 60 per cent
(to turret top) 1.865 m (6 ft 5 in);	**Vertical obstacle:** 0.7 m (2 ft 3 in)
Powerplant: one V-8 diesel	**Trench:** 2.7 m (8 ft 10 in)
developing 179 kW (240 hp)	

FV432 Armoured personnel carrier

After the end of World War II various prototypes of full-tracked armoured personnel carriers were built in the UK, but it was not until 1962 that one of these, the **FV432**, was accepted by the British Army. The FV432 is member of the **FV430** series of vehicles which also includes the FV433 Abbot 105-mm (4.13-in) self-propelled gun built by Vickers at its Elswick facility in Newcastle between 1964 and 1967, and discussed separately. The **FV431 Light Tracked Load Carrier** did not enter service.

Production of the FV432 and its many variants was undertaken by GKN Sankey between 1963 and 1971, about 3,000 being built in all. Although offered overseas it was not

purchased by any other country as by that time the very similar American M113 APC was already in volume production for the US Army, and this was much cheaper than the FV432. For a short period the FV432 was commonly known as the **Trojan**.

Transportation

Replacing the Saracen 6x6 APC, the basic role of the FV432 is to transport British infantry across the battlefield to a location close to its objective, where the men dismount and continue the assault on foot. The main difference between the M113 and the FV432 is that the latter has a hull of welded steel construction while the former has a hull of welded aluminium.

The FV432's tracked running gear with torsion-bar suspension comprises, on each side, five rubber-tyred dual road wheels, a forward-mounted drive sprocket, a rear-mounted idler and two track-return rollers. In later service many of the vehicles were fitted with a Peak Engineering turret armed with a single machine-gun.

The driver is seated at the front on the right, with the commander to his rear and the

powerpack to his left. The troop compartment is at the rear of the hull, with entry to this compartment via a large single door in the hull rear. Hatches are provided over the top of the troop compartment, but there is no provision for the infantry to use their weapons from within the vehicle. The 10 embarked infantry are seated five on each side of the hull, facing each other on seats that can be quickly folded up to enable cargo to be carried. The vehicle is fitted with night vision equipment and was also one of the first vehicles of its type to be fitted with an NBC protection system, which supplies clean air to the crew and troops.

When introduced to service the FV432 was fitted with a flotation screen attached to the top of the hull; when this had been erected, the vehicle could propel itself across lakes and rivers with its tracks. These screens were later removed as they were easily damaged and prone to combat damage from small arms fire and shell splinters. The basic vehicle is fitted with a 0.3-in (7.62-mm) machine-gun in an unprotected mount, but many vehicles were then retrofitted with a turret-

The FV432 is often fitted with a one-man turret armed with a 0.3-in (7.62-mm) machine-gun and four electrically operated smoke dischargers on either side. When fitted with this turret the roof hatches over the troop compartment cannot be used. The FV432 is in service only with the British Army.

mounted 0.3-in machine-gun over the troop compartment.

Versatility

In addition to being used as a troop carrier, the FV432 was or still is employed for a wide range of other roles including ambulance, command with extensive communications equipment installed, 81-mm (3.19-in) mortar carrier, minelayer towing the Bar minelaying system and fitted with the Ranger anti-personnel mine scatterer on the roof, carrier of radar such as the ZB

SPECIFICATION	
FV432	engine developing 179 kW (240 bhp)
Crew: 2 + 10	
Weight: 15280 kg (33,686 lb)	**Performance:** maximum road speed
Dimensions: length 5.25 m (17 ft 7 in); width 2.8 m (9 ft 2 in); height (with machine-gun) 2.29 m (7 ft 6 in)	52.2 km/h (32 mph); maximum range 483 km (300 miles)
	Fording: 1.07 m (3 ft 6 in)
	Gradient: 60 per cent
	Vertical obstacle: 0.61 m (2 ft)
Powerplant: one Rolls-Royce K60 liquid-cooled 6-cylinder multi-fuel	**Trench:** 2.05 m (6 ft 9 in)

298 surveillance or Cymbeline mortar/artillery-locating systems, artillery fire-control vehicle with FACE (Field Artillery Computer Equipment), and **FV439** specialised Royal Signals vehicles. The maintenance

carrier is called the **FV434 Armoured Fitter's Vehicle** and can change tank engines in the field, while the anti-tank member of the family was the now retired **FV438** with Swingfire heavyweight missiles.

A British Army FV432 APC operational in Macedonia. In many respects this vehicle is similar to the American M113, but it has steel rather than aluminium armour and, as built, was fitted with a multi-fuel engine and a complete NBC system.

M113 Lightweight APC family

By the mid-1950s the US Army was paying increased attention to light vehicles that could easily be transported by transport aircraft to any part of the world. A decision was taken to build prototypes of a new APC whose mechanical components would also be used to form a complete family of vehicles. Prototypes of steel (designated **T117**) and aluminium (designated **T113**) vehicles were built and tested. The latter was standardised for service in 1960 as the **M113**, and was soon in production at San Jose, where it continued until 1992, with production totalling almost 75,000.

Vehicle export

Since then the production line has been periodically reopened in order to fulfil export orders. The vehicle has been constantly improved to meet changing requirements, and has served with 50 countries, current operators including Argentina, Australia, Bahrain, Belgium, Bolivia, Bosnia, Brazil, Cambodia, Canada, Chile, Colombia, DR Congo, Denmark, Ecuador, Egypt, Ethiopia, Guatemala, Germany, Greece, Haiti, Iran, Iraq, Israel, Italy, Jordan, Kuwait, Lebanon, Libya, Macedonia, Morocco, New Zealand, Norway, Pakistan, Peru, Philippines, Portugal, Saudi Arabia, Singapore, Somalia, South Korea, Spain, Sudan, Switzerland, Taiwan, Thailand, Tunisia, Turkey, United States, Uruguay, Vietnam and Yemen. The Italian company Otobreda built almost 4,500 M113s for the Italian army, Chile and Turkey, and further development resulted in the much improved **Infantry Armoured Fighting Vehicle** (**VCC-1**) which is used by the Italian army and by Saudi Arabia in the anti-tank role fitted with the same twin TOW launcher as installed on the M113-derived **M901 Improved TOW Vehicle** (**ITV**). Belgium also maunfactured the

The standard US Army APC until the arrival of the M2 Bradley from the early 1980s, the M113 has been the subject of numerous improvement programmes undertaken both in the US and overseas.

M113A2 version under licence for its army.

The original model to enter service was powered by a Chrysler 75M V-8 petrol engine that developed 156 kW (209 bhp), giving the vehicle a maximum road speed of 64 km/h (40 mph) and a cruising range of 322 km (200 miles). Subsequently, a decision was made to power all future armoured vehicles with diesel rather than petrol engines, both to increase their operating range (diesels being more fuel-efficient than petrol engines) and to reduce the risk of fire. Trials with a diesel-powered model designated **T113E2** were successful and from 1964, the petrol-powered M113 was replaced on the production lines by the diesel-powered **M113A1**. This was powered by the proven General Motors Corporation Detroit Diesel Model 6V-53 six-cylinder diesel which develops 160 kW (215 bhp) to give a cruising range of 483 km (300 miles).

M113A2 production

The next model to enter production (in 1979) was the

The M125 mortar carrier is armed with an 81-mm (3.19-in) mortar and 114 mortar bombs. The 0.5-in (12.7-mm) machine-gun installation is retained.

M113A2, which was essentially the M113A1 with an improved cooling system and improved suspension. This model retained the same engine as the M113A1 but the increased weight slightly lowered its power-to-weight

vehicles up to the new M113A2 standard, additional vehicles being purchased from FMC as the requirement for M113A2s was almost 20,000 vehicles, including variants. These conversions were carried out both in the US as well as

SPECIFICATION	
M113A2	height (overall) 2.82 m (8 ft 3 in)
Crew: 2+11	**Performance:** maximum road speed
Weight: 11341 kg (25,002 lb)	67.59 km/h (42 mph); maximum
Powerplant: one GMC Detroit	water speed 5.8 km/h (3.6 mph);
Diesel Model 6V-53 six-cylinder	maximum range 483 km (300
water-cooled diesel developing	miles)
160 kW (215 bhp)	**Fording:** amphibious
Dimensions: length 2.69 m (8 ft	**Gradient:** 60 per cent
9 in); width 2.54 m (8 ft 4 in);	**Vertical obstacle:** 0.61 m (2 ft);
height (hull top) 1.85 m (6 ft 1 in);	**Trench:** 1.68 m (5 ft 6 in)

ratio. At this time the US Army still had over 5,000 of the original petrol-powered M113s in service as well as almost 13,000 of the diesel-powered M113A1s, and a decision was taken to bring all of these

overseas in West Germany and South Korea.

The next version to enter production was the **M113A3**, which was the M113A2 fitted with the more powerful 6V-53T turbocharged diesel engine

An Israeli M113 series APC, one of an estimated 6,000 in IDF service, fitted with an experimental two-man turret armed with a 60-mm hyper-velocity medium support weapon.

developing 205 kW (275 bhp), new transmission and new driver's controls. These improvements led to enhanced acceleration, superior cross-country performance, better fuel consumption and generally upgraded reliability.

M113 variants

There are probably more variants of the M113 family than any other vehicle in existence in the world today, and these can be divided into two series. First are those that use the hull of the M113 itself, modified in many applications, and second are those that use the chassis of the unarmoured **M548** tracked load carrier that is also a member of the M113 family and is discussed in a separate entry. In addition, many countries have carried out extensive modifications to meet their own particular requirements.

There are two mortar-carriers, the **M106/M106A1** and the **M125/M125A1**, the A1 models being powered by the diesel engine. The first of these has a 107-mm (4.2-in) mortar mounted in the rear, the M125 has the 81-mm (3.19-in) mortar mounted on a turntable that can be traversed through 360°. In both cases the mortar can be dismounted and fired away from the vehicle if required.

The anti-aircraft member of the family is the **M163**, which is fitted with a power-operated turret armed with a six-barrelled 20-mm Vulcan cannon. A flamethrower version was deployed to Vietnam, but it is no longer used.

The command version is the **M577**, which entered production in 1962. This is easily distinguishable from the basic M113 as it has a much higher roof to allow the command staff to work in an upright position. It also has extensive communications equipment as

Right: The Norwegian army's fleet of upgraded M113A1 vehicles are fitted with a Hägglunds one-man turret armed with a Rheinmetall 20-mm MK Rh 202 cannon.

Below: A US Army M113 APC prepares to pull an armoured 'Humvee' from the mud in Bosnia during IFOR's Operation Joint Endeavour in May 1996.

well as a tent that can be erected at the rear to increase the work area.

TOW Vehicle

The M901 Improved TOW Vehicle (or ITV) was developed for the US Army from 1976. This is the basic vehicle fitted on the full roof with an Emerson power-operated launcher that can be elevated from behind cover and carries two Hughes TOW ATGWs in the ready-to-launch position; an additional 10 missiles are carried inside for rapid reloading. A standard ground TOW launcher is also carried so missiles can be launched away from the vehicle if required. Now retired from front-line US Army service on the M113A1/A2, the ITV is used by Egypt, Greece, Jordan, Kuwait, Pakistan (all on the M113A1 chassis), the Netherlands (on **AIFV** chassis), Thailand (M113A1 chassis) and Saudi Arabia (VCC-1 chassis). The latest **M901A1** is capable of firing any of the basic

Raytheon Systems TOW missiles. The **M981 Fire Support Team Vehicle** (**FISTV**) is similar in appearance to the ITV except that it does not carry missiles in the launcher; these have been replaced by surveillance equipment and a laser. This vehicle is used to locate targets for the artillery and to direct Cannon-Launched Guided Projectiles (CLGPs) onto enemy tanks.

M113 progress

Further development of the M113 by FMC Corporation has resulted in the **Armoured Infantry Fighting Vehicle** (AIFV) operated by Bahrain, Belgium, Egypt, the Netherlands, Philippines and Turkey. The basic chassis has also been selected for a number of private-venture weapons developments including Canada's **M113 ADATS** (Air Defence Anti-Tank System), which has eight Oerlikon missiles in the ready-to-launch position.

SIBMAS Armoured personnel carrier

In the mid-1970s the Belgian company B N Constructions Ferroviaires et Métalliques started the development, as a private venture, of a 6x6 armoured personnel carrier which would have a number of common and proven commercial components. The first of two **SIBMAS** prototypes was completed in 1976, and one of these was tested by the Royal Malaysian army.

Malaysia selected two vehicles, namely the Thyssen Henschel Condor 4x4 type from West Germany and the SIBMAS 6x6 type. The first SIBMAS vehicles were delivered in 1983, and the order comprised 24 and 162 examples respectively of the **SIBMAS ARV** armoured recovery vehicle version with winch and crane, and the **SIBMAS Armoured Fire Support**

Malaysia is the sole operator of the SIBMAS, its 162 Armoured Fire Support Vehicle 90s being armed with the 90-mm (3.54-in) Cockerill Mk III gun in a CM 90 two-man turret. These were delivered in 1983-85.

Vehicle 90. The latter has a two-man Cockerill turret armed with a 90-mm (3.54-mm) Cockerill Mk III gun, 7.62-mm (0.3-in) co-axial and 7.62-mm anti-aircraft machine-gun, and fitted with an OIP fire-control system.

The hull of the SIBMAS is of all-welded steel construction providing the crew with complete protection from small arms fire and shell splinters. The driver is seated at the front of the vehicle, with the crew compartment in the centre and the engine at the rear of the vehicle on the left side, an aisle connecting the troop compartment with a door in the hull rear fitted on the right side.

Troop access

Doors are provided in each side of the hull, and there

The SIBMAS was a private-venture design, and was intended to accommodate a wide number of turrets and weapon systems, from a 105-mm (4.13-in) low-recoil anti-tank gun to a 7.62-mm (0.3-in) GPMG.

are hatches over the troop compartment. Depending on the model, firing ports and/or vision blocks can be fitted in the sides and rear of the troop compartment. If required, the vehicle can be fitted with a hydraulically operated winch to assist in self-recovery or the recovery of other vehicles. The basic model is fully amphibious without preparation, being propelled in the water by its wheels at a speed of 4 km/h (2.4 mph), or optionally

two rear-mounted propellers for a maximum water speed of 11 km/h (6.8 mph). Other optional equipment includes night-vision equipment, an air-conditioning system, a heater and an NBC system.

There were a number of other armament options, most of them based on French turrets and fire-control systems, but none of them had been ordered before the SIBMAS was taken out of production.

SPECIFICATION	
SIBMAS	**Powerplant:** one MAN D 2566 MK liquid-cooled 6-cylinder diesel developing 239 kW (320 hp)
Crew: 3 + 11	
Weight: 14500 kg to 16500 kg (31,967 to 36,376 lb) depending on role and armament	**Performance:** maximum road speed 100 km/h (62 mph); maximum road range 1000 km (621 miles)
Dimensions: length 7.32 m (24 ft); width 2.5 m (8 ft 2½ in); height (hull) 2.24 m (7 ft 4 in)	**Fording:** amphibious **Gradient:** 70 per cent **Vertical obstacle:** 0.6 m (1 ft 11½ in) **Trench:** 1.5 m (4 ft 11 in)

ENGESA EE-11 Urutu Armoured personnel carrier

In 1970 ENGESA turned its attention to the development of a range of 6x6 wheeled vehicles to meet the needs of the Brazilian armed forces, and it was in 1970 that the **ENGESA EE-11 Urutu** APC appeared, production following from 1974.

The driver is seated at the front on the left side with the engine to his right and the troop compartment to his rear. Sitting on seats down each side of the hull facing each other, the troops enter the vehicle via a door in the side of the hull

or through two doors in the hull rear.

Basic armament

Over the top of the troop compartment are four roof hatches, two on each side, which open outward, while

forward of this is the main armament. This can range from a pintle- or ring-mounted 12.7-mm (0.5-in) M2HB machine-gun, via a turret armed with a 20-mm cannon and 7.62-mm (0.3-in) co-axial machine-gun, to a two-man

The ENGESA EE-11 Urutu armoured personnel carrier has a crew of two and can carry up to 12 fully armed infantrymen. The basic armament is one 12.7-mm (0.5-in) M2HB heavy machine-gun.

turret armed with a 90-mm (3.54-in) gun, 7.62-mm co-axial and 7.62-mm anti-aircraft machine-gun. Firing ports and/or vision blocks can be installed in the troop compartment. The EE-11 is amphibious, being propelled in the water at 8 km/h (5 mph) by two propellers at the hull rear.

Sharing automotive components with the EE-9 Cascavel, the EE-11 was produced in seven marks differentiated by their engines and transmissions, and optional equipment includes a winch, night-vision equipment, an NBC system and various radio installations.

A whole range of versions of the basic vehicle has now been designed by the company, including ambulance, mortar carrier and cargo vehicles. When fitted with the 90-mm (3.54-in) two-man turret the EE-11 is known as the **Urutu Armoured Fire Support Vehicle** (**AFSV**), operated by Tunisia. Other operators include Bolivia, Chile, Colombia, Ecuador, Jordan, Libya and UAE.

SPECIFICATION	
EE-11 Urutu	developing 158 kW (212 hp)
Crew: 2 + 12	**Performance:** maximum road speed
Weight: 13000 kg (28,660 lb)	90 km/h (56 mph); maximum road
Dimensions: length 6.15 m (20 ft 2 in); width 2.59 m (8 ft 6 in); height (without armament) 2.09 m (6 ft 10 in)	range 850 km (528 miles)
	Fording: amphibious
	Gradient: 60 per cent
	Vertical obstacle: 0.6 m (1 ft 11½ in);
Powerplant: one Detroit Diesel 6V-53N liquid-cooled 6-cylinder diesel	

OT-64 Armoured personnel carrier

Rather than employ the Soviet BTR-60P series of 8x8 APCs, Czechoslovakia and Poland decided to develop their own vehicle. This entered service in 1964, and in addition to being used by Czechoslovakia and Poland it was also exported.

OT64- advantages

The main advantages of the **OT-64** over the Soviet vehicle are that the former is powered by one diesel instead of two petrol engines and that the troop compartment is enclosed.

The hull of the OT-64 is of all-welded steel construction providing protection from small arms fire and shell splinters, the maximum hull armour thickness being 10 mm (0.39 in). The commander and driver are seated at the front of the vehicle with the engine to their immediate rear. At the rear is the troop compartment, which is accessed by two rear doors. Roof hatches are provided over the troop compartment, and firing ports are located in the sides and rear. The OT-64 is amphibious, being driven in the water by two propellers at 9 km/h (5.6 mph). All vehicles have night-vision equipment, a front-mounted winch and an NBC system.

OT-64 varaints

The original member of the family, the **OT-64A** (or **SKOT** in Poland) was sometimes fitted with a roof-mounted 7.62-mm (0.3-in) machine-gun. The **OT-64B** (**SKOT-2**) used by Poland has on the roof behind the engine compartment a plinth carrying a 7.62-mm (0.3-in) or 12.7-mm (0.5-in) machine-gun.

The unarmed OT64A APC in Czech Republic service. The OT-64C(1) has the same one-man turret as fitted to the Soviet BRDM-2 4x4 and BTR-60PB 8x8 vehicles.

The **OT-64C(1)** or **SKOT-2A** has a one-man turret identical to that fitted to the BTR-60PB 8x8 APC and BRDM-2 4x4 scout car, and carrying a 14.5-mm (0.57-in) and 7.62-mm machine-gun. The **OT-64C(2)** or **SKOT-2AP** used by Poland has a new turret with a distinctive curved top which has the same armament as the turret of the OT-64C(1) but with an elevation of +89.5° to facilitate the engagement of aerial targets. Other more specialised versions include a recovery vehicle and at least three command vehicles, designated **R-2M** and **R-3MT** and **R-4MT**.

Czechoslovakia also used the **OT-810** halftrack. In World War II the Germans made the SdKfz 251 halftrack at the Skoda plant in Pilsen, where production continued after the war. In the 1950s many of these OT-810 vehicles were rebuilt and fitted with a diesel and overhead armour protection for the troop compartment. Most were fitted with an 82-mm (3.23-in) M59A recoilless gun.

SPECIFICATION	
OT-64C(1)	
Crew: 2 + 15	**Performance:** maximum road speed 94.4 km/h (59 mph); maximum road range 710 km (441 miles)
Weight: 14500 kg (31,967 lb)	
Dimensions: length 7.44 m (24 ft 5 in); width 2.55 m (8 ft 4½ in); height (overall) 2.06 m (6 ft 9 in)	**Fording:** amphibious
	Gradient: 60 per cent
	Vertical obstacle: 0.5 m (1 ft 7½ in)
Powerplant: one Tatra 928-18 V-8 diesel developing 134 kW (180 hp)	**Trench:** 2 m (6 ft 7 in)

Panhard VCR *Armoured personnel carrier*

Following the success of its AML and M3 range of 4x4 armoured vehicles, Panhard developed the **VCR** 6x6 APC. The first VCR (*Véhicule de Combat à Roues*, or wheeled combat vehicle) prototype was shown in 1977, the initial production vehicles being completed just two years later. The VCR was designed specifically for the export market, and known sales have been made to Argentina, Gabon, Iraq, Mexico and the UAE.

The VCR has an all-welded hull which varies in thickness from 8 to 12 mm (0.315 to 0.47 in), the very front of the vehicle being almost identical to that of the Panhard M3 4x4 APC. The driver is seated at the front with the engine to his right rear and the commander to his left rear. Both have a single-piece hatch cover and periscopes for observation. The troop compartment is at the rear and has twin doors in the hull rear, with roof hatches and firing/observation ports.

Main armament

The main armament is normally mounted over the forward part of the troop compartment and can consist of a pintle-mounted 7.62- or 12.7-mm (0.3- or 0.5-in) machine-gun, or a turret with similar weapons or a 20-mm cannon. An unusual feature of the VCR is its wheel arrangement as all six wheels are powered, with power-assisted steering on the front wheels only. When the VCR is travelling on roads, the central pair of road wheels is normally raised off the ground. The VCR is fully amphibious, being propelled in the water by its wheels at 4 km/h (2.5 mph). Optional equipment includes an airconditioning system, passive night-vision equipment, an NBC system and a front-mounted winch.

The first model to enter production was the four-man **VCR/TH** anti-tank vehicle, of which 106 were supplied to Iraq. This is fitted with the Euromissile UTM 800 turret with four HOT missiles in the ready-to-fire position and a further 10 missiles in the hull. Mounted over the rear part of the troop compartment is a remotely controlled 7.62-mm machine-gun.

The ambulance version is the **VCR/IS** with a higher roof. This can carry six seated and two stretcher patients or four stretcher patients plus the three-man crew consisting of commander, driver and medical orderly. The command post version is the **VCR/PC**, which has communications equipment and mapboards.

The repair vehicle is the **VCR/AT**, fitted with a block and tackle for lifting engines and other components; it carries a full range of spares and tools, but no winch.

There is also a **VCR/TT** 4x4 model of which 24 were delivered to the Argentine marines. This is propelled in water by two waterjets at 7.2 km/h (4.5 mph).

SPECIFICATION	
VCR	
Crew: 3 + 9	**Performance:** maximum road speed 100 km/h (62 mph); maximum range 800 km (497 miles)
Weight: 7000 kg (15,432 lb)	
Dimensions: length 4.565 m (14 ft 11½ in); width 2.495 m (8 ft 2 in); height (without armament) 2.03 m (6 ft 8 in)	**Fording:** amphibious
	Gradient: 60 per cent
	Vertical obstacle: 0.8 m (2 ft 7½ in)
Powerplant: one Peugeot PRV V-6 petrol developing 116 kW (155 hp)	**Trench:** 1.1 m (3 ft 7⅓ in)

Below left: This Panhard VCR/TT APC is fitted with a one-man turret armed with a 20-mm cannon. All VCRs are fully amphibious without preparation.

Below: A VCR/TT 6x6 APC in service with Gabon is seen in company with an AML 90 armoured car (left). Note the opened firing ports in the side of the VCR.

Panhard M3
Armoured personnel carrier

The **Panhard M3** APC was a private venture, and the first production vehicles were completed in 1971. More than 25 countries purchased the vehicle, some for army use and some for police use. For example, Algeria took delivery of 44 vehicles for its *gendarmerie* fitted with a one-man turret armed with a machine-gun. Algeria also has the VPC, VAT, VLA and VTS variants in service.

Front-mounted engine

The hull of the M3 is of all-welded steel armour construction varying in thickness from 8- to 11-mm (0.315- to 0.43-in). The driver is seated at the front of the hull, with the engine immediately to his rear. The engine is coupled to a manual gearbox with six forward and one reverse gear, and power is transmitted to the four road wheels by drive shafts that run inside the hull. The troop compartment is at the rear of the hull, a single door being provided in each side of the hull and twin doors in its rear. In the upper part of the hull side, which slopes inward, are three hatches hinged at the top, these enabling troops to use their small arms from within the vehicle. The main armament is normally mounted in the roof to the rear of the

engine compartment: this armament ranges from a turret with single or twin 7.62-mm (0.3-in) machine-guns to a power-operated turret with a 20-mm cannon. Over the rear of the troop compartment is a small hatch on which is normally installed a rail mount with a 7.62-mm machine-gun.

The M3 is fully amphibious, being propelled in the water by its wheels at a speed of 4 km/h (2.48 mph), but it can operate only in lakes and rivers with a slow current. Many vehicles are fitted with channels which can be quickly removed and placed in front of the vehicle to allow it to cross ditches and other battlefield obstacles. If required, the M3 can be fitted with passive night-vision equipment for the driver, an air-conditioning system (essential for Middle Eastern operators) and smoke dischargers. The basic M3 has also been adopted with particular equipment for a number of more specialised roles.

Role specialisation

The anti-aircraft model is called the **M3 VDA** and is fitted with a power-operated turret armed with twin 20-mm cannon. The **M3 VAT** repair vehicle has a full range of tools and is fitted with a jib for lifting engines in the field.

This Panhard M3 armoured personnel carrier has the driver's hatch open and is fitted with a Creusot-Loire STB shield with a 7.62-mm (0.3-in) machine-gun. Designed as a private venture, the M3 has been purchased by more than 25 countries, with more than 4,000 vehicles delivered.

The **M3 VPC** command vehicle has extensive communications equipment. The ambulance model of the family is called the **M3 VTS** and is unarmed. The

engineer vehicle version is the **M3 VLA**, and this is fitted with a hydraulically operated dozer blade at the front of the hull for the clearing of obstacles.

SPECIFICATION	
M3	**Performance:** maximum road speed
Crew: 2+10	90 km/h (56 mph); maximum range
Weight: 6100 kg (13,448 lb)	600 km (373 miles)
Dimensions: length 4.45 m (14 ft 7⅛ in);	**Fording:** amphibious
width 2.40 m (7 ft 10½ in); height	**Gradient:** 60 per cent
(without armament) 2.00 m (6 ft 6.7 in)	**Vertical obstacle:** 0.3 m (11¾ in);
Powerplant: one Panhard Model 4	**Trench:** with one channel 0.80 m
HD air-cooled 4-cylinder petrol	(2 ft 7½ in) or with three channels
engine developing 67 kW (90 hp)	3.10 m (10 ft 2 in)

ACMAT Armoured personnel carrier

A builder of cross-country trucks, ACMAT (Ateliers de Construction Mécanique de l'Atlantique) realised that there was a market for an APC on the same chassis, and therefore introduced the **ACMAT TPK 4.20 BL**, which is now in service with a number of African states and also Saudi Arabia.

Truck-derived design

The layout of the TPK 4.20 BL is similar to that of a truck, with

the engine at the front, commander and driver in the centre and the troop compartment at the rear. The commander and driver each have a windscreen to their front which can be quickly covered by an armoured shutter, a side door with a bullet-proof window in its upper part, and a single-piece hatch cover above their position.

The troops are seated on bench seats down each side of

the vehicle, and can exit quickly through the two doors in the hull rear. If required, firing ports and/or vision blocks can be provided in the sides and rear of

the troop compartment, and a 12.7- or 7.62-mm (0.5- or 0.3-in) machine-gun turret can be mounted on the roof of the vehicle to give covering fire

SPECIFICATION	
TPK 4.20 BL	**Powerplant:** one Perkins Model
Crew: 2+8	6.354.4 6-cylinder diesel
Weight: 7800 kg (17,196 lb)	developing 93 kW (125 hp)
Dimensions: length 5.98 m (19 ft 7½	**Performance:** maximum road speed
in); width 2.07 m (6 ft 9½ in);	95 km/h (59 mph); maximum range
height 2.21 m (7 ft 3 in)	1600 km (994 miles); fording 0.80
	m (2 ft 7½ in); gradient 60 per cent;
	trench not applicable

while the infantry dismount from the vehicle. Another model of the vehicle has an open-topped rear troop compartment with sides that can quickly be folded down on the outside.

Mechanical reliability

The well-proven Perkins six-cylinder diesel engine is coupled to a manual gearbox with four forward and one reverse gear and a two-speed transfer case. Steering is of the worm and nut type, and the exceptional operating range of 1600 km (994 miles) results from the large-capacity fuel tank which holds 370 litres (81.4 Imp gal). A spare wheel and tyre are normally carried on the wall to the immediate rear of the commander's and driver's position. Optional equipment includes an air-conditioning

An ACMAT TPK 420 light APC with all its hatches closed and fitted with a Creusot-Loire one-man turret armed with one machine-gun.

system, essential in many parts of the world if the infantry are to arrive at their objective in any condition to fight, and different radio systems. Other armament options include a Euromissile MILAN anti-tank missile system with additional missiles carried internally in the troop compartment, and an 81-mm (3.2-in) Brandt mortar firing to the rear. In most infantry battalions six or eight mortars are normally issued to provide immediate and close-range support for the infantry. Artillery support is normally not organic to an infantry battalion, although for some

missions (for example a long-range patrol in North Africa by a battalion of infantry in ACMAT trucks), it would often have a battery of four 105-mm (4.13-in) howitzers.

Transportpanzer 1 Armoured personnel carrier

In the mid-1960s the West German army decided to develop a complete new range of vehicles sharing many common components; the range included 4 x 4, 6 x 6 and 8 x 8 trucks, an 8 x 8 armoured reconnaissance vehicle and 4 x 4 and 6 x 6 APCs. The 8 x 8 armoured reconnaissance vehicle emerged as the Spahpanzer Luchs, of which 408 were built between 1975 and 1978. In the end only the 6 x 6 APC entered production as the **Transportpanzer 1**: it was in 1977 that Rheinstahl (now Rheinmetall Landsys-teme) was contracted for an eventual 1,125 vehicles, the first of which was completed in 1979. In 1983 Venezuela ordered 10 Transportpanzer 1 vehicles fitted with a 12.7-mm (0.5-in) and a 7.62-mm (0.3-in) machine-gun, and these were delivered late in 1983.

When used as an APC, the **TPz 1/Standard** can carry 10 troops in addition to the com-mander and driver. In German service, though, the TPz 1 is normally used for more

Rheinstahl Wehrtechnik, which became Henschel Wehrtechnik and is now Rheinmetall Landsysteme, built 1,125 Transportpanzer 1 6 x 6 amphibious vehicles for the German army, and these are operated in a wide range of roles including NBC reconnaissance, load carrying and engineer support.

specialised roles. The **TPz 1A3/ABC** or **Spurpanzer Fuchs** NBC reconnaissance vehicle, of which 140 were built, is fitted with NBC detection equipment, and devices for taking soil samples and for marking the ground. The engineers received 220 vehicles for carrying mines and demolition equipment about the battlefield. The electronic

warfare version is the **TPz-1 Eloka**, of which 87 were delivered, has a large number of antennae on the roof and a generator to provide sufficient power to run the equipment. The supply units have 220 vehicles to supply forward units with ammunition and other essential supplies, and this model can also be used as a

forward ambulance carrying up to four stretcher patients. The **TPz 1A2/Funk**, of which 265 were delivered, is operated in two subvariants as the **TPz 1A2/FuFu** command and control model with extensive communications equipment and a generator at the rear, and the **TPz 1A2/PARA** radar carrier with RASIT battlefield surveillance radar mounted on a hydraulic arm which is raised above the roof of the vehicle and can be operated up to 30 m (98 ft) from the vehicle by remote control. The German army vehicles are normally armed with a 7.62-mm (0.3-in) machine-gun above the commander's position but other weapons can be fitted on the roof of the troop compartment. Mounted on the hull is a bank of six smoke dischargers.

Internal layout

The commander and driver are seated at the front of the TPz 1 with the engine immediately behind them on the left and the troop compartment at the rear; a small aisle connects the front and rear compartments. The latter has seats on each side, and these seats can be folded to allow cargo to be carried. The compartment has two doors in the rear, roof hatches and three vision blocks. The TPz 1 is amphibious, being propelled in

water by two propellers at 10.5 km/h (6.5 mph). All German vehicles have an NBC system and passive night-vision equipment.

For the export market a wider range of variants is offered, such as anti-tank vehicles with HOT, TOW or MILAN missiles, mortar carriers and a recovery vehicle. The USA bought 110 **M93** vehicles to the Fuch standard for use in the NBC reconnaissance role.

SPECIFICATION	
Transportpanzer 1	(7 ft 6½ in)
Crew: 2+10	**Powerplant:** one Mercedes-Benz
Weight: 17000 kg (37,479 lb)	OM 402A diesel developing
Dimensions: length 6.76 m (22 ft 1	239 kW (320 hp)
in); width 2.98 m (9 ft 9⅓ in);	**Performance:** speed 105 km/h (65
height (without armament) 2.30 m	mph); range 800 km (497 miles)

UR-416 and Condor Armoured personnel carriers

In the first part of the 1960s Rheinstahl (now Rheinmetall) saw that there was a considerable overseas market for an armoured personnel carrier based on the chassis of the Unimog 4 x 4 truck and the first **UR-416** prototype was completed in 1965. Production got under way four years later, and by the time production ended some 1,030 vehicles had been delivered mainly to countries in Africa, South America, and the Far East.

The all-welded hull provides protection against small arms fire and shell splinters. The commander and driver are seated at the front with eight troops to their rear, three down each side facing outward and two at the rear facing the rear. Firing ports are provided in the

hull sides and rear to allow the troops to fire their rifles from inside the vehicle, and if required these standard ports can be replaced by spherical firing ports and an observation block which allows each man to fire his rifle or submachine gun from within the vehicle in complete safety. The UR-416 has two roof hatches, the forward one normally being fitted with a 7.62-mm (0.3-in) machine-gun that can also be provided with a shield.

As with most vehicles of this type, the UR-416 can be fitted with a wide range of optional equipment and also a roof-mounted turret.

Condor wheeled APC

Following the success of the UR-416, the manufacturer

The UR-416 is based on the chassis of the Mercedes-Benz Unimog 4 x 4 vehicle, which has exceptional cross-country mobility and is easy to maintain and operate.

developed a new vehicle with improved armour protection, greater speed and range, increased load carrying capability, amphibious capability and the ability to mount heavier armament installations. The first prototype of this **Condor** was completed in 1978, and just under 600 are in service.

The Condor has an all-welded steel hull and a three-man crew (driver, gunner and commander) and carries nine infantry who can use their weapons from within the vehicle. The main armament turret is normally in the centre of the hull, and can carry a machine-gun or 20-mm cannon.

This Condor 4 x 4 armoured personnel carrier has a Rheinmetall TUR-1 one-man turret armed with twin 7.62-mm (0.3-in) machine-guns. In 1981 Malaysia ordered a total of 459 Condors, which was by far the largest single order for the type. The vehicle is fully amphibious and can carry several types of turret.

SPECIFICATIONS	
UR-416	**Condor**
Crew: 2+8	**Crew:** 3+9
Weight: 7600 kg (16,755 lb)	**Weight:** 12000 kg (26,455 lb)
Dimensions: length 5.21 m (17 ft 1 in); width 2.30 m (7 ft 6 ½ in); height (without armament) 2.225 m (7 ft 3 in)	**Dimensions:** length 6.05 m (19 ft 10 in); width 2.47 m (8 ft 1 in); height (without armament) 2.10 m (6 ft 10¾ in)
Powerplant: one Daimler-Benz OM 352 6-cylinder diesel developing 89.5 kW (120 hp)	**Powerplant:** one Daimler-Benz OM 352A 6-cylinder diesel developing 125 kW (168 hp)
Performance: maximum road speed 85 km/h (53 mph); maximum range 600 to 700 km (373 to 435 miles)	**Performance:** maximum road speed 100 km/h (62 mph); maximum range 900 km (559 miles)
Fording: 1.40 m (4 ft 7 in)	**Fording:** amphibious
Gradient: 75 per cent	**Gradient:** 60 per cent
Vertical obstacle: 0.55 m (1 ft 9 ½ in)	**Vertical obstacle:** 0.55 m (1 ft 9 in); **Trench:** not applicable

TM 170 Armoured personnel carrier

Thyssen Maschinenbau (now Rheinmetall Landsysteme) developed three light wheeled APCs, all based on common commercial components to keep procurement and operating costs to an absolute minimum. The vehicles are the **TM 170, TM 125** and **TM 90**. The largest is the TM 170, which has a two-man crew and can carry 10 fully equipped infantrymen, although more often than not it is used in the internal security role for the rapid and safe transport of riot squads to spots at which they are needed.

Internal security role

Germany's border police and state police selected the TM 170 under the designation **SW4**. At least 250 examples of the SW4 were required, though funding problems meant that the initial order was for only 87 vehicles, the first of these being delivered in 1983.

The TM 170 has a hull of all-welded steel construction with the engine at the very front of the hull and coupled to a manual gearbox with four forward and one reverse gear. For road use the driver normally selects 4 x 2 (rear wheels only) drive, while for cross country the front axles are also engaged for 4 x 4 (all-wheel) drive.

The commander and driver have bulletproof windows to their front, and in combat these are covered by armoured

A Thyssen Maschinenbau TM 170 4 x 4 armoured personnel carrier with the hatches over the windscreen in the lowered position. The TM 170 was selected by the West German Border Guard and State Police to replace a miscellany of older vehicles.

shutters, observation then being obtained through roof-mounted periscopes. An entry door is provided in each side of the hull and rear, and firing ports and/or vision blocks enable the troops or police to aim their weapons safely from inside the vehicle. The basic vehicle is amphibious, being propelled in the water by its wheels; before the vehicle enters the water a trim vane is erected at the front of the hull. For increased water speed the TM 170 can be fitted with waterjets, which give a maximum speed of 9 km/h (5.6 mph). A variety of armament

stations can be fitted on the roof including turret- or pintle-mounted 7.62-mm (0.3-in) machine-guns or even 20-mm cannon. Specialised equipment for the riot-control role includes a front-mounted hydraulically operated dozer blade for clearing street barricades

and other obstacles out of the way, and a special observation cupola.

The TM 125 is slightly smaller than the TM 170, has a crew of two and can carry 10 men. The TM 90 is an armoured patrol vehicle rather than an APC and has a crew of four.

SPECIFICATION	
TM 170	developing 125 kW (168 hp)
Crew: 2+12	**Performance:** maximum road speed
Weight: 9500 kg (20,944 lb)	100 km/h (62 mph); maximum
Dimensions: length 6.10 m (20 ft	range 670 km (416 miles)
0 in); width 2.45 m (8 ft ½ in);	**Fording:** amphibious
height 2.22 m (7 ft 3½ in)	**Gradient:** 80 per cent
Powerplant: one Daimler-Benz	**Vertical obstacle:** 0.50 m
OM 352 supercharged diesel	(1 ft 7½ in);

PSZH-IV Armoured personnel carrier

In the 1960s Hungary developed the FUG 4x4 amphibious scout car for service in place of the Soviet BRDM. Development led to the appearance in the mid-1960s of what became known in the West as the **FUG-70**. After some time it was discovered that the new vehicle was in reality the **PSZH-IV**, not a scout car, but an APC.

Orthodox concept

The hull of the PSZH-IV is of all-welded steel construction with a maximum thickness of 14 mm (0.55 in). The commander and driver are seated at the front of the vehicle, forward of each being a windscreen that can be quickly covered by an armoured shutter with an integral periscope. Above their position is a single-piece roof hatch and

to each side is a vision block. Mounted in the centre of the roof is a one-man Hungarian

turret armed with a 14.5-mm (0.57-in) KPVT machine-gun and a 7.62-mm (0.3-in) PKT co-axial

SPECIFICATION	
PSZH-IV	**Performance:** maximum road speed
Crew: 3+6	80 km/h (50 mph); maximum range
Weight: 7500 kg (16,535 lb)	500 km (311 miles)
Dimensions: length 5.695 m (18 ft	**Fording:** amphibious
8½ in); width 2.50 m (8 ft 2½ in);	**Gradient:** 60 per cent
height 2.31 m (7 ft 7 in)	**Vertical obstacle:** 0.40 m (1 ft
Powerplant: one Csepel D.414.44	3½ in)
diesel developing 74.6 kW (100 hp)	**Trench:** 0.60 m (1 ft 11½ in)

machine-gun. Both weapons have an elevation of +30° and a depression of -5°, turret traverse being 360°. Totals of 500 14.5-mm and 2,000 7.62-mm ammunition are carried.

Full equipment

The troops enter and leave the PSZH-IV through a door in each side of the hull; each door is in two parts, upper and lower, and opens towards the front of the vehicle. The engine is mounted at the rear of the hull. The PSZH-IV is amphibious, being propelled in the water at a speed of 9 km/h (5.6 mph) by two waterjets. Like most Warsaw Pact vehicles of its period, the PSZH-IV is fitted with a central tyre-pressure regulation system (allowing the driver to adjust the tyre pressure to suit the type of ground being crossed), an NBC system

When the PSZH-IV was first seen in the early 1960s it was believed to be a scout car, but it was later discovered that the vehicle was in fact an armoured personnel carrier and carried six troops in addition to its three-man crew, the latter consisting of the commander, gunner and driver.

and IR night-vision equipment for the gunner and commander.

Variants

There are a number of variants of the PSZH-IV including two command vehicles (one with and the other without the turret), an ambulance model (although loading of stretchers cannot be considered to be an easy occupation), and an NBC reconnaissance vehicle. The last can detect NBC agents and then drop pennants into the ground to mark a path through these contaminated areas.

BDX and Valkyr Armoured personnel carriers

In the early 1970s Technology Investments of Ireland designed and built the **Timoney** 4 x 4 APC prototype, and after trials with several prototype vehicles the Irish army finally ordered 10 vehicles in two batches of five.

In 1976 Beherman Demoen of Belgium obtained a licence from Technology Investments to manufacture the APC. The Belgian government ordered 123 vehicles under the designation **BDX**, and these were all

built between 1978 and 1981. Of the 123, 43 were delivered to the Belgian air force for air-base defence, and the others were supplied to the Gendarmerie. All of the air force vehicles have a 7.62-mm (0.3-in) machine-gun,

The Vickers Valkyr, while based upon the Timoney/BDX design, was of significantly improved capability. The Valkyr could be fitted with a range of weapon systems, but it is thought that only two were sold to Kuwait.

while the Gendarmerie vehicles comprise 13 fitted with an 81-mm (3.2-in) mortar, 41 APCs, and 26 with a front-mounted dozer blade.

Limited sales

The BDX was also tested in a number of other countries but the only other operators have been Argentina (five vehicles) and Mexico (95 ex-Belgian vehicles).

Vickers Defence Systems of the UK further developed the BDX as the considerably

improved **Valkyr**, whose first two prototypes were completed in 1982 and the third in 1984. The Valkyr is powered by a General Motors Model 4-53T diesel coupled to an automatic transmission.

Two basic models of the Valkyr were offered as an APC and a weapons platform with a slightly lower profile and options for weapons stations such as a French turret armed with a 90-mm (3.54-in) gun and the Belgian CM-90 Cockerill turret armed with the 90-mm Cockerill

Mk III gun, 7.62-mm (0.3-in) co-axial and 7.62-mm (0.3-in) anti-aircraft machine-guns.

As an APC the vehicle normally had a two-man crew and could carry 10 troops, who

could leave rapidly via twin doors in the hull rear. If required the Valkyr could be fitted with firing ports and/or vision blocks and a range of equipment and role-specific options.

SPECIFICATION	
BDX	**Performance:** maximum road speed 100 km/h (62 mph); maximum road range 500 to 900 km (310 to 560 miles)
Crew: 2+10	
Weight: 10700 kg (23,590 lb)	
Dimensions: length 5.05 m (16 ft 7 in); width 2.50 m (8 ft 2½ in); height (hull top) 2.06 m (6 ft 9 in)	**Fording:** amphibious
	Gradient: 60 per cent
Powerplant: one Chrysler V-8 water-cooled petrol engine developing 134 kW (180 hp)	**Vertical obstacle:** 0.40 m (1 ft 4 in);
	Trench: not applicable

Tipo 6614 Armoured personnel carrier

Some years ago Fiat and OTO-Melara designed and built prototypes of the Tipo 6616 4 x 4 armoured car and the **Tipo 6614** 4 x 4 APC with identical automotive components, mostly from standard commercial vehicles, although their layouts were quite different. The Tipo 6616 is used in small numbers by the Italian police, and known export customers included Peru and Somalia.

It is estimated that by 2002 slightly more than 1,000 examples of the Tipo 6614 had been delivered to operators in seven countries, including South Korea, where licensed production has been undertaken by Asia Motors Incorporated, which calls the vehicle the **KM900**.

The hull of the Tipo 6614 is of all-welded steel construction that varies in thickness from 6 mm (0.24 in) to 8 mm (0.315 in), providing protection against 7.62-mm (0.3-in) small arms fire and light artillery splinters. The driver is seated at the very front of the vehicle on the left side with the engine to his right. The

troop compartment is toward the rear, and the 10, including the commander, sit on individual bucket seats that can be quickly folded up. The troops enter and leave via a door in each side of the hull, or a power-operated ramp in the hull rear. A total of 10 firing ports is provided. Over the troop compartment is a two-part hatch, while to the front of this is the main armament installation. This is normally an M113-type cupola with a single-piece hatch cover that opens to the rear, periscopes for all-round vision and a 12.7-mm (0.5-in) M2HB machine-gun. A turret armed with twin 7.62-mm (0.3-in) machine-guns can also be installed. Variants include a

mortar carrier, a command vehicle and an ambulance.

The Tipo 6614 is amphibious, being propelled in the water by its wheels at 4.5 km/h (2.8 mph), and before the vehicle enters the water four bilge pumps are switched on.

Optional equipment

A range of optional equipment is available apart from the different weapon stations, these

including various types of passive night vision equipment, a spare wheel and holder (often mounted on the roof of the troop compartment), smoke dischargers, an air-conditioning system, a fire extinguishing system, and a front-mounted winch with a capacity of 4500 kg (9,221 lb) and 40 m (131 ft) of cable. This last is designed for use in the recovery of other vehicles or for self-recovery.

SPECIFICATION	
Tipo 6614	diesel developing 119 kW (160 hp)
Crew: 1+10	**Performance:** maximum road speed 100 km/h (62 mph); maximum range 700 km (435 miles)
Weight: 8500 kg (18,739 lb)	
Dimensions: length 5.86 m (19 ft 2½ in); width 2.50 m (8 ft 2½ in); height (hull top) 1.78 m (5 ft 10 in)	**Fording:** amphibious
	Gradient: 60 per cent
Powerplant: one Iveco Model 8062.24 liquid-cooled supercharged	**Vertical obstacle:** 0.40 m (1 ft 4 in);
	Trench: not applicable

Seen fording a stream, the Type 6614 APC shares many components with the Type 6616 armoured car. The APC can transport 10 men in addition to the driver, and the usual armament is a 12.7-mm (0.5-in) machine-gun.

YP-408 Armoured personnel carrier

In 1958 DAF built prototypes of an eight-wheeled APC. With a number of modifications and the replacement of the Hercules JXLD petrol engine by a more powerful DAF diesel, this was accepted for Dutch service as the **YP-408**, the first production vehicles were delivered in 1968. A total of 750 vehicles were built for the Dutch army and five are used by Surinam. The YP-408 has been replaced in Dutch service by the YPR-765, which is the Dutch version of the FMC Armored Infantry Fighting Vehicle.

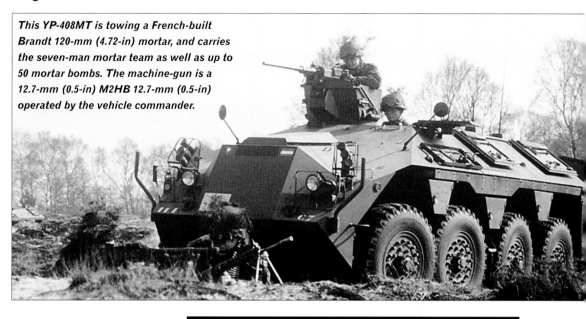

This YP-408MT is towing a French-built Brandt 120-mm (4.72-in) mortar, and carries the seven-man mortar team as well as up to 50 mortar bombs. The machine-gun is a 12.7-mm (0.5-in) M2HB 12.7-mm (0.5-in) operated by the vehicle commander.

Armoured hull

The hull of the YP-408 is of all-welded steel construction varying in thickness from 8 mm (0.315 in) to 15 mm (0.59 in). The engine is at the front, the commander and driver are to the rear of the engine compartment and the troop compartment is at the rear. The YP-408 has four road wheels on each side, but only six of these are powered, making the YP-408 an 8 x 6 vehicle; it is the second pair of road wheels which is unpowered.

Steering is power-assisted on the front four wheels, and the tyres have reinforced side walls that enable the vehicle to be driven 50 km (31 miles) at a reduced speed after they have been punctured. The driver is seated on the left with the commander/ machine-gunner to his right. The 12.7-mm (0.5-in) M2 machine-gun can be traversed through 360° and elevated from -8° to +70°.

The 10 troops enter and leave through two doors in the hull rear, and are seated five down each side facing each other. Hatches are provided over the troop compartment. Standard equipment includes a heater, but the YP-408 lacks an NBC system and amphibious capability. If required, IR equipment can be fitted for the driver and the machine-gunner.

The basic armoured personnel carrier is called the **PWI-S(GR)**, this standing for **Pantser Wagen Infanterie Standaard (Groep).**

The platoon commander's vehicle was the **PWI-S(PC)**, and had a crew of nine and extra communications equipment; and the battalion or company commander's vehicle was the **PWCO** with a crew of six, extra communications equipment and map boards. The **PW-GWT** ambulance was unarmed and can carry two litters and four seated patients plus its crew of a driver and two medical attendants. The **PW-V** cargo carrier could transport 1500 kg (3,307 lb) of freight. The **PW-MT** had a seven-man mortar team and towed a French 120-mm (4.72-in) Brandt mortar and 50 mortar bombs. Later versions were the **PWRDR** fitted with the Marconi ZB 298 ground surveillance radar, and the **PWAT** anti-tank vehicle (with TOW).

SPECIFICATION	
YP-408	**Performance:** maximum road speed
Crew: 2+10	80 km/h (50 mph); maximum road
Combat weight: 12000 kg (26,455 lb)	range 500 km (311 miles)
Powerplant: one DAF Model DS	**Fording:** 1.2 m (3 ft 11 in)
575 6-cylinder diesel developing	**Gradient:** 60 per cent
165 hp (123 kW)	**Vertical obstacle:** 0.7 m (2 ft 4 in);
Dimensions: length 6.23 m (20 ft 5½ in); width 2.40 m (7 ft 10½ in); height (inc. MG) 2.37 m (7 ft 9½ in)	**Trench:** 1.2 m (3 ft 11 in)

Ratel 20 Infantry fighting vehicles

For many years the British-supplied 6 x 6 Alvis Saracen was the South African army's standard APC. When it became apparent that future supplies of armoured vehicles and their all-essential spare parts were in some doubt, the South Africans decided to build a new vehicle to meet their own requirements. Sandock-Austral (now Alvis OMC) was building a modified version of the Panhard AML 4 x 4 armoured car with the name Eland, and received the task of designing and building the new vehicle.

The first production vehicles were completed in 1978. More than 1,350 examples of the Ratel were built for the home market and for export to Morocco. The South African army used the type operationally for the first time in May 1978, and after that Ratels were used on many deep strikes into Angola, where the type's large operating range proved to be very useful. The Moroccans have used their Ratels against Polisario fighters in the Sahara desert.

Internal layout

The basic vehicle is the **Ratel 20** and carries the commander and gunner in the turret, the driver at the front, the anti-

SPECIFICATION	
Ratel 20	developing 210 kW (282 hp)
Crew: 11	**Performance:** maximum road speed
Weight: 19000 kg (41,888 lb)	105 km/h (65 mph); maximum
Dimensions: length 7.212 m (23 ft 8 in); width 2.516 m (8 ft 3 in); height (overall) 2.915 m (9 ft 6⅔ in)	range 1000 km (621 miles)
	Fording: 1.20 m (3 ft 11 in)
	Gradient: 60 per cent
Powerplant: one Bussing Model D 3256 BTXF 6-cylinder diesel	**Vertical obstacle:** 0.35 m (1 ft 1½ in);
	Trench: 1.15 m (3 ft 9½ in)

aircraft machine-gunner at the rear and seven infantry. The two-man turret is armed with a 20-mm dual-feed cannon and 7.62-mm (0.3-in) co-axial machine-gun, a similar weapon being located on the turret roof for AA defence. Mounted on each side of the turret are two smoke-dischargers, and there is another 7.62-mm AA machine-gun at the right rear of the hull roof.

The **Ratel 60** has a similar crew, but has a two-man turret armed with a 60-mm (2.36-in) breech-loaded mortar and 7.62-mm co-axial and AA machine-guns.

The **Ratel 90** is the fire-support vehicle and has a two-man turret armed with the same 90-mm (3.54-in) gun as fitted to the Eland light armoured car, together with 7.62-mm co-axial and AA machine-guns. Some 69 rounds of 90-mm ammunition are carried (29 in the turret and 40 in the hull). The command member of the family has a

nine-man crew consisting of the commander, driver, main gunner and six command staff, and is armed with a turret-mounted 12.7-mm (0.5-in) M2HB machine-gun and two 7.62-mm AA machine-guns. This variant has map boards, a pneumatically operated mast, intercom, internal loudspeakers, public address system and three radios for communication with other vehicles and higher command staff.

Other variants are a repair vehicle, 81- and 120-mm (3.2- and 4.72-in) mortar carriers, a model carrying the ZT-3 Swift anti-tank missile system, and an enhanced artillery observation post. An 8 x 8 logistic support variant was evaluated but not put into production.

The Ratel series of infantry fighting and special-purpose vehicles was designed to meet the exacting requirements of the South African army, and has proved very successful.

Buffel Personnel carrier

The **Buffel** 4 x 4 vehicle, designed by Armscor on the basis of the Mercedes-Benz Model 416/162 Unimog high-mobility truck, has been the standard mine-protected APC of the South African army since 1978, and estimates suggest that some 2,400 vehicles of the series were completed. In layout the type is fairly conventional, with the engine at the front, and the driver above and to the left of the engine in a fully armoured cab characterised by a bulletproof combination of a windscreen and side windows. The hull's belly is V-shaped to offer the best possible protection against the effect of mines.

Troop compartment

The troop compartment over the rear of the vehicle has an open top and carries 10 infantry seated five down each side in a

The Buffel has the driver's cab and engine at the front of the vehicle on the left and right respectively, and the V-shaped belly helps to divert the blast of any mine detonation outward and upward.

back-to-back arrangement. The only means of entry and exit is over the compartment's sides, which can be hinged down. Two machine-guns can be pintle-mounted on top of the hull, most generally on the right-hand

front and left-hand rear corners of the troop compartment. Recently the Buffel has been marketed with paired machine-guns with a gunner's shield.

Specialised variants include a mortar carrier, and the **Buffel**

Mk I tractor with a fully armoured cab at the front but fitted with a cargo area at the rear with a drop tailgate to carry 2500 kg (5,511 lb). This has also been used as a prime mover towing various equipment, for example, a 20-mm light anti-aircraft gun.

During the 1995 International Countermine Conference in Copenhagen, Denmark, a request was made for a cheap MPV (Mine Protected Vehicle). Armscor responded with the combat-proved Buffel, and numbers of remanufactured Buffels are now being made available for use in worldwide de-mining operations. Before being delivered for use in this

task, each Buffel is completely rebuilt to create what is in effect a new vehicle offering protection against small arms fire, the detonation of one Russian TM57 anti-tank mine (or equivalent) anywhere under the vehicle, and the detonation of two TM57 mines under any wheel.

The **Buffel Mk II** has been developed in two basic subvariants, namely the **Buffel Mk IIA** and **Buffel Mk IIB** with

SPECIFICATION	
Buffel	**Powerplant:** one Mercedes-Benz
Crew: 1+10	OM 352 liquid-cooled 6-cylinder
Weight: 6140 kg (13,536 lb)	diesel developing 93 kW (125 hp)
Dimensions: length 5.10 m (16 ft 8¾	**Performance:** maximum road speed
in); width 2.05 m (6 ft 8¾ in);	96 km/h (59.5 mph); maximum
height 2.995 m (9 ft 10 in)	road range 1000 km (621 miles)

drum and disc brakes respectively. The Buffel Mk II is a rebuild of an earlier Buffel by No. 61 Base Workshop of the South African National Defence Force with a new and fully

enclosed rear troop compartment accessed by a large rear door with steps below it. To the front, sides and rear are bulletproof windows, each provided with firing ports.

BMR-600/BLR-600 Armoured fighting vehicle/personnel carrier

In the early 1970s the Spanish army issued a requirement for a 6 x 6 infantry fighting vehicle which was developed by ENASA and the Spanish army under the designation **Pegaso 3.500**, later **BMR-600** (*Blindado Medio de Ruedas*, or wheeled medium armoured vehicle). The type was accepted for service against a requirement for at least 500. The company has now developed a complete family of vehicles using the same basic chassis, namely the **Pegaso 3560.1** APC, **Pegaso 3560.53E** 81-mm (3.2-in) mortar carrier, **Pegaso 3560.54E** 120-mm (4.7-in) mortar towing vehicle, **Pegaso 3560.5** battalion command vehicle, **Pegaso 3564** fire-support vehicle, which can be fitted with armament such as the French TS-90 two-man

turret with a 90-mm (3.54-in) gun, and the **Pegaso 3562.03 VEC** cavalry scout vehicle.

The hull of the BMR-600 is of all-welded aluminium construction. The driver is at the front on the left with the machine-gunner/radio operator to his rear and the engine compartment to their right. The troop compartment at the rear carries 10 troops who enter and leave the vehicle over a power-operated rear ramp. The main armament is normally a 12.7-mm (0.5-in) external machine-gun. The vehicle is amphibious, and when fitted with waterjets has a max water speed of 10 km/h (6.2 mph).

BLR-600 4 x 4

The **BLR-600** (*Blindado Ligero de Ruedas*, or wheeled light

The BMR (Blindado Medio de Ruedas) was designed for a battlefield role, and in addition to its embarked infantry, who can fire their weapons from inside the troop compartment, has a forward-mounted turret armed with a single cannon.

armoured vehicle) is a 4 x 4 vehicle designed mainly for internal security operations and used in this role by the Spanish army and civil guard. The BLR's layout is unusual, the commander and driver being seated at the front of the vehicle with excellent observation to the

front and sides, and 12 troops to the rear of the commander and driver and along the sides of the hull at the rear with four doors and four roof hatches. The 164-kW (220-hp) engine is in the centre of the hull at the rear. A cupola carries one 7.62-mm machine-gun.

The BLR (Blindado Ligero de Ruedas) was designed by the Empresa Nacional de Autocamiones (which also builds the BMR-600 IFV) for use mainly in the internal security role. It is now used by the Spanish.

SPECIFICATIONS	
BMR-600	**BLR-600**
Crew: 2+10	**Crew:** 3+12
Weight: 14000 kg (30,864 lb)	**Weight:** 12000 kg (26,455 lb)
Dimensions: length 6.15 m (20 ft 2¼in); width 2.50 m (8 ft 2½ in); height (to hull top) 2.00 m (6 ft 6¾ in)	**Dimensions:** length 5.65 m (18 ft 6½ in); width 2.50 m (8 ft 2½ in); height (without armament) 2.00 m (6 ft 6¾ in)
Powerplant: one Pegaso 9157/8 liquid-cooled 6-cylinder diesel developing 228 kW (306 hp)	**Powerplant:** one Pegaso 9220 liquid-cooled 6-cylinder diesel developing 164 kW (220 hp)
Performance: maximum road speed 100 km/h (62 mph); maximum road range 700 km (435 miles)	**Performance:** maximum road speed 86 km/h (53.4 mph); maximum road range 800 km (497 miles)
Fording: amphibious	**Fording:** 1.10 m (3 ft 7½ in)
Gradient: 68 per cent	**Gradient:** 75 per cent
Vertical obstacle: 0.80 m (2 ft 7½ in)	**Vertical obstacle:** 0.60 m (1 ft 11⅔ in)
Trench: 1.20 m (3 ft 11¼ in)	

MOWAG Roland Armoured personnel carrier

The **MOWAG Roland** 4x4 was the smallest vehicle produced by MOWAG in Switzerland before production ended in 1980, and is used mainly for internal security. The first production vehicles were completed in 1964, and known operators have included Argentina, Bolivia, Chile, Ghana, Greece, Iraq, Liberia, Mexico, Peru and Sierra Leone.

The hull is of all-welded steel armour providing the crew with protection from 7.62-mm (0.3-in) small arms fire. The driver is at the front, the crew compartment (with two side doors) in the centre, and the engine at the rear on the left side; there is also an aisle in the hull leading to a door in the hull rear.

In the centre of the roof is the main armament, normally a simple cupola with a 12.7-mm (0.5-in) or 7.62-mm machine-gun. One of the alternative weapon stations is a turret above which is a remotely controlled 7.62-mm machine-gun.

The petrol engine is coupled to a manual gearbox with four

The basic Roland was designed from the outset for relatively easy conversion to a number of role. This Argentinian Grenadier has been re-engined with a Deutz diesel. Argentina's army and marines operate some 60 Grenadiers.

forward and one reverse gears and a two-speed transfer case, though the Roland was later offered with an automatic gearbox.

Internal security task

For the internal security (IS) role the Roland is normally fitted with an obstacle-clearing blade at the front of the hull, a public address system, wire mesh protection for the head lamps and sometimes the vision blocks as well, a siren and flashing lights. Another option is MOWAG bulletproof cross-country wheels. These consist of metal discs on each side of the tyre, the outside ones having ribs which assist the vehicle when crossing through mud.

SPECIFICATION	
Roland	developing 151 kW (202 hp)
Crew: 3 + 3	**Performance:** maximum road speed
Weight: 4700 kg (10,362 lb)	110 km/h (68 mph); maximum road
Dimensions: length 4.44 m (14 ft 6⅔	range 550 km (341 miles)
in); width 2.01 m (6 ft 7 in); height	**Fording:** 1 m (3 ft 3½ in)
(with turret) 2.03 m (6 ft 8 in)	**Gradient:** 60 per cent
Powerplant: one V-8 petrol engine	**Vertical obstacle:** 0.4 m (1 ft 4 in)

In the late 1960s the company built another 4x4 APC as the **Grenadier**, with provision for nine men including the commander and driver. This model was sold to a number of countries but is no longer offered, having been replaced by the Piranha range of 4x4, 6x6

and 8x8 vehicles. The Grenadier's typical armament included a one-man turret armed with a 20-mm cannon and a turret with twin 80-mm (3.15-in) rocket launchers. The vehicle is amphibious, being propelled in the water by a propeller located under the rear of the hull.

BTR-152 Armoured personnel carrier

The USSR did not employ a tracked or wheeled APC in World War II, and Soviet infantry normally went in on foot or were carried on tanks.

Simple yet effective

The **BTR-152** was accepted for service in 1950 and was first seen in public during 1951. The vehicle is basically the ZIL-151 truck chassis fitted with an armoured body, though later production vehicles from the **BTR-152V1** were based on the ZIL-157 chassis. From the early 1960s the BTR-152 was replaced in front-line Soviet motorised rifle

A BTR-152 6x6 APC fitted with a central tyre pressure-regulation system, allowing the driver to adjust the pressure to suit the type of ground being crossed.

divisions by the BTR-60 series of 8x8 APCs, which offered better cross-country capabilities. The BTR-152 and its variants were widely exported, and even in 2002 remained in service with some 24 countries. The type has seen action in the Middle East (with Syria, Iraq and Egypt), Africa and the Far East.

The first model to enter service was the BTR-152 with an open-topped compartment for 17 troops on bench-type seats running across the hull. The

second model was the BTR-152V1 still with the open-topped troop compartment but fitted with a front-mounted winch and a central tyre pressure-regulation system with external air lines, enabling the driver to adjust the tyre pressure to suit the type of ground being crossed. The **BTR-152V2** was not fitted with a winch, but did have a tyre pressure-regulation system.

The **BTR-152V3** had a winch, IR night-vision equipment and a central tyre-pressure regulation system with internal air lines more robust than those of the external system.

The main drawback of these versions was the open-topped troop compartment, which left the infantry vulnerable to overhead shell bursts, and this was rectified in the **BTR-152K**

with full overhead protection. In all versions of the BTR-152 firing ports are provided in the sides and rear of the troop compartment.

Specialist models

The command version is the **BTR-152U** and has a much higher roof so the command staff can work while standing; it also has an armoured roof. The anti-aircraft model is the **BTR-152A**, which has at its rear a mount

with twin 14.5-mm (0.57-in) KPV machine-guns that can be elevated from -5° to +80° with turret traverse through 360°. During the fighting in the Lebanon in 1982, the Israeli army captured a number of BTR-152s from the PLO: these vehicles had the towed ZU-23 twin 23-mm mounted for weightier firepower.

It is worth noting that the first APC deployed by the USSR after World War II was in fact the

SPECIFICATION	
BTR-152V1	developing 82 kW (110 hp)
Crew: 2 + 17	**Performance:** maximum road speed
Weight: 8950 kg (19,731 lb)	75 km/h (47 mph); maximum road
Dimensions: length 6.83 m (22 ft 5	range 780 km (485 miles)
in); width 2.32 m (7 ft 7½ in);	**Fording:** 0.8 m (2 ft 7½ in)
height 2.05 m (6 ft 8½ in)	**Gradient:** 55 per cent
Powerplant: one ZIL-123 liquid-	**Vertical obstacle:** 0.6 m (1 ft 11½ in)
cooled 6-cylinder petrol engine	**Trench:** 0.69 m (2 ft 3 in)

BTR-40 4x4 vehicle, which was based on a modified GAZ-63 truck chassis. This could carry eight troops, and was also used as a recon vehicle until the

introduction of the BRDM-1 in the 1950s. Both the BTR-40 and BTR-152 were normally armed with a pintle-mounted 7.62-mm (0.3-in) machine-gun.

BTR-60P series Armoured personnel carrier

The BTR-152 6x6 armoured personnel carrier introduced into the Soviet army during the 1950s had a number of major shortcomings, including poor cross-country mobility and a lack of amphibious capability.

Enhanced capabilities

In the late 1960s these deficiencies were largely overcome by the introduction of the **BTR-60P**, and this and later variants replaced the BTR-152 force used by the Soviet army: in Soviet service the BTR series and its improved variants were usually used by the motorised rifle divisions, while the tank divisions were allocated the BMP series tracked MICVs. The BTR-60 series was exported to some 30 countries, the number of operator countries rising to 42 after the dissolution of the USSR, and Romania has produced a modified version under the designation **TAB-72**. The BTR-60 has seen action in many parts of the world, and the type was even encountered in Grenada during the American operation of 1984.

The members of the BTR-60 series are all fully amphibious, being propelled in water by a

single waterjet under the rear of the hull at a speed of 10 km/h (6.2 mph), and all based on essentially the same configuration with the commander and driver at the front, troop compartment in the centre and the two petrol engines at the rear. Each of these engines drives one side of the vehicle. Power-assisted steering is provided on the front two axles.

The first model to enter service was the BTR-60P, and this is characterised by an open-topped troop compartment for 16 infantry seated on bench seats across the hull. Armament normally consisted of one 12.7-mm (0.5-in) and two 7.62-mm (0.3-in) machine-guns. This was soon replaced in production by the **BTR-60PA**, which has a fully enclosed troop compartment and carries a maximum of 16 troops, although its normal complement is 12. This model is generally armed with a pintle-mounted 7.62-mm machine-gun. The **BTR-60PB** is similar to the BTR-

SPECIFICATION	
BTR-60PB	each developing 67 kW (90 hp)
Crew: 2 + 14	**Performance:** maximum road speed
Weight: 10300 kg (22,708 lb)	80 km/h (50 mph); maximum road
Dimensions: length 7.56 m (24 ft 9½	range 500 km (311 miles)
in); width 2.825 m (9 ft 3 in); height	**Fording:** amphibious
(to top of turret) 2.31 m (7 ft 7 in)	**Gradient:** 60 per cent
Powerplant: two GAZ-49B liquid-	**Vertical obstacle:** 0.4 m (1 ft 3⅔ in)
cooled 6-cylinder petrol engines	**Trench:** 2 m (6 ft 7 in)

60PA but fitted with the same one-man manual turret as installed on the BRDM-2 4x4 scout car and the Czechoslovak OT-64C(1) armoured personnel carrier, which was used by Czechoslovakia and Poland (as the SKOT-2A) in place of the Soviet vehicle. The infantry carried by the BTR-60PA and the BTR-60PB can aim and fire their weapons from within the vehicle, although they normally have to dismount by climbing through the roof hatches. The command version of the vehicle is called the **BTR-60Pu**, and this has additional communications equipment. In excess of 60 specialist command and control versions have been identified, including a forward air control vehicle, basically the BTR-60PB

with the armament removed, an observation window in the forward part of the turret, and probably different radio equipment.

Successor

The BTR-60PB was replaced in first-line Soviet formations by the **BTR-70**, which is very similar in appearance and has the same turret but introduced a slightly more powerful engine and has improved seating and exit arrangements for the infantry. The roof hatches are supplemented by a small door in the lower part of the hull between the second and third road wheels. The BTR-70 saw action in Afghanistan, where some were fitted with an AGS-17 30-mm grenade launcher.

The BTR-60PB 8x8 APC has the same turret as that fitted to the BRDM-2 4x4 amphibious scout car and the Czechoslovak OT-64C 8x8 vehicle. This is armed with a single 14.5-mm KPV and a co-axial 7.62-mm PKT machine-gun.

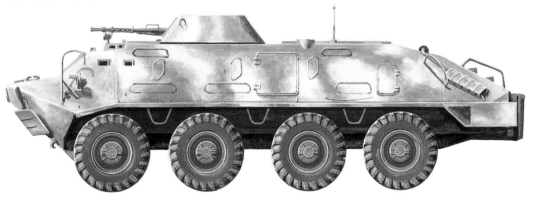

Humber 'Pig'

Armoured personnel carrier

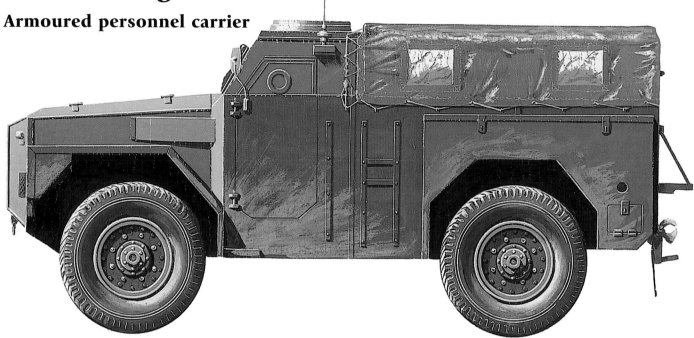

When World War II was over, the British army drew up its requirements for a complete new generation of wheeled military vehicles including a 1-ton truck which was eventually produced by Humber/Rootes.

Wheeled APC

In the early 1950s the Alvis Saracen 6 x 6 armoured personnel carrier entered service, but as there would clearly be insufficient of these to go around it was decided to build another wheeled APC on the basis of the chassis of **Humber FV1600** series of trucks. This APC was not designed to operate with tanks, but rather to transport the infantry from one part of the battlefield to another, where they would dismount and fight on foot. About 1,700 vehicles were eventually built, the bodies being provided by GKN Sankey and the Royal Ordnance Factory at Woolwich.

By the 1960s the FV432, also designed and built by GKN Sankey, was entering service in increasing numbers so the **'Pigs'** were phased out of service and placed in reserve or scrapped. The flare-up in Northern Ireland in the late

1960s meant that many of these vehicles were returned to service, remaining operational in Northern Ireland for some years.

Many of the Pigs in Northern Ireland were specially modified for the requirements of the internal security role, being fitted with additional armour protection to stop 7.62-mm (0.3-in) armour-piercing rounds and barricade-removal equipment at the front of the hull.

Related models

The basic armoured personnel carrier model was the **FV1611**, and this was normally outfitted for the carriage of six or eight fully equipped men in the rear, with the commander and driver sitting at the front to the rear of the engine. Both the commander and driver were provided with a door in the side of their cab, and there were twin doors in the rear for the embarked infantry. A total of six firing ports/observation blocks are provided in the rear troop compartment (two in each side and one in each of the rear doors). The ambulance member of the family was the **FV1613**, which had a two-man crew and could carry three litter or eight seated patients, and the radio

The FV1609 model of the Humber 1-ton armoured personnel carrier entered service in the early 1950s. With an open top, capacity was two crew and up to eight troops.

vehicle was the **FV1612**. The anti-tank version was designated as the **FV1620**, otherwise known as the **Hornet/Malkara**, and this

model had two Malkara long-range anti-tank guided missiles in the ready-to-launch position. The missile's obsolescence led to the FV1620's retirement.

SPECIFICATION	
FV 1611 'Pig'	**Powerplant:** one Rolls-Royce B60
Crew: 2+6 (or 2+8)	Mk 5A liquid-cooled 6-cylinder
Weight: 5790 kg (12,765 lb)	petrol engine developing 89.5 kW
Dimensions: length 4.926 m (16 ft	(120 bhp)
2 in); width 2.044 m (6 ft 8½ in);	**Performance:** maximum road speed
height 2.12 m (6 ft 11½ in)	64 km/h (40 mph); maximum road
	range 402 km (250 miles)

The 'Pig', as it became known, had been withdrawn from service before worsening civil disorder in Northern Ireland required its return to major service in the internal security role.

Alvis Saracen

Armoured personnel carrier

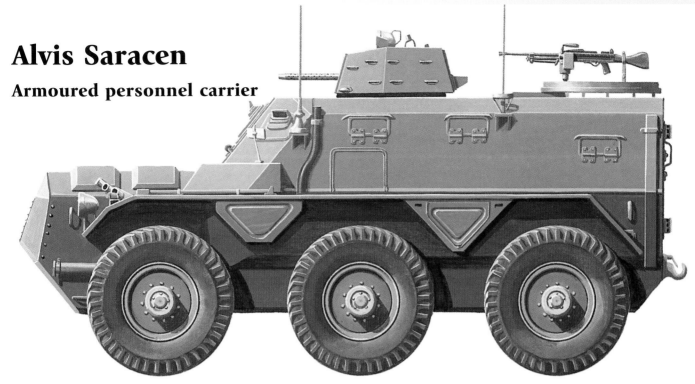

After the end of World War II the UK's Fighting Vehicles Research and Development Establishment (FVRDE) designed a complete family of wheeled armoured vehicles known as the **FV600** series which included the FV601 Saladin armoured car and the **FV603 Saracen** APC. The requirement for the latter was much more urgent because of the 'emergency' in Malaya, so the first production vehicles appeared by December 1952.

Production of the FV600 series was undertaken by Alvis at Coventry, and 1,838 vehicles had been completed by the end of production in 1972. Throughout the 1950s the Saracen was the only real APC in British army service, and was used in the Far East and Middle East (for example Aden and Libya) as well as in the UK and with the British Army of the Rhine.

Tracked replacement

From the early 1960s the Saracen was replaced in the BAOR by the FV432 fully racked APC, which has better performance across country, improved armour protection and longer operational range. The last Saracens were retired from British service during 1993 in Hong Kong. Sales of the Saracen were also made to Indonesia, Jordan, Kuwait, Lebanon, Libya, Mauritania, Nigeria, Qatar, South Africa, Sri Lanka, Sudan, Thailand, UAE and Uganda, and it is still serving with seven of these.

Although the FV603 Saracen has the same automotive components as the FV601 Saladin armoured car, its layout is quite different, with the engine at the front and troop compartment at the rear. The driver is seated in the centre, with the section commander to his left rear and radio operator to his right rear. To their rear are the eight infantrymen, who are seated on individual seats (four down each side of the hull facing inward). The troops enter and leave via twin doors in the hull rear, and firing ports are provided in the sides and rear.

First produced in 1952, the FV603 Saracen APC was part of a family of 6x6 vehicles. The turret mounts a 7.62-mm (0.3-in) machine-gun.

On the forward part of the roof is a manually operated turret with a 7.62-mm (0.3-in) machine-gun, and over the rear part of the troop compartment is a 7.62-mm (0.3-in) light machine gun for air defence.

Steering is hydraulically assisted on the front four wheels, and the vehicle can be driven with one wheel missing from each side.

Small-scale family

There were not many variants of the Saracen as the FV602 ambulance was cancelled early in the family's programme. The **FV604** was a command vehicle, while the **FV610** was another command vehicle with a much higher roof to allow the command staff to work standing up. The **FV611** was an ambulance model and also had a higher roof. The FV610 was also fitted with the Robert surveillance radar but this did not enter service; the same fate befell the 25-pdr self-propelled gun version and a roller-type mineclearing vehicle.

Versions of the Saracen included the FV604 command vehicle, seen landing from a Mexefloat while on exercise with the 13th/18th Hussars in Cyprus. Notice the extensive external stowage, the auxiliary generator on the front wing and the lack of the machine-gun turret.

SPECIFICATION	
Saracen	engine developing 119 kW (160 hp)
Crew: 2+10	**Performance:** maximum road speed
Combat weight: 8640 kg (19,048 lb)	72 km/h (44.7 mph); maximum
Dimensions: length 5.233 m (17 ft	road range 400 km (248 miles);
2 in); width 2.539 m (8 ft 4 in);	**Fording:** 1.07 m (3 ft 6 in)
height (overall) 2.463 m (8 ft 1 in)	**Gradient:** 42 per cent
Powerplant: one Rolls-Royce B80 Mk	**Vertical obstacle:** 0.46 m (1 ft 6 in);
6A liquid-cooled 8-cylinder petrol	trench 1.52 m (5 ft)

GKN Sankey Saxon
Armoured personnel carrier

The AT105P has a commander's cupola with a pintle-mounted 7.62-mm (0.3-in) GPMG. The cupola can be replaced by one of a number of alternative armament installations.

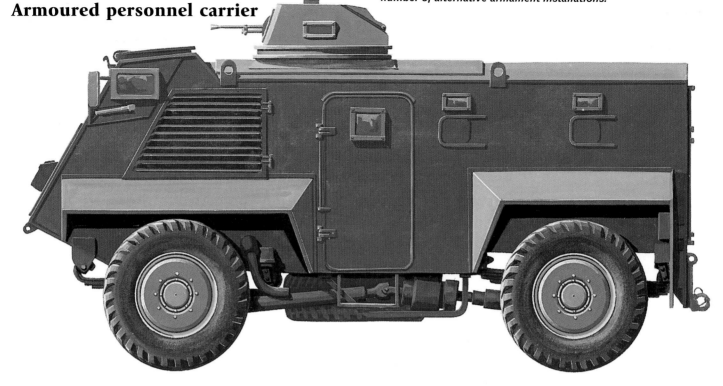

As a private venture in the early 1970s, GKN Sankey built the **AT100** 4x2 and **AT104** 4x4 vehicles aimed mainly at the internal security role. The former secured no production order, but about 30 AT104s were built for the Dutch state police and Royal Brunei Malay Regiment.

Fresh design

These were followed by the **AT105** which later received the name **Saxon**. This was a completely new design using many automotive components of the Bedford MK 4-tonne 4x4.

Production of the AT105 started by 1976, and by the programme's end 832 vehicles had been delivered to Bahrain, Hong Kong, Malaysia, Nigeria, Oman, UAE and UK. The British army purchased an initial three for evaluation purposes in the 1970s, and in 1983 ordered 50 further vehicles. The first of these were delivered early in 1984 and issued to infantry battalions in the UK which, in time of war, would have been sent to West Germany to reinforce the British Army of the Rhine. The British army requirement was for up to 1,000 AT105s, but procurement reached just 664.

The AT105 has a hull of all-welded steel construction providing complete protection against small arms fire and shell splinters. Both left- and right-hand drive models were offered, the driver being seated right at the front of the vehicle with the engine to his left or right. The troop compartment is at the rear of the hull, and twin doors are provided in the hull rear and a single door in each side to allow for the rapid exit of troops. British army vehicles do not have the left-hand door as external bins are fitted for the stowage of kit and supplies.

The commander's roof-mounted cupola is fixed and fitted with an observation block in each of the four sides for all-round observation; a 7.62-mm (0.3-in) machine-gun is mounted on a DISA mount for ground and AA fire. A range of other armament installations can be fitted, including turret-mounted 12.7- and 7.62-mm (0.5- and 0.3-in) machine-guns or anti-riot weapons. Firing ports and/or vision blocks can be installed in the troop compartment. An unusual feature is the mud-guards are of light sheet steel construction that will blow off in the event of the vehicle hitting a mine so that the blast is not contained under the hull. Proposed Saxon variants included a command vehicle, mortar carrier, armoured ambulance and anti-riot versions.

The Saxon is certainly a beast of completely unlovely appearance, but it is a thoroughly utilitarian vehicle, offering good overall capabilities and excellent levels of reliability.

SPECIFICATION	
Saxon	122 kW (164 bhp)
Crew: 2+8	**Performance:** maximum road speed
Weight: 10670 kg (23,523 lb)	96 km/h (60 mph); maximum road
Dimensions: length 5.169 m (16 ft	range 510 km (317 miles)
11½ in); width 2.489 m (8 ft 2 in);	**Fording:** 1.12 m (3 ft 8 in)
height 2.86 m (9 ft 4½ in)	**Gradient:** 60 per cent
Powerplant: one Bedford 500 liquid-	**Vertical obstacle:** 0.41 m (1 ft 4 in);
cooled 6-cylinder diesel developing	**Trench:** not applicable

Verne Dragoon

Armoured personnel carrier

SPECIFICATION	
Dragoon	Model 6V-53T liquid-cooled V-6
Crew: typically 3+6	diesel developing 224 kW (300 hp)
Weight: typically 12700 kg	**Performance:** maximum road speed
(27,998 lb)	116 km/h (72 mph); maximum road
Dimensions: length 5.588 m (18 ft 4	range 1045 km (650 miles)
in); width 2.438 m (8 ft); height	**Fording:** amphibious
(hull top) 2.133 m (7 ft) but varies	**Gradient:** 60 per cent
with weapon fit	**Vertical obstacle:** 0.99 m (3 ft 3 in)
Powerplant: one Detroit Diesel	**Trench:** not applicable

In the late 1970s the US Army Military Police issued a requirement for an air base protection and convoy escort vehicle air-portable in a Lockheed C-130 Hercules transport. The requirement lapsed, but the Verne Corporation (now AV Technology) built two private-venture prototypes of a vehicle which was eventually called the **Verne Dragoon**. In appearance the Dragoon is very similar to the Cadillac Gage V-100 and V-150 range of 4x4 multi-mission vehicles, but shares many common components with the M113A2 tracked APC and M809 6x6.5-ton truck, offering obvious logistical advantages.

The hull of the Dragoon is of all-welded steel construction providing protection from 7.62- and 5.56-mm (0.3- and 0.22-in) small arms fire and shell splinters. The driver is seated at the front on the left with another crew member to his right, the main crew compartment is in the centre, the engine is at the rear of the hull on the right-hand side, and an aisle connects the main crew compartment with the door in the hull rear. The troops normally enter and leave the vehicle via a door in each side of the hull, the lower part of each door folding down to form a step while the upper part hinges to one side. Firing ports with vision blocks above are provided

in the sides and rear of the crew compartment. The diesel engine is coupled to an automatic transmission with five forward and one reverse gear and a single-speed transfer case, and steering is hydraulic on the front axle. The Dragoon is amphibious, being propelled in the water by its wheels at a speed of 4.8 km/h (3 mph), with three bilge pumps extracting any water that seeps in through the door and hatch openings.

When being used as a basic armoured personnel carrier the Dragoon is normally fitted with

an M 113 type cupola with a pintlemounted 12.7-mm (0.5-in) or 7.62-mm machine-gun to allow the maximum number of troops to be carried. Other and, indeed, considerably more powerful weapon installations are available, however, these including power-operated two-man turrets armed with a 25-mm cannon or a 90-mm (3.54-in) gun and 7.62-mm co-axial and anti-aircraft/local defence machine-guns. More specialised versions include command, engineer, anti-tank (with TOW heavyweight missiles), recovery and internal security vehicles.

In 1982 six Dragoons were supplied to the US Army and a smaller number to the US Navy. The former is operated by the 9th Infantry Division High Technology Test Bed in two roles, electronic warfare and video optical surveillance. The first of these has extensive communications equipment and a hydraulically operated mast which can be quickly extended for improved communications. The US Navy uses its vehicles for the armed patrol of nuclear weapons storage areas in Alaska and the continental USA.

The electronic warfare Dragoon was operated for trials purposes by the US 9th Infantry Division, its roles including the jamming of high-speed communications and advanced battlefield direction finding.

LAV-150 Commando

Armoured personnel carrier

In the early 1960s Cadillac Gage designed a multi-purpose armoured vehicle revealed in 1963 as the **V-100 Commando** with a Chrysler petrol engine. Trials were so successful that the type entered production the following year for the export market. The war in South

Vietnam revealed an urgent need for a wheeled vehicle to patrol high-value sites and escort road convoys, so large numbers of vehicles were shipped to Vietnam.

There followed the much larger **V-200** with a more powerful engine, greater weight

and increased loadcarrying capability. The V-200 was sold only to Singapore. In the 1970s there emerged the **V-150**, which is still the current production model. The V-150 introduced a number of improvements, including a diesel engine providing much greater range.

So far well over 3,000 V-150 vehicles have been built for 29 countries. The **LAV-150 S** 'stretched' model secured no US order but has scored limited export sales.

The V-150 is called a multi-mission vehicle as it can be used for a range of roles. In the

Developed from the V-100 of 1962, the V-150 entered production in 1971. A wide range of armament can be fitted, including a two-man gun turret.

basic APC model it has a three-man crew (commander, gunner and driver) and can carry nine troops, who enter and leave the vehicle via doors in the hull sides and rear. A very wide range of armament installations can be fitted, including a one-man turret with various combinations of 12.7- and 7.62-mm (0.5- and 0.3-in) machine-guns; a power-operated two-man turret with 90-mm (3.54-in) or 76-mm (3-in) gun and 7.62-mm co-axial and AA machine-guns; and a turret with 20-mm cannon and 7.62-mm co-axial and AA machine-guns. There is also an AA vehicle with a

20-mm Vulcan six-barrel cannon, 81-mm (3.2-in) mortar carrier, anti-tank vehicle with TOW missiles, command vehicle with raised roof for greater head room, riot control vehicle with special equipment, and recovery vehicle.

SPECIFICATION	
LAV-150 Commando	**Performance:** maximum road speed
Crew: 3+9	88. 5 km/h (55 mph); maximum
Weight: 9888 kg (21,800 lb)	range 643 km (400 miles)
Dimensions: length 5.689 m (18 ft 8	**Fording:** amphibious
in); width 2.26 m (7 ft 5 in); height	**Gradient:** 60 per cent
(hull top) 1.98 m (6 ft 6 in)	**Vertical obstacle:** 0.61 m (2 ft)
Powerplant: one V-504 V-8 diesel	**Trench:** not applicable
developing 151 kW (202 bhp)	

Cadillac Gage V-300 Commando Armoured personnel carrier

The V-300 was developed as a private venture. The heaviest of the wide range of weapons operable is the 90-mm (3.54-in) Cockerill Mk III gun, mounted in a two-man Cadillac Gage turret. A 7.62-mm (0.3-in) machine-gun is pintle-mounted for air defence.

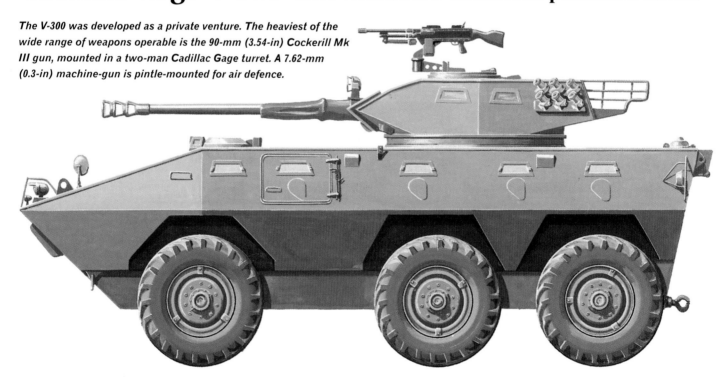

In 1979 Cadillac Gage built two **V-300 Commando** 6x6 prototypes usable for a wide range of roles. In 1982 Panama ordered 12 V-300s all delivered in the following year. Four different models were selected by Panama: a fire-support vehicle with 90-mm (3.54-in)

Cockerill gun, a recovery vehicle, and two types fitted with different machine-gun installations. Cadillac Gage also supplied three V-300s for the US Army and US Marine Corps Light Armoured Vehicle (LAV) competition: one was fitted with a two-man turret armed with a

90-mm Cockerill gun, while the other two had a two-man turret carrying the 25-mm Chain Gun.

The driver is seated at the front left with the engine to his right. The troop compartment is at the rear, the troops entering and leaving via the two doors in the hull rear; in addition there

are hatches in the roof and firing ports with a vision block in the sides and rear.

The V-300 can be fitted with a wide range of armaments in a turret designed and built by Cadillac Gage. Among the two-man installations is a turret armed with the 90-mm Cockerill

Mk III, or 76-mm (3-in) ROF gun or 25-mm Chain Gun, or 20-mm cannon; there is also a one-man turret with a 20-mm cannon or a machine-gun. In all of these there is a 7.62-mm (0.3-in) co-axial machine-gun, and a similar weapon can usually be mounted on the roof for anti-aircraft defence.

Variants of what is now the **LAV-300** include an ambulance with a higher roof, anti-tank vehicle fitted with a TOW missile launcher, and an 81-mm (3.2-in) mortar carrier.

The LAV-300 is fitted with a winch and is amphibious, propelled in the water by its wheels at 5 km/h (3 mph).

SPECIFICATION	
V-300 Commando	175 kW (235 hp)
Crew: 3+9	**Performance:** maximum road speed
Weight: 13137 kg (28,962 lb)	105 km/h (65 mph); maximum road
Dimensions: length 6.40 m (21 ft);	range 925 km (585 miles)
width 2.54 m (8 ft 4 in); height (hull	**Fording:** amphibious
top) 1.981 m (6 ft 6 in) but varies	**Gradient:** 60 per cent
with weapon fit	**Vertical obstacle:** 0.61 m (2 ft);
Powerplant: one VT-504 liquid-	**Trench:** not applicable
cooled V-8 diesel developing	

Cadillac Gage Commando Ranger

Armoured personnel carrier

Developed to meet US Air Force base security requirements, the Commando Ranger is also tasked with the escort of ordnance convoys.

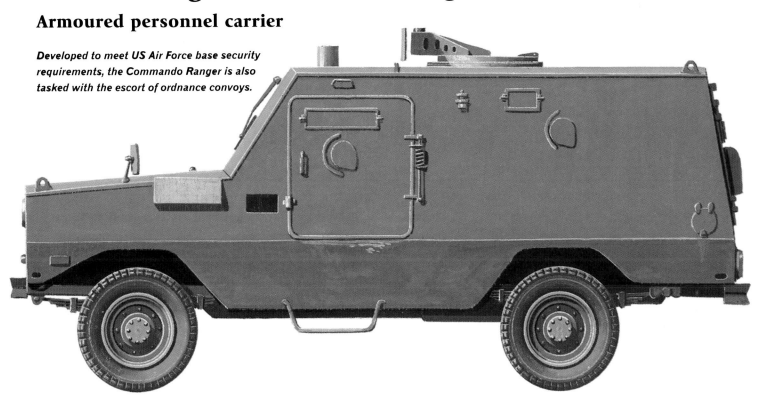

The US Air Force has hundreds of vast bases spread all over the world, and in recent years these have become possible targets for terrorists and other fringe groups. To protect these assets the USAF issued a requirement for a vehicle which it called a Security Police Armored Response/ Convoy Truck that would, in addition to carrying out patrols on air bases, also escort convoys carrying ordnance to and from bases,

or even from the storage dump on the airfield to the aircraft themselves.

After studying proposals, early in 1979 the USAF selected the **Commando Ranger** APC to meet its requirements as the **Peacekeeper**. The first of these vehicles was handed over in the following year, and by 1994 some 708 had been delivered to the USA and allied states.

The Commander Ranger is based on a standard Chrysler

truck chassis with a shorter wheelbase. The armoured body provides the crew with protection from small arms fire and shell splinters. The engine is at the front of the vehicle and coupled to an automatic transmission with three forward and one reverse gear and a two-speed transfer case.

The commander and driver are seated to the rear of the engine, each being provided with a bulletproof window to his front and a rearward-opening side door that has a bulletproof vision block and a firing port underneath; in addition there is a firing port between the driver's and commander's windscreens.

The six troops sit three down each side in the rear, and enter

via two doors in the hull rear. Each of these doors has a firing port, and the left one also has a vision block. In each side of the troop compartment is a vision block and a firing port. In the roof is a hatch on which a variety of light armament installations can be fitted, including a shield with a 7.62-mm (0.3-in) machine-gun or a turret with twin 7.62-mm machine-guns.

Standard equipment includes an air-conditioning system and heater, while optional equipment includes 24-volt electrics in place of the normal 12-volt system, and a winch. Specialised versions of the Commando Ranger include a command vehicle and an ambulance.

SPECIFICATION	
Commando Ranger	developing 134 kW (180 hp)
Crew: 2+6	**Performance:** maximum road speed
Weight: 4536 kg (10,000 lb)	112.5 km/h (70 mph); maximum
Dimensions: length 4.70 m (15 ft	road range 556 km (345 miles);
5 in); width 2.02 m (6 ft 7½ in);	**Fording:** 0.457 m (1 ft 6 in)
height 1.98 m (6 ft 6 in)	**Gradient:** 60 per cent
Powerplant: one Dodge 360 CID	**Vertical obstacle:** 0.254 m (10 in);
liquid-cooled V-8 petrol engine	**Trench:** not applicable

Steyr SK 105 Light tank/tank destroyer

The **Jagdpanzer SK 105** was designed by Steyr in the mid-1960s to an Austrian requirement. The first prototype was completed in 1967, with production beginning during the early 1970s. Some 652 examples were built – 286 for the Austrian army and the remainder for export to Argentina, Bolivia, Botswana, Brazil, Morocco and Tunisia. Over the years some updates, such as a stabilised turret on the **SK 105/A2**, were introduced. Many of the SK 105's automotive components are identical to those of the Saurer 4K 4FA tracked armoured personnel carrier.

An SK 105 climbs an incline, showing the French TCV 29 laser rangefinder on the turret roof at the rear with an IR/white light search-light above it. The 105-mm main gun is fed by two six-round revolver magazines.

Limited protection

Over its frontal arc the vehicle has protection from attack by all weapons up to 20-mm calibre, protection against small aims fire being provided over the remainder of the vehicle. The turret is a modified version of that installed on the AMX-13 light tank. It is of the oscillating type, with the gun fixed to the upper part and pivoting on the lower part. The main armament comprises a 105-mm (4.13-in) gun, and ammunition stowage is provided for 44 main gun rounds as well as 2,000 rounds for the 7.62-mm (0.3-in) co-axial machine-gun. The main gun is fed by two revolver-type magazines in the turret bustle, enabling the gun to fire until the ammunition is exhausted. One of the crew then has to leave the vehicle to reload the magazines. Empty cartridge cases are ejected from the turret through a small trap in the bustle. Fire control includes telescopes for the commander and gunner with an IR/white light searchlight above this.

Transmissions

The diesel engine and transmission are at the rear, the latter being a ZF manual box replaced in the **SK 105/A1** by an automatic transmission. The suspension is of the torsion-bar type, consisting on each side of five dual rubber-tyred road wheels with the drive sprocket at the rear, idler at the front and three track-return rollers. The standard equipment includes an NBC system and a heater.

SK 105 variants include the **Greif** armoured recovery vehicle, the **Pionier** combat engineer vehicle, and the **Fahrschulpanzer** driver training vehicle. The Greif is fitted with a 6-tonne hydraulic crane, a dozer/stabiliser blade at the front of the hull, a winch with a pulling capacity of 20 tonne and full provision for spare parts.

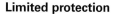

SPECIFICATION	
Steyr SK 105	**Powerplant:** one 239-kW (320-hp) Steyr liquid-cooled 6-cylinder diesel
Crew: 3	**Performance:** maximum road speed 65 km/h (40 mph); maximum road range 520 km (325 miles)
Weight: 17.7 tonnes	
Dimensions: length (including gun) 7.76 m (25 ft 5½ in) and (hull) 5.58 m (18 ft 3½ in); width 2.5 m (8 ft 2½ in); height 2.53 m (8 ft 3½ in)	**Fording:** 1 m (3 ft 3 in)
	Gradient: 75 per cent
	Vertical obstacle: 0.8 m (2 ft 7½ in)
	Trench: 2.41 m (7 ft 11 in)
Armament: one 105-mm (4.13-in) 105 G1 main gun, and one 7.62-mm (0.3-in) Steyr MG 74	

ENGESA EE-9 Cascavel Armoured car

During the late 1960s the Sao Paulo company ENGESA, formerly a truck manufacturer, developed two 6x6 armoured vehicles to meet the requirements of the Brazilian army. These were the **EE-9 Cascavel** armoured car and the EE-11 Urutu APC, which shared many automotive components even though their layouts were different. The EE-9 prototype, named after a Brazilian snake, was completed in 1970 and was followed by a batch of pre-production vehicles before the first production examples were completed at what was then the company's new facility at Sao Jose dos Campos during 1974. Large numbers were built, not only for the Brazilian army but also for many other countries, including Bolivia, Burkina Faso, Chad, Chile, Colombia, Cyprus, Ecuador, Gabon, Ghana, Iraq, Libya, Nigeria, Paraguay, Surinam, Togo, Tunisia, Uruguay and Zimbabwe.

The Cascavel was deployed operationally by Iraq during their war with Iran, which captured a number of vehicles. Although ENGESA is no longer trading, many Cascavels remain in service.

A least six different Cascavel marks were produced, although the layout of all EE-9s remains essentially the same. The driver is seated at the front of the vehicle on the left, with the two-man turret in the centre, and the engine and transmission at the rear. The engine is either a Detroit Diesel or a Mercedes-Benz diesel, coupled to an automatic or manual transmission. Spare parts for both the engine and transmission are available from commercial sources all over the world. All six wheels are powered, and power-assisted steering is provided on the front two wheels. The armour is of a locally designed type with a hard steel outer shell and a softer inner layer designed to provide the maximum protection within the vehicle's weight limitations.

Armament variations

The **Cascavel Mk II** initial production model had the same 37-mm (1.46-in) gun as the M3 Stuart light tank, then still in service with the Brazilian army, but all of these vehicles were rebuilt with an ENGESA turret armed with a 90-mm (3.54-in) gun. The **Cascavel Mk III** was only for export, having a French Hispano-Suiza H-90 turret armed with a 90-mm GIAT gun. The other models, the **Cascavel Mks IV, V, VI** and **VII** have a two-man ENGESA ET-90 turret armed with a 90-mm Cockerill Mk III gun made under licence in Brazil by ENGESA as the EC-90, a 7.62-mm (0.3-in) co-axial machine-gun and a 12.7-mm (0.5-in) or 7.62-mm machine-gun on the roof for AA defence.

The later production variants of the ENGESA EE-9 Cascavel armoured car carry a laser rangefinder mounted externally over the 90-mm (3.54-in) gun and a 7.62-mm (0.3-in) machine-gun mounted externally at the commander's station. The EE-9 was widely used by the Iraqi army during the 1980s war with Iran.

As in most modern armoured cars, a wide range of optional equipment could (and still can) be fitted or retrofitted to the Cascavel, including a fire-control system, a laser rangefinder mounted externally over the main armament or operating through the gunner's sight, day/night sights for the commander and gunner, an NBC system and a ventilation system. A characteristic of all the models is a central tyre pressure regulation system to enable the driver to adjust the pressure to suit the nature of the terrain being crossed.

SPECIFICATION	
ENGESA EE-9 Cascavel	7.62-mm AA machine-gun
Crew: 3	**Powerplant:** one 158-kW (212-hp)
Weight: 13.4 tonnes	Detroit Diesel 6V-53 liquid-cooled
Dimensions: length (gun forward)	6-cylinder diesel
6.22 mm (20 ft 5 in) and (hull)	**Performance:** maximum road speed
5.19 m (17 ft ¼ in); width 2.59 m	100 km/h (62 mph); maximum road
(8 ft 6 in); height 2.29 m (7 ft 6 in)	range 1000 km (620 miles)
Armament: (Mk IV) one 90-mm	**Fording:** 1 m (3 ft 3 in)
(3.54-in) EC-90 gun, one 7.62-mm	**Gradient:** 60 per cent
(0.3-in) co-axial machine-gun, and	**Vertical obstacle:** 0.6 m (1 ft 11½ in)
one 12.7-mm (0.5-in) M2 HB or	

Panhard EBR Heavy armoured car

The origins of the Panhard **EBR** (**Engin Blinde de Reconnaissance** or armoured reconnaissance vehicle) can be traced to 1937, when Panhard et Levassor of Paris started design work on a new armoured car that would have superior cross-country mobility to the 4x4 armoured cars then in use by the French army. The first prototype was completed in 1939 with the armament of one 25-mm cannon and one 7.5-mm (0.295-in) co-axial machine-gun. Its most unusual feature was that of its eight road wheels, the four centre ones (two on each side) were fitted with steel rims for improved traction: during road movement, these were raised clear of the ground by a hydro-pneumatic unit operated by the driver, and then lowered again for cross-country travel.

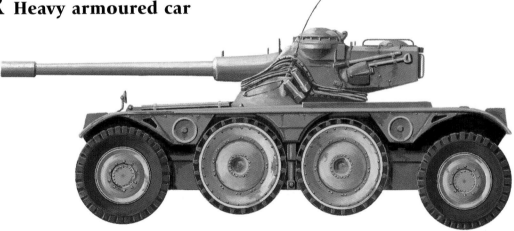

Revived effort

After the end of World War II the French army issued a requirement for a new heavy armoured car and, after a number of proposals from French companies had been studied, Panhard et Levassor was awarded a contract for an 8x8 vehicle while Hotchkiss was awarded a contract for a 6x6 vehicle. Each company built

The Panhard EBR 8x8 vehicle was the standard heavy armoured car of the French army from 1950, although its design dated back to before World War II. An unusual feature of the vehicle was that its centre pairs of road wheels, which had steel rims, were normally raised when travelling on roads and lowered only when going across country, so improving ground traction in mud and soft soils.

prototypes for evaluation by the French army, and the Panhard et Levassor vehicle was subsequently selected for service as the EBR. The first production vehicles were completed in 1950, and in a manufacturing programme that lasted to 1960, some 1,200 vehicles were built. In addition to the French army, the type was also exported to Mauritania, Morocco and Tunisia. An armoured personnel carrier version, the **EBR VTT**, was also developed by Panhard on the same chassis, and a few of these were exported to Portugal, where they were used mainly for internal security duties. The EBR was finally phased out of French Army service in 1987, some 50 years after its design.

The driver was seated at the front, with the commander and gunner in the centre of the vehicle, the engine in the floor and the second driver at the rear. The EBR had an FL-11 oscillating

turret armed with a 90-mm (3.54-in) gun, 7.5-mm co-axial machine-gun and two banks of electrically operated smoke dischargers. In an oscillating turret the gun was fixed in the upper part of the turret, which pivoted on the lower part of the turret. The 90-mm gun fired the following types of fixed ammunition: HEAT (muzzle velocity 640 m/2,100 ft per second), HE (muzzle velocity 635 m/2,085 ft per second), smoke (muzzle velocity 750 m/2,460 ft per second) and canister for close defence. Ammunition totals were 43 rounds of 90-mm and 2,000 of 7.5-mm.

Another unusual feature of the EBR was that the drivers at the front and rear were each provided with a 7.5-mm fixed machine-gun. Some vehicles were fitted with the FL-10 turret of the AMX-13 light tank armed with a 75-mm (2.95-in) gun fed by two revolver-type magazines, each holding six rounds of

ammunition. These allowed 12 rounds to be fired very quickly, after which the magazines had to be reloaded manually from outside the vehicle. The main drawback of this combination was that the weight of the vehicle went up to over 15 tonnes, while overall height was also increased.

SPECIFICATION	
EBR	Panhard liquid-cooled 12-cylinder petrol engine
Crew: 4	**Performance:** maximum road speed 105 km/h (65 mph); maximum road range 650 km (404 miles)
Weight: 13.5 tonnes	
Dimensions: length (gun forward) 6.15 m (20 ft 2 in); width 2.42 m (7 ft 11¼ in); height 2.32 m (7 ft 7¼ in)	**Gradient:** 60 per cent
	Vertical obstacle: 0.4 m (1 ft 3¾ in)
Powerplant: one-149 kW (200-hp)	**Trench:** 2 m (6 ft 7 in)

GIAT AMX-13 Light tank

The **AMX-13** light tank was one of three armoured vehicles designed in France immediately after World War II, the other being the Panhard EBR heavy armoured car and the AMX-50 MBT. The AMX-13 was designed by the Atelier de Construction d'Issy-les-Moulineaux, the numeral 13 in the designation being the specified design weight in tonnes.

The first prototype was completed in 1948 and production had begun at the Atelier de Construction Roanne (ARE) by 1952. The AMX-13 continued in production at the ARE until the 1960s, when space was needed for the AMX-30 MBT and AMX-10P IFV families. Production of the whole AMX-13 family, including the light tank, was transferred to Creusot-Loire at Chalon-sur Saône. The AMX-13 finally became a GIAT Industries product before production ceased. Over 7,700 vehicles were built and the type remains in service with several nations, many of them updated in various ways, including a conversion to diesel power. The chassis of the AMX-13 (extensively modified in many cases) was used as the basis for one of the most complete families of AFVs ever

An AMX-13 light tank fitted with an FL-10 two-man turret armed with the original 75-mm (2.95-in) gun. Other versions were armed with 90-mm (3.54-in) or 105-mm (4.13-in) guns.

developed. It included the 105-mm (4.13-in) Mk 61 self-propelled howitzer, 155-mm (6.1-in) Mk F3 self-propelled gun, AMX-13 DCA twin 30-mm self-propelled anti-aircraft gun system, and the AMX VCI infantry fighting vehicle and its countless variants (all discussed elsewhere), the AMX VCG engineer vehicle, AMX-13 ARV armoured recovery vehicle and the AMX-13 CPP armoured bridgelayer. Many further variants were produced for export.

Light armament

The original model of the AMX-13 was fitted with the FL-10 turret armed with a 75-mm (2.95-in) gun and a 7.62-mm (0.3-in) co-axial machine-gun. This turret is of the oscillating type and the 75-mm gun is fed by two revolver-type magazines, each of which holds six rounds of ammunition. This model was

used in some numbers by Israel during the 1967 Six-Day War, but the gun was found to be ineffective against the frontal armour of the Soviet T-54 and T-55 MBTs operated by Syria and Egypt, so it was phased out of service, most going to Singapore or Nepal.

At a later date all 75-mm models of the French army were fitted with a 90-mm (3.54-in) gun which could fire canister, HE, HEAT and smoke projectiles, later supplemented by an APFSDS projectile capable

of penetrating a triple NATO tank target at an incidence of 60 degrees at a range of 2000 m (2,195 yards). The 105-mm (4.13-in) gun model was designed specifically for the export market and had the heavier FL-12 turret, which is also fitted to the SK 105 light tank/tank destroyer.

The basic AMX-13 had a petrol engine offering an operative range up to 400 km (250 miles), but later Creusot-Loire offered a package to replace this with a Detroit Diesel unit.

SPECIFICATION	
AMX-13 (90-mm gun)	**Powerplant:** one 186-kW (250-hp) SOFAM 8Gxb liquid-cooled 8-cylinder petrol engine
Crew: 3	
Weight: 15 tonnes	
Dimensions: length (gun forward) 6.36 m (20 ft 10¼ in) and (hull) 4.88 m (16 ft); width 2.5 m (8 ft 2½ in); height 2.3 m (7 ft 6½ in)	**Performance:** maximum road speed 60 km/h (37 mph); maximum road range 350–400 km (220–250 miles)
	Fording: 0.6 m (1 ft 11½ in)
Armament: one 90-mm (3.54-in) main gun, one 7.62-mm (0.3-in) machine-gun, and one optional 7.62-mm AA machine-gun	**Gradient:** 60 per cent
	Vertical obstacle: 0.65 m (2 ft 11/4 in)
	Trench: 1.6 m (5 ft 3 in)

Shorland Armoured patrol car

In the 1960s, Short Brothers and Harland developed the **Shorland** armoured patrol car to meet the urgent requirements of the local Royal Ulster Constabulary.

The vehicle is based on a modified Land Rover (4x4) long-wheelbase chassis and is fitted with a fully armoured body that provides the occupants with protection from small-arms fire and shell splinters. The floor provides further protection against nail bombs, and special attention has been provided to protect the occupants against similar improvised devices, including petrol bombs.

The vehicle normally has a crew of three consisting of the driver, commander and gunner. Mounted on top of the hull is a one-man manually operated turret armed with a 0.3-in (7.62-mm) machine-gun. The turret can also be fitted with a searchlight and electrically operated smoke-grenade launchers.

Since its introduction, the Shorland has been continuously developed as technology has evolved. A wide range of optional equipment was offered including air conditioning, a fire-suppression

An early example of the Shorland armoured patrol car fitted with a 0.3-in (7.62-mm) machine-gun turret. The vehicle's Land Rover origins are apparent.

system, run-flat tyres and various types of communications systems.

There were a number of specialised versions of the Shorland including an anti-tank vehicle fitted with the Vigilant wire-guided anti-tank missile, an anti-hijack vehicle and another fitted with Javelin lightweight surface-to-air missiles. The same company also built a complimentary Shorland armoured personnel carrier (APC), which is also referred to as the **SB 301**. This has a similar hull to the earlier vehicle but is extended to the rear. The APC normally has a crew of two and carries six.

Large quantities of the Shorland series of 4x4 vehicles were built, most for export. The production and sales rights were subsequently sold to the then British Aerospace Australia, who in turn sold the complete Shorland product range to Tenix Defence Systems.

To meet emerging requirements for a vehicle with

increased payload and capabilities, the **S600** was developed. This is based on a Mercedes-Benz (4x4) Unimog chassis. First prototypes were completed in Northern Ireland

but all production has since been undertaken in Australia by Tenix Defence Systems, with sales being made to Belgium and Kuwait. The S600 can carry up to 10 people.

Bottom: A late production Shorland armoured patrol car fitted with a machine-gun turret, the front of which mounts electrically operated smoke-grenade launchers.

Below: The Shorland armoured patrol car (left) is seen in company with the armoured personnel carrier. The latter has an extended hull with seating for six.

SPECIFICATION	
Shorland Mk 2	**Powerplant:** one Rover petrol
Crew: 3	engine developing 67 kW (91 hp)
Weight: 3360 kg (7,407 lb)	coupled to manual transmission
Dimensions: length 4.597 m (15 ft);	**Performance:** maximum road speed
width 1.778 m (5 ft 10 in); height	88 km/h (54.7 mph); maximum
2.286 m (7 ft 6 in)	range 260 km (162 miles)
	Fording: 0.4 m (1 ft 4 in)
	Gradient: 60 per cent

EE-3 Jararaca Scout car

To complement the EE-9 Cascavel and EE-11 Urutu 6x6 light armoured vehicles, ENGESA developed the smaller **EE-3 Jararaca** 4x4 scout car. Unlike the EE-9 and EE-11 vehicles, the EE-3 was not adopted by the Brazilian army. About 100 examples were built

for the export market before production was completed.

The main role of the EE-3 Jararaca is reconnaissance and it relies on its speed and compact shape to avoid detection. The driver is seated at the front with the commander and weapons

SPECIFICATION	
EE-3 Jararaca	**Powerplant:** one Mercedes-Benz
Crew: 2/3	diesel developing 89 kW (120 hp)
Weight: 5800 kg (12,787 lb)	**Performance:** maximum road speed
Dimensions: length 4.16 m	100 km/h (62 mph); maximum
(13 ft 8 in); width 2.23 m (7 ft 4 in);	range 700 km (435 miles)
height 2.3 m (7 ft 7 in)	**Fording:** 0.6 m (2 ft)

operator in the centre and the engine and transmission are located at the rear of the vehicle.

Armour protection

The hull of the EE-3 is of all-welded steel armour similar to that used on the other ENGESA wheeled vehicles and provides the occupants with protection from small-arms fire and shell splinters.

The EE-3 can be fitted with a wide range of weapon stations depending on particular mission requirements. These include a MILAN ATGW on a pintle mount, a turret armed with various combinations of 7.62-mm (0.3-in) and/or 12.7-mm (0.5-in) machine-guns, and a cupola-mounted 20-mm cannon.

Standard equipment includes power steering and a central tyre-pressure regulation system that allows the driver to adjust the tyre pressure to suit the terrain being crossed. As usual, the EE-3 Jararaca can be fitted with a wide range of optional equipment such as an NBC system, passive night-vision equipment and various radios.

Two armament options for the EE-3 Jararaca include a cupola-mounted 12.7-mm (0.5-in) M2 machine-gun (right) and MILAN anti-tank guided weapon system (below). A wide range of specialised EE-3 versions were proposed, including an NBC reconnaissance vehicle.

BRM-23 Reconnaissance vehicle

The BMP-23 infantry fighting vehicle (IFV) was developed during the Cold War to meet the operational requirements of the Bulgarian army and fulfils a similar mission to the widely deployed Soviet-built BMP-2 IFV.

The BMP-23 IFV has a crew of three and can carry seven fully-equipped troops. It is fitted with a two-man turret armed with a 23-mm cannon, a 7.62-mm (0.3-in) co-axial machine-gun and the Russian-designed 9M14 Malyutka (AT-3 'Sagger') wire-guided anti-tank weapon (ATGW).

IFV armament

The 23-mm cannon is not stabilised and so the BMP-23 has to come to a halt to enable targets to be engaged. Maximum range of the 23-mm cannon is about 2000 m (2,187 yards) in the direct-fire mode, but it can also be used against slow and low-flying aircraft and helicopters. The ATGW has a maximum range of 3000 m (3,281 yards) and is fitted with a HEAT warhead.

Right: The BRM-23 is seen with the high-frequency radio antenna erected over the hull roof at the rear. The vehicle is based on the BMP-23, operated by Bulgaria instead of the BMP-2 IFV.

Below right: Armament of the BRM-23 includes the 9M14 Malyutka (AT-3 'Sagger') ATGW which is seen here mounted on the roof of vehicle.

To meet more specialised reconnaissance requirements, Bulgaria developed the **BRM-23** reconnaissance vehicle that is very similar to the earlier BMP-23 IFV.

Externally, the BRM-23 reconnaissance vehicle can be recognised by the different arrangement of firing ports in the hull and associated vision devices. Above the hull at the rear of the vehicle is a large frame-type antenna. When erected in the vertical position this allows the high-frequency radio to achieve a range of 100 km (62 miles) under ideal conditions. This enables the

vehicle to pass detailed information on to the next chain of command.

Mission equipment

The BRM-23 reconnaissance vehicle has a crew of five and a similar weapon fit to that of the BMP-23 IFV, but it is also fitted with a variety of more specialised equipment to enable it to carry out its demanding reconnaissance mission.

This equipment includes an extensive suite of communications equipment, a laser rangefinder with a maximum range of 9000 m

(9,843 yards), a passive night observation device, a portable mine detector, as well as chemical and radiation detectors.

The laser rangefinder and passive night observation device can also be dismounted from the vehicle and installed on a tripod if required. A land navigation system determines the exact position of the vehicle.

Amphibious capability

Standard equipment for the BRM-23 includes an NBC protection system and night-vision equipment. The vehicle is fully amphibious, being propelled in the water by its tracks at a speed of 5 km/h (3.1 mph).

Before entering the water the bilge pumps are switched on and a trim vane is erected at the front of the vehicle. Special slotted devices are fitted to each side of the BRM-23, above the forward part of the suspension, to improve the water flow. While the BRM-23 has adequate mobility, the sensor suite no longer meets the future operational requirements. Many armies now fit their reconnaissance platforms with thermal observation devices coupled to advanced GPS (global positioning system) navigation equipment. Some such vehicles are also fitted with a surveillance radar to allow the detection of ground targets at extended ranges.

Snezka Reconnaissance vehicle

To meet the operational requirements of the Czech army for an advanced day/night reconnaissance platform, the **Snezka** reconnaissance vehicle was developed under the leadership of the Czech Military Institute for Weapon and Ammunition Technology. This facility was assisted by a number of other civil and military establishments in the Czech Republic, as well as a smaller number of overseas contractors.

Stretched chassis

Snezka consists of a heavily modified and stretched BMP-2 infantry fighting vehicle (IFV) chassis fitted with an advanced sensor package which is mounted on top of a hydraulically operated scissors-type mast.

The standard BMP-2 chassis has six road wheels on each side, while the Snezka has a stretched hull with seven road wheels on each side. The hull rear is extended upwards to provide greater internal volume for the highly specialised equipment carried, together with its crew.

Like the BMP-2, Snezka is fully amphibious, being propelled in the water by its tracks at a maximum speed of about 7 km/h (4.3 mph). It is also fitted with an NBC system and armament comprises a 12.7-mm (0.5-in) machine-gun. Laser detectors are fitted to alert the crew when they have been detected by laser rangefinders or laser designators.

Mounted at the rear of the hull is the scissors-type mast on top of which is installed the advanced sensor suite. This can be raised to a maximum height of 14 m (46 ft) above ground level. When not required, the mast is lowered into the horizontal position to reduce the profile of the vehicle.

The sensor pod includes a day/night TV system, thermal camera, battlefield surveillance radar and a laser rangefinder. This information is fed into the operators' displays inside the vehicle.

Snezka is also fitted with an advanced inertial navigation system (INS) which enables it to determine its exact position.

The sensor suite enables targets to be detected and identified at long range. This information is then passed on to the next chain of command for immediate action. This could include calling for artillery, or other types of fire support such as rocket launchers, mortars or close air support.

Operational role

To work with the advanced Snezka reconnaissance vehicle, the Czech Republic has developed the **Light Observation System** (**LOS**) which is also based on the BMP-2 IFV chassis.

In a typical operational situation, the LOS vehicles would be forward-deployed, with the longer-range Snezka vehicles deployed to the rear. The LOS has a fixed turret with the original 30-mm cannon replaced by a mock-up, providing more room inside the vehicle.

Integrated into the rear part of the LOS turret is the mast-mounted sensor pod that includes a laser rangefinder, laser target designator and day/night cameras. The LOS also has GPS and INS equipment.

The Snezka reconnaissance vehicle is seen with the mast-mounted sensor pod in the elevated (below) and lowered (below left) positions. The Snezka is based on a lengthened BMP-2 IFV chassis, with an additional road wheel on each side.

LAV-25 Coyote Reconnaissance vehicle

The Canadian **LAV-25 Coyote** is typical of modern battlefield reconnaissance vehicles in which the 'eyeball mk 1' is augmented by electronic surveillance sensor systems. It was selected as the Coyote platform in 1992, a production order for 203 vehicles being placed in 1993 for service with the Canadian Armed Forces. The vehicle is externally similar to other members of the LAV-25 family, but has several improvements. One is an increase in protection with the option of add-on armour providing protection against 14.5-mm (0.57-in) projectiles all round and 30-mm cannon shells over the frontal arc. The armament is that of other LAV-25s, namely an electrically driven two-man turret with a fully stabilised 25-mm M242 Bushmaster cannon, a 7.62-mm (0.3-in) co-axial machine-gun and provision for a similar machine-gun on the roof for local and air defence. The main gun is used with a computer-based fire-control system including a laser rangefinder.

The vehicle is air portable, the C-130 and C-5 being able to carry one and eight respectively. Unlike other LAV-25 series vehicles, the Coyote is not amphibious. For normal road conditions the vehicle's drive is connected to the rear two axles, the 8x8 capability being selected for rough terrain. The driver has night driving equipment and laser-protected vision devices.

Two sensor packages

The Coyote was made in three forms described as the battle group kit, the fixed brigade kit and a form that can be configured for either role. The sensor suite is the responsibility of General Dynamics Canada (formerly Computing Devices Canada), and the surveillance systems operator is seated at a monitoring and display console in a compartment at the rear of the hull. The commander in the turret has a display duplicating the operator's visual display and also seven laser-protected periscopic day vision devices and a target acquisition sight in the turret roof, complete with

In travelling layout with its turret aligned straight to the front, there is little to distinguish the Coyote from other LAV-25 series vehicles.

an image intensification system for use at night.

The battle kit consists of at least two man-portable ground tripods that are dismounted from the vehicle and emplaced as necessary with the vehicle up to 200 m (220 yards) from the sensors but connected to them by a fibre-optic link. One tripod carries the British Thales MSTAR (Man-portable Surveillance and Target Acquisition Radar) battlefield surveillance radar with 180° scan. The second tripod has 360° scan using an optronic package based on a long-range video camera, laser rangefinder and thermal imager. The commander can also monitor the image through the gunner's sight.

For the fixed brigade kit an extending mast can be raised through one of two roof hatches to a height of 10 m (33 ft). At the top of the mast is a package carrying much the same sensors as the battle kit but providing greatly enhanced performance, derived in part from the height of the sensor package above the ground. The battlefield

surveillance radar still has 180° scan but can detect moving targets at ranges of up to 24 km (14.9 miles), the long-range video camera provides day/night target detection and recognition imagery to 18 km (11.2 miles), the laser rangefinder has a range of 10 km (6.2 miles) with an accuracy of ±5 m (16.4 ft), and the thermal imager can detect targets out to a range of 12 km (7.5 miles).

Extra capability

To extend the Coyote's reconnaissance capabilities, the four crew members have hand-held chemical warfare agent detectors and a nuclear radiation detector. The land navigation equipment includes a digital compass system. Needless to say, a comprehensive communication system provides a link to command centres, including visual images.

To add to the general level of vehicle and crew protection there is a full NBC protection system providing each crew member with a ventilated face mask.

This LAV-25 Coyote has its sensor mast in the raised position, which provides full operational capability even as the vehicle enjoys the protection of cover.

SPECIFICATION	
LAV-25 Coyote	**Performance:** maximum road speed 100 km/h (62 mph); road range about 660 km (410 miles)
Crew: 4	**Fording:** not available
Weight: 13400 kg (29,541 lb)	**Gradient:** 60 per cent
Dimensions: length 6.93 m (22 ft 9 in); width 2.5 m (8 ft 2 in); height 2.692 m (8 ft 10 in)	**Vertical obstacle:** not available
Powerplant: one Detroit Diesel 6V-53T diesel developing 205 kW (275 hp)	**Trench:** 2.057 m (6 ft 9 in)

Stryker Mobile Gun System

The **Stryker Mobile Gun System** was originally known as the **105-mm LPT Assault Gun**, LPT denoting Low Profile Target as a result of the vehicle's somewhat lower-than-usual silhouette. The first prototype appeared during 1999 and was adopted by the US Army as the Stryker Mobile Gun System (MGS) to provide direct fire support for the service's BCTs (Brigade Combat Teams).

LAV chassis used

The chassis of the LAV-III has been modified for the MGS role, mainly by the installation of a lower top deck with a race ring support for the gun turret. Changes have also been made to the hull sides and rear, while the roof has a re-loading hatch for the main gun's autoloader. The steel armour is proof against 12.7-mm (0.5-in) armour-piercing projectiles. In addition to this exterior protection, the vehicle is also provided with an internal layer of composite materials at critical points to minimise spalling in the event that a projectile defeats the outer armour. Further protection for the vehicle and crew is provided by an automatic fire detection/suppression system for the engine compartment (to the right of the driver at the front of the hull) and the crew compartment. Also provided is a collective NBC protection system. Fixed vertical posts over the turret and driver's position act as anti-tank missile guidance wire cutters. Full production vehicles will carry two banks of four smoke grenade launchers.

Air portability

The Stryker MGS is air portable, the C-130 Hercules transport aircraft being just capable of accommodate its weight and bulk. Unlike most other vehicles in the Stryker BCTs, the MGS is not amphibious, although it can negotiate water obstacles up to 1.7 m (5 ft 7 in) deep. For normal road conditions the vehicle has full-time drive connected only to the rear two axles, the full 8x8 capability being selected when crossing rough terrain. Power steering is applied to the front two axles. A central tyre pressure-regulation system allows the driver to vary tyre pressures to suit the terrain being traversed, even when on the move.

The heart of the Stryker MGS is the low, roof-mounted 105-mm (4.13-in) electrically powered gun turret, which is remotely controlled and aimed from within the hull. The low silhouette arrangement makes the external turret more difficult to detect, and the unmanned turret is also considerably lighter than any conventional tank turret with the same-calibre gun. The ordnance involved is a 105-mm M68A2 rifled gun, and its turret provides 360° traverse and an elevation arc between -8° and +18°. The gun is equipped with a hydraulically operated autoloader in a bustle behind the breech. This autoloader can hold up to eight ready-use rounds, and can be replenished from within the hull via a roof hatch. A complete reload cycle takes about six seconds. It is anticipated that a full main gun ammunition load will be from 24 to 32 rounds. The gun is also provided with an integral pepperpot-pattern muzzle brake, a bore evacuator, a muzzle reference system and a thermal sleeve. The main gun mounting also carries a 7.62-mm (0.3-in) co-axial machine-gun, and another 7.62-mm or 12.7-mm (0.5-in) machine-gun can be mounted over the commander's station for local and AA defence.

The M68A2 can fire the complete range of NATO standard 105-mm tank gun ammunition, including kinetic-energy AP projectiles, but it has to be stressed that

The Stryker MGS is designed to provide an effective fire support capability for the US Army's new Brigade Combat Teams in combination with high ground mobility, an excellent level of survivability, great mechanical and systems reliability, and easy air portability.

the primary operational role of the Stryker MGS is the provision of direct fire support for BCT infantry units, not engagement of AFVs.

Remote gun control

The main gun is aimed from under the turret roof using a computerised fire-control system supplied by General Dynamics Canada (formerly Computing Devices Canada). The commander, seated below and to the right of the turret, selects a target either by using his six periscopic vision devices, or the image presented by a stabilised panoramic camera complete with a low light and night vision capability, or by monitoring the image seen through the gunner's roof-mounted sights. The fire mission is then passed to the gunner, located below and to the left of the gun, allowing the commander to search for other targets. If necessary the commander can override the gunner to aim and fire the gun using his duplicate set of gun controls. The sights and the gun are fully stabilised, allowing the vehicle to engage targets while on the move.

SPECIFICATION	
Stryker MGS (provisional) **Crew:** 3 **Weight:** 18730 kg (41,292 lb) **Dimensions:** length (hull) 6.984 m (22 ft 11 in); width 2.717 m (8 ft 11 in); height 2.692 m (8 ft 10 in) **Powerplant:** one Caterpillar 3126A diesel developing 298 kW (400 hp)	**Performance:** maximum road speed 96.5 km/h (60 mph); maximum range about 483 km (300 miles) **Fording:** 1.7 m (5 ft 7 in) **Gradient:** 60 per cent **Vertical obstacle:** 0.6 m (2 ft) **Trench:** 2 m (6 ft 7 in)

The most notable external feature of the Stryker MGS is the use of a powerful gun with an autoloader in a wholly unmanned but powered mounting installed over an 8x8 hull based on that of the LAV-III light AFV.

AMX-10RC Reconnaissance vehicle

The first unit to equip with the AMX-10RC was the 2éme Régiment de Hussards based at Sourdon in 1981-82.

During the 1960s the French army issued a requirement for an amphibious armoured car with a powerful gun, advanced fire-control system and good cross-country mobility. The resulting **AMX-10RC** was placed in production at the Atelier de Construction Roanne for service from 1981.

The AMX-10RC has two major drawbacks: it is more expensive than some MBTs, and is too sophisticated for many potential users. For these reasons the French army trimmed its original requirements to 337 units, and export sales were made only to Morocco (108) and Qatar (12). The type saw action in Chad and played an active part during Operation Desert Storm. Production has now ceased and planned update programmes were abandoned, although a battlefield management system and improved thermal cameras have been installed.

Structural details

The hull and turret of the AMX-10RC are of all-welded aluminium construction, with the driver at the front left, the turret in the centre and the engine and transmission at the rear. The 6x6 suspension is unusual in that the driver can adjust its ground clearance to suit the type of ground being crossed and tilt it from side to side. Many

automotive components, including the engine and transmission, are identical with those of the AMX-10P tracked MICV. The vehicle is amphibious, being propelled in the water by two waterjets imparting a speed of 7.2 km/h (4.5 mph).

The commander and gunner are seated on the right of the turret, with the loader on the left. The main armament comprises a special-to-type 105-mm (4.13-in) F2 gun and a 7.62-mm (0.3-in) co-axial machine-gun with 40 and 4,000 rounds respectively. Two electrically operated smoke dischargers are mounted on each side of the turret rear.

The fire-control system includes a laser rangefinder, a computer and a low-light thermal imager. The system allows the engagement of stationary and moving targets by day or night. The three types of main-gun ammunition, APFSDS, HEAT and HE, are unique to this powerful F2 gun.

Below: The AMX-10RC, seen here in desert operations, is very capable but also very expensive. The type has moderately good armament and advanced fire control.

SPECIFICATION	
AMX-10RC	8-cylinder diesel
Crew: 4	**Performance:** maximum road speed
Weight: 15.88 tonnes	85 km/h (53 mph); maximum road
Dimensions: length (gun forward)	range 800 km (500 miles)
9.15 m (30 ft ¼ in) and (hull) 6.35 m	**Fording:** amphibious
(20 ft 10 in); width 2.95 m (9 ft	**Gradient:** 60 per cent
8 in); height 2.68 m (8 ft 9½ in)	**Vertical obstacle:** 0.7 m (2 ft 3¼ in)
Powerplant: one 194-kW (260-hp)	**Trench:** 1.15 m (3 ft 9 in)
Baudouin 6F 11 SRX liquid-cooled	

Panhard AML 90 Light armoured car

The French army used large numbers of British-built Daimler Ferret 4x4 scout cars in North Africa during the 1950s, and then decided to procure a similar vehicle with a wider range of armament installations. After evaluation of prototype vehicles, the design from Panhard was selected. Production began in 1960

under the designation **AML**, (**Auto-Mitrailleuse Légère**, or light armoured car), and since then well over 4,000 vehicles have been built in several variants, with production continuing to this day for export. The type was also built in South Africa by Sandock Austral for the South African army, which calls the type the **Eland**. The AML, which

is in service with 40 countries, shares 95 per cent of its automotive components with the Panhard M3 APC, and many countries operate M3 and AML fleets with the obvious financial, logistical and training advantages.

The layout of all variants is similar, with the driver at the front, the two-man turret in the

centre (with an entry door in each side of the hull) and the engine and transmission at the rear.

One of the most common models is the **AML 90**. The AML's original H 90 turret with a 90-mm (3.54-in) gun was replaced by a Lynx 90 two-man turret also designed and built by Hispano-Suiza and armed with a

90-mm GIAT gun, a 7.62-mm (0.3-in) co-axial machine-gun and a 7.62-mm anti-aircraft machine-gun. The 90-mm gun can fire a wide range of fixed ammunition, including HEAT, HE, smoke and canister. The HEAT round will penetrate 320 mm (12.6 in) of armour at an incidence of 0° or 120 mm (4.72 in) of armour at an incidence of 65°. Totals of 21 rounds of 90-mm and 2,000 rounds of 7.62-mm ammunition are carried. Optional equipment for this turret includes passive night-vision equipment, powered controls and a laser rangefinder.

Mortar versions

The **HE 60-7** turret has a 60-mm (2.36-in) breech-loaded mortar and two 7.62-mm machine-guns, the **HE 60-12** turret a similar mortar and a 12.7-mm (0.5-in) machine-gun, and the **HE 60-20** turret has the 60-mm mortar and a 20-mm cannon. The breech-loaded mortar is used both in the indirect and direct fire modes, and is useful in guerrilla-type actions as it can be fired over hills and buildings.

One of the more recent turrets is the **HE 60-20 Serval**

The AML 90 has been one of the most successful wheeled AFVs of the period after World War II, with over 4,000 built in France and South Africa. This model has a 90-mm (3.54-in) gun.

with a 60-mm long-barrel mortar mounted in its front with a 20-mm cannon and 7.62-mm machine-gun mounted externally at the turret rear. For the export market an AA model of the AML was developed with a two-man **SAMM S 530** turret armed with twin 20-mm cannon, each with 300 rounds of ready-use ammunition. Turret traverse and weapon elevation are powered for enhanced engagement capability.

Lighter armament

More recently, scout car versions of the AML have been developed with various

combinations of 7.62-mm and 12.7-mm machine-guns on pintle mounts or in turrets. These have a lower profile than the 90-mm gun models and are well suited for light reconnaissance.

As usual a wide range of optional equipment can be

fitted, including passive night vision equipment, an air-conditioning system and a complete NBC system. An amphibious kit was also developed, but as far as is known this was not produced in any significant quantity.

SPECIFICATION	
Panhard AML-90 **Crew:** 3 **Weight:** 5.5 tonnes **Dimensions:** length (including gun) 5.11 m (16 ft 9¼ in) and (hull) 3.79 m (12 ft 5¼ in); width 1.97 m (6 ft 5½ in); height 2.07 m (6 ft 9½ in) **Powerplant:** one Panhard 4 HD liquid-cooled 4-cylinder petrol	engine developing 67 kW (90 hp) **Performance:** maximum road speed 90 km/h (56 mph); maximum road range 600 km (375 miles) **Fording:** amphibious **Gradient:** 60 per cent **Vertical obstacle:** 0.3 m (1 ft) **Trench:** 0.8 m (2 ft 7½ in) with one channel

Panhard ERC Sagaie Armoured car

For many years the backbone of Panhard production of armoured vehicles was the AML 4x4 light armoured car and the M3 4x4 APC with which the AML shares many common components. In 1970 the French army issued a requirement for a VAB (Véhicule de l'Avant Blinde, or front-line armoured vehicle), and Panhard and Renault built prototype vehicles in both 4x4 and 6x6 configurations, all of them amphibious. The competition was won by Renault, and since then large numbers of 4x4 and 6x6 vehicles have been built.

Using the technology gained in this competition Panhard then started design work on a new range of 6x6 vehicles that would include both an armoured car and an APC. The former made its first appearance in 1977 as the **ERC** (**Engin de Reconnaissance Canon**, or cannon-armed reconnaissance machine), while the APC is

known as the VCR (Véhicule de Combat à Roues, or wheeled combat vehicle). Production began in 1979, and the ERC was ordered by Argentina, Chad, Gabon, Ivory Coast, Mexico and Niger. The French army also obtained a batch of 192.

The driver is seated at the front of the hull, the turret is in the centre and the engine and

transmission are at the rear. All six road wheels are powered, and power-assisted steering is provided on the front two wheels. The centre pair of wheels can be raised off the ground for road travel and lowered again for cross-country travel. The basic vehicle is amphibious, being propelled in the water at 4.5 km/h (2.8 mph)

This Panhard ERC Sagaie armoured car carries the GIAT TS-90 turret with a 90-mm (3.54-in) gun.

by its wheels, or by two optional waterjets at 9.5 km/h (5.9 mph). Before the vehicle enters the water a trim vane is erected at the front of the hull and two snorkels are erected at the rear.

Turret options

The basic vehicle has been offered with a wide range of turrets including the **GIAT TS-90** and **Hispano-Suiza Lynx 90** units with a 90-mm (3.54-in) gun, the **Hispano Suiza 60-20 Serval** and **EMC** units with a 60 or 81-mm (2.36- or 3.2-in) mortar respectively, and a two-man unit with twin 20- or 25-mm cannon for use in the AA role.

The model selected by the French army, for the use of its rapid intervention force, is fitted with the TS-90 turret and called the **ERC-90 F4 Sagaie**. This turret is armed with a long-barrel 90-mm gun with an elevation of +15 degrees and a depression of -8 degrees. The gun can fire the following types of fixed ammunition: canister, HE, HEAT, smoke and APFSDS. The last has a muzzle velocity of 1350 m (4,430 ft) per second and its projectile will penetrate 120 mm (4.72 in) of armour. A 7.62-mm (0.3-in) machine-gun is mounted co-axial with the main armament, and two electrically

operated smoke-dischargers are mounted on each side of the turret. Twenty rounds of 90-mm and 2,000 rounds of 7.62-mm machine-gun ammunition are carried. Optional equipment includes an air-conditioning system, additional ammunition stowage, a laser rangefinder,

passive night vision equipment, an NBC system, an anti-aircraft machine-gun, additional elevation of the 90-mm gun to +35 degrees, various types of fire-control system and a land navigation system. Production is now undertaken only on the receipt of an order.

SPECIFICATION	
Panhard ERC Sagaie	**Performance:** maximum road speed 100 km/h (62 mph); maximum road range 800 km (500 miles)
Crew: 3	
Weight: 8.3 tonnes	**Fording:** amphibious
Dimensions: length (including gun) 7.7 m (25 ft 2¾ in) and (hull) 5.08 m (16 ft 8 in); width 2.5 m (8 ft 2¼ in); height 2.3 m (7 ft 4¾ in)	**Gradient:** 60 per cent
	Vertical obstacle: 0.8 m (2 ft 7½ in)
	Trench: 1.1 m (3 ft 7½ in)
Powerplant: one 116-kW (155-hp) Peugeot V-6 petrol engine	

Panhard Sagaie 2 Armoured car

In 1977 Panhard unveiled its private venture range of 6x6 armoured vehicles, including families of armoured cars and APCs using identical automotive components in a process providing the operator with obvious training, logistical and cost advantages.

The armoured car family is commonly known as the Engin de Reconnaissance Cannon (ERC) and includes the ERC 90 F4 Sagaie 1, ERC 90 F1 Lynx, ERC 60/20 Serval, ERC 20 Kriss, and ERC 60/12 Mangouste. These were all originally developed specifically for the export market, although the Sagaie 1 was subsequently adopted by the French army.

In 1985 Panhard revealed that it had developed the **Sagaie 2** or **ERC-2** armoured car. It

subsequently emerged that Gabon had placed an order for the vehicle, and this nation remains the only customer although extensive marketing has been undertaken elsewhere. The type is no longer in production, and is no longer marketed.

Improved turret

The Sagaie 2 has a slightly longer and wider hull than the Sagaie 1, and instead of the 90-mm GIAT TS-90 turret it is fitted with the **SAMM TTB-190** turret, which has the same gun as the TS-90 turret. The SAMM turret provides much improved armour protection, however, and is offered with a wide range of turret controls, fire control systems and optical devices. Two types of ammunition

Panhard's private venture range of 6x6 armoured cars has attracted a number of export orders as well as interest from the French army. The Sagaie 2 has a longer, wider hull than the Sagaie 1, and was selected by Gabon with the TTB 190 90-mm gun turret.

stowage are available, one having 35 rounds of 90-mm ammunition, 13 of them ready for use, and the other having 32 rounds, with 10 ready for use.

Greater power

The original Panhard Sagaie 1 was powered by a single Peugeot V-6 petrol engine developing 116 kW (155 hp), but the Sagaie 2 is powered by two

Peugeot XD 3T turbo-charged diesels developing a total of 146 kW (196 hp). Twin V-6 petrol engines were also offered an an option. The Sagaie 1 and 2 both have full 6x6 drive with powered steering on the front road wheels only. An unusual feature is that when travelling on roads the centre wheels can be raised clear of the ground, reducing resistance and saving tyre wear.

The Sagaie 2 was unveiled in 1985 and was ordered only by Gabon, which received 10 vehicles – six with the TTB 190 turret (pictured) and the remaining four with the ERC 20 Kriss anti-aircraft turret with two 20-mm cannon.

SPECIFICATION	
Panhard Sagaie 2	liquid-cooled 4-cylinder diesels developing a total of 146 kW (196 hp)
Crew: 3	
Weights: loaded 10000 kg (22,046 lb)	**Performance:** maximum road speed 100 km/h (62 mph); maximum road range 600 km (373 km)
Dimensions: length (overall with gun forward) 7.97 m (26 ft 1¾ in) and hull 5.57 m (19 ft 3⅓ in); width 2.7 m (8 ft 10⅓ in); height 2.3 m (7 ft 6½ in)	**Fording:** 1.2 m (3 ft 11 in)
	Gradient: 50 per cent
	Vertical obstacle: 0.8 m (2 ft 7½ in)
Powerplant: two Peugeot XD 3T	**Trench:** 0.8 m (2 ft 7½ in)

Panhard VBL Scout car

In 1978 the French army issued a requirement for a light and fast armoured vehicle to carry out two combat roles: anti-tank with an armament of missiles, and reconnaissance/scout. Panhard and Renault were contracted to deliver prototypes for French army trials. Following these trials the **Panhard VBL** (**Véhicule Blindé Léger**) was accepted for service, and 1,250 such vehicles have been delivered to the French army. Panhard also undertook intensive overseas marketing. Mexico placed an order for 40 VBLs in 1984, and these were followed by significant orders from 13 other nations including Greece, Indonesia and Kuwait.

The Panhard VBL light armoured vehicle was designed as a reconnaissance scout car and anti-tank guided weapons platform carrying Milan missiles. It is fully amphibious and is fitted with an NBC system.

Armoured protection

The VBL's hull provides protection from small arms fire and shell splinters, and to reduce procurement and life cycle costs, proven commercial automotive parts are incorporated. The layout is conventional, with the engine and transmission forward, the driver and commander in the centre and space for a third soldier, weapons or other equipment in the rear. Bullet-proof windows are provided for all occupants. 'Runflat' tyres allow the VBL to travel 50 km (31 miles) at 30 km/h (19 mph) after being hit.

Anti-tank missiles

The anti-tank model has a crew of three with a Milan anti-tank guided missile launcher, six missiles and a 7.62-mm (0.3-in) machine-gun. The VBL can also mount a TOW or HOT anti-tank missile launcher. The scout model normally has extra communications equipment, a two-man crew and a 7.62-mm or 12.7-mm (0.5-in) machine-gun.

Panhard offers a wide range of VBL variants including a police/internal security version, a battlefield surveillance model carrying various radars, a version armed with a 20-mm cannon and an AA vehicle carrying Mistral surface-to-air missiles.

In the anti-tank role the VBL carries a three-man crew and, over the rear of the vehicle, a traversing and elevating launcher for anti-tank missiles stowed in the hull. This French VBL is seen in Afghanistan.

SPECIFICATION	
VBL	Peugeot XD 3T liquid-cooled 4-cylinder diesel engine
Crew: 2 or 3	**Performance:** maximum road speed
Weight: 3550 kg (7,826 lb)	95 km/h (59 mph); road range
Dimensions: length (with additional fuel can) 3.87 m (12 ft 8½ in); width 2.02 m (6 ft 7½ in); height (hull top) 1.7 m (5 ft 7 in)	800 km (497 miles) with extra fuel **Fording:** amphibious **Gradient:** 50 per cent **Trench:** 0.5 m (1 ft 7¾ in)
Powerplant: one 78-kW (105-hp)	

Spähpanzer Luchs Reconnaissance vehicle

During the mid-1960s a complete family of 4x4, 6x6 and 8x8 trucks, 4x4 and 6x6 (later to become the Transport-panzer 1, or Fuchs) armoured amphibious load-carriers, and an 8x8 amphibious armoured reconnaissance vehicle were developed specifically for the West German army. These all shared automotive components already in production for civilian applications. Prototypes of the 8x8 amphibious armoured reconnaissance vehicle were designed and built by Daimler-Benz and a consortium of companies known as the Joint Project Office (JPO) in 1968. In 1971 the Daimler-Benz model was selected for production by Thyssen Henschel, and 408 examples of the **Spähpanzer Luchs** (lynx) were built between 1975 and 1978. The Luchs was offered for export, but proved too expensive for all potential customers for this capable type.

Armour protection

Its all-welded steel turret and hull front provides the Luchs with protection against attacks from 20-mm projectiles, and the remainder of the vehicle is proof against small arms fire and shell splinters. The driver is at the front left, the turret with a crew of two in the centre, the engine at the rear on the right side and a co-driver is towards the rear on the left side, seated facing the rear. In an emergency the co-driver can take control and drive the vehicle out of trouble. The drivers have powered steering and can select either steering on the front four wheels or on all eight wheels: the latter's turning radius is only 11.5 m (37 ft 8¾ in). The Luchs has the same maximum speed in both directions and also possesses an exceptionally large operating range of 800 km (497 miles).

The Rheinmetall TS-7 turret is armed with a 20-mm Rheinmetall MK 20 Rh 202 dual-feed cannon with 375 rounds of ammunition, and a 7.62-mm (0.3-in) MG3 machine-gun is also mounted on the turret for anti-aircraft defence. On each side of the turret is a

The Spähpanzer 2 Luchs continues the German tradition of 8x8 reconnaissance vehicles. The vehicle has a four-man crew and is fully amphibious.

bank of four electrically operated smoke dischargers, all firing forward.

The Luchs is amphibious, being propelled in water at 9 km/h (5.6 mph) by two steerable propellers under the hull rear. Before the vehicle enters the water the trim vane is erected at the front of the hull and the three bilge pumps are switched on. The Luchs also has an NBC system, and the

original range of IR night-vision equipment has been replaced by the passive type. Standard equipment includes a heater for

the batteries, engine and transmission oil and cooling liquid, all essential for winter operations in Germany.

SPECIFICATION	
Spähpanzer Luchs	liquid-cooled 10-cylinder diesel
Crew: 4	**Performance:** maximum road speed
Weight: 20 tonnes	90 km/h (56 mph); maximum road
Dimensions: length 7.74 m (25 ft 4¾	range 800 km (497 miles)
in); width 2.98 m (9 ft 9¼ in); height	**Fording:** amphibious
(with MG) 2.9 m (9 ft 6¼ in)	**Gradient:** 60 per cent
Powerplant: one 291-kW (390-hp)	**Vertical obstacle:** 0.6 m (1 ft 11½ in)
Daimler-Benz OM 403 A	**Trench:** 1.9 m (6 ft 3 in)

Fennek Multi-purpose carrier

The **Fennek** multi-purpose carrier is an international venture under order by Germany and the Netherlands. It was originally known as the **Multi-Purpose Carrier** (**MPC**), an early 1990s Dutch private venture from SP aerospace and vehicle systems, centred around a modular design that allows the vehicle to be configured for numerous battlefield tasks. A total of 612 has been ordered as 410 and 202 for the Dutch and German armies respectively, with production carried out by the ARGE Fennek consortium comprising SP and Krauss Maffei Wegmann of Germany (SP is now part of RDM Technology, also of the Netherlands). Fennek deliveries are scheduled to take place between 2003 and 2007.

Combat roles vary from battlefield reconnaissance and surveillance, a mobile command and communications centre, an

anti-tank missile carrier, front area supply carrier and many other tasks such as combat engineer reconnaissance.

The Fennek has an all-welded aluminium armour hull with permanent 4x4 drive powered by a Deutz diesel. Power steering and an automatic transmission are provided to ease the driver's workload. The interior layout can be varied considerably to suit specific roles. For instance, the interior can be all seating for carrying troops, or completely bare apart from handling aids for supply missions, while space and seating can be arranged to suit any electronics carried. The flat roof is designed to allow a

The Fennek is a versatile light vehicle in which modular design concepts have been fully exploited to multiply the vehicle's suitability for use in any of several roles. Note the sensor pod in the operating position.

small turret to be installed. For some roles a machine-gun or grenade launcher can be carried

on an electrically powered and remotely controlled weapon station on the hull roof. For the

anti-tank role, missiles can be launched from the roof, via remote weapon stations or manually from hatches, or from dismounted launchers some distance from the carrier vehicle. The armour protection levels can also be varied to suit the intended role. For most roles the armour is proof against small arms fire and shell splinters, with extra protection, including floor protection against land mines, added by modular armour panels. A fully amphibious version also exists.

Work in the field

One of the primary roles planned for the Fennek is battlefield reconnaissance and surveillance. For this the vehicle carries a sensor pod on a telescopic mast that allows day and night surveillance without exposing the vehicle when behind suitable cover. The pod contains thermal imaging and day cameras as well as a laser rangefinder. Other sensors include Global Positioning System (GPS) for land navigation and survey purposes.

Data from the sensors can be directly and automatically integrated into battle area command and control systems via an on-board communications suite.

SPECIFICATION	
Fennek	**Powerplant:** one 179-kW (240-hp) Deutz BF6M 2013C liquid-cooled 6-cylinder diesel
Crew: 3 or according to role	
Weight: 10.2 tonnes	**Performance:** maximum road speed 112 km/h (69 mph); maximum road range 1,000 km (621 miles)
Dimensions: length 5.58 m (18 ft 3 in); width 2.55 m (8 ft 4 in); height 1.79 m (5 ft 10½ in)	
	Fording: 1 m (3 ft 3 in)
	Gradient: 60 per cent

FIAT-Otobreda Tipo 6616 Armoured car

During the early 1970s, FIAT and OTO-Melara (now Otobreda) jointly developed the **Tipo 6616** armoured car and the Tipo 6614 APC used by the Italian army and air force. In both cases FIAT was responsible for the powerpack and automotive components, plus final assembly, while OTO-Melara supplied the armoured hull and turret. The first prototype of the Tipo 6616 was ready for tests in 1972, and 40 vehicles were later ordered by the Italian government for the Carabinieri. Sales were also made to Peru (15) and Somalia (30). The Tipo 6616 is no longer in production.

The hull of the Tipo 6616 is of all-welded steel construction with a uniform thickness of 8 mm (0.315 in), somewhat thinner than the figure for other vehicles in its class. The driver is seated at the front of the vehicle on the left, with vision blocks giving good vision to the front and sides. The two-man turret is in the centre of the vehicle, and the engine and transmission are at the rear.

The Tipo 6616 is amphibious, being propelled in the water by its wheels at 5 km/h (3.1 mph); the only preparation that is required before entering the water is to switch on the bilge pumps and pressurise the submerged mechanical components. Unlike most other comparable vehicles, the Tipo 6616 requires no trim vane at the front of the hull.

The Tipo 6616 armoured car was a collaborative development between FIAT and OTO-Melara (now IVECO and Otobreda), and shares components with the Tipo 6614 APC. It is underarmed, however, and for this reason a model with a two-man turret was developed with a Belgian gun, the 90-mm (3.54-in) Cockerill Mk III weapon used in many other AFVs.

Conventional layout

The commander is seated on the left and gunner on the right of the turret, each on an adjustable seat and with observation equipment and a single-piece hatch cover. The communications equipment is mounted in the turret bustle. The main armament comprises a German weapon, the 20-mm Rheinmetall MK 20 Rh 202 cannon. Turret control is all electric, with traverse at a maximum of 40° per second and weapon elevation at a maximum of 25° per second; 400 rounds of 20-mm ammunition are carried, of which 250 are for ready use and 150 in reserve. Empty cartridge cases are ejected outside the turret automatically, and therefore do not clutter up the crew compartment. A 7.62-mm (0.3-in) MG 42/59 machine-gun is mounted co-axial with the cannon, and 1,000 rounds are carried for this. Mounted on each side of the turret is a bank of three electrically operated forward-firing smoke dischargers.

One of the main drawbacks of this vehicle on the export market was its small-calibre gun. FIAT (now IVECO Military Vehicles Division) therefore offered the basic Tipo 6616 chassis in upgraded form with a new two-man OTO-Melara turret armed with a 90-mm (3.54-in) Cockerill Mk III gun and a 7.62-mm co-axial machine-gun. No sales of this version resulted.

Standard equipment includes a front-mounted recovery winch with a capacity of 4500 kg (9,921 lb), while optional equipment includes an NBC protection system and a full range of passive night-vision equipment for the commander, gunner and driver.

SPECIFICATION	
FIAT-Otobreda Tipo 6616	**Performance:** maximum road speed 100 km/h (62 mph); maximum range 700 km (435 miles)
Crew: 3	
Weight: 8 tonnes	**Fording:** amphibious
Dimensions: length 5.37 m (17 ft 7½ in); width 2.5 m (8 ft 2½ in); height 2.03 m (6 ft 8 in)	**Gradient:** 60 per cent
	Vertical obstacle: 0.45 m (1 ft 5¾ in)
Powerplant: one FIAT 8062.24 diesel developing 119 kW (160 hp)	

VBC-90 Armoured car

Following extensive trials with prototype vehicles submitted by Panhard and Saviem, the latter company was selected to build a new 4x4 armoured personnel carrier (APC) for the French army designated as the VAB (Véhicule de l'Avant Blindé).

Saviem was subsequently taken over by Renault, and, using many of the automotive parts of the 6x6 model of the VAB, the VBC (Véhicule Blindé de Combat) 6x6 armoured car was built.

This had a different layout to the VAB for its intended battlefield mission of reconnaissance. On the **VBC-90**, the driver's compartment is at the front, the fighting compartment and turret are in the centre and the powerpack is at the rear. The hull is of all-welded steel armour which provides the occupants with protection from both shell splinters and small-arms fire.

All production Renault VBC-90 armoured cars are fitted with a Giat Industries TS-90 two-man turret armed with a 90-mm (3.54-in) main gun and a 7.62-mm (0.3-in) co-axial machine-gun.

The turret is also fitted with a computerised fire-control system and day/night sights. A total of 45 rounds of 90-mm ammunition is carried plus 4,000 rounds of 7.62-mm machine-gun ammunition. Types of main gun ammunition carried include armour-piercing fin-stabilised discarding sabot tracer (APFSDS-T).

Limited production

Eventually some 5,000 VABs in 6x6 and 4x4 versions were built for the home and export markets, but the VBC-90 was not a commercial success and was sold to only two customers, the French Gendarmerie (28 units in total)

Top: The Renault VBC-90 armoured car fitted with the standard TS-90 90-mm (3.54-in) turret as supplied to the French Gendarmerie.

Above: The Renault VBC-90 armoured car was fitted with a wide range of turrets for trials purposes including this MECAR 90-mm (3.54-in) gun turret.

SPECIFICATION	
VBC-90	**Powerplant:** one 163-kW (220-hp) Renault MIDS 06.20.45 6-cylinder diesel engine
Crew: 3	
Weight: 13500 kg (29,762 lb)	
Dimensions: length (with turret forwards) 8.08 m (26 ft 6 in) and (chassis) 5.63 m (18 ft 6 in); width 2.5 m (8 ft 2½ in); height 2.55 m (8 ft 4 in)	**Performance:** maximum road speed 92 km/h (57 mph); maximum range 1000 km (621 miles)
	Fording: 1.2 m (3 ft 11 in)
	Gradient: 50 per cent

and the Royal Guard of Oman (six units).

The French Panhard ERC Sagaie 6x6 armoured car (discussed separately) was a much more successful design, and 350 of these were built for the home and export markets.

For the export market a wide range of alternative turret types were installed on the VBC armoured car for trials purposes. These included one with an externally mounted 90-mm gun, a MECAR turret armed with a 90-mm gun and a SAMM turret

also armed with a 90-mm gun. Standard equipment includes power-steering and a central tyre-pressure regulation system. Mounted internally at the front of the hull is a power-operated winch with 60 m (66 yards) of cable which can be used for self-recovery operations, or to recover other damaged or disabled vehicles.

As with most vehicles developed in recent times, the VBC-90 armoured car can be fitted with a wide range of optional equipment.

The VBC-90 demonstrates its ditch-crossing capability. The vehicle can cross a trench measuring 1 m (3 ft 3 in).

R-400 Armoured car

In the 1980s the German company of Thyssen Henschel commenced development of a complete family of 4x4, 6x6 and 8x8 AFVs. Wherever possible, many sub-systems, including diesel engines and automatic

transmissions, were standard production models.

Only the 6x6 model reached the prototype stage, and this **R-400** is fitted with a three-man turret armed with a stabilised 105-mm (4.13-in) rifled gun. This

is coupled to an advanced day/night computerised fire-control system enabling it to engage stationary and moving targets while crossing rough terrain, with a high first-round hit probability.

A 7.62-mm (0.3-in) machine-gun is mounted co-axially with the main armament, and a similar weapon is mounted on the roof of the vehicle for local protection and self-defence purposes.

The layout of the vehicle is conventional with the driver at the front, power-operated turret in the centre and the powerpack at the rear. The latter can be rapidly removed as a complete unit. Steering is power-assisted on the front wheels and standard equipment includes a central tyre-pressure regulation system. A wide range of optional equipment can be fitted, including an NBC crew protection system. In addition to being marketed fitted with a three-man 105-mm turret, more recently the R-400 has been offered with other weapons stations developed by the Rheinmetall group who took over Thyssen Henschel in the late 1990s.

These include the latest E8 turret armed with 30-mm Mauser MK 30 cannon, and the E4 two-man turret that can be fitted with various automatic cannon up to 30-mm in calibre. These turrets can be fitted with various types of advanced sighting systems, ranging from image intensification devices to the more expensive but more effective thermal type.

Above: Despite extensive trials and marketing, the Rheinmetall Landsysteme R-400 6x6 armoured car currently remains at the prototype stage.

SPECIFICATION	
R-400	**Performance:** maximum road speed
Crew: 4	105 km/h (65 mph); maximum
Weight: 24000 kg (52,910 lb)	range 1000 km (621 miles)
Dimensions: length (without	**Fording:** 1.2 m (3 ft 11 in)
weapon) 6.36 m (20 ft 10 in); width	**Gradient:** 60 per cent
2.98 m (9 ft 9 in); height 2.735 m	**Vertical obstacle:** 0.6 m (2 ft)
(8 ft 11½ in)	

Above: Armed with 105-mm gun, the R-400 has the firepower of a 40-tonne Leopard 1 MBT but offers far greater strategic mobility, enabling rapid deployment.

RAM Light armoured vehicle

In the early 1970s the RAMTA Division of Israel Aircraft Industries (IAI) developed a low-cost family of light armoured vehicles designated RBY. This series of 4x4 vehicles was of a modular design to enable the baseline vehicle to be adopted for a wide range of battlefield missions, ranging from reconnaissance to troop carrier and anti-tank weapons carrier.

The RBY is powered by a Chrysler petrol engine coupled to a manual transmission and a two-speed transfer case. The hull is of special all-welded steel to provide the occupants with protection from small-arms fire and shell splinters.

Mine protection

Combat experience in the Middle East demonstrated that mines were one of the greatest threats, and for this reason special attention is paid to provide a high level of protection against mines, especially anti-tank mines. The underside of the hull has a V-shape to help deflect the force of a mine blast, with the wheels being located at the extreme ends of the vehicle, away from the crew compartment in the centre of the vehicle. The powerpack is situated at the rear of the vehicle.

Further development of the RBY in the late 1980s resulted in the improved **RAM** family of vehicles. These have a longer wheelbase than the earlier models and have been marketed as two distinct families, the **RAM V-1** (open) and the **RAM V-2** (closed). The RAM-V1 has a crew of two, and with the roof of the

The RAM is seen in APC configuration with the roof hatches closed. Mine protection makes the RAM suitable for UN operations.

The RAM armoured personnel carrier with the roof hatches seen in the open position. Seven troops are carried.

vehicle open can carry seven fully equipped troops. The RAM-V2 has a fully enclosed troop compartment that increases the weight of the vehicle to 6000 kg (13,228 lb). Both versions are powered by a more fuel-efficient diesel engine coupled to a fully automatic transmission, which makes the vehicle easier to drive as well as reducing incidences of driver fatigue.

Armament options

The RAM-V1 can have a number of 5.56-mm (0.219-in), 7.62-mm (0.3-in) or 12.7-mm (0.5-in) machine-guns mounted around the upper part of the hull to provide suppressive firepower through a full 360°. A number of anti-tank versions of the RAM are available including one with the 3750-m (4,100-yard) range Raytheon TOW anti-tank guided missile (ATGM) system, and another with the older 106-mm (4.17-in) M40 recoilless rifle.

The prototype of a self-propelled anti-aircraft gun (SPAAG) has also been built and tested. This is fitted with an IAI power-operated turret armed with twin 20-mm cannon, with the gunner being seated in the turret between the two weapons. The mount is a modified version of a US system developed during World War II and originally armed with four 0.5-in heavy machine-guns to provide formidable anti-aircraft or ground fire.

The RAM self-propelled anti-aircraft gun system is fitted with a two-man IAI turret armed with twin 20-mm cannon.

SPECIFICATION	
RAM	**Performance:** maximum road speed 96 km/h (60 mph); maximum range 800 km (497 miles)
Crew: 2+7	
Weight: 5800 kg (12,787 lb)	**Fording:** 1 m (3 ft 3 in)
Dimensions: length 5.52 m (18 ft 1 in); width 2.03 m (6 ft 8 in); height 1.72 m (5 ft 7 in)	**Gradient:** 65 per cent
	Vertical obstacle: 0.8 m (2 ft 7 in)
Powerplant: one 98-kW (132-hp) Deutz 6-cylinder diesel engine	

Type 87 Reconnaissance vehicle

For many years the Japanese Ground Self-Defence Force (JGSDF) used mainly fully tracked armoured fighting vehicles (AFVs), but in recent years has also started to develop and deploy wheeled AFVs, as these offer a number of advantages over their tracked counterparts.

Two 6x6 AFV types have been developed in Japan, the Komatsu **Type 87** reconnaissance and patrol vehicle, and the Mitsubishi Heavy Industries Type 82 command and communications vehicle. Both of these share a number of components, such as the Isuzu 10-cylinder diesel engine, but their overall layout and design is very different due to their different missions.

The Type 87 reconnaissance vehicle has a crew of five, comprising the driver and radio operator at the front, commander and gunner in the two-man turret in the centre and the powerpack and observer located at the rear.

The power-operated turret is armed with a 25-mm Oerlikon Contraves KBA cannon which is manufactured under licence in Japan, with a 7.62-mm (0.3-in) machine-gun being mounted co-axially. These weapons are aimed using roof-mounted day/night observation devices, and it is understood that they can be laid onto the target by the gunner and vehicle commander.

Smoke equipment

Mounted on either side of the turret is a bank of four electrically operated smoke-

SPECIFICATION	
Type 87	**Powerplant:** one 225-kW (305-hp) Isuzu 10-cylinder diesel engine
Crew: 5	
Weight: 15000 kg (33,069 lb)	**Performance:** maximum road speed 100 km/h (62 mph); maximum range 500 km (311 miles)
Dimensions: length 5.99 m (19 ft 8 in); width 2.48 m (8 ft 1⅘ in); height 2.8 m (9 ft 2¼ in)	**Fording:** 1 m (3 ft 3 in)

grenade launchers. These fire smoke-grenades over the frontal arc, and when activated the vehicle would normally withdraw or move to another position under cover of the smoke.

Standard equipment includes powered steering and passive night-vision equipment for all of the crew members. In common with many JGSDF AFVs, the Type 87 has no amphibious capability.

While the Type 87 reconnaissance vehicle is well armed, it is somewhat large for the scope of its mission and lacks the longer-range reconnaissance suite installed on more recent and modern vehicles of this type.

Above: The Type 87 shares many common components with the Type 82 command and communications vehicle.

Right: The Type 87 reconnaissance vehicle is fitted with a two-man turret armed with a 25-mm cannon.

BRDM-1 Amphibious scout car

In the period immediately after World War II the BA-64 light armoured car remained the standard reconnaissance vehicle of its type in the Soviet army. From the late 1950s this was rapidly replaced by the **BRDM-1** 4x4 amphibious scout car.

The layout of the BRDM-1 is similar to that of a car, with the engine and transmission at the front, the driver and commander in the centre and a small crew compartment at the rear. The only means of entry are hatches in the roof and rear of the crew compartment. Between the front and rear wheels on each side of the hull are two belly wheels, which are powered and lowered to the ground by the driver when the vehicle is crossing ditches or rough terrain. A central tyre pressure-regulation system is standard, and this allows the driver to inflate or deflate the tyres according to the conditions.

The BRDM-1 is fully amphibious, being propelled in water at a speed of 9 km/h (5.6 mph) by a single waterjet at the rear of the hull. Before the vehicle enters the water, a trim vane is erected at the front and the bilge pumps are switched on. The BRDM-1 is normally armed with a single 7.62-mm

(0.3-in) SGMB machine-gun mounted on the forward part of the roof with a total traverse of 90° (45° left and right) elevation being from -6° to +23.5°. A total of 1,070 rounds of ammunition is carried. Some vehicles were observed with a similar weapon at the rear and a 12.7-mm (0.5-in) DShKM machine-gun at the front of the roof.

Specialised models

The **BRDM-U** command vehicle has additional communications equipment, while the **BRDM-1RKhb** radiological/chemical reconnaissance vehicle was designed to mark lines through contaminated areas. Mounted at the rear of the hull are two racks that contain the marking poles and pennants; when required, these racks swing through 90° over the rear of the vehicle, allowing the poles and attached pennants to be planted.

There were three versions of the BRDM-1 fitted with anti-tank missiles. The first model had three 3M6 Shmel (AT-1 'Snapper') ATGWs with a range of 2500 m (2,735 yards). The missiles on their launcher arms were carried under armour protection and raised above the roof of the vehicle for launching. The second model was similar

Soviet BRDM-1 4x4 amphibious scout cars, with roof hatches open, ford a stream. The vehicle is propelled in water by a single waterjet at the rear of the hull, which gives it a maximum speed of 9 km/h (5.6 mph). For travel across rough country, belly wheels are lowered between the front and rear axles.

but had four 3M11 Falanga (AT-2 'Swatter') missiles with a range of 3000 m (3,280 yards); for some reason this mounting was not exported outside the Warsaw Pact nations. The last model to enter service had six 9M14 Malyutka (AT-3 'Sagger') ATGWs with a maximum range of 3000 m (3,280 yards);

additional missiles were carried in the hull. This wire-guided missile, which proved to be highly effective in the 1973 Middle East War, could be launched from within the vehicle itself or up to a distance of 80 m (87.5 yards) away from it with the aid of a separation sight/control unit.

SPECIFICATION	
BRDM-1	**Performance:** maximum road speed
Crew: 5	80 km/h (50 mph); maximum road
Weight: 5.6 tonnes	range 500 km (311 miles)
Dimensions: length 5.7 m (18 ft	**Fording:** amphibious
8½ in); width 2.25 m (7 ft 4 in);	**Gradient:** 60 per cent
height 1.9 m (6 ft 2¾ in)	**Vertical obstacle:** 0.4 m (1 ft 3¾ in)
Powerplant: one 6-cylinder petrol	**Trench:** 1.22 m (4 ft)
engine developing 67 kW (90 hp)	

BRDM-2 Amphibious scout car

The **BRDM-2** 4x4 amphibious scout car was developed as the successor to the earlier BRDM-1, and was first seen in public in 1966, although it entered service some years before that date. The most significant improvements of the BRDM-2 over the earlier vehicle can be summarised as better vision for the commander and driver, a more powerful armament mounted in a fully enclosed turret, a more powerful engine for higher speeds, an NBC protection system and longer range.

Most BRDM-2 ATGW versions carried six Malyutka (AT-3 'Sagger') missiles in the ready-to-launch position, but some were armed with a quadruple launcher for the earlier 3M11 Falanga (AT-2 'Swatter') or five 9M113 Konkurs (AT-5 'Spandrel' missiles.

International service

The BRDM-2 replaced the BRDM-1 in most Soviet units. At one time it was in service with almost 40 countries all over the world, seeing action in such places as Angola, Egypt, Iraq, Syria

and Vietnam. It is still in wide-spread service.

The all-welded steel hull of the BRDM-2 is only 7 mm (0.275 in) thick, apart from the nose plate which is 14 mm (0.55 in) thick, and the under-side of the belly which is only 2 or 3 mm (0.08 or 0.12 in) thick. This leaves the vehicle vulnerable to land mine explosions.

Limited access

The driver and commander are seated at the front of the vehicle. Each has a windscreen covered in combat by an armoured hatch. Over each position is a single-piece hatch

cover that opens vertically; these are the only means of entry into the vehicle for the four-man crew. The turret, with no roof hatch, is armed with a highly effective 14.5-mm (0.57-in) KPVT heavy machine-gun, and a 7.62-mm (0.3-in) PKT co-axial machine-gun.

As with the earlier BRDM-1, the BRDM-2 has two belly wheels that can be lowered to the ground to enable ditches and rough country to be crossed with ease.

The basic BRDM-2 chassis formed the basis for a family of more specialised vehicles including the **BRDM-2 RKhb**

NBC reconnaissance vehicle and the **BRDM-2U** command vehicle without a turret. The first ATGW model carried six 9M14 Malyutka ('Sagger') ATGWs with a range of 3,000 m (3,280 yards). A version with 3M11 Falanga ('Swatter') ATGWs appeared, but the latest model is armed with five 9M113

Konkurs ('Spandrel') ATGWs in the ready-to-launch position on the hull top. These missiles have a range of at least 4000 m (4,375 yards).

The 9M31 Strela-1 (SA-9 'Gaskin') SAM system also uses the BRDM-2 chassis, with four missiles carried in the ready-to-launch position.

SPECIFICATION	
BRDM-2	**Performance:** maximum road speed 100 km/h (62 mph); maximum road range 750 km (465 miles)
Crew: 4	
Weight: 7 tonnes	**Fording:** amphibious
Dimensions: length 5.75 m (18 ft 10⅓ in); width 2.35 m (7 ft 8½ in); height 2.31 m (7 ft 7 in)	**Gradient:** 60 per cent
	Vertical obstacle: 0.4 m (1 ft 3¾ in)
Powerplant: one GAZ-41 petrol engine developing 104 kW (140 hp)	**Trench:** 1.25 m (4 ft 1 in)

PT-76 Amphibious light tank

The **PT-76** light amphibious tank was designed in the immediate post-war period by the design team responsible for the IS series of heavy tanks. For many years the PT-76 was the standard reconnaissance vehicle of the Soviet army, and was used alongside the BRDM-1 and BRDM-2 4x4 amphibious scout cars. In Soviet units the type was replaced by MBTs such as the T-72 and variants of the BMP. Although production of the PT-76 was completed many years ago, the tank is still likely to be encountered.

Versatile vehicle

The chassis of the PT-76 was subsequently used for a number of other vehicles, including the BTR-50 amphibious APC and the launcher for the FROG (Free Rocket Over Ground) artillery rocket system.

The driver is seated at the front in the centre, the two-man turret is in the centre of the vehicle and the engine and transmission are at the rear. The torsion-bar suspension consists on each side of six single road wheels, with the drive sprocket at the rear and the idler at the front.

The main armament consists of a 76.2-mm (3-in) D-56T gun. A 7.62-mm (0.3-in) SGMT machine-

gun is mounted co-axial with the main armament; many vehicles have a 12.7-mm (0.5-in) DShKM machine-gun on the turret roof. Totals of 40 rounds of 76-mm and 1,000 rounds of 7.62-mm ammunition are carried. Several types of fixed ammunition can be fired, namely APT, API-T, HE-FRAG, HEAT and HVAP-T.

The most useful feature of the PT-76 is its amphibious capability, which is the reason why the type was also used by Polish and Soviet marines. In water the tank is powered by two waterjets at up to 10 km/h (6.2 mph). The only preparation required before entering the water is the raising of the trim vane at the front of the hull, the activation of the bilge pumps and the engagement of the waterjets. The maximum waterborne range is about 65 km (40 miles). To enable the driver to see forward when afloat, his centre periscope can be raised above the hatch cover, and equipment includes IR lights, but no NBC system.

The PT-76 light tank was replaced in many Soviet units by special models of the BMP-1 reconnaissance vehicle.

SPECIFICATION	
PT-76	diesel developing 179 kW (240 hp)
Crew: 3	**Performance:** maximum road speed 44 km/h (27 mph); maximum road range 260 km (160 miles)
Weight: 14.6 tonnes	
Dimensions: length (gun forward) 7.63 m (25 ft ¼ in) and (hull) 6.91 m (22 ft 8 in); width 3.14 m (10 ft 3⅔ in); height 2.26 m (7 ft 4¾ in)	**Fording:** amphibious
	Gradient: 60 per cent
	Vertical obstacle: 1.1 m (3 ft 7⅓ in)
Powerplant: one V-6B 6-cylinder	**Trench:** 2.8 m (9 ft 2 in)

PT-76 Model 2 light amphibious tanks come ashore from landing craft of the Red Banner Northern Fleet. Note the open turret hatch cover and the trim vane at the front in the raised position. The main armament comprises a 76.2-mm (3-in) gun and 7.62-mm (0.3-in) co-axial machine-gun.

Daimler Ferret Scout car

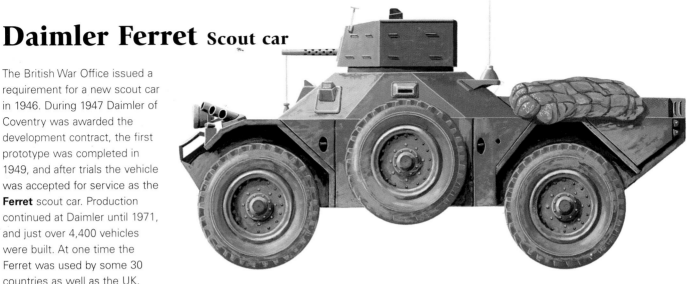

The British War Office issued a requirement for a new scout car in 1946. During 1947 Daimler of Coventry was awarded the development contract, the first prototype was completed in 1949, and after trials the vehicle was accepted for service as the **Ferret** scout car. Production continued at Daimler until 1971, and just over 4,400 vehicles were built. At one time the Ferret was used by some 30 countries as well as the UK.

All Ferrets have the same layout: the driver at the front, the commander/gunner in the centre and the engine and transmission at the rear. The all-welded steel hull has a maximum thickness of 12 mm

A Ferret Mk I (left) armed with a Bren light machine-gun, and a Ferret Mk 2/3 (right) armed with a 0.3-in machine-gun. Some 4,409 vehicles were built for home and export markets when production ended in 1971.

The Ferret Mk 2/3 has a one-man turret armed with a 0.3-in machine-gun. In addition to being used as a scout car, it is operated in the internal security role.

(0.47 in), providing the crew with protection from small arms fire and shell splinters.

Ferret variants

The **Ferret Mk 1** had an open top and a pintle-mounted 0.3-in (7.62-mm) machine-gun The **Ferret Mk 1/2** had a crew of three and a low-profile turret with an externally mounted machine-gun. The **Ferret Mk 2/3**

had a one-man turret armed with a 0.3-in machine-gun. The **Ferret Mk 2/2** was developed locally in the Far East, being a Ferret Mk 2 with an extension collar between the hull top and turret base to improve all-round observation. The **Ferret Mk 2/6** was the Ferret Mk 2/3 with a Vigilant anti-tank missile on each side of the turret. The wire-guided Vigilant had a maximum range of 1375 m (1,500 yards). The **Ferret Mk 3** and **Ferret Mk 4** were essentially earlier versions rebuilt with stronger suspension units, larger tyres and a flotation screen carried

collapsed around the top of the hull. This screen could be quickly erected by the crew to make the vehicle fully amphibious. The **Ferret Mk 5** was the final version, a rebuild of earlier marks. It had a turret in each of whose sides were two launcher bins for the Swingfire anti-tank missile with a range of 4000 m (4,380 yards). The Ferret Mk 5 was also armed with a 0.3-in machine-gun and, like all Ferrets, smoke dischargers. The Ferret is no longer in service with the British Army although many remain in service elsewhere.

SPECIFICATION	
Daimler Ferret Mk 2/3	**Performance:** maximum road speed
Crew: 2	93 km/h (58 mph); maximum road
Weight: 4.4 tonnes	range 306 km (190 miles)
Dimensions: length 3.835 m (12 ft	**Fording:** 0.91 m (3 ft)
10 in); width 1.905 m (6 ft 3 in);	**Gradient:** 46 per cent
height 1.879 m (6 ft 2 in)	**Vertical obstacle:** 0.41 m (1 ft 4 in)
Powerplant: one 96-kW (129-hp)	**Trench:** 1.22 m (4 ft) with one
Rolls-Royce liquid-cooled 6-cylinder	channel
petrol engine	

Fox Light armoured car

During the late 1960s the British Army decided to build two new reconnaissance vehicles, one tracked and the other wheeled. These became known as the Combat Vehicle Reconnaissance (Tracked), or Scorpion, and the **Combat Vehicle Reconnaissance (Wheeled)**, or **Fox**. Daimler of Coventry gained

the development contract for the Fox, the first prototype appearing in 1967. Following service acceptance as the **FV721**, the Fox entered production in 1972 at Royal Ordnance Leeds. The final deliveries were made in 1979.

In British service the Fox was used for reconnaissance duties.

Driver training had to be carefully conducted as the vehicle's centre of gravity was high, resulting in a propensity to turn over when cornering. The Fox was therefore withdrawn from British Army service, never quite replacing the Ferret scout cars it was meant to supplant. Most Fox turrets were removed

and transferred to redundant Scorpion reconnaissance vehicle chassis to produce the Sabre, which is still in service. About 13 turrets were mounted on FV432 APC chassis and issued to the Berlin Brigade, and these have now been withdrawn. Export sales were made to Nigeria (55) and Malawi (20), but the exact status of these vehicles is now uncertain.

Modernised Ferret

The Fox was basically an updated Ferret with a two-man turret armed with a 30-mm RARDEN L21 cannon firing an APDS-T round. The accuracy of the RARDEN is enhanced by being designed to fire only rapid single shots or short bursts. Ammunition types include armour piercing and high explosive. A 0.3-in (7.62-mm) co-axial machine was the only other weapon carried. An L2A1 passive night sight was provided for area surveillance or gun aiming. Smoke grenade

The Fox is a Jaguar-powered development of the late production Ferret family. Capable of 104 km/h (64.6 mph) on roads, the Fox is armed with the 30-mm RARDEN cannon.

launchers were provided for rapid concealment of the vehicle when necessary.

Structural details

The Fox had a relatively large all-welded aluminium hull and turret. The driver was seated centrally at the front while the commander and gunner occupied the centrally mounted turret. The militarised Jaguar XK petrol engine and transmission

were at the rear. A full 4x4 drive configuration was employed, coupled with a coil spring independent suspension. A flotation collar around the hull periphery was originally a fixture, providing the Fox with full amphibious capability. This was little used so the collar was later removed from British Army Foxes. Without the collar the

Fox could wade through water obstacles 1 m (3 ft 3 in) deep. The Fox could also be paradropped, the Hercules transport aircraft being able to carry two Foxes prepared for para-dropping or three for normal air transport. The Fox could carry several recon aids such as a portable battlefield surveillance radar.

SPECIFICATION	
Fox	**Performance:** maximum road speed
Crew: 3	104 km/h (64.6 mph); maximum
Weight: 6.12 tonnes	road range 434 km (270 miles)
Dimensions: length 5.08 m (16 ft	**Fording:** 1 m (3 ft 3 in)
8 in); width 2.134 m (7 ft); height	**Gradient:** 60 per cent
1.981 m (6 ft 6 in)	**Vertical obstacle:** 0.5 m (1 ft 7¾ in)
Powerplant: one 142-kW (190-hp)	
Jaguar XK petrol engine	

Alvis Saladin Armoured car

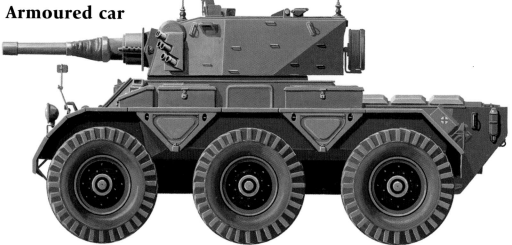

Following the success of the AEC Mk III and Daimler Mk II armoured cars during World War II, the British Army issued a requirement for a new armoured car with a 2-pdr (40-mm/1.57-in) gun. It was then decided that this gun would be ineffective against future armoured vehicles, and it was replaced by the new 3-in (76-mm) L5 gun.

The chassis of the **Saladin** (**FV601**) is similar to that of the FV603 Saracen APC, also under development by Alvis at the same time. The Saladin was accepted for service with the British Army in 1956. Production started two years later at Alvis in Coventry and continued until 1972, by which time 1,177 vehicles (including many for export) had been completed.

Although it has been replaced in British service by the Alvis Scorpion tracked vehicle, the Saladin remains in military and internal security service (or in reserve) with 11 countries.

The Saladin armoured car shares many common automotive components with the Saracen APC. The last examples in British service were based in Cyprus. Kuwaiti Saladins were used against Iraq in 1990.

Steel construction

The hull of the Saladin is of all-welded steel armour construction that varies in thickness from 8 mm (0.31 in) to 16 mm (0.63 in); the turret has a maximum thickness of 32 mm (1.25 in) at the front and 16 mm (0.63 in) at the sides and rear. The driver sits at the front of the vehicle with excellent vision to his front and sides. The

other two crew members are seated in the turret with the

commander/loader on the right and the gunner on the left. The

SPECIFICATION	
Alvis Saladin	**Performance:** maximum road speed
Crew: 3	72 km/h (45 mph); maximum road
Weight: 11.59 tonnes	range 400 km (250 miles)
Dimensions: length (including gun)	**Fording:** 1.07 m (3 ft 6 in)
5.28 m (17 ft 4 in) and (hull) 4.93 m	**Gradient:** 46 per cent
(16 ft 2 in); width 2.54 m (8 ft 4 in);	**Vertical obstacle:** 0.46 m (1 ft 6 in)
height 2.93 m (9 ft 7½ in)	**Trench:** 1.52 m (5 ft)
Powerplant: one 127-kW (170-bhp)	
Rolls-Royce B80 petrol engine	

engine and transmission are at the rear. All six wheels of the Saladin are powered, with steering on the front four wheels. The vehicle is driveable with one wheel blown off.

Ammunition total

A total of 42 rounds of fixed ammunition is carried for the turret-mounted 3-in gun. A 0.3-in (7.62-mm) machine-gun is mounted co-axially, and there is a similar weapon mounted on the turret roof for air defence. Six electrically operated smoke dischargers are mounted each side of the turret.

There were few variants of the Saladin, one being an amphibious model. This had a flotation screen around the top of the hull, and when this had been erected the vehicle could propel itself in water with its wheels.

The Saladin is armed with a 3-in (76-mm) L5 rifled gun; a lightened version was fitted in the more recent Scorpion, firing the same range of fixed ammunition. Between 1958 and 1972 Alvis of Coventry built a total of 1,177 Saladin armoured cars.

Alvis Scorpion Reconnaissance vehicle

In the late 1960s the British Army decided to build two new reconnaissance vehicles, one tracked and the other wheeled. These became known as the **Combat Vehicle Reconnaissance (Tracked)** or **Scorpion** and the Combat Vehicle Reconnaissance (Wheeled), or Fox. In 1967 Alvis was awarded a contract to build prototypes of the Scorpion, the first completed in 1969. Trials were so successful that it was accepted for service the following year. Late in 1970 the Scorpion was also ordered by Belgium and an assembly line was established in that country. The first production Scorpions were delivered to the British Army in 1972, but this was

only one of a large family of vehicles based on the same chassis, production of which continues for export sales to many countries.

The Scorpion has an all-welded aluminium hull and turret. The driver is seated at the left front with the engine to his right, and the two-man turret is at the rear. The suspension is of the torsion-bar type, and on each side comprises five road wheels with the drive sprocket at the front and the idler at the rear; there are no track-return rollers.

Indifferent main gun

The basic Scorpion has a 3-in (76-mm) gun with 40 rounds of ammunition. A 0.3-in (7.62-mm) machine-gun is mounted

The original Scorpion light tank was armed with a 3-in (76-mm) main gun, but this was withdrawn from British service at a comparatively early date.

co-axially with the main armament to be used as a ranging as well as a secondary weapon. Export vehicles may have a diesel engine in place of the standard petrol engine, and some have a 90-mm (3.54-in) gun.

The Scorpion is no longer used by the British Army as the

L23 gun was withdrawn from service. Existing Scorpion chassis were then allied with 30-mm RARDEN cannon turrets taken from FV721 Fox reconnaissance vehicles. These hybrids are known as the **Sabre**, being similar to the FV107 Scimitar but with the machine-gun replaced by a Boeing 0.3-in chain gun.

The original L23 gun of 3-in calibre was distinguishable from the 30-mm RARDEN cannon that replaced it by its thicker but shorter barrel. The Scorpion can be airlifted by Hercules tyransport aircraft.

SPECIFICATION	
Alvis Scorpion	**Performance:** maximum road speed
Crew: 3	80 km/h (50 mph); maximum road
Weight: 8.073 tonnes	range 644 km (400 miles)
Dimensions: length 4.79 m (15 ft 8¾ in); width 2.235 m (7 ft 4 in); height 2.102 m (6 ft 10¾ in)	**Fording:** 1.067 m (3 ft 6 in)
	Gradient: 60 per cent
	Vertical obstacle: 0.5 m (1 ft 8 in)
Powerplant: one Jaguar petrol engine developing 142 kW (190 hp)	**Trench:** 2.06 m (6 ft 9 in)

The Scorpion has good cross-country mobility and is notably agile, but its decidedly limited armour protection dictates the avoidance of more heavily armed AFVs. This Scorpion is seen waiting for the order to move on during night manoeuvres in Saudi Arabia, just prior to the 1991 invasion of Iraq.

Scorpion
In action

The Scorpion is built of structural armour, which helps maximise the volume of this small AFV for the crew and essential systems. Located in a semi-reclining position in the front of the vehicle, the driver is provided with overhead cover by a hatch that lifts and rotates, while the commander and gunner seated in the turret are shielded by hatches that open upward and to the rear.

Commander
Seated on the left of the turret, the commander has a roof-mounted sight and seven persicopes. The sight allows an 85° horizontal field of view and has a magnification of x1 and x10. Since there are only three crew members, the commander must also load the main armament.

Hull armour
The Scorpion's all-welded aluminium front armour is proof against machine-gun bullets up to 14.5-mm (0.57-in) calibre (as fitted to the Russian BRDM-2 amphibious scout car and the BTR-60PB wheeled armoured personnel carrier). In addition, both the side and rear armour is proof against 7.62-mm (0.3-in) bullets.

Engine compartment
The Scorpion is powered by a 4.2-litre Jaguar engine, de-rated from 198 to 142 kW (265 to 190 bhp) and with a reduced compression ratio to allow the use of military fuel. Specially designed for a long life at high engine revolutions, the engine is cooled by a fan drawing air through the radiator, over the gearbox and out via the louvres.

Suspension
The torsion bar suspension consists of five aluminium road wheels with rubber tyres; the first and last wheels have hydraulic shock absorbers. This causes the track to exert less pressure than a man and so allow the Scorpion to safely cross areas that foot soldiers cannot.

Tracks
The Scorpion is steered by locking one track and allowing the other to continue, thus turning the vehicle. Vertical obstacle clearance is 50 cm (1 ft 7 in). The tracks are light steel and have an average life of 4828 km (3,000 miles).

SPECIFICATION

Alvis FV101 Scorpion CVR(T)

Type: tracked reconnaissance vehicle
Crew: driver, commander and gunner

Dimensions

Length: (overall) 4.79 m (15 ft 9 in) and (hull) 4.572 m (15 ft); **width:** (overall) 2.235 m (7 ft 4 in); **height:** 2.102 m (6 ft 11 in)

Combat weight

8073 kg (17,798 lb)

Powerplant

One Jaguar J60 No. 1 Mk 100B 4.2-litre liquid-cooled six-cylinder petrol engine developing 142 kW (190 hp) at 4,750 rpm

Fuel capacity

423 litres (93 Imp gal)

Performance

Maximum road speed: 80 km/h (50 mph)
Maximum water speed: 6.5 km/h (4 mph) driven by its tracks or 9.65 km/h (6 mph) driven by an optional propeller kit
Maximum road range: 644 km (400 miles)
Fording: 1.07 m (3 ft 6 in) without preparation and amphibious with preparation
Gradient: 60 per cent
Vertical obstacle: 0.5 m (1 ft 8 in)
Trench: 2.06 m (6 ft 9 in)

Armament

One 3-in (76.2-mm) L23A1 gun with 40 rounds of ammunition, one 0.3-in (7.62-mm) L43A1 co-axial machine-gun with 3,000 rounds, and two triple or quadruple smoke-dischargers

The Scorpion is a notably compact AFV optimised for the reconnaissance role, which emphasises the need for mobility, largely in terms of speed and agility, rather than firepower and protection. In British service, the Scorpion was manned by the Royal Armoured Corps and deployed in Belize, the UK and in West Germany with the BAOR. It could be airlifted to any part of the world by RAF Hercules transport aircraft.

Smoke dischargers
On each side of the turret is a bank of three or four electrically operated smoke dischargers. These are normally used to cover an emergency withdrawal.

Gunner
The gunner has two periscopes, a roof-mounted sight and a passive night sight which can detect enemy/infrared devices. The gun control include hand elevation and a manual, two-speed traverse.

External stowage
One of the problems with the original Scorpion was a lack of external stowage. A characteristic of British Army vehicles is how many unofficial 'bins' can be fitted on to carry as much extra kit as possible. Turret and hull back bins are standard, but extra boxes are often fitted.

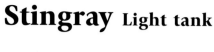

Stingray Light tank

Cadillac Gage Textron (now Textron Marine & Land Systems) produced its **Stingray** light tank for the export market, and to date the only sale has been to Thailand (106 vehicles). The Stingray programme started in 1983, the first prototype was completed in August 1984, and Thailand's order was fulfilled in 1988–90.

Limited protection

The Stingray is too lightly protected for any real battlefield role, and in is effect a reconnaissance tank. The vehicle is of steel construction offering protection against 14.5-mm (0.57-in) and 12.7-mm (0.5-in) armour-piercing rounds over the frontal arc and the rest of the vehicle respectively, and is orthodox in its layout, with the driver at the front, the three-man turret in the centre, and the powerplant (diesel engine and automatic transmission) at the rear. The

The Stingray light tank is the heaviest, largest and most capable of the vehicles offered in Cadillac Gage's series of private-venture AFVs, and is a light or reconnaissance tank providing good firepower and mobility, but only indifferent protection as a result of its thin armour.

suspension is of the torsion-bar type, and the running gear comprises, on each side, six dual rubber-tyred road wheels, drive sprocket at the rear, idler at the front, and three track-return rollers.

The primary armament is an LRF (Low Recoil Force) version of the British L7 series 105-mm (4.13-in) rifled gun installed in the well angled and electro-hydraulically powered turret with optional stabilisation and eight rounds; another 24 rounds

SPECIFICATION	
Stingray	diesel engine developing 399 kW
Crew: 4	(535 hp)
Weight: 21.205 tonnes	**Performance:** maximum road speed
Dimensions: length (gun forward)	67 km/h (42 mph); maximum road
9.30 m (30 ft 6 in); length (hull)	range 483 km (300 miles); fording
6.448 m (21 ft 2 in); width 2.71 m	1.07 m (3 ft 6 in); gradient 60 per
(8 ft 10 in); height 2.55 m (8 ft 4 in)	cent; vertical obstacle 0.76 m (2 ft
Powerplant: one Detroit Diesel	6 in); trench 2.13 m (7 ft 0 in)
Model 8V-92TA liquid-cooled V-12	

are stowed in the hull. The main armament can be elevated through an arc of 27.5° (-7.5° to +20°). The secondary armament comprises a 7.62-mm (0.3-in)

co-axial machine-gun with 2,400 rounds and a 12.7-mm (0.5-in) AA machine gun with 1,100 rounds on the commander's hatch. The tank's fire-control system is not notably advanced, but includes a laser rangefinder and night-vision equipment, and there is provision for this fire-control system to be upgraded and an NBC system to be fitted.

The company's marketing is now concentrated on the **Stingray II**. This has the same armament system as the Stingray, but a more capable digital fire-control system and NBC equipment are standard. The other improvements offered by the Stingray II, which is based on proven automotive elements and in-production turret and armament, lie in its maximised survivability through the use of armour offering protection against rounds up to 23-mm calibre, enhanced mobility, and superior target-engagement capability.

The sides of the Stingray's pointed turret slope inwards with a turret basket at the rear. A bank of four smoke grenade dischargers are carried on each side, with a 12.7-mm gun on the right side of the roof.

Lynx Command and reconnaissance vehicle

When the M113 armoured personnel carrier entered production at FMC's facility at San Jose in 1960, it was realised that in addition to being used for a wide range of roles, its automotive component could also be used in other armoured vehicles. At that time the US Army had already selected the M114 vehicle to carry out the role of command and reconnaissance, but the M114 did not prove a successful design and has long since been phased out of service; moreover, it was never sold overseas. FMC then designed and built a command and reconnaissance vehicle using automotive components of the diesel-powered M113A1, and this was subsequently selected by Canada, which ordered 174 vehicles under the name **Lynx**, and also by the Netherlands, which ordered 250 vehicles; all of these were delivered by 1968. The vehicle is often called the 'M113 and a half'!

In comparison with the M113, the Lynx has a lower-profile hull, the powerpack repositioned to the rear, and one road wheel less on each side. The hull is of all-welded aluminium armour construction that provides the crew with complete protection from small arms fire and shell splinters. The driver is seated at the front of the vehicle, with the

A Lynx Command and Reconnaissance vehicle of the Canadian Armed Forces, armed with a 12.7-mm (0.5-in) M2HB machine-gun forward and a 7.62-mm (0.3-in) machine-gun at the rear. A bank of three electrically operated smoke dischargers is mounted on each side of the hull front.

commander to his rear and right. The radio operator/observer is seated to the left rear of the commander. The engine compartment is at the rear of the hull on the right side, with access hatches in the roof and hull rear.

Amphibious capability

The suspension is of the torsion-bar type, and consists of four dual rubber-tyred road wheels on each side with the drive sprocket at the front and the idler at the rear; there are no track-return rollers. The Lynx is fully amphibious, being propelled in the water by its tracks at a

speed of 5.6 km/h (3.5 mph). Before the vehicle enters the water, a trim vane is erected at the front of the hull, and electric bilge pumps are switched on. Rectangular covers are also erected around the air inlet and exhaust louvres on the hull top to stop water entering the engine compartment, the vehicle having very limited freeboard. Vehicles such as the M113 and the Lynx can cross only calm rivers and lakes; open-sea landings almost inevitably resulting in swamping.

Turret cannon

The commander of the Lynx has an M26 hand-operated turret, with vision blocks for all-round observation and an externally mounted standard 12.7-mm M2HB machine-gun for which 1,155 rounds of ammunition are carried. The radio operator/ observer has a pintle-mounted 7.62-mm (0.3-in) machine-gun

with 2,000 rounds. A bank of three electrically operated smoke-dischargers is mounted at the front of each side of the hull.

The Dutch vehicles have a slightly different internal layout, and as originally supplied were slightly lighter. More recently all of these vehicles have been fitted with a Swiss Oerlikon-Contraves GBD-AOA one-man turret carrying a 25-mm KBA-B cannon. This has three rates of fire: single-shot, 175 rounds per minute and 570 rounds per minute. Some 200 rounds of ready-use ammunition (120 HE and 80 AP) are carried for the cannon. An added advantage for the Dutch is that this Oerlikon cannon (in a one-man power-operated turret) is also installed in the FMC-designed armoured infantry fighting vehicles of the Dutch army, so providing a very useful element of ammunition commonality.

All Dutch vehicles have now been fitted with a Swiss Oerlikon-Contraves one-man turret armed with a 25-mm KBA-B cannon. This is also fitted to the Dutch army's Armoured Infantry Fighting Vehicles, thus facilitating ammunition resupply on the battlefield.

SPECIFICATION	
Lynx	160 kW (215 hp)
Crew: 3	**Performance:** maximum road speed
Weight: 8.775 tonnes	70.8 km/h (44 mph); maximum
Dimensions: length 4.597 m (15 ft 1 in);	range 523 km (325 miles)
width 2.413 m (7 ft 11 in); height	**Fording:** amphibious
(including armament) 2.17 m (7 ft 1½ in)	**Gradient:** 60 per cent
Powerplant: one Detroit Diesel Type	**Vertical obstacle:** 0.61 m (2 ft 0 in);
6V53 6-cylinder diesel developing	**Trench:** 1.524 m (5 ft 0 in)

M41 Walker Bulldog Light tank

In 1949 the US Army decided to develop new tanks to replace all its World War II types. The light tank was placed under development as the **Light Tank T41**, based on the T37 whose design as a development model had been launched shortly after World War II. The T37 Phase I prototype with the 76.2-mm (3-in) M32 gun was completed in 1949. Already the T37 was involved in a development programme whose fruits were the T37 Phase II with a redesignated cast/welded turret, a new mantlet, revised ammunition stowage and a fire-control system that integrated a coincidence rangefinder with a Vickers stabiliser for the gun mounting, and the T27 Phase III with an automatic loader for the main armament and an IBM stabiliser for the gun mounting. The T37 Phase II led to the T41, which was standardised in 1950 as the **Light Tank M41 Little Bulldog**, although the name was subsequently changed to **Walker Bulldog** in honour of the US commander killed in Korea during 1951. Production by Cadillac Gage began in 1950, and some 5,500 M41 series vehicles were built before the production line closed.

Classic layout

In design the M41 made full use of US combat experience in World War II but is in many ways similar to the M24 it was designed to replace. The all-welded hull is divided into the standard three compartments, with the driver in the forward compartment, the commander, gunner and loader in the turret/basket assembly over the central compartment, and the powerplant at the rear. The running gear consists on each side of five road wheels with independent torsion-bar suspension, and there are three track-return rollers, a rear sprocket and a front idler. The electro-hydraulically powered

turret is mainly of cast construction with a welded roof and bustle, and accommodates the M32 unstabilised gun with an elevation arc of 29° 30' (-9° 45' to +19° 45') but only a primitive optical fire-control system; there are also 7.62-mm (0.3-in) co-axial and 12.7-mm (0.5-in) AA machine guns. Later variants were the **M41A1**, **M41A2** and **M41A3** which differed only in detail, including an increase in main armament stowage from 57 to 65 rounds. The last variants also had a fuel-injected rather than normally aspirated engine. Subsequent variants were to have had a 90-mm (3.54-in) or even 105-mm (4.13-in) main gun, but these were not procured. Variants that did appear, however, were the **M42 Duster** with twin 40-mm anti-aircraft guns, the **M44** 155-mm (6.1-in) self-propelled howitzer, the **M52** 105-mm (4.13-in) self-propelled howitzer and the **M75** armoured personnel carrier. The M41 and its derivatives are still in extensive service, update packages centring on the engine and armament – a diesel and a 90-mm main gun.

The M41 series was widely exported to American allies for whom a readily available and cheap light tank, offering reconnaissance and counter-insurgency capabilities of a high order, was more important than a costlier battle tank offering unwanted capability.

For its size and weight the M41 offered good capability, but the type was not best suited to operations in any form of high-intensity battlefield, where it might be engaged by battle tanks or large-calibre artillery firing armour-penetrating projectiles.

SPECIFICATION	
M41 Walker Bulldog	895-3 air-cooled 6-cylinder petrol
Crew: 4	engine developing 373 kW (500 hp)
Weight: 23.496 tonnes	**Performance:** maximum road speed
Dimensions: length (gun forward)	72 km/h (45 mph); maximum road
8.20 m (26 ft 11 in); length (hull)	range 161 km (100 miles)
5.82 m (19 ft 1 in); width 3.20 m	**Fording:** 1.02 m (3 ft 4 in)
(10 ft 6 in); height (including AA	**Gradient:** 60 per cent
machine-gun) 3.07 m (10 ft 1 in)	**Vertical obstacle:** 0.71 m (2 ft 4 in);
Powerplant: one Continental AOS-	**Trench:** 1.83 m (6 ft 0 in)

M551 Sheridan Light tank

An M551 Sheridan, as deployed to Vietnam, showing extensive external turret stowage and additional protection for the commander.

In the mid-1950s the only mobile weapons with a direct-fire capability in the US airborne divisions were the 76-mm (3-in) M41 light tank and the 90-mm (3.54-in) M56 self-propelled anti-tank gun. In 1959 a requirement was issued for a new airportable vehicle to replace both the M41 and M56, and development of such a vehicle started under the name **Armored Reconnaissance/ Airborne Assault Vehicle (AR/AAV)** and the designation **XM551**. The Allison Division of General Motors was subsequently awarded the development contract, and a total of 12 proto-types was built. In 1965, a four-year production contract was awarded to the company, although at that time the vehicle had not been fully accepted for service.

New vehicles

Production continued until 1970, when a total of 1,700 vehicles had been built. The XM551 was officially classified fit for service in 1966 and called the **M551 General Sheridan**. Although it was evaluated by a number of countries the type was never sold overseas, though it was deployed with the US Army to

Europe, South Korea and Vietnam. In the last theatre the M551 earned itself a bad reputation, many faults soon becoming apparent, especially with the 152-mm (6-in) main armament, the powerpack and the very thin belly armour, which provided little protection from mines, one of the more common Vietcong weapons.

In the late 1970s the M551 was withdrawn from most front-line units, its problematic MGM-51 Shillelagh missiles never having been used in anger, and by early 1983 it remained in service only with the tank battalion attached to the 82nd Airborne Division, though a few remained in service with the Arkansas National Guard into the 1980s. Large numbers are also used by the National Training Center at Fort Irwin, California, where they have been modified to resemble Soviet vehicles such as the ZSU-23-4 23-mm self-propelled anti-aircraft gun, BMP series MICV and the 122-mm (4.8-in) 2S3 self-propelled howitzer.

The hull of the M551 was of welded aluminium construction while the turret was of steel construction. The driver was

seated at the front in the centre, the turret was in the centre of the hull, and the engine and transmission were at the rear. Suspension was of the torsion-bar type, and consisted of five

A standard Sheridan during tests at Fort Knox. About 1700 of these vehicles were built between 1966 and 1970, and the last operational battalion, the 82nd Airborne Division, gave up its vehicles in the mid 1990s. Other vehicles have been converted to resemble Soviet vehicles such as the ZSU-23-4 and BMP for use at the National Training Center, Fort Irwin, California.

SPECIFICATION	
M551 Sheridan	0.5-in (12.7-mm) M2 machine-gun
Crew: 4	**Powerplant:** one Detroit Diesel 6V-53T 6-cylinder diesel developing 224 kW (300 hp)
Weight: 15.83 tonnes	
Dimensions: length 6.3 m (20 ft 8 in); width 2.82 m (9 ft 3 in); height (overall) 2.95 m (9 ft 8 in)	**Performance:** maximum road speed 70 km/h (43 mph); maximum range 600 km (310 miles)
Armament: 152-mm (6-in) M81 gun/missile launcher with 20 conventional rounds and eight Shillelagh missiles, co-axial 0.3-in (7.62-mm) M240 machine-gun,	**Fording:** amphibious
	Gradient: 60 per cent
	Vertical obstacle: 0 84 m (2 ft 9 in)
	Trench: 2.54 m (8 ft 4 in)

dual rubber-tyred road wheels with the drive sprocket at the rear and idler at the front; there were no track-return rollers. A flotation screen was carried collapsed around the top of the hull and when this was erected

the M551 was fully amphibious, being propelled in the water by its tracks.

Armament

The main armament consisted of an M81 152-mm (6-in)

gun/missile launcher that could fire a Shillelagh missile or one of four types of combustible-case conventional ammunition, namely HEAT-T-MP, WP, TP-T and canister. The last was of some use in Vietnam for beating off massed guerrilla attack at close quarters. The mix of conventional ammunition and missile depended on the mission being undertaken, but was typically 20 conventional

rounds and eight missiles. A 0.3-in (7.62-mm) machine-gun was mounted co-axial with the main armament and a 0.5-in (12.7-mm) machine-gun, with a shield, was mounted on top of the commander's cupola for local and anti-aircraft defence. Space was so cramped inside the M551 that much of the machine-gun ammunition was often carried externally on the sides of the turret.

Faults encountered with the Shillelagh anti-tank missile and a poor combat record meant that the Sheridan was only retained by the US Airborne service on account of its air-portability. It did, however, survive in service long enough to see action in Panama in 1989 and in support of Desert Shield.

Rooikat Armoured car

Development of the **Vickers OMC Rooikat** armoured car began in 1976 when three 8x8 vehicles were built to verify platform concepts. This was followed by a further three vehicles which were built and evaluated by the South African Defence Force in the early 1980s.

The main role of the Rooikat is combat reconnaissance during high-mobility operations, using its speed to outmanoeuvre the enemy and strike at his flanks and deep into the rear. Its secondary role is that of hunter/killer against a variety of battlefield targets including AFVs, with its third role being interdiction.

The hull is of all-welded steel armour with the driver seated at the front, three-man

power-operated turret in the centre and the power pack at the rear. Over the frontal arc protection is provided against penetration from the 23 mm AP rounds fired from the Russian ZU-23-2 LAAG.

Powerplant

The Rooikat has a V-10 turbocharged water-cooled engine driving through a six-speed fully automatic transmission, drop down gearbox and high/low-range transfer gearbox. This can be field exchanged in 60 minutes. The engine compartment is fitted with an automatic fire detection and suppression system. The driver can select full 8x8 drive or 8x4 drive, depending on the tactical situation. Steering is power

assisted on the front four wheels. The driver, seated on the centreline of the vehicle,

enters through the fighting compartment or the single-piece hatch cover that opens to the

Trials have demonstrated that the hull of the Rooikat provides a high degree of protection against anti-tank mines. The Rooikat remains mobile with two same-side wheels blown off by landmine explosion.

left. The driver's station (including essential controls) is fully adjustable and when closed down forward observation is via three day periscopes, the centre one of which can be replaced by a passive night periscope. The driver's periscopes can be cleaned by a compressed air cleaning system.

A hull escape hatch is on each side of the hull, between the second and third axles, thus protecting the crew from small arms fire if they evacuate. The commander sits on the right of the turret with the gunner forward and below his position, and the loader on the left. The commander is provided with eight day vision blocks to give observation through 360°. Mounted in the roof, forward of the commander's station, is a x12 day panoramic sight. This enables the commander to observe through a full 360° without moving his head. The sight can also be slaved to the main gun or uncoupled.

Observation

The loader has a single-piece hatch cover that opens to the rear, and is provided with two day periscopes that can be traversed to observe on the left side of the vehicle. The gunner has a roof-mounted periscopic sight that has x8 day and night (image intensification) channels and an integral laser rangefinder. The gunner also has an auxiliary day sight. If required, the commander can override the gunner.

Turret traverse and weapon elevation features solid-state electric controls for both gunner

The 76-mm Rooikat is shown here during camouflage trials. Smoke-laying equipment includes eight 81-mm (3.19-in) smoke grenade launchers (with two rounds each) as well as an exhaust smoke screen generator.

and commander, with manual emergency back up. Traverse is through a full 360° with elevation limits from -10 to +20°. The commander has a single control handle and the gunner twin control handles.

The digital fire-control system receives information from a laser rangefinder and a number of sensors including cant and windspeed. Ammunition type is set manually. The Rooikat can engage and hit targets with a high probability while it is moving across rough terrain.

The fire-control system provides automatic fire control by computing and implementing

SPECIFICATION	
76-mm Rooikat **Crew:** 4 **Combat weight:** 28 tonnes **Dimensions:** length (including gun) 8.2 m (26 ft 11 in); width 2.9 m (9 ft 6 in); height 2.8 m (9 ft 2½ in) **Armament:** 76-mm (3-in) GT4 rifled gun with 48 rounds, coaxial 7.62-mm (0.3-in) machine-gun, 7.62-mm AA machine-gun **Powerplant:** one V-10 water-cooled diesel engine developing 420 kW (563 hp)	**Performance:** maximum road speed 120 km/h (74.57 mph); cross-country speed 60 km/h (37.28 mph); maximum road range 1000 km (621 miles) **Gradient:** 70 per cent **Fording depth:** 1.5 m (4 ft 11 in); **Vertical obstacle:** 1 m (3 ft 4 in) **Trench:** 2 m (6 ft 7 in) at crawl speed; 1 m (3 ft 4 in) at 60 km/h (37.28 mph)

the ballistic offsets for the ammunition type selection. It takes into account target range, target speed, manually entered environmental data, crosswind speed, weapon tilt, and gun jump characteristics of the main weapon. A ready to fire indication appears in the gunner's field advising him to fire. Total reaction time from lasing to firing is typically less than two seconds.

GT4 gun

Main armament comprises a 76-mm (3-in) GT4 gun. The 76-mm gun was chosen because of the larger number of rounds that could be carried compared to a 105-mm (4.13-in) gun, the ease of handling ammunition when moving across country and crew comfort when firing. The 76-mm stabilised gun has a vertical sliding semi-automatic breech block, a thermal sleeve and concentric glass fibre fume

extractor. The recoil system consists of a concentric hydrospring with an external replenisher with maximum recoil being 370 mm (14.6 in). Two types of fixed 76-mm ammunition have been developed, HE-T and APFSDS-T with a total of 48 rounds of ammunition being carried, nine for ready use stowed vertically below the turret ring on the left side. For safety reasons no main gun ammunition is stowed above the turret ring. Rate of fire is stated to be 6 rds/min, with the APFSDS-T projectile having an effective range of 2,000 to 3,000 m (2,187 to 3,281 yds). It will penetrate the T-54/55 and T-62 from all angles of attack. The HE-T round has a maximum range of 12,000 m (13,123 yds) in the indirect fire role and 3,000 m in the direct fire role.

It is understood that production of the 76-mm Rooikat is now complete with about 240 vehicles being built.

Configured for the export market, the 105-mm Rooikat has been built in prototype form only. Development was completed in 1997 and the turret has been offered for installation on other tracked and wheeled vehicles.

Eland Armoured car

Anxious to update its armed forces' armoured vehicle fleet, late in 1961 the South African government concluded a contract for 100 Panhard AML 4x4 armoured cars (the **Eland Mk 1**) and, in the following year, a licence to manufacture the design locally as the **Eland Mk 2**. Some 1,300 vehicles were manufactured by Sandrock-Austral (now Vickers OMC), late production vehicles having 95 per cent local content and South African engines.

There were two main types of Eland; the **Eland 60** with a turret-mounted 60-mm (2.36-in) gun-mortar and the **Eland 90** with a Giat 90-mm (3.54-in) DEFA gun. Both armament types and their ammunition were licence-made in South Africa, the 90-mm rounds being fin-stabilised. Both vehicles could also have a locally developed 7.62-mm (0.3-in) co-axial machine-gun, with another

Light and handy, the Eland 90 is also well armed but suffers from poor protection, a comparatively cramped interior and limited cross-country mobility.

on the turret roof. In addition, two 81-mm (3.2-in) smoke grenade launchers were provided. Apart from their armament, the two basic vehicles were the same, but during their manufacturing life numerous design detail changes were introduced to suit local conditions and preferences.

For instance, the first four marks were powered by Panhard petrol engines characterised by steadily increasing power. The **Eland Mk 5** introduced a South African 2.4-litre diesel engine developing 77 kW (103 hp), together with a locally developed engine access arrangement that allowed the engine and cooling system to

slide out on rails for maintenance and repair. Eland production ended in 1975, but the production lines were kept busy rebuilding the earlier marks up to Eland Mk 5 standard. Over 1,000 vehicles were updated, resulting in the **Eland Mk 6**. The final variant was the **Eland Mk 7** with local extras such as more powerful brakes, a larger fresh water tank and changes to the commander's cupola vision devices.

There was also a more powerful diesel-engined model produced for export (possibly to the Congo) as the **Eland Mk 7 DT**. Another export model option was the installation of a 20-mm cannon in place of the

usual main armament: this was a variant delivered to Morocco. Other Eland vehicles were exported to Malawi and Zimbabwe.

Elands of all marks saw extensive action, mainly in the light reconnaissance role, in the course of South Africa's various border campaigns with its northern neighbours. By the end of the 1990s nearly all of the vehicles had been phased out of service as they were gradually replaced by the more powerful and better-armed Rooikat 8x8 reconnaissance vehicle. At least 120 of the phased-out vehicles were sold to a Belgian concern for resale to an unspecified South American state.

While the Eland 60 carries 54 60-mm (2.36-in) mortar rounds, the Eland 90 has accommodation for just 29 90-mm (3.54-in) rounds fired from an unstabilised gun.

SPECIFICATION	
Eland 90 Mk 5	
Crew: 3	**Performance:** maximum road speed 85 km/h (53 mph); road range about 450 km (280 miles)
Weight: 6000 kg (13,228 lb)	
Dimensions: length overall 5.12 m (16 ft 9½ in); width 2.015 m (6 ft 7⅓ in); height 2.5 m (8 ft 2½ in)	**Fording:** 0.615 m (2 ft)
	Gradient: 51 per cent
	Vertical obstacle: 0.3 m (12 in)
Powerplant: one 4-cylinder diesel developing 77 kW (103 hp)	**Trench:** 0.5 m (1 ft 8 in)

VEC Cavalry scout vehicle

VEC stands for **Vehiculo de Exploration de Caballeria** (cavalry scout vehicle) and was designed by Santa Barbara Sistemas (now owned by General Dynamics of the US). The first prototypes appeared during 1977. The VEC shares many components with the BMR-600 infantry combat

vehicle, also from Santa Barbara. VEC production was undertaken for the Spanish army, which received 340 units. Despite extensive marketing, including the offer of several specialised variants such as an air-defence vehicle, no export sales were secured. The VEC is no longer made, but production

could be restarted on the receipt of further orders.

Three main types of VEC can be encountered. The first 32 production examples had the Italian TC20 Type 6616 armoured car turret armed with a 20-mm Rheinmetall Rh 202 cannon. Then followed 100 examples armed with the Panhard H90

turret (taken from Panhard AML-90 armoured cars as they were withdrawn from Spanish service) armed with a Giat 90-mm (3.54-in) DEFA gun to provide direct fire support during scouting missions. The remaining 208 late production units were fitted with an Italian Otobreda turret armed with a

25-mm Boeing M242 Chain Gun and 7.62-mm (0.3-in) co-axial machine-gun. All three turret types are fitted centrally between the first and second axles, and may be equipped with external smoke grenade launchers. All six wheels have independent hydro-pneumatic suspension.

The VEC has a 6x6 drive configuration and is protected by aluminium armour. From 1996 onwards the original Pegaso diesel engine was gradually replaced by a Swedish Scania diesel unit produced in Spain under licence. Both engines deliver 231 kW (310 hp), and the re-engined vehicles have the designation **VEC 2**. Other changes incorporated at the same time

included an increased level of armoured protection and enlarged external stowage capacity.

Of the five-man crew, two are located in the turret, and the others are the driver and two observers provided with periscopes, one located at the right rear of the vehicle. An NBC system is optional, as is the rendering of the VEC fully amphibious by the installation of a sealing kit, a trim vane and two rear-mounted waterjet units. Even if the waterjets are not fitted, the VEC can be propelled by its wheels, albeit at much lower speeds. Further options include an air-conditioning and a recovery winch. Also on offer is a land navigation system.

Above: One of the VEC's three turret options is the Otobreda TC25 carrying a 25-mm Chain Gun cannon with 170 rounds and a 7.62-mm (0.3-in) co-axial machine-gun with 250 rounds.

Below: The VEC has good cross-country mobility, and can be made fully amphibious with a kit that can also add waterjet propulsion.

SPECIFICATION

VEC 2
Crew: 5
Weight: 13750 kg (30,313 lb)
Dimensions: length overall 6.1 m (20 ft); width 2.5 m (8 ft 2½ in); height 2 m (6 ft 6¾ in)
Powerplant: one Scania D9 water-cooled diesel developing 231 kW (310 hp)

Performance: maximum road speed 103 km/h (64 mph); water speed 9 km/h (5.6 mph); road range about 800 km (497 miles)
Fording: optionally amphibious
Gradient: 60 per cent
Vertical obstacle: 0.6 m (2 ft)
Trench: 1.5 m (4 ft 11 in)

LAV-600 Armoured car

The **LAV-600** 6x6 was originally a Cadillac Gage private venture for the export market, and was known as the **V-300A1** when launched in 1985. It was renamed as the LAV-600 in

1986, and is made by Textron Marine & Land Systems. The type remains at the pre-production prototype stage even though it has been stated that development is complete.

The LAV-600 uses many automotive and other components of the Cadillac Gage LAV-300 family of combat vehicles sold to several nations. The main difference from the

LAV-300 series is that the LAV-600 is armed with a 105-mm (4.13-in) gun, as installed on the Cadillac Gage Stingray light tank type sold to the Thai army. As far as is known no export sales of the LAV-600 have yet been made, although the vehicle underwent extensive mobility and firepower testing in Egypt during 1988.

Compared with the LAV-300 series, the provision of the Stingray turret reduces the crew to four, three of them in the armoured steel turret. The gun is produced by British Aerospace, Royal Ordnance Defence, as its 105-mm Low Recoil Force lightweight gun, and is capable of firing all NATO standard 105-mm tank gun ammunition with no loss of armour penetration or other ballistic performance. Only eight

The LAV-600 has good mobility and performance, and carries the Stingray light tank turret with a 105-mm (4.13-in) Low Recoil Force main gun, co-axial machine-gun, and roof-mounted machine-gun for local and AA defence.

105-mm rounds are carried in the turret, the remaining 28 rounds being carried in the hull. The replenishment of the ammunition is effected through two doors in the hull rear. There are also a 7.62-mm (0.3-in) co-axial machine-gun and a 7.62-mm or 0.5-in (12.7-mm) machine-gun on the turret roof. Fire control is provided by a computerised system closely related to that employed by the M1 Abrams tank, complete with a night vision capability. Two banks of four smoke

grenade launchers (one on each side of the turret) are an optional extra, and a laser warning system can also be fitted.

A wide range of other optional equipment is available according to customer requirements. These include an NBC protection system and a chemical-resistant paint finish to assist decontamination, night driving lights, and an automatic fire-suppression system for the engine compartment. Run-flat inserts can be supplied for all

six wheels, as can a central tyre pressure-regulation system. This last enables the driver to vary the tyre pressure to suit the type of terrain being traversed. A 9000-kg (19,841-lb)

capacity self-recovery winch is fitted as standard, as is an engine-driven air compressor.

The suspension is based on front coil springs and rear torsion bars.

SPECIFICATION	
LAV-600	
Crew: 4	**Performance:** maximum road speed 100 km/h (62 mph); road range about 600 km (373 miles)
Weight: 18500 kg (40,785 lb)	**Fording:** not available
Dimensions: hull 6.3 m (20 ft 8 in); width 2.667 m (8 ft 9 in); height 2.74 m (9 ft)	**Gradient:** 60 per cent
	Vertical obstacle: 0.61 m (3 ft)
Powerplant: one Cummins 6CTA 8.3-litre 6-cylinder inline diesel developing 205 kW (275 hp)	**Trench:** not available

LAV-105 Light armoured vehicle

The **LAV-105** light armoured vehicle has undergone a somewhat varied development career dating back to 1988. At that time the US Marine Corps had a requirement for 130 LAV-AGs (Light Armoured Vehicles - Assault Guns) armed with a 105-mm (4.13-in) lightweight gun in a two-man turret. The gun was to be mounted on a suitably modified variant of the LAV 8x8 family, based around an armoured personnel carrier produced by the Diesel Division, General Motors of Canada (now General Motors Defense). The LAV family is based upon the Swiss Mowag Piranha 8x8 amphibious chassis.

Cadillac Gage was awarded a contract to produce the turret,

The all-welded hull of the LAV-105 is basically that of the 8x8 LAV armoured personnel carrier, and carries a two-man welded steel turret over its rear.

The LAV-105's turret carries a 105-mm (4.13-in) low-recoil gun and two 7.62-mm (0.3-in) machine-guns (one co-axial and the other on the roof).

which was to be armed with a 105-mm XM35 (now M35) lightweight gun developed by the Watervliet Arsenal and characterised by recoil forces 40 per cent less than those produced by conventional 105-mm tank guns. The provision of an auto-loading system, holding eight ready-use rounds, in the turret bustle meant that no loader was necessary, the only other member of the crew of three being the driver. Even so, the weight of the turret and gun meant that extra buoyancy measures had to be provided.

Before the three prototypes were fully developed the USMC was forced to cancel the programme for purely financial provisions reasons during 1991. During 1993 some funds were released to allow development and testing of the three prototypes to be completed, and there the programme rested for some time. Eventually Textron Marine & Land Systems (formerly Cadillac Gage) leased back the three prototypes as demonstrators for an export sales drive. There were no immediate results from this marketing effort. By 2002 the LAV-105 was once again under active consideration by the US, however, in this instance for possible procurement for the US Army's new BCTs (Brigade

Combat Teams). In the event this requirement was met by the Stryker Mobile Gun System, also with a 105-mm gun.

Although the 105-mm M35 lightweight gun can fire the full array of NATO standard tank gun ammunition, including kinetic-energy armour-penetration projectiles, its main function is to act as a direct fire support platform. For this role the gunner is provided with a General Dynamics Canada fire-control system incorporating a day or night ranging sight and capable of engaging moving targets. The commander is provided with a video monitor to observe gunnery proceedings so that he can override fire missions and select new targets as this becomes necessary.

SPECIFICATION	
LAV-105	
Crew: 3	**Performance:** maximum road speed 100 km/h (62 mph); water speed 9.65 km/h (6 mph); road range about 668 km (415 miles)
Weight: 13864 kg (30,565 lb)	**Fording:** amphibious
Dimensions: length overall 7.835 m (25 ft 8½ in); width 2.49 m (8 ft 2 in); 2.625 m (8 ft 7⅓ in)	**Gradient:** 60 per cent
	Vertical obstacle: 0.5 m (1 ft 8 in)
Powerplant: one Detroit Diesel 6V-53T 6-cylinder diesel developing 205 kW (275 hp)	**Trench:** 2.057 m (6 ft 9 in)

MOWAG Piranha IIIC Armoured combat vehicle

Based on its experience in the design, development and production of the Piranha family of 8x8 light armoured vehicles, the MOWAG company decided in the early 1990s to start the development of a larger **Piranha IIIC** 10x10 model.

By comparison with the Piranha 8x8, the 10x10 model has greater volume and a heavier payload capability, which allow it to undertake a much wider range of operational roles. When used as a weapons platform, for example, it can be fitted with various turrets and weapon stations up to a three-person turret armed with a stabilised 105-mm (4.13-in) gun coupled to a computerised fire-control system.

By 2003 the only customer for the Piranha IIIC was Sweden, which originally ordered a batch for use as command post vehicles for its coastal artillery units. Sweden then decided to use the vehicle as a platform for air- and coast-defence radars with their antennae on a scissors-type hydraulic arm. For greater stability, four stabilisers are hydraulically lowered to the ground before the arm is raised.

To provide greater working space for the crew, the roof line behind the driver's and commander's position has been raised. The vehicle is also fitted with an integrated auxiliary power unit, which allows all of the electronic devices onboard to be powered with the main engine off. As usual with a vehicle of this type, a wide range of optional equipment can be fitted to customer requirement.

Some of Sweden's Piranha IIIC vehicles are operated in the radar-carrying role, the antennae being elevated on a hydraulically powered arm to lengthen the radar's search range. Outriggers provide stability on the ground.

The 10x10 Piranha III has been trialled in a number of forms. This is a weapon platform with the Giat TML 105 turret armed with a 105-mm (4.13-in) stabilised gun. A 40-mm gun turret has also been evaluated.

SPECIFICATION	
MOWAG Piranha IIIC ACV (with 105-mm turret)	**Powerplant:** one Detroit Diesel or Scania water-cooled diesel engine
Crew: 1 + 3	**Performance:** maximum road speed 100 km/h (62 mph); maximum range 800 km (497 miles)
Weight: 18000 kg (39,683 lb)	
Dimensions: length (hull) 7.45 m (24 ft 5⅓ in); width 2.6 m (8 ft 6⅓ in); height 2.99 m (9 ft 9¾ in)	**Fording:** 2 m (6 ft 7 in)
	Gradient: 60 per cent
	Trench: 2 m (6 ft 7 in)

MOWAG SPY & Eagle Reconnaissance vehicles

Although it is known mainly for its highly successful Piranha series of 6x6, 8x8 and 10x10 light armoured vehicles, the Swiss company MOWAG (later bought by the Diesel Division of General Motors of Canada, which was then incorporated into General Motors Defense of the US) has also developed and placed in production a number of 4x4 reconnaissance vehicles including the **SPY** and more recently the **Eagle**.

MOWAG developed the SPY during the late 1970s, and this type was purchased by only one undisclosed customer in Asia. The vehicle has an all-welded hull of steel armour, and carries a crew of three. The vehicle can be fitted with any of several turrets or remotely controlled weapon stations armed with a machine-gun or a cannon.

The more recent Eagle is based on the US AM General High Mobility Multi Purpose Wheeled Vehicle (HMMWV) chassis fitted with an armoured body that protects the occupants from small arms fire and anti-personnel mines.

The Swiss army has received 154 **Eagle I** and 175 slightly

The artillery observation post variant of the Eagle series derives its capability from a mast-mounted pod carrying a TV camera, IR imaging system and laser rangefinder.

upgraded **Eagle II** vehicles fitted with a one-man turret carrying a 7.62-mm (0.3-in) machine gun and a day/night sight. Denmark has received 36 Eagle I vehicles.

In production for the Swiss army in 2003 was the **Eagle III** artillery observation vehicle with a mast-mounted sensor pod that contains a day camera, thermal camera and laser rangefinder. This is coupled to

an onboard land navigation system. Targets can be rapidly detected and target information

passed onto the artillery for accurate and devastating engagement.

SPECIFICATION	
MOWAG Eagle I	cooled V-8 diesel coupled to an
Crew: 1 + 3	automatic transmission and two-speed transfer case
Weight: 5100 kg (11,243 lb)	**Performance:** maximum road speed
Dimensions: length 4.9 m (16 ft 1 in); width 2.28 m (7 ft 6 in); height 1.75 m (5 ft 9 in)	125 km/h (78 mph; maximum range 450 km (280 miles)
Powerplant: one 119-kW (160 hp) General Motors Type 6.5 water-	**Fording:** 0.76 m (2 ft 6 in) **Gradient:** 60 per cent

This SPY reconnaissance vehicle has a MOWAG one-man turret carrying an external 7.62-mm (0.3-in) machine-gun.

Alvis Vickers Scarab Reconnaissance vehicle

Based on its very extensive experience in the design, development and production of light tracked and wheeled armoured fighting vehicles, the Alvis company (now Alvis Vickers) in the mid-1990s developed the **Scarab** light armoured vehicle.

Reconnaissance role

The Scarab was created primarily for the reconnaissance role, and in keeping with the requirements of this specialised task features a high level of cross-country mobility, high speed, a low profile and a suite of advanced reconnaissance equipment. The Scarab's hull is fabricated of all-welded steel armour, and to this can be attached additional armour for the provision of a higher level of protection.

The driver is seated at the front of the vehicle with excellent fields of vision over the frontal arc. The other two members of the three-man crew, typically the commander and the weapons operator, are seated in the middle of the vehicle with the diesel powerpack (diesel engine and Allison six-speed automatic gearbox with torque converter) to their rear.

SWARM

For trials purposes the Scarab has been fitted with the Thales AFV Systems SWARM (Stabilised Weapon And Reconnaissance Mount) armed with a 0.5-in (12.7-mm) M2 machine-gun. This weapon is aimed and fired from under armour protection by the gunner, who uses an advanced day/night optical suite incorporating day and thermal cameras, an eye-safe laser rangefinder and, below these, electrically operated launchers for smoke grenades.

As well as being used as a reconnaissance vehicle, for which a remotely controlled and

Fast, agile and well protected for a vehicle of its class, the Scarab has a roof hatch for each member of the vehicle's standard three-man crew, although up to five men can be carried. This vehicle is armed with a roof-mounted machine-gun.

elevating mast-mounted sight system (day and thermal cameras supplemented by a laser rangefinder) is offered as the primary equipment, the Scarab can be outfitted for the utility role fitted with a variety of heavier weapons 2nd cannon, 40-mm grenade launchers, and anti-tank guided missiles.

The Scarab is also fitted with a navigation and battle management system allowing it

to make real-time detailed reports on threats.

Development of the Scarab was completed in 2001, but as

of late 2003 quantity production had yet to start even though the type has been demonstrated to several countries.

SPECIFICATION	
Alvis Vickers Scarab	diesel developing 179 kW (240 hp)
Crew: 1 + 2	**Performance:** maximum road speed
Weight: 10000 kg (22,046 lb)	110 km/h (68 mph); maximum
Dimensions: length 5.283 m (17 ft 4	range 600 km (373 miles)
in); width 2.405 m (7 ft 10½ in);	**Fording:** 1.1 m (3 ft 7 in)
height 1.95 m (6 ft 5¾ in)	**Gradient:** 100 per cent
Powerplant: one Mercedes-Benz	
OM906 water-cooled 6-cylinder	

The Scarab has a single door in each side, and the reconnaissance sensors are carried in a mast-mounted pod.

RG-32 Scout General-purpose patrol vehicle

An RG-32M seen here on trials with the British Army. It is fitted with an observation system mounted on top of its roof.

The **RG-32 Scout** patrol vehicle was originally developed to provide a commercial vehicle that came somewhere between a partially armoured security vehicle and the expensive, large and heavy bullion or high-value cargo carriers. The first example of the Scout resembled a bulky commercial saloon car, complete with bulletproof side windows, but gradually evolved into the armoured general-purpose patrol vehicle and personnel or weapon carrier, now in service with numerous military and para-military organisations. Small numbers of the Scout have been sold to purely civilian organisations to carry high-value cargoes or personnel in troubled or mine-infested areas.

The Scout has been produced in both petrol- and diesel-engined forms. A closely related vehicle, the slightly larger **RG-31 Nyala** (Charger), is configured as a lightly-armoured and mine-hardened personnel carrier with a crew of two and seating for up to 10 passengers.

The first RG-32 Scout was developed during the early 1990s by what was then TFM Defence and Security Division. Since then several corporate changes have resulted in that concern becoming Alvis OMC who continue to market the Scout in several forms from their headquarters in Benoni.

The RG-32 Scout in its present form was first manufactured in 1998 and since then well over 730 examples for over 12 countries have been built, with large orders coming from the United Nations (UN), numerous police forces around southern Africa and even the US Army which obtained two for patrol duties in Kosovo. The UN order was for over 160 four-door vehicles to be deployed in some of their more dangerous areas of operation, such as the Balkans.

FCLV

The military version of the RG32 Scout is the **RG-32M**, first

Not dissimilar in appearance to a civilian sports recreation vehicle, the RG-32 has been popular with organisations working in troubled areas.

Seen here with a mortar system mounted towards the rear of the vehicle, this RG-32M is pictured in bush camouflage.

shown in 2001; there is also a **RG-31M** Nyala. Two examples of the RG-32M have undergone trials for the British Army's requirement for their Future Command and Liaison Vehicle (FCLV). The FCLV model is typical of the many military or para-military forms of the Scout in that it is a 4x4 vehicle (some models of the Scout have a 4x2 drive configuration) and has a fully armoured body. The body armour can withstand rifle calibre armour-piercing bullets coming from all directions and is mine hardened, being capable of protecting the occupants against the blast effects of most anti-tank mines. The windscreen and other vision panels provide protection against rifle-calibre bullets.

Should a customer require a higher level of protection, extra steel or ceramic armoured panels can be provided and further provision can be made against land mines. Up to three fully-loaded RG-32M vehicles can be carried in a C-130 Hercules transport aircraft.

Stowage space

The RG-32M has a payload of one tonne and space is available

for the driver and up to six passengers (five being more typical), plus stowage space and bins for the occupants' equipment and provisions to last through a 48-hour mission. Numerous internal configurations can be adopted, a typical example being a mobile command or communications post but the most widely used layout is as a light patrol vehicle. Provision can be made in the body walls for weapon stations or vision ports. A roof hatch is usually provided on the RG-32M, with provision for mounting a weapon, such as a machine-gun, under manual or remote control. A standard accessory is an electrically-driven self-recovery winch with a capacity of 4000 kg (8,818 lb).

The RG-32M can also be configured as a weapons carrier, usually in 4x4 form and with larger wheels. In this role the area behind the armoured cab is an open flat bed for numerous types of weapon. To date, weapon installations have included a 12-barrel 107-mm (4.2-in) rocket launcher, a standard or long-range 60-mm (2.3-in) mortar, a 106-mm (4.17-in) recoilless rifle, a 20-mm

(0.7-in) cannon and various forms of anti-tank missile launchers.

Tyre inflation

While the RG-32MS is intended for the Middle East market and thus has air-conditioning and other provisions for hot weather operations, there is also a kit available for very cold operational conditions. To assist traction across soft terrain the driver can be provided with a manually-operated central tyre inflation system, while run-flat inserts can be added to the tyres. Although a strong conventional leaf spring suspension is usually provided, a coil spring suspension option is available.

During late 2001 a more streamlined version with a muted military appearance was unveiled as the Scout 2. Intended primarily for the

paramilitary market, the diesel-engined Scout 2 is available as a mine-hardened patrol vehicle or as a more general-purpose personnel or supply carrier.

To keep unit and maintenance costs to a minimum, the RG-32M makes extensive use of commercial components, a typical installation being a Mercedes-Benz diesel engine and drive train, with strengthened beam axles to bear the extra weights. Left- or right-hand powered steering is provided to assist the driver, while an automatic transmission is optional. A conventional chassis is not provided as the all-welded armoured steel body acts as the load-bearing structure and attachment point for the various vehicle sub-assemblies, greatly extending the life of the vehicle compared with conventional construction methods.

SPECIFICATION	
RG-32M Scout	**Max road speed:** 120 km/h (74 mph)
Crew: up to 6	**Powerplant:** 600 km (372 miles)
Configuration: 4x4	**Engine (typical):** diesel developing
Combat weight: 4600 kg (10,141 lb)	110 kW (148 hp) at 2,000 rpm
Length overall: 4.6 m (15 ft)	**Transmission:** automatic
Width: 1.8 m (5 ft 10 in)	**Steering:** power assisted
Height: 1.91 m (6 ft 2 in)	**Electrical system:** 12 or 24 volt
Wheelbase: 3.05 m (10 ft)	**Armament:** to customer
Ground clearance: 200 mm (7.8 in)	requirements

Between 1989 and 1992 the German army took delivery of 345 **Wiesel 1** (Weasel 1) armoured weapon carriers, armed with a 20-mm (0.7-in) cannon or TOW anti-tank guided missiles. These vehicles were deployed in the light reconnaissance or tank-killer roles. During the late 1990s some Wiesel 1s were converted to the battlefield reconnaissance role by the removal of the armament which was replaced by a telescopic mast carrying

sensors such as day and night video cameras. The small size of the Wiesel 1 prevented it being adapted for other roles but what is now Rheinmetall Landsysteme perceived that a slightly larger version of the vehicle could be converted into a helicopter-portable and versatile multi-purpose carrier. The result was the **Wiesel 2**.

By lengthening the hull and adding an extra road wheel each side, the Wiesel 2 gained internal space and a higher

payload. The prototype was completed during mid-1994 and since 1998 it has been delivered to the German army. Despite demonstrations held in several other nations, no export sales have yet been announced.

The first Wiesel 2 was configured as a light armoured personnel carrier, the crew being the commander and driver, with seating for a four-man half squad of infantry. In an armoured vehicle weighing only 4100 kg (9,038 lb), the armoured protection is light although tactical mobility is high – a CH-53G helicopter can carry two vehicles. The light weight also produces a very low ground pressure so the vehicle can go where many others cannot.

Ambulance

The Wiesel 2 personnel carrier was not adopted by the German army so it evolved into a multi-

purpose carrier. One of the first versions was as a front-line ambulance capable of carrying the driver and a medical attendant plus two seated casualties or a single stretcher. The German army ordered 20 of this model.

Around the same time the Wiesel 2 was selected as the basis for the Atlas Short Range Air Defence (ASRAD) low-level air defence system based on the Stinger ground-to-air missile. This system is known to the German army as the LeFlaSys. The electronic command and control section of the system uses three Wiesel 2 versions. The most numerous is a launch vehicle known as the Ozelot (Ocelot) with a retractable launcher mast for four Stinger missiles. The launcher can also be used with the former East German army Igla missiles during training. A platoon command Wiesel 2 carries a target detection and tracking radar while a further Wiesel 2 variant is employed as a battery commander's vehicle with extra communications equipment. The German Army has 50 Ozelot launch vehicles, 10 platoon command vehicles and seven battalion command vehicles.

Combat role

The Wiesel 2 was also developed in combat engineer reconnaissance form to support airborne formations, and as a command and control vehicle with a raised roof to provide more internal space to accommodate additional radio and other command equipment. The latter is also intended for airborne forces. There is also an ammunition carrier intended primarily to support the Wiesel 1 weapon carriers still in service with the German army. This carrier has a 1000-kg (2,294-lb) payload.

A prototype of a self-propelled 120-mm (4.7-in) mortar on a surplus Wiesel 1 chassis

SPECIFICATION	
Base Wiesel 2	**Ground clearance:** 300 mm (11 in)
Crew: up to 6	**Max road speed:** 70 km/h (43 mph)
Combat weight: 4100 kg (9,038 lb)	**Road range:** 550 km (341 miles)
Length, overall: 4.2 m (13 ft)	**Engine:** Diesel developing 81 kW
Width, overall: 1.852 m (6 ft)	(109 hp)
Height: 1.7–2.11 m (5 ft 6 in–6 ft	**Main armament:** according to model
10 in), according to model	**Secondary armament:** 1 x 7.62-mm
	(0.3-in) MG3 machine-gun

The small size of the Wiesel is indicated here by the comparative size of the troops on top of the vehicle.

A graphic display of the air-portability of the Wiesel as it is seen here driving past Luftwaffe C-160 Transall aircraft. The vehicle is also air-portable via helicopter.

has also been developed as the German army has expressed a requirement for about 65 such vehicles, later enlarged to 94. During transport the mortar is carried over the top of the carrier vehicle. For firing, the smooth-bore mortar barrel is pivoted at the rear and is lowered to the upright position for firing. After firing, the barrel resumes the horizontal position for muzzle reloading from within the carrier hull. The prototype of this mortar carrier was trialled during 1997. It is anticipated that two further pre-production prototypes based on the Wiesel 2 chassis will be manufactured by Rheinmetall Landsysteme during 2004 before the series production run begins. Rheinmetall also supplies the mortar.

The Wiesel 2 has also been used as an experimental platform for several advanced concepts. One is known as the ARGUS and is an air transportable armoured surveillance and reconnaissance vehicle which can carry a suite of battlefield sensors developed by STN Atlas Elektronik, some of them mounted upon a telescopic mast.

Robotic control

Wiesel 2 chassis have been used as experimental platforms for at least two robotic control systems where no personnel actually travel in the carrier vehicle. One is the German Programme for Intelligent Mobile Unmanned Systems (PRIMUS), with a second Wiesel 2 as the control vehicle. A Wiesel 2 is also used as a technology demonstrator for the essentially similar French Syrano remote control project.

Further Wiesel 2 test platforms have investigated digitally controlled drive-by-wire control systems, and the employment of all-electric drive and control systems. A light armoured recovery vehicle based on the Wiesel 2 was proposed, but it has not appeared. A NBC reconnaissance variant has also been proposed, but has not yet reached prototype stage.

A Wiesel pictured with a TOW anti-tank missile launcher mounted on top of the hull. This gives the vehicle significant tank-killing ability.

The Modern Era

New technology has revolutionised armoured vehicle design. Most modern tanks are armed with smoothbore cannon. Rifled guns are inherently more accurate, but smoothbore guns can fire fin-stabilised rounds at a higher pressure, which means greater velocity and greater penetration. Protection has been improved by the use of incredibly tough composite armour made from layered laminates of plastics, ceramics, steel and exotic but very dense metals like depleted uranium.

As a result, tank weights have increased dramatically, but developments in engine technology have more than compensated for the increase. Multi-fuel diesels or gas turbines now deliver up to 1500 horsepower, which is enough to drive a 60-tonne tank at more than 70 kilometres per hour on roads. Sophisticated suspension systems make them almost as fast across country. Similar improvements have enhanced the capabilities of other armoured fighting vehicles, which are tougher, more mobile and more effectively armed than they have ever been before.

Left: Since 1945 the tank has been joined by a wide variety of other armoured vehicles, with troop carriers probably being the most numerous. The original, fairly simple armoured personnel carrier has been supplemented by infantry fighting vehicles like the M2 Bradley, which are more heavily armed and armoured than their predecessors.

Types 59/69 Main Battle Tanks

In the early 1950s China was supplied with a quantity of Soviet T-54 main battle tanks. These were used as a basis for a Chinese-built tank, the **Type 59**, which entered service in the 1950s. The original model is a straight copy of the T-54, armed with a 100-mm (3¾-in) rifled gun as its main armament.

Modernised

Most People's Liberation Army (PLA) equipment is based on Soviet designs of the 1950s, but many of its main weapons have been substantially upgraded, often utilising Western technology. The **Type 59II** is an upgraded version of the original tank, incorporating several Western improvements into the basic vehicle. The main improvement is in fitting a rifled 105-mm (4-in) gun based on the long-serving and highly effective British L7. Stabilised in both planes, it gives the Type 59 a major increase in striking power.

Iran has developed an upgraded variant of the Type 59 which has a broad range of Western and Soviet upgrades to fire-control, protection and main gun.

First seen in public in 1982, the **Type 69** main battle tank is a modified Type 59, roughly equivalent to the Soviet T-55.

It is a relatively inexpensive and easy to operate tank but it is of an outdated design by modern standards. The interior is cramped and can be difficult to operate in. The 36-ton Type 69 main battle tank has improved armour, a gun stabiliser, a fire control system including a laser range finder, infra-red search-lights, and a 105-mm smooth-bore gun.

The **Type 69II MBT Command Tank Type B** is fitted with additional radio sets for the command and control function at Regimental level.

At least 6,000 Type 59 and 59II MBTs served in the PLA and many will remain in service until China decides on a next-generation tank. A new GEC-Marconi Centaur fire control system is available, and British Barr and Stroud thermal based FCS (fire control system) can also be fitted.

Worldwide use

Type 59 and Type 69 MBTs have seen combat all over the world. Operators include Vietnam, Cambodia, North Korea and Pakistan (more than 1,300). Chinese Type 59s were also sold or given to Albania, Bangladesh, the Congo, Tanzania, and Zimbabwe. Type 69 tanks saw combat with both sides during the Iran-Iraq war; with the Iraqi Army in the 1991 Gulf War and by the Sri Lankan Army.

Over 6,000 Type 59 and Type 69 tanks have been manufactured for the PLA. This is a Type 69II, a tank which was still in production in the late 1990s. It is equipped with a rifled 105-mm gun.

SPECIFICATION	
Type 59II	one 7.62-mm MG in ball mount on
Crew: 4	bow, one 12.7-mm (0.5-in) AA MG
Combat weight: 36 tons	on turret cupola
Dimensions: chassis length	**Powerplant:** one 380-kW (520 hp)
6.04 m/19.8 ft (9 m/29 ft 6 in with	V-12 diesel piston engine
gun forward); height 2.59 m	**Performance:** max road speed
(8 ft 6 in); width 3.27 m (10 ft 9 in)	50 km/h (31 mph); max off road
Armour: 203 mm maximum	speed 25 km/h (16 mph); range
thickness on turret front	400 km (240 miles)
Armament: one 105-mm rifled gun,	**Fording:** 5.5 m (18 ft) with snorkel
one co-axial 7.62-mm (0.3-in) MG,	**Vertical obstacle:** 0.79 m (2 ft 7 in)

A regiment of Type 69 tanks parades at a military review outside Beijing. The Type 69 is an improved Type 59; many have been upgraded with advanced fire control systems and more powerful guns.

Types 85/90 Main Battle Tanks

Although the new-generation of Chinese tanks like this Type 85 is based on the mechanical features of the ancient Soviet-era T-54, it is clear that their changed hulls, guns and turrets make them almost entirely new designs.

Although the Type 59 and Type 69 tanks have been the mainstay of Chinese tank forces for more than 40 years, they are very much products of 1940s and 1950s Soviet technology. In spite of modernisation programmes, they would stand little chance in combat against state-of-the-art Western or Russian tanks.

New tanks

In the 1980s, the Chinese began the development of a new, more competitive tank. First revealed outside China in 1987, the Type 80 MBT is a further development of the long-serving Type 59. However, the chassis has been so extensively modified it is a virtually new design.

A new welded turret mounting a new fire-control system and the standard Chinese 105-mm (4-in) gun is used in place of the cast turret of earlier tanks. The gun can fire APFSDS-T, HEAT-T, HESH, and HE (armour-piercing fin-stabilised discarding sabot-tracer, high-explosive anti-tank-tracer, high-explosive practice-tracer and high-explosive) rounds.

Production of the Type 80 began in 1988, but in 1991 it was succeeded by the further improved **Type 85**. Variants include the **Type 85IIAP** which can be produced from Type 59s and Type 69IIs using upgrade kits. The newest model, the **Type 85III** with a 746-kW (1,000-hp) engine, incorporates features also found in the latest Chinese designs. These include a larger 125-mm (43⁄4-in) smooth bore main gun capable of firing APFSDS, HEAT, and HE-FRAG (HE-fragmentation). A Soviet-style autoloader means that the crew has been reduced to three men. The Type 85III uses modular composite armour, and has been seen fitted with explosive reactive armour. A stabilised image intensification sight allows the tank to engage moving targets while in motion.

Further development has resulted in the **Type 90**, which incorporates significant improvements over the Type 85. Powered by an 895-kW (1,200 hp) eight-cylinder turbo-charged diesel, the Type 90 comes with an autoloading, smooth bore 125-mm gun capable of firing APFSDS, HEAT, and HE-FRAG rounds. The gun is mounted in a stabilised turret with passive thermal imaging. Reactive armour panels, an improved laser rangefinder, and increased mobility make the Type 90II the most advanced MBT ever built in China.

The PLA ordered 100 Type 90IIs to be delivered in 1999. Completed without fire-control systems, their main purpose was to take part in parades celebrating the 50th anniversary of the People's Republic of China.

SPECIFICATION	
Type 85IIM	**Powerplant:** one V-12 supercharged
Crew: 3	diesel delivering (544 kW) 730 hp
Combat weight: 40 tons	**Performance:** road speed 57 km/h
Dimensions: overall length 10.28 m	(35 mph); range 500 km (311
(33 ft 9 in); hull length 7.30 m (23 ft	miles)
11 in); height to turret top 2.30 m	**Fording:** 1.40 m (4 ft 7 in)
(7 ft 6 in); width 3.45 m (11 ft 4 in)	unprepared; 2.4 m (7 ft 10 in) with
Armament: one 2A46M/D-81TM	snorkel)
125-mm gun with 22 rounds in	**Vertical obstacle:** 0.80 m (2 ft 8 in)
autoloader and 23 stowed, one	**Trench:** 2.7 m (8 ft 10 in)
7.62-mm (0.3-in) co-axial MG, one	
12.7-mm (0.5-in) AA MG on turret	

Types 62/63 Light tanks

China is one of the last countries to use large numbers of light and medium tanks in a non-reconnaissance combat role. The diminutive 21-ton **Type 62** is classed as a medium tank. Obviously based on the Type 59, it resembles a scaled-down version of the main battle tank. The cast and welded Type 62 turret is slightly smaller, but it has nearly identical hatches and fittings. Similarly, the wheels and tracks resemble smaller

and lighter copies of those used on the Type 59.

The Type 62 mounts an 85-mm (3.25-in) gun. Its armour protection is limited, offering little resistance to modern anti-tank munitions. North Korea has manufactured a Type 62 variant armed with a 115-mm (4.5-in) main gun.

Amphibian

The **Type 63** light tank was an attempt to get near-MBT

firepower onto a light, amphibious chassis. It uses the

same turret and 85-mm gun as the Type 62, mounted on a

SPECIFICATION	
Type 62	(0.5-in) AA MG, two 7.62-mm
Crew: 4	(0.3-in) MGs
Weight: 21 tons	**Powerplant:** one 321-kW (430 hp)
Dimensions: length gun forwards	diesel engine
7.90 m (25 ft 11 in); hull 5.55 m	**Performance:** maximum road speed
(18 ft ½ in); height 2.25 m	50 km/h (31 mph); range 450 km
(7 ft 4½ in); width 2.86 m	(280 miles);
(9 ft 4½ in)	**Fording:** 1.40 m (4 ft 7 in)
Armour: 15- to 100-mm hull;	**Vertical obstacle:** 0.70 m (2 ft 3½
200-mm turret front	in)
Armament: one 85-mm (3¼-in)	**Trench:** 2.55 m (8 ft 4½ in)
smooth bore gun, one 12.7-mm	

Chinese/Russian hybrid
Although the hull design of the Type 63 is based on that of the Soviet PT-76, its automotive components are adapted from the indigenous Chinese Type 77 armoured personnel carrier.

The Type 63 is fully amphibious. It is propelled in the water to a maximum of 12 km/h (7.5 mph) by two water jets mounted to the rear.

Chinese copy of the Soviet PT-76 light amphibious tank hull. The Chinese version has higher sides, a nearly horizontal front glacis plate and different engine grilles. There are three vertical slot side inlets on the Type 63, in contrast to the single inlet on the PT-76.

Obsolete and vulnerable to advanced anti-tank munitions, the Type 62 tank has largely been relegated to secondary defence and training, though it remains in service with the PLA in large numbers. Type 63 tanks by contrast are very much in the front-line, deployed with PLA Navy Marine units. Both were supplied to regular Chinese customers in Africa and Asia, and both saw combat service with the North Vietnamese at the end of the Vietnam War.

A Type 63 lays its own smokescreen by injecting diesel fuel into the exhaust.

Light battle tank
In essence a scaled-down Type 59 MBT, the Type 62 light/medium tank was designed for use in rugged terrain not suitable for heavier armour. Although not currently being manufactured, production can be restarted as and when required.

Layout of the Type 62 is identical to the Type 59. The driver is seated front left, the three-man turret is centred (commander and gunner left, loader right) and the engine and transmission are to the rear.

Type 80 Main battle tank

The Chinese **Type 80** main battle tank is based on design studies that began during 1978. It differs from its predecessor, the Type 69, mainly in its armament, fire control and automotive improvements; at one point the project was known as the **Type 69-III**. The main developer and manufacturer was Norinco (China North Industries Corporation), which began production late in 1988 at its Factory No. 617. Over 500 were manufactured for the People's Liberation Army, and about 20 were exported to Myanmar (Burma). Despite extensive marketing campaigns, no further export sales were accomplished. Production was completed some years ago.

The Type 80 is armed with a 105-mm (4.13-in) rifled gun closely related to the NATO M68/L7 gun so it can fire both NATO- and Chinese- produced ammunition, including the latest generation of high-performance APFSDS types; 44 rounds are carried. The gun is used with stabilisation and computer-based fire-control systems (the latter with a laser range-finder), which impart a high first-round hit probability, although firing against moving targets has to be carried out from a stationary position. Image-intensifying night vision and driving systems are standard. A new torsion-bar suspension was introduced, and a new diesel engine provides more power. Early examples had a 520-kW (697-hp) engine, but later models had an engine

By comparison with the Type 69 MBT, the Type 80 has a 105-mm (4.13-in) rifled gun with stabilisation and a moderately advanced fire-control system, more power and new torsion-bar suspension.

uprated to 540 kW (731 hp). A snorkel is an optional extra for fording deep water. In addition a complete NBC protection system was incorporated as standard. As with the Type 69, extra range can be achieved by adding two fuel tanks over the rear of the vehicle, and these can be jettisoned when necessary. Another mobility-enhancement device, carried as standard, is an unditching beam. Extra kit and equipment can be carried in a turret bustle that also acts as stand-off protection for the turret rear.

An enhanced fire-control computer system was introduced on the **Type 80-II** model, known to the People's Liberation Army as the **Type 88B**. For this variant the transmission's former manually controlled gearbox

was replaced by a semi-automatic system. The new fire-control system can be retro-installed in the standard Type 80. Also installed on the updated model were new and improved radios. The Type 80-II's weight is increased to 38500kg (84,877lb).

The secondary armament on all Type 80 models is a 7.62-mm (0.3-in) co-axial machine-gun, and a roof-mounted 12.7-mm (0.5-in) machine-gun is fitted for local and air defence. Also provided are eight smoke discharger projectors, four on each side of the turret.

Among the items available to the Type 80 for enhanced battlefield range and mobility are jettisonable fuel tanks, an unditching beam and a snorkel tube for the fording of deep water obstacles.

SPECIFICATION	
Type 80	**Performance:** maximum road speed
Crew: 4	65 km/h (40.5 mph); range 430 km
Weight: 38000 kg (83,774 lb)	(267 miles)
Dimensions: length (overall) 9.33 m	**Fording:** 1.4 m (4 ft 6 in) without
(30 ft 6 in) and (hull) 6.33 m (20 ft 8	preparation and 5 m (16 ft 5 in)
in); width 3.33 m (11 ft 1 in); height	with snorkel
2.29 m (7 ft 5 in) to the turret roof	**Gradient:** 60 per cent
Powerplant: one Model VR36 water-	**Vertical obstacle:** 0.8 m (2 ft 8 in)
cooled diesel developing 540 kW	**Trench:** 2.7 m (8 ft 10 in)
(731 hp)	

Type 98 Main battle tank

The **Type 98** main battle tank is the latest known Chinese tank from Norinco, first seen during 1999 although it entered service with the People's Liberation Army during 1998. It is an updated and generally improved version of the earlier Type 90, a vehicle based along the same general lines as the Soviet/Russian T-72 and developed specifically for export sales. The only known customer for the Type 90 is Pakistan, where it is made under licence as the **Khalid** or **MBT-2000**. At one time the Type 98 was known as the **Type 90-III** (industrial designation **WZ 123**).

Although many of its details have yet to be confirmed, the Type 98 appears to be an amalgam of several recent armoured vehicle developments that originated outside China. For instance, the smoothbore main gun has a calibre of 125-mm (4.92 in) and is almost certainly based on the Russian D-81 gun series, complete with an autoloader holding 22 rounds of ready-to-load ammunition. The tank also has single 7.62-mm (0.3-in) co-axial and 12.7-mm (0.5-in) roof-mounted machine-guns. Although the precise nature of the diesel powerpack installed has yet to

The Type 98 is notable for its high power/weight ratio, and therefore probably possesses high performance and considerable agility. The tank is also well protected by its armour.

be confirmed, this appears to have been imported from an outside source (possibly Ukraine) and could be rated at up to 1120 kW (1,502 hp).

The fire-control system is of Chinese origin, and is of the latest technical generation giving the tank an ability to engage targets while moving, but even here some outside influences can be detected. The Type 98 can fire the Russian 9K119 Reflecks laser-guided missile, effective against tanks out to a range of about 5000 m

(5,470 yards), where it can penetrate 700 mm (27½ in) of steel. The fire-control system had to be modified to accommodate this round. Other rounds fired are locally produced and match the latest Russian ammunition in both range and armour penetration performance.

Also present on the Type 98 is a passive armour suite built into the outer surfaces of the conventional armoured protection over the frontal arc. This provides a good measure of protection against incoming shaped-charge projectiles. Other survival measures incorporated

in the Type 98 include an IR jammer and a laser dazzler device, both intended to confuse anti-tank missile guidance and launcher systems. Other protective features include a state-of-the-art NBC protection system, a fire-suppression system and a satellite-based ground navigation system. External options include a front-mounted dozer blade and a snorkel tube for deep wading through deep water obstacles.

The combat weight of the Type 98 has been estimated at from 52000 (114,638 lb) to 54000 kg (119,048 lb), but no further data is available.

Left: The Type 98 main battle tank significantly closes the technical gap between Chinese armoured fighting vehicles and those of the Western nations and also the CIS.

Below: Possessing an advanced computer-based fire-control system, the Type 98 is able to tackle targets while it is on the move. The 125-mm (4.92-in) main gun can also fire a laser-guided projectile.

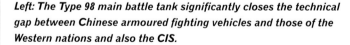

Arjun Main battle tank

The development history of the Indian **Arjun** (lion) main battle tank can be seen as an example of just how not to develop a tank. The project began as long ago as 1974 after the Indian government issued a requirement for between 1,500 and 2,000 tanks to be developed and manufactured indigenously. To assist the modest Indian armoured vehicle infrastructure along the tank design and production learning curves, considerable technical assistance was obtained from Germany and the Netherlands. Various concerns supplied technical know-how and advice regarding the powerpack, transmission, suspension and tracks. Further assistance was used to develop the fire-control system.

Unfortunately the Arjun programme has been constantly beset by delays and cost escalations to the extent that in 2004 series production has yet to start despite the construction of a series of 32 prototypes and pre-production models by the Heavy Vehicles Factory at Avardi. An initial order for 125 units was placed during 1999, although none of these has yet appeared. Despite the expenditure of vast amounts of money, it appears that the Arjun is still

The Arjun main battle tank has many good features of modern concept, but has been bedevilled by problems in the integration of the various systems to make an effective and affordable whole.

beset by automotive, suspension and system integration troubles. Although firing trials of the 120-mm (4.72-in) rifled main gun (39 rounds) were completed in 1993, integration with the advanced technology fire-control system is still problematic. There are also single 7.62-mm (0.3-in) co-axial and 12.7-mm (0.5-in) local defence/AA machine-guns.

Numerous Arjun variants have been forecast, from combat engineer vehicles to air-defence platforms. To date the prototype of only one such type, an armoured recovery vehicle, has appeared.

The point has been reached at which the Indian government has had to acquire significant numbers of Russian-built tanks to maintain a combat parity with Pakistan. It is still possible that the Arjun tank project might be redirected along two separate lines. It has been proposed that the gun and turret could be placed on the T-72 tank chassis, already in licensed production as the Ajeya. Prototypes of this combination have appeared in technology demonstration and trials form with the designation of Tank EX. The second line is to utilise the Arjun chassis and hull for a 155-mm (6.1-in) artillery system known provisionally as the Bhim. It is possible that the 155-mm gun will be of South African origin, but the Bhim still awaits confirmation, despite having been under consideration for at least a decade. It seems the Arjun saga is set to continue for some time to come. The data is provisional.

The Indian army's long experience with tanks of Soviet design is reflected in the Arjun by the provision of two jettisonable extended-range fuel drums on the upper rear of the hull.

SPECIFICATION	
Arjun	1036 kW (1,400 hp)
Crew: 4	**Performance:** maximum road speed
Weight: 58500 kg (128,968 lb)	72 km/h (45 mph); road range
Dimensions: length (overall) 10.19 m	about 450 km (280 miles)
(33 ft 4 in); width 3.84 m (12 ft 6	**Gradient:** 77 per cent
in); height 2.32 m (7 ft 6 in)	**Vertical obstacle:** 0.9 m (3 ft)
Powerplant: one MTU 838 Ka 501	**Trench:** 2.43 m (8 ft)
water-cooled diesel developing	

Leclerc
Main battle tank

Above: For many years the French Army had to depend on the ageing AMX-30 main battle tank to provide its armoured punch. The introduction in the 1990s of the Leclerc, with its powerful 120-mm (4.7-in) gun, composite armour and advanced fire control electronics, has provided a quantum leap in the capability of France's spearhead formations.

Left: Named after the Free French liberator of Paris in 1944, it is appropriate that Leclerc main battle tanks should head the parade down the Champs Elysées on Bastille Day. General Leclerc would probably have been proud of the immensely capable machine which bears his name into the 21st century.

The history of tank development is littered with failed multinational projects which have nevertheless provided the impetus for the production of new fighting vehicles. The current French main battle tank arose out of a failed French/German MBT project of the 1980s. Originally known as the **Engin de Combat Principal**, it was renamed the **Leclerc** in January 1986.

In service with the armies of France since 1992 and of the United Arab Emirates since 1996, the Leclerc is a thoroughly modern weapon system, being well-protected, highly mobile and well armed with a very powerful gun.

The 120-mm (4.7-in) smoothbore main armament is longer than the gun on the Leopard 2 and the M1 Abrams, but fires the same combustible cartridge ammunition. It is fully stabilised to allow firing on the move across country, and has an automatic loader which enables the Leclerc to sustain a rate of fire of 12 rounds per minute.

The autoloader can quickly switch between APFSDS and HEAT, the two principal types of projectile carried. Normal ammunition load is 22 ready-use rounds in the turret, with a further 18 in the hull. For self-protection the tank has a 12.7-mm (0.5-in) heavy machine

gun mounted co-axially, together with a 7.62-mm (0.3-in) anti-aircraft gun mounted on the turret roof. Nine 80-mm smoke launchers can also deploy infra-red decoys or anti-personnel grenades.

Leclerc is powered by a SACM V8 high-pressure diesel

engine, delivering 1119 kW (1,500 hp) via an automatic hydrostatic transmission. Suspension is hydropneumatic, and cross-country performance is excellent.

As with all of the current generation of MBTs, the Leclerc has an extensive sensor and

SPECIFICATION	
Leclerc	developing 1119 kW (1,500 hp)
Type: Main battle tank	**Performance:** maximum road speed
Crew: 3	71 km/h (44 mph); max cross-
Weight: 54500 kg (120,175 lb)	country c.45 km/h (28 mph); road
Dimensions: length (including	range 550 km (342 miles) or 650
armament) 9.87 m (32 ft 4½ in);	km (404 miles) with auxiliary tanks;
length (hull) 6.88 m (22 ft 6¾ in);	**Fording:** 1.00 m (3 ft 3 in) without
width 3.71 m (12 ft 2 in); height	preparation, over 2.00 m with preparation
2.53 m (8 ft 3½ in)	**Gradient:** 60 per cent
Powerplant: one SACM V8X-1500	**Vertical obstacle:** 1.00 m (3 ft 3 in)
12-cylinder hyperbar diesel engine	**Trench:** 3.20 m (7 ft 3 in)

computerised fire-control fit. The commander's panoramic sight incorporates a laser rangefinder and an image intensifier. The gunner's sight incorporates a thermal imager, while the driver's vision system also has night capability. Leclerc is fitted with the FINDERS battle management system, which has a coloured map display onto which the positions of allied and opposition forces can be projected. It can be used for route and mission planning.

The United Arab Emirates are the only export customer for the Leclerc. A squadron of the UAE tanks has served in Kosovo, where it reinforced the French Leclerc brigade already on the ground.

Leopard 2 Main battle tank

The **Leopard 2** was a product of the abortive West German/US MBT-70, incorporating the engine, transmission and certain other components developed for the earlier tank. In 1977 the Bundeswehr (German army) placed an order for a total of 1,800 Leopard 2 MBTs, of which Krupp MaK was to build 810 and Krauss-Maffei of Munich the remaining 990. The first produc-tion tanks were handed over to the West German army in 1979, with the balance delivered through the 1980s.

In 1979 the Netherlands selected the Leopard 2 to replace its ageing Centurion and AMX-13 tanks, and since then the Leopard 2 has been sold widely to several major European armies. More than 3,000 Leopard 2s have been delivered or are being constructed.

120-mm gun

The Leopard 2 is armed with a powerful fully-stabilised Rheinmetall 120-mm (4.7-in) smooth-bore gun. A total of 42 rounds of 120-mm ammunition is carried, compared with 60 rounds for the first-generation Leopard 1 with its 105-mm (4.1-in) gun. This is not a great drawback as the 120-mm round has greater penetration and the fire-control system gives a much greater hit probability. A 7.62-mm (0.3-in) machine gun is mounted co-axially with the main armament for local defence and ranging use, and a very similar weapon is mounted on the turret roof for anti-aircraft defence.

The Leopard 2's 120-mm (4.7-in) gun ammunition was among the first to have combustible cartridge cases. After the gun is fired, all that remains of the cartridge is the base stub which is ejected into a bag under the breech of the gun.

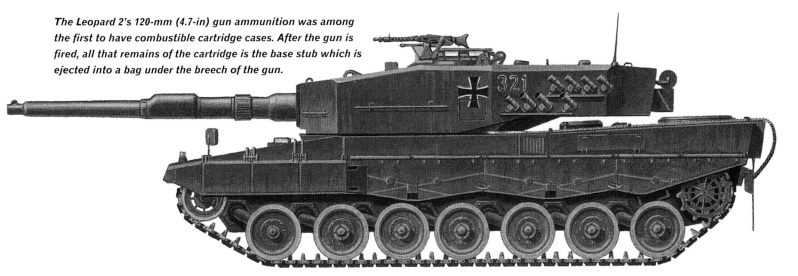

Advanced armour

From the start, the hull and turret of the Leopard 2 had advanced laminated armour for a high degree of battlefield survivability, especially against anti-tank weapons with HEAT warheads. The improved **Leopard 2 A5** currently in service with the Bundeswehr

has upgraded armour, heavily reinforced in the turret front and with add-on modules. The next-generation **Leopard 2 A6 EX** is armed with a longer 55-calibre gun; this has a higher muzzle velocity and increased armour penetration.

Both commander and gunner have stabilised roof-mounted sights with thermal imaging: the gunner's sight incorporates a laser range-finder linked to the fire-control system. Standard equipment includes passive night-vision equipment,

inertial/GPS navigation, an NBC system, a fire extinguishing system and a schnorkel for wading.

High mobility

The Leopard 2 is powered by a multi-fuel engine developing 1119 kW (1,500 hp), which gives a power-to-weight ratio of 20 kW (27 hp) per tonne compared with just under 15 kW (20 hp) per tonne for the final production models of the Leopard 1. This gives the tank greater acceleration and mobility.

SPECIFICATION	
Leopard 2	**Powerplant:** one MTU MB 873
Crew: 4	12-cylinder multi-fuel engine
Weight: combat weight 55150 kg	developing 1119 kW (1,500 hp)
(121,725 lb)	**Performance:** max road speed
Dimensions: length (with gun	72 km/h (45 mph); max range
forward) 9.67 m (31 ft 8⅔ in);	550 km (342 miles)
length (hull) 7.77 m (25 ft 6 in);	**Gradient:** 60 per cent
width 3.70 m (12 ft 1⅗ in); height	**Fording:** (schnorkel) 4 m (13 ft 1½ in)
(overall) 2.79 m (9 ft 1¾ in)	**Vertical obstacle:** 1.10 m (3 ft 7¼ in)
	Trench: 3.00 m (9 ft 10 in)

Left: Leopard 2 operators include Austria, Denmark, the Netherlands, Sweden, Switzerland and Spain.

Below: The Leopard 2 A6EX has the improved armour of the Bundeswehr's A5, allied to a longer 55-calibre gun. The higher muzzle velocity gives AP rounds even greater penetration.

Leopard 2 in operation
Potent main battle tank

First delivered in 1978 and being radically upgraded early in the 21st century, the Leopard 2 is one of the finest MBTs of its generation, and as such offers a unique blend of firepower, protection and mobility.

The Rheinmetall 120-mm (4.72-in) gun carried by the Leopard 2 is more than 5 m (16.4 ft) long. It fires an armour-piercing projectile to a useful range of 3500 m (3,830 yards) with a muzzle velocity of more than five times the speed of sound.

The Leopard 2 is a third-generation MBT incorporating what was, for its time, the latest in weapons technology. Protected by advanced armour which can defeat the warheads of most infantry anti-tank weapons, and fitted with a new powerplant and suspension system, the Leopard 2 is tougher and has more battlefield mobility than its predecessors. Great use of computers and automated equipment enable the Leopard to hit first, hit hard and keep on hitting with its 120-mm (4.72-in) smooth-bore gun.

The earlier models of the Leopard are armed with a 105-mm (4.13-in) gun, but Rheinmetall calculated that only a 120-mm weapon would be able to defeat the frontal armour of the latest-generation Soviet tanks. The Leopard 2's 120-mm gun fires APFSDS-T ammunition: the projectile is fired at very high velocity, 1650 m (5,413 ft) per second, and contains a very dense core of tungsten alloy. By striking the target with such ferocity the core can penetrate the heaviest tank armour.

This specialised round has only vestigial capability against infantry and, in particular, the tank crew's great enemy, the anti-tank guided missile. The Leopard's secondary ammunition is thus a dual-purpose HEAT round: it relies on the chemical energy of its explosion to burn a hole through armour plate, and its fragmentation effect gives it more value than APFSDS against infantry targets. Its lower velocity and high trajectory make it less accurate, however.

Smooth-bore gun
The Leopard 2 was the first Western tank to have a smooth-bore gun, 20 years after the Soviets pioneered the use of smoothbore tank armament with the U-5TS 115-mm (4.53-in) gun of the T-62. Where a rifled gun gives a spin to the shell, whose flight is thus stabilised, the projectile from a smooth-bore gun has stabilising fins that are exposed as the projectile leaves the barrel.

The Soviets encountered some difficulties with their first smooth-bore gun: at long ranges a crosswind would alter the course of a shell as the fins turned the projectile into the wind. But they firmly believe that most tank gunnery takes place at under 2000 m (2,185 yards), where this is not a severe drawback.

The British 120-mm rifled gun, carried by Chieftain and Challenger tanks, has better theoretical performance at longer ranges, but after testing the British and German 120-mm guns the US Army selected the German weapon for the M1A1 Abrams. The Rheinmetall gun has a barrel life of over 1,000 rounds and is chromium-plated to cope with the immense strain of firing large projectiles at four times the speed of sound. Tests showed that accuracy began to deteriorate after 400 rounds.

The Arab-Israeli tank battles of 1967–73 demonstrated the importance of mobility: a

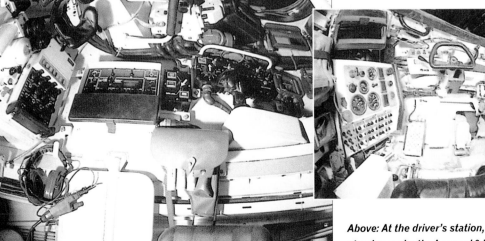

Above: At the driver's station, the automatic transmission and variable steering make the Leopard 2 less tiring to drive than any other tank.

Left: Inside the Leopard 2's large turret one can see the loader's seat on the left-hand side. Having this fourth crewman is thought better than using an auto-loader.

LEOPARD 2: PASSIVE DEFENCE MEASURES

The Leopard 2 relies primarily for the protection of its core on its armour, which is of the spaced multi-layer type able to defeat most types of modern anti-tank weapon. However, this leaves the upper part of the suspension and tracks vulnerable, opening the possibility of the tank suffering a mobility kill. To reduce the chances of this happening, this area is protected by steel-reinforced rubber or, in later vehicles, composite skirts over its rear two-thirds, and by special armoured boxes over the front one-third. The latest Leopard 2A5 upgrade enhances the frontal-arc protection.

tank must be able to travel across country at a fair speed, to accelerate away from a firing position quickly, and to have a long range. The Leopard 2 is one of the fastest MBTs in the world, with a top road speed of over 70 km/h (43.5 mph), its only rivals being the M1 and the T-72/80.

Battlefield mobility

On rough ground the Leopard 2 is surprisingly mobile, throwing its great weight across the battlefield with the agility of an armoured personnel carrier, thanks to its 12-cylinder turbocharged diesel engine. This gives the Leopard 2 a power/weight ratio equalled only by the Abrams.

It is all very well for an armoured vehicle to crash across country at high speed, but if the journey is too exhausting, the crew members will not put up a good performance when they meet opposition. Driver fatigue has been a problem for armoured forces since tanks were invented, but the Leopard 2 has an advanced automatic transmission that saves the driver from having to fight with a clutch pedal throughout the journey.

Driver fatigue

The double clutching required on the earlier T-54/55 and T-62 Soviet tanks was a source of endless trouble, particularly in the Middle East, where the heat and effort of more than half an hour's driving seriously affected the driver's performance. By contrast, the Leopard's transmission and suspension allow it to travel across country faster than most crews can react.

The fire-control computer receives the range of the target from the rangefinder and guides the main armament to the line-of-sight of the gunner's periscope. It aims the gun to allow for the tilt of the vehicle; the relative speeds and courses of the Leopard and its target; any crosswind that may affect the path of the projectile; and the flight characteristics of the type of ammunition being fired. The system allows the Leopard 2 to shoot with considerable accuracy even while moving across country.

Under their armoured skins tanks contain an alarming mixture of flammable fuel and explosive ammunition: if an enemy shell punches through the armour the crew are often doomed to burn to death where they sit. Like the M1, the Leopard protects its crew from an ammunition explosion by having 'blow-off' panels positioned above the shells stored in the turret rear. A hit on this area simply blows away the panels and the force of the explosion passes upward while the crew are on the other side of armoured doors. The rest of the ammunition is stored in the hull, which is far less vulnerable to enemy fire.

To protect the crew against the consequences of a penetrative hit through the hull, the Leopard 2 is fitted with an inert gas fire-suppression system designed to put out a fire in one-fifth of a second. Otherwise a penetration of the fuel tanks by a shaped-charge warhead can result in a fatal mixture of fuel, air and heat.

Front-line service

The Leopard 2, the US M1 and the British Challenger represent the latest in Western tank design. They are expected to serve in the front line into at least the second decade of the 21st century. Further improvements in armament, ammunition, fire-control systems and automation can be expected, but the overall 'classic' layout of the tank is unlikely to disappear in the immediate future.

New ammunition is continually being developed, and further improvements to the 120-mm weapons will inevitably follow. One possibility for the future is an anti-helicopter round.

The front and sides of the Leopard 2's turret are protected by thick slabs of advanced armour, and the hull front is very well sloped to provide maximum protection. The lump mid-way along the gun barrel is the GRP (glass-reinforced plastics) fume extractor.

Ariete Main battle tank

Despite Italy's increasing involvement in peacekeeping and low-intensity operations, the Italian army is still prepared to fight more conventional set-piece land battles. To this end, a second generation MBT, the **Ariete** (ram) has been developed. Delivery of the Ariete began in December 1995. The Italian Army procured 200 of the tanks and final deliveries were completed in 2002.

The Ariete sensor suite includes a stabilised panoramic periscope incorporating an infra-red capability for night operations. Moreover, the tank features a digital fire control system. This computes firing patterns for the main gun based on meteorological data, positioning, ammunition, and targeting information.

The Ariete can engage targets during the day or night with its 120-mm smoothbore gun. The gun contains a fume extraction system, a muzzle reference system and a thermal sleeve. The gun can fire APFDS (Armour-Piercing, Fin-stabilised, Discarding Sabot) and HEAT (High-Explosive Anti-Tank) rounds. The turret accommodates 15 rounds of ammunition, with a further 27 rounds being stored in the hull of the vehicle.

Mounted on each side of the turret are four forward-firing smoke grenade launchers. These can be automatically launched by a laser warning system.

Additional armament includes a 7.62-mm (0.3-in) machine-gun, which is mounted co-axially with the main gun. The tank also features a 7.62-mm air-defence gun mounted on the turret, which is operated by the commander. The Ariete carries 2,500 rounds of 7.62-mm machine-gun ammunition.

Protective measures

Ariete is protected by a comprehensive suite of protective measures. These include electrically operated smoke grenades and a laser-warning receiver. The hull and turret are of all-welded steel construction.

SPECIFICATION	
Ariete	**Powerplant:** one IVECO V-12
Crew: 4	turbocharged 12-cylinder diesel
Combat weight: 54 tonnes	developing 969-kW (1,300-hp)
Dimensions: length 9.7 m (31 ft 9½ in) including main armament; overall width 3.6 m (11 ft 9½ in); height 2.50 m (8 ft 3 in) to turret roof	**Performance:** maximum cruising speed in excess of 65 km/h (40 mph); maximum cruising range over 550 km (342 miles)
Armament: one Otobreda 120-mm smoothbore gun with 42 rounds, 7.62-mm (0.3-in) co-axial machine-gun on left of turret, 7.62-mm AA machine-gun on turret roof	**Fording:** 1.2 m (3 ft 11 in) unprepared
	Gradient: 60 per cent
	Vertical obstacle: 1 m (3 ft 3⅓ in)
	Trench: 3 m (9 ft 10 in)

*The Ariete incorporates a layer of additional advanced armour over the frontal arc, offering protection against modern **HEAT** warheads.*

Sabra M60 upgrade

Originally based on the US M60 MBT, Israel Military Industries has up-gunned and upgraded the M60A3 to **Sabra** standard using highly advanced indigenous technology. As well offering an upgrade for Israeli Defence Force M60s, the manufacturer is also expected to upgrade 170 Turkish M60A1s. These upgrades improve on the M60's Cold War technology, whilst extending its operational life and enabling it to destroy most contemporary MBTs.

The Sabra features a powerful 120-mm smoothbore gun, the same weapon developed for the Merkava Mk 3. The gun is fitted with a fume extraction unit and a thermal sleeve, which reduces barrel wear. This also increases

From a standing start, the Sabra can accelerate from to 32 km/h (20 mph) in 9.6 seconds. Upgraded suspension improves cross country mobility and ride for the crew.

accuracy by reducing the distortion of the barrel. The gun has greater accuracy compared to the 105-mm model originally installed on Israel's M60s. The new gun fires NATO standard 120-mm smoothbore ammunition, which can also include APFDS rounds. In common with the Merkava, the Sabra can carry a single 60-mm mortar for infantry suppression.

The crew are protected with a fire and explosion suppression system, and a threat suppression system. The hull is covered with modular passive armour protection; however, this has been upgraded to an explosive-reactive standard. A smoke grenade launcher also helps to mask the tank.

The Sabra's fire control system manages the dynamics of the turret. It also stabilises the gun, increasing its accuracy and the probability of a 'first hit' against moving and stationary targets. The gun can be slaved to the line of sight; it can also be used in a non-stabilised mode and has an emergency back-up mode for manual operation.

SPECIFICATION	
Sabra	machine-guns on roof operated by
Crew: 4	commander and gunner, and one
Combat weight: around 55 tonnes,	60-mm mortar
depending on level of armour	**Powerplant:** one General Dynamics
protection	AVDS-1790-5A twin-turbocharged
Dimensions: length 9.4 m (30 ft 9½	diesel developing 677-kW (908-hp)
in) gun forward; width 3.63 m (11	**Performance:** maximum road speed
ft 11 in) without skirts; height 3.05	48 km/h (30 mph); range 450 km
m (10 ft) to commander's cupola	(280 miles)
Armament: one Israeli Military	**Fording:** 1.4 m (4 ft 7 in) unprepared
Industries 120-mm smoothbore	**Gradient:** 60 per cent
gun with 40 rounds, 7.62-mm (0.3-	**Vertical obstacle:** 0.91 m (3 ft)
in) co-axial machine-gun, two	**Trench:** 2.6 m (8 ft 6 in)
pintle-mounted 7.62-mm AA	

Merkava Mk 3 Main battle tank

Design work on the **Merkava Mk 3** began in 1983, and the variant entered Israeli Armour Corps service with the 188th Armoured Brigade in early 1990. Since then earlier Merkava Mk 1

Mounted on each side of the Merkava Mk 3's turret is an instantaneous self-screening system for the identification of 'friendly' combat vehicles.

and Mk 2 MBTs have been given certain Mk 3 features during overhaul, although this has not included the 120-mm smoothbore gun, one of the key features of the Mk 3. The Merkava Mk 3 essentially constitutes a new design, with a lengthened hull and increased fuel capacity. The turret is also lengthened and incorporates modular armour, which may be quickly replaced or upgraded.

The 105-mm main armament of the earlier Merkavas has been substituted for a 120-mm thermal-sleeved weapon, similar to that fitted to the M1A1/M1A2 and Leopard 2. The gun has an elevation of +20° and a depression of -7°. The heavily-armoured turret compartment houses some of the 48 rounds for the main gun. A supplemen-

tary 60-mm mortar is operated from within the turret and can fire HE or illuminating rounds. Three 7.62-mm (0.3-in) machine-guns are provided with a total of 10,000 rounds of ammunition.

The Merkava Mk 3 has all-electric turret controls and can be operated by the commander or gunner. The Merkava Mk 3 is capable of engaging moving targets while it is on the move, using an advanced fire-control system and an Automatic Target Tracker (ATT). The commander's panoramic sight is relayed to the gunner's stabilised day/night sight. The gunner's sight features a laser range-finder and an automatic target tracker. The fire-control system offers line of sight stabilisation for the gunner and commander, and is integrated to the turret- and gun-control equipment. Further Merkava Mk 3 systems improvements include a new threat warning system. The NBC protection system is similar to that of its predecessors, but has a new central filter and air-conditioning.

The 'Hawk'

A increased degree of protection compared to the Merkava Mks 1 and 2 is offered by modular hull and turret armour 'packages'. The **Merkava Mk 3 Baz** (hawk) adds elliptical turret armour providing improved ballistic protection. In addition, the Baz carries an automatic target tracking system that holds the sight on target after acquisition by either TV (daytime engagements) or infra-red (night/adverse weather) camera. The system is claimed to be capable of engaging high-speed ground targets and helicopters, irrespective of temporary terrain masking.

Optional equipment for the Merkava Mk 3 includes turret-mounted grenade launchers and a counter-measures system. The latter, mounted either side of the main gun, is similar to the Shtora-1 system fitted to Russian tanks, and is designed to decoy anti-tank guided weapons (ATGWs) prior to impact.

SPECIFICATION	
Merkava Mk 3 **Crew:** 4 **Combat weight:** 65 tonnes **Dimensions:** length 9.04 m (29 ft 8 in) gun forward; width 3.72 m (12 ft 2½ in); height 2.66 m (8 ft 9 in) to turret roof **Armament:** one Israeli Military Industries 120-mm smoothbore gun with 48 rounds, 7.62-mm (0.3-in) co-axial machine-gun, two roof-mounted 7.62-mm AA machine-guns and one 60-mm mortar fired from within turret	**Powerplant:** one General Dynamics AVDS-1790-9AR V-12 air-cooled diesel developing 895-kW (1,200-hp) **Performance:** maximum road speed 60 km/h (37 mph); range 500 km (311 miles) **Fording:** 1.4 m (4 ft 7 in) unprepared **Gradient:** 70 per cent **Vertical obstacle:** 1.05 m (3 ft 4¾ in) **Trench:** 3.55 m (11 ft 7 in)

Type 90 Main battle tank

Despite having an advanced self-defence force, Japan is not well known for its defence industry. However, the **Type 90** is considered one of the most advanced MBTs in its class, incorporating composite armour for the hull and turret. The Type 90 project was originally launched in 1977, and the tank was finally accepted for service by the Japanese Self-Defence Force in 1990. In late 1999 some 172 vehicles were in service, with production continuing at around 17 annually.

The Type 90 uses the same smoothbore 120-mm Rheinmetall gun which is fitted to the German Leopard 2 MBT, and in a modified form, the M1A1/M1A2. The main gun can deliver several different types of ammunition, including armour-piercing projectiles, anti-tank howitzer shells and adhesive HE projectiles.

Type 90 details

The Type 90 tank features a highly automated systems suite. This enables operations with a crew of three, due to the installation of an automated ammunition feeder for the main gun. The gun is guided by laser and thermal imaging technology. The commander's targeting periscope affixed to the turret can be independently rotated, increasing visibility. The tank's fire control system has an integrated laser range finder, which uses the infra-red rays of the target to fix the gun. This enables the tank to engage targets in high-precision attacks while on the move; while allowing the Type 90 to effec-tively engage mobile targets. An NBC system is fitted as standard, and a mineclearing roller system, recovery crane and winch or dozer blade can be fitted to the front of the hull. A scissor-bridge can also be carried on the vehicle front of the **Type 91 AVLB**.

SPECIFICATION	
Type 90 **Crew:** 3 **Combat weight:** 50 tonnes **Dimensions:** overall length 9.76 m (32 ft); overall width 3.43 m (11 ft 3 in); height 3 m (9 ft 9½ in) **Armament:** one Rheinmetall 120-mm smoothbore gun, 7.62-mm (0.3-in) co-axial machine-gun, 12.7-mm (0.5-in) AA machine-gun	**Powerplant:** one Mitsubishi 10ZG 10-cylinder diesel developing 1119-kW (1,500-hp) **Performance:** maximum road speed 70 km/h (43 mph); maximum range 400 km (249 miles) **Fording:** 2 m (6 ft 7 in) **Gradient:** 60 per cent **Vertical obstacle:** 1 m (3 ft 3⅓ in) **Trench:** 2.7 m (8 ft 10 in)

With vertical front, sides and rear, the Type 90 turret is similar to that of the Leopard 2, and combines that tank's Rheinmetall 120-mm smoothbore gun with an indigenous recoil system and gun mount.

K1 and K1A1 Main Battle Tanks

For many decades, the Republic of Korea has relied on American weaponry to equip its military. However, since the 1970s the country's rapid industrial expansion has fostered the development of a significant indigenous armaments industry. One of the first major products of that industry was the **K1 Main Battle Tank**, originally known as the **Republic of Korea Indigenous Tank** or **ROKIT**.

The preliminary design was based on the US M1 Abrams tank but the K1 was modified to meet the requirements of the Korean armed forces. The tank has been optimised for maximum manoeuvrability in the muddy off-road conditions of Korea, and is intended to cope with the wide variety of terrain, including rugged mountains, jungles, paddy fields and swamp.

Based on the American M1 tank, but with a diesel powerplant, the K1A1 is a thoroughly modern main battle tank. Its firepower, protection and mobility are as good as any fighting vehicle in the world.

The K1 is conventional in layout, with its four-man crew of commander, gunner, loader and driver. It is powered by a turbo-charged 895-kW (1200-hp) diesel engine. The main gun is a 105-mm rifled high velocity cannon, with a coaxial 7.62-mm (0.3-in) machine gun. A 12.7-mm (0.50-in) calibre machine gun is mounted on the turret for the commander's station, while the loader also has a 7.62-mm machine gun.

The relationship between the K1 and the American M1 seen here is obvious. However, the Korean tank is optimised for operations in its own challenging home terrain.

The original K1 tank was armed with the American version of the long-serving British L7 105-mm gun. It is more than capable of dealing with any North Korean or Chinese opposition.

<table>
<tr><td colspan="2">SPECIFICATION</td></tr>
</table>

K1A1	**Maximum speed:** road 65 km/h
Type: Main Battle Tank	(40 mph)
Crew: four	**Trench:** 2.60 m (8 ft 6 in)
Dimensions: length with gun	**Fording:** 2.20 m (7 ft 2 in)
forward 9.71 m (31 ft 10 in); width	**Vertical obstacle:** 1.0 m (3 ft 3 in)
3.59 m (11 ft 9 in); height to top of	**Armament:** one M256 120-mm
turret 2.25 m (7 ft 5 in)	(4.7-in) smoothbore rifled main gun
Combat weight: 54.5 tonnes	with 32 rounds; one co-axial
Powerplant: MB 871 ka-501 turbo-	7.62-mm (0.3-in) M60E1 MG, one
charged diesel engine delivering	M60 7.62-mm, one M2 12.7-mm
895 kW (1200 hp)	(0.5-in) MG on turret

K1 in service

The K1 has been operational with the ROK Army since 1986 and the army plans to keep it in service for the next 30 years. It forms the basis for a family of AFVs, including the **K1 ARV** armoured recovery vehicle, and the **K1 AVLB** armoured bridge layer.

The **K1A1** is an upgraded version of the K1 MBT, equipped with the 120-mm M256 smoothbore cannon, also used by the M1A2 and the German Leopard 2. The A1 has a new ballistic computer and a Korean- developed fire control system which includes laser rangefinders and a dual field of view day TV camera. The K1A1 completed testing in 1997 and has been ordered by the Republic of Korea Army.

Challenger 2 Main Battle Tank

The British **Challenger** tank was developed from an upgraded Chieftain design known as the **Shir 2**, ordered by the Shah of Iran in the 1970s. Much faster than its ageing predecessor, thanks to its more powerful diesel engine and greatly improved suspension, its major advance was in protection.

Chobham armour

Challenger was one of the first main battle tanks to be fitted with Chobham laminated armour, a quantum leap in tank protection against both armour-piercing and HEAT rounds.

Its 120-mm (4.7-in) rifled gun was the same as that fitted to the Chieftain, but although it was extremely powerful, the Challenger performed badly in NATO tank gunnery competitions. This was primarily because of serious problems with its modernised fire control system. The British Army actually ceased to enter the annual NATO tank shoot because Challenger kept coming in last place!

By the time of the Gulf War in 1991, most of the problems had been ironed out, and the Challenger performed creditably in combat – not one vehicle was lost while being credited with destroying over 300 Iraqi

Oman is the only export customer for the Challenger 2 to date. The final batch of 38 vehicles ordered were shipped late in 2000, equipping the Royal Oman 1st Main Battle Tank Regiment.

main battle tanks and armoured vehicles.

Challenger 2

In the 1980s, Vickers began development of a much improved variant of the Challenger, and in June 1991 the UK government placed an order for 127 **Challenger 2** MBTs, followed by an order for a further 259 in 1994. Production commenced in 1993 and the Challenger 2 was accepted for service with the British Army on 16 May 1994.

Although the Challenger 2 looks very much like the original Challenger, it is in essence a new MBT. Over 150 improvements were made to the hull alone. The turret, which incorporates second-generation Chobham armour, is also a new design. The L30A1 120-mm rifled gun is chrome-lined, giving longer life and greater accuracy. The gun fires all current 120-mm ammunition, including a new depleted uranium APFSDS round. Normal ammunition stowage is 50 rounds.

Digital fire control

A fully digital system handles fire control, and both commander and gunner are

provided with stabilised thermal sights. The driver is equipped with an image-intensifying Passive Driving Periscope (PDP) for night driving.

Under the Strategic Defence Review, the Royal Armoured Corps will have six Challenger 2 MBT regiments, each equipped with 38 tanks. So far, the only export customer is Oman, which has ordered 38 tanks.

Reliability

Early in 1999, the UK MoD published the results of a demanding series of trials under battlefield conditions, which confirmed that Challenger 2 had

The first regiment to be fully equipped with the Challenger 2 was the Royal Scots Dragoon Guards, in June 2000.

SPECIFICATION	
Challenger 2 **Type:** Main Battle Tank **Crew:** 4 – commander, gunner, loader, driver **Dimensions:** length (hull) 8.327 m (27 ft 4 in); length with gun forward 11.50 m (37 ft 8 in); width: 3.52 m (11 ft 7 in); height to top of turret 2.49 m (8 ft 2 in) **Weight:** 62500 kg (137,500 lb) **Powerplant:** 12-cylinder Perkins	diesel delivering 895 kW (1200 hp) **Performance:** road speed 56 km/h (35 mph); cross-country 40 km/h (25 mph); range 450 km (280 miles); cross-country 250 km (155 miles) **Armament:** one L30 120-mm (4.7-in) rifled main gun with 50 rounds; one co-axial 7.62-mm (0.3-in) chain gun and one L37 7.62-mm anti-aircraft MG

exceeded the most rigorous reliability targets ever set.

Challenger 2E, the latest development model, has been

designed for the export market and is capable of operating in harsh environmental and climactic conditions.

The Challenger 2 test squadron fired 2,850 rounds of 120-mm ammunition during 84 simulated battlefield days.

T-72 Main Battle Tank

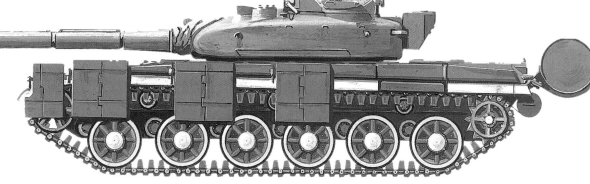

The **T-72** is, by a considerable margin, the most widely used of all modern main battle tanks. Entering production in 1971, it was not seen in public until the late 1970s. Developed in parallel to the more advanced (and considerably more troublesome) T-64, the T-72 was the main Soviet export tank into the 1990s, and is still in production at the Malyshev HMB Plant, Kharkov, Ukraine, and at UKBM Nizhny Tagil in the Russian Federation.

Export tank

While the T-64 was deployed only with front-line Soviet units, the T-72 was exported to non-Soviet Warsaw Pact armies and to other countries. In addition to production in the USSR it has been built under licence in Czechoslovakia, India, Poland and Yugoslavia. At least 50,000 have been built over the last

Eyes right! T-72 tanks drive through Moscow streets during a rainy May Day procession. These tanks would provide the vanguard of the Red Army.

Provisional drawings of the T-72, with the commmander's cupola fitted with a 12.7-mm (0.5-in) AAMG traversed rear. Side skirts provide defence against ATGWs with their HEAT warheads.

three decades, and T-72s are in service with as many as 30 armies.

The T-72 retains the characteristic low silhouette of earlier Soviet battle tanks. Since 1988, Explosive Reactive Armour (ERA) has been fitted to all variants. Its main armament is a 125-mm D-81 smoothbore gun with automatic loader. The tank carries 45 rounds of main ammunition, of which 22 are in the automatic loading carousel. The gun fires APDS, HEAT and HE-FRAG projectiles.

Later variants can also fire the 9K119 Refleks (NATO codename AT-11 'Sniper') anti-armour missile. This is intended to engage tanks fitted with ERA as well as low-flying air targets. The gun has a range of 100-4000 m (328-13,123 ft) but firing requires the tank to be stationary. The

SPECIFICATION	
T-72S	MG on turret
Crew: 3	**Powerplant:** one V-84 12-cylinder
Combat weight: 44.5 tonnes	liquid-cooled four-stroke multi-fuel
Dimensions: length (with gun	diesel engine developing 618 kW
forward) 9.53 m (31 ft 3 in); length	(840 hp)
(hull) 6.86 m (22 ft 6 in); width	**Performance:** maximum road speed
3.59 m (11 ft 9 in); height (to turret	60 km/h (37.25 mph); maximum
roof) 2.19 m (7 ft 2 in)	road range on internal fuel 500 km
Armour: laminate plus ERA	(310 miles), 900 km (560 miles)
equivalent to 950 mm plate against	with external tanks
HEAT, 520 mm against APFSDS	**Gradient:** 30 per cent
Armament: 125-mm 2A46M	**Fording:** 1.20 m (3 ft 11 in) unprepared,
smoothbore with 45 rounds; co-	5 m (16 ft 5 in) with schnorkel
axial PKT 7.62-mm (0.3-in) MG;	**Vertical obstacle:** 0.85 m (2 ft 9 in)
NSVT 12.7-mm (0.5-in) heavy AA	**Trench:** 2.90 m (9 ft 6 in)

gun's automatic loader will feed both ordnance and missiles.

Variants

Variants of the T-72 include the **T-72A**, which has a laser rangefinder and additional armour. The **T-72B** has thickened frontal turret armour and is commonly known in the USA as

the Dolly Parton. The **T-72BK** is a command tank with additional radios.

The current **T-72BM** has second generation Kontakt-5 explosive reactive armour similar to that fitted to the T-90. The **T-72S** is the export variant of the BM. A number of upgrade packages are available for T-72 series tanks. Ukraine is offering the **T-72MP** with SAGEM SAVAN sights. It is also developing a version fitted with a NATO-standard 120-mm smoothbore gun. The Czech Republic is upgrading 140 **T-72M1** tanks to **T-72CZ** standard, which will include Western fire control systems and an Israeli powerpack incorporating a Perkins diesel engine and Allison transmission. Poland has begun an upgrade programme, and India and Croatia are considering modernising their T-72 tanks.

T-72s have seen action in the conflicts that have afflicted a number of post-Soviet republics. This Armenian example is seen in the troubled enclave of Nagorno-Karabakh in 2003.

T-72 in operation
Soviet MBT success story

The T-72 is one of the great success stories of modern tank history. Fast and reliable yet relatively cheap to construct, the T-72 has also been widely built under licence and formed the core of Iraq's much-vaunted Republican Guard during the 1991 Gulf War.

Since the advent of the T-34/85 during World War II, Soviet main battle tanks have typically been built to a cheap, rugged design encompassing good firepower, mobility and armoured protection. Easy to maintain, they have required little support and only a minimum of crew training.

The T-72 has considerable potential firepower. The 2A46 125-mm smoothbore main gun fires APFSDS, HEAT and HE projectiles, is fully stabilised, and unlike earlier Soviet tank guns can fire accurately on the move. The BM-42M APFSDS-T projectile has a maximum range of 3000 m (3,281 yards).

Fire control

An integrated fire-control system with a laser rangefinder and onboard ballistic computer is fitted to all but the earliest T-72 models. This not only relieves the gunner and commander of

some of their traditional tasks, but greatly increases the probability of a first-round hit.

Most revolutionary of all is the carousel-type automatic loader, which enables a reduction in the crew to three men. Twenty-two rounds of assorted ammunition, designed with separate propellant cartridges and projectiles, are carried in the carousel itself, while a further 23 rounds are stored uncomfortably in the already cramped crew compartment.

The commander selects the required round by pressing a button, after which the carousel rotates to the nearest suitable projectile and stops. The gunner then lifts the cassette and the round is rammed into the breech. An automatic ejection system for the propellant casing completes the cycle.

Although simple in design, this system is not without its problems. The autoloader is unreliable and when it fails manual loading takes a great deal of time, and can only be carried out at some risk to the gunner's fingers. During the Cold War, NATO designers steadfastly ignored all temptations to reduce crew size by the introduction of automatic loading despite acute shortages of trained manpower, as they considered manual loading to be far more reliable and, in the case of a good crew, only a little slower. It is likely that the Soviets removed the loader only because it would otherwise have been impossible to fit so large a gun into so small a turret, and not for reasons of efficiency.

Although the T-72 tank operated by Iraq was no match for the coalition's armour, its low profile and powerful gun could have presented a serious threat.

T-72 IN DESERT STORM: TWO SIDES, ONE TANK

The T-72 featured on both sides during the 1991 Gulf War; this Kuwaiti example displays the prominent tactical markings carried by all coalition armoured vehicles. Prior to the war, Iraq was thought to have possessed around 1,000 T-72s, the principal operator being elite divisions of the Republican Guard. Kuwait, meanwhile, ordered 200 M-84s (the Yugoslavian-built T-72) in 1989, including 15 command tanks and 15 ARVs. About 12 were delivered before the Iraqi invasion in 1990, and more were delivered during the war. These served alongside standard T-72s and first saw action with the 35th Kuwaiti Armoured Brigade 'Fatah'. Soviet tanks sold to non-Warsaw Pact armies had all their classified equipment removed, including the complex integrated fire-control system, which was replaced with a more traditional coincidence rangefinder. Although the T-72's smoothbore gun was theoretically capable of penetrating an M1 Abrams at 1000 m (1,094 yards), Iraqi tank crews often failed to achieve the decisive first shot in an engagement. Furthermore, the 120-mm (4.72-in) smoothbore gun of the M1A1 was more than capable of carving through the armour of the T-72.

Mobility

Weighing 41 tonnes or more, the T-72 was one of the largest and heaviest tanks in Soviet service, but its wide tracks and improved suspension allow it to traverse all but the boggiest of terrain.

All T-72s are fitted with a dozer blade under the glacis plate and can be fitted with the KMT-4/6 mine roller/ plough system, three of which were carried with each Soviet tank company.

The T-72 formed the backbone of the Warsaw Pact's armoured forces in the last years of that organisation's existence. This example, operated by East Germany, is seen crossing a pontoon bridge.

A schnorkel can be fitted to enable the tank to ford rivers to a depth of 5 m (16 ft 4 in), but preparation takes up to 20 minutes and extensive engineering preparation to the banks is needed.

Designed during the Cold War to operate in an NBC environment, the T-72 is protected by the PAZ system. A radiation detector, located on the right-hand side of the turret compartment, senses the initial pulse of radiation from a blast and activates a number of explosive squibs or spring-loaded shutters which close the engine louvres, sight apertures, vents and air intakes to the blower/dust separator.

Personal protection

Although notionally this relieves the crew from the necessity of wearing hot and cumbersome protective suits, many personnel would still choose to do so in case any part of the chassis was holed or the airtight seal broken. Also, the commander would not be able to operate the anti-aircraft machine-gun and his vision would be severely limited.

Successive versions of the T-72 were up-armoured, and the tank was fitted with explosive reactive armour (ERA) from 1988. A glacis plate set at a very shallow angle directly below the driver's hatch is designed to defeat short-fused TOW 1 or LAW rounds and may cause a sabot round to bounce off the front of the hull, but would have little effect against a clean strike.

Track protection

Early model T-72s incorporated spring-loaded 'gull wings' along the side of the chassis to protect the wheels and tracks. Theoretically these steel plates would stick out at an angle of 45° from the side of the tank, causing the premature detonation of an incoming TOW round before it hit the hull, but although sound in theory this was found to be ineffective in practice and full-length skirts were later fitted to most tanks.

During the 1982 war in the Lebanon several Syrian T-72s were destroyed with comparative ease by Israeli tanks and anti-tank missiles, and like any tank, the T-72 remains vulnerable to a direct hit. The improved T-72A model has smoke-grenade launchers and an enlarged view finder.

T-80 Main Battle Tank

The most advanced tank in widespread use with the Russian army in 2002, the **T-80** has been in service since the late 1970s. It was originally produced by the Kirov Plant in Leningrad, where the prototype was known as **Obiekt 219**. A modification of the T-64, the T-80 was the first Soviet production tank to be gas-turbine powered. The engine was developed by the Isotov design bureau and built by the Klimov factory, both having had extensive experience with helicopter powerplants.

The GTD-1000T provided more power than contemporary diesels, but with a much higher fuel consumption. The hull had to be redesigned to take twice as much fuel as the T-64. At the same time, a new auto-loader and torsion-bar suspension were fitted since both items had proved unreliable in the T-64.

Build problems

From the start, the manufacturers and the Soviet army encountered problems with the T-80. Manufacturing costs were high, and the engines were unreliable. Nevertheless, the tank went into production in the mid-1970s, and it was accepted for service in 1976 (much earlier than previously believed in the West, and four years before production of the M1 Abrams).

The T-80UK is a command tank variant. This example is fitted with the laser detectors, aerosol mortars and reactive armour of the Shtora-1 defensive system.

The gas-turbine-powered T-80 is faster and more agile than other former Soviet tanks, but it is incredibly fuel-thirsty and has a very poor range.

Meanwhile, the Kharkhov design bureau in the Ukraine had developed the much improved T-64B, and used its new armour, Kobra guided missile system and improved fire control on the T-80 to produce the **T-80B**. More upgrades were introduced to the T-80B in 1980, including the adoption of the T-64B turret, to reduce logistics problems, and a forced-air version of the GTD-1000 which boosted power to 820 kW (1,100 hp) and doubled service life to 1,000 hours. In 1985, the first-generation Kontakt ERA was fitted.

In the mid-1980s, the Shipunov design bureau at Tula developed a new generation of laser-beam-riding missile. The 9K112 (NATO designation AT-8 'Songster') has a range of 5 km (3 miles) and can penetrate 700 mm (27.6 in) of armour. It can also engage helicopters.

The system was fitted into the **T-80U**, which was the first

SPECIFICATION	
T-80U	**Powerplant:** one GTD-1250T gas turbine developing 932 kW (1,250 hp)
Crew: 3	
Combat weight: 46 tonnes	**Performance:** maximum road speed 70 km/h (43.5 mph); maximum road range on internal fuel 325 km (202 miles), and c.500 km (310 miles) with external tanks
Dimensions: length (gun forward) 9.65 m (31 ft 8 in); length (hull) 7 m (22 ft 11 in); width 3.60 m (11 ft 10 in); height 2.20 m (7 ft 2½ in)	
Armour: laminated plus ERA, over 1000 mm armour plate equivalent	**Gradient:** 30 per cent
Armament: one 125-mm 2A46M smoothbore gun with 45 rounds; co-axial PKT 7.62-mm (0.3-in) MG; NSVT 12.7-mm (0.5-in) heavy AA MG on turret	**Fording:** 1.80 m (5 ft 11 in) unprepared, 5 m (16 ft 5 in) with schnorke
	Vertical obstacle: 1 m (3 ft 3¼ in)
	Trench: 2.90 m (9 ft 6 in)

model of the T-80 to be appreciably more capable than the T-64 from which it was descended.

Reactive armour

The T-80U is fitted with new-generation Kontakt-5 reactive armour. It has an advanced fire control system incorporating an optical sight and laser rangefinder paired with a stabilised image intensifier and active infra-red sight.

Production of the T-80 in Leningrad ceased in 1990. Low-rate production continues at Omsk and at Kharkhov in the Ukraine. The 2002 production version is the **T-80UM-1 Bars (Snow Leopard)**. This can be fitted with advanced Shtora and Arena defences. Arena's turret-mounted radar detects incoming anti-tank missiles at 50 m (164 ft) or more, and detonates one of a number of

outward-facing fragmentation charge launchers arranged in a semicircle around the turret front. Future versions of Shtora will include radar and electronic jammers.

T-80 in combat

T-80s were used extensively in the Chechen war, where their fuel consumption was unacceptably high, and they proved vulnerable to RPG strikes from above. Former Defence Minister Pavel Grachev therefore ordered the redesign of ammunition storage in all Russian MBTs. The first result of his order is the Black Eagle, a mock-up of which was shown by the Omsk plant in 1997. This mounts a completely new turret with highly sloped front and a bustle-mounted autoloader which permits a likely rate of fire of 10-12 rounds per minute, on a standard T-80U hull.

T-90 Main Battle Tank

Curiously, for a nation that finds itself in a perpetual state of financial crisis, Russia maintains two main battle tank programmes. In addition to the expensive turbine-powered T-80, the Russian army also operates the **T-90** – initially a simpler and cheaper diesel-powered machine, but which has been upgraded with new weapons systems and has nominally replaced the T-80 as the standard army tank.

The original T-90 was a modestly upgraded T-72. In 1988 the Uralvagon plant in Nizhni-Nagil, builder of the T-72, developed the T-72BM or **Obiekt 187**. This was fitted with Kontakt-5 third-generation ERA, giving similar protection to the T-80. Although the T-72 carried a less sophisticated fire-control system than the T-64 or the T-80, the design bureau planned to fit more advanced electronics to make its design more competitive. The **T-72BU**, which appeared in the early 1990s, carried a full T-80 fire-control system.

Marketing ploy

In 1992, after the fall of the USSR, it was decided to redesignate the tank T-90. This was partly to indicate its increased fighting power, and partly a marketing measure. The poor showing of Iraqi T-72s in the Gulf War reflected badly on Russian attempts to export the type, so the designation change was approved personally by President Boris Yeltsin.

The T-90 entered low-rate production in 1994. The first unit to be fully re-equipped was the tank regiment of the 21st Motor Rifle Division in Siberia in 1995.

In 1996, following T-80 losses in Chechnya, the T-90 was selected as the Russian army's new standard battle tank. The T-90 had not been used in the Chechen war, so it avoided the bad reputation the turbine-engined tank gained. In many

Although the T-90 is being marketed as a new tank, it is in fact an upgrade of the T-72. This example is fitted with Kontakt-5 reactive armour on the turret.

respects this was an illusion – large numbers of virtually identical T-72s were lost in the conflict, and there is nothing to say that the T-90 would have fared any better.

Army objection

There was considerable opposition to the move in the Russian army, since the T-80 is faster and more agile. But as a stopgap, until more advanced tanks can be developed (and until economic conditions in the bankrupt former Soviet Union allow), the T-90 has one great advantage. Each tank costs about $1.6 million against the T-80's $2.2 million. But both continue in production – probably to prevent economic hardship in areas of tank production.

The current **T-90S** has similar offensive and defensive power to the T-80. It has the same stabilised 125-mm smoothbore gun which can fire the 9M119 Refleks missile. Missiles weigh 23.40 kg (51.59 lb) each, and are treated like any other round of ammunition by the automatic loader.

The T-90 tank is protected by both conventional armour and explosive reactive armour (ERA). These provide a substantial increase in protection over the T-72, especially against HEAT and kinetic energy projectiles.

T-90 can be equipped with the the Arena active counter-measures system and with the with the TShU-1 Shtora-1 defensive aids suite. Shtora-1 is intended to provide protection against command and semi-active laser-guided anti-tank and air-to-ground missiles, and against guided artillery projectiles.

Active defence

The two main components are the Electro-Optical Countermeasures Station (EOCS), and the Quick-Forming Aerosol Screening System. The EOCS includes two IR emitters, two modulators and a control panel. It is designed to disrupt the guidance of enemy anti-tank guided missiles with flare feedback, by confusing the guidance system's co-ordinator. The aerosol screening system

detects laser illumination, determines its direction and type and generates warning signals. In two to three seconds the launchers can lay a quick-forming aerosol cloud up to 80 m (262 ft) from the tank. This disrupts hostile guidance lasers.

The T-90S is in service with the Russian Army. In February 2001, the Indian Army signed a contract for 310 T-90S tanks.

A new Russian MBT reportedly started State acceptance trials at the Kubinka Proving Ground in 1998. Very little is known about this vehicle, apart from the fact that it was designed at Nizhniy Tagil. Any future Russian tank is likely to weigh around 50 tonnes, and be armed with a large-calibre fully automatic weapon externally mounted, while the crew will be housed in the hull.

SPECIFICATION	
T-90S	coaxial PKT 7.62-mm (0.3-in) MG;
Crew: 3	NSVT 12.7-mm (0.5-in) heavy AA
Combat weight: 50 tonnes	MG on turret
Dimensions: length (with gun forward) 9.53 m (31 ft 3 in); length (hull) 6.86 m (22 ft 6 in); width 3.37 m (11 ft 1 in); height (overall) 2.23 m (7 ft 4 in)	**Powerplant:** one V-84MS multi-fuel diesel engine developing 618 kW (840 hp)
	Performance: maximum road speed 60 km/h (37.28 mph); maximum range on internal fuel 500 km (310 miles), 650 km (404 miles) with external tanks
Armour: 520 mm on turret plus Kontakt ERA offering a total of 1220 mm equivalent against HEAT and 810 mm equivalent against APFSDS	**Gradient:** 30 per cent
	Fording: (schnorkel) 5 m (16 ft 5 in)
Armament: 125-mm 2A46M smoothbore with 43 rounds;	**Vertical obstacle:** 0.85 m (2 ft 9 in)
	Trench: 2.90 m (9 ft 6 in)

T-84 Main battle tank

Within the former Soviet Union, one of the largest main battle tank (MBT) facilities was the Malyshev factory in the Ukraine where the T-64 MBT was designed and built. The Malyshev plant then built the diesel-powered T-80 while the Omsk facility built the turbine-powered version. With the breakup of the Soviet Union, development of the diesel-powered T-80UD, under the gaze of Mykhaylo D. Borysyuk, continued in the Ukraine and this resulted in the **T-84**.

The T-84 is armed with a 125-mm (4.92-in) smoothbore gun fed by an automatic loader, and is also fitted with a day/night computerised fire-control system. A 7.62-mm (0.3-in) machine-gun is mounted co-axially with the main armament and there is also a roof-mounted 12.7-mm (0.5-in) AA machine-gun.

Over the frontal arc the T-84 is fitted with explosive reactive armour (ERA) to provide an enhanced level of protection against anti-tank weapons. It is fitted with an NBC system, and like most ex-Soviet tanks can carry fuel drums at the rear.

This Ukrainian army T-84, seen with its turret traversed to the front and right, was conducting cold weather trials in Turkey during February 2000.

Export model

Further development of the T-84 resulted in the **T-84-120 Oplot** which has a number of further enhancements for the export market. The most important of these is the replacement of the 125-mm smoothbore gun by a NATO standard 120-mm (4.72-in) smoothbore gun for which ammunition is available from many sources. This weapon is fed by a bustle-mounted automatic loader that holds 22 rounds of ready-use ammunition. The tank is fitted with a new all-welded turret, ERA, a thermal imaging system, a digital fire-control system, an 895-kW (1,200-hp) engine, an auxiliary power unit, an automatic muzzle reference system, and navigational equipment.

The transmission is automatic, while the driver steers the tank with a yoke as opposed to control levers. The first T-84 prototype was unveiled in 1994 and the type immediately began an exhaustive series of tests. The T-84 entered service with the Ukrainian army in 1999.

A Ukrainian army T-84 main battle tank mounted on a flatbed railcar for transport. The armour skirts on the side of the tank are removed to ease transportation.

SPECIFICATION	
T-84	machine-gun
Crew: 3	**Powerplant:** one 6TD-2 diesel
Combat weight: 46000 kg (101,411 lb)	developing 895 kW (1,200 hp)
Dimensions: length (to turret front) 9.72 m (31 ft 10⅝ in); length (chassis) 7.085 m (23 ft 3 in); width 3.775 m (12 ft 4⅝ in); height (including AA MG) 2.74 m (9 ft)	**Performance:** maximum road speed 65 km/h (40 mph); maximum road range 540 km (336 miles)
	Fording: normal 1.8 m (5 ft 11 in)
	Gradient: 60 per cent
Armament: one 125-mm (4.92-in) smoothbore gun, one co-axial 7.62-mm (0.3-in) machine-gun, and one 12.7-mm (0.5-in) anti-aircraft	**Vertical obstacle:** 1 m (3 ft 3⅓)
	Trench: 2.85 m (9 ft 4 in)

PT-91 Main battle tank

For many years Poland manufactured the Soviet T-72M1 series main battle tank (MBT) for the home and export markets, as well as developing a number of specialised versions based on this chassis.

The latter include an armoured recovery vehicle (ARV), armoured vehicle-launched bridge (AVLB), armoured engineer vehicle (AEV) and a twin 35-mm self-propelled anti-aircraft gun (SPAAG) system.

Further development of the T-72M1 in Poland resulted in the much enhanced **PT-91** which is fitted with explosive reactive armour (ERA). This protects against a variety of battlefield threats including anti-tank guided missiles (ATGMs) fitted with high-explosive anti-tank (HEAT) warheads.

Main armament of the PT-91 consists of a 125-mm (4.92-in) gun fed by an automatic loader which first loads the projectile

SPECIFICATION	
PT-91	(0.5-in) anti-aircraft machine-gun
Crew: 3	**Powerplant:** one S-12U V-12 diesel
Combat weight: 45500 kg (100,309 lb)	developing 633 kW (850 hp)
Dimensions: length (hull) 9.53 m (31 ft 3 in); width 3.59 m (11 ft 9⅓ in); height (without AA MG) 2.18 m (7 ft 2 in)	**Performance:** maximum road speed 60 km/h (37 mph); maximum range 650 km (404 miles)
Armament: one 125-mm (4.92-in) gun, one co-axial 7.62-mm (0.3-in) machine-gun, and one 12.7-mm	**Fording:** 5 m (16 ft 5 in)
	Gradient: 60 per cent
	Trench: 2.8 m (9 ft 2¼ in)

and then the charge. A 7.62-mm (0.3-in) machine-gun is mounted co-axially with the main armament and there is also a roof-mounted 12.7-mm (0.5-in) AA machine-gun.

More recently Poland has developed an enhanced version of the PT-91 which incorporates many Western sub-systems including a French SAVAN-15 computerised fire-control system that has a stabilised day/ thermal sighting system incorporating a laser rangefinder. It also has a defensive aids suite that includes laser detectors and grenade launchers.

Following an international competition, Malaysia selected the enhanced PT-91 MBT to meet its future requirements and placed a contract for enough PT-91 gun tanks and variants to enable it to form its first tank regiment. This contract covered the supply of 48 PT-91 MBTs, five AVLBs

fitted with a German bridging system, six WZT-4 ARVs and three MID engineer vehicles which can also be used to breach minefields.

Standard equipment for the PT-91 includes an NBC system and a snorkel for deep-fording operations. Long-range fuel tanks are normally carried at the rear and diesel fuel can be injected into the exhaust to create a local smokescreen.

Above: The PT-91 is seen here with its hull and turret covered by explosive reactive armour (ERA). Note also the turret-mounted smoke-grenade launchers.

Below: This PT-91 MBT is fitted with alternative pattern ERA plates on the turret, and carries front and side skirts to protect against HEAT projectiles.

M-84 Main battle tank

To supplement its large existing fleet of T-55 series main battle tanks (MBTs) supplied by the Soviet Union and armed with 100-mm (3.94-in) main guns, the then Yugoslavia negotiated a licence deal with the Soviets for local production of the T-72M1 series vehicle. Prior to the beginning of licence production in Yugoslavia, an initial batch of T-72M1 series MBTs was supplied direct from the USSR to enable crew training to get underway.

The Yugoslavian **M-84** MBT has many detail improvements

over the original T-72M1 MBT design, and incorporates a more advanced computerised fire-control system of local origin. The latter enables the M-84 to engage stationary or moving targets with a high first-round hit probability.

Firepower

The main armament of the M-84 is essentially the same as that of the T-72M1 MBT and consists of a 125-mm (4.92-in) smoothbore gun which is fed by an automatic loader, a 7.62-mm (0.3-in) co-axial machine-gun and

a roof-mounted 12.7-mm (0.5-in) heavy machine-gun for anti-aircraft purposes. Electrically operated smoke-grenade

launchers are fitted to the sides of the turret, and the tank can also lay its own smokescreen by injecting diesel fuel into the

SPECIFICATION	
M-84	machine-gun
Crew: 3	**Powerplant:** one V-46 series V-12 diesel developing 746 kW (1,000 hp)
Combat weight: 42000 kg (92,593 lb)	
Dimensions: length (with turret forwards) 9.53 m (31 ft 3 in); length (chassis) 6.86 m (22 ft 6 in); width 3.57 m (11 ft 8½ in); height (without AA MG) 2.13 m (7 ft)	**Performance:** maximum road speed 65 km/h (40 mph); maximum range 550 km (342 miles)
	Fording: 5 m (16 ft 5 in) with preparation
Armament: one 125-mm (4.92-in) smoothbore gun, one co-axial 7.62-mm (0.3-in) machine-gun, and one 12.7-mm (0.5-in) anti-aircraft	**Gradient:** 58 per cent
	Vertical obstacle: 0.85 m (2 ft 9½ in)
	Trench: 2.8 m (9 ft 2¼ in)

A Yugoslavian M-84 is seen in profile, with the anti-aircraft machine-gun in the deployed position. The jettisonable auxiliary fuel tanks which greatly extend the range of the tank can be seen at the rear of the hull.

exhaust outlet on the left side of the hull. Standard equipment includes an NBC crew protection system and a dozer blade that is normally retracted under the nose of the vehicle.

M-84 in action

In addition to being built in quantity for the former Yugoslavian army, a significant number of M-84s was also built for the Kuwait army and some of these were involved in the recapture of Kuwait from Iraqi forces during early Operation Desert Storm in 1991. It is estimated that at least 500 M-84 MBTs were built prior to the outbreak of hostilities within the borders of Yugoslavia, but many of these were lost in the subsequent fighting. With the break-up of Yugoslavia and its civil war in the early 1990s, production of the M-84 came to a halt as parts of the tank had previously been fabricated all over the country.

More recently Croatia has re-started production and developed the new **M-84A4 Degman** version. This features hull and turret of welded armour and is fitted with a ballistic computer and a meteorological system.

The vehicle can be fitted with explosive reactive armour and also possesses an integral Geiger counter. A laser detection system automatically launches the tank's smoke grenades.

A 'desertised' M-84 in Kuwaiti service. These tanks were used by the remnants of the Kuwaiti army against Iraq during Operation Desert Storm in 1991.

a

Stridsvagn 122 Main battle tank

By the early 1990s the Swedish army was well aware that it would soon need a new main battle tank (MBT) and comparative trials were conducted with the French Leclerc, the US M1A2 Abrams and the German Leopard 2A5. The result was that the Leopard 2A5 was selected during early 1994 and an industrial co-operation contract was signed by the Swedish defence equipment procurement authorities and what is now Krauss-Maffei Wegmann of Germany. The contract was for 120 tanks to equip two mechanised brigades. The new vehicles were specially modified to suit Swedish requirements, and were initially known as the **Leopard 2(S)** but are now designated by the Swedish army as the **Stridsvagn 122**. An option for a further 90 units was included in the contract but is now unlikely to be exercised.

The Stridsvagn 122 at speed during trials. Note the armoured skirts over the tracks on the side of the hull. The Stridsvagn 122 provides the Swedish defence forces with a very advanced main battle tank which will endure for some years to come.

Despite its modifications, many features of the Stridsvagn 122 remain unchanged from the basic Leopard 2A5, such as the 120-mm (4.72-in) main gun, the MTU main powerplant and the fire-control system.

The costs involved in the original contract were considerable, coming to DM 1,020 million, and were increased still further by the procurement of specialised support vehicles, including 10 (the original requirement was for

29) Krauss-Maffei Wegmann Büffel (buffalo) armoured recovery vehicles.

As a more immediate measure until the new tanks could be supplied, a total of 160 Leopard 2A4 tanks was supplied direct from German army stocks,

sufficient to equip three mechanised brigades. These are known as the **Stridsvagn 121** and it is anticipated that many features of the upgraded Stridsvagn 122 will gradually be incorporated into these earlier

vehicles. With the introduction of the Stridsvagn 121 and the enhanced Stridsvagn 122 complete, all other types of Swedish army tank, including the Stridsvagn 103 (S-tank), were withdrawn from service.

Local components

The contract for the new Stridsvagn 122 tanks ensured that most of the special requirements would come from Swedish sources and that series manufacture would be conducted under licence in Sweden. As a result the Swedish tanks were increasingly manufactured and supported by Bofors Defence (part of the United Defence Group) and Alvis Hägglunds, formerly Hägglunds Vehicles, and numerous other Swedish concerns, including electronic systems manufacturer SaabTech. The latter licence-manufactured much of the fire-control system (FCS) originally developed in Germany by STN ATLAS Elektronik. In broad terms, Bofors Defence supplied the turret and all its systems, including about 50 per cent of the 120-mm (4.72-in) main gun, and Alvis Hägglunds supplied the chassis. The first 'all-Swedish' tank was delivered during early 1998. All contracted

Stridsvagn 122s have since been completed and delivered to their customers.

Ultimate Leopard

As a result of the various Swedish requirement changes, the Stridsvagn 122 is the most advanced and well protected of all the models in the already formidable Leopard 2 family.

Numerous Swedish components were incorporated. These include the radio and crew inter-communications suite, together with many relatively minor items such as seat belts for the crew of four and batteries for the 24-volt electrical system. Also involved in the initial contract were locally produced gunnery and other simulators plus the necessary interfaces for all parts of the vehicle to utilise existing Swedish army support and other equipment.

Although all the armour protection of the standard Leopard 2A5 was retained, extra add-on protection was added to the turret roof to defend against artillery-delivered top-attack bomblets. Further protection for the sides was provided by heavy track-skirt plates. In addition, a passive armour system developed by Akers provides a

SPECIFICATION	
Stridsvagn 122 **Crew:** 4 **Combat weight:** 62000 kg (136,684 lb) **Dimensions:** length (overall) 9.97 m (32 ft 8½ in); width 3.81 m (12 ft 6 in); height (overall) 2.64 m (8 ft 8 in) **Armament:** one 120-mm (4.72-in)	smoothbore gun and two 7.62-mm (0.3-in) MG3 machine-guns **Powerplant:** one MTU diesel engine developing 1118.5 kW (1,500 hp) at 2,600 rpm **Performance:** maximum road speed 72 km/h (45 mph); road range around 470 km (292 miles)

high degree of protection from attack by both kinetic and chemical energy projectiles.

In addition, the Stridsvagn 122 is provided with the French Giat Industries Galix vehicle protection system which automatically detects and then counters incoming missiles by launching screening smoke or explosive grenades. In time Galix may be replaced by a locally developed warning and countermeasures system.

While the tank retains the NATO-standard Rheinmetall 120-mm smoothbore gun, the ammunition it fires is supplied mainly by Israel Military Industries (IMI) and includes advanced armour-piercing fin-stabilised discarding sabot (APFSDS) projectiles with con-ventional (rather than depleted uranium) penetrator rods. One

non-standard round, not employed outside Sweden, is a high-explosive tracer (HE-T). This is a joint IMI-Swedish development and consists of a Swedish 120-mm fin-stabilised mortar bomb combined with an Israeli consumable-propellant charge.

Command and control

The combat efficiency of the Stridsvagn 122 is enhanced by an advanced command and control system from STN ATLAS/SaabTech. This presents the crew with map displays, land navigation data, enemy and friendly force locations and dispositions, and other combat support functions, including routine logistic information. The system also processes and records all data and enables data interchange from individual tank

up to local and battalion level. The Stridsvagn 122 was the first European tank to feature such a system.

While the diesel power unit and drive train for the Stridsvagn 122 remain much the same as for the original Leopard 2A5, some modifications were introduced, mainly concerned with engine and cooling. Some

changes were also made to the braking system. The suspension also had to be altered to accommodate the weight of all these extra items, especially the add-on armour, and combat weight is now quoted as a nominal 62000 kg (136,684 lb), compared to 59700 kg (131,614 lb) for the German army Leopard 2A5.

In addition to new armour protection for the turret roof area and tracks, extra armour modules are added to the front plate of the Stridsvagn 122 MBT.

CV90120-T Lightweight battle tank

The Swedish **CV90120-T** lightweight battle tank was originally developed as a private venture by Hägglunds Vehicles, now Alvis Hägglunds, during the mid-1990s. The intention was to meet forecast requirements which indicated that an

air-portable lightweight tank with a far greater degree of strategic and tactical mobility would be needed for many future combat scenarios.

Most current battle tanks weigh between 55000 and 60000 kg (121,252 and 132,275

The Swiss-designed 120-mm (4.72-in) L/50 fully stabilised high-pressure smoothbore gun of the CV90120-T has a maximum rate of fire of 12 rounds per minute.

lb) and are thus difficult to transport by air when needed by rapid deployment forces. In addition, many nations lack the road or rail infrastructure to accommodate such weights. Although the required lighter weight could be achieved, it was recognised that this would be at the expense of protection. However, no compromises were to be contemplated regarding firepower – this had to be maintained at existing levels.

IFV origins

The Alvis Hägglunds solution was to combine the hull and chassis of their existing CV90 infantry fighting vehicle (IFV) with a steel turret housing a crew of three and carrying a compact 120-mm (4.72-in) gun. Numerous combat sensors and

electronic measures were introduced to enhance survival on the battlefield. The CV90 is already in production for Sweden (CV9040) and Norway, Finland and Switzerland (CV9030) armed with either a 40-mm or 30-mm main gun. By introducing a 120-mm gun turret the CV90 becomes the CV90120-T lightweight tank. Some observers would rate the CV90120-T as a tank destroyer.

The CV90120-T is based around the fully stabilised 120-mm smoothbore gun and its turret. The gun is a Swiss product from RUAG Land Systems, so designed that it has virtually the same space and weight requirements as existing 105-mm (4.13-in) tank guns, such as the NATO standard L7/M68 series.

Main gun

Known as the 120-mm Compact Tank Gun, the gun, which has a length of 50 calibres, manages to remain within its space and weight limits mainly by the introduction of an extended recoil system, with recoil forces further reduced by the addition of an integral 'pepper pot' pattern muzzle-brake. A thermal sleeve and fume evacuator for the barrel are also standard. Being smooth-bored the Compact Tank Gun can fire the latest and future generations of ammunition produced by Rheinmetall DeTec of Germany and the many other nations who manufacture similar combustible case rounds. The gun's projectile dispersion pattern performance is stated to be 'at least equal to that of the most modern battle tanks'.

Magazine

The gun is loaded from a semi-automatic magazine holding 12 ready-use rounds. A load-assist device enables a rate of fire of up to 12 rounds a minute. A further 33 rounds are carried in a compartment at the hull rear. Reloading of this compartment is via a hatch in the hull rear that also doubles as a crew escape hatch. Co-axial with the main gun is a 12.7-mm (0.5-in) heavy machine-gun.

The electrically driven, fully traversing turret has a crew of three: commander, gunner and loader, the latter also acting as the second commander. The fourth member of the crew is the driver at the front left, next to the engine compartment. All crew members are well supplied with vision devices and video displays for combat information ranging from land navigation to fire-control data. The gunner is provided with a SaabTech day and night sight and fire-control unit with a laser rangefinder, while the commander has a stabilised sighting system from Thales to detect and acquire targets. Also mounted on the turret roof is a multi-sensor SaabTech Panoramic Low-Signature Sight (PLSS) operated by either the commander or loader to acquire and track targets until the gunner can take over the fire mission. If required the commander can also take over a fire mission. The provision of three independent sighting systems is claimed to impart a high level of battlefield awareness and considerably improve combat efficiency.

The CV90120-T hull is protected by modular armour and internal spall liners that can be varied as required. The basic CV90 hull, already provided with extra passive armour over the frontal arc, is proof against 14.5-mm (0.57-in) armour-piercing ammunition, but this can be increased by extra passive or reactive applique

The CV90120-T combines an armoured steel turret mounted on the latest CV90 IFV chassis. The vehicle can also operate as a tank hunter/killer, using the turret-mounted sight.

armour panels that protect against 30-mm projectiles. Further protection is provided by laser warning sensors on the turret, radar and missile approach warning systems, and a top-attack warning radar that can detect the descent of autonomous top-attack submunitions delivered by artillery or aircraft. In addition to this sensor suite are 12 grenade launchers that produce rapid aerosol screens. The overall turret shape produces a low radar signature, and radar detection is further reduced by radar energy-absorbing track skirts. Overall, the thermal signature of the vehicle is low. Full NBC protection and fire detection and suppression systems are also installed.

Sensor suite

Despite the current provision of modern warning and sensor systems, the CV90120-T is so designed that it can be easily modified to accommodate any future equipment or technological advances, including battle management and combat data systems. There is no standard communications suite as this can be varied to suit user requirements.

Powerplant

The Scania V-8 diesel engine powering the CV90120-T produces 500 kW (670 hp). Coupled to an automatic transmission, this gives the vehicle a maximum road speed of 70 km/h (43 mph) in its basic form, with the combat weight at a nominal 26000 kg (57,319 lb). The extra weight imposed by add-on armour degrades this performance slightly.

To date, the CV90120-T remains at the prototype stage, although the Swedish armed forces may procure a batch of four vehicles for trials.

SPECIFICATION	
CV90120-T	**Armament:** one 120-mm (4.72-in)
Crew: 4	Compact Tank Gun and one
Combat weight: 26000 to 27700 kg	12.7-mm (0.5-in) co-axial heavy
(57,319 to 61,067 lb)	machine-gun
Dimensions: length (overall) 8.95 m	**Powerplant:** one Scania V-8 diesel
(29 ft 4 in); length (hull) 6.45 m (21	engine developing 500 kW (670
ft 2 in); width 3.19 m (10 ft 5½ in);	hp) at 2,200 rpm
height 2.4 m (7 ft 10 in)	**Performance:** maximum road speed
	70 km/h (43 mph); road range
	around 600 km (373 miles)

M60A3 Upgraded Main Battle Tank

A further development of the M48 series, just over 15,000 examples of the **M60** MBT family had been built for the home and export market when manufacture was completed in 1987. As the final production variant for the US Army, the **M60A3** featured a computerised day/thermal sighting system incorporating a laser rangefinder and passive night vision equipment for improved 'first round' hit probability under most weather conditions.

Enhanced features

A number of features of the M60A3 were originally introduced to the **M60A1**, including add-on stabilisation systems, RISE (Reliability Improved Selected Equipment) engine and smoke grenade

The M60A3 MBT was fitted with a thermal sleeve for the 105-mm gun, designed to increase the number of shots able to be fired before needing a barrel change.

The M60 is one of the world's most successful Main Battle Tanks, having served with more than 20 armies since its introduction in 1960.

SPECIFICATION	
M60A3	width 3.63 m (12 ft); height 3.27 m
Crew: 4	(10 ft 8 in)
Weight: 52617 kg (116,000 lb)	**Performance:** max road speed
Powerplant: one 12-cylinder	48 km/h (30 mph); road range
Continental air-cooled diesel	480 km (298 miles)
developing 559 kW (750 hp)	**Fording:** 1.22 m (4 ft)
coupled to a fully automatic	**Gradient:** 60 per cent
transmission	**Vertical obstacle:** 0.914 m (3 ft)
Dimensions: length 9.44 m (31 ft);	**Trench:** 2.59 m (8 ft 6 in)

launchers. In addition, many M60A1s were effectively brought up to M60A3 standard after the addition of thermal night vision equipment. Out of a total of 5,400 M60A3 tanks delivered to the US Army from 1978, 3,600 were converted from earlier models, while 144 were improved M60A1 tanks retrofitted to **M60A3 TTS** standard. The remaining tanks were new-build M60A3s.

The principal advantage of the M60A3 over its predecessors lies in its fire control system, incorporating a Raytheon laser rangefinder with a range of 5000 m (16,000 ft) in place of the original optical device. This is coupled to an M21 ballistic computer, which replaced the earlier mechanical computer. This system receives range data, as well as information on wind speed, air temperature and density, altitude, target tracking rate and ammunition ballistics, providing firing commands for

the gunner and commander.

The gunner or commander are responsible for selecting one of up to six different types of ammuntion for the 105-mm M68 gun, which on the M60A3 variant is fitted with a thermal sleeve. In addition, the coaxial 0.50-in (12.7-mm) machine-gun mounted to the left of the main gun on the original M60 was replaced by a 0.3-in (7.62-mm) M240 weapon. The AN/VGS-2 TTS was included from 1980, improving all-weather capability and allowing the tank to 'see' through smoke and ground cover. Several years later, a new air filtration system was fitted to the fleet.

Reserves

No longer in service with the US armed forces, large numbers are retained in reserve, although many of these are now being passed on to other operators. A total of 100 M60A3 tanks were ordered by Saudi Arabia in 1983, followed by a further 150 conversion kits (with TTS) for existing M60A1 models – these saw service during Desert Storm. M60A3 production was scheduled to end in 1985, however, a further 94 orders from Egypt meant that production continued for another two years.

M60s served in large numbers during the Gulf War, primarily with the USMC and with Saudi forces.

M1 Abrams series Main Battle Tank

In the early 1970s the US Army embarked on a programme for a new Main Battle Tank to replace the 105-mm M60 series, as by that time it had reached the end of its development potential. In mid-1973, the then Chrysler Corporation (which was subsequently taken over by General Dynamics) and General Motors were each awarded a contract to design and build prototypes of a new MBT designated **XM1**, and armed with the 105-mm M68 series gun as fitted to the M60 series. Following trials, the Chrysler design was selected and a production contract placed. Production was undertaken at the Detroit Tank Plant and the Lima Army Tank Plant but eventually production was concentrated at the latter facility.

Above: All Abrams since the M1A1 have been equipped with the Rheinmetall 120-mm smoothbore, one of the most powerful tank guns in the world.

Right: From its earliest days, the M1 has been equipped with sophisticated fire control systems, incorporating day/night sights and laser rangefinders.

Improved M1

The first production **M1 Abrams** was armed with the 105-mm M68 rifled gun, and this was followed by the **Improved M1** with a higher level of armour protection. The next model was the **M1A1** which had many improvements including a 120-mm smooth bore gun which was a further development of the weapon installed in the German Leopard 2 MBT. All versions of the M1 series have a 0.3-in (7.62-mm) co-axial machine-gun with a similar weapon at the loader's station, while the tank commander has a 0.5-in (12.7-mm) machine-gun.

Final model

The final model of the M1A1

incorporated depleted uranium armour in its hull and turret. The current production model is the **M1A2** which has many improvements. There is currently a programme to upgrade older M1 to the latest M1A2 standard, and in a further development 240 tanks are to be upgraded to **M1A2 SEP** (Sytem Enhancement Package) standard. In the future the AGT 1500 gas turbine is expected to be replaced by a more fuel efficient unit, and there have also been significant improvements in 120-mm tank ammunition in recent years. The standard equipment on the Abrams includes a NBC system and a fire detection and suppression system.

Export

So far there have been three export customers for the M1 series, Egypt (M1A1 assembled under licence at the Egyptian Tank Plant near Cairo), Kuwait (M1A2) and Saudi Arabia (M1A2). One of the more recent developments is the General Dynamics **120S** which is an upgraded M60 chassis with the complete combat-proven M1A2 turret. An M1A2 has also been tested with a German 1119-kW (1,500-hp) MTU EuroPowerPack.

The M1 chassis is also used as the basis of a series of engineer vehicles, including the **Heavy Assault Bridge** (**HAB**) that is now in service with the US Army. The private venture **Abrams Recovery Vehicle** remains at the prototype stage, while the **Grizzly** Counter Obstacle Vehicle (COV), fitted with a mine clearance blade, has been cancelled.

Below: The M1A2 version of the Abrams has upgraded sights and fire control systems.

SPECIFICATION	
M1A2	height 2.89 m (9 ft 6 in)
Crew: 4	**Performance:** max road speed 68
Weight: 63036 kg (138,968 lb)	km/h (42 mph); max range 426 km
Powerpack: gas turbine developing	(265 miles)
1119 kW (1,500 hp) coupled to a	**Fording:** 1.22 m (4 ft)
fully automatic transmission	**Gradient:** 60 per cent
Dimensions: length 9.83 m	**Vertical obstacle:** 1.067 m (3 ft 6 in)
(32 ft 3 in); width 3.66 m (12 ft);	**Trench:** 2.743 m (9 ft)

M1 Abrams
Main Battle Tank

To the US Army, the Abrams has one prime function, which is 'to provide heavy armour superiority on the battlefield'. The Abrams tank is designed to close with and destroy enemy forces in combat, using superior mobility and firepower to shocking effect. The Abrams proved its ability in the Gulf War, when it provided the mailed fist of the Coalition effort to destroy Saddam Hussein's armies.

Fire control: The gunner places the aiming mark in his sight on the target and fires a laser. The range data from the laser is fed into the fire-control computer, which also takes into account air pressure and temperature, wind speed, ammunition type, barrel wear, and the angle of tilt of the tank. Within seconds it has calculated and applied the correct elevation and aim-off to ensure a first-round hit. All the gunner now has to do is to squeeze the trigger.

Suspension: Suspension is important, not only for providing a comfortable ride for the crew, but more importantly for providing a stable platform for the gun. The Abrams has torsion bar suspension – each wheel is on its own mini-axle. This allows the tank to operate with the loss of some road wheels; it also gives 381 mm (15 in) of vertical travel. There are shock absorbers on the first, second and seventh road wheels, which allow the vehicle to travel at speed, with the force of the bumps being taken up by the shock absorbers rather than the crew.

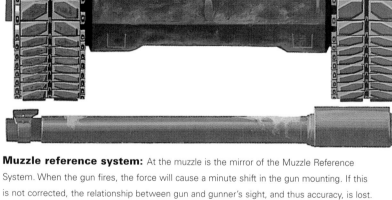

Turret crew: The tank and turret are commanded by the track commander, who sits above and to the left of the gun. He controls all aspects of the tank, from selecting targets and controlling the gun through map-reading and giving instructions to the driver. The loader stands to the right of the turret. His main task is to ensure that the gun is kept loaded and ready to fire. The gunner sits in front of and below the loader, and is the man who actually fires the gun.

Muzzle reference system: At the muzzle is the mirror of the Muzzle Reference System. When the gun fires, the force will cause a minute shift in the gun mounting. If this is not corrected, the relationship between gun and gunner's sight, and thus accuracy, is lost. The MRS works by projecting a light from a fixed source along the barrel off the mirror at the muzzle; the reflected beam is directed back into the gunner's sight. If the gun/sight relationship is OK, the spot of light will be shining in the centre of the aiming mark. If not, the gunner can realign his sight quickly.

Fume extractor: The swelling on the barrel about halfway down is a fume extractor, which evacuates the fumes caused by firing. As the round moves down the barrel it causes a vacuum behind it. When it passes the fume extractor, fresh air is drawn in behind it, forcing the fumes out of the muzzle as the round leaves, rather than back into the turret as the breech opens. The only time it will not work is when the barrel faces directly into the wind.

Above: The original M1 Abrams was armed with the M68E1 105-mm (4-in) gun, an effective and combat-tested weapon derived from the long-serving British L7 gun. However, new armour developments promised to make it less effective, and it was always envisaged that the gun would be replaced by a more powerful weapon.

Above: Deliveries of the improved M1A1 began in 1985. The new tank had a number of detail changes, but the most notable change was in its armament. The 120-mm (5-in) gun is a Rheinmetall design, which has a smooth bore, optimised for firing high-density, fin-stabilised, discarding sabot rounds.

Turret visibility: The commander has six periscopes to provide 360° vision and a sight for the .50 Browning anti-aircraft gun. He is also linked to the gunner's primary sight. This has a magnification of x10 (narrow field of view) or x3 (wide field of view). The sight is fully stabilised, so allowing accurate firing on the move. It has night vision capability.

SPECIFICATION

M1A1 Abrams
Manufacturer: General Dynamics Land Systems
Type: Main Battle Tank
Crew: 4

Dimensions

Length: (hull) 3.657 m (11.9 ft); (gun forwards) 9.828 m (32.2 ft); (gun to rear) 9.033 m (29.6 ft); **width:** 3.657 m (11.9 ft); **height:** 2.886 m (9.5 ft); **track width:** 0.635 m (2.1 ft)

Combat weight

57154 kg (126,002 lb);

Powerplant

Lycoming AGT-1500 gas turbine developing 1500 hp (1119 kW)
Transmission: Automatic, 4 forward and 2 reverse gears;
Steering: hydrostatic
Braking: hydro-mechanical
Suspension: advanced torsion bar suspension

Fuel capacity

1900 litres (502 US gal)

Performance

Max speed: 67 km/h (42 mph) on road; 48 km/h (30 mph) cross-country; 7 km/h (4 mph) up a 60° slope
Acceleration: 6.8 secs 0–32 km/h (0–20 mph)
Max road range: 460 km (286 miles)
Fording depth: 1.219 m (3.9 ft); 2.375 m (7.8 ft) with preparation)
Gradient: 60°
Vertical obstacle: 1.1 m (3.6 ft)
Trench: 2.75 m (9.0 ft)

Armament

Main armament: 1 x 120-mm (5-in) Rheinmetall smoothbore cannon, stabilised
Barrel length: 5.3 m (17.3 ft)

Gun weight: 1905 kg (4,200 lb)
Normal effective range: 3500 m (11,483 ft)
Barrel life: 700 rounds
Muzzle velocity: 1750 m (5,741 ft)/sec (AP); 1100 m (3,609 ft)/sec (HEAT)
Turret traverse: electro-hydraulic with manual back-up
Traverse rate: 42°/sec
Elevation: +20°/-9°

Ammunition

Semi-combustible cartridge cases firing APFSDS (Armour-Piercing, Fin-Stabilised Discarding-Sabot) or HEAT (High-Explosive Anti-Tank) fin-stabilised projectiles

Secondary armament

1 x 7.62-mm (0.3-in) co-axial MG plus 1 x 12.7-mm (0.5-in) and 1 x 7.62-mm (0.3-in) anti-aircraft MGs on turret roof

Ammunition load

40 rounds main; 1,000 rounds 12.7-mm; 11,400 rounds 7.62-mm;

Smoke dischargers

Six either side of turret; 24 smoke grenades; engine smoke-generation system

M1: 3,273 built for US Army, first manufactured in 1978
M1A1: 4796 built for US Army from 1985; 221 built for the USMC; 555 co-produced with Egypt
M1A2: 77 built for US Army from 1986; 315 built for Saudi Arabia; 218 built for Kuwait.

Upgrades

1,079 M1 tanks are being upgraded to M1A2 standard for the US Army; 1,150 M1A2 SEP (System Enhancement Package) being installed for US Army

Powerplant: The gas turbine engine on the M1 was unique in the MBT world until the introduction of the T-80 by the Soviets. One of the advantages of a gas turbine is that it is twice as efficient (weight for weight) as a conventional engine. This means twice as much power for the same weight. It is also very quiet; compared to deafening noise of a conventional diesel; this gives the relatively noiseless Abrams a very significant tactical advantage.

AMX-10P Infantry combat vehicle

The **AMX-10P** was created as the replacement for the AMX-VCI, and was designed by the Atelier de Construction d'Issy-les Moulineaux in the mid-1960s, production being undertaken from 1972 at the Atelier de Construction Roanne (ARE), where production of the AMX-30 MBT was undertaken together with that of the AMX-10RC 6x6 reconnaissance vehicle which is automotively related to the AMX-10P despite the fact that it is a wheeled vehicle. The first production vehicles were completed in 1973, and up to the end of manufacture in 1994 more than 1,800 vehicles were completed for the French army and for export to countries such as Greece, Indonesia, Iraq, Qatar, Saudi Arabia, Singapore and the United Arab Emirates.

Aluminium hull

The AMX-10P has a hull of all-welded aluminium, with the driver at the front left, engine to his right, two-man turret in the centre and troop compartment at the rear. The eight troops enter and leave the vehicle via a power operated ramp in the hull rear; there is a

The AMX-10P has a two-man power-operated turret armed with a 7.62-mm machine-gun and a dual-feed 20-mm cannon. It is possible that the latter will be replaced by a 25-mm weapon, offering improved penetration characteristics against more recent vehicles, to create the AMX-10P 25.

two-part roof hatch above the troop compartment. Apart from the roof hatches and two firing ports in the ramp, there is no provision for the troops to use their rifles from within the vehicle. The power-operated turret is armed with a 20-mm dual-feed (HE and AP) cannon with a 7.62-mm (0.3-in) co-axial machine-gun; mounted on each side of the turret are two smoke dischargers. The weapons can be elevated

SPECIFICATION	
AMX-10P	developing 209 kW (280 hp)
Crew: 3 + 8	**Performance:** maximum road speed
Weight: 14200 kg (31,305 lb)	65 km/h (40 mph); maximum range
Dimensions: length 5.78 m (18 ft 11 in); width 2.78 m (9 ft 1 in); height (hull top) 1.92 m (6 ft 4 in) and (overall) 2.57 m (8 ft 5 in)	600 km (373 miles)
	Fording: amphibious
	Gradient: 60 per cent
	Vertical obstacle: 0.7 m (2 ft 4 in)
Powerplant: one Hispano-Suiza HS 115 water-cooled V-8 diesel	**Trench:** 1.6 m (5 ft 3 in)

between -8° and +50°, and the turret traverse is 360°. Ammunition totals are 800 20-mm and 2,000 7.62-mm rounds.

The AMX-10P is fully amphibious, being propelled in the water by waterjets at the rear of the hull, and is also fitted with an NBC system and night vision equipment for the commander, gunner and driver.

Variants of the AMX-10P include an ambulance, a driver training vehicle, **AMX-10 ECH** repair vehicle with a crane for lifting engines, **AMX-10 HOT** anti-tank vehicle with four HOT missiles in the ready-to-fire position, **AMX-10 PC** command vehicle, a RATAC radar vehicle, **AMX-10 SAO** and **VAO** artillery

The AMX-10P is a useful infantry combat vehicle of a fairly early generation, but is still effective and could be made more so by the retrofit of a one-man turret armed with a 25-mm cannon offering longer stand-off range and the ability to penetrate harder targets.

observation vehicles, **AMX-10 SAT** artillery survey vehicle, **AMX-10 SAF** artillery fire-control vehicle, AMX-10 TM mortar tractor towing the 120-mm (4.72-in) Brandt mortar and carrying 60 mortar bombs, AMX-10P Marines vehicle for Indonesia and Singapore, and AMX-10 PAC 90 fire-support vehicle. The last has been adopted by the Indonesian marines and has a GIAT TS-90 two-man turret armed with a 90-mm (3.54-in) gun, for which 20 rounds of ammunition are carried, and a 7.62-mm co-axial machine-gun. As with most turrets today, a wide range of options is offered including an AA machine-gun and various types of fire-control equipment. In addition to its three-man crew of commander, gunner and driver, the AMX-10 PAC 90 carries four infantrymen in the rear. The vehicles delivered to Indonesia have improved amphibious characteristics and they are meant to leave landing

craft offshore rather than just cross rivers and streams, as is the basic vehicle. Indonesia also took delivery of a number of AMX-10P Marines with the original two-man turret replaced by a new one-man turret at the rear armed with a M2HB MG.

The AMX-10P MICV forms the basis of a complete family of vehicles including command post, HOT anti-tank, mortar tractor, fire control, artillery observation, repair, ambulance, radar and fire-support variants. This AMX-10 is seen in the artillery observation role.

Marder Infantry combat vehicle

When the West German army was re-formed in the 1950s, its first mechanised infantry combat vehicle was the **Schützenpanzer 12-3**, based on a Swiss chassis, and subsequently manufactured both in the UK and West Germany. A decision was taken at an early stage that a complete family of vehicles would be developed on the same basic chassis. The first members of this family to enter service were the **Jagdpanzer Kanone** with a 90-mm (3.54-in) gun and the **Jagdpanzer Rakete** armed with SS.12 anti-tank missiles that were later replaced by HOT missiles. After

Many Marders have been fitted with new passive night vision equipment and a Euromissile MILAN ATGW system. The retrofit of a larger-calibre cannon was planned to enable the vehicle to defeat the latest light combat vehicles such as the Russian BMP-3.

many different prototypes had been built and subjected to extensive tests, one of these was finally adopted by West Germany as the **Marder Schützenpanzer Neu M-1966**, and Rheinstahl was selected as prime contractor with MaK of Kiel as the second source: both companies are now part of Rheinmetall Landsysteme. The first production vehicles were delivered late in 1970 and production continued until 1975, by which time 2,136 had been built. The Marder (marten) was not exported.

High-speed vehicle

At the time of its introduction the Marder was the most advanced MICV in the West, and today is still an effective type whose primary failings are the cost and difficulty of its maintenance. The Marder has good armour protection and a high cross country speed to enable it to operate with the Leopard 1 and Leopard 2 MBTs within the context of the German army's combined arms team.

The driver is seated at the front left with one infantryman to his rear and the engine to his right. The power-operated turret (commander and gunner) is in the centre of the vehicle, and the troop compartment is at the rear. The infantry enter and leave via a power operated ramp in the hull rear, and on each side of

The Marder is still a powerful mechanised infantry fighting vehicle, but is now showing the age of its design and manufacture. Faced with rising maintenance costs and lower operational requirements, Germany has ordered the creation of a lighter and cheaper replacement.

the troop compartment are two spherical firing ports, each surmounted by a roof-mounted periscope to enable infantrymen to aim and fire their rifles from within the vehicle. The turret is armed with a 20-mm MK 20 Rh 202 dual-feed cannon and a 7.62-mm (0.3-in) MG3 co-axial machine-gun. These can be elevated from -17° to +65°, turret traverse being 360°. From the later part of the 20th century there was considerable discussion of the idea of upgrading the

Marder in a number of ways, including the replacement of the MK 20 Rh 202 cannon with a larger and more modern cannon, but in the event Germany has opted for the development of a new infantry fighting vehicle. Most Marders were retrofitted with a Euromissile MILAN anti-tank missile launcher on the turret to enable them to engage MBTs out to a range of 2000 m (2,190 yards). Mounted above the rear troop compartment is a remotely controlled 7.62-mm machine-gun.

The Marder was the first MICV to enter service in the West, and is fitted with a power-operated two-man turret armed with a 20-mm cannon and a 7.62-mm (0.3-in) machine-gun. No export orders were received.

Variants

Variants of the Marder in service with the German army include the Roland SAM system with two missiles in the ready to fire position and a further eight in reserve, and a model with a surveillance radar on a hydraulically operated arm that can be raised above the top of the vehicle for increased radar coverage.

The Marder was produced for Germany as the **Marder 1A1**, and upgrades include the **Marder 1A2** with thermal imaging sight equipment and the **Marder 1A3** with upgraded protection. There are also a number of intermediate upgrade standards, differentiated mostly by their radio equipment, and the **Marder 1A5** is the Marder 1A3 fitted with better mine protection.

SPECIFICATION	
Marder	447 kW (600 hp)
Crew: 4 + 6	**Performance:** maximum road speed
Weight: 28200 kg (62,169 lb)	75 km/h (46.6 mph); maximum
Dimensions: length 6.79 m (22 ft 3	range 520 km (323 miles)
in); width 3.24 m (10 ft 8 in); height	**Fording:** 1.5 m (4 ft 11 in)
(overall) 2.95 m (9 ft 8 in)	**Gradient:** 60 per cent
Powerplant: one MTU MB 833	**Vertical obstacle:** 1 m (3 ft 3 in)
6-cylinder diesel developing	**Trench:** 2.5 m (8 ft 2 in)

Below: Marder on the move with hatches open; the position behind the driver is occupied by one of the infantrymen, who dismounts to fight. The height of Marder (nearly 3 m/9 ft 9 in) is apparent. The Soviet BMP is just 2.15 m (7 ft) high.

Marder in operation
The marauding Marder

When the Marder entered service with the West German army in 1971, it represented not only a breakthrough in military technology, but also an enormous improvement in the capabilities of the Bundeswehr.

The Marder was the first Mechanised Infantry Combat Vehicle (MICV) to enter NATO service. The Marder enabled West German infantry to fight supported by the heavy armament of their vehicle.

Development

Marder took nearly 15 years to develop. In the late 1950s a chassis was developed which could be utilised for a number of basic vehicles including the Jagdpanzer Kanone and Jagdpanzer Rakete tank destroyers, a light reconnaissance tank and an MICV.

Priority was given to the Jagdpanzer Kanone, which entered production in 1965, and then to the Jagdpanzer Rakete so that construction of the MICV was delayed until 1967, and the reconnaissance tank was eventually abandoned.

Troop trials for the MICV ran from October 1968 to April of the following year, after which the vehicle was formally adopted and named Marder. Production lines were established at Kassel and MaK of Kiel, and an initial order for 2,801 vehicles was placed. However, by the time that production ceased in 1975 this number had been increased to 3,111.

The hull of the Marder provides the four-person crew and six passengers with protection from small arms fire and shell splinters. The front of the vehicle affords protection up to 20-mm (0.7-in) projectiles.

Driver's position

The driver, seated at the front left of the hull, has a single-piece hatch-cover opening to the

Infantrymen fire G3 rifles from their roof hatches. They can also fire from within the vehicle, using the firing ports in the hull side. A ventilation system clears away the fumes far more efficiently than in the Soviet BMP

right and is equipped with three periscopes, the centre of which can be replaced by a passive night-driving device for operating closed down. An infantryman, usually the section commander, equipped with a single hatch-cover opening to the right but supported by a single periscope capable of 360° traverse, is seated behind the driver.

The six infantrymen in the troop compartment at the rear are carried in comparative comfort, seated three aside and back-to-back to enable them to fire on the move. Two MOWAG-designed spherical firing ports are built into each side of the troop compartment, as are two circular hatches and three periscopes on the roof.

Mobility

Powered by an MTU MB 833 Ea-500 six-cylinder liquid-cooled diesel engine positioned to the right of the driver, the Marder can develop a useful 447 kW (600 hp) at 2,200 rpm. This gives the Marder a top speed of 75 km/h (47 mph) forwards or backwards.

With a maximum road range of 520 km (325 miles), coupled with the ability to climb

MARDER GERMAN INFANTRY FIGHTING VEHICLE

Marder has a unique sting in the tail: the box above the hull (above left) rear houses a remote-controlled MG3 7.62-mm (0.3-in) machine-gun. This traverses 180° to cover the whole rear arc and can elevate to +60°. A top view of Marder (above right) reveals the three roof periscopes which allow everyone

in the troop compartment to see out. The commander's hatch on the right-hand side of the turret is also clearly visible. It has been announced that the Marder will be replaced by the 'Igel' ('Hedgehog') Armoured Personnel Carrier, which is due to enter service with the German army in 2008.

Left: Marder at speed, with the commander clinging to the rim of his hatch. Despite being two or three times as heavy as many APCs, the Marder has a good power-to-weight ratio and excellent battlefield mobility.

Below: Marder is not amphibious but can ford up to 1.5 m (4 ft 10 in) without preparation. Here, it uses its deep wading kit, distinguished by the snorkel to the right of the turret. This copes with a depth of 2.5 m (8 ft 2 in).

gradients of 60 per cent and to ford to depths of 2.5 m (8 ft), the Marder has excellent mobility, despite its size.

Firepower

Produced by KUKA of Augsburg, the two-man forward-mounted turret Rh-202 is among the most advanced of its type. The commander and gunner, mounted on the left and right respectively, each have a single-piece hatch-cover and adjustable seat. Turret traverse and gun elevation are operated electro-hydraulically, while loading and unloading, cocking, firing and reloading are all executed under armour protection.

The 20-mm Rheinmetall Mk 20 cannon is fed via a series of rigid and flexible chutes from three different belts to give the gunner a choice of either armour- piercing (AP) or high- explosive (HE) shells. A

dual control system enables the commander to over-ride the gunner in the case of an emergency.

Marders have also been improved by the retro-fitting of a double belt feed for the 20-mm cannon, improved night capabilities and an enhanced image intensifier with thermal pointer.

A MOWAG-designed remote-controlled 7.62-mm (0.3-in) MG3 machine-gun mounted above the rear of the crew compartment gives the Marder a unique sting in its tail. With the exception of command vehicles, all Marders in German service are fitted with a Euromissile MILAN ATGW launcher.

Variants

Numerous prototype variants of the Marder were designed, although these never entered production.

Several production variants of the Marder exist. The Radarpanzer TUR is a Marder chassis with an air defence radar dish mounted on a hydraulically-operated arm which replaced the turret.

The Marder 1 A1(+) had a double-feed for its 20-mm cannon along with an image intensification night sight and a thermal pointer; new water can ranks were added together with flaps for the periscope. The Marder 1 A1(-) was similar to its predecesor, but did not feature a laser pointer. The

Marder 1 A1A underwent a comprehensive upgrade although this did not extend to the vehicle's night vision equipment.

The Marder 1 A2 was the result of an upgrade undertaken on all German Marders and featured an improved chassis and suspension system. The final version, the Marder 1 A3, also featured improved armour and comprehensive upgrades in other areas. The driver training version saw the turret replaced with a fixed cuppola.

Dardo Armoured infantry fighting vehicle

In 1992 the Italian army awarded Otobreda and IVECO a contract for the construction of three prototypes of an advanced armoured infantry fighting vehicle capable of operating successfully on the modern high-intensity battlefield. These were completed by 1988 for official evaluation with the designation **VCC-80**. The type was fitted with a two-man turret carrying a 25-mm cannon and a 7.62-mm (0.3-in) co-axial machine gun, controlled by means of a fire-control system similar to that of the Ariete MBT and Centauro 8x8 tank destroyer.

New model

It was then decided to use the VCC-80's chassis as the basis of a harder-hitting AIFV with a turret in which the cannon and machine-gun were supplemented by launchers for the TOW heavyweight anti-tank missile. This led in the later stages of 1988 to a production order being placed with the Consorzio Iveco Oto for 200 **Dardo** AIFVs, including the standard version (with a two-man turret carrying the 25-mm cannon and 7.62-mm co-axial machine gun) as well as four specialised models. These latter were anti-tank, 120-mm (4.72-in) mortar, command post and ambulance variants. The anti-tank model has a one-tube launcher for the TOW missile on each side of the turret, and provision for the Galileo Avionica (originally Officine Galileo) HIT-FIST integrated fire-control system as an alternative to the Kollsman Day/Night Range Sight specified for Italian army variants. All Dardo turrets are

The embarked infantry can enter and exit the Dardo's rear troop compartment via a large power-operated ramp, which has an inset manually operated door for emergency use in the event that the ramp mechanism is disabled.

fitted to accept the TOW launchers and guidance system, and the variant with the Italian rather than American fire-control system is known as the **Dardo HITFIST**.

Armour and turret

The Dardo's hull and turret are of all-welded aluminium armour construction, with an additional layer of ballistic steel armour bolted to the hull and turret for greater protection. The driver sits at the front of the vehicle on the left-hand side. The engine compartment is to the driver's right and is occupied by the IVECO diesel engine developing 388 kW (520 hp). The same engine that powers the Centauro.

Main armament

The electrically operated Otobreda TC 25 turret is in the centre of the vehicle with the commander on the left and the gunner on the right, but can be operated by just one man. The main armament comprises one 25-mm Oerlikon Contraves Type KBA dual-feed cannon, and a 7.62-mm MG 42/59 machine-gun co-axial with this. These weapons have 200 and 700 ready-use rounds respectively,

The Dardo AIFV can be operated with or without a pair of single-tube launchers for the TOW heavyweight anti-tank missile on the sides of its turret, the use of these missiles providing the ability to destroy a tank out to 3430 m (3,750 yards).

and the cannon also has two-axis stabilisation. The cannon can be elevated through an arc of 70° (-10° to +60°). Mounted on each side of the turret is a one-tube launcher for the TOW anti-tank missile, which can be elevated through an arc of 37.5° (-7.5° to +30°), and also a bank of four 80-mm (3.15-in) smoke grenade launchers.

The six infantrymen sit at the rear of the vehicle, entering and leaving by means of a power-operated rear ramp with an inset door: two are seated on each side facing the front, and the other two in the centre as one facing left and one facing the rear. The troop compartment has five firing ports each with an associated vision block allowing

five of the infantrymen to fire their weapons from inside the vehicle. Above the troop compartment is a single rearward-opening roof hatch that is also employed when TOW missiles are being loaded into the launcher units.

The torsion-bar suspension on each side comprises dual road wheels, a front-mounted drive sprocket and a rear-mounted idler; there are three track-return rollers. The upper part of the suspension is covered by skirts. The standard equipment includes passive night-vision equipment, air-conditioning system, NBC system, automatic fire-extinguishing system for the crew and engine compartments, and equipment permitting the vehicle to ford to a depth of 1.5 m (4 ft 11 in).

Potential

At present there are no other in-production variants of the Dardo, although the chassis could be the basis for a complete family of vehicles including air defence, engineer, command post and specialised liaison vehicles. Among the other turret options available to buyers are the Otobreda T 60/70A two-man all-welded unit carrying a 60-mm (2.36-in) High-Velocity Gun System and, as a highly potent alternative to the 25-mm turret version, the Otobreda HITFIST turret which carries the 30-mm Bushmaster II cannon.

The construction of the Dardo from aluminium armour helps to keep basic weight down to a minimum, but also opens the spectre of vulnerability. Thus, the Dardo has provision for the attachment of steel armour over several of its most vulnerable areas.

SPECIFICATION	
Dardo Hitfist	**Performance:** maximum road speed
Crew: 2 + 7	70 km/h (43.5 mph); maximum
Weight: 23 tonnes rising to	road range 500 km (311 miles)
26 tonnes with maximum armour	**Fording:** 1.5 m (4 ft 11 in) without
Dimensions: length 6.71 m (22 ft);	preparation
width 3 m (9 ft 10 in); height	**Gradient:** 60 per cent
(overall) 2.64 m (8 ft 8 in)	**Vertical obstacle:** 0.85 m (2 ft 9½ in)
Powerplant: one IVECO 8260 liquid-	**Trench:** 2.5 m (8 ft 2 in)
cooled V-6 diesel developing 388	
kW (520 hp)	

ASCOD Armoured infantry fighting vehicle

The **ASCOD** armoured infantry fighting vehicle, which first ran in prototype form in 1990, is a collaborative Austrian and Spanish programme by the Austrian Spanish Co-Operative Development undertaking created by Steyr-Daimler-Puch and Santa Barbara.

The first customer was the Spanish army with a contract for 144 **Pizarro** vehicles to be manufactured by a Santa Barbara subsidiary, and comprising 123 AIFVs and 21 command posts. The Spanish army's total requirement is for 463 vehicles including variants such as armoured command post, communications, 81- and 120-mm (3.2- and 4.72-in) mortar carriers, anti-tank guided missile, armoured engineer, armoured recovery, artillery forward observation post and tank-destroyer vehicles, the last with a 105-mm (4.13-in) gun.

Austrian contract

In May 1999, the Austrian defence ministry contracted with Steyr-Daimler-Puch for 112 **Ulan** AIFVs for delivery in 2002–04 as partial successor to the 4K 4FA family of tracked

The ASCOD vehicle is offered with the choice of two engines and several armament fits. The standard arrangement is a turret offset to the right and providing 360° traverse for guns that can be elevated between -10° and +50°.

APCs. The Ulan contract does not currently include any variants of the baseline model, and the Austrians will operate the tracked type alongside the Pandur 6x6 wheeled APC. Late in 1999, the Thai marine corps selected the ASCOD, of which 17 are to be delivered as 15 **ASCOD 105** light tanks and single command post and recovery vehicles.

The ASCOD's hull and turret are of all-welded steel construction providing protection against 7.62-mm (0.3-in) armour-piercing projectiles everywhere except the frontal arc, where protection is offered against 14.5-mm (0.57-in) rounds. The ASCOD can also be fitted with additional steel armour on the front and sides of the turret, glacis plate and hull sides.

The driver is seated at the front of the hull on the left with the powerpack to his right. This powerpack is based on the German MTU 8V-183 TE22 V90 liquid-cooled diesel developing 447 kW (600 hp). The Ulan is powered by an MTU 8V 199

The ASCOD's baseline weapon is the 30-mm Mauser Model F cannon, which is fitted with two-axis stabilisation and controlled via a Kollsman Direct Night Range Sight with optical and thermal sights, a digital computer and a laser rangefinder.

diesel developing 529 kW (710 hp). The complete powerpack can be removed in approximately 15 minutes.

Offset to the right in the centre of the hull is the

SPECIFICATION	
Pizarro	**Performance:** maximum road speed
Crew: 3 + 8	70 km/h (43.5 mph); maximum
Weight: 27.5 tonnes	road range 600 km (373 miles)
Dimensions: length 6.99 m (22 ft 11	**Fording:** 1.2 m (3 ft 11¼ in) without
in); width 3.15 m (10 ft 4 in); height	preparation and 1.5 m (4 ft 11 in)
(overall) 2.65 m (8 ft 8½ in)	with preparation
Powerplant: one MTU 8V 153 TE22	**Gradient:** 75 per cent
8 V-90 liquid-cooled V-8 diesel	**Vertical obstacle:** 0.95 m (3 ft 1½ in)
developing 447 kW (600 hp)	**Trench:** 2.5 m (8 ft 2 in)

---

electrically operated SP-30 two-man turret. The main armament comprises a 30-mm Mauser Model F dual-feed cannon with 200 rounds of ready-use ammunition together with 202 reserve rounds. On the cannon's left is a 7.62-mm MG3 co-axial machine-gun, and this has 700 rounds of ready-use ammunition together with 2,200 reserve rounds.

Troop compartment

The troop compartment is at the rear with eight men seated on individual fold-up seats (five and

three along the left- and right-hand sides respectively). The troops enter and leave their compartment by means of a large power-operated rear door. Above the left-hand side of the troop compartment's roof is a cupola with day periscopes and a rearward-opening hatch.

The suspension is of the torsion-bar type with seven dual road wheels on each side, the drive sprocket at the front and the idler at the rear; there are three track-return rollers. Standard equipment includes a fire detection/suppression system for the engine compartment, a centralised environmental suite based on an NBC/ventilation system with optional air conditioning and water heating system, and a driver's passive night-vision device.

The ASCOD at speed. This is the standard armoured infantry fighting vehicle version with a 30-mm cannon as its main armament, but there is also a considerably more potent light tank variant armed with a 105-mm (4.13-in) main gun in a different turret.

CV 90 Infantry combat vehicle family

For many years the standard armoured personnel carrier (APC) of the Swedish army was the then Hägglund & Söner Pbv 302 which was fitted with a manually operated one-man turret armed with a 20-mm cannon.

To supplement the Pbv 302 the Swedish army issued a requirement for a new ICV (Infantry Combat Vehicle) and awarded the development contract to a very small company called HB Utveckling.

This company in turn awarded contracts to what was then Hägglunds Vehicle for development of the chassis and to Bofors for development of the turret and its associated weapon system. Final vehicle integration, for example the mating of the hull and turret, was carried out by what is now Bofors Defence.

Early production

Following extensive trials with prototype vehicles, a production contract was placed and the first production vehicle was handed over to the Swedish army in November 1993 with final deliveries following in September 2002. By this time, total production for the Swedish army amounted to almost 700 vehicles including related variants.

The basic **CV 9040** is fitted with a power-operated two-man turret armed with a Bofors Defence 40-mm 40/70B cannon characterised by ammunition feed from the bottom and empty cartridge case ejection out of the roof.

The 40/70B is a further development of the famous 40-mm L/70 anti-aircraft gun and fires a variety of ammunition types, these including APFSDS-T (Armour-Piercing Fin-Stabilised Discarding Sabot – Tracer), the advanced 3P which is programmed as it leaves the muzzle, pre-formed high explosive and a tracer.

Above: The CV 9040 of the Swedish army is typical of current ICV thinking in all but its primary armament, which is of larger calibre than that of most other ICVs. This 40-mm Bofors turreted weapon can be elevated between -8 and +35 degrees. The gun is supplied with 238 rounds of ammunition, and the 7.62-mm (0.3-in) co-axial machine-gun has 3,000 rounds.

Right: Infantrymen disembark from the troop compartment of the CV 9030 during trials. This is accessed by a large rear door that opens to the right.

An M/39 7.62-mm (0.3-in) machine-gun is mounted co-axial with the main gun, and a computerised day/night fire-control system is fitted as standard. The French Galix grenade launching system is fitted. This can fire several types of grenade including smoke and screening.

The crew of the CV 90 consists of the driver, commander and gunner, and eight fully equipped infantrymen can be carried in the rear compartment, where they are seated four down each sidefacing inward. The troops can enter and leave the vehicle rapidly by means of a power-operated ramp in the hull rear.

In addition to the CV 9040, the Swedish army operates several specialised variants including a **CV 90 FCV** forward command vehicle, **CV 90 FOV** forward observation vehicle and **CV 90 ARV** armoured recovery vehicle. Finally there is the **TriAD** air-defence vehicle with a turret similar to that of the CV 9040 but carrying to its rear a large dome over the Thales air-defence radar.

Upgrade programme

An upgrade programme has been under way for some time to upgrade early production vehicles to the enhanced **CV 9040A** and **CV 9040B** configurations. The latest CV 9040 upgrade includes additional hull and turret armour for increased battlefield protection. A number of improvements have also been undertaken to enhance the lower part of the

SPECIFICATION	
CV 9040	X-300-5N automatic transmission
Crew: 3 + 8	**Performance:** maximum road speed
Weight: 22800 kg (50,265 lb)	70 km/h (43.5 mph); maximum
Dimensions: length 6.47 m (21 ft 2¾	range 600 km (373 miles)
in); width 3.19 m (10 ft 5¾ in);	**Fording:** 1.4 m (4 ft 7 in)
height 2.5 m (8 ft 2½ in)	**Gradient:** 60 per cent
Powerplant: one 410-kW (550-hp)	**Vertical obstacle:** 1 m (3 ft 3½ in);
Scania diesel coupled to a Perkins	**Trench:** 2.4 m (7 ft 10½ in)

hull against the effects of anti-tank mines, which have proved to be a problem in Balkan peacekeeping operations. In the future the Swedish army will procure another version of the CV 90 fitted with the twin 120-mm (4.72-in) Advanced MOrtar System (AMOS) turret, which has already been successfully demonstrated on a number of other chassis, tracked and wheeled.

Using its own funding, Hägglunds Vehicle, which late in 2002 became Alvis Hägglunds, developed the **CV 9030** ICV. This has a hull similar to that of the Swedish army's CV 9040 but carrying a Hägglunds Vehicle turret armed with an American ATK Gun Systems Company 30-mm Chain Gun. The first customer for this was Norway, which took delivery of 104 vehicles. A further development

The two-man turret of the CV 9030 can be electrically traversed though 360 degrees. There is a moderately advanced Celsius Tech Electronics Universal Tank and Anti-Aircraft System fire-control system, but no stabilisation of the gun.

of the CV 9030 fitted with the Boeing 30-mm/40-mm MK 44 cannon has been adopted by Finland (first order for 57 **CV 9030FIN** units) and Switzerland (first order for 186 **CV 9030CH** units). Alvis Hägglunds has also

developed the **CV 90120-T** light tank for the export market. This is essentially an upgraded CV 90 chassis fitted with a new three-man turret armed with a Swiss RUAG Land Systems 120-mm (4.72-in) smooth-bore gun fitted

with a muzzle brake. This is coupled to an advanced computerised fire control system that enables targets to be engaged and hit while the CV 90120-T is either stationary or moving.

BMP-3 Infantry combat vehicle

The **BMP-3** infantry combat vehicle (ICV) was developed by the Kurgan Machine Construction Plant, which was also responsible for the earlier BMP-1 and BMP-2. Production of the BMP-3 began in 1989, and the type was first shown in public during 2000. It is estimated that since then about 1,000 have been built. The Russian army had hoped to replace the older BMP-2 with the BMP-3 on a one-for-one basis, but funding problems mean that production for the Russian army is estimated to have reached only 200 to 300 vehicles.

Export successes
The BMP-3 has also been offered on the export market

and in recent years it has been one of the best-selling Russian ICVs with almost 600 examples sold to Cyprus, Kuwait, South Korea and the UAE.

The BMP-3 is the best armed ICV in the world as it has a power-operated two-man turret fitted with a 100-mm (3.94-in) gun, a 30-mm co-axial cannon and a 7.62-mm (0.3-in) co-axial machine-gun, all coupled to a computerised day/night fire-control system so that targets can be engaged with a high first-round hit probability, regardless of whether the vehicle is stationary or moving. In addition to HE-FRAG projectiles, the rifled main gun can also fire laser-guided 9M117 (AT-10 'Stabber') projectiles to a range of 5000 m (5,470 yards)

or more. Early examples of this missile carried a HEAT warhead with a claimed capability to penetrate more than 650 mm (25.6 in) of conventional steel armour. More recently a new missile with a tandem HEAT warhead has been developed to counter tanks fitted with Explosive Reactive Armour.

The driver is seated at the front of the vehicle with an

additional crew member on each side, and mounted on each side of the hull front is a 7.62-mm machine-gun to provide suppressive fire.

The remaining five troops are seated to the rear of the turret under very cramped conditions as the engine compartment is at the rear of the hull. The troops can enter or leave by two rear doors or roof hatches. Firing

SPECIFICATION	
BMP-3	
Crew: 3 + 7	**Performance:** maximum road speed 70 km/h (43.5 mph); maximum water speed 10 km/h (6.25 mph); maximum range 600 km (373 miles)
Weight: 18700 kg (41,226 lb)	
Dimensions: length 7.14 m (23 ft 5 in); width 3.23 m (10 ft 6¾ in); height 2.65 m (8 ft 8½ in)	
Powerplant: one UTD-29M diesel developing 373 kW (500 hp) and coupled to a transmission with four forward and two reverse gears	**Fording:** amphibious
	Gradient: 60 per cent
	Vertical obstacle: 0.8 m (2 ft 7½ in)
	Trench: 2.5 m (8 ft 2½ in)

ports and associated vision devices allow the infantry to fire their weapons from within the vehicle.

The BMP-3 is amphibious, being propelled in the water by two hydrojets. Before entering the water a trim vane is erected at the front of the vehicle and the electrically operated bilge pumps are activated. A special marinised version of the BMP-3, the **BMP-3F,** has been developed for service with marine forces.

Standard equipment includes an NBC system and night-vision equipment for the commander,

gunner and driver. To enhance the fighting capabilities of the BMP-3 still further, thermal vision equipment can be fitted.

Battlefield survivability can be enhanced by the installation of ERA, which defeats HEAT warheads, and this has already been adopted by one export customer. The Arena active defence system can also be installed on the BMP-3.

Family of variants

A complete family of vehicles has been developed on the chassis of the BMP-3, although most of these have so far only

The BMP-3 is notably well armed, its turret alone carrying a 100-mm (3.94-in) gun, 30-mm cannon and 7.62-mm (0.3-in) machine-gun. The main gun has 40 rounds including 22 within an automatic loader, as well as eight laser-guided anti-tank projectiles, and the cannon has 500 rounds. The machine-gun armament, including the two fixed weapons, has 6,000 rounds.

reached the prototype stage as a result of Russia's funding problems.

The armoured recovery vehicle is the **BREM-L,** and it is known that this has been built in small numbers. Anti-tank missile platforms include the **BMP-3 Kornet-E** and **BMP-3 Krizantema**, neither of which has entered quantity production.

There is also the **2S31 Vena** 120-mm (4.72-in) self-propelled mortar system, but this too is still only a prototype.

The dedicated reconnaissance vehicle is the **BRM-3** or **Rys** (lynx) with a specialised optronic suite for day/night reconnaissance under all weather conditions. The **BMP-3K** is a command vehicle with radio equipment. There is also a driver training vehicle with the turret removed. The baseline BMP-3 chassis has been offered with Western turrets such as the German Wildcat air-defence system which can be armed with a system of 30-mm cannon and/or guided missiles.

The BMP-3 chassis has been used as the basis of an extensive AFV family including that seen here, the BREM-L recovery vehicle with a dozer blade, winch, crane with a telescopic jib, cargo bed, and a mass of specialised equipment.

Warrior The 'battle taxi'

A British Army Warrior in the Middle East configured for desert combat with additional applique armour, supplies and a special camouflage scheme.

In the late 1960s and early 1970s the British Army carried out a number of studies to field a more capable vehicle to replace the FV432 armoured personnel carrier (APC) and, in the late 1970s, GKN Sankey (now Alvis Vehicles) was selected to develop a new vehicle which was referred to as **MCV-80 (Mechanised Combat Vehicle 80)**.

Following extensive trials with prototypes, a production order was placed and eventually a total of 789 was built for the British Army with final deliveries made in 1995.

The basic Warrior is designated **FV510** and is fitted with a two-person Vickers Defence Systems turret, armed with a 30-mm RARDEN cannon and 0.3-in (7.62-mm) co-axial machine-gun. It has a crew of three consisting of commander, gunner and driver, and carries seven fully-equipped troops that can rapidly dismount via the rear door. The interior is also fully insulated against nuclear, biological and chemical (NBC) attack.

Warrior variants

Variants of the Warrior used by the British Army include the **FV511** command vehicle, **FV512** repair vehicle, **FV513** recovery vehicle, **FV514** artillery observation vehicle, **FV515** artillery battery command vehicle and **FV516** anti-tank vehicle.

Despite many overseas trials, so far there has been only one export customer. In 1993 Kuwait placed an order for a total of 254 **'Desert Warriors'**. These vehicles were completed to a much higher standard than the Warriors delivered to the British Army and featured a US Delco Defense two-person turret armed with an ATK Gun Systems Company 25-mm M242 cannon with a 0.3-in (7.62-mm) co-axial machine gun. Mounted either side of the turret is a TOW launcher, which is used in with a day/thermal fire control system.

More recently, Alvis has developed an advanced **Warrior 2000** for export, which features a new two-person turret armed with a 30-mm cannon with three rates of fire.

The Warrior 2000 was developed for the Swiss Army, which ultimately ordered the rival Hägglunds CV 9030CH. The two-crew turret is armed with a 30-mm Bushmaster cannon.

SPECIFICATION	
British Army Warrior	**Performance:** maximum road speed
Crew: 3 + 7	75 km/h (47 mph); maximum range
Weight: 28000 kg (61,730 lb)	660 km (410 miles)
Powerpack: diesel developing	**Fording:** 1.13 m (3 ft 8½ in)
410 kW (550 hp) coupled to fully	**Gradient:** 60 per cent
automatic transmission	**Vertical obstacle:** 0.75 m (2 ft 6 in)
Dimensions: length 6.34 m (21 ft);	**Trench:** 2.5 m (8 ft 2½ in)
width 3.03 m (10 ft); height 2.74 m	
(9 ft)	

Warrior in operation
British 'battle taxi'

Fast, heavily armed and superbly agile, the British Army's Warrior mechanised combat vehicle takes the infantry into battle safely and at speed.

In the late 1980s, the FV510 Warrior began to replace the FV432 APC that had served the British Army since the early 1960s. The FV432 followed the successful design pioneered by the US M113 APC. Armoured infantry philosophy at the time had demanded a vehicle that could move a section of infantry over the battlefield in comparative safety. In other words it was an armoured 'taxi' designed to deliver troops somewhere short of their objective. Then, they would debus and continue the assault on foot.

British military doctrine changed considerably during the years of the Cold War. One result was the Warrior, which

is essentially a fighting vehicle. It has the power and mobility to keep up with the Challenger tank and is armed with a 30-mm RARDEN cannon and a Chain Gun, although unlike many contemporaries, it does not have firing ports. The British Army doubts their value in combat, so the section still have to dismount short of the objective and continue on foot.

Fire support

However, Warrior can provide powerful covering fire during the assault. In defence, Warrior can be dug in, hull-down, behind an infantry position so that it can add its weight of fire to the section's defence. Warrior weighs nearly twice the weight

Warrior was specifically designed to stay in action under NBC conditions. If infantry have to stay masked up, their combat efficiency is quickly reduced. Warrior's filtration system allows troops to remove their respirators while inside, helping to keep them fit for action.

of the FV432. It is also longer, wider and higher. But the important difference is in the performance. Whereas the FV432 had a theoretical top speed of 50 km/h (31 mph) – this was nearer 40 km/h (25 mph) in later service – Warrior's top road speed is around 80 km/h (50 mph).

Agility, mobility and acceleration are also impressive: the 25-ton Warrior can reach 48 km/h (30 mph) in around 18 seconds.

The combination of aluminium alloy armour, a powerful engine and a remarkable suspension system means that infantry can move quickly between cover on the battlefield, and reduce their

The British Army took delivery of a number of Warrior variants. This is the repair and recovery vehicle, seen in action during Desert Storm in 1991. The hydraulically-operated crane mounted on the left side of the vehicle has a capacity of 6500 kg (14,330 lb) and can lift out a complete Challenger tank powerpack.

DESERT DEBUT: THE WARRIOR IN DESERT STORM

The Warrior's combat debut came in 1991, when infantry battalions of the British 1st Armoured Division went into action against the Iraqi army. Desert sand and heat caused few mechanical problems, although Warrior crews complained of being somewhat cramped. The Warrior's mobility enabled it to keep up with tanks, but it did create another problem. Many infantry support elements, such as ambulances and mortars, were mounted in FV432s (right), and they could not keep up with the fast-moving armoured columns as they pushed into Kuwait and southern Iraq.

time and visual exposure to enemy fire.

Modern anti-tank guided missiles fly quite fast out to their maximum range (MILAN, for instance, takes 13 seconds to reach 2000 m/2,187 yards). Thus, infantry located approximately 1500 m (1,640 yards) from an enemy ATGW system probably have about 10 seconds (including acquisition time) to move from one piece of cover to the next. In the Warrior, depending on the terrain, that might be possible. In the FV432 it almost certainly was not.

Armament

In addition, Warrior can return fire. The 30-mm L21 RARDEN cannon is capable of firing APDS and HE rounds out to 2000 m (2,187 yards) and 225 rounds are carried inside the turret. The 0.3-in (7.62-mm) M242 Chain

Gun, mounted co-axially in the turret, can fire to 1100 m (1,203 yards).

Despite this considerable firepower, Warrior is not intended for use as a tank: no APC or MICV can offer the same sort of protection as an MBT. The RARDEN is designed to engage enemy APCs, not tanks, and the Chain Gun is designed to support dismounted infantry.

The vehicle does have some anti-tank capability; LAW 80s are carried in the troop compartment and can be fired from the roof hatches (although normally the section will be dismounted when firing them). They can even be fired from the turret by the commander or gunner. Firing from the vehicle can be a useful tactic in close country or built-up areas.

Warrior is also equipped with multi-barrel smoke dischargers,

which are mounted either side of the turret and fire forwards. They discharge a pattern of smoke grenades to create an instant smoke screen. This is useful if Warrior is under fire and needs to extricate itself quickly. The turret is equipped with a x8 day sight and a fully integrated image intensifier night-sight.

Battlefield tactics

Warrior is designed to carry a total of 10 troops, including a vehicle commander and driver. Because Warrior is designed to support the section when it dismounts, the vehicle commander remains with the vehicle, acquiring targets and loading the cannon. In a typical battlefield assault scenario, two fire-teams, one of four men and one of three, will normally debus from the vehicle, both armed with an LSW. The vehicle itself will then act as a third fire-team. The section commander will lead one team, the section second-in-command will command the other, and an additional JNCO will command the vehicle.

Warrior could have been made as low as the Soviet BMP series, but the decision was made to increase the headroom in the troop compartment. This makes life much more comfortable for the infantry in the rear.

The Warrior's crew compartment is inevitably cramped but has been carefully designed to give more head-room. The suspension system is good, but infantry still need individual harnesses during high-speed cross-country driving. The vehicle is also fitted with a highly efficient air filtration system. In addition to the basic aluminium armour, which is proof against 14.5-mm (0.57-in) AP rounds, 155-mm (6.1-in) air-burst shell fragments and 9-kg (20-lb) anti-tank mines, additional protection can be fitted to the Warrior in the form of appliqué armour panels.

Most new armoured vehicles form the basis of a range of variants. Warrior has been designed so that it can easily be adapted for any number of roles. Thirteen variants were originally planned, including two versions of an APC, a command vehicle, a recovery vehicle, a combat repair vehicle, mortar, ATGW, recce and anti-aircraft vehicles, rocket-launcher and even a 30-tonne light battle tank with a 105-mm (4.13-in) gun.

Six Warrior variants were deployed in Operation Desert Storm, and since then the British Warrior has seen action on UN duties in Bosnia and in Operation Iraqi Freedom. A total of 789 Warriors were delivered to the British Army between 1987 and 1995.

Stormer Multi-role armoured personnel carrier

The origins of the **Alvis Vehicles Stormer** armoured personnel carrier can be traced back to the late 1970s, when the Fighting Vehicle Research and Development Establishment (FVRDE) developed a prototype vehicle designated **FV4333**. This used some automotive components from the Alvis Scorpion Combat Vehicle Reconnaissance (Tracked) series of vehicles. However, the FV4333 was longer and wider, and therefore had greater internal volume and could undertake more battlefield roles.

The design and marketing rights for the FV4333 were subsequently purchased by what is now Alvis Vehicles, and the concept was developed into a family of light tracked vehicles ranging from an APC to a light tank.

The largest customer to date is the British Army, which

currently uses it in a number of specialised versions. These

include a flatbed carrier fitted with the US ATK Volcano anti-tank mine scattering system, a troop reconnaissance vehicle for use with Starstreak High Velocity Missile (HVM) units and the actual Stormer-based HVM launcher.

The first export customer for the Stormer was Mayalsia, which has two APC versions,

Using a single chassis design, the Stormer can be configured for several different duties, such as this mobile command/control vehicle for Indonesia.

one fitted with a one-person turret armed with a 20-mm cannon and the other with machine-guns. Oman has a command post version for use by its Challenger 2 tank regiments.

The most recent export customer for the Stormer is Indonesia, which has taken delivery of a large number of variants including APC, logistics carrier, command post vehicle, ambulance, recovery and bridgelayer versions, the latter fitted with a scissors bridge system.

A new minelaying Stormer variant, to be known as **Shielder**, is being developed in cooperation with Alliant Technosystems Volcano.

Stormer can be tailored to specific customer requirements. The ambulance version, fitted with a higher roof, has been bought by Indonesia.

SPECIFICATION	
Stormer APC	m (8 ft 2 in)
Crew: 3 + 8	**Performance:** Maximum road speed
Weight: 12700 kg (28,000 lb)	80 km/h (50 mph); maximum range
Powerpack: diesel developing	664 km (412 miles)
186 kW (250 hp) coupled to semi-automatic transmission	**Fording:** 1.10 m (3 ft 7 in)
	Gradient: 60 per cent
Dimensions: length 5.27 m (17 ft 3½ in); width 2.76 m (9 ft); height 2.49	**Vertical obstacle:** 0.60 m (1 ft 11 in)
	Trench: 1.75 m (5 ft 8 in)

M2 Bradley Infantry fighting vehicle

The M6 Bradley Linebacker is intended to replace the M163 Vulcan air defence system, equipped with a four-round Stinger SAM launcher with six reloads. The main armament is retained, with a reduced ammunition capacity.

Following a competition, the company which became United Defense Ground Systems Division was awarded a contract in the spring of 1972 to develop a new Mechanised Infantry Fighting Vehicle (MICV) to meet the requirements of the US Army as a successor to the M113 series APC. The requirement was for a vehicle with with greater armour and mobility, and improved firepower.

Variants

After a protracted development period, two vehicles were finally type classified: the **M2 Bradley Infantry Fighting Vehicle** (**IFV**) and the **M3 Bradley Cavalry Fighting Vehicle** (**CFV**). The former carries seven fully equipped troops, while the latter has a smaller crew and is used principally in the reconnaissance/ scout role. The M2 and M3 are both air, land and sea portable. This enables them to undertake rapid deployment.

The M2 and M3 are very similar and both are fitted with an advanced two-person turret armed with an ATK Gun Systems Company stabilised 25-mm M242 cannon, 0.3-in (7.62-mm) co-axial machine-gun

The M2A3 Bradley Modernisation Plan was initiated following Operation Desert Storm. This view of the M2A3 shows the applique armour, and Commander's Independent Viewer mounted on the right rear.

and have a twin launcher on the left side of the turret for a Raytheon Systems Company TOW anti-tank guided weapon (ATGW). An advanced day/night fire control system has also been installed.

First production Bradley vehicles were completed in 1981 and production continued through to 1995 with just under 6,800 units being built, including 400 for Saudi Arabia, which is the only export customer.

Over the years the Bradley has been continuously enhanced through the **A1**, **A2** and **A3** standards, with the latest models being fitted with

explosive reactive armour. Automotive components of the Bradley vehicle are used in the Multiple Launch Rocket System (MLRS).

SPECIFICATION	
M2A3 Bradley IFV	
Crew: 3 + 7	**Performance:** maximum road speed 61 km/h (38 mph); maximum range 400 km (249 miles)
Weight: 30391 kg (67,000 lb)	
Powerpack: 447-kW (600-hp) diesel coupled to automatic transmission	**Fording:** amphibious
	Gradient: 60 per cent
Dimensions: length 6.55 m (21 ft 6 in); width 2.97 m (9 ft 8 in); height 3.38 m (11 ft 1 in)	**Vertical obstacle:** 0.91 m (2 ft 11 in)
	Trench: 2.54 m (8 ft 4 in)

The M2 Bradley's embarked infantry enter and leave the vehicle at the rear by means of the large hydraulically powered ramp, which has an inset manually operated door for emergency use.

M2 Bradley
Infantry Fighting Vehicle

Below: The M2 Bradley is laid out with the driver in the front, commander and gunner in the central power-operated turret, and infantry in the rear compartment. The turret is the core of the Bradley's fighting capabilities with its 25-mm 'Chain Gun' cannon and 7.62-mm (0.3-in) co-axial machine-gun, and a two-tube TOW missile launcher.

The M2 Bradley infantry fighting vehicle succeeded the M113 armoured personnel carrier in the US Army's first-line mechanised divisions, and offers not just the ability to deliver its infantry to any spot on the high-intensity battlefield, but to fight its way to the required location with the aid of its onboard missile system to defeat tanks and its cannon to defeat thinner-skinned AFVs. The M2 can also use its cannon and machine-gun to provide fire-support for its infantry squad after these personnel have disembarked.

Above: The steady growth of the M2's weight as additional equipment and protection were worked into the vehicle inevitably meant a reduction in speed and mobility, and this was only partially restored in the M2A2 by the introduction of a new version of the Cummins VTA-903T turbocharged V-8 diesel engine delivering 447.5 kW (600 hp) rather than the 373 kW (500 hp) provided in the M2's first production form. The engine and its associated systems are located at the front of the hull on the right-hand side.

Above and below: The M2 Bradley can ford to a useful depth and with some preparation can be made amphibious, being propelled in the water by its tracks at a speed of 6.4 km/h (4 mph). The erection of the special water barrier before the vehicle enters the water takes a well-trained crew some 30 minutes, but this is reduced in the M2A3 by the use of a compartmentalised pontoon system that can be attached in less than 15 minutes to the front and sides of the vehicle and is inflated by an onboard system. Much of the Bradley's operational use has been confined to Middle Eastern areas in which an amphibious capability is not really useful.

SPECIFICATION

M2A3 Bradley

Crew
driver, commander, gunner and seven infantrymen

Weight
36886 kg (81,318 lb)

Dimensions
Length: 6.55 m (21 ft 6 in)
Width: 3.28 m (10 ft 9 in) over the hull and 2.97 m (9 ft 9 in) over the tracks
Height: 2.57 m (8 ft 5 in) to the top of the turret and 3.38 m (11 ft 1 in) to the top of the commander's sight

Suspension
torsion-bar type with six rubber-tyred dual road wheels with hydraulic shock absorbers on the first, second, third and sixth units; three track-return rollers, front-mounted drive sprocket, and rear-mounted idler on each side

Tracks
single-pin type with replaceable rubber pads replaced from 1991 by larger and longer-lasting 'bigfoot' pads; the tracks are 0.533 m (21 in) wide, the length of track on the ground is 3.91 m (12 ft 10 in), and the ground clearance is 0.46 m (18 in)

Powerplant
one Cummins VTA-903T water-cooled V-8 turbocharged diesel engine delivering 447.5 kW (600 hp) at 2,600 rpm

Fuel capacity
662 litres (175 US gal)

Performance
maximum road speed 61 km/h (38 mph); maximum water speed 6.4 km/h (4 mph); maximum road range 402 km (250 miles); fording amphibious with preparation; gradient 60 per cent; side slope 40 per cent; vertical obstacle 0.91 m (3 ft); trench 2.54 m (8 ft 4 in)

Armour
top and front slopes 5083 aluminium alloy of an unrevealed thickness and reinforced with additional steel armour and ERA; vertical sides and rear spaced laminate armour of an unrevealed thickness and reinforced by additional steel armour and ERA; belly 5083 aluminium alloy of an unrevealed thickness and reinforced by applique anti-mine armour

Armament
one 25-mm M242 Bushmaster 'Chain Gun' cannon with 300 ready-use and 600 reserve rounds, one 7.62-mm (0.3-in) M240C co-axial machine-gun with 800 ready-use and 3,600 reserve rounds, and one two-tube anti-tank missile launcher with two ready-use and five reserve BGM-71 TOW missiles

INFANTRY AND CAVALRY FIGHTING VEHICLES

There are two versions of the Bradley: the M2, which is the basic Infantry Fighting Vehicle carrying a full squad of infantry, and the M3, which is a reconnaissance vehicle with a smaller complement but a larger number of anti-tank missiles.

M2: The M2 (right) carries seven infantrymen and the driver in its hull. The gunner sits in the left-hand side of the turret and the vehicle commander, who dismounts with the infantry, in the right-hand side. Six firing ports are provided so that the infantry can fire their personal weapons from inside the vehicle.

M3: Looking all but identical to the M2 from the outside, the M3 (far right) carries a crew of only five but nearly twice as much ammunition, including 15 TOW anti-tank missiles, 1,200 25-mm cannon rounds and 4,500 7.62-mm (0.3-in) machine-gun rounds.

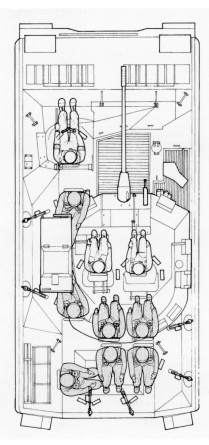

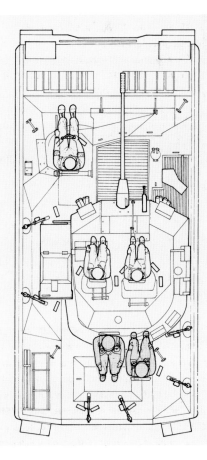

Fahd

Armoured personnel carrier

Designed and built in prototype form in Germany by Thyssen Henschel (now Rheinmetall Landsysteme) as the **TH 390**, this 4x4 APC was created to meet a requirement of the Egyptian army. The type was then placed in production during 1985 by the Kader Factory for Developed Industries (part of the Arab Organisation for Industrialisation) as the **Fahd** and entered service in the following year with the Egyptian army as successor to obsolescent types such as the Soviet BTR-40 and indigenous Walid wheeled APCs. It was estimated that by a time early in 2001 more than 1,000 examples of the family had been completed for Egypt and export customers such as Algeria, Democratic Republic of Congo, Kuwait, Oman and Sudan.

The Fahd is based on the chassis and automotive system of the Mercedes-Benz LAP 1117/32 4x4 truck, on which an armoured body is installed.

This body is of all-welded steel construction offering protection against shell splinters as well as small arms fire up to 7.62-mm (0.3-in) calibre. The driver (on the left) and commander are seated side by side in the front of the body and behind bullet-proof windscreen halves that can be covered by top-hinged armoured shutters. There is a door, with a bullet-proof window and shutter, in each side, and above the commander is a hatch.

Embarked infantry

The hull's rear is occupied by the troop compartment. This is

The AFV Fahd 240/30, used only by Egypt and then just in small numbers, has boosted firepower in the form of the BMP-2's two-man turret with a 30-mm cannon and 7.62-mm (0.3-in) co-axial machine-gun.

The Fahd is a thoroughly unexceptional 4x4 wheeled APC, with the advantage of being based on a well-proved commercial chassis, facilitating logistic support for the type. This example is seen in Bosnia.

laid out for the carriage of up to 10 infantry, who sit on two longitudinal rows of outward-facing seats along the centreline of the compartment. These troops enter and leave their compartment by means of a two-part rear door: the upper part hinges up and to the rear, and the lower part down to form a step. Above the troop compartment are two rectangular hatches hinged along the centreline. The troops can fire their weapons from inside the Fahd, for their compartment has 10 pairs of firing ports and superimposed vision blocks (four along each side and one on each side of the rear door). There is also provision for the installation of three machine-guns on the Fahd's roof.

The engine is mounted toward the front of the vehicle, and the tyres (of the run-flat type) are improved in all-terrain capability by the incorporation of

a central tyre pressure-regulation system. Optional equipment includes a front-mounted winch, an NBC and ventilation system, passive night vision equipment, and a bank of four smoke dischargers on each side of the troop compartment, at either the front or rear.

There is provision over the hull for a one-man turret carrying one 12.7-mm (0.5-in) or alternatively one or two 7.62-mm (0.3-in) machine-guns, or one 20-mm cannon. Kader has also proposed the Fahd as

the basis of a complete family of derivatives in the whole gamut of battlefield and internal security roles.

The only two developments to have entered production are the **Fahd 240** and its **AFV Fahd 240/30** derivative. Announced in 1996, the former is similar to the basic Fahd except for being mounted on the chassis of the Mercedes-Benz LAP 1424/32 truck, while the latter carries the complete turret of the Russian BMP-2 IFV complete with its 30-mm cannon.

SPECIFICATION	
Fahd	turbocharged diesel engine
Crew: 2 + 10	delivering 125 kW (168 hp)
Weight: 10.9 tonnes	**Performance:** maximum road speed
Dimensions: length 6 m (19 ft	90 km/h (56 mph); maximum road
8¼ in); width 2.45 m (8 ft ½ in);	range 800 km (497 miles)
height to the top of the hull 2.1 m	**Fording:** 0.7 m (2 ft 3½ in)
(6 ft 10⅔ in)	**Gradient:** 70 per cent
Powerplant: one Mercedes-Benz	**Vertical obstacle:** 0.5 m (1 ft 7¾ in)
OM 352A liquid-cooled 6-cylinder	**Trench:** 0.9 m (2 ft 11½ in)

Centauro Tank destroyer

Designed by FIAT and OTO Melara (now IVECO and Otobreda respectively), the **Centauro** 8x8 tank destroyer is a member of the AFV generation that the Italian army requested in the 1980s, the other three types being the Ariete MBT, Dardo IFV and Puma 4x4 and 6x6 light vehicles. FIAT was responsible for the hull and automotive system, and OTO Melara for the armament system.

The Italian army's 1984 requirement demanded a highly capable tank destroyer armed with a 105-mm (4.13-in) rifled gun firing the standard range of NATO ammunition and employing an advanced fire-control system and possessing a high road speed, long range and good cross-country mobility.

First run in prototype form during 1987, the Centauro was delivered from 1991, and by 1996 some 400 vehicles had been completed for the Italian army. The only other operators of the type are Spain (22 vehicles) and the US Army, which loaned 16 vehicles for trials.

Steel protection

The Centauro is built of all-welded steel armour providing protection against 20-mm projectiles over the frontal arc and 12.7-mm (0.5-in) projectiles elsewhere. The front of the vehicle is occupied by the powerpack (on the right) with the driver to its left under a hatch that can be fitted with night vision devices. This forward compartment is separated from the rest of the vehicle by a fireproof bulkhead. Located over the rear of the hull is the fighting compartment with its low-silhouette turret. The turret carries the commander on the left and the gunner (with his own dedicated sight unit including day optics, a thermal imaging device and a laser rangefinder) and loader on

the right. The commander has his own roof hatch, four day periscopes and a stabilised sight, while the other two members of the turret crew have a single hatch above the loader's position.

The turret armament comprises an Otobreda 105-mm gun with 40 rounds (14 of them in the turret for ready use), 7.62-mm (0.3-in) co-axial and 7.62-mm AA machine-guns with 1,400 rounds, and smoke dischargers on each side of the turret. The TURMS fire-control system is the same as that of the Ariete MBT.

Further equipment

Standard features include an NBC system, central tyre pressure-regulation system, front-mounted winch, fire and explosion detection and suppression systems, and provision for passive armour. The latter has been fitted to Centauros deployed to Bosnia.

Several variants have been proposed, and those to have reached hardware form are a close-defence vehicle with provision for four infantry using the door in the rear of the hull, a

A Centauro is pictured during main armament firing trials. Evident in this photograph are the overall layout and the low-silhouette turret with a large bustle.

SPECIFICATION	
Centauro	**Powerplant:** one 388-kW (520-hp)
Crew: 4	IVECO VTCA liquid-cooled V-6
Weight: 25 tonnes	turbocharged diesel engine
Dimensions: length (with gun	**Performance:** maximum road speed
forward) 8.555 m (28 ft ¾ in) and	105 km/h (65 mph); maximum road
(hull) 7.85 m (25 ft 9 in); width	range 800 km (497 miles)
3.05 m (10 ft); height (overall)	**Fording:** 1.5 m (4 ft 11 in)
2.735 m (8 ft 11¾ in)	**Gradient:** 60 per cent
	Vertical obstacle: 0.55 m (1 ft 9½ in)
	Trench: 1.2 m (3 ft 11 in)

longer and wider model with the 60-mm (2.36-in) Otobreda gun, a 155-mm (6.1-in) self-propelled howitzer testbed and a Centauro VBC APC with a turreted 25-mm cannon.

The Centauro's turret has 360° electrohydraulic traverse, and the main armament can be elevated between -6° and +15°. The sights and fire-control system are both comprehensive.

Puma APC

The smallest of the new generation of vehicles requested by the Italian army in the mid-1980s (the others being the Ariete MBT, Dardo IFV and Centauro tank destroyer), the **Puma** was developed by FIAT and OTO Melara (now IVECO and Otobreda respectively) as an APC to operate with the Centauro. The origins of the type can in fact be traced back to the early 1980s, when FIAT built its 4x4 Armoured Vehicle Light as the starting point of a proposed 4x4 and 6x6 series of wheeled AFVs.

The Italian army wanted something larger than the AVL, and the result was the Puma that initially ran, in the form of the first of five prototypes, in 1988. The Italian army also asked for the creation of six specialised models as three four-crew weapons carriers (TOW and MILAN anti-tank missiles and Mistral SAM), a four-crew 81-mm (3.2-in) mortar carrier, a two-crew ambulance with provision for two litters and a five/six-man light armoured command post.

Development of the Puma series of 4x4 and 6x6 vehicles was completed in 1999, and the Consorzio Iveco Oto received

The Puma 4x4 vehicle is sized for air transport inside machines such as the Boeing CH-47 Chinook twin-rotor helicopter, with obvious mobility advantages.

The Puma has a very well sloped upper nose, and an unusual feature is the use of a single side plate rather than two plates welded together along the angle.

orders for 580 vehicles in the form of 330 4x4 and 250 6x6 APCs to be delivered from the first half of 2001 to 2004. The 4x4 vehicles are used by five reconnaissance regiments to work in concert with the Centauro tank destroyer, and the 6x6 vehicles are distributed among light infantry, mountain, paratroop and light amphibious regiments. The 4x4 vehicles carry six persons, allowing them to deploy a pair of two-man scout teams, and the 6x6 vehicles carry seven persons in the form of a driver and a six-man combat team.

Conventional layout

The Puma is of all-welded steel armour construction providing protection against small arms fire and shell splinters. From front to rear, the vehicle

comprises the engine compartment, the position for the driver on the left-hand side under a domed hatch and with three day periscopes of which the central unit can be replaced by a passive night periscope, and the troop compartment. This last is accessed by a single inward-opening door in each side of the one-piece hull side, and by an outward-opening door in the rear of the hull. There is a firing port and, above it, a vision block in each of the three doors. Above the troop compartment is the commander's cupola with a circular hatch, five day periscopes and provision for one 12.7- or 7.62-mm (0.5- or 0.3-in) machine-gun. On each side of the rear hull, aligned to fire forward, is a bank of three smoke dischargers.

Standard equipment includes an NBC system, a fire detection

and suppression system, an integrated air-conditioning system and a rear-mounted winch. The vehicle has run-flat tyres, and while the early vehicles have the IVECO 8141.47 diesel engine delivering 93 kW (125 hp) via a manual transmission, later machines have a more powerful engine with an automatic transmission.

Larger variant

It was in 1990 that the first prototype of the Puma's 6x6 version first ran, and among the variants that have been proposed for this model are an 81-mm mortar carrier and a command post. The prototype was completed with an externally mounted 12.7-mm machine-gun and a bank of three forward-firing smoke dischargers on each side of the commander's turret.

SPECIFICATIONS	
Puma (4x4)	**Puma (6 x 6)**
Crew: 1 + 6	**Crew:** 1 + 8
Weight: 5.7 tonnes	**Weight:** 7.5 tonnes
Dimensions: length 5.108 m (16 ft 9 in); width 2.09 m (6 ft 10¼ in); height (hull top) 1.678 m (5 ft 6 in)	**Dimensions:** length 5.526 m (18 ft 1½ in); width 2.284 m (7 ft 6 in); height (hull top) 1.678 m (5 ft 6 in)
Powerplant: one IVECO 8042.45 liquid-cooled 4-cylinder diesel delivering 134 kW (180 hp)	**Powerplant:** one IVECO 8042.45 liquid-cooled 4-cylinder diesel delivering 134 kW (180 hp)
Performance: maximum road speed 105 km/h (65 mph); range 800 km (497 miles)	**Performance:** maximum road speed 100 km/h (62 mph); range 700 km (435 miles);
Fording: 1 m (3 ft 3 in)	**Fording:** 1 m (3 ft 3 in)
Gradient: 60 per cent	**Gradient:** 60 per cent

BTR-80 Armoured personnel carrier

For many years the Soviet and now Russian army has employed a mix of tracked and wheeled infantry fighting vehicles (IFVs) and armoured personnel carriers (APCs). Each offers several significant advantages: wheeled vehicles have greater strategic mobility, while the tracked vehicles generally have better cross-country mobility and can be fitted with a more powerful weapon system.

Early service

The first 8x8 APC to enter service with the Soviet army was the BTR-60, and this was followed by the BTR-70 and more recently the **BTR-80**. All of

The BTR-80A variant displays its rough-terrain capabilities. The tyre pressure of these vehicles can be centrally altered to suit terrain requirements.

these were designed and built by GAZ (Gorky Automobile Plant) which today is known as the Arzamas Construction Plant. Development of the BTR-80 began in the late 1970s, and the first production vehicles were completed and deployed in the early 1980s.

The layouts of all the BTR series vehicles are very similar, with the commander and driver at the very front and the weapon station on the roof to their immediate rear. The troop compartment is in the middle of the hull with the powerpack at

the very rear. When compared to Western vehicles such as the Swiss-designed MOWAG Piranha 8x8 APC, the overall design of the BTR-80 has significant limitations as a result of the powerpack's location at the rear of the hull.

The infantry have to dismount via the roof hatches or via the door in the side of the hull between the second and third road wheels. The lower part of the door folds down to form a step, while the upper part forms a door that opens to the front.

The manually operated turret is armed with a 14.5-mm (0.57-in) KPVT machine-gun and a 7.62-mm (0.3-in) PKVT machine-gun.

Small arms

A bank of six electrically operated 81-mm (3.2-in) smoke grenade launchers, firing forward over the front of the vehicle, is

The BTR-80A is armed with the same 30-mm 2A72 gun as the BMP-3. This weapon has a range of 4000 m (4,374 ft) firing HE incendiary projectiles.

SPECIFICATION	
BTR-80	in); width 2.9 m (9 ft 5 in); height
Crew: 3 + 7	2.46 m (8 ft 1 in)
Weight: 13600 kg (29,982 lb)	**Performance:** maximum road speed
Powerplant: one V-8 turbocharged	90 km/h (56 mph); maximum water
diesel developing 179 or 194 kW	speed 5.1 kts (9.5 km/h; 5.9 mph);
(240 or 260 hp)	maximum road range 600 km (373
Armament: one 14.5-mm (0.57-in)	miles)
KPVT machine-gun and one	**Fording:** amphibious
7.62-mm (0.3-in) coaxial PKVT	**Gradient:** 60 per cent
machine-gun	**Vertical obstacle:** 0.5 m (1 ft 8 in)
Dimensions: length 7.65 m (25 ft 1	**Trench:** 2 m (6 ft 7 in)

mounted on the rear of the turret. The crew can also fire their small arms from within the vehicle with a high level of safety as firing ports and associated vision devices are provided in the sides of the hull.

Like the BTR-60 and -70, the BTR-80 is amphibious, being propelled in the water by a water jet at the rear of the hull. Before the vehicle enters the water, a trim vane is erected at the front and the electrically operated bilge pumps are activated.

The BTR-80's standard equipment includes night vision gear for the commander, driver and gunner, and steering is powered on the front four road wheels. A central tyre inflation system allows the driver to adjust the tyre pressure to suit the terrain, and an NBC system is standard. A winch is mounted internally at the front of the hull, and this can be used for self-recovery or the recovery of other vehicles on the battlefield.

Some BTR-80 vehicles have been fitted with explosive reactive armour to provide the occupants with some protection from attack by anti-tank weapons with a HEAT (high explosive anti-tank) warhead.

Variants

As usual with Russian vehicles, a whole family of variants has been developed on the same basic chassis. These include **BTR-80K** series of armoured command posts, **BMM** series of armoured battlefield ambulances, the **BTR-80 SPR-2** electronic warfare vehicle, and the **BREM-K** armoured recovery vehicle. The chassis of the BTR-80 is also used as the basis for the **BTR-80 2S23** 120-mm (4.72-in) self-

Right: The standard BTR-80 APC is operated in the largest numbers by Hungary, Kazakhstan, Russia, Turkey, Turkmenistan, Ukraine and Uzbekistan.

propelled gun/mortar system The BTR-80 chassis has also been marketed for a number of civilian applications, these including a fire-fighting conversion of the vehicle. On this version, the turret is removed and the top of the vehicle is instead fitted with 22 launchers which are

The BREM-K armoured recovery vehicle is based on the BTR-80 armoured personnel carrier. The vehicle is fitted with an 'A' frame jib and towbars.

designed to launch fire suppressant cartridges.

Further development of the BTR-80 has resulted in the **BTR-80A**, which is based on the same hull as the earlier vehicle but in this application fitted with a new one-person turret. This is a power-operated unit armed with

an externally mounted 30-mm 2A72 cannon and a 7.62-mm co-axial machine-gun.

Weapon stations

The BTR-80 has also been marketed with a number of other weapon stations, including the Russian Kliver turret armed with

four Kornet laser-guided anti-tank missiles and a 30-mm cannon. This turret is also offered for installation on Western vehicles, as well as on the Russian BMP-1 and BMP-2 IFVs. A version of the vehicle fitted with a Western diesel engine, of Cummins manufacture, is also available.

ARTEC MRAV Multi-Role Armoured Vehicle

As with many European armoured fighting vehicle (AFV) programmes, the **ARTEC Multi-Role Armoured Vehicle (MRAV)** has had a very chequered development history. The MRAV was originally conceived in an effort

to meet the operational requirements of France, Germany and the United Kingdom. In the end, France pulled out and went its own way with the development of the Satory Military Vehicles Véhicule Blindé de Combat

d'Infanterie (VBCI) infantry combat vehicle (ICV). This is slated to replace the AMX-10P tracked ICV, currently operating in the French army, later in the first decade of the 21st century.

Germany and the United

Kingdom were not looking for an IFV, but wanted a vehicle that could be used for a variety of roles including armoured personnel carrier (APC) and as a command post vehicle (CPV). While the British army calls the vehicle the MRAV, the German army designates it as the **GTK (Gepanzertes Transport Kraftfahrzeug)**.

Development

Late in 1999, Germany and the UK went ahead and awarded a development contract for the MRAV to a new industrial consortium based in Munich called ARTEC (ARmoured TEChnology). This company comprises Krauss-Maffei Wegmann and Rheinmetall Landsysteme of Germany and what is now Alvis Vickers of the UK. Under the terms of this contract a total of eight prototypes was to be built, four for each country.

Subsequently, the Netherlands joined the programme and the number of prototypes to be built has increased to 12, with each country now having four prototype vehicles. It is expected that the first production contract will be for 600 vehicles to provide each country with 200 units. As with any programme of this type, there have been delays and the first prototype was not completed until early 2002, with the second following in late 2002.

There are some who believe that MRAV is now too heavy and large for many future potential operational requirements and that greater emphasis should be placed on a type for rapid-deployment forces. There is now an emphasis on equipment that can be rapidly transported by air in tactical transport aircraft such as the Lockheed Martin C-130 Hercules.

The MRAV is designed to be air-portable and also retains low-observable characteristics. Deliveries are expected to take place between June 2006 and March 2009.

When the MRAV enters production, it is expected that there will be production lines in Germany, the Netherlands and the UK, with each country feeding subsystems to each other. Some parts, such as communications and weapon stations, will be unique to each country.

Unusual design

The design of the MRAV is unusual in that the vehicle consists of two key parts; the chassis complete with the powerpack and driver's station, and a dedicated mission module at the rear which can be detached from the vehicle.

MRAV features a high level of protection against not only small arms fire but also shell splinters, anti-tank mines and top attack munitions; the vehicle is also fitted with an NBC system. Stealth characteristics are also incorporated into the design. The vehicle's protection is enhanced through the reduction of both its thermal and acoustic signatures.

To reduce overall life cycle costs, the MRAV uses proven and off-the-shelf components wherever possible – including the engine, transmission and drive line. The basic vehicle has a crew of three, consisting of commander, driver and gunner, and will typically carry eight fully equipped infantry plus supplies for 24 or 48 hours. The infantry will be able to rapidly dismount via the power-operated ramp at the rear of the vehicle.

Armament

It is expected that the armament of the vehicle will be a 40-mm (1.57-in) automatic grenade launcher, and a 12.7-mm (0.5-in) or 7.62-mm (0.3-in) machine-gun in a turret

or remotely controlled from within the vehicle. If the latter were fitted, it would not only reduce the height and overall weight of the vehicle but also make more space available within the hull for additional troops or supplies.

Standard equipment on the MRAV will include a full range of passive night vision equipment, a central tyre inflation system, powered steering and an anti-skid braking system.

Several specialised mission modules are already under development. The UK and the Netherlands have a requirement for an **Armoured Treatment and Evaluation Vehicle**, which will be able to stabilise injured troops in the forward area and then transport them to the rear. This model will have a module with a higher roof line to provide greater volume for litters and medical personnel. Other variants include communications and cargo vehicles.

Other MRAV variants are projected included command and control, electronic warfare and mortar carriers.

SPECIFICATION

MRAV
Crew: 3 + 8
Weight: 33000 kg (72,751 lb)
Powerplant: one MTU diesel developing 530 kW (711 hp) and coupled to Allison fully automatic transmission
Armament: one 40-mm (1.57-in) grenade launcher and one 12.7-mm (0.5-in) or 7.62-mm (0.3-in) machine-gun

Dimensions: length 7.88 m (25 ft 10 in); width 2.99 m (9 ft 10 in); height 2.38 m (7 ft 10 in)
Performance: maximum road speed 103 km/h (64 mph); maximum range 1000 km (621 miles)
Fording: 1.5 m (4 ft 11 in)
Gradient: 60 per cent
Vertical obstacle: 0.8 m (2 ft 7½ in)
Trench: 2 m (6 ft 7 in)

Pandur Armoured personnel carrier

Dating in concept from 1979, when the Austrian company Steyr-Daimler-Puch Spezialfahrzeug AG began work on this private-venture type using commercial and 'off-the-shelf' components wherever possible, the **Pandur** is a 6x6 APC that was first revealed in 1985 after the company had started trials with two prototypes (2 + 8 seats), which were followed in the period to December 1986 by six pre-production vehicles.

Manufacture

The Pandur vehicle family is manufactured by the parent company and also by AV Technology International (a General Dynamics company) in the US. The Pandur has been operational with the Austrian army since 1996 (68+ vehicles) and is also used by Kuwait (70 vehicles), Belgium (54 vehicles) and Slovenia (10+ **Valuk** vehicles). The US Army has awarded a contract for up to 50 Pandur vehicles with new applique armour to form a possible basis for the Armored Ground Mobility System.

All variants are based on the same chassis but configured in two basic forms, namely the 'A' and 'B' models with an

extended centre and flat roofs respectively, and the variants include APCs with cupolas and turrets (including the AV-30 and US Marine Corps' Upgunned Weapon Station) carrying machine-gun armament, an MICV with a more powerfully armed turret, a reconnaissance vehicle with the Multi-Gun Turreted System mounting a 25-, 30- or 35-mm cannon, combat support vehicles mounting a 90-mm (3.54-in) anti-tank gun or any of several mortar types. The service support vehicles include ambulance, engineer, logistics and command/control variants.

Upgraded model

Steyr-Daimler-Puch has also developed the **Pandur II**, trialled from September 2001. This has a longer wheel base and a modified hull, is offered in 6x6 and 8x8 versions, and is powered by a higher-rated engine, the 265-kW (355-hp) Cummins ISC 350 diesel. The first 8x8 prototype is an IFV armed with a 30-mm cannon, and the type's standard equipment includes a central tyre pressure-regulation system.

For the reconnaissance and fire support role the vehicle is equipped with a Cockerill LCTS turret with a 90-mm Mk 8 gun

The Pandur can be fitted with a large number of sensor and weapon fits – this 6x6 vehicle carryies a machine-gun and two Euromissile UTM 800 launchers for HOT anti-tank missile as well as an elevating sensor head. The Pandur's hull was designed with the aid of a computer for the smallest possible radar cross section.

and two 7.62-mm (0.3-in) machine-guns, one mounted co-axially and the other on the overhead cupola. Four smoke grenade dischargers are fitted on each side of the turret.

The turret is electro-mechanically powered with manual back-up. The 90-mm gun can be elevated from -9° to +20°, and the turret can be traversed through 360°. The gunner's station has a combined day and thermal imaging sight with a stabilised head mirror and an integrated laser rangefinder. The commander has a panoramic day sight featuring a gyro-stabilised line of sight, and a monitor displays the gunner's thermal channel.

The APC is armed with one 12.7-mm (0.5-in) M2HB

machine-gun mounted with a shield on a ring providing 360° traverse, and one 7.62-mm (0.3-in) MG3 general-purpose machine-gun. For vision in the closed-down state the driver has three episcopes, and the commander's observation cupola has five episcopes. Six smoke grenade dischargers are fitted on each side of the turret. The amphibious version of the Pandur has a lengthened exhaust and is driven in the water by two waterjets. Protection against 12.7-mm projectiles over the frontal 60° arc, and the rest of the vehicle is proof against the effects of 7.62-mm rounds. Other defensive features also include engine and exhaust silencing, and IR absorbent paint.

A 6x6 amphibious Pandur emerges from a river crossing with its right-hand waterjet evident under the hull. The embarked infantry leave the vehicle by means of two outward-opening rear doors as well as three roof hatches.

SPECIFICATION	
Pandur (6x6 amphibious model)	**Performance:** maximum road speed 100 km/h (62 mph); maximum road range 700+ km (435+ miles)
Crew: 2 + 10	
Weight: 14000 kg (30,864 lb)	**Fording:** amphibious
Dimensions: length 6.297 m (20 ft 8 in); width 2.6 m (8 ft 6½ in); height 1.82 (6 ft) to top of hull	**Gradient:** 70 per cent
	Vertical obstacle: 0.5 m (1 ft 8 in)
Powerplant: one Steyr WD 612.35 6-cylinder diesel engine delivering 212.5 kW (285 hp)	**Trench:** 1.1 m (3 ft 8¼ in)

XA series Armoured personnel carriers

To meet the requirements of the Finnish forces for a 6x6 wheeled APC, in 1982 SISU (now Patria Vehicles) and Valmet built prototypes of their **XA-180** and Model 1912-16 respectively. The former was selected by the Finnish defence ministry, which ordered 59 XA-180s in December 1983. There followed the **XA-185** and **XA-186** variants, the former with a more powerful engine and stronger axles, and the latter optimised for UN-led operations with extra passive armour, a weapon mount in the front, weapon ports in the sides, a one-man turret carrying a 12.7-mm (0.5-in) machine-gun and omission of the XA-185's waterjets. A variant that has not found a customer is the **XA-186/ALT** with the Kvaerner Armoured Launching

Turret carrying four TOW anti-tank missiles.

Standard layout

The vehicle's hull is welded from steel armour, and the modular construction of the hull's armour helps to provide protection against small arms ammunition up to 14.5-mm (0.57-in) calibre, shell fragments and mines. The commander and driver sit at the front, the engine is a turbocharged diesel (behind the driver on the left-hand side of the vehicle with a passage to its right) driving the wheels via an automatic gearbox. The troop compartment is at the rear and has bench seats for 10 infantrymen who enter and exit the vehicle by means of two rear doors and two roof hatches. The troop compartment has 10

The XA-180 series comprises a number of multi-role APC variants of Finnish design, and can be fitted with a number of different role-specialised turrets. This version carries a cupola-mounted 12.7-mm (0.5-in) machine-gun.

vision blocks and firing ports (two in the doors and four on each side), and its roof has provision for a ring-mounted machine-gun or any of several turret types.

Patria plans to build the XA-180 series up to 2004 or later, and currently has orders for more than 700 vehicles

including more than 500 for Finland as well as substantial orders from the Netherlands (**XA-188** with improved protection but no amphibious capability), Norway (XA-186) and Sweden; Ireland has also ordered two vehicles.

The later orders are for the **XA-200** series, whose current

The hydraulically operated telescopic mast of the command variant of the XA-180 series has hydraulic support legs and an automatic guy rope system with hydraulic tightening, and can be erected by two persons in 10 minutes.

Below: Armoured shutters with vision slots can be closed over the windscreen and side windows of the XA-180 series' driving compartment in high-threat conditions.

SPECIFICATION	
Patria Vehicles XA-180	engine delivering 202 kW (271 hp)
Crew: 3 + 10	**Performance:** maximum road speed
Weight: 15500 kg (34,171 lb)	100 km/h (62 mph); maximum road
Dimensions: length 7.35 m (24 ft 2	range 800 km (497 miles)
in); width 2.9 m (9 ft 6 in); height	**Fording:** amphibious
2.3 m (7 ft 6 in)	**Gradient:** 70 per cent
Powerplant: one Valmet 612WIBIC	**Vertical obstacle:** 0.6 m (2 ft)
liquid-cooled 6-cylinder diesel	**Trench:** 1 m (3 ft 3½ in)

variants are the **XA-202** mainly for the weapons platform role and the **XA-203** with a higher roof line over the troop compartment for enhanced APC capability.

Further variants in the family include command and communication, anti-aircraft missile (**XA-181/Crotale NG**), anti-tank missile, ambulance, folding-mast radar carrier, mine scatterer, mortar carrier, recovery and repair, and NBC reconnaissance vehicles. A number of different turrets can be added, these turrets offering the choice of armament between a 7.62-mm (0.3-in) machine-gun and a 30-mm cannon. Other options available include night sights, an air-conditioning system and an NBC package.

The command vehicle's hull is divided into operator, driver/commander, engine and auxiliary power unit compartments. The 10-kW (13.4-hp) diesel APU provides power for the equipment in the operator's compartment.

VBCI Armoured personnel carrier

After it had pulled out of the Multi-Role Armoured Vehicle programme with Germany and the UK, France undertook its own programme to find a successor to the AMX-10P tracked APC of its army's current generation of wheeled and tracked APCs. The programme envisaged a production total of at least 700 and ultimately more than 1,000 vehicles in the form of an initial 550 AIFVs and 150 command post vehicles.

In 2000, after a design competition, the Délégation Générale pour l'Armement issued a contract to Satory Military Vehicles (formed by GIAT Industries and Renault Véhicules Industriels) for the design, development, manufacture and complete logistic support of what had by now been designated as the **VBCI (Véhicule Blindé de Combat d'Infanterie**, or infantry combat armoured vehicle). The programme envisaged the construction and evaluation of four prototypes leading to the delivery of the first production vehicles in 2005 and the completion of sufficient vehicles for the equipment of an initial battalion in 2006.

The overall concept of the VBCI reflects the modern concern for modest initial procurement cost and low life-cycle cost, and is one reason that the type was schemed as a wheeled rather than tracked vehicle, and another aspect of the programme is the use of 'off-the-shelf' components.

Unexceptional design

The VBCI is based on a 8x8 configuration with steering on the front four wheels and, as standard, a central tyre pressure-regulation system. In its layout the vehicle is orthodox, with the driver in a compartment at the front left of the vehicle with the powerpack to his right and the commander to his rear, the power-operated turret in the centre and the eight infantrymen in a compartment at the rear with a rear-set ramp/door arrangement as their primary means of entering and exiting the vehicle. There are vision blocks and firing ports in the sides as well as the rear of the vehicle to allow the embarked infantrymen to use their personal weapons from inside the troop compartment.

The VBCI is being developed as an 8x8 wheeled APC in both AIFV and command post forms as a low-cost and durable successor to the AMX-10P. The French army has a requirement for an initial 700 units.

The turret selected for the AIFV version of the VBCI is the GIAT Dragar unit, which is a one-man turret armed with a 25-mm cannon and a 7.62-mm (0.3-in) co-axial machine-gun with possibly some 620 and 1,400 rounds of ammunition respectively. Variants with the Eryx and MILAN anti-tank missiles are also proposed.

The command post variant will weigh some 23300 kg (51,367 lb), carry a crew of two in addition to the command staff of five, and will also be provided with a local defence capability by the installation of an off-the-shelf remotely controlled weapon station armed with a 0.5-in (12.7-mm) machine-gun.

SPECIFICATION	
Satory Military Vehicles VBCI	**Powerplant:** one Renault liquid-cooled 6-cylinder diesel engine delivering 410 kW (550 hp)
Crew: 3 + 8	
Weight: 25600 kg (56,437 lb)	
Dimensions: length 7.6 m (24 ft 11¼ in); width 2.98 m (9 ft 9½ in); height 2.2 m (7 ft 2½ in) to the top of the hull and 3.06 m (10 ft ½ in) to the top of the turret	**Performance:** maximum road speed 100 km/h (62 mph); maximum road range 750 km (466 miles)
	Fording: 1.2 m (3 ft 11 in)
	Vertical obstacle: 0.7 m (2 ft 4 in)
	Trench: 2 m (6 ft 7 in)

Renault VAB Armoured Personnel Carrier

To meet a French army requirement for a wheeled APC (Armoured Personnel Carrier) for its infantry units, prototypes of the **VAB (Véhicle de l'Avant Blindé**, or front-line armoured vehicle) were built by Panhard and Saviem/Renault in both 4x4 and 6x6 configurations. In May 1974 the Renault design was selected, and the first production vehicles were delivered to the French army in 1976. The total French army requirement was for some 4,000 vehicles, and production quickly rose as high as 50 vehicles per month. Large numbers of VABs were used during Desert Storm, and the vehicle has been deployed on peacekeeping missions in Bosnia, Cambodia, Croatia, Lebanon, Rwanda and Somalia.

World sales

The VAB was a major export success, over 1,000 having been sold to the armies of at least 16 countries, including Argentina, Brunei, Central African Republic, Cyprus, France, Indonesia, Ivory Coast, Kuwait, Lebanon, Mauritius, Morocco, Norway, Oman, Qatar and the United Arab Emirates. Of these, Morocco is the largest operator, having purchased over 400 vehicles; a number were lost in the fighting in the Sahara against the Polisario guerrillas.

The VAB is a conventional wheeled APC, offering greater road mobility than tracked vehicles. It is protected against small arms fire and shell splinters.

The VAB has a hull of all-welded steel armour construction, with the driver and commander at the front. The latter also operated the roof-mounted 7.62-mm (0.3-in) machine-gun. The engine compartment is behind them, with the troop compartment at the rear of the hull; an aisle con-nects the front of the vehicle with the troop compartment. The infantry enter and leave via two doors in the hull rear, and the troops are seated five down each side facing the centre. The VAB is fully amphibious, being propelled in the water by its wheels or, as an option, by two waterjets at the rear of the hull. Standard equipment on French army vehicles includes an NBC system and passive night-vision gear.

The basic vehicle has also been adapted to a wide range of other roles and, since 1976, more than 30 different versions of the VAB have been produced. These include a forward ambulance, internal security vehicle, command vehicle,

A VAB of the 1st Regiment Etrangere Cavalrie (Foreign Legion Cavalry Regiment) crests a sand dune in Djibouti. This vehicle is equipped with the Mephisto turret, carrying four HOT heavy anti-tank missiles. Eight reloads are carried inside the VAB.

repair vehicle, 81-mm (3.2-in) mortar carrier, 120-mm (4.7-in) mortar tractor, NBC reconnaissance vehicle, anti-aircraft vehicle (with twin 20-mm rapid-fire cannon or short range SAMs) and anti-tank vehicle. The latter includes VABs fitted with UTM 800 or Mephisto turrets, equipped with HOT ATGWs (Anti-Tank Guided Weapons). Standard French army VABs are fitted with a cupola-mounted 7.62-mm machine-gun, but a wide range of other armament options is available, including turret-mounted 12.7-mm (0.5-in) machine-guns and stabilised 20- or 25-mm cannon.

Improved VAB

Combat and operational experience over three decades in places as far afield as Chad, Djibouti, Iraq and French Guiana has seen the Armée de Terre carrying out numerous VAB enhancement programmes. More than 1,100 improvements have been implemented in the **VAB New Generation**.

SPECIFICATION	
VAB	in); width 2.49 m (8 ft 2 in); height
Type: Wheeled armoured personnel carrier	without armament 2.06 m (6 ft 9 in)
Crew: 2+10 troops	**Performance:** maximum road speed 110 km/h (68.4 mph); maximum
Combat weight: 4x4 version 13600 kg (29,980 lb); 6x6 version 14800 kg (32,630 lb)	road range 1000 km (621 miles); **Fording:** unlimited – vehicle is amphibious; maximum water speed
Powerplant: Renault MIDR 062045 intercooled Turbo-Diesel delivering 219 kW (300 hp)	8.50 km/h (5 mph) **Gradient:** 60 per cent **Vertical obstacle:** 0.60 m (2 ft)
Dimensions: length 5.98 m (19 ft 7½	**Trench:** (6x6) 1.50 m (4 ft 11 in)

A six-wheeled VAB carrying an experimental winter/urban camouflage scheme. It is possible to convert 4x4 VABs to this configuration, the hulls of the two vehicles being of the same size.

MOWAG Piranha Armoured Personnel Carrier

The **Piranha** range of 4x4, 6x6 and 8x8 APCs was designed by the Swiss firm of MOWAG (now owned by General Dynamics Land Systems) in the late 1960s, the first prototype being completed in 1972.

The hull of the Piranha is of welded steel, providing protection from small arms fire. All members of the Piranha family are fully amphibious, being propelled in the water by two propellers. Optional equipment includes night vision sights, an NBC system, and an air-conditioning system.

Piranha armament depends on the role, but can range from a single machine-gun turret up to a power-operated turret armed with a 105-mm low-recoil gun.

Canada

In 1977 Canada decided to adopt the 6x6 version and production was undertaken by the Diesel Division of General Motors Canada, 491 being built for the Canadian Armed Forces between 1979 and 1982.

Canada initially built three versions of the 6x6 Piranha. The Cougar Fire Support Vehicle has a 76-mm (3.0-in) gun, while the Grizzly APC is armed with 12.7-mm (0.5-in) and 7.62-mm

(0.3-in) MGs. The Husky is a Wheeled Maintenance and Recovery Vehicle.

After evaluating a number of different vehicles, both tracked and wheeled, the USA selected

the 8x8 version of the Piranha to meet its requirement for a **Light Armored Vehicle (LAV)**. The first of these was completed for the US Marine Corps in late 1983. The basic **LAV-25** has a two-man power-operated turret armed with a 25-mm cannon and a co-axial 7.62-mm machine-gun. Other Marine variants include logistics support vehicles, command vehicles, repair vehicles, mortar carriers, anti-tank and anti-aircraft platforms and electronic warfare vehicles.

Marine combat

LAVs played an important part in the Gulf War, and were the first American armoured vehicles flown into Afghanistan when the Marines established their forward base near Kandahar.

In 1983 the 6x6 model was evaluated by the Swiss army as an anti-tank vehicle fitted with the TOW anti-tank system, entering service in the late 1980s.

Piranha III

The current **Piranha III** features a new lightweight hull, higher payloads, improved hydropneumatic suspension, and quick-change powertrains. Available in 6x6, 8x8, and 10x10 versions, the Piranha III incorporates lessons learned in peacekeeping operations all over the world, and is well protected against mines.

The US Army withdrew from the original LAV programme early in 1984, but recent operational experience of rapid reaction and peacekeeping missions has shown the value of air mobility and cost-efficiency. The US Army's future combat system (FCS) was launched in 1999 as a result of the experience of the Kosovo conflict when it took several weeks for Task Force Hawk to deploy to Albania. Since the FCS is not due to enter service until after 2010, there is a need to field seven interim brigade combat teams equipped with off-the-shelf wheeled vehicles.

In November 2000, the US Army ordered 2,131 Piranha IIIs, with the first interim brigade to be equipped by the end of 2001. Several different versions

are being acquired, including a mobile gun with a 105-mm cannon, infantry carrier, reconnaissance, anti-tank guided missile platform, ambulance, mortar carrier, engineer, command post, fire support co-ordination and NBC reconnaissance.

Piranha IV

The latest vehicle in the Piranha family is the 8x8 **Piranha IV**. With increased armour and mine protection, and an upgraded MTU powerplant delivering 406 kW (544 hp), the Piranha IV is fitted with hydropneumatic suspension, ABS and a traction control system. Combat weight is up to 24 tonnes with a 10 tonne payload and the vehicle is air transportable in Lockheed C-130 Hercules aircraft. Also known as the **LAV III**, it is expected to supplement and replace earlier models in Canadian service.

In addition to Canada, the USA and Switzerland, the Piranha range of vehicles is used or has been ordered by Australia, Chile (licence production), Denmark, Ghana, Ireland, Liberia,

The latest Piranha IV has thicker armour, an upgraded MTU powerplant delivering 406 kW (544 hp), hydropneumatic suspension, ABS and a traction control system.

SPECIFICATION	
Piranha III 8x8	Caterpillar 3126
Crew: 2+14	**Dimensions:** length 6.93 m (22 ft
Combat weight: 16500 kg	8 in); width 2.66 m (8 ft 9 in);
(36,380 lb); payload 6000 kg	height 1.98 m (6 ft 6 in)
(13,230 lb)	**Performance:** maximum road speed
Powerplant: will accept numerous	100 km/h (62 mph); maximum
diesel engines in the range of	range 800 km (497 miles); fording
260-331 kW (350-450 hp),	amphibious; maximum water
including Scania DSJ9-48A, Detroit	speed 10 km/h (6.2 mph); gradient
Diesel 6V53TA, MTU 6V183 TE 22,	60 per cent; vertical obstacle 0.60
Cummins 6CTAA 8.3-T350 or	m (1 ft 11 in); trench 2 m (6 ft 7 in)

New Zealand, Nigeria, Oman, Saudi Arabia, Sierra Leone and Sweden. Canada is the main licence manufacturer,

but production licences are also held in the UK by Vickers Defence Systems and Alvis Vehicles.

Since its entry into service in the 1980s, the LAV used by the US Marine Corps has seen action all over the world, most recently in Afghanistan.

Internal security vehicles

Tracked APCs such as the American M113 are not suited to the IS role for a variety of reasons, including the high cost of procuring, maintaining and operating a tracked vehicle, their size and lack of manoeuvrability in confined spaces, lack of doors for rapid entry and exit, poor observation for the driver and commander, and the political consequences of bringing 'tanks' onto the streets.

Design planning

Ever since the requirement for specialised IS vehicles emerged, many companies have devoted considerable effort to the design and development of wheeled vehicles for use in IS operations. The hull of such vehicles must provide protection against attack with 7.62-mm (0.3-in) rifle projectiles. In some countries the terrorist's most commonly employed weapon is the mine, often laid in culverts under roads in remoter areas and intended for detonation when a vehicle runs over it. More often than not, such mines are exploded by remote control so that the terrorist can hit just a military or paramilitary vehicle, leaving civilian traffic to pass in safety.

If the mine is a standard anti-personnel mine or small anti-tank mine, the vehicle designer can help to minimise the amount of damage inflicted on the vehicle by careful design of the hull armour so that the blast is deflected sideways and upward, and thus not contained under the hull of the vehicle, which would lead to the vehicle being lifted and turned over, or alternatively to having its lower surface penetrated by the blast. For example, the British Saxon vehicle has an integral hull with the areas above the wheels manufactured of sheet steel so that they blow should a mine detonate under the vehicle. The South African **Rhino** and **Bulldog** APCs have a V-shaped lower hull raised well above the wheels so that if the vehicle runs over a mine, it is the wheels and suspension that take the blast, and not the hull.

Preference for diesel

The designers and users of IS vehicles prefer diesel engines to petrol engines because diesel fuel is of lower volatility than petrol and therefore does not catch fire as easily. The position of the fuel tank is also critical in any IS vehicle, whether it is petrol- or diesel-engined.

The commander, driver and troops must have excellent

The Alvis Saxon 4x4 APC is typical of wheeled vehicles for the IS role. This vehicle has a mast-mounted TV camera and a turret armed with a machine-gun and grenade launchers.

all-round fields of vision through windows that must provide the same degree of protection as the rest of the hull. The commander's and driver's windows must have wipers and a reservoir of special cleaning liquids to ensure that paint thrown by demonstrators is removed speedily and efficiently.

Entry and exit points

The means of entry and exit must be as numerous and large as possible. If the main door is at the rear and the vehicle is ambushed from the rear, for example, the occupants cannot leave the vehicle in safety unless they also have access to side doors. Moreover, the doors and handles must be designed so that unauthorised entry is not possible, and there should be no external fittings that rioters could use to help them climb on to the vehicle.

The tyres must be of the run-flat type to enable the vehicle to be driven some distance after the tyres have been damaged by bullets. The vehicle should also have a fire detection and suppression system, especially around the wheel arches as rioters often throw petrol bombs at IS vehicles' rubber tyres,

which catch fire easily. The roof of the IS vehicle must be sloped so that grenades that land on the roof can roll off before exploding. The openings around the doors and the engine compartment must be carefully designed so that any flaming liquid from petrol bombs runs down to the ground and not into the vehicle.

As the troops or police may have to stay inside the vehicle for considerable periods, the interior must be insulated and provided with a heating/cooling system. The seats must have belts because if the vehicle does run over a mine many of the casualties could result from occupants being thrown around the vehicle's interior. Adequate stowage space must be provided for riot shields, weapons and other essential equipment.

Some IS vehicles are fitted with turret-mounted 12.7-mm (0.5-in) or 7.62-mm machine-guns, while others have a simple armoured observation cupola for the commander. Specialised equipment such as a barricade remover at the front of the vehicle is standard on some vehicles, while others have provision to be outfitted as specialised command post

An army patrol approaches the explosion of a booby-trapped car in Northern Ireland. The two vehicles, fitted with wire mesh screens to protect the following soldiers against stone-throwers and petrol bombs, are Humber 'Pig' APCs.

vehicles or as ambulances. The type can also be used to carry EOD (explosive ordnance disposal) teams and their equipment, such as remote-control devices fitted with TV cameras and other appliances, and it is common for IS vehicles to be fitted with water cannon or launchers for tear gas grenades.

Some countries use standard military wheeled APCs for the IS role while others, perhaps faced with financial problems and/or a more persistent need for IS capability, prefer to operate cheaper vehicles based on standard light truck chassis such as those from Mercedes Benz and Land Rover.

Some wheeled APCs are used in an internal security role. These include the MOWAG Roland and Piranha ranges of 4x4, 6x6 and 8x8 vehicles, AV Technology Dragoon, Cadillac Gage Commando family and Commando Ranger, Humber 'Pig', Alvis Saracen, GKN Sankey AT 105 Saxon, ENGESA EE-11 Urutu, Fiat Tipo 6614, Renault VAB, Panhard VCR and M3, ACMAT, BMR-600 and BLR-600, Ratel, TM 170 and Soviet BTR series.

Specialist IS vehicles

IS vehicles based on a Mercedes Benz chassis from Germany include the UR-416 delivered from 1969, and also the more recent TM 170 and TM

The Cadillac-Gage V-150 Commando series of APCs have been produced in a number of variants; the police and riot-control versions carry much lighter armament than combat vehicles.

125. Since 1965 Shorts of Northern Ireland has built very substantial numbers of its **Shorland** armoured patrol car, and in 1974 introduced the **Shorland SB 401** APC. Hotspur of Wales has also developed APCs in 4x4 and 6x6 configurations based on the Land Rover chassis.

The **Fiat 11A7 A Campagnola** 4x4 light vehicle is used by many countries, so the Advanced Security Agency SpA of Milan developed the **Guardian** range of 4x4 IS and now offers such vehicles not only on the original Fiat chassis, but also on the Land Rover One Ten and Mercedes Benz 280 GE chassis.

In addition to making the Piranha range of 4x4 and 6x6 vehicles under licence, Chile also builds the **VTP 2** which is similar in some respects to the German **Thyssen IS** vehicle, and the **Multi 163** APC that is also used to patrol airports and other high-risk areas. The Bravia company of Portugal has built the **Chaimite** range of 4x4 APCs in variants almost identical to the V-100 family by Cadillac

Gage, which has built for the US Army National Guard the **Commando Mk III** APC that is similar in basic concept to the Shorland vehicles, although somewhat larger.

Up to the time of its collapse the Warsaw Pact countries in general and the USSR in particular did not develop vehicles specifically for the IS role. Events in Afghanistan, however, revealed that the

BTR-60 and BTR-70 series of 8x8 APCs suffered from a number of drawbacks in the IS role. Some vehicles were fitted with extra armour protection and more firepower, including an AGS-17 grenade launcher.

Some time ago the former East Germany built two types of vehicles for IS operations in the form of the **SK-1** armoured car and the **SK-2** armoured water cannon.

France's Gendarmerie operates both the VBC-90 6x6 armoured car with a 90-mm (3.54-in) gun (background) and the 4x4 VBRG. The latter is a version of the VXB-170 APC, and carries a turret-mounted 7.62-mm machine-gun or grenade launcher.

Below: The South African Buffel APC is typical of that nation's mine-protected IS vehicles, developed during the Apartheid era. The hull floor is V-shaped to offer maximum protection against mines. A mortar carrier version also exists.

SPECIFICATION	
Alvis OMC Casspir Mk III	developing 127 kW (170 hp)
Crew: 2 + 10	**Performance:** maximum road speed
Weight: 12.58 tonnes	90 km/h (56 mph); maximum road
Dimensions: length 6.87 m (22 ft 6½ in); width 2.45 m (8 ft ½ in); height 3.125 m (10 ft 3 in)	range 850 km (528 miles); maximum cross-country range 564 km (350 miles)
Armament: between one and three 7.62-mm (0.3-in) machine-guns	**Fording:** 1 m (3 ft 3¾ in)
	Gradient: 65 per cent
Powerplant: one ADE-352T liquid-cooled 6-cylinder diesel	**Vertical obstacle:** 0.5 m (1 ft 7½ in)
	Trench: 1.06 m (3 ft 5¾ in)

M37 Light vehicle

The 'Beep' (4x4) light vehicle, or to give its official designation, the T214, was widely used as a command/radio vehicle and forward ambulance during World War II, and was placed back in production to meet Korean War requirements. This vehicle was replaced by the **M37**, also produced by Dodge, who built over 125,000 vehicles between 1950 and 1970 for the US Army and many other countries. The M37 was replaced in many units in the 1970s by the M715 series, but insufficient numbers of these were built to replace the M37.

An M37 (4x4) cargo truck complete with bows and a tarpaulin cover over the rear compartment. The latter was provided with a drop tailgate and fold-up troop seats.

Basic design

The basic M37 truck was designed to carry 907 kg (2,000 lb) of cargo on roads or 680 kg (1,500 lb) of cargo across country, and could also tow a trailer weighing 2722 kg (6,000 lb) on roads or 1815 kg (4,000 lb) across rough terrain.

In layout the M37 was similar to a standard commercial pick-up, with the engine at the front, the driver and two passengers in the centre and the cargo area at the rear. The last had a drop tailgate, folding troop seats down each side, removable front rack bows and a tarpaulin cover. The cab has a windscreen that could be folded forward onto the bonnet. On each side was a door from

which the top could be removed. The cargo area also had a removable tarpaulin cover. Some vehicles were fitted with a front-mounted winch for recovery operations, and a deepfording kit could be fitted enabling the M37 to ford 2.133 m (7 ft).

There were a number of variants of the M37, including the **M43** ambulance which had a fully enclosed steel body and could carry eight seated or four stretcher patients and a medical attendant. The rear compartment was provided with a heater and a light. The command post model was similar to the basic cargo model but had side windows, and internally had a folding table and map light, and could be fitted with comms equipment.

The telephone maintenance truck was the **M201** which had an all-steel body with compartments for tools and spare equipment. The M37 was also made under licence in Canada in the 1950s by Chrysler at Windsor, Ontario, these being called the **M37CDN** cargo vehicle, **M43CDN** ambulance and **M152CDN** fully enclosed panel truck. One of the more unusual Canadian models was an M37CDN with a pedestal mounted to the rear of the cab for launching anti-tank guided weapons.

Japananese models

In the 1950s Japan produced

two vehicles very similar to the M37. These were the **Nissan Q4W73** (4x4) 750-kg (1,653-lb) truck and the **Toyota 2FQ15L** (4x4) with a similar carrying capability. Both of these were used by the Japanese Self-Defence Force, and the Nissan vehicle was also built under licence in India for the Indian army. The Toyota model was also used by United States forces in the Far East, South Vietnam and South Korea. The South Vietnam military forces fitted many of their vehicles with armour protection for convoy escort work and for the patrol of airbases and other targets.

Right: Between 1950 and 1970 Dodge built more than 130,000 of these M37 (4x4) cargo trucks for the US armed forces.

Below: The ambulance member of the family was designated the M43, and could carry either four stretcher patients or eight seated patients.

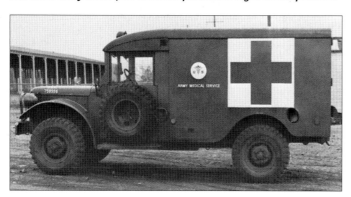

SPECIFICATION	
M37 **Crew:** 1+ 2 (plus 6/8 in rear) **Weight:** empty 2585 kg (5,699 lb) and loaded 3493 kg (7,700 lb) **Powerplant:** one Dodge T245 six cylinder petrol engine developing 58 kW (78 bhp)	**Dimensions:** length 4.81 m (15 ft 9 in); width 1.784 m (5 ft 10 in); height 2.279 m (7 ft 6 in) **Performance:** maximum road speed 88.5 km/h (55 mph); maximum range 362 km (225 miles) **Gradient:** 68 per cent **Fording:** 1.066 m (3 ft 6 in)

M38 Light vehicle

At the outbreak of the Korean War in 1950, the standard American light vehicle was still the Jeep. But the rapid expansion of the US Army meant that there were insufficient Jeeps, even when units in Europe and elsewhere were robbed of their vehicles. To meet this urgent need the civilian **Willys CJ3A** was fitted with a 24-volt electrical system (to enable it to be fitted with radios), semi-floating rear axle and a deep-fording kit (enabling it to ford to a depth of 1.879 m/6 ft 2 in), and this was standardised as the **M38**. In appearance it was similar to the Jeeps of World War II, and could carry a payload of 544 kg (1,200 lb) on roads or 363 kg (800 lb) across country, and could tow a trailer weighing 907 kg (2,000 lb) on roads or 680 kg (1,500 lb) across country. It could also be fitted with a front-mounted winch.

The M38 was in production from 1950 to 1952, when it was replaced by the **M38A1**, which was powered by a four-cylinder petrol engine developing 53.69 kW (72 bhp), had a longer wheelbase, possessed greater operational range thanks to the provision of a larger-capacity fuel tank, and had the same payload capability as the basic M38. The M38A1 is distinguishable from the M38 as the former has distinct curved sides to the bonnet, while the latter has a flat bonnet that is almost identical to that of the World War II Jeep.

The layout of the M38 was conventional, with the engine at the front, the driver and one passenger in the centre, and a bench seat for a further two passengers at the rear. The windscreen folded forward onto the bonnet and a canvas top, stowed at the rear when not required, could be quickly erected when the windscreen was raised. Variants of the later

M38A1 included the **M38A1C** which carried a 106-mm (4.17-in) recoilless rifle in the rear that could be fired from the vehicle or dismounted for ground use, and also had a split windscreen so that the barrel could be locked along the centre of the vehicle for travelling. The ambulance model of the M38A1 was the **M170**, which could carry three stretcher or six seated patients.

Canadian production

The M38 and M38A1 were replaced in the US Army by the M151 light vehicle, but they remained in service with many other countries around the world, and the type was also made under licence in Canada as the **M38CDN** and **M38A1CDN**, both of which were be replaced by the West German Volkswagen Iltis light vehicle built under licence.

Jeep Corporation

In the early 1960s Willys-Overland became Kaiser Jeep, which later became the Jeep Corporation, a subsidiary of the American Motors Corporation, which manufactures a wide range of 4x4 vehicles for the

An M38A1 (4x4) light vehicle was used by the Spanish marines, and is fitted with radio equipment for use in the command role.

civilian market. Military versions of some of these vehicles are also produced for export including the **AM7**, **AM8** and

AM10, which all have different wheelbases and payloads, although they are all powered by the Model 258 engine.

The forward ambulance version of the M38 was the M170, which had a longer wheelbase and could carry three stretcher or six seated patients.

SPECIFICATION	
M38	**Dimensions:** length 3.377 m (11 ft 1 in); width 1.574 m (5 ft 2 in); height 1.879 m (6 ft 2 in)
Crew: 1 + 1 (plus 2 in rear)	
Weight: empty 1247 kg (2,749 lb) and loaded 1791 kg (3,948 lb)	**Performance:** maximum road speed 88.5 km/h (55 mph); maximum range 362 km (225 miles)
Powerplant: one Willys MC 4-cylinder petrol engine developing 44.7 kW (60 bhp)	**Gradient:** 65 per cent
	Fording: 0.939 m (3 ft 1 in)

M151 Light vehicle

The **M151**'s development can be traced back to a requirement issued in 1950 for a new ¼-ton vehicle to replace the M38 which was then entering production at Willys.

Development of the new vehicle was undertaken by the Ford Motor Company, the first prototypes being completed in 1952 and further prototypes in 1954 under the designation **XM151**. Further development of the latter resulted in the **XM151E1** of steel construction, and in the **XM151E2** of aluminium construction. The former was eventually selected for production, and the first vehicles came off the production line at Ford's Highland Park Plant in 1960 under the designation M151.

By 1984 the vehicle was in service with some 100 armies in almost every corner of the world, with production undertaken by AM General Corporation at its Sound Bend Facilities. This company produced over 100,000 vehicles, however, the US Army abruptly curtailed its orders after it was revealed that the vehicle did not meet stringent emission standards. Thus all subsequent production was chiefly for export. The M151 saw action with American forces in Vietnam, where the vehicle

An M151 (4x4) light vehicle with the canopy erected. AM General Corporation produced this vehicle to meet foreign military sales after the US Army stopped purchasing the vehicle because of emission concerns.

was used for a wide range of roles – some even being fitted with armour protection.

M151 variants

The original M151 was followed in production by the **M151A1**, which has improved suspension, while the **M151A2** that followed in 1970 has modified lighting, two-speed wipers, modified rear suspension, a collapsible steering wheel and a dual brake system. The **M151A2LC** has a different gearbox, transfer box and suspension. There are many variants of the M151 including the **M107/M108** communications vehicles, the **M718** ambulance which can carry one stretcher and three seated patients (or various combinations of

stretcher patients and sitting patients), and the **M825** fitted with the M40 106-mm (4.17-in) recoilless rifle.

The basic M151 series can carry 554 kg (1,221 lb) on roads or 362 kg (798 lb) across country, and can tow a trailer weighing 970 kg (2,138 lb) on roads or 680 kg (1,499 lb) across country. A variety of kits can be fitted including a heater, a fully enclosed hard top, searchlight, front-mounted

winch, 100-amp alternator and a kit to enable the vehicle to ford to a depth of 1.524 m (5 ft), the latter was widely used by the USMC when driving out of landing craft during amphibious operations.

Vehicle layout

The layout of the vehicle is similar to other vehicles of this type, with the engine at the front, the driver and one passenger in the centre and a bench seat at the rear. The engine is coupled to a manual gearbox with four forward and one reverse gear and a single-speed transfer box that enables the driver to select either 4x4 or 4x2 drive. The suspension, front and rear, consists of coil springs and hydraulic shock absorbers.

The M151 was widely used by the US Army to mount such weapons as 0.3-in (7.62-mm) or 0.5-in (12.7-mm) machine-guns or the Hughes TOW ATGW system. The M151 was replaced by the High Mobility Multi-purpose Wheeled Vehicle (HMMWV or 'Hummer') – also built by AM General Corporation.

SPECIFICATION	
M151	**Dimensions:** length 3.352 m (11 ft); width 1.58 m (5 ft 2 in); height 1.803 m (5 ft 11 in)
Crew: 1 + 1 (plus 2 in rear)	
Weight: empty 1012 kg (2,231 lb) and loaded 1575 kg (3,472 lb)	**Performance:** maximum road speed 106 km/h (66 mph); maximum range 483 km (300 miles)
Powerplant: one 4-cylinder petrol engine developing 53.69 kW (72 bhp)	**Gradient:** 60 per cent
	Fording: 0.533 m (1 ft 9 in)

From 1960, the M151 was the standard light vehicle of the US Army and many other armies around the world. From 1984 it was replaced by the 'Hummer'.

HMMWV High Mobility Multi-purpose Wheeled Vehicle

For many years the US Army operated a bewildering range of light vehicles including the M274 (4x4) Mechanical Mule, M151 (4x4) ¼-ton light vehicle, M37 (4x4) ¾-ton light vehicle and the M715 (4x4) 1¼-ton and M561 (6x6) Gama Goat vehicles. By the early 1980s these vehicles were becoming increasingly difficult to maintain. Moreover, in many cases there were insufficient vehicles to meet requirements: in 1981, for example, the US Army had a requirement for some 30,000 M561 type vehicles but had only 11,000 on strength. In the same year the situation for the M151 was even more acute: the US Army had not purchased any such vehicles since 1978, as its petrol engine no longer met the government's stringent emission-control standards. Some 60,000 of these vehicles remained in service into the 1980s, the majority built between 1966 and 1969.

These vehicles were replaced by two main types, the Commercial Utility Cargo Vehicle (CUCV) and the **High Mobility Multi-purpose Wheeled Vehicle (HMMWV)**. To meet the requirement for the CUCV, 26 commercial vehicles were put

through an exhaustive series of trials at Aberdeen Proving Ground, Maryland, located just north of Washington, DC. The US Army then selected the General Motors Model K and placed an order worth just under $700 million for over 53,000 vehicles, the first of these being delivered in 1983. This vehicle is a standard commercial vehicle with the minimum of modifications to suit it for military use, for example military paint, tow hooks, slave kit, 28-volt electrical system and so on. All versions are powered by the same 6.2-litre diesel coupled to an automatic transmission and two-speed transfer case. Five basic 4x4 versions were procured, namely utility, cargo, ambulance, truck and cargo shelter carrier.

'Hummer' arrives

To meet the requirement for the HMMWV (invariably shortened to 'Hum-Vee' or 'Hummer'), five companies (out of 61 approached) submitted proposals to the Tank Automotive Command in early 1981, and in July the same year AM General Corporation, Chrysler (by then the Land Systems Division of General Dynamics) and Teledyne

Above: An HMMWV during the 1991 Gulf War. Independent arm suspension on each wheel station means the vehicle can traverse almost any terrain.

Below: An HMMWV in the desert of central Iraq during Operation Iraqi Freedom and armed with a Mk 19 40-mm grenade launcher.

Continental were each awarded a contract for the supply of 11 prototype vehicles. After these vehicles had been put through tests at various locations in the US, the AM General entry was selected for standardisation early in 1983, with first production vehicles to be completed in 1984. The initial contract was for some 53,973 vehicles worth

$1,184 million with a 100 per cent option. Of the initial order, 38,085 vehicles were for the US Army, 13,196 for the USMC and the remaining 2,692 for the USAF.

Compared with the vehicles that it replaced, the HMMWV has a greatly increased carrying capability, improved cross-country performance, higher speed and longer range of operation. The engine is at the front, four individual seats in the centre and a cargo carrying area at the rear, with roll-over protection provided as standard. The basic model is unarmoured, although an appliqué armour kit is available, as is a wide range of other equipment such as winches.

Variants

Variants of the HMMWV include the basic **M998** cargo/troop carrier without winch; **M1038** cargo/troop carrier with winch; **M966** TOW missile carrier, basic armour, without winch; **M1036** TOW missile carrier, basic armour, with winch; **M1045** TOW missile carrier, supplemental armour, without winch; **M1046** TOW missile carrier, supplemental armour, with

US Marines in an HMMWV equipped with a 0.5-in (12.7-mm) heavy machine-gun move in to support fellow Marines involved in a fire-fight at Nasiriyah, Iraq, during Iraqi Freedom in April 2003.

winch; **M1025** armament carrier, basic armour, without winch; **M1026** armament carrier, basic armour, with winch; **M1043** armament carrier, supplemental armour, without winch; **M1044** armament carrier, supplemental armour, with winch; **M996** mini-ambulance, two litters, basic armour; **M997** maxi-ambulance, four litters, basic armour; **M1035** soft-top ambulance, two litters; **M1037** S-250 communications shelter carrier, without winch; **M1042** S-250 carrier, with winch;

and **M1069** tractor for M119 105-mm (4.13-in) light gun. The HMMWV also carries the

Avenger light anti-aircraft system. The vehicle has been widely exported.

SPECIFICATION	
M998 HMMWV	
Crew: 1 + 3	**Performance:** maximum road speed 105 km/h (65 mph) at maximum gross weight; maximum road range on internal fuel 500 km (311 miles)
Weight: empty 2295 kg (5,060 lb)	
Powerplant: one liquid cooled 6.2-litre fuel injected V8 Detroit Diesel engine delivering 96.9 kW (130 hp) at 3,600 rpm via a three-speed automatic transmission	
Dimensions: length 4.57 m (15 ft); width 2.16 m (7 ft); height 1.83 m (6 ft) reducible to 1.37 m (4 ft 6 in)	**Fording:** 0.76 m (2 ft 6 in) without preparation or 1.5 m (5 ft) with deep water fording kit
	Gradient: 60 per cent

Fast attack vehicles FAV, RST-V and IFAV

The idea of using light vehicles on fast, highly mobile strike operations is hardly new. Britain's SAS and LRDG made epic raids through the desert in such vehicles during World War II, and much of the success of Israel's armed forces is based on tactics evolved by Jeep columns which outmanoeuvred Arab columns during the War of Independence. However, the US Army did little in the field until the emergence of the Special Forces in the 1960s.

The initial fast attack vehicle used by the US Armed Forces was the M151. Never entirely successful – the M151 was notoriously unstable and drivers had to take great care over rough terrain – it was nevertheless available in large numbers and was small enough to be transported by cargo

aircraft and helicopters. The M151's replacement, the HMMWV, was far more able to sustain long-range reconnaissance patrol, but it lacked the performance that

was required for Special Forces operations.

Civilian design

In 1982 Emersion Electric was awarded a contract worth $2

million for 80 **Fast Attack Vehicles**, based on a Chenowth Racing Products cross-country racer. The **FAV** has no armour protection and relies for its survival on its speed and small

Powered by a hybrid diesel/electric drive, the RST-V Shadow developed by General Dynamics offers excellent cross-country capability combined with certain 'stealth' features.

size. The chassis is essentially a tubular frame with an integral roll-over cage. The driver is seated in the centre of the vehicle on the left with the gunner/passenger/commander to his right, both crew members being provided with seat belts which are essential when the vehicle is travelling at speed across country. Mounted at the rear is the air-cooled petrol engine developing 70 kW (94 hp). Maximum road speed is almost 129 km/h (80 mph). The FAV can be fitted with a variety of weapons, including 40-mm grenade launchers, 0.3-in (7.62-mm) or 0.5-in (12.7-mm) machine-guns, a 30-mm Chain Gun or TOW anti-tank missiles.

Hybrid drive

The FAV is very fast across country and can pack a considerable punch, but it lacks the capacity for sustained operations. The US Marine Corps needs more capable vehicles, moreover, and the **Reconnaissance, Surveillance and Targeting Vehicle**, or **RST-V**, is currently under

development. An advanced hybrid-drive vehicle featuring in-hub hybrid electric motors, the **Shadow** has demonstrated maximum road speeds of 113 km/h (70 mph). It is also capable of significant cross-country speeds. The hybrid drive lets the Shadow run silently – on batteries alone – for more than 32 km (20 miles). The Shadow is designed to be carried by the V-22 Osprey tiltrotor aircraft, which is unable to accommodate vehicles as large as the HMMWV. Shadow is also readily

deployable in helicopters like the CH-53 and CH-46.

Until the RST-V comes into service in the next decade, the Marines have acquired an

First deployed to a USMC unit in 1999, the Interim Fast Attack Vehicle (right) replaces the petrol-driven M151, offering far greatly improved capability.

Interim Fast Attack Vehicle in the Mercedes-Benz MB 290 GD 1.5-ton off-road vehicle. The **IFAV** can be carried internally by Marine helicopters.

Below left: The Light Strike Vehicle is the British Army's FAV equivalent and can carry MILAN (pictured) and LAW80 anti-tank weapons. This example is deployed with 24 Airmobile Brigade.

Below: A US Army 9th Infantry Division FAV on exercise in South Korea. Based on a highly successful off-road racing vehicle, the FAV is modified to carry military equipment such as radios and armament.

SPECIFICATION	
RST-V Shadow	(reduced for air transportation) 1.674 m (5 ft 6 in); maximum height 1.674 m (5 ft 6 in); minimum height 1.397 m (4 ft 7 in); ground clearance 0.457 m (1 ft 6 in) or (for air transportation) 0.1 m (4 in)
Crew: up to 6	
Weights: combat weight 3629 kg (8,000 lb); payload 1361 kg (3,000 lb)	
Powerplant: one 114-kW (153-hp) Detroit Diesel 2.5-litre DI-4V turbocharged diesel engine, powering a 110-kW (148-hp) generator driving four 50-kW (67-hp) permanent magnetic hub motors	**Performance:** speed 112 km/h (70 mph); range on main engine 758 km (471 miles); range on batteries 32 km (20 miles)
	Fording: 0.92 m (3 ft)
	Gradient: 60 per cent
Dimensions: length 5.45 m (17 ft 10 in); width 2.057 m (6 ft 9 in); width	

Land Rover Light utility vehicle

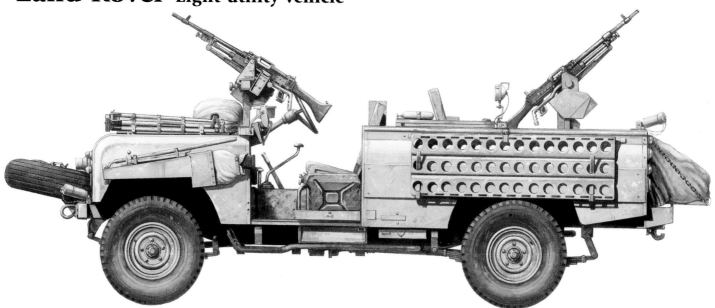

A long wheelbase Land Rover as used by the British Special Air Service (SAS) Regiment for reconnaissance in the Middle East. These 'Pink Panthers' were fitted with 0.3-in (7.62-mm) General-Purpose Machine-Guns, smoke dischargers, sand channels, water and fuel cans, and external stowage.

In the early 1990s the British Ministry of Defence drew up its requirements for a new family of more capable wheeled vehicles to replace its then-current fleet of Land Rover 4x4 vehicles. In the end three different vehicles were required: these were the Truck Utility Light, Truck Utility Medium, and Truck Utility Medium Heavy Duty.

Several different vehicles were tested before it was announced that Land Rover had won the competition for the first two vehicles and Steyr-Daimler-Puch the contest for the Truck Utility Medium Heavy Duty with its Pinzgauer vehicle.

The Truck Utility Light requirement was met by a modified version of the **Land Rover Defender 90** while the Truck Utility Medium requirement was met by the **Land Rover Defender 110** in

the **XD** versions. These British Army vehicles include a number of modifications, and are easily differentiated from their civilian counterparts as the spare wheel/tyre unit has been removed from the bonnet and fitted on the side of the vehicle.

There was also a competition for an ambulance, and this requirement was met by the **Land Rover Defender 130** in the XD vehicle with the relevant body designed and built by Marshall Specialist Vehicles.

Above right: This Syrian long wheelbase (LWB) Land Rover has been modified for special forces use with a 30-mm cannon fitted at the rear.

Right: Developed to meet a British Army requirement for a medium utility truck, these Land Rover Defender 110s are seen on patrol in the streets of Kabul, Afghanistan.

In all just under 8,000 new Land Rover vehicles were supplied to the UK MoD before the final deliveries were effected in 1998.

Specialist variants

The Land Rover has also been assembled in a number of other countries. Australia, for example, has a 6x6 model. The baseline Land Rover is also used for a wide range of special applications, for example fitted with an armoured body for service in the internal security role.

The Land Rover vehicle has also been adopted in optimised forms for use by police and special forces. For the

important export market Land Rover developed the **Special Operations Vehicle (SOV)** based on a modified Land Rover 110 chassis, and a number of other companies have developed special add-on equipment to enhance the core capabilities of the basic Land Rover.

In British service, the Special Air Service Regiment makes use of a special version of the Land Rover optimised for the regiment's particular and exacting requirements, and thus capable of carrying a variety of weapons such as machine-guns of various makes and calibres, and a launcher for the MILAN anti-tank guided missile.

SPECIFICATION	
Land Rover XD 110 **Crew:** 1 + 1 front and 8 rear **Weight:** 3350 kg (7,385 lb) **Dimensions:** length 4.55 m (14 ft 11 in); width 1.79 m (5 ft 10½ in); height 2.08 m (6 ft 10 in) **Powerplant:** one 4-cylinder turbocharged diesel developing 83 kW (111 hp) and coupled to	manual transmission with five forward and one reverse gears and a two-speed transfer case **Performance:** maximum road speed 90 km/h (56 mph); maximum range 600 km (373 miles) **Fording:** 0.7 m (28 in) **Gradient:** 60 per cent

Below: Well proven in action over many years, the latest Land Rover Defender 4x4 vehicle is rugged and reliable.

Below left: The multinational International Security Assistance Force is tasked with assisting the Afghan government in maintaining security. Note the spare wheel stowage and canvas tilt on this ISAF Land Rover.

Land Rover 1-Tonne Light utility vehicle/artillery tractor

When the long wheelbase Land Rover was introduced to service in the 1950s, it was more than adequate to tow weapons such as the 105-mm (4.13-in) pack howitzer used by the Royal Artillery from 1960. It was realised that in the future heavier weapon systems would be introduced into service, however, so a requirement was drawn up for a 4x4 vehicle with a cross-country payload of 1000 kg (2,205 lb) and also the ability to tow a powered trailer carrying 1500 kg (3,307 lb). This vehicle was subsequently designed by Land Rover in co-operation with the Military Vehicles and Engineering Establishment at Chertsey in Surrey. The first prototypes were completed in the

The Land Rover 1-Tonne 4x4 vehicle was too specialised to find civilian buyers, but was sold to Australia, Egypt and Luxembourg as well as the British forces.

The Land Rover 1-Tonne was created to carry passengers or freight (including mortar and anti-tank missile teams) in its open but coverable rear payload area, and also to serve as a tractor for lighter weapons such as the 105-mm (4.13-in) Light Gun and the Rapier surface-to-air missile system.

mid-1960s, but as a result of trials a number of modifications had to be carried out and it was not until 1975 that the first **Land Rover 1-Tonne** production vehicles were issued to British Army units.

Limited production

For a variety of reasons less than 3,000 of these vehicles were built, most of them being supplied to the British Army and the Royal Air Force, although overseas sales were made to Australia (for the Rapier SAM), Egypt (for the Swingfire anti-tank missile system) and Luxembourg. The main reason for this relative short production run, almost insignificant by Land Rover standards, was that the vehicle was designed specifically for military use, whereas the basic Land Rover

was developed as a commercial vehicle but later adopted by the military.

In the British Army the Land Rover 1-Tonne has been used to tow the 105-mm Light Gun, to carry the 81-mm (3.2-in) mortar teams of British-based infantry battalions, to carry MILAN anti-tank teams (two launchers and 14 missiles), and to tow the Rapier SAM launcher, its missile resupply trailer and the Blindfire radar system.

There is also a model with a fully enclosed body for use in the ambulance role, and this can carry four litters or six seated casualties in addition to its crew. Another version with an enclosed body is used in the communications and EW roles.

The Land Rover 1-Tonne is of the forward control type, with the driver at the front right and

passenger on the left with the engine between and below their seats. The engine is basically a standard commercial model (but with a reduced compression ratio to enable it to run on low-octane fuels) and is coupled to a manual gearbox with four forward and one reverse gears. The transfer box is of the two-speed type with permanent

four-wheel drive. The cargo area is at the rear

Air transport

For air transport the complete hood, body sides, windscreen, bumpers, doors, bows and tarpaulin cover can be removed, reducing the overall weight of the vehicle to only 1580 kg (3,483 lb).

The Land Rover 1-Tonne was developed to meet the needs of the British armed forces by Land Rover and the Military Vehicles and Engineering Establishment.

SPECIFICATION	
Land Rover 1-Tonne	**Powerplant:** one Rover V-8 petrol
Crew: 1 + 1 front and 8 rear	engine developing 95.5 kW
Weight: empty 1924 kg (4,242 lb)	(128 bhp)
and loaded 3120 kg (6,878 lb)	**Performance:** maximum road speed
Dimensions: length 4.127 m (13 ft 6	120 km/h (74 mph); maximum
in); width 1.842 m (6 ft 1 in); height	range 560 km (348 miles)
2.138 m (7 ft)	**Gradient:** 60 per cent

Land Rover Perentie Heavy-duty light truck

These Land Rover Perentie 6x6 light trucks undertake long-range patrol and are reconnaissance units for the Australian army. They offer good cross-country mobility and excellent reliability, and are here seen with pintle-mounted 0.5-in (12.7-mm) M2 machine-guns.

In 1981, faced with an increasingly urgent need to replace its existing fleet of all-terrain light vehicles, the Australian army started the Perentie programme that eventually resulted in the production of more than 4,200 Land Rover vehicles, in 4x4 and 6x6 configurations, by Rover Australia starting in 1987.

The 6x6 model can be traced back to a development that took place as a private venture in the UK in the 1980s by a company called SMC Engineering. This first step in the process was further developed within Australia, and the vehicle that eventually emerged is the **Land Rover Perentie** heavy-duty 6x6 light truck based on the chassis of the Land Rover 110 and later Land Rover Defender 110.

The Perentie vehicle is wider than the standard Land Rover and, of course, is lengthened to carry the third powered axle and

the much increased payload. It is, however, similarly configured with the engine (manual transmission (four forward and one reverse gears) and two-speed transfer box at the front, two-person cab in the centre and, at the rear, cargo area with

Right: The Land Rover Perentie 6x6 vehicle, seen here in armed form, is highly capable and can also tow a 1500-kg (3,307-lb) trailer.

Seen with a rear-mounted motorcycle and pintle-mounted 0.3-in (7.62-mm) FN general-purpose machine-gun, the Land Rover Perentie has a front-mounted Thomas T9000M winch for self-recovery and the aid of other vehicles when they become stuck.

drop sides, a drop tailgate, bows and a removable cover, and capacity for 12 equipped troops.

Variants

As usual there are numerous variants including a winch-equipped light cargo truck, air-defence truck with the Rapier or RBS 70 SAM, four-litter ambulance, general maintenance truck with a box body, and electronic repair truck. A special version, which has seen service in Afghanistan, was developed for the Australian SAS Regiment. This is the **Long-Range Patrol**

Seen without the machine-gun that is generally standard, this is a 4x4 Land Rover of the Australian army used for long-range patrol.

Vehicle, and has additional specialised equipment including mounts for weapons including a machine-gun of up to 0.5-in (12.7-mm) calibre. The vehicles were originally supplied with a frame on the rear to carry a motorcycle.

SPECIFICATION	
Land Rover 110 Perentie	diesel engine developing 90 kW (121 hp)
Crew: 1 + 1 (front)	
Weight: 5660 kg (12,478 lb) loaded	**Performance:** maximum road speed 100 km/h (62 mph); maximum range 600 km (373 miles)
Dimensions: length 6.14 m (20 ft 1¾ in); width 2.2 m (7 ft 2½ in); height (canopy) 2.76 m (9 ft ⅓ in)	**Fording:** 0.6 m (2 ft)
Powerplant: one Isuzu 4BDI liquid-cooled 4-cylinder turbocharged	**Gradient:** 70 per cent

ENGESA EE-12 Light utility vehicle and weapons carrier

Although known primarily for its extensive family of wheeled armoured fighting vehicles, including the EE-9 Cascavel 6x6 armoured car and EE-11 Urutu 6x6 armoured personnel carrier, the ENGESA company of Brazil also developed a complete range of 4x4 and 6x6 military trucks.

The smallest of these was the **ENGESA EE-12** 4x4 light vehicle, which was developed as a private venture and aimed at the export market. It has seats for the driver and three passengers and a nominal cross-country payload of 500 kg (1,102 lb) and can also tow a trailer weighing up to 250 kg (551 lb).

The layout of the EE-12 is similar to most vehicles of this type, and therefore has the engine with a manual transmission (five forward and one reverse gears) at the front, driver and one passenger in the centre, and the other persons in the cargo area at the rear.

EE-12 is provided with a single door in each side and at the rear there is a tailgate that

The ENGESA EE-12 4x4 light vehicle was built exclusively for the export market, and is thought to have found only one buyer before ENGESA failed.

swings open to the right. The spare wheel/tyre is also at the

rear. The windscreen can be folded forward onto the bonnet,

and the sides, top and rear can also be folded down.

As usual, a wide range of EE-12 variants was offered, these including an ambulance with a fully enclosed body and a weapons carrier that could be fitted with various machine-guns and/or anti-tank weapons. ENGESA ceased trading some years ago, and the only customer for the EE-12 was Angola.

SPECIFICATION	
ENGESA EE-12	engine developing 63.5 or 52 kW
Crew: 1 + 3	(85 or 70 hp) respectively
Weight: 2100 kg (4,630 lb)	**Performance:** maximum road speed
Dimensions: length 3.57 m (11 ft 8½	110 km/h (68.5 mph); maximum
in); width 1.77 m (5 ft 9⅔ in); height	range 600 km (373 miles)
(cab) 1.9 m (6 ft 2¾ in)	**Fording:** 0.6 m (2 ft)
Powerplant: one General Motors	**Gradient:** 70 per cent
4-cylinder petrol or Perkins diesel	

An ENGESA EE-12 4x4 light vehicle is put through its paces during trials in Brazil.

Automotive Industries M-462 Abir Light utility vehicle

In the 1960s Automotive Industries developed the **M-325** 4x4 truck, which had a nominal payload of 1800 kg (3,968 lb). This was built in numerous configurations for the Israel Defence Force, which took cargo, troop carrier, ambulance, box body and special mine protected vehicles.

Further development

Development of the M-325 resulted in the much enhanced **M-462 Abir**, which is marketed as a multi-purpose tactical vehicle. The layout of the vehicle is conventional, and therefore has the engine and its associated transmission at the front, the driver and up to two passengers in the centre, and the cargo area at the rear.

The baseline vehicle has been offered with a choice of two different types of V-8 engine in the forms of a petrol engine or a diesel engine coupled to a manual or fully automatic transmission and two-speed transfer case. The suspension consists of semi-elliptical springs and hydraulic shock absorbers. The steering is power assisted.

The M-462 Abir is normally delivered with a soft-top cab and the rear cargo area fitted with a drop tailgate, removable bows and a tarpaulin cover. However, the vehicle can be supplied in specialised models such a reconnaissance vehicle or internal security machine.

Fully enclosed version

A fully enclosed armoured personnel carrier version of the M-462 Abir was developed with an all-welded body providing the occupants with protection from small arms fire and shell splinters. As far as it is known this did not enter quantity production. The vehicle can also be used to tow weapons and can be configured as a weapons carrier, for example for the 106-mm (4.17-in) M40 recoilless rifle.

The Automotive Industries M-462 Abir 4x4 multi-purpose tactical vehicle is seen here in its form with central seats for use in the police role.

SPECIFICATION	
Automotive Industries M-462 Abir	**Performance:** maximum road speed
Crew: 1 + 2	110 km/h (68.5 mph); maximum
Weight: 4700 kg (10,362 lb)	range 600 km (373 miles)
Dimensions: length 5.03 m (16 ft	**Fording:** 0.76 m (2 ft 6 in)
6 in); width 2.04 m (6 ft 10½ in);	**Gradient:** 60 per cent
height 2.1 m (6 ft 10⅔ in)	
Powerplant: one General Motors	
diesel developing 127 kW (170 hp)	

Hotchkiss M 201 Light vehicle

The Free French Forces used the American-supplied Jeep in large numbers during World War II, and these proved so successful that in the early 1950s Hotchkiss-Brandt of Paris obtained a licence to start production in France, for both the civilian and military markets. The first production models of this **Hotchkiss M 201** were completed in 1953 and production continued until 1969, by which time over 40,000 had been built. In addition to being used by the French armed forces the M 201 was supplied to many countries in North Africa and also to Belgium. In the French armed forces its replacement by the Peugeot P4 (4x4) vehicle. which has greater load-carrying capability, began in the mid-1980s. The M 201 will be around for some years yet, however, and surplus vehicles also found their way onto the civilian market.

Jeep similarities

The M 201 is almost identical to the wartime Jeep with the engine at the front, driver and one passenger in the centre, and a seat for a further two passengers at the rear. With the windscreen erected a canopy can be fitted to the M 201 to provide protection for the crew. The engine is coupled to a manual gearbox with three forward and one reverse gear and a two-speed transfer box. Suspension consists of semi-elliptical springs and hydraulic shock absorbers. The vehicle can carry a maximum load of 400 kg (882 lb) and tow a trailer weighing up to 500 kg (1,102 lb).

Weapons carrier

The M 201 has been used as a weapons carrier and fitted with 7.62-mm (0.3-in) or 12.7-mm (0.5-in) machine-guns, 106-mm (4.17-in) M40 type recoilless rifles (which can also be dismounted for use in the

ground role) and ENTAC ATGWs. In the last model a total of four missiles were carried in the ready-to-launch position, a further three missiles being carried in reserve; this model was used by France and Belgium, but the missiles were replaced by the longer-range MILAN system. The vehicle has also been fitted with extensive communications equipment for use in the command role, and some have even been fitted with battlefield surveillance radars to detect enemy movements at some distance away. The basic military model has a wheelbase of 2.03 m (6 ft 8 in), but a longer model was built with a wheelbase of 2.53 m (8 ft 4 in) and greater carrying capability.

Once the M 201 had gone out of production, a number of manufacturers proposed vehicles to fill this gap: at the time there was no French army requirement for a new vehicle, but new countries that were previously French colonies or who had a strong French bias still looked to France for their requirements. This gap was eventually filled by the **SAMO** light vehicle, which is available in both standard-and long-wheelbase configurations, with a petrol or diesel engine, and

with a wide range of optional equipment such as heavy-duty axles, 24-volt electrical system, long-range fuel tanks and a

winch. This has been exported to a number of countries including the Central African Republic, and Chad.

Above: The M 201 4x4 light vehicle was in production by Hotchkiss-Brandt in Paris from 1953 to 1969 for both the civilian and military markets. It is almost identical to the Jeep used by the Allied armies during World War II, and it was only replaced in the French army in the 1980s by the Peugeot P4 4x4 light vehicle, which is based on a West German design.

Below: A Hotchkiss M 201 light vehicle of the French army fitted with four Aérospatiale ENTAC wire-guided anti-tank missiles. For travelling, these missiles were retracted to the rear of the driver and missile operator. In the French army ENTAC was replaced by the MILAN ATGW.

SPECIFICATION	
Hotchkiss M 201	1.77 m (5 ft 10 in)
Crew: 1 + 1 (plus 2 in rear)	**Performance:** maximum road speed
Weight: empty 1120 kg (2,469 lb) and loaded 1520 kg (3,351 lb)	100 km/h (62 mph); maximum range 348 km (216 miles)
Powerplant: one 4-cylinder petrol engine developing 61 hp (46 kW)	**Gradient:** 65 per cent
Dimensions: length 3.36 m (11 ft); width 1.58 m (5 ft 2 in); height	**Fording:** 0.533 m (1 ft 9 in)

Citroën Méhari Armée Light vehicle

The **Citroën Méhari Armée** is typical of the many standard commercial vehicles that have been adopted to meet military requirements with a minimum of changes. In times of peace light vehicles, apart from the periods when they are on exercises, spend much of their time on normal roads and have little occasion to use their all-wheel drive. The 4x4 vehicles are not only expensive to procure, but also tend to be uneconomic on fuel load.

Operators

After looking at a number of vehicles on the market the French army chose the Méhari to meet its requirements for a vehicle suitable for use in rear areas where little cross-country capability is required, and at least 10,000 were delivered, not only to the French army, but also the *gendarmerie*, air force and navy, with additional export sales being made. Typical roles include cargo carrying with a maximum load of 405 kg (894 lb), and command when fitted with radios. The type is not used to mount any type of weapon system.

Plastic body

The civilian model is produced in such exotic colours as TP orange and beige, but the military vehicles are in various shades of sand or green. The Méhari Armée has an all-steel chassis with a plastic body. This requires hardly any maintenance as it will not rust. The basic model has the engine at the front, seats for the driver and one passenger in

A basic Citroën Méhari Armée (4x2) light vehicle, with the hood folded down at the rear. An unusual feature of this vehicle is that its body is of all-plastic construction, which is rust free and therefore requires little or no maintenance. The vehicle has been used by all three arms of the French forces.

A Citroën Méhari Armée (4x2) light vehicle, used in the command role with a radio fitted in the rear of the vehicle. This vehicle was originally developed for the civilian market, but was then found to be suitable for a wide range of rear area duties where all-wheel drive is not considered essential.

the centre (each with a safety door chain), and an additional two-man seat that folds down at the rear to provide a large cargo area. The windscreen folds forwards onto the bonnet and a black cotton canopy can be fitted over the body; if required, a complete hood with transparent side panels and doors can be installed. The utility model is similar, but to the rear of the front seats is a flat load area. It has a windscreen and canopy, and can

be fitted with a complete hood.

The engine is coupled to a manual gearbox with four forward and one reverse gear, there being no transfer box as it is only a 4x2 vehicle. The front

and rear axles are suspended by arms with lateral interplay on spiral springs, with hydraulic shock absorbers at each wheel station. Even though this is only a 4x2 vehicle the Méhari Armée

SPECIFICATION	
Citroën Méhari Armée	**Dimensions:** length 3.52 m (11 ft 7 in); width 1.53 m (5 ft); height 1.635 m (5 ft 4 in)
Crew: 1 + 1	
Weight: empty 585 kg (1,290 lb) and loaded 990 kg (2,183 lb)	
Powerplant: one AK 2 2-cylinder air-cooled petrol engine developing 19.4 kW (26 hp)	**Performance:** maximum road speed 100 km/h (62 mph); maximum range 300 km (186 miles)
	Gradient: 40 per cent
	Fording: 0.3 m (1 ft)

does have some cross-country capability, and it is so light that it can be easily manhandled in the field. The Citroën company more recently developed another light vehicle that is available in both 4x4 and 4x2 configurations. This is the **A FAF** and has a maximum payload of 400 kg (882 lb). It is powered by a petrol engine developing 21 kW (28.5 hp) in the 4x2 configuration, or 25.3 kW (34 hp) in the 4x4 configuration. Both versions use automotive components from the civilian A type 4x2 vehicle, of which many millions have been built. The 4x4 model was selected by Burundi and in 1981 by the French army which placed an order for 5,000 vehicles, while the 4x2 model has been produced under licence in Greece by the National Motor Company (NAMCO) as the **Pony**, which is used by the Greek army in a number of roles.

Peugeot P4 Light vehicle

Five variants of the Peugeot P4 range of vehicles are (left to right) short-wheelbase; short-wheelbase with 7.62-mm (0.3-in) machine-gun; long-wheelbase command vehicle; short-wheelbase with MILAN ATGW; and long-wheelbase troop carrier. The French army ordered only the short-wheelbase version.

From the 1950s until the mid-1980s, the standard light vehicle of the French army was the Hotchkiss M 201, and to find a replacement for this type the French army held a competition for which three manufacturers each provided four vehicles. Each of the three French manufacturers selected foreign vehicles, Peugeot selecting a Mercedes-Benz vehicle, Renault the Italian Fiat 1107 AD which it renamed the TRM 500, and Citroën the West German Volkswagen Iltis (already in service with the West German army at the time) which it renamed the C 44. In 1981 the **Peugeot P4** was selected, and the first of 15,000 vehicles were delivered in the following year.

Vehicle layout

In the basic model the engine is at the front, the driver and one passenger in the centre, and the cargo area at the rear. The last has a two-man bench seat down each side, and this can be folded down to provide more space; the opening tailgate also carries the spare tyre. The engine is coupled to a manual gearbox with four forward and one reverse gear and a two-speed transfer box is fitted. The suspension front and rear consists of coil springs and double-action shock absorbers. The basic model is powered by the XN8 four-cylinder inline petrol engine, but the P4 is also offered with the XD3 four-cylinder diesel which develops 56 kW (75 hp) and gives a much better fuel consumption when being driven at a speed of 60 km/h (37 mph), though at 90 km/h (56 mph) fuel consumption is identical with that of the petrol engine. Standard equipment includes inertia seat belts, towing eyes at the front, a trailer hook at the rear and a 24-volt electrical system. Optional equipment includes a 15-litre (3.3 Imp gal) fuel can, power take-off front and rear, power-assisted steering, front locking differential and a front-mounted winch. Winches are available on most light vehicles as an optional extra and can be used for self recovery or for recovering other vehicles. In the former case the end of the cable is attached to a tree or other solid object and the vehicle winches itself out of trouble.

Armed versions

In French army service some vehicles are fitted with twin light machine-guns for use in the reconnaissance role, while others can be used to carry MILAN anti-tank teams around the battlefield, each team having one launcher and four missiles.

There is also a long-wheelbase version, which has not been adopted by the French army; this can carry 10 men (two in the front as normal and a further eight in the rear seated four down each side). Fully enclosed versions of both the standard- and long-wheelbase models are available for use in the command and also ambulance roles.

Peugeot has also built a 4x4 version of the standard civilian Peugeot 504 pick-up truck, and some of these were ordered by the French marines as it has a useful payload of 1110 kg (2,448 lb), good ground clearance and also a high road speed. In addition to the basic pick-up model, station wagon and ambulance versions have also been offered.

SPECIFICATION	
Peugeot P4	**Dimensions:** length 4.12 m (13 ft 6 in); width 1.7 m (5 ft 7 in); height 1.95 m (6 ft 5 in)
Crew: 1 + 1 (plus 4 in rear)	
Weight: empty 1680 kg (3,704 lb) and loaded 2280 kg (5,026 lb)	**Performance:** maximum road speed 122 km/h (76 mph); maximum range 500 km (311 miles)
Powerplant: one XN8 4-cylinder petrol engine developing 62 kW (83.5 hp)	**Gradient:** 70 per cent
	Fording: 0.6 m (2 ft)

Volkswagen Iltis Light utility vehicle

The standard light vehicle of the West German armed forces for many years was the Auto-Union Lkw (4x4), which could carry 250 kg (552 lb) of cargo. Between 1958 and 1968 over 55,000 of these were built at Ingolstadt for both civil and military use. The Lkw was to have been replaced by the so-called Europe Jeep designed to carry 500 kg (1,102 lb) of cargo and also have an amphibious capability, but after prototypes had been built by two competing teams (each having one manufacturer from West Germany, Italy and France), the whole project was dropped.

New requirement

The West German army then issued a new requirement for a vehicle that would carry 500 kg (1,102 lb) of cargo across country, but which was not required to be amphibious. To meet this requirement prototype vehicles were built by Daimler-Benz and Volkswagen, and in 1977 the latter type was selected and an order placed for 8,800 **Volkswagen Iltis** vehicles. The first of these were handed over in 1978 and by 1981 8,800 had been built.

The Iltis (polecat) was entered in the French army competition for a new light vehicle by Citroën under the designation **Citroën C 44**, but this competition was eventually won by the Peugeot P4 based on a Mercedes-Benz design. The Iltis was also selected by the Canadian

Armed Forces to replace its obsolete M38 vehicles which had been in service for some 30 years. Production of a further 2,500 vehicles for the CAF (plus 2,637 for Belgium and others for Oman and Cameroon) was undertaken in Canada by Bombardier.

Iltis in detail

The Iltis has a pressed steel body with the engine at the front, driver and one passenger in the centre, and cargo area at the rear. The last has a seat which can be folded down to increase the load area. In inclement weather the windscreen is raised and the folding hood and removable sidescreens are fitted. The engine is coupled to a manual gearbox with five forward and one reverse gear and a two-speed transfer box. When driving on roads the front axle is normally disengaged so the vehicle becomes a 4x2.

A Volkswagen Iltis (4x4) vehicle with the hood folded down at the rear. In the 1980s, this became the standard vehicle in its class in the West German armed forces, and has also been manufactured under licence in Canada by the Bombardier corporation.

SPECIFICATION	
Volkswagen Iltis	**Dimensions:** length 3.887 m (12 ft 9 in); width 1.52 m (5 ft); height 1.857 m (6 ft 1 in)
Crew: 1 + 1 (plus 2 in rear)	
Weight: empty 1550 kg (3,417 lb) and loaded 2050 kg (4,520 lb)	**Performance:** maximum road speed 130 km/h (80 mph); maximum range 500 km (311 miles)
Powerplant: one four-cylinder petrol engine developing 75 hp (56 kW)	**Gradient:** 70 per cent
	Fording: 0.6 m (2 ft)

Suspension front and rear consists of semi-elliptical leaf springs and also features double-acting hydraulic shock absorbers.

The basic vehicle is used for normal duties in the front-line area, but more specialised versions include a cablelayer for use by signal units, a command vehicle with communications equipment, an artillery survey vehicle, an ambulance and an anti-tank vehicle with MILAN ATGWs. This last model is the replace-

ment for the Lkw with Cobra ATGWs that were launched over the rear of the vehicle.

The German army also used a number of **Volkswagen 181** (4x2) light vehicles for general duties where a 4x4 capability is not essential, and numbers of these vehicles were supplied to Austria, Denmark and France for military use. Other variants were also marketed for civilian uses such as forestry and hunting and also for recreation.

Steyr-Puch Haflinger High-mobility light utility vehicle

The **Steyr-Puch 700 AP Haflinger** light vehicle was designed in the early 1950s specifically for use in mountainous terrain, and was in production between 1959 and 1974, by which time the Pinzgauer was firmly established

as its successor with its much improved cross-country perform-ance and increased load-carrying capability. The Haflinger has an unusual layout, with the driver at the very front on the left, with one passenger to his right and a further two passengers to the

rear. At the rear is a very small cargo carrying area, which can be increased by folding flat the back two seats. When the vehicle is being used for troop-carrying the windscreen is normally erected with a canvas top.

Manual gearbox

The engine is mounted under the very rear of the hull which has enabled the load-carrying area to be retained, but it has also meant that the fording capability of the vehicle is limited. The engine is coupled to

a manual gearbox (with four forward and one reverse gears) which transmits power to all four wheels. All of the vehicles produced after 1967 have a manual gearbox with five forward and one reverse gear, a significant improvement over the earlier model as no transfer box is fitted. From 1967 the vehicle was produced with a slightly more powerful engine. Optional equipment included a winch

with a capacity of 1500 kg (3,307 lb), a power take-off for running accessories such as a power saw, and a snow plough. There was also a model of the Haflinger with a slightly longer wheelbase and also a slightly greater load-carrying capability. In its military role, the Haflinger was often used as a weapons platform. The Austrian army has used the vehicle to mount the standard 12.7-mm (0.5-in)

Two Haflinger (4x4) light vehicles of the Austrian army. The one on the left is armed with a 12.7-mm (0.5-in) M2 HB machine-gun, and that on the right with a 57-mm (2.24-in) recoilless rifle for use in the anti-tank role. This vehicle was in production between 1959 and 1974.

M2 HB machine-gun on a pintle in the centre of the vehicle, or the old American 57-mm (2.24-in) M18A1 recoilless anti-tank rifle. Both the Swiss and Swedish armies have

used the vehicle as an anti-tank platform with six Bofors Bantam wire-guided anti-tank missiles facing the front and another eight missiles facing the rear.

A Steyr-Puch Haflinger (4x4) light vehicle with a canvas top and the side removed to show the seating arrangements. The two-cylinder petrol engine is under the rear and is coupled to a manual gearbox with four forward and one reverse gears.

SPECIFICATION	
Steyr-Puch Haflinger	**Dimensions:** length 2.85 m (9 ft
Crew: 1 + 3	4 in); width 1.4 m (4 ft 7 in); height
Weight: empty 645 kg (1,422 lb)	1.74 m (5 ft 8 in)
and loaded 1200 kg (2,645 lb)	**Performance:** maximum road speed
Powerplant: one Model 700 AP two	75 km/h (46.6 mph); maximum
cylinder petrol engine developing	range 400 km (248 miles)
18 kW (24 hp)	**Gradient:** 65 per cent
	Fording: 0.4 m (1 ft 4 in)

Fiat 1107 AD Light utility vehicle

When the Italian army was reformed its specific requirement for a light vehicle was met by the **Fiat AR-51,** which received power from a four-cylinder petrol engine

developing 39.5 kW (53 hp); this was ultimately succeeded in production by the **AR-55** and finally by the **AR-59**. All these vehicles have a similar layout with the engine at

the front, driver and one passenger in the centre, and cargo area at the rear, the last having a bench seat down each side for two men. An interesting feature of these vehicles was that

the side doors could be swung back through 180° and clipped to the sides, therefore allowing the crew to leave from the vehicle rapidly during an emergency.

New model

The AR-59 was replaced in production by the **Fiat 1107 AD** (4x4) light vehicle which has a maximum payload of 750 kg (1,653 lb) across country and can tow a 1740-kg (3,836 lb) trailer on roads or a 900-kg (1,984-lb) trailer across country.

The Fiat 1107 AD entered production in 1974 for both the civilian and military markets. It was also produced under licence in Yugoslavia for the army (as was the earlier AR-59 under the name of the **Zastava**) and was entered in the French army's competition for a new light vehicle by Renault under the designation **Renault TRM 500**, although this competition was won by Peugeot.

All-steel construction

The body of the Fiat 1107 AD is of all-steel construction with the engine at the front, driver and two passengers in the centre (with a door on each side opening to the front) and the cargo area at the rear. The last has a bench seat down each side for two men, and can be loaded via the tailgate, on which the spare wheel is carried. The basic model has a windscreen that folds forward onto the bonnet and a removable canvas top and side curtains. The Fiat 1107 AD is also produced with a fully enclosed hard-top body and there is also a long-wheelbase version that can carry a total of nine men.

The petrol engine is coupled to a manual gearbox with five forward and one reverse gear and a two-speed transfer box. Suspension is of the independent McPherson type with longitudinal torsion bar. Each front wheel station has a single hydraulic shock absorber while each rear wheel station has two hydraulic shock absorbers, because the loaded vehicle has more weight on the back of the vehicle than at the front.

More recently the company has offered the type with a diesel engine for longer operational range. Standard equipment for the military model includes a pintle towing hook at the rear to enable trailers and light weapons to be towed, towing eyes at the front, pick and shovel, a fire extinguishing system, and a heating and defrosting system; options include a petrol engine that will run on low-octane fuel and special equipment such as engine protection and a fuel filter between the pump and the vehicle's carburettor.

The vehicle can be adapted as a communications vehicle or ambulance, and a number of companies in Italy have made use of the chassis for other applications, one such being ASA for the **Guardian** internal security vehicle, used by Italian peacekeepers in the Lebanon. Variants have also been constructed for civilian use, such as airport fire and rescue appliances.

SPECIFICATION	
Fiat 1107 AD	**Dimensions:** length 3.775 m (12 ft 5 in); width 1.58 m (5 ft 1 in); height 1.901 m (6 ft 3 in)
Crew: 1 + 2 (plus four in rear)	
Weight: empty 2420 kg (5,335 lb) and loaded 1670 kg (3,682 lb)	**Performance:** maximum road speed 120 km/h (74.5 mph); maximum range 400 km (249 miles)
Powerplant: one 4-cylinder petrol engine developing 59.7 kW (80 hp)	**Fording:** 0.7 m (2 ft 3 in)

The Fiat 1107 AD (4x4) chassis is used for a number of applications, such as this forward ambulance with bodywork by Grazia. In addition to the military, civilian authorities such as ambulance and fire brigades use the military-type chassis where an off-road capability is required.

Volvo L3314 Laplander Light cross-country vehicle

The **Volvo L3314 Laplander** 4x4 cross-country vehicle was developed in the late 1950s, the first prototype being completed in 1961. Trials revealed that the company's objectives had been fully met, and large numbers were then built for the home and export markets.

The Swedish army operated two basic models of the vehicle: the model with a fully enclosed hard top was designated as the **Personlastterrüngbil 903B**, and the pick-up model was known as the **Pltgbil 903**. The hard-top model was typically used as a command post and troop carrier, while the soft-top model could also be used as a troop or general cargo carrier. The Swedish army had a number of specialised versions of the vehicle such as ambulance and command post.

The powerpack was mounted at the front of the vehicle and standard equipment included a transfer box. The suspension consisted of semi-elliptical

This is the L3314 Laplander cross-country vehicle in pick-up configuration with a soft top (Pltgbil 903 in Swedish service), which could be rapidly removed.

springs and hydraulic double-acting shock absorbers at each wheel station. The steering was of the cam and roller type on the front wheels. As usual a number of options were available, such as special tow hooks, a power take-off and a side-mounted power-operated winch.

An improved version of the Laplander was subsequently manufactured in Hungary by Csepel under the local designation **C202**.

The Laplander was phased out of service with the Swedish army some years ago, its replacement being the Volvo 4140 series of 4x4 and 6x6 v vehicles, which offered a significant increase in both performance and payload over the L3314 series.

SPECIFICATION	
Pltgbil 903	**Dimensions:** length 3.985 m (13 ft 1 in); width 1.66 m (5 ft 5 in); height 2.09 m (6 ft 10 in)
Crew: 1 + 1	
Weight: 2455 kg (5,412 lb)	
Powerplant: one Volvo B18A 4-cylinder water-cooled petrol engine developing 55.9 kW (75 bhp)	**Performance:** maximum road speed 90 km/h (56 mph); maximum range 330 km (205 miles)

GAZ-69 series Light cross-country vehicle

The **GAZ-69** series was created as the Soviet equivalent of the Jeep and entered production at the Gorky Motor Vehicle Plant in 1952. Production was transferred to the Ulyanovsk Motor Vehicle Plant in 1956, and the vehicle was subsequently redesignated as the **UAZ-69**. Manufacture continued well into the 1960s, and the UAZ-469B entered production in 1972 as the type's definitive replacement.

The basic GAZ-69 has a conventional layout with the engine at the front, the driver and one passenger in the centre, and the cargo at the rear, where there is a bench seat down each side. The windscreen can be folded forward on to the bonnet, and the crew and cargo/passenger area can be covered by a quickly

The GAZ-69 4x4 light vehicle has seats for the driver and one passenger at the front and a bench seat down each side at the rear. The windscreen is seen in the raised position, but the cover is not erected. On the left side of the vehicle are the spare wheel and tyre.

removable cover that is stowed at the rear when not in use. The GAZ-69 can carry a maximum load of 500 kg (1,102 lb) and tow a trailer weighing a maximum of 850 kg (1,874 lb).

The M-20 petrol engine is coupled to a manual gearbox

with three forward and one reverse gear, a two-speed transfer box being standard. The suspension consists of semi-elliptical springs with hydraulic shock absorbers.

Late-production vehicles were of the **UAZ-69M** standard with

a more powerful engine. The **GAZ-69A** (later **UAZ-69A**) has four doors, two on each side, and can carry five men and 100 kg (220 lb) of cargo.

As with most vehicles of this type the chassis has been used for a number of applications.

The GAZ-69 anti-tank vehicle was rebuilt to the rear of the driver/passenger area for the carriage of four Shmel (AT-1 'Snapper') wire-guided anti-tank missiles launched to the rear of the vehicle with the operator either a short distance away from the vehicle (controlling the missiles with a separation sight and controller) or in the cab (a window in the right-hand side being provided for this purpose). This variant has seen combat in the Middle East. The chassis was also used as the basis for the **GAZ-46** or **MAV** amphibious vehicle, which is similar in concept to the American Ford GPA 4x4 vehicle supplied to the USSR in World War II and based on a Jeep chassis.

SPECIFICATION	
GAZ-69	
Crew: 1 + 1 and 4 in the rear	**Dimensions:** length 3.85 m (12 ft 8 in); width 1.85 m (5 ft 2 in); height 2.03 m (6 ft 8 in)
Weight: empty 1525 kg (3,362 lb) and loaded 2175 kg (4,795 lb)	**Performance:** maximum road speed 90 km/h (56 mph); maximum range 530 km (330 miles)
Powerplant: one M-20 4-cylinder water-cooled petrol engine developing 39 kW (52 hp)	**Gradient:** 60 per cent
	Fording: 0.55 m (1 ft 10 in)

A GAZ-69 4x4 light vehicle with the top in the raised position. This vehicle entered service with the Soviet armed forces in 1952, but was largely replaced in most units by the UAZ-469B, which has a slightly greater payload.

UAZ-469B Light cross-country vehicle

In 1960 the Ulyanovsk Motor Vehicle Plant, which was then manufacturing the UAZ-69 and UAZ-69A series of 4x4 light cross-country vehicles, built the prototype of the **UAZ-469**, a new vehicle of the same basic type based on the use of many components from the UAZ-450 range of 4x4 forward control vehicles designed mainly for civilian use. The UAZ-69 was not placed in production, however, and further development was then undertaken to produce the **UAZ-469B**. This entered production in 1972 and generally replaced almost all of the UAZ-69 and UAZ-69A light vehicles in the armies of the USSR and of most other Warsaw Pact members.

The UAZ-469B uses the engine, transmission, axles, brakes and other parts of the UAZ-452 series of 4x4 light vehicles, which are used in both civilian and military roles. The vehicle was widely exported outside the USSR, especially to the Arab countries of the Middle East, and was also made available on the civilian market as the **Tundra**.

The main improvements over the earlier vehicle provided by the UAZ-469B include a slight increase in the payload, greater road speed and, perhaps most important of all, much longer operational range.

Orthodox layout
The layout of the UAZ-469B is conventional, with the engine at the front, the driver and one passenger in the centre each with a side door, and a rear payload compartment. This last has a three-man bench seat with a door on each side, and a further two men can sit at the rear, one on each side facing each other. The windscreen can be folded forward on to the bonnet, the tops of the doors removed and the canvas top folded down. When carrying the maximum number of personnel, the vehicle has a freight payload of only 100 kg (220 lb), but when only the driver and one passenger are carried this payload is increased to 600 kg (1,323 lb). The vehicle can also tow a 600-kg (1,323-lb) unbraked or 2000-kg (4,409-lb) braked trailer.

The four-cylinder petrol engine is coupled to a manual gearbox with four forward and one reverse gear, and there is a two-speed transfer case. The suspension consists of semi-elliptical springs and hydraulic shock absorbers; 8.40 x 15 tyres

The UAZ-469B 4x4 light vehicle entered production at the Ulyanovsk Plant in 1972. It entered service with every arm of the Soviet forces and was also exported on a large scale to allies, satellites and clients. This example is seen in service with Hungary.

are fitted all round; a spare wheel and tyre are carried on the rear.

Ambulance variant
In addition to the basic model, there is also a **UAZ-469G** ambulance model that can carry four litters in addition to the driver, a fully enclosed van-type vehicle used for a variety of roles, and another that has rear-mounted equipment to dispense pennants into the ground to mark clear lanes in NBC-contaminated areas.

SPECIFICATION	
UAZ-469B	
Crew: 1 + 1 and 7 in the rear	**Dimensions:** length 4.025 m (13 ft 2 in); width 1.785 m (5 ft 10 in); height 2.02 m (6 ft 7 in)
Weight: empty 1540 kg (3,395 lb) and loaded 2290 kg (5,048 lb)	**Performance:** maximum road speed 100 km/h (62 mph); maximum range 750 km (466 miles)
Powerplant: one ZMZ-4151M 4-cylinder water-cooled petrol engine developing 56 kW (75 hp)	**Gradient:** 62 per cent
	Fording: 0.8 m (2 ft 8 in)

CAMANF Amphibious truck

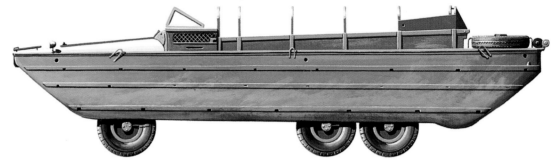

Having used the DUKW for many years, the Brazilian replacement is virtually identical, but with minor modifications to suit Brazilian maritime requirements. Maximum water speed is 14 km/h (8.7 mph).

The Brazilian marines come under the operational control of the Brazilian navy, and number about 15,000 men organised into one amphibious division, one reinforcement command and an internal security force. Its vehicles are mostly of Brazilian origins, such as the ENGESA EE-11 Urutu amphibious armoured personnel carriers, EE-9Cascavel armoured cars, LARC-5 4x4 amphibious cargo carriers, and **CAMANF** amphibious trucks. Also in use, however, are a small number of AAV7A1 amphibious armoured assault vehicles from the US.

Problematic vehicles

After the end of World War II Brazil was supplied with a number of American DUKW 6x6 amphibious vehicles, but by the 1970s these were becoming difficult to maintain and operate, and there was also the problem, as is the case with all petrol-engined vehicles, of the ever-present risk of fire as a result of the use of a high-volatility fuel.

By this time the Biselli Viaturas e Equipamentos Industriais company of São Paulo had already for some time been supplying the Brazilian armed forces with non-combat motor equipment, including tank transporters, and in the mid-1975s started design work on the CAMANF (**Caminhao anfibio**, or amphibious truck). During the late 1970s the first batch of 15 vehicles was delivered to the Brazilian

marines for service evaluation pending the issue of contracts for a larger number of vehicles. The CAMANF vehicle is essentially a 6x6 version of a Ford F-7000 chassis fitted with a watertight body. Some sources have indicated that it is almost identical to the original American body with modifications to suit the particular operational requirements of the Brazilian marines, including a much stronger bow to enable the vehicle to operate in rougher water and to push beached landing craft back into the water.

Layout

In appearance the CAMANF is almost identical to the American DUKW designed in the early days of World War II, with the engine compartment at the front and the crew and troop compartment toward the rear. The cargo area is provided with removable bows and a tarpaulin cover, and a ring-mounted 0.5-in (12.7-mm) Browning M2HB anti-aircraft machine-gun can be fitted over the right side of the crew compartment. The vehicle can carry a load of 5000 kg (11,023 lb) on land and

The CAMANF's 5000-kg (11,203lb) payload is somewhat reduced in rough water, but the bow is strengthened so that handling in such conditions is improved.

very calm water, but in rougher water it is limited to 2500 kg (5,511 lb). Before entering the water a trim vane is erected at the front of the vehicle and the bilge pumps are switched on, and the CAMANF is propelled in the water by a single propeller mounted under the rear of the hull.

All of the six wheels are fitted with a tyre pressure-regulation system which allows the commander to adjust the tyre pressure to suit the different types of ground being crossed. The tyres are all 9.00 x 20, and a spare wheel and a tyre are carried on the rear of the vehicle.

SPECIFICATION	
CAMANF	**Performance:** maximum road speed
Crew: 1 + 2	72 km/h (45 mph); maximum water
Combat weight: 13500 kg (29,762 lb)	speed 14 km/h (8.7 mph);
Dimensions: length 9.5 m (31 ft	maximum road range 430 km
2 in); width 2.5 m (8 ft 2½ in);	(267 miles)
height 2.65 m (8 ft 8⅓ in)	**Gradient:** 60 per cent
Powerplant: one Detroit Diesel	**Vertical obstacle:** 0.4 m (1 ft 3¾ in)
Model 40-54N diesel engine	

Pegaso VAP 3550/1 Amphibious vehicle

The Spanish marines come under operational control of the navy, and currently number about 12,000 men organised into five garrison regiments and one regiment that comprises two infantry, one support and one logistics battalion. Equipment includes the M48

tank, AAV7 amphibious assault vehicle, 106-mm (4.17-in) recoilless rifle, 105-mm (4.13-in) OTO Melara pack howitzer, 105-mm M52 self-propelled howitzer and **Pegaso VAP 3550/1** amphibious vehicle. The last was designed by ENASA to meet a requirement for an

amphibious wheeled vehicle that could be launched from an LST while carrying a payload of 3000 kg (6,614 lb), reach the coast under its own power and then travel inland to a point where the cargo would be unloaded with the assistance of an onboard crane.

The VAP 3550/1 uses many of the automotive components from the Pegaso 3045 4x4 and Pegaso 3050 6x6 series of trucks produced in large numbers for the Spanish forces over the last 15 years. This makes for easier training and reduced maintenance.

Construction

The VAP 3550/1's hull is of all-welded steel construction to a maximum thickness of 6 mm (0.24 in), and is divided into a number of watertight compartments, any one of which can be punctured without the vehicle sinking. The crew compartment is toward the front of the vehicle, with the driver on the left and the other two crew members to his right; the top, front and sides of the crew compartment are covered, but the back is open. The cargo compartment is in the centre and normally fitted with removable bows and a tarpaulin cover; there is no provision for loading wheeled vehicles, the normal role of the vehicle being the carriage of bulk cargo. To the rear of the cab is a hydraulic crane with an extending jib which can lift 350 kg (772 lb).

The engine compartment is at the rear with the air inlet/air outlet louvres and exhaust pipe mounted above it. The engine is coupled to a manual gearbox with six forward and one reverse gears and a two-speed transfer case. The steering is power-assisted on the front wheels.

Many amphibians are moved in the water by propellers, but the VAP 3550/1 is propelled by two waterjets, one on each side of the hull rear, and these give excellent waterborne manoeuvrability. The vehicle is also fitted with two automatic bilge pumps with a maximum capacity of 3600 litres (792 Imp gal) per hour and two pumps with a maximum capacity of 6000 litres (1,320 Imp gal) per hour, while at the very front is a 4500-kg (9,921-lb) capacity winch for self-recovery operations.

Export

In addition to serving with the Spanish navy and marines, the type has been exported: seven

Designed to operate from Spanish navy LSTs, the Pegaso VAP 3550/1 is powered in water by two waterjets driving the vehicle at some 5.5 kts when afloat. The standard payload is 3000 kg (6,614 lb). The vehicle has also been exported to Mexico and Egypt.

were delivered to Mexico in 1982, and a quantity to Egypt.

Astra, an Italian company, has a manufacturing licence.

SPECIFICATION	
Pegaso VAP 3550/1	**Powerplant:** one Pegaso 9125/5
Crew: 1 + 2	diesel delivering 142 kW (190 hp)
Combat weight: 12500 kg (27,558 lb)	**Performance:** maximum road speed
Dimensions: length 9.058 m (29 ft	87 km/h (54 mph); maximum water
8½ in); width 2.5 m (8 ft 2½ in);	speed 10 km/h (6.2 mph); range on
height to top of cab 2.5 m (8 ft	land 800 km (497 miles); range on
2½ in)	water 80 km (49.7 miles)
	Gradient: 60 per cent

EKW Bison Amphibious truck

The **EKW Bison** 4x4 amphibious truck was developed as a private venture by the Eisenwerke Kaiserslautern Goppner company of Germany for both civil and military applications, and was seen in public for the first time in 1982. EWK had considerable experience in the development of amphibious vehicles, having already designed the ALF-2 amphibious fire tender, the M2 amphibious bridge/ferry systems used by the British, German and Singaporean armies, and more recently the APE (Amphibische Pionier-Erkuindungsfahrzeug) 4x4 amphibious armoured reconnaissance vehicle. The last was developed to meet the requirements of the West German army but did not enter production because of a shortfall in defence funding.

Truck detail

The Bison has a fully enclosed forward control cab with the engine to its rear. The engine is coupled to a fully automatic transmission with six forward and one reverse gears. The load area is at the rear and provided with drop sides, bows and a tarpaulin cover. The normal load is 5000 kg (11,023 lb), but in an emergency a total of 7000 kg (15,432 lb) of cargo can be carried. Before the vehicle enters the water a trim vane is erected at the front and, to provide an additional margin of buoyancy, flotation bags are extended to each side and inflated with the aid of a pump powered by an auxiliary power unit. The APU also provides the power for the two propellers which are mounted at the rear of the hull. These propellers were designed by Schottel and can be traversed through 360° for increased waterborne manoeuvrability. (Schottel propellers are fitted to many

The 5000-kg (11,023-lb) capacity Bison is driven in the water by two steerable Schottel propellers at speeds of up to 12 km/h (7.4 mph). The private-venture Bison was not ordered for military purposes, but its development is complete.

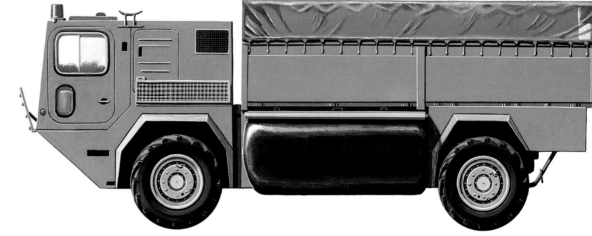

SPECIFICATION	
Bison	**Performance:** maximum road speed
Crew: 1 + 1	80 km/h (49.7 mph); maximum
Combat weight: 16000 kg (35,274 lb)	water speed 12 km/h (7.4 mph);
Dimensions: length 9.34 m (30 ft 7¾	maximum road range 900 km (559
in); width 2.5 m (8 ft 2½ in); height	miles)
to cab roof 2.96 m (9 ft 8½ in)	**Gradient:** 60 per cent
Powerplant: one KHD air-cooled V-8	
diesel delivering 239 kW (320 hp)	

of the armoured fighting vehicles ordered by what was then the West German army, including the Transportpanzer 6x6 and the Luchs 8x8 reconnaissance vehicles.) The Bison's steering is power-assisted to reduce driver fatigue, and dual brakes (hydraulic on the front wheels and pneumatic on the rear) are fitted as standard. The Bison is also fitted with a central tyre pressure-regulation system that allows the driver to adjust the tyre pressure to suit the type of terrain being crossed. The Soviets fitted such a system to most of their wheeled armoured vehicles and many of their cross-country trucks since shortly after the end of World War II, but they started to become standard in the West only at somewhat a later time.

Other designs

Another German designer of

The Bison was originally intended for civil use in under-developed regions, but the capabilities of the vehicle soon to led to the interest of armed forces.

amphibious vehicles is Hans Trippel, who has been working on such vehicles for some 50 years and in the 1980s designed the 550-kg (1,212-lb) Trippel 4x4 light vehicle which was propelled in the water by two propellers (mounted at the hull rear), each of which could be traversed through 360°. A bilge pump was fitted as standard, and this was activated automatically activated when the vehicle entered the water, so there was no possibility of the driver forgetting to switch it on. The vehicle did not enter production for military use.

Komatsu Type 60 & Type 61 Oversnow vehicles

The northernmost of the main islands comprising the Japanese homeland is Hokkaido, which is often covered in snow, and it was this factor which led the Japanese Ground Self-Defence Force (JGSDF) to consider and then implement the procurement of two fully tracked oversnow vehicles, the **Type 60** and **Type 61**, both designed and built by the Komatsu Manufacturing Company and the Ohara Ironworks. The Type 60, which is also called the **Medium Snow Mobile**, was designed for the carriage of a total complement of 10 men (including the driver) or 900 kg (1,984 lb) of cargo, and to tow a trailer or weapon weighing 1500 kg (3,307 lb). The engine is at the front of the Type 60 and coupled to a manual gearbox with four forward and one reverse gears. The suspension is based on the use of torsion bars and bogies with eight dual road wheels, track-return rollers, drive sprockets and idler. The cargo area is at the rear, behind the enclosed cab, and is for ease of loading and unloading is provided with a drop tailgate; this cargo area is normally covered with removable bows carrying a weatherproof tarpaulin cover tied at its lower edges to the sides and rear of the vehicle.

The Type 61 oversnow vehicle, also called the **Large Snow Mobile**, is similar in appearance to the Type 60, but its combination of a more powerful engine and greater size makes it possible the the vehicle to carry 1280 kg (2,822 lb) of cargo or tow a maximum load of 3200 kg (7,055 lb). This capability is not infrequently exploited for the towing of ski-fitted artillery such as the 105-mm (4.13-in) M101 medium howitzer, which is the standard weapon of its type in the Japanese Ground Self-Defence Force. The Type 61 is powered by an Isuzu DA-120T water-cooled 6-cylinder diesel engine delivering 116 kW (155 hp) and coupled to a manual gearbox.

SPECIFICATION	
Komatsu Type 60	delivering 78 kW (105 hp)
Crew: 1 + 9	**Performance:** maximum road speed
Combat weight: 3770 kg (8,311 lb)	36 km/h (22 mph); maximum range
Dimensions: length 4.07 m (13 ft 4¼	135 km (84 miles)
in); width 1.98 m (6 ft 6 in); height	**Gradient:** 60 per cent
2.05 m (6 ft 8¾ in)	**Trench:** 1.066 m (3 ft 6 in)
Powerplant: one Toyota water-	**Vertical obstacle:** 0.5 m (1 ft 7¾ in)
cooled 6-cylinder petrol engine	

Evolved from the civilian Komatsu KC-20 designed for use in the northern Japanese island of Hokkaido, the Type 60 was adopted in 1960 by the JGSDF, largely for use in the same location.

The Industrial Division of Bombardier Limited of Quebec has for many years involved itself in the design and production of a variety of tracked and semi-tracked oversnow vehicles for the civilian market. More recently it has undertaken production of some 2,000 M35 CDN 6x6 2½-ton trucks for the Canadian Armed Forces (CAF), and built the German Iltis 4x4 light vehicle for both the Belgian and Canadian forces. The **Bombardier Bombi** is a very small oversnow vehicle that has seen service with the Canadian Armed Forces as part of the United Nations forces operating in the Sinai desert, where the type's very low ground pressure makes it at home on sand as much as on snow. The **Bombardier Ski Doo Elite Snowmobile**, which can carry two passengers, was tested by the US Marine Corps as a reconnaissance vehicle for possible use in Norway and elsewhere. The fully tracked **Bombardier Skidozer**, which is available with either a petrol or a diesel engine, has been used by a number of countries in a military role, although it was not originally designed for this purpose.

The **Bombardier Snowmobile** oversnow vehicle has seen use with the Canadian Armed Forces in northern Canada as a general utility vehicle, and in appearance is very similar to a coach but with the engine at the rear and coupled to an automatic gearbox with three forward and one reverse gears. The front suspension consists of coil springs and hydraulic shock absorbers and it normally carries tyred wheels, although these can be replaced by skis.

Purchased by the CAF for use in northern Canada, the Bombardier Snowmobile was designed for civil use.

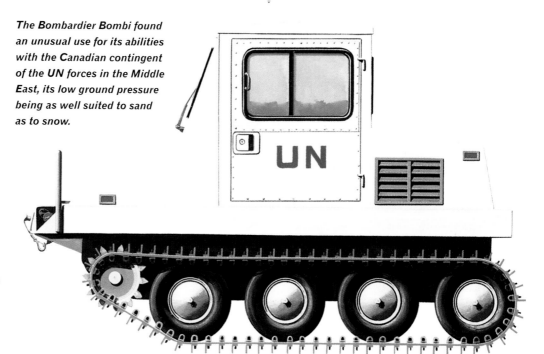

*The **B**ombardier **B**ombi found an unusual use for its abilities with the **C**anadian contingent of the **UN** forces in the Middle East, its low ground pressure being as well suited to sand as to snow.*

The rear suspension on each side of the vehicle consists of four rubber-tyred road wheels on trailing arms, fitted with tracks, 420 mm (16.5 in) wide, of rubber belts with steel crosslinks.

The personnel enter via a large door in the forward part of the vehicle, and there is also a door in the rear and an emergency roof hatch.

Steering is of the power-assisted rack-and-pinion type, and standard equipment includes a powerful heater and also a defroster system, two fuel tanks and a dry-type paper air cleaner.

SPECIFICATION	
Bombardier Snowmobile	**Dimensions:** length 5.38 m (17 ft 7¾ in); width 1.95 m (6 ft 4¾ in); height 2.06 m (6 ft 9 in)
Crew: 1 + 11	
Combat weight: 2337 kg (5,152 lb)	
Powerplant: one Chrysler Model 318 V-8 petrol engine delivering 139 kW (187 bhp)	**Performance:** maximum road speed 64 km/h (40 mph); maximum range 320 km (199 miles)

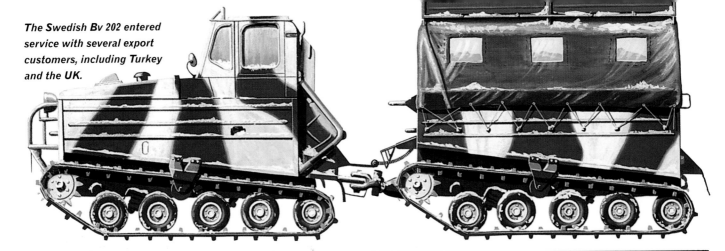

The Swedish Bv 202 entered service with several export customers, including Turkey and the UK.

The first oversnow vehicle used in any numbers by the Swedish army was the US Weasel, which was developed by Studebaker during World War II for service in both Europe and the Far East. By the mid-1950s these vehicles were becoming difficult to maintain and operate, so the Swedish army approached a number of national companies with a proposal to build a new vehicle. As none of them showed any real interest, the Swedish army itself built prototypes which were completed in 1958. These were followed by additional vehicles incorporating improvements as a result of trials with the original test rigs and prototypes. Once the design had been finalised, the complete production programme was put out to tender, and in 1961 Bolinder -Munktell was awarded the first production contract for the vehicle, which was designated as the **Bv 202**.

The Bv 202 remained in production for almost 20 years, final deliveries being made in 1981. In addition to those for the Swedish army, sales were also made to Finland, the Netherlands, Norway, Turkey and the UK. The UK uses its vehicles for a wide range of roles such as command, cargo-carrying and towing the 105-mm (4.13-in) Light Gun on skis. The Royal Marines and Royal Artillery used the vehicle during the 1982 Falklands campaign, where it

proved to be one of the few vehicles able to traverse the boggy terrain.

In the Swedish army the Bv 202 was supplemented by the much improved Bv 206 built by Hägglund & Söner. The Bv 202 has also been used for a number of civil roles in Sweden and countries where its low ground pressure enables it to cross with ease soft-surfaced terrain such as swamp, mud and snow.

The Bv 202 consists of two distinct units, front and rear, connected together by an articulated joint. The front unit contains the engine, transmission, driver and commander, while the rear unit carries the load which can be

800 kg (1,764 lb) across country or 1000 kg (2,205 lb) on roads.

The commander and driver are seated in a fully enclosed cab provided with a potent heater, but the rear unit has only a tarpaulin cover for the troops sitting on a bench seat down each side; if required, however, the rear unit can also be fitted with a heater. The vehicle is fully amphibious, being

propelled through the water by the motion of its tracks.

When in production the vehicle was offered with a number of options such as a fully enclosed rear unit with stowage rack on top, a torque converter, a cold starting device and a tropical kit. Late production vehicles had a slightly more powerful engine and a different transmission.

SPECIFICATION	
Bv 202	
Crew: 2 (front unit) + 8 (rear unit)	**Performance:** maximum road speed 39 km/h (24 mph); maximum water speed 3.3 km/h (2 mph); maximum range 400 km (249 miles)
Combat weight: 4200 kg (9,259 lb)	
Powerplant: one Volvo B18 4-cylinder petrol engine delivering 68 kW (91 bhp)	**Fording:** amphibious
Dimensions: length 6.172 m (20 ft 3 in); width 1.759 m (5 ft 9⅓ in); height 2.21 m (7 ft 3 in)	**Gradient:** 60 per cent
	Vertical obstacle: 0.5 m (1 ft 7¾ in)

Bv 202 in service with the British Army, which has found the type to offer exceptional capabilities. Although unarmoured, the Bv 202 saw combat service in the Falklands.

Bv 206 Tracked oversnow vehicle

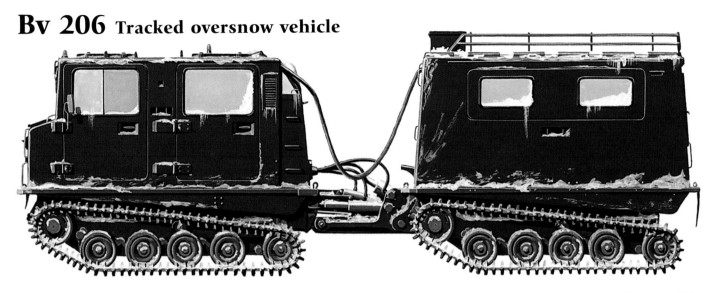

Larger and more capable than the Bv 202, the Bv 206 replaced this vehicle in Swedish army service. It was proposed that the Bv 206 could be fitted with the Giraffe surveillance radar on a hydraulically operated mast for use with the Swedish army's RBS 70 SAM.

The **Bv 206** was developed from 1974 by Hägglund & Söner to meet the requirements of the Swedish army for a vehicle to replace the Bv 202 tracked oversnow vehicle. After trials with three batches of prototypes, the Swedish army placed an initial order for production vehicles in 1979, and the first of these were delivered in 1981. The Swedish army had a requirement for some 4,000 Bv 206s, and export orders were placed by Finland, Norway, the UK and the US, while trials vehicles were ordered by Canada and Italy. In the US Army the Bv 206 is known as the **Small Unit Support Vehicle M973**, and 268 vehicles were ordered to replace the old M116 oversnow vehicles which had been in service in Alaska.

Bv 206 units

Like the Bv 202, the Bv 206 consists of two units, front and rear, connected by a steering unit. The front unit contains the engine and transmission and has seats for five or six, while the rear unit has seating for 11. When used in the cargo-carrying role, the Bv 206 can move a maximum of 600 kg (1,323 lb) in the front unit and 1400 kg (3,086 lb) in the rear unit.

The basic Bv 206 has fully enclosed front and rear bodies of fire-resistant glass fibre reinforced plastic. The basic vehicle is fully amphibious, being propelled in the water by its tracks. The anti-tank member of the family is the **Pvbv 2062**, which has an open-topped front body in which is mounted a Bofors 90-mm (3.54-in)

This is a Bv 206 vehicle, with a roof-mounted Milan anti-tank missile launcher, of the type used by the Royal Marines in countries such as Norway.

recoilless rifle, the rear unit being used for ammunition. The front unit has special roll-over protection bars which can be quickly lowered in action to allow the gun to be used. The gun was later replaced by the

BILL anti-tank missile, while for trials purposes the vehicle was fitted with the TOW, also used by the Swedish army. The command post version of the Bv 206 is the **Rabv 2061**, which has extensive radio equipment.

The Bv 206 has a notably low ground pressure and good traction, making it ideal for forces such as these French army mountain troops.

SPECIFICATION	
Bv 206	height 2.4 m (7 ft 10½ in)
Crew: 5 or 6 (front unit) + 11 (rear unit)	**Performance:** maximum road speed 55 km/h (34 mph); maximum water speed 3 km/h (1.86 mph); maximum range 330 km (205 miles)
Combat weight: 6340 kg (13,977 lb)	
Powerplant: one Ford Model 2658E V-6 petrol engine or Mercedes 5-cylinder diesel engine delivering 101 or 93 kW (136 or 125 bhp)	
	Fording: amphibious
Dimensions: length 6.86 m (22 ft 6 in); width 1.85 m (6 ft ¾ in);	**Gradient:** 60 per cent
	Vertical obstacle: 0.5 m (1 ft 7¾ in)

PTS Amphibious vehicle

The PTS has seen considerable use in Egyptian service, its amphibious carrying capacity having been used to good effect during the Yom Kippur War of 1973.

The **PTS** amphibian entered service with the Soviet army in the mid-1960s, and in comparison with the earlier K-61 amphibian has a greatly increased load-carrying capability, slightly higher speed on both land and water, and can also tow a trailer when afloat. The PTS has a steel hull with the crew compartment at the very front of the hull and the cargo area stretching back right to the rear. The crew compartment, unlike those on the earlier K-61 and BAV-485, is fully enclosed, the two-man crew entering via two circular roof hatches. An NBC protection system is provided to enable the vehicle to operate in an NBC-contaminated area. The engine is beneath the vehicle, with the exhaust pipes on top of the cargo compartment on each side, a configuration which in certain conditions could permit exhaust fumes to be blown back into the cargo area, an unfortunate situation when troops are being carried. The

PTS can carry a maximum of 5000 kg (11,023 lb) of cargo on land and 10000 kg (22,046 lb) on water, or up to 70 or so fully equipped troops. Cargo and vehicles such as a Ural-375D 6x6 4000-kg (8,818-lb) truck can be loaded into the PTS via the rear tailgate, which has two integral loading ramps. The suspension of the vehicle is of the torsion-bar type with six dual rubber-tyred road wheels, plus a drive sprocket at the front and an idler at the rear; there are no track-return rollers. The vehicle is driven in the water by two propellers mounted in tunnels under the rear of the hull, and steered by two rudders. Before the vehicle enters the water a trim vane is erected at the front to stop water swamping the forward part of the vehicle, and the bilge pumps are switched on. All vehicles have a front-mounted winch (to recover other vehicles and equipment, or to assist in self-recovery), night driving equipment, a searchlight

mounted on top of the crew compartment, radios and an intercom. The PTS can also tow the specially developed **PKP** boat-shaped two-wheel trailer, which is provided with ramps to enable cargo to be loaded. This has two sponsons, one on each side: for land travel these are folded on top of the trailer, but before entering the water they are swung through 180° and locked in position to provide additional buoyancy. The trailer can be used to carry a 122-mm (4.8-in) D-30 howitzer while the

PTS vehicle carries the associated truck, ammunition and crew for the weapon.

Improved model

The latest production version is the **PTS-M**, which has minor differences including increased fuel capacity. A variant used by Poland has a rocket-propelled mine-clearing system mounted in the rear. In addition to being used by most members of the Warsaw Pact, the PTS has also seen service with the armed forces of Egypt, Iraq and Syria.

SPECIFICATION	
Crew: 1 + 1	**Performance:** maximum road speed 42 km/h (26 mph); maximum water speed 10.6 km/h (6.5 mph); range 300 km (186 miles)
Combat weight: on land 22700 kg (50,045 lb); on water 27700 kg (61,068 lb)	**Gradient:** 60 per cent
Powerplant: one 350-hp (261-kW) V-54P diesel engine	**Vertical obstacle:** 0.65 m (2 ft 1⅜ in)
Dimensions: length 11.5 m (37 ft 8¾ in); width 3.3 m (10 ft 10 in); height 2.65 m (8 ft 8½ in)	**Trench:** 2.5 m (8 ft 2½ in)

Water-driven by twin tunnel-mounted propellers at the rear, the large PTS is capable of carrying up to 10000 kg (22,046 lb) on water, or up to 70 personnel. The crew compartment is fully sealed against NBC contaminants.

BAV-485 Amphibious carrier

Derived directly from the wartime 6x6 DUKW provided under Lend-Lease, the BAV-485 is a watertight boat-like body on a Soviet truck chassis.

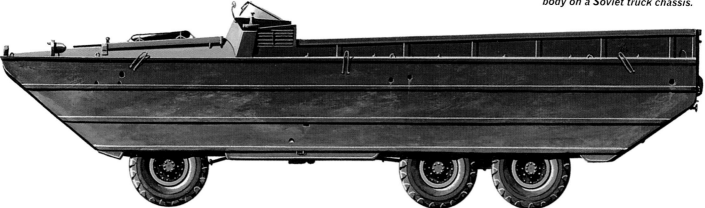

Soviet military doctrine stressed the importance of marine landings in wartime, with marines coming ashore at selected points, to establish bridgeheads and hold until regular reinforcements could arrive. As a result, amphibious vehicles were afford a high priority. Following the successful use of American-supplied DUKW 6x6 amphibious vehicles by the Soviet army during World War II, it was decided to build a similar vehicle but based on a Soviet truck chassis. This finally appeared in the early 1950s as the **BAV-485**, sometimes called the **ZIL-485**.

'Duck' origins

The layout of the BAV-485 is similar to that of the American DUKW with the engine and transmission at the front, crew seats to the rear of the engine compartment, and the cargo area at the rear. A maximum of 2500 kg (5,511 lb) of cargo or 25 fully equipped troops can be carried.

The crew at the front are provided with a windscreen which can be folded forwards, and if required bows and a tarpaulin cover can be erected over the crew and troop compartments. A major improvement over the original American DUKW is the installation of a drop-down tailgate at the very rear of the cargo compartment, which enables light vehicles, mortars and light artillery weapons to be loaded very quickly. The engine

is coupled to a manual gearbox with five forward and one reverse gear, and a two-speed transfer case. The main brakes are pneumatic, with a mechanical parking brake that operates on the rear wheels only. The BAV-485 is powered in the water by a single three-blade propeller mounted under the rear of the hull.

The basic BAV-485 was based on the ZIL-151 6x6 2500-kg

(5,511-lb) truck chassis built by the Likhachev Motor Vehicle Plant in Moscow between 1947 and 1958. Later production vehicles were based on the ZIL-157 6x6 2500-kg truck chassis built at the same plant between 1958 and 1961, this model being designated the **BAV-485A**. The major difference between the BAV-485 and the later BAV-485A is that the former has external air lines for the central tyre pressure-regulation system while the latter has internal air lines which are less easily damaged. The central tyre pressure-regulation system is a common feature on Soviet wheeled armoured vehicles and military trucks, and enables the driver to adjust the ground pressure to suit the ground being crossed. It is by no means a new idea, however, as the Americans had a similar system on their DUKWs during World War II. Some BAV-485s have been observed with a 12.7-mm (0.5-in) DShKM heavy machine-gun for anti-aircraft defence, this being mounted on the forward right side of the troop compartment.

SPECIFICATION	
BAV-485	2.66 m (8 ft 8¾ in)
Crew: 1 + 1	**Performance:** maximum road speed
Combat weight: on land and on	60 km/h (37.3 mph); maximum
water 9650 kg (21,275 lb)	water speed 10 km/h (6.2 mph);
Powerplant: one ZIL-123 6-cylinder	maximum road range 480 km (298
petrol engine developing 110 hp	miles)
(82 kW)	**Gradient:** 60 per cent
Dimensions: length 9.54 m (31 ft 3⅔	**Vertical obstacle:** 0.4 m (1 ft 4 in)
in); width 2.85 m (9 ft 4 in); height	

Based upon ZIL trucks, the BAV-485 amphibious carriers largely served with second-line units of the Warsaw Pact during the Cold War. This example is armed with a 12.7-mm (0.5-in) machine-gun.

GT-S Tracked oversnow vehicle

Wartime experience with fighting in the snow led to the developent of the GT-S oversnow vehicle. The 1000-kg (2,205-lb) payload makes the GT-S equivalent to a light truck.

The **GT-S**, sometimes called the **GAZ-47**, is believed to have been the first tracked amphibious oversnow vehicle to enter service with the Soviet army after World War II. During this conflict the Soviet army used a number of oversnow vehicles including several sled-type vehicles with a propeller at the rear. The GT-S was designed to carry a maximum payload of 1000 kg (2,205 lb) and to tow a trailer. Alternatively a weapon such as a 120-mm (4.72-in mortar) weighing up to 2000 kg (4,409 lb) could be towed.

Powerplant

The engine, more commonly the GAZ-61, is at the very front of the vehicle and coupled to a manual gearbox with four forward and one reverse gear. Some vehicles were fitted with the less powerful GAZ-47 powerplant. The commander and driver are seated to the immediate rear of the engine, and behind them is the cargo area extending to the very rear of the vehicle. This cargo area is normally covered by a tarpaulin cover with small windows in the sides and rear. The tracks are 300 mm (11.81 in) wide and give a ground pressure of 0.24 kg/cm² (3.4 lb/sq in) loaded. The suspension is of the torsion-bar type and consists of five large

rubber-tyred road wheels, the last road wheel on each side acting as the idler, and a drive sprocket at the front; there are no track-return rollers. As with the later oversnow vehicles, the GT-S is fully amphibious without preparation, being propelled in the water by its tracks.

Pontoon version

One of the more interesting versions of the GT-S is the **LFM-RVD-GPI-66**, on which the tracks are replaced by cylindrical steel pontoons powered by the main engine. This model has a much higher water speed of 20 km/h (12.4 mph), but is wholly impractical on hard surfaces such as roads.

The GT-S was replaced in production by the **GT-SM**, which has a longer chassis with six instead of five road wheels, and is powered by a more powerful GAZ-71 V-8 water-cooled petrol engine developing 115 hp (86 kW). This gives the GT-SM higher road and water speeds, and the vehicle's wider tracks give a lower ground pressure and therefore better mobility across soft ground.

Widely employed by the Soviet military, the more capable GT-SM version has six road wheels per side instead of the five of the earlier model.

SPECIFICATION	
GT-S	**Performance:** maximum road speed
Crew: 1 + 1	35 km/h (21.7 mph); maximum
Combat weight: 4600 kg (10,141 lb)	water speed 4 km/h (2.5 mph);
Powerplant: one 85-hp (63-kW)	maximum range 725 km (450 miles)
GAZ-61 6-cylinder water-cooled	**Fording:** amphibious
petrol engine	**Gradient:** 60 per cent
Dimensions: length 4.9 m (16 ft 1 in);	**Trench:** 1.3 m (4 ft 3¼ in)
width 2.44 m (8 ft); height 1.96 m (6	**Vertical obstacle:** 0.6 m (1 ft 11⅔ in)
ft 5⅜ in)	

Above: Fully amphibious without prior preparation, the GT-S entered service in 1955, and was manufactured until 1970. It was replaced by the enlarged GT-SM model, with a more powerful engine and enhanced performance over both land and water.

LARC-5, LARC-15, LARC-60 Amphibious cargo carriers

In the 1950s, the US Transportation Engineering Command issued a requirement for vehicles capable of transporting cargo from ships lying offshore, across the beach and then inland.

This resulted in the **Lighter Amphibious Resupply Cargo** (**LARC**) family of vehicles. The **LARC-60**, weighing 60000 kg (132,276 lb) was the first to be developed (in the early 1950s) by the Pacific Car and Foundry Company. Production of the 5000 kg (11,023 lb) **LARC-5** was carried out by the Condiesel Mobile Equipment. The final production of the larger 15000 kg (33,069 lb) **LARC-15** was undertaken by the Fruehauf Corporation.

The LARC-5 is in service with the US, Australia, West Germany and Argentina. The only known operators of the LARC-15 are the US and West Germany. Argentina used the LARC-5 during its invasion of the Falklands.

The LARC-5 hull is all-welded aluminium. The cab is located at the front of the vehicle, the cargo area is in the centre and the engine is positioned at the rear.

Cargo capacity

The cargo area is open at the top, but fabric curtains can be installed to protect the cargo from spray. In place of cargo, up to 20 fully equipped troops can be carried. Some vehicles were fitted with a hydraulically-operated boom that can lift a maximum load of upto 2495 kg (5,500 lb).

The LARC-5 power plant compartment is fully water-protected and is provided with a fire extinguisher operated from the cargo-deck rear bulkhead.

On roads the 4x2 drive is normally used, the 4x4 drive being engaged when the vehicle is being driven across country. The LARC-5 is powered in the water by a three-blade propeller mounted under the hull at the rear. Bilge pumps are also fitted. The LARC vehicles have no suspension and therefore the tyres absorb all of the shock. The vehicle's steering is power-assisted on the front wheels only. A major difference between the LARC-5 and the LARC-15 is that the latter has the engine compartment and cab at the rear to make possible the incorporation of a hydraulically-operated bow ramp for the loading of vehicles.

Engines

An unusual feature of the LARC-60 is that it is powered by four engines, one powering each wheel. When afloat, the vehicle is powered by two propellers, each of these being driven by two engines. The vehicle's steering system allows for driving at an oblique angle, particularly useful when crossing beaches. The LARC-60 tyres are fitted with a pressure-regulation system, a feature useful for crossing deep sand as the pressure can be decreased for improved traction over rough ground.

SPECIFICATION	
LARC-15	**Performance:** maximum road speed
Crew: 1+1	50 km/h (31 mph); maximum water
Combat weight: 34100 kg (75,177 lb)	speed 8 kts (15 km/h; 9.3 mph);
Powerplant: two Cummins V8	maximum road range 482 km (300
diesels each developing 224 kW	miles)
(300 hp)	**Fording:** amphibious
Dimensions: length 13.7 m (45 ft);	**Gradient:** 40 per cent
width 4.4 m (14 ft 6 in); height	**Trench:** not applicable
(with cab) 4.7 m (15 ft 6 in)	**Vertical obstacle:** not known

SPECIFICATION	
LARC-5	48.2 km/h (30 mph); maximum
Crew: 1+2	water speed 8.6 kts (16 km/h; 10
Combat weight: 14038 kg (30,948 lb)	mph); maximum road range 402
Powerplant: one Cummins V8	km (250 miles)
diesel developing 224 kW (300 hp)	**Fording:** amphibious
Dimensions: length 10.6 m (35 ft);	**Gradient:** 60 per cent
width 3.1 m (10 ft 4 in);	**Trench:** not applicable
height (with cab) 3 m (9 ft 11 in)	**Vertical obstacle:** 0.5 m (1 ft 7 in)
Performance: maximum road speed	

AAV7 Amphibious Assault Vehicle

For many years the LVTP-5 (Landing Vehicle Tracked Personnel 5) was the standard vehicle of the US Marine Corps and was used to transport Marines from ship to the beach and, in some cases, inland as well.

The LVTP-5 had a number of drawbacks. United Defense LP, Ground Systems Division, was selected to develop a new vehicle under the designation of the **LVTPX12**.

Following extensive user trials with prototypes, a vehicle was selected for service and classified as the **Landing Vehicle Tracked Personel 7** (**LVTP7**). A total of 942 vehicles were built for the US Marine

With a seven-hour waterborne endurance, the AAV7A1 amphibious assault vehicle can be launched from up to 26 nm (50 km; 31 miles) from the beach.

Corps between 1971 and 1974. The vehicle was subsequently redesignated the **Amphibious Assault Vehicle 7** (**AAV7**). The US Marine Corps subsequently upgraded their vehicles to the **AAV7A1** standard, and more recently a Product Improvement Program was completed during the late 1980s/early 1990s, to enable the vehicles to remain effective until the new Advanced Amphibious Assault Vehicle (AAAV) enters service between 2012 and 2014.

Foreign sales

A number of foreign countries have purchased the vehicle, including Argentina, Brazil, Italy, South Korea (co-production programme), Spain, Thailand and Venezuela. It has seen active service with the US Marine Corps and was also used by Argentina during the invasion of the Falkland Islands in 1982.

The AAV7A1 has an all-welded aluminium hull that provides the occupants with protection from small arms fire and shell splinters. The US Marine

USMC AAV7 vehicles on beach manoeuvres. Supplies for the Marine detachment inside can be seen on the left side of the vehicle at the front.

Corps vehicles have been fitted with an appliqué passive armour package developed by the RAFAEL Armament Development Authority of Israel to provide a higher level of ballistic protection.

The basic vehicle has a crew of three consisting of

31st Marine Expeditionary Unit AAV7A1 vehicles move across Freshwater Beach at the Shoalwater Bay Training Area, Queensland, Australia.

The turret-mounted 0.5-in (12.7-mm) machine-gun and 40-mm (1.5-in) grenade launcher are clearly visible as this AAV7A1 traverses the beach.

commander, gunner and driver and can carry 25 fully equipped Marines who normally enter and leave the vehicle via a power operated ramp at the rear. The one man turret is armed with a 0.5-in (12.7-mm) machine- gun and a 40-mm (1.5-in) automatic grenade launcher. The vehicle has a maximum water speed of 7 kts (13 km/h; 8 mph) when being propelled by the two water jets mounted either side of the hull at the rear. The vehicle can also be propelled by its tracks at a maximum speed of 3.7 kts (7 km/h; 4.3 mph).In addition to the basic troop carrier there are a number of specialised versions which are operated, including the **AAVC7A1** command and control vehicle and the **AAVR7A1**

recovery vehicle. The latter version is fitted with a crane and winches for its specialised recovery and repair missions. There have also been prototypes of a 105-mm (4.1-in) assault gun and a mine clearing vehicle.

Two AAV7 vehicles emerge from the sea onto the beach. The vehicle on the left has been fitted with the RAFAEL Enhanced Appliqué Armor Kit.

AAV7 in action

US Marine Corps 'battle bus'

The original LVTP7 and its current AAV7A1 counterpart have served the US Marine Corps well since the first vehicles were taken into service in 1972. The original concept was the ship-to-shore movement of 25 men or 4536 kg (10,000 lb) of cargo and then the support of landed troops as they secured the bridge-head. The vehicle therefore emerged as a tall, slab-sided machine with protection limited to the halting of small arms fire and shell splinters. Since that time, however, the vehicle has been extensively used in land warfare, and gained greater protection and firepower.

Hull
The design of the original LVTP7 was dictated by the requirement to carry no fewer than 25 fully equipped men of the US Marine Corps (or a large freight payload) over the surface of the water to an assault landing. This demanded considerable size in a hull that had also to be optimised, so far as was possible, for good stability and adequate speed through the water.

Suspension and track
The AAV7 is based on tube-over-bar suspension with six dual rubber-tyred roadwheels, a front-mounted drive sprocket and a rear-mounted idler in each side; there are no track-return rollers. The track is 533 mm (21 in) wide, and the length of track on the ground is 3.94 m (12 ft 11 in). The vehicle's ground clearance is 0.406 m (16 in), and it can negotiate a 60 per cent gradient and a 40 per cent side slope as well as surmount a vertical obstacle 0.914 m (3 ft) high and pass safely over a trench 2.44 m (8 ft) wide.

Above: CH-53E Super Stallions conduct low-level operations over Pattaya Beach, Thailand, while AAV7s undertake a beach assault training exercise. Helicopters such as the CH-53 and CH-46 Sea Knight are used to move men and, more importantly in the case of the CH-53, heavier weapons and equipment.

Left: An AAV7 attached to the 31st Marine Expeditionary Unit launches from the well deck of the amphibious transport dock USS Juneau. Any water that enters the vehicle is removed by the system of two electric and two hydraulic bilge pumps.

VARIANTS

AAV7

AAVC7A1

Command vehicle with the turret replaced by a simple hatch cover, and armament limited to a pintle-mounted 0.3-in (7.62-mm) M240G machine-gun.

AAVR7A1

Recovery vehicle with the armament turret replaced by a 0.3-in (7.62-mm) M240G machine-gun. There is also a roof-mounted hydraulic crane with a 2722-kg (6,000-lb) lift, a two-speed recovery winch with a pull of 22045 kg (48,600 lb), and a mass of specialised equipment and tools.

AAV7A1 with VEMASID

Vehicle Magnetic Signature Duplicator for trials purposes.

AAV7A1 mine clearance

Modified M125 mine-clearing system bolted into the rear compartment to fire a linear explosive charge out to 550 m (600 yards) before detonation, clearing about 80 per cent of the mines for a distance of 7 m (23 ft) on each side of the line.

AAV7A1 mine plough

Demonstration model with track-width mine-clearance system.

AAV7A1 with UGW

The Cadillac Gage Up-Gunned Weapons Station has been installed on 240 AAV7A1s and consists of a 40-mm Mk 19 grenade launcher and a 0.5-in (12.7-mm) M2HB machine-gun. The turret has electric traverse and the weapons have manual elevation. Neither the turret nor the weapons are stabilised, and fire-control is of the simple optical type.

Electric Drive AAV7A1

Test-bed for an all-electric propulsion arrangement.

Limited firepower provision

The LVTP7 reveals the age of its basic design in its lack of provision for the embarked troops to see the outside world via vision blocks, and also in the absence of firing ports through which the troops might have contributed a measure of suppressive fire before they disembarked. By modern standards, another failing was the omission from the vehicle of any type of NBC protection.

Troop accommodation

The AAV7 was designed for the delivery of 25 fully equipped marines from their ships into an assault landing. Unlike assault craft, which beach at the water's edge and disgorge their troops over a bow ramp, the AAV7 was designed to move up on to the beach and still farther forward, and was therefore designed with a rear troop compartment with a large power-operated ramp/door (with an inset door) at the extreme back of the vehicle. The troops sit on three benches extending along the sides and centre of the compartment.

AAAV Advanced Amphibious Assault Vehicle

After a competition between United Defense and General Dynamics Land Systems, the latter was selected to design and develop the **Advanced Amphibious Assault Vehicle** (**AAAV**) for the US Marine Corps as a replacement for the United Defense AAV7A1 which entered service in 1971.

When compared to the 30 year old AAV7 series, the new Advanced Amphibious Assault Vehicle has a number of significant advantages, including increased firepower, better protection, three times the water speed and the ability to operate with the US Marine Corps M1A1 series main battle tank. This will make the AAAV a much more effective system and more more survivable.

Under the Program Definition and Risk Reduction (PDRR) phase, General Dynamics Amphibious Systems built three prototypes of the AAAV with the first of these being completed in 1999. This contract was followed in 2001 by the Systems Development and Demonstration (SDD) contract under which an additional nine prototypes are now being built as well as additional improvements to the first prototypes.

Under current plans, the US Marine Corps hopes to procure a

total of 1,013 AAAV series vehicles with first deliveries expected in 2006. Of this order, 935 will be in the troop carrier configuration with the remaining 78 in the command and control role. At the present time there are no plans to procure a recovery version of the AAAV.

The AAAV incorporates many advanced features with the hull being of welded aluminium armour to which an additional later of advanced ceramic armour has been added.

The powerpack consists of a NITU diesel coupled to an Allison transmission which develops 634 kW (850 hp) in the land mode and 2013 kW (2,700 hp) in water mode. When afloat the vehicle is propelled by two large water jets situated one either side of the hull low down at the rear.

High water speed

The high water speed is not only achieved by the use of the powerful waterjets but also by retracting the hydropneumatic suspension to reduce drag, and the planing hull design. When

Prior to the first production model of the AAAV being built, this prototype Automotive Test Rig was built in order to prove automotive aspects of the design.

One of the development models of the Advanced Amphibious Assault Vehicle demonstrates its capabilities.

afloat the vehicle's brow plate opens automatically.

The AAAV is fitted with a two person powered turret armed with a ATK Gun Systems Company MK 44 30-mm/40-mm cannon and a 0.3-in (7.62 mm) co-axial machine gun.

Armament is coupled to an advanced fire control system, including day/thermal sighting with integrated laser rangefinder; enabling targets to be engaged when the AAAV is stationary or moving, with a high first round hit probability.

SPECIFICATION	
AAAV	cannon, one 0.3-in (7.62-mm)
Crew: 3+18	machine-gun
Weight: 34,500 kg (76,058 lb)	**Performance:** maximum road speed
Powerpack: MTU MT 883 diesel	72 km/h (44.7 mph); maximum
developing 634 kW (850 hp) (in	water speed 24 kts (44 km/h; 27
land mode)	mph)
Dimensions: length 9.27 m (30 ft	**Fording:** amphibious
4 in); width 1.63 m (5ft 3 in); height	**Gradient:** 60 percent
1.20 m (3 ft 9 in)	**Vertical obstacle:** 0.92 m (3 ft)
Armament: one 30-mm/40-mm	**Trench:** 2.3 m (7.5 ft)

AMX-30 family CCP and EBG

The Engin Blindé du Génie, can carry out a wide range of combat engineer roles, including clearing battlefield obstacles and laying small minefields.

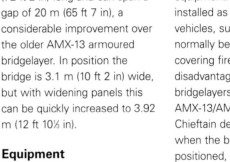

For many years the only armoured bridgelayer in service with the French army was the AMX-13 Char Poseur de Pont (CPP). This is essentially an AMX-13 light tank chassis with turret removed and fitted with a scissors bridge which is laid hydraulically over the rear of the vehicle. Opened out the bridge is 14.3 m (46 ft 11 in) long and can take vehicles up to Class 25, well below the weight of the American M47 tanks which were the standard tanks of the French army at the time of the CPP's debut. To allow the M47 tank to cross, two bridges were laid side by side.

Prototype

The prototype of a new bridgelayer based on the chassis of the AMX-30 tank was completed in the mid-1960s, but for a variety of reasons it was some 10 years before the first production **AMX-30 CPP** vehicles were delivered to the French army. The chassis of this AMX-30 bridgelayer is built by the Atelier de Construction Roanne (ARE), the only MBT plant in France, while the bridge

itself is made by Titan, which also builds many of the trailers used by the French army.

The overall layout of the AMX-30 armoured bridgelayer is almost identical to that of the MBT, with the driver seated at the front, the commander and bridge operator accommodated in the centre, and the engine and transmission located at the rear. Like that of the older AMX-13 CPP, the scissors bridge of the AMX-30 CPP is laid hydraulically over the rear of the vehicle and takes about 5 minutes to position and a similar time to be recovered. Like most bridges of this type it can be laid and recovered from either end. Opened out, the bridge is 22 m

The EBG features a pivoted crane on the right-hand side of the hull that can lift obstacles. Pincers or an auger can also be fitted to the crane arm.

(72 ft 2 in) long and can span a gap of 20 m (65 ft 7 in), a considerable improvement over the older AMX-13 armoured bridgelayer. In position the bridge is 3.1 m (10 ft 2 in) wide, but with widening panels this can be quickly increased to 3.92 m (12 ft 10½ in).

Equipment

Standard equipment for the AMX-30 armoured vehicle-launched bridge includes an NBC system and night-vision

equipment. No armament is installed as other armoured vehicles, such as tanks, would normally be in a position to give covering fire. A major disadvantage of armoured bridgelayers such as the French AMX-13/AMX-30 and British Chieftain derivatives is that when the bridge is being positioned, i.e. being laid through 180°, its position can be easily detected by the enemy. Other bridgelayers, such as the Soviet MTU-20 and the

SPECIFICATION	
AMX-30 CPP	(with bridge) 4.29 m (14 ft 1 in)
Crew: 3	**Performance:** maximum road speed
Weight: 42500 kg (93,696 lb)	50 km/h (31.1 mph); maximum
Powerplant: one Hispano-Suiza HS-110 12-cylinder multi-fuel diesel	range 600 km (373 miles)
developing 522 kW (700 hp)	**Fording:** 1 m (3 ft 4 in)
Dimensions: length (with bridge)	**Gradient:** 60 per cent
11.4 m (37 ft 4¾ in); width (with	**Vertical obstacle:** 0.93 m (3 ft ½ in)
bridge) 3.95 m (12 ft 11½ in); height	**Trench:** 2.9 m (9 ft 6¼ in)

German Biber, lay their bridges horizontally to aid their concealment.

EBG

From the late 1960s the AMX-13 Engineer Combat Vehicle (Véhicule de Combat du Génie, or VCG) was the standard vehicle of its type in the French army. The VCG was based on the AMX VCI infantry combat vehicle, and was fitted with a front-mounted hydraulically-operated dozer blade, an A-frame pivoted at the front of the hull which when in position could lift a maximum load of 4500 kg (9,921 lb), mine detectors, a hammer drill, a power saw and demolition equipment.

The VCG was replaced by the **Engin Blindé du Génie** (**EBG**) or **AMX-30 Combat Engineer Tractor** based on the chassis of the AMX-30 main battle tank, of which over 1,000 entered service with the French army.

Versatile vehicle

The EBG is a much more versatile vehicle, can carry out a wide range of combat engineer roles including laying small minefields, preparing fire positions, clearing battlefield obstacles and so on. Mounted at the front of the EBG is a hydraulically-operated dozer blade which is used for clearing and earthmoving operations. When its six scarifying teeth are

Developed for use by the French army engineers, the EBG features a front-mounted dozer blade, hydraulic winch and a demolition projector.

Right: The DT mineclearing version of the AMX-30 has its armament removed, a plough-type mine-clearing system and a magnetic field generator.

lowered and the vehicle is driven in reverse the dozer blade can be used to rip up road surfaces to make them impassable to wheeled vehicles. Located internally at the front of the hull is the main hydraulic winch with a capacity of 15000–20000 kg (33,069–44,092 lb), which can be used to recover other vehicles.

Fitted at the front of the hull on the right side is a hydraulic arm that can be traversed through 360°. In addition to lifting a maximum load of 15000 kg (33,069 lb), the arm can also be fitted with an auger for boring

holes in the ground to a depth of 3 m (9 ft 10 in) or a pincer which can be used to rip trees from the ground.

Mounted on the hull top is a one-man turret armed with a 7.62-mm (0.3-in) machine-gun, for which 4,000 rounds of ammunition are carried, and located on each side of the turret are electrically-operated smoke dischargers. The vehicle is also fitted with a 142-mm (5.6-in) demolition-charge launcher, for which five charges

are carried. Each of the charges weighs about 17 kg (37.48 lb) and has a maximum range of 300 m (328 yards). Typically these would be used to destroy bunkers and other battlefield targets. On each side of the demolition-charge projector are two mine-launching tubes, each of which has a container of five mines which fall to the ground and will be activated by any vehicle over 1500 kg (3,307 lb). Standard equipment for the EBG includes an NBC system.

Over 1,000 EBGs were built for the French army, the last example being delivered in 1993. The vehicle can be fitted with a scissors-type folding assault bridge. Deployed with the aid of the crane, this bridge can span a gap of up to 12 m (39 ft 4 in) in width.

SPECIFICATION	
AMX-30 EBG	**Performance:** maximum road speed
Crew: 3	65 km/h (40.4 mph); maximum
Weight: 38000 kg (83,776 lb)	range 500 km (311 miles)
Powerplant: one Hispano-Suiza HS	**Fording:** (without preparation) 2.5 m
110-2 12-cylinder multi-fuel engine	(8 ft 2½ in)
developing 522 kW (700 hp)	**Gradient:** 60 per cent
Dimensions: length 7.9 m (25 ft 11	**Vertical obstacle:** 0.9 m (2 ft 11½ in)
in); width 3.5 m (11 ft 5¾ in); height	**Trench:** 2.9 m (9 ft 6½ in)
2.94 m (9 ft 7⅗ in)	

PAA Self-propelled bridge system

The origins of the French army's **Pont Automoteur d'Accompagnement (PAA)** can be traced back to a time when the West German company EWK built three prototype vehicles to meet the requirements of the French army engineers. In the late 1960s the Etablissement d'Expériences Techniques d'Angers and the Direction des Constructions et Armes Navales carried out a complete redesign of the vehicle, after which two prototypes were built, the latter being completed in 1970. Two years later the PAA was accepted for service with the French army, and production got under way at Lorient in 1973. First production vehicles were delivered to the French army in 1974 and production completed by the mid-1980s. The PAA was offered overseas but no sales were made.

A French army PAA self-propelled bridge system unfolds its scissors bridge. The PAA can either help make a longer span, or leave the bridge in position while it moves to the rear.

Dual roles

The PAA can be used in two roles: it can lay its bridge in position in the same way as a conventional bridgelayer and then withdraw to the rear, or it can lay its bridge in position and remain to the rear and act as the ramp, especially when the far bank is higher.

The hull consists of a large aluminium box-type structure with the crew compartment at the front, engine in the centre and fuel tanks at the rear. Steering is power-assisted on the front wheels, and there are independent brake systems for front and rear. NBC and air-conditioning systems are fitted as standard.

Seen with a GCT self-propelled gun, the PAA bridge system was built for the French army engineers by the Direction des Constructions et Armées Navales at Lorient, although the first prototypes were built by the West German company of EWK during the 1960s.

In action

After reaching the obstacle to be crossed, the PAA raises its four wheels clear of the ground and rests on shoes under its hull. The scissors-type bridge is then launched hydraulically over the front of the vehicle. When opened out this has a total length of 21.72 m (71 ft 3 in) and is 3.05 m (10 ft) wide. With the aid of special widening panels carried on a 6x6 truck the width of the bridge can be increased to 3.55 m (11 ft 7¾ in). If required the widening panels can be carried attached to the bridge, but in practice they are normally removed to reduce the overall width of the vehicle. With the launch vehicle remaining in position as a ramp, soft-banked gaps of up to 17.4 m (57 ft 1 in) can be crossed, while the hard-banked gap capability stands at 22.4 m (73 ft 6 in).

In a combat scenario, the PAA was designed to replace bridges launched by AMX-30 armoured bridgelayers, which would then move forward. As soon as possible bridges laid by the PAA would be replaced by more permanent and durable structures.

Bridging systems

The French army has a number of other bridging systems in service, including the **Castor** light river crossing equipment and the later **CNIM Pont Flottant Motorisé Modèle F1**. The latter is perhaps the French equivalent of the PMP heavy floating bridge, but it has several different advantages: it can be used as a bridge, as a raft or as a pontoon. No pontoon boats are required due to the fact that each centre section has two outboard motors installed.

SPECIFICATION	
PAA	3.99 m (13 ft 1 in)
Crew: 4	**Performance:** maximum road speed
Weight: 34500 kg (76,059 lb)	60 km/h (37.3 mph); maximum
Powerplant: one Deutz V-12 diesel	range 800 km (497 km)
developing 223.7 kW (300 hp)	**Fording:** 1.5 m (4 ft 11 in)
Dimensions: length (travelling) 13.15	**Gradient:** 50 per cent
m (43 ft 1⅞ in); width (travelling)	**Trench:** no capability
3.05 m (10 ft); height (travelling)	

Bar and Ranger Mine systems

For many years the Mk 7 was the standard anti-tank mine of the British Army. This circular anti-tank mine was then replaced by the **Bar Mine**, which was designed by the Royal Armament Research and Development Establishment at Fort Halstead to disable even the heaviest tanks by blowing off one if not both of its tracks. Production was then undertaken by Royal Ordnance.

The Bar Mine system is composed of two main parts, the mine itself and its mechanical layer. The Bar Mine is of virtually all-plastic construction with just a few metallic components in its fuse. This feature makes it very difficult to detect with standard mine detectors. The Bar Mine's long shape not only doubles the chance of it being run over by a tank and therefore being activated, but also means that less mines are required than of the older Mk 7. The Bar Mine is normally fitted with an impulse fuse activated by the pressure of a vehicle.

Multiple fuse options

To make the Bar Mine even more effective, Marconi Command and Control Systems and Royal Ordnance developed a number of add-on fuses (double-impulse type designed to defeat the efforts of mine rollers and flails, L127 mast-operated sensor to ensure that the tank is right over the mine before the explosive is detonated and L128 electronic type initiated by the specific radiation signal of a nearby tank). With these the Bar Mine becomes the **Full Width Attack Mine**. In combat, Bar Mines with different fuses would be laid to hinder clearance.

The Bar Mine can be laid by hand but is normally laid by the **Bar Minelayer** that was manufactured by Royal Ordnance. This is towed by a truck or an armoured vehicle such as the FV432 armoured personnel carrier. The mines are placed on a loading chute and armed as they pass through this, and are then buried under the ground, thereby making detection more difficult. The laying rate depends on the type of soil, but is normally between 600 and 700 mines per hour.

Anti-personnel mine

The **Ranger** anti-personnel mine system was developed to meet a specific requirement of the

A view of the FV432 minelaying system of the Royal Engineers with the Bar Minelayer at the rear and the Ranger anti-personnel system above the hull.

SPECIFICATION	
Bar Mine	**Dimensions:** length 1.194 m (3 ft 11
Weight: total 11 kg (24.25 lb);	in); width 108 mm (4¼ in); height
explosive 8.39 kg (18.5 lb)	82.6 mm (3¼ in)

British Army by the Royal Armament Research and Development Establishment at Fort Halstead and Thorn EMI Electronics Ltd, and has since been retired from British Army service. The Ranger system consisted essentially of 72 tubes mounted on a frame which could be carried on top of a vehicle such as the FV432, or mounted in the back of a truck or other load carrier. The tubes were mounted in magazines of

four, each tube containing 18 circular **L10A1** anti-personnel mines: each of them was 62 mm (2.44 in) in diameter and 32 mm (1.26 in) in depth, and carried a 0.01-kg (0.022-lb) charge of RDX high explosive within an overall weight of 0.11 kg (0.22 lb). The operator had a firing unit connected to the launcher and each time he pressed a button a cartridge was fired and 18 anti-personnel mines were ejected to a

This FV432 APC is towing a Bar Minelayer for anti-tank mines and carrying on its roof a Ranger dispersal system for L10A1 anti-personnel mines. The combination could quickly create a minefield that was very effective and difficult to clear.

distance of up to 100 m (328 ft) depending on wind conditions. The launcher could be elevated and traversed as required. The mine itself was not armed until 20 seconds after its launch, and then lay on the ground until activated by pressure. Special training mines of compressed peat were also available.

In the Royal Engineers an FV432 was generally used to tow a Bar Minelayer, while a Ranger anti-personnel minelayer system was mounted on the roof, making it possible to create a combined anti-tank/personnel minefield.

Below: Each of the 72 tubes (grouped in reloadable four-tube magazines) of the Ranger system was loaded with 18 L10A1 anti-personnel mines.

Above: Bar mines are fed to the minelayer by hand from the rear of the APC. Laying rates of up to 700 mines per hour are possible. The minelayer's chute arms the mine, buries it and replaces the soil to prevent dectection.

Alvis Moelv Leopard 1 AEV Armoured Engineer Vehicle

The Norwegian army operates a large fleet of Leopard 1 series main battle tanks (MBTs) which are supported by armoured recovery vehicles (ARVs) and armoured vehicle-launched bridges (AVLBs) based on variants of the same basic chassis for ease of maintenance and matched operational speed and mobility.

To support these vehicles based on the Leopard 1, the Norwegian company Alvis Moelv designed and built the **Leopard 1 Armoured Engineer Vehicle** (AEV), which is based on a rebuilt Leopard 1 MBT chassis.

Following extensive trials with prototype vehicles, the Leopard 1 AEV was accepted for service with the Norwegian army, and 22 such vehicles were delivered. The Leopard 1

AEV has already seen service in the Balkans as part of Norway's commitment to the peacekeeping forces deployed in that region. Typical roles undertaken by the Leopard 1 AEV include the preparation of river crossing points, the

The Alvis Moelv Leopard 1 AEV is seen with its dozer blade lowered and excavator arm traversed to the front.

removal of battlefield obstacles, the preparation of fire positions for armour and infantry units, and general engineer work.

The process of creating the Leopard 1 AEV involved stripping down the surplus Leopard 1 MBT chassis before a new superstructure of all-welded armour construction was installed over the vehicle's forward part. The superstructure provides the occupants with protection against small arms fire and shell splinters, and its interior is fitted with an anti-spall liner. The chassis is also fitted with an enhanced mine protection package.

Role equipment

Mounted under the nose is an hydraulically operated dozer blade that can also be used as a stabiliser while the winch or excavator is being used. The dozer blade can be rapidly fitted with two rippers to tear up roads and other hard surfaces.

Pivoted at the front of the hull is the hydraulically operated excavator, which is normally traversed to the rear

With its dozer blade lifted and excavator arm traversed to the rear, the Leopard 1 AEV has much the same cross-country capability as the Leopard 1 MBT.

for travelling. The excavator carries a bucket that can be used to a maximum depth of 4 m (13 ft 1 in). The underside of the excavator arm is fitted with a grabbing claw so that timber logs can be lifted.

The Leopard 1 AEV is also fitted with two hydraulically powered constant-pull capstan winches, which can be used for a variety of missions such as self-recovery or the recovery of damaged or disabled vehicles.

The vehicle is fitted with a weapon station, of German design and manufacture, armed with a 12.7-mm (0.5-in) machine-gun that can be aimed and fired from within the safety of the vehicle. Banks of 76-mm (3-in) smoke grenade launchers are also provided. The vehicle can also be fitted with the Mineclearing Line Charge, which is used to neutralise anti-tank minefields.

SPECIFICATION	
Alvis Moelv Leopard 1 AEV	**Performance:** speed 60 km/h
Crew: 2	(37 mph); range 450 km (280
Weight: 46000 kg (101,410 lb)	miles)
Powerplant: one MTU 10-cylinder	**Fording:** 2.2 m (7 ft 3 in)
diesel delivering 620 kW (832 hp)	**Gradient:** 60 per cent
Dimensions: length 10 m (32 ft	**Vertical obstacle:** 1.3 m (4 ft 3 in)
10 in); width 3.6 m (11 ft 9½ in);	**Trench:** 2.5 m (8 ft 2 in)
height 3 m (9 ft 10 in)	

Following its big success with the Leopard 1 AEV, Alvis Moelv was awarded a contract for the design, development and production of a flail-type armoured mineclearing

vehicle based on the same basic chassis. Prototype trials proved to be unsuccessful, however, and therefore the whole programme was cancelled.

The weapon station mounted on the upper part of the superstructure's right-hand part gives the Leopard 1 AEV a capacity to protect itself against infantry equipped with nothing but short-range anti-tank weapons.

Leopard 1 engineers Armoured Engineer Vehicle and Biber AVLB

The **Leopard 1 Armoured Engineer Vehicle** was developed by Krupp MaK of Kiel specifically to meet the requirements of the West German army, the first production vehicles being completed in 1968. The company subsequently built six for Belgium, nine for Canada, 36 for West Germany, 12 for Italy and 25 for the Netherlands. OTO-Melara of Italy later built an additional 28 Leopard 1 AEVs for the Italian army.

The Leopard 1 AEV is almost identical to the Leopard 1 Armoured Recovery Vehicle (Bergepanzer 2), the major difference being that the AEV carries demolition charges and fuses but does not carry a spare powerpack.

Mounted at the front of the hull is a hydraulically operated dozer blade that can be used for preparing fire positions, or for clearing roads and other obstacles. The width of the blade can be extended by adding sections to each end, and four scarifiers can be fitted to the blade for ripping up the surface of roads when the tank is being driven in reverse. The dozer blade is also used to stabilise the vehicle when the winch or crane is being used.

Fitted at the front of the hull on the right-hand side is a hydraulically operated crane which can lift a maximum load of 20000 kg (44,092 lb). It can also be fitted at one end with an auger that can drill holes in the ground to a maximum depth of 2 m (6 ft 7 in). Mounted in the lower part of

Seen behind a Biber (Leopard 1 armoured bridgelayer), the Leopard 1 Armoured Engineer Vehicle is extensively equipped for its battlefield role.

the crew compartment at the front of the hull is the main winch with a capacity of 35000 kg (77,162 lb), a figure which can be doubled with the aid of a pulley.

Demolition capability

Standard equipment includes demolition blocks and detonators, tow bars and shackles, and electric welding and cutting gear.

Installed in the front of the hull on the left-hand side is a ball-mounted 7.62-mm (0.3-in) machine-gun, a similar weapon being located on the roof for anti-aircraft defence. A bank of

six electrically operated smoke dischargers is fitted on the left of the hull, firing forward.

The Leopard 1 AEV is used for a wide range of roles such as preparing fire positions, recovery of bogged-down vehicles, preparing bridges and other high-value targets for

demolition, filling in holes and keeping roads clear, to name but a few.

For many years the West German army has had a requirement for a GPM Engineer Vehicle which would be used during river-crossing operations to keep vehicle entry

The Leopard AEV is identical to the Leopard ARV in all significant details other than the fact that it carries no powerpack and is fitted with a heat exchanger and auger. The dozer blade is also fitted with special scarifiers to rip up the surfaces of roads.

SPECIFICATION	
Leopard 1 AEV	**Powerplant:** one MTU MB 838
Crew: 4	Ca.M500 10-cylinder diesel
Weight: loaded 40800 kg	developing 619 kW (830 hp)
(89,949 lb)	**Performance:** maximum road speed
Dimensions: length overall 7.98 m	65 km/h (40.4 mph); maximum
(26 ft 2¼ in); width overall 3.75 m	road range 850 km (528 miles)
(12 ft 3⅔ in); height with machine-	**Fording:** 2.1 m (6 ft 11 in)
gun 2.69 m (8 ft 10 in)	**Gradient:** 60 per cent
	Vertical obstacle: 1.15 m (3 ft 9½ in)
	Trench: 3 m (9 ft 10 in)

SPECIFICATION	
Biber	engine developing 619 kW (830 hp)
Crew: 2	**Performance:** maximum road speed
Weight: 45300 kg (99,869 lb)	62 km/h (38.5 mph); maximum
Dimensions: (with bridge) length	range 550 km (342 miles)
11.82 m (38 ft 9½ in); width 4 m	**Fording:** 1.2 m (3 ft 11 in)
(13 ft 1½ in); height 3.57 m (11 ft	**Gradient:** 60 per cent
8⅔ in)	**Vertical obstacle:** 0.7 m (2 ft 3⅔ in)
Powerplant: one MTU MB 838	**Trench:** 2.5 m (8 ft 2 in)
Ca.M500 10-cylinder multi-fuel	

points clear. Prototypes were built by EWK and Krupp MaK, but a shortage of funds prevented production. EWK also built prototypes of a 4x4 Amphibious Engineer Reconnaissance Vehicle called the APE, but this too fell victim to defence cuts.

Armoured bridgelayer

As had been the case with the Leopard 1 MBT programme, the West German army decided to build two different bridgelayers for comparative trials, these being known as the Type A and the Type B. After troop trials the latter was selected by the West German army, and the first production vehicles were completed by Krupp MaK Maschinenbau in 1975. In addition to the 105

such **Brückenlegepanzer Biber** (**BRLPZ-1**) armoured bridgelayers built for the West German army, five were made for Australia, nine for Canada and 25 for the Netherlands. In Italy OTO-Melara produced 64 such vehicles for the Italian army.

The hull of the Biber is virtually identical to that of the Leopard 1 MBT, but with its turret replaced by a two-part aluminium bridge. When opened out the bridge has a total length of 22 m (72 ft 2 in) and can be used to span gaps up to a maximum of 20 m (65 ft 7 in). As with all bridges of this type, the actual gap depends largely on the height and condition of the banks. The bridge can take vehicles up to 50000 kg (110,229 lb) under

standard conditions or 60000 kg (132,277 lb) in emergencies.

The standard equipment carried by the Biber includes night-vision equipment, an NBC system and four electrically operated smoke dischargers mounted on each side firing forward. The Biber can ford to a depth of 1.2 m (3 ft 11 in) without preparation, though with some preparation this can be increased to 1.65 m (5 ft 5 in). Mounted at the front of the hull is a support blade which is normally lowered before the bridge is placed in position, although it can be used as a dozer to ensure that the surface under the bridge is level. Normally such levelling and grading operations would be carried out by other specialised vehicles.

The Biber bridge is normally employed as follows. Forward elements know that ahead of them is a gap that has to be crossed with the aid of a Biber. Tanks are deployed as far forward as possible to give covering fire as the Biber is being brought up. On arriving at the river, the Biber first lowers its support blade. The lower half of the bridge then slides forward until its end is lined up with the end of the upper half. The two sections of the bridge are then locked together and the complete bridge is extended across the gap and lowered into position. Finally, the cantilever arms are withdrawn, the support blade is raised, and the vehicle is driven away so that the tanks can cross.

A West German army Biber AVLB extends the lower part of its bridge. The two parts are then locked together and the complete bridge is extended across the gap. Under the nose of the Biber is a hydraulic blade, which can be used as a stabiliser or as a dozer blade to prepare the bridge launch area.

M2 Amphibious Bridge and Ferry System

In the 1950s the West German company Eisenwerke Kaiserslautern Göppner GmbH undertook production of the Gillois bridge and ferry system based on the design of the French General J. Gillois.

The Gillois system, which is still used by the French army, consists of two basic units, the bridge and ramp: each of these is mounted on a 4x4 vehicle fitted with large 18x25 cross-country tyres and powered by a 164-kW (220-hp) Deutz V-12 diesel engine. Before the equipment enters the water a pneumatic float is attached on each side and inflated to provide additional buoyancy. When the units are in the water, the roadway or ramp units are rotated through 90° and coupled to form a bridge or ferry. When afloat, each unit is propelled by a propeller unit. The major disadvantages of this system are that it takes almost 30 minutes to prepare each unit

for water use, and that the pneumatic floats are prone to damage, not only from small arms fire and shell splinters but from river debris.

Into service

In the 1960s EWK and Klockner-Humboldt-Deutz developed the **M2 Amphibious Bridge and Ferry System** to meet the requirements of the West German army. After successful evaluation on the usual type of intensive troop trials, this equipment was accepted and entered service in 1968. The M2 system has also been used by the British Army and Singapore, the latter having a version with slightly more powerful engines.

The M2 is based on a 4x4 chassis with 16.00x20 cross-country tyres; steering can be on all four wheels, and the ground clearance can be adjusted from within the cabin to suit the ground being

An M2 amphibious bridging and ferry system, with its hydraulically operated buoyancy tanks in position on each side of the hull, prepares to enter the water. Each M2 has three propellers, one for steering and two for sideways propulsion, and the maximum water speed is 14 km/h (8.7 mph).

SPECIFICATION	
M2	**Powerplant:** two Deutz Model F 8 L
Crew: 4	714a V-8 diesel engines each
Weight: 22000 kg (48,502 lb)	developing 133 kW (178 hp)
Dimensions: length (travelling)	**Performance:** maximum road speed
11.315 m (37 ft 1½ in); width	60 km/h (37.3 mph); maximum
(travelling) 3.579 m (11 ft 9 in);	range 1000 km (621 miles); water
height (travelling) 3.579 m (11 ft	endurance 6 hours
9 in)	**Fording:** amphibious
	Gradient: 60 per cent

crossed. Before the M2 enters the water, a hydraulically operated buoyancy tank is unfolded on each side of the hull and the decking positioned by an onboard crane. This gives

Left: British Army M2s were modified in order to accept the increased-weight Challenger MBT, this being accomplished by the fitting of inflatable bags along the sides.

a total roadway length of 7.62 m (25 ft) and a width of 5.486 m (18 ft). The units then enter the water, where they are coupled together to form a ferry or bridge. The latter is to Class 50 standard, although introduction of the Challenger MBT meant that British Army M2s had to be strengthened to take the additional weight.

The M2 has two engines. When afloat, one of these drives two propellers for lateral propulsion while the other powers a single steering propeller.

The main advantages of the M2 over the original Gillois system are that it can be brought into action more quickly and is also considerably less susceptible to damage.

The Japanese Ground Self-Defence Force uses a system similar to the M2: this is called the **Type 70 Self-Propelled Pontoon Bridge**, but this is a less capable system with a capacity of only 40000 kg (88,183 lb).

Below: Three M2 amphibious bridging and ferry units are coupled together in the water to form a three-bay ferry with the capability for carrying heavyweight MBTs such as the Leopard 2 and the Challenger.

MTU-20 Armoured vehicle-launched bridge

After the end of World War II at least three armoured bridgelayers based on the chassis of the T-34 tank were developed and placed in service, two by the Soviet Union and one by Czechoslovakia (MT-34). In the 1950s the Soviet T-34 armoured bridgelayers were replaced by the **MTU** system based on a T-54 or T-55 tank chassis with its turret replaced by a cantilever launching mechanism and a bridge. The latter is launched over the front of the vehicle, and is 12.3 m (40 ft 4 in) long and can span a gap of up to 11 m (36 ft 1 in).

In the late 1960s this was replaced by the **MTU-20** in front-line Soviet units. The main difference between the original MTU and the more recent MTU-20 is that the latter has a bridge that when opened out is 20 m (65 ft 7 in) long and can span a gap of 18 m (59 ft 1 in). To reduce the overall length of the system for travelling, the front and rear parts of the bridge are swung upwards through 180° so that they rest on top of the central portion. The bridge is launched as follows. The MTU-20 approaches the obstacle to be crossed and comes to a halt. The stabilisers are lowered at the front of the vehicle and the ends of the bridge are unfolded and locked into position. A chain system

An MTU-20 armoured bridgelayer of the Finnish army approaches its launch position on an exercise in the 1980s. When fully open the bridge is 20 m (65 ft) long and can span a gap of up to 18 m (59 ft), representing a considerable improvement over the older MTU.

then moves the complete bridge along the cantilever launching girder until the end of the bridge reaches the far bank. The launching girder is then depressed and the end of the bridge is lowered onto the far bank. The tank then withdraws and vehicles can cross. The bridge can be recovered from either end in a similar time. The MTU-20 and older MTU were built in significant numbers and exported to many countries across the world.

Alternative designs

Two members of the Warsaw Pact, Czechoslovakia and East Germany, built their own armoured bridgelayers. The East German system is called **BLG-60** and was developed with the assistance of Poland.

It has a scissors-type bridge that is launched over the front of the vehicle. In position this is 21.6 m (70 ft 10 in) long and can span a gap of up to 20 m (65 ft 7 in). The Czech system is the **MT-55** and is based on a T-55 chassis. This has a scissors-type bridge that is launched over the front of the vehicle. In position this is 18 m (59 ft 1 in) long and can span a gap of 16 m (52 ft 6 in). The bridge takes about 3 minutes to be positioned and

6 minutes to be recovered. The MT-55 has an NBC system, night-vision equipment and a system to ensure that the bridge is long enough to span the obstacle. In addition to being used by Czechoslovakia and the USSR, it was exported to a number of countries including the Yugoslavia. The Israeli army captured a significant quantity of MT-55 armoured bridgelayers during the 1973 Middle East conflict.

SPECIFICATION	
MTU-20	(with bridge) 3.4 m (11 ft 2 in)
Crew: 2	**Performance:** maximum road speed
Weight: 37500 kg (82,673 lb)	50 km/h (31.1 mph); maximum
Powerplant: one V-55 12-cylinder	range 500 km (311 miles)
diesel developing 432.5 kW	**Fording:** 1.4 m (4 ft 7 in)
(580 hp)	**Gradient:** 40 per cent
Dimensions: length (with bridge)	**Vertical obstacle:** 0.8 m (2 ft 8 in)
11.64 m (38 ft 2½ in); width (with	**Trench:** 2.7 m (8 ft 10 in)
bridge) 3.3 m (10 ft 10 in); height	

TMM Truck-mounted treadway bridge

The **TMM** treadway bridge was initially carried and launched from the KrAZ-214 6x6 truck. In most front-line units the truck itself was replaced by the KrAZ-255B 6x6 truck, resulting in the revised vehicle designation of **TMM-3**.

The TMM truck-mounted treadway bridge consists of four spans, each of which are launched and recovered over the rear of a KrAZ-214 truck chassis. Three of the spans have

adjustable trestle legs while the fourth does not as it is the link between the third span and the far bank.

Employment

The TMM can be used to span both wet and dry gaps and is employed as follows. First the height of the treadway legs are carefully adjusted for the correct height so that when the bridge is laid in position it is level. (If the exact depth of water is not

known in advance or if the bottom is muddy this can be a major problem). When travelling the treadway legs are folded up

and stored under the folded scissors bridge, while the treadways are closed up to reduce the overall width of the

SPECIFICATION	
TMM	bridge) 3.15 m (10 ft 4 in)
Crew: 3	**Performance:** maximum road speed
Weight: 19500 kg (42,990 lb)	55 km/h (34.2 mph); maximum
Powerplant: one YaMZ M206B	road range 530 km (329 miles)
6-cylinder water-cooled diesel	**Fording:** 1 m (3 ft in)
developing 152.9 kW (205 bhp)	**Gradient:** 60 per cent
Dimensions: length (with bridge) 9.3	**Vertical obstacle:** 0.4 m (1 ft 4 in)
m (30 ft 6 in); width (with bridge)	**Trench:** no capacity
3.2 m (10 ft 6 in); height (with	

vehicle. Once the treadways have been extended, and the trestles fitted and adjusted for height, the truck backs up to the edge of the gap. A hydraulically-operated launching girder raises the folded span into the vertical position, where it is opened and locked. As it is lowered down by the winch system the integral trestle legs swing into place.

Multiple spans

Once the trestle legs are emplaced the cables are disconnected, the launching girder retracted into the travelling position on the rear of the truck, the truck is driven off to pick up the next span and the same procedure is repeated until the far shore span is emplaced. As mentioned previously a basic unit consists

A KrAZ-255B truck lays its opened scissors bridge. A complete TMM system consists of three spans with adjustable legs, and a shore span which does not have an adjustable leg and is the link between the third span and the far bank of the gap to be crossed.

A Soviet TMM truck-mounted treadway bridge system in the travelling mode is mounted on the rear of the older KrAZ-214 (6x6) cross-country truck. More recent models are mounted on the more powerful KrAZ-255B (6x6) truck chassis, which is also used to carry and launch the PMP system.

of three spans and one shore span, but more can be used if required. A basic unit can span a gap of 40 m (131 ft 3 in) in between 45 and 60 minutes under good conditions. Each bridge section weighs about 7000 kg (15,432 lb), has a

capacity of 6000 kg (13,228 lb) and is 10.5 m (34 ft 5 in) long.

The older **KMM** truck-mounted treadway bridge system is similar in concept but is carried on the rear of ZIL-157 6x6 truck chassis, with one unit consisting of four spans and one

shore span. The KMM unit can, however, span a gap of only about 34 m (111 ft 7 in) and has a capacity of about 12000 kg (26,455 lb), which severely restricts the type of vehicle, especially armoured, that can traverse the bridge.

PMP Heavy floating bridge

The **Pomtommo Mostovoy Park** (**PMP**) heavy folding pontoon bridge entered service with the Soviet Union in the 1960s and was subsequently adopted by every member of the Warsaw Pact except Poland (which uses the locally produced PP-64 system) and Romania (which uses the RR-60). The PMP has also been exported on a large scale and was successfully used by the Egyptian army while crossing the Suez Canal in 1973.

The PMP originally entered service mounted on the rear of the KrAZ-214 6x6 chassis, but Soviet PMP systems were later mounted on the KrAZ-255 6x6 chassis, although many foreign countries use local chassis: for example Egypt has fitted its

The Soviet PMP heavy folding pontoon bridge system consists of river and shore pontoons that are carried and launched from 6x6 KrAZ-214 or the more recent KrAZ-255B truck.

systems onto the rear of West German Magirus-Deutz 6x6 chassis while Czechoslovakia used the Tatra-813 8x8 chassis. Some of the latter were fitted at the front of the hull with a hydraulically operated dozer blade that can be used to clear

obstacles or prepare river banks before the launching of the pontoons.

System elements

The PMP system consists of two main elements, both of which are carried folded on the

rear of the truck. The two pontoon types are the river and shore, each of them of all-steel construction and launched in the same manner. The truck backs up to the water's edge, the catches are released and the pontoon rolls off the back of the truck into the water, where it automatically unfolds. Once the pontoons have been locked they are coupled up to form a bridge. A complete PMP pontoon set consists of 32 river pontoons, four shore pontoons and 12 bridging boats. This is sufficient to make a pontoon with a capacity of 20000 kg (44,092 lb) some 389 m (425 yards) long or a 60000-kg (132,277-lb) bridge 227 m (248 yards) long. The former takes about 50 minutes to position, while the latter takes about 30 minutes. The bridging boats are used to hold the pontoon bridge in position. The pontoons can also be used to form ferries which are then pushed across wide rivers by bridging boats. A 60000-kg ferry can be constructed from three pontoons in around ten minutes.

The US reverse-engineered the PMP into the **Ribbon Bridge**, entering service with the US Army in the mid-1970s. The American version has many improvements and is much lighter as it is made of aluminium rather than steel. It was made under licence by EWK in West Germany as the **Bundeswehr Ribbon Bridge**. This model has been used by Belgium, Egypt, the Netherlands and Sweden.

A KrAZ-214 cross-country truck carries a PMP shore pontoon. A standard set consists of 32 river pontoons, four shore pontoons and 12 bridging boats which are used to hold the completed pontoon bridge in position or to push rafts of PMP pontoons.

SPECIFICATION	
River Pontoon **Weight:** 6676 kg (14,718 lb) **Dimensions:** length (open) 6.75 m (22 ft 1¾ in); width (open) 7.1 m (23 ft 3½ in); depth (open) 0.915 m (3 ft)	**Shore Pontoon** **Weight:** 7252 kg (15,988 lb) **Dimensions:** length (open) 5.58 m (18 ft 3⅔ in); width (open) 7.02 m (23 ft ½ in); depth (open) 0.73 m (2 ft 4¾ in)

IMR Combat engineer vehicle

The **IMR** combat engineer vehicle was introduced into the Soviet army in the early 1970s, and was also used by some members of the Warsaw Pact as well as by Yugoslavia. The IMR consists essentially of a T-55 tank with its standard turret replaced by a new turret with a hydraulic crane and an armoured cupola for the crane operator. The crane has a telescopic jib, and when travelling is normally traversed to the rear to reduce the overall length of the vehicle. The crane is usually fitted with a pincer-type device for ripping trees out of the ground. The pincer can be replaced by a bucket which is normally carried on the left side of the hull when not required. This bucket is quite small, and so has only limited earthmoving capabilities.

This IMR combat engineer vehicle has its turntable-mounted hydraulic crane traversed to the rear and its pincer-type grab in travelling lock. Lowered at the front of the IMR is the dozer blade which can be used in either straight or angle configuration.

Dozers and ditchs

Mounted at the front of the hull is the hydraulically operated dozer blade, which is controlled from within the safety of the IMR by the driver. The dozer blade can be used in the normal straight configuration or at a V-angle. The IMR has night-vision equipment, and like most vehicles based on the chassis of the T-54/T-55 tank can also lay its own smoke screen. Mounted at the rear of the hull is an undiching beam, another common feature on Soviet tanks, although such a device was pioneered by the British during World War I: if the vehicle becomes stuck in the mud the undiching beam is removed from the rear and attached under the lower forward part of the tracks to improve traction.

Compared with Western vehicles, the Soviet IMR has very limited capabilities as it has no demolition device (as is fitted to the EBG, Chieftain Mk 5 AVRE and M728 CEV), cannot lay a minefield (as can the EBG) and would require some time to prepare fire positions for other vehicles. In the Soviet Union many of these roles were undertaken by other vehicles, and in any case the Soviet army was more offensively minded than most Western armies.

The Soviet army did have a wide variety of specialised trench diggers, these normally being mounted on full-tracked chassis such as that of the AT-T heavy tracked artillery tractor. One of these is the BTM ditching machine, which is essentially the AT-T fitted with the ETR-409 ditching machine. This machine is capable of digging a trench 1.5 m (4 ft 11 in) deep and 0.8 m (2 ft 7½ in) wide at the rate of about 1100 m (1,203 yards) per hour.

SPECIFICATION	
IMR **Crew:** 2 **Weight:** 34000 kg (74,957 lb) **Powerplant:** one Model V-55 V-12 diesel developing 432.5 kW (580 hp) **Dimensions:** length (overall) 10.6 m (34 ft 9⅓ in); width (overall) 3.48 m (11 ft 5 in); height (cupola) 2.48 m (8	ft 1⅗ in) **Performance:** maximum road speed 48 km/h (29.8 mph); maximum range 400 km (249 miles) **Fording:** 1.4 m (4 ft 7 in) **Gradient:** 60 per cent **Vertical obstacle:** 0.8 m (2 ft 7½ in) **Trench:** 2.7 m (8 ft 10⅓ in)

Centurion Mk 5 AVRE Armoured assault vehicle

A Centurion Mk 5 AVRE is shown with the dozer blade at the front of the hull in the raised position. Later in their lives the vehicles became known by the name Centurion AVRE 165, as Centurion guns tanks were also taken into service by the Royal Engineers.

During World War II, the British 79th Armoured Division employed a large number of specialised armoured vehicles which were successfully used during the D-Day landings and the subsequent push through France and on into Germany. One of these vehicles was the Churchill AVRE (Assault Vehicle Royal Engineers), which was fitted with a demolition gun for the destruction of battlefield fortifications such as pillboxes; it could also carry on its hull front a short assault bridge or a fascine. The latter was a large bundle of wood which could be dropped into enemy anti-tank ditches so that tracked armoured vehicles could then cross.

The Churchill AVRE continued in service with the British Army after the end of World War II, but by the mid-1950s these vehicles were becoming difficult to maintain and operate as the basic Churchill tank had been phased out of service.

Churchill successor

The Churchill AVRE was replaced in the 1960s by the **Centurion Mk 5 AVRE**, otherwise known as the **FV4003** and based on the chassis of the Centurion Mk 5 tank. The main armament of the Centurion Mk 5 AVRE was a 165-mm (6.5-in) demolition gun, which fired a HESH (High Explosive Squash-Head) projectile to a maximum range of about 2400 m (2,625 yards), although its effective range was a good deal less than this figure. Co-axial with the 165-mm gun was a 0.3-in (7.62-mm) machine-gun, and a similar weapon was located on the turret roof for anti-aircraft defence. Mounted at the front of the hull was a hydraulically operated dozer blade which could be used to clear battlefield obstacles and prepare fire positions. The vehicle could also carry and lay a length of Class 30 or 60 aluminium trackway across muddy ground so that following wheeled vehicles would not become bogged down. A fascine could also be carried on the front of the hull, and the Centurion Mk 5 AVRE could also tow a special trailer carrying additional engineer supplies, for example explosives or extra 165-mm rounds, or a trailer for the Royal Ordnance Giant Viper explosive system for the clearing of mines.

Later in its career the Centurion Mk 5 AVRE was fitted with mine-clearing ploughs at the front of the hull: when a

A key element of the Centurion Mk 5 AVRE's equipment was the 165-mm (6.5-in) short-barrel demolition gun, which fired a large projectile over short range for the destruction of hard targets.

minefield was detected, the ploughs were lowered hydraulically to the ground in front of each track and the tank was driven forward, the ploughs then ripping up the ground and pushing any anti-tank mines to one side. These mine ploughs were later fitted also to Chieftain Armoured Vehicle-Launched Bridges of the Royal Engineers.

Centurion Mk 5 AVREs were used up to October 1993 by armoured engineer squadrons of the British Army of the Rhine.

As a total of only 40 Centurion Mk 5 AVREs were produced, some Centurion tanks with 105-mm (4.13-in) guns were fitted with mine-clearing ploughs and issued to the Royal Engineers for service with the designation **Centurion AVRE 105**. The Centurion Mk 5 AVRE also became known as the **Centurion AVRE 165**, when the Centurion gun tank entered service with the Royal Engineers.

SPECIFICATION	
Centurion Mk 5 AVRE	petrol engine delivering 484.7 kW (650 bhp)
Crew: 5	**Performance:** maximum road speed 34.6 km/h (21.5 mph); maximum road range 177 km (110 miles)
Weight: loaded 51809 kg (114,220 lb)	
Dimensions: length 8.69 m (28 ft 6 in); width 3.96 m (13 ft); height 3 m (9 ft 10 in)	**Fording:** 1.45 m (4 ft 9 in)
	Vertical obstacle: 0.94 m (3 ft 1 in)
Powerplant: one Rolls-Royce Meteor Mk IVB water-cooled V-12	**Trench:** 3.35 m (11 ft)

Although produced only in small numbers, the Centurion Mk 5 AVRE was a key element in British Army planning for possible high-intensity warfare operations on the European mainland.

Combat Engineer Tractor

Multi-role armoured engineer vehicle

The **Combat Engineer Tractor** (**CET**) or **FV180** was designed by the Military Engineering Experimental Establishment to meet the requirements of the Royal Engineers for a vehicle combining the characteristics of an armoured vehicle and an earthmover. At one time France, the UK and West Germany were to have worked together on such a type, but each country then went its own way. Two test rigs to prove the basic concept were built in the late 1960s by the Royal Ordnance Factory Leeds, and these were followed by seven prototype vehicles in 1973–74. In 1975 the CET was accepted for service with the Royal Engineers, and 141 vehicles were then built at the Royal Ordnance Factory

Nottingham between 1977 and 1981, entering service in 1978. In 1984 India placed an order for a quantity of CETs.

The CET can carry out a wide range of roles such as the recovery of damaged and disabled vehicles (especially at river-crossing points), the clearance of fire positions, the preparation and clearance of obstacles, the preparation of river banks, and so on.

The vehicle is normally driven with its hydraulically operated bucket to the rear. This bucket can be used for normal earthmoving duties or bulldozing, or as an earth anchor when the 8000-kg (17,637-lb) winch is being used.

Rocket anchor

Mounted on top of the hull is a rocket-propelled self-emplacing earth anchor, which is fired in the event that the CET becomes stuck in mud or a river. The anchor falls to the ground about 90 m (295 ft) from the vehicle, and the CET can then winch itself out of trouble.

The vehicle can ford to a depth of 1.83 m (6 ft) but with some preparation can be made fully amphibious, making it especially useful during water

crossings. When afloat the CET is propelled by two water-jets mounted one on each side of the hull. Standard equipment includes six smoke dischargers, provision for a 0.3-in (7.62-mm) local-defence machine-gun, and an NBC system, the latter allowing the vehicle to work in a contaminated area.

The CET can also tow the trailer-mounted Giant Viper mine-clearing system, and

Designed to meet the requirements of the Royal Engineers, the FV180 CET can be used for a wide range of battlefield roles such as clearing debris and preparing fire positions for AFVs.

SPECIFICATION	
CET	**Performance:** maximum road speed
Crew: 2	56 km/h (35 mph); maximum water
Weight: 18000 kg (39,683 lb)	speed 8 km/h (4.9 mph); maximum
Dimensions: length overall 7.54 m	range 322 km (200 miles)
(24 ft 9 in); width overall 2.9 m (9 ft	**Fording:** 1.83 m (6 ft) or amphibious
6 in); height overall 2.67 m (8 ft	with preparation
9 in)	**Vertical obstacle:** 0.61 m (2 ft)
Powerplant: one Rolls-Royce C6TFR	**Trench:** 2.06 m (6 ft 9 in)
water-cooled 6-cylinder diesel	
delivering 238.6 kW (320 hp)	

Mounted on the roof of the Combat Engineer Tractor is a rocket-propelled earth anchor. If the vehicle gets stuck, the rocket is fired and the earth anchor falls to the ground, the vehicle then using its onboard winch to haul itself out of the obstacle or mud.

can also be fitted with a number of kits for different roles. These kits include a jib crane attachment installed in the bucket, Class 30 or 60 aluminium trackway, and also a pusher bar for launching pontoons, which are pushed onto water during amphibious operations.

The CET was used by the Royal Engineers for a wide range of roles during the Falklands and Gulf War campaigns, and parts of the chassis were used for the

One of the many roles performed by the CET is the preparation of river banks for bridging by pontoons. Here the CET, having done its job, waits as the pontoon bridge is fitted into position.

122-mm (4.81-in) D-30 self-propelled gun developed by the ROF Leeds in an effort to meet an Egyptian requirement. The

CET is considered to be one of the most useful vehicles in service with the Royal Engineers.

A Combat Engineer Tractor uses its hydraulically operated bucket to move soil. The bucket can also be used as an earth anchor when the winch is being deployed. When afloat, the CET is powered by a waterjet on each side.

BARV Beach Armoured Recovery Vehicle

In the UK the Royal Marines have always placed great emphasis on their ability to undertake amphibious operations, in which men and equipment are transported from ships lying offshore onto the beach by various types of landing craft. The landing craft are run onto the beach and their bow ramps are lowered to allow the men and vehicles to disembark rapidly onto the beach.

Beached craft

Very often the landing craft can become stuck on the beach, especially in rough water. A specialised vehicle called the **Beach Armoured Recovery Vehicle** (**BARV**) is then used to push the landing craft into deeper water. For many years the Royal Marines' standard BARV has been based on a much modified Centurion tank chassis. This was developed in the late 1950s and entered service in the early 1960s.

The BARV has two main roles, first to push landing craft into deeper water and second to recover onto land any vehicles that have been stuck or disabled while trying to come ashore.

The **Centurion BARV** can ford to a depth of 2.97 m (9 ft 9 in), is fitted with a push bar on

Above: A Centurion Beach Armoured Recovery Vehicle (BARV) comes ashore during amphibious operations.

Right: A Centurion Beach Armoured Recovery Vehicle of the Royal Marines prepares to assist a beached landing craft pushed broadside to the waves.

the front of its hull, and is also equipped with tow cables.

Toward the future

The Centurion BARV is the last member of the Centurion tank to serve with the UK armed forces, and in 2000 the Norwegian company Alvis Moelv was awarded a contract to design and build a **Future Beach Recovery Vehicle** (**FBRV**) based on the much modified chassis of the Leopard 1 tank.

The modifications have been extensive, and include the complete removal of the turret and the installation of a new

superstructure to enable the vehicle to ford to a depth of 2.9 m (9 ft 6 in). The suspension and hull have also been optimised for use in a salt water environment.

A total of four FBRVs was ordered, the first vehicle being delivered for trials purposes in 2001 and the remaining three following by 2003, after which the elderly Centurion BARV will finally be phased out of service.

The new Alvis Moelv Future Beach Recovery Vehicle, based on the chassis of the Leopard 1 main battle tank, seen during trials in Norway.

SPECIFICATION	
Centurion BARV	**Powerplant:** one Rolls-Royce
Crew: 4	Meteor water-cooled V-12 petrol
Weight: 40597 kg (89,500 lb)	engine delivering 484.5 kW
Dimensions: length 8.076 m (26 ft 6	(650 hp)
in); width 3.402 m (11 ft 2 in);	**Performance:** maximum speed
height 3.453 m (11 ft 4 in)	34 km/h (21 mph)

Husky Wheeled Maintenance and Recovery Vehicle

In the late 1970s, following an international competition, the Canadian Armed Forces selected a version of the Swiss MOWAG Piranha series of 6x6 light armoured vehicles to meet their future operational requirements.

In the end a total of 491 vehicles were manufactured in Canada by the now General Dynamics Land Systems – Canada (at the time called the Diesel Division, General Motors Canada). Three versions were supplied, all of them sharing the same basic hull and drive train. These were the 76-mm (3-in) Cougar Wheeled Fire Support Vehicle (WFSV), Grizzly Wheeled Armoured Personnel Carrier (WAPC) and the **Husky Wheeled Maintenance and Recovery Vehicle (WMRV)**.

Some 27 examples of the WMRV were built to support the other members of the family, and the type is operated by a crew of four. The hull is similar to that of the Cougar and Grizzly except that the roof line of the rear section is raised to provide additional volume for

The hydraulically operated crane installed on the Husky Wheeled Maintenance and Recovery Vehicle is used to lift complete powerpacks. The vehicle also carries a kit of specialised equipment.

the carriage of the specialised equipment required for the Husky's task.

Mounted in the centre of the hull roof on a turntable is a HIAB Model 650 hydraulic crane with a telescopic jib, and this is capable of lifting a complete powerpack. When the crane is used, a hydraulically operated stabiliser is normally lowered to

the ground on either side of the vehicle between the first and second road wheel stations.

SPECIFICATION	
Husky WMRV	**Powerplant:** one Detroit Diesel
Crew: 4	diesel delivering 160 kW (215 hp)
Weight: 10500 kg (23,148 lb)	**Performance:** max road speed
Dimensions: length 5.97 m (19 ft 10	100 km/h (62 mph); max road
in); width 2.5 m (8 ft 2½ in); height	range 600 km (373 miles)
1.85 m (6 ft 1 in) excluding crane	

The Husky is fully amphibious, and it is propelled in the water by two propellers mounted one at each side of the rear. Before entering the water a trim vane is erected at the front of the vehicle, and the electric bilge pumps are then activated.

The vehicle is armed with a 7.62-mm (0.3-in) machinegun and carries two banks of electrically operated smoke grenade launchers. Standard equipment includes powered steering and automatic transmission.

With the introduction into service of Piranha 8x8 vehicles, some of the 6x6 vehicles are being retasked, the remaining 23 WMRVs being re-designated as the Mobile Repair Team. The vehicles' amphibious capability is being completely removed, and some versions, including the 76-mm Cougar, are being wholly phased out of Canadian service.

The Husky Wheeled Maintenance and Recovery Vehicle is armed with a 7.62-mm (0.3-in) machine-gun. The crane has a capacity of 4536 kg (10,000 lb).

LAV-E Light Armored Vehicle – Engineer

Following extensive trials of a number of tracked and wheeled armoured vehicles, the US Army selected a version of what is now General Dynamics Land Systems – Canada Light Armoured Vehicle III (LAV-III) for its new Interim Brigade Combat Teams (IBGT).

A total of six of these IBCTs are being formed to give the US Army an interim rapid deployment capability before the introduction of the Future Combat System.

For the US Army application the LAV-III has been modified in a number of areas and is called the Stryker. The first version to enter service was the Infantry Carrier Vehicle (ICV) in the spring of 2002, other versions then following. These others are the engineer squad, medical evacu- ation, anti-tank guided missile, fire-support, mortar

carrier, commander's, NBC reconnaissance, reconnais- sance, and 105-mm (4.13-in) mobile gun system vehicles.

All of these have the same powerpack and suspension, and most also have the same all-welded steel hull that provides the occupants with protection from small arms fire and shell splinters.

The engineer squad vehicle, otherwise the **LAV-E**, provides the squad with a highly mobile protected transport to decisive locations on the battlefield to provide the required mobility and limited counter-mobility support to the IBCT. Current obstacle neutralisation, lane marking and mine detection systems are integrated into the LAV-E. The relevant obstacle neutralisation equipment is pro- vided by Pearson Engineering of the UK, and includes a surface

The Engineer Squad Vehicle, or LAV-E, is based on the Infantry Carrier Vehicle (ICV) version of the Stryker, and can be fitted with a variety of specialised attachments, suiting the vehicle to specific tasks.

mine plough and a roller system. Either of these can be rapidly attached to the vehicle depending on the threat.

Weapon station

Mounted on the roof of the vehicle is a remotely controlled weapon station that can be armed with a 0.5-in (12.7-mm) M2 machine-gun or a Mk 19 automatic grenade launcher. Standard equipment on all members of the Stryker family

includes powered steering, hydro-pneumatic suspension, a power-operated braking sys- tem and a central tyre pressure- regulation system that allows the driver to adjust the vehicle's tyre pressure to suit the terrain being crossed.

The vehicle is also fitted with an NBC system and a complete climate-control system. The Stryker is not amphibious, however, as the US Army had no requirement for this.

SPECIFICATION	
LAV	**Powerplant:** one Detroit Diesel 6V-53T diesel delivering 205 kW (275 hp)
Crew: 2 + 8	
Weight: 17400 kg (38,360 lb)	
Dimensions: length 6.98 m (22 ft 11 in); width 2.717 m (8 ft 11 in); height 2.64 m (8 ft 8 in)	**Performance:** maximum road speed 97 km/h (60 mph); maximum road range 540 km (335 miles)

M728 Combat Engineer Vehicle

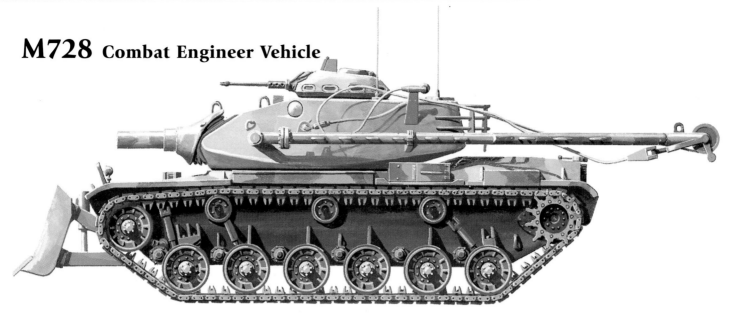

In the 1950s the standard MBT of the US Army was the M48, which was to have been replaced by a new vehicle called the T95. Using the same chassis, a combat engineer vehicle was developed under the designation T118. In the end the whole T95 project was cancelled along with the T118, and further development of the M48 took place. The result was the M60, which entered production in 1960. A decision was then taken to develop a combat engineer vehicle on this chassis under the designation **T118E1**. After trials with prototype vehicles, this type was finally accepted in 1963 for service as the **M728 Combat Engineer Vehicle**. Some 300 M728s were built at the Detroit Tank Plant, which was then operated for the US Army by

General Dynamics Land Systems. In addition to being used by the US Army the M728 was also sold to the armies of Oman, Saudi Arabia and Singapore.

Squash-head round

The M728 is essentially an M60A1 MBT with its 105-mm (4.13-in) M68 gun replaced by a short-barrel 165-mm (6.5-in) demolition gun for destroying battlefield fortifications; 30 rounds of high explosive squash-head (HESH) ammunition are carried for this gun. A 0.3-in (7.62-mm) machine-gun is mounted co-axial with the main armament, and the commander has a cupola-mounted 0.5-in (12.7-mm) machine-gun.

Pivoted at the front of the hull is an A-frame which can lift

The standard combat engineer vehicle of the US Army was the M728, which was the M60A1 tank with its 105-mm gun replaced by a 165-mm demolition gun, an A-frame for lifting at the front of the hull and a hydraulically operated dozer blade for obstacle clearing. It has also been used by Singapore and Saudi Arabia.

a maximum load of 15876 kg (35,000 lb). When the vehicle is travelling the A-frame is normally swung through about 120° to lie back on the rear engine decking. The winch to operate with the A-frame is mounted at the rear of the turret and controlled by the vehicle commander. Mounted at the

front of the hull is a hydraulically operated dozer blade which can be used for filling-in holes, clearing obstacles and preparing fire positions. Standard equipment on all vehicles includes night-vision equipment (including a searchlight mounted above the main armament) and an NBC system.

The M728 Combat Engineer Vehicle was designed for use by engineers in forward areas to clear and prepare battlefield obstacles. In addition to its 165-mm demolition gun it also had a 0.3-in (7.62-mm) co-axial machine-gun and a cupola-mounted 0.5-in (12.7-mm) machine-gun.

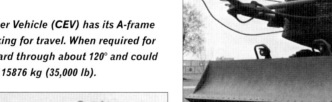

Below: This M728 Combat Engineer Vehicle (CEV) has its A-frame lowered over the rear engine decking for travel. When required for use, the A-frame was swung forward through about 120° and could be used to lift a maximum load of 15876 kg (35,000 lb).

SPECIFICATION	
M728 CEV	m (10 ft 6 in) Performance:
Crew: 4	maximum road speed 48.3 km/h
Weight: 53200 kg (117,285 lb)	(30 mph); maximum range 451 km
Powerplant: one Continental AVDS-1790-2A V-12 diesel delivering 559 kW (750 hp)	(280 miles)
	Fording: 1.22 m (4 ft 10 in)
Dimensions: length (travelling) 8.92 m (29 ft 3 in); width (overall) 3.71 m (12 ft 2 in); height (travelling) 3.2	**Gradient:** 60 per cent
	Vertical obstacle: 0.76 m (2 ft 6 in)
	Trench: 2.51 m (8 ft 3 in)

Grizzly Combat Mobility Vehicle

For many years the standard Combat Engineer Vehicle (CEV) of the US Army was the M728 which was based on a much modified M60 series tank. To replace the M728 CEV a new vehicle was developed under the leadership of the now United Defense LP, Ground Systems Division which eventually merged as the **Combat Mobility Vehicle** (**CMV**), or **Grizzly** as it is also known.

This is based on automotive components of the General Dynamics Land Systems M1 series of main battle tanks, and thus has similar cross-country mobility and a very high level of armour protection as it is required to operate in the forward battle area. It is also fitted with smoke grenade launchers and a remotely controlled 0.5-in (12.7-mm) machine-gun.

The vehicle is operated by a crew of two (commander and driver), either of whom can control all functions of the vehicle. The Grizzly is based on a new all-welded steel armour hull, and mounted at the front of the hull on the right-hand side is a telescopic arm which is

The Grizzly CMV with its mine-clearing blade in V-configuration and telescopic arm (complete with earth-moving bucket) on the right-hand side of the hull traversed partially toward the vehicle's rear.

traversed to the rear when not required. This is fitted with a bucket and used to dig holes and trenches. The bucket can be removed, allowing the arm to be fitted with other attachments. Mounted at the front of the vehicle is a full-width mine-clearing blade with extendible side elements. This advanced blade can clear a path 4.2 m (13 ft 9 in) wide and 305 mm (12 in) deep, and is fitted with replaceable tines.

Two prototypes of the Grizzly Combat Mobility Vehicle were

built and tested, but in the end the whole programme was cancelled in order to release funding for the the US Army's Future Combat System (FCS). The M728 CEV was

subsequently retired without the adoption of a wholly compatible replacement, and as a result the US Army today lacks a dedicated combat engineer vehicle type for its heavy forces.

SPECIFICATION	
Grizzly CMV	**Dimensions:** length 10.62 m (38 ft 10 in); width (hull) 3.66 m (12 ft); height 3.6 m (11 ft 10 in)
Crew: 2	
Weight: 64005 kg (141,100 lb)	
Powerplant: one AGT 1500 gas turbine delivering 1118 kW (1,500 hp) and coupled to an Allison fully automatic transmission with four forward and two reverse gears	**Performance:** road speed 66 km/h (41 mph); range 402 km (250 miles)
	Fording: 1.22 m (4 ft)
	Gradient: 60 per cent
	Trench: 2.28 m (7 ft 6 in)

This view of the Grizzly CMV reveals the mine-clearing blade being used in its V-configuration, and the vehicle's telescopic arm in its stowed position aligned rearward along the right-hand side of the hull.

M9 Armored Combat Earthmover

The **M9 Armored Combat Earthmover** (**ACE**) is used by the US Army engineers in the forward combat area for a variety of missions, such as preparing fire positions and river crossings, filling in trenches and clearing roads and battlefield obstacles.

The vehicle began life as the **Universal Engineer Tractor** (**UET**) in the late 1950s, but development was slow as at that time the US Army had higher priorities. Prototypes were built by a number of contractors, and final development was undertaken by Pacific Car and Foundry. The UET was later redesignated as the **M9 Tractor, Full Tracked, High Speed, Armored Dozer-Scraper Combination** before finally becoming the ACE.

Into production

As usual in the US, production was put out to competitive tender and the BMY Corporation (now part of United Defense) was awarded the M9 ACE production contract in 1986, with the first production vehicles delivered several years later. The M9 is air-transportable in many of the US Air Force's logistic transport aircraft, and can also be carried by heavy-lift helicopters.

Almost 600 M9s were built for the US Army and US Marine Corps, and additional vehicles were manufactured for a number of export customers.

Foreign service

The South Korean army has more than 200 examples of the M9 in service, and these were produced under a co-production programme between Samsung and United Defense. The M9 saw extensive use with the American armed forces in Middle Eastern operations during the 1991 and 2003 Gulf War campaigns against Iraq.

The M9 is of all-welded aluminium armour that provides

Above: The M9 ACE's hull is of welded and bolted construction with a towing pintle and air-brake connections so that heavy loads can be towed.

Below: Two M9 ACE vehicles in the Middle East show off the raised position of the hydro-pneumatic suspension, this being used for normal travel and the lowered position for scraping or dozing.

the driver/operator (seated under a cupola with eight vision blocks for all-round fields of vision) with protection against small arms fire and shell splinters, and is fitted as standard with an NBC protection system. When operating the vehicle with the cupola hatch open, the driver/operator is provided with a rectangular windscreen which is characterised by round-off corners.

The M9 is unarmed but is normally fitted with smoke grenade launchers. The M9 is fully amphibious, being

propelled in the water by its tracks at 4.8 km/h (3 mph), but this capability is no longer supported in US Army vehicles. Standard equipment includes a power-operated winch, bilge pump and periscopes for the driver and operator.

The front part of the vehicle is occupied by the scraper bowl, which has a capacity of more than 6 m³ (212 cu ft), and the driver is seated to the rear on the left side with the powerpack to his right. The dozer blade is mounted at the front.

SPECIFICATION	
M9 ACE	**Dimensions:** length 6.248 m (20 ft 6 in); width 3.2 m (10 ft 6 in); height 3 m (9 ft 10 in)
Crew: 1	
Weight: 16400 kg (36,155 lb)	
Powerplant: one Cummins water-cooled 8-cylinder diesel delivering 220 kW (295 hp) and coupled to a Clark transmission with six forward and two reverse gears	**Performance:** maximum road speed 48 km/h (30 mph); maximum range 322 km (200 miles)
	Fording: 1.83 m (6 ft)
	Gradient: 60 per cent

M88 Armoured Recovery Vehicle

To support its expanding fleet of M60 series tanks, the US Army awarded a contract to BMY for the development of a new purpose-built armoured recovery vehicle (ARV) which would, where possible, use many of the M60 tank's automotive components. The resulting **M88 ARV** was specifically designed to help recover tanks from the battlefield while under enemy fire. The M88 was also designed to replace the earlier series of M74 medium-duty recovery vehicle which had previously been tasked with recovering front-line US Army M48 tanks.

While developing the M88 ARV, the BMY company was instructed, as noted above, to make use of as many standard M60 MBT components as possible to save time and costs.

Bowen-McLaughlin-York Inc., as BMY was then known, signed a contract in 1959 with the US Army to supply 1,075 M88 vehicles.

An M88A2 ARV prototype lifts the turret of an M1 Abrams tank using the hoist associated with the frame boom mounted on the hull front.

The resulting ARV entered production in 1960 and featured a hull of all-welded construction with steel armour for the crew, with its complement of specialised equipment located at the front, and the powerpack at the rear. However, it was claimed that the armoured protection offered by the hull design fell short of what was required to ensure the crew's safety.

Special equipment

The M88 ARV was fitted with a front-mounted dozer/stabiliser blade, a frame pivoted at the front of the hull for lifting vehicles and powerpacks, and winches to recover damaged and disabled vehicles.

The vehicle's main winch could be used to drag a disabled tank to safety, while the boom could be used to change a tank's turret or its powerpack. The M88 could also be used to move mechanics and a full collection of tools and parts to the site of a disabled or damaged vehicle in order to carry out field repairs.

The M88 was powered by a petrol engine, and was followed by the diesel-engined **M88A1** and finally the **M88A2** with many improvements for the recovery of the heavier M1 Abrams series of tank.

All M88A2 ARVs are conversions of older M88A1s, and also have additional armour protection on the hull front and sides, and are powered by a 783-kW (1,050-hp) diesel engine. The vehicle is normally armed with a roof-mounted 0.3-in (7.62-mm) M240 or 0.5-in (12.7-mm) M2 machine-gun and electrically operated smoke grenade launchers. The M88A2 was exported to Egypt, Kuwait and Thailand.

SPECIFICATION	
M88A2	**Powerplant:** one diesel delivering
Crew: 3	783 kW (1,050 hp)
Weight: 63000 kg (138,889 lb)	**Performance:** speed 48 km/h
Dimensions: length 8.58 m (28 ft 2 in); width 3.67 m (12 ft); height 2.97 m (9 ft 9 in)	(30 mph); range 483 km (300 miles)

AAVR7 Amphibious recovery vehicle

To support its fleet of LVTP7 (Landing Vehicle Tracked Personnel 7) series of amphibious assault vehicles, the US Marine Corps drew up a requirement for the development of a recovery vehicle on a similar chassis.

This was developed by the FMC Corporation, which is today part of United Defense. The result was the **LVTR7 (Landing Vehicle Tracked Recovery 7)**, a designation later changed to **AAVR7 (Assault Amphibian Vehicle Recovery 7)** or, in upgraded form, the **AAVR7A1**.

The vehicle is based on the standard LVTP7/AAV7 hull but modified for its specialised role. The changes from the amphibious assault vehicle variant include the addition of a telescopic arm attached to the right-hand side of the roof. This crane is able to extend to 6.55 m (21 ft 3 in) and can lift up to 2722 kg (6,000 lb). The AAVR7 is also fitted with a winch capable of hauling vehicles and equipment weighing up to 13608 kg (30,000 lb). The

This AAVR7A1 recovery vehicle is seen in travelling configuration with its crane stowed. An extensive range of recovery and repair equipment is carried.

vehicle is also boosted in capability by several other items of equipment that can be carried. These include an air compressor, a 5-kW (6.7-hp) generator, work benches, welding equipment and a complete range of tools for field repair tasks. Furthermore, a tent can be extended to the rear of the vehicle to provide a shelter for mechanics while they undertake field repairs of damaged vehicles.

SPECIFICATION	
AAVR7A1	3.28 m (10 ft 8 in)
Crew: 5	**Powerplant:** one Cummins VT400
Weight: 23600 kg (52,028 lb)	diesel delivering 298 kW (400 hp)
Dimensions: length 8.14 m (26 ft 8	**Performance:** speed 72 km/h
in); width 3.27 m (10 ft 8 in); height	(45 mph); range 483 km (300 miles)

The rear turret and crane arrangement is clearly visible on this M578. The 0.3-in (7.62-mm) defensive machine-gun is also visible on top of the turret. The vehicle was replaced in US Marine Corps service by the AAVR7 derivative of the AAV7 assault vehicle.

SPECIFICATION	
M578	**Powerplant:** one Detroit Diesel
Crew: 3	diesel delivering 302 kW (405 hp)
Weight: 24000 kg (52,910 lb)	**Performance:** speed 53 km/h
Dimensions: length 6.43 m (21 ft 1	(33 mph); range 724 km (450
in); width 3.15 m (10 ft 4 in); height	miles)
2.91 m (9 ft 6 in)	

M1059 Smoke-generating vehicle

The US Army's **M1059** smoke-generating vehicle is based on a standard United Defense M113A3 series armoured personnel carrier (APC) chassis that has been modified specifically for its new role.

The M1059 was developed in the 1980s and entered service with the US Army in 1988, and almost 300 were created as conversions of existing M113A3 series vehicles.

Battlefield role

The official US Army designation for the system is **Smoke Generator M58 Wolf**. Its role is to deny the enemy information, protect friendly forces and dominate the manoeuvre battle by generating mobile large-area obscuration screens in the visual through to the IR regions of the electro-magnetic spectrum.

Mounted on the roof of the vehicle are two M54 smoke generators, which are operated from a control panel located inside the vehicle's hull.

The operator can select both smoke generators or just one smoke generator. The system provides mobile battlefield obscurant screens for at least 90 minutes of visual and 30 minutes of IR protection at maximum output. With lower material flows, longer-duration screens are possible.

The vehicle is fitted with a driver's thermal viewer to allow the driver to see through the visual smoke clouds created by the M58 Wolf, which is also fitted with a gas-particle filter unit for operations in any area of nuclear, chemical or biological contamination and, for local defence, a roof-mounted 0.5-in (12.7-mm) M2 machine-gun.

The system has undergone an upgrade known as the RISE (Reliability Improvement Selected Equipment) programme. This saw the addition of a 205-kW (275-hp) Detroit Diesel engine which is coupled to a four-speed hydrostatic transmission. Under RISE, external fuel tanks have also been added to the M58 Wolf, in addition to a new driver's station.

Together with a new suspension system, these additions enable the M58 to keep pace with M1 Abrams main battle tanks and M3 Bradley fighting vehicles. Future additions should include a millimetric-wavelength obscuration module. The entire M58 system is operated by a three-person crew and is fully able to provide shielding against threats from most current and future visual sensors.

A view inside the the rear of the M1059 vehicle reveals the equipment which produces the smoke screen. The two M54 smoke generators exhaust through a pair of ducts located above the rear of the hull.

SPECIFICATION	
M1059	**Powerplant:** one Detroit Diesel
Crew: 3	diesel delivering 205 kW (275 hp)
Weight: 12500 kg (27,557 lb)	**Performance:** speed 65 km/h
Dimensions: length 5.3 m (17 ft	(40 mph); range 470 km (292
4 in); width 2.686 m (8 ft 8 in);	miles)
height 2.52 m (8 ft 1½ in)	

Glossary

AA Anti-Aircraft.

AAMG Anti-Aircraft Machine Gun, usually mounted on top of the turret of armoured vehicles.

AAV Assault Amphibian Vehicle. US term for armoured tracked amphibians used by marine corps, formerly called landing vehicle tracked or LVT.

AAVC Assault Amphibian Vehicle, Command. AAV with additional communications fit for unit commanders.

ACP Armoured Command Post. Armoured vehicle with extra communications gear used by commanders in the field.

AFD Automatic Feeding Device. System for feeding ammunition from magazine into breech mechanically.

AFV Armoured Fighting Vehicle. Generic term for military vehicles with armour protection and armament.

AMX Atelier de construction d'Issy-les-Moulineaux. Primary postwar constructor of French tracked and wheeled AFVs.

AP Armour Piercing. Ammunition designed to penetrate and destroy armoured targets. Term usually reserved for solid shot fired at high velocity.

APAM Anti-Personnel, Anti-Materiel. Dual-purpose round for use against soft targets.

APC Armoured Personnel Carrier. APCs, usually armed with machine guns, generally transport infantry to the battle before the troops dismount to fight on their own.

APDS Armour-Piercing Discarding Sabot. APDS projectiles are smaller than the diameter of the gun's barrel. Sabots (French for 'shoe') are placed around the projectile and fill the space between the projectile and barrel walls. Once the projectile clears the gun tube, the sabots fall away. APDS projectiles have a higher muzzle velocity than comparable full-bore projectiles.

APDS-T Armour-Piercing Discarding Sabot Tracer. APDS round fitted with tracer compound in base.

APFSDS Armour-Piercing Fin-Stabilized Discarding Sabot. Unlike APDS projectiles, APFSDS penetrators are stabilized by fins, rather than spinning. Designed to be fired from smoothbore guns.

APHE Armoured Piercing High Explosive. Thick-walled, hardened casing and small HE filling. Detonates inside tank.

Ballistics The science of studying projectiles and their paths. Ballistics can be 'interior' (inside the gun), 'exterior' (in-flight), or 'terminal' (at the point of impact).

CFV Cavalry Fighting Vehicle. M3 reconnaissance variant of the M2 Bradley infantry fighting vehicle.

Ditched A tank is ditched when the trench it is being driven across is too wide or the ground beneath is too soft or waterlogged to allow the tracks to grip.

DP Dual-purpose. When a weapon is intended for more than one job, or a round of ammunition has more than one effect, it is said to be dual-purpose.

FAV Fast Attack Vehicle. Light vehicle carrying MGs, cannon, grenade launchers or missiles. Used by Special Forces making raids behind enemy lines.

FCS Fire Control System. Computers, laser rangefinders, optical and thermal sights and gunlaying equipment designed to enable a fighting vehicle to engage the enemy accurately.

FEBA Forward Edge of the Battle Area. Loosely, what used to be called the front line.

Female WWI British tank (Mk 1 to Mk V) armed with machine guns in right and left sponsons.

Fording Depth of water which a military vehicle can wade through without flooding engine. Usually quoted as without preparation and with preparation.

FV Fighting Vehicle. Term used by the British army to identify vehicles accepted for service. For example,the FV432 was Britain's standard APC for nearly 30 years.

GP General-Purpose

GPMG General-Purpose Machine Gun. MG used as both infantry LMG and for sustained fire. Variants adapted as coaxial guns for tanks and as anti-aircraft guns on many different kinds of armoured vehicle.

Gradient Degree of slope up which a tank can travel.

Grenades Originally hand-thrown high-explosive and fragmentation bombs, but also applied to weapons delivered by grenade launchers. Tanks usually have some kind of grenade-launching system to deliver smoke grenades.

HE High Explosive.

HEAP High Explosive Anti-Personnel. Dual-purpose HE round which destroys by a combination of blast and anti-personnel effects.

HEAT High Explosive Anti Tank. Tank round or guided missile with shaped-charge warhead designed to burn through the thickest of armour.

HE-Frag High Explosive-Fragmentation. Dual-purpose munition suitable for dealing with troops and soft-skin targets.

HEP High Explosive Plastic.

HESH High Explosive Squash Head. British term for HEP.

HVAP High Velocity Armour Piercing. Armour piercing round fired at very high velocity, relying on kinetic energy to break through enemy armour.

LARS Light Artillery Rocket System. Multiple rocket system developed for the German Bundeswehr.

LAV Light Armoured Vehicle. Canadian-built wheeled APC based on a Swiss design and used by the US Marine Corps.

Light tanks One of the original classes of tanks. Thinly armoured fast tanks designed primarily for reconnaissance.

LRV Light Recovery Vehicle.

Male WWI designation of the British heavy tank equipped with 6pdr guns rather than machine guns.

MG Machine gun

Muzzle Brake Device attached to the gun muzzle to reduce recoil force without seriously limiting muzzle velocity.

Muzzle velocity Speed of projectile as it leaves the muzzle. Air friction means velocity drops rapidly once in flight.

NATO North Atlantic Treaty Organization. Western alliance established to counter Soviet threat in Europe after World War II.

RMG Ranging Machine Gun. A machine gun coaxial with the main armament. The bullets have the same ballistic performance as the main gun.

Round One complete piece of ammunition.

RP Rocket propelled. Applied to tank ammunition, artillery rounds and antitank grenades.

RPG Rocket Propelled Grenade Launcher. Soviet-made infantry antitank weapons.

RPV Remote-Piloted Vehicle. Now equipped with real-time datalinks used to provide reconnaissance information.

RTC Royal Tank Corps. The world's first armoured formation.

Running Gear The transmission, suspension, wheels and tracks of a tank.

Shell Hollow projectile normally fired from a rifled gun. Shell can have a number of fillings, including HE, submunitions, chemical and smoke.

SLAP Saboted Light-Armour Penetrator. Machine-gun calibre high-velocity weapon designed to penetrate light armour.

Shot Solid projectile, usually armour-piercing.

Sloped Armour Angled armour – projectiles will either ricochet or be forced to penetrate diagonally.

SMG Sub machine-gun. Small fully automatic weapon often carried as personal arm by armoured crewmen.

Trajectory The curved path of a projectile through the air.

Transmission Means by which the power of the engine is converted to rotary movement of wheels or tracks. Transmission can be hydraulic mechanical or electrical.

Traverse The ability of a gun or turret to swing away from the centreline of a vehicle. A fully rotating turret has a traverse of 360 degrees.

Tread Distance between the centrelines of a vehicle's tracks or wheels.

Trench Field fortification which the tank was developed to deal with. Expressed as a distance in feet or metres in a tank's specification, trench indicates the largest gap a tank can cross without being ditched.

Turret Revolving armoured box mounting a gun. Usually accommodates commander and other crew.

Turret ring Ring in the hull on which the turret rides supported by bearings. The size of the turret ring affects the size of the gun which can be fitted: the larger the ring, the larger the gun.

TRV Tank Recovery Vehicle

Unditching beam Heavy wooden beam carried on early tanks. Mounted transversely across the tracks, it was used to gain extra grip when the tank was bogged down.

VDU Visual Display Unit.

Velocity The speed of a projectile at any point along its trajectory, usually measured in feet per second or metres per second.

Vertical volute spring Suspension with road wheels mounted to a bogie in pairs on arms, pivoting against a vertically mounted volute spring, it is protected from damage by the bogie frame.

Index Page numbers in *italics* refer to illustrations

1-Tonne light utility vehicle/artillery tractor (UK) 389–90

2S9 120-mm self-propelled gun (USSR) 248

8-cwt Lorry utility and command truck (UK) 158

1107 AD Campagnola light vehicle (Italy) 381, 396, 398–9

A FAF light vehicle (France) 396

AAAV (Advanced Amphibious Assault Vessel) (US) 416

AAV7 amphibious assault vehicle (US) 411–15, 416, 439

AAV7A1 amphibious assault vehicle (US) 402, 412–13, 416

AAVR7 assault amphibian vehicle recovery (US) 439–40

Abbot FV433 105-mm self-propelled gun (UK) 252

ACMAT armoured personnel carrier (France) 259–60, 381

Advanced Amphibious Assault Vessel (AAAV) (US) 416

AEC armoured cars (UK) 99, 296

Afghanistan 40, *234*, 246, 248, 269, 379, 381, *388*, 392

Albania 219, 318, 379

Alvis Moelv (Norway)
    FBRV (Future Beach Recovery Vehicle) 433
    Leopard 1 AEV (Armoured Engineer Vehicle) 421–2

Alvis (UK)
    MRAV multi-role armoured vehicle 372–3
    Saladin armoured car 271, 296
    Saracen armoured personnel carrier 252, 265, 270, 271, 296, 381
    Saxon armoured personnel carrier 272, *380*, 381
    Scarab reconnaissance vehicle 311
    Scorpion reconnaissance vehicle 295, 297–9, 364
    Stormer multi-role armoured personnel carrier 364

AM7, AM8 and AM10 light vehicles (US) 383

AML 90 light armoured car (France) *258*, 265, 284–5, 306

amphibious vehicles
    Cold War 180, 294
    Modern Era 374, 401, 402–4, 406–16
    World War II *34*, 51, 165, 172–83, 401, 402, 406, 409
    see also tracked infantry fighting vehicles

AMX-10P infantry combat vehicle (France) 241, 245, 249, 278, 284, 350–1, 372, 376

AMX-10RC reconnaissance vehicle (France) 284, 350

AMX-13 CPP bridgelayer (France) 417

AMX-13 light tank (France) 241, 276, 278, 325

AMX-30 CPP bridgelayer (France) 417–18, 419

AMX-30 EBG combat engineer tractor (France) *417*, 418, 428

AMX-30 main battle tank (France) 219–20, 221, 224, 241, 278, 324, 350, 418

AMX-32 main battle tank (France) 221

AMX VCG combat engineer vehicle (France) 418

AMX VCI infantry combat vehicle (France) 241–2, 278, 350, 418

Angola 40, 41, 265, 293, 393

Archer tank destroyer (UK) 72, 142

Argentina
    amphibious vehicles 412
    armoured cars 285
    armoured personnel carriers 241, 254, 258, 264, 268, 377
    tanks 218, 276
    see also Falklands War

Ariel motorcycles (UK) 169, *171*

Ariete main battle tank (Italy) 329, 369, 370

Arjun main battle tank (India) 323

Armored Utility Car M20 (US) 103, 105, 109

Armoured Car, AEC (UK) 99

Armoured Car, Daimler (UK) 100, *101*

Armoured Car, Humber (UK) 98, *101*, 102

Armoured Car, Marmon Herrington (UK) 97–8

armoured cars
    Cold War 9, 88, 100, *258*, 265, 271, 276–8, 284–6, 289–91, 295–6, 304–6, 307–8
    World War I 9, 12–13, 18–20, 24–5, 27
    World War II 9, 18, 49, 88–109, *171*
    see also reconnaissance vehicles

armoured personnel carriers
    Cold War 9, 203, 204, 216, 218, 256–75, 279, 291–2, 312, 371
    Gulf War, 1991 *362*, 363, 377, 379
    Modern Era 265, 368–81, 434
    Vietnam War 273
    see also tracked infantry fighting vehicles

ARTEC MRAV multi-role armoured vehicle (Germany/UK) 372–3

ASCOD armoured infantry fighting vehicle (Austria/Spain) 356–7

Austin-Putilov armoured car (Russia) 13

Austin (UK)
    8HP Series AP light utility car (UK) 157
    10HP HP Series G/KG light utility car (UK) 157

Australia
    armoured personnel carriers 254, 279, 379
    combat engineer vehicles 424
    light vehicles *163*, 389, 390, 391–2
    tanks 71, 74, 77, 211, *213*, 224

Austria
    armoured personnel carriers 240, 356–7, 374
    light vehicles 397–8
    tanks 48, 214, 276, 326

Auto Union Lkw light vehicle (Germany) 397

Autoblinda 40 and 41 armoured cars (Italy) 96

Autoblindé Peugeot armoured car (France) 24–5

Autoblindo Mitragliatrice Lancia Ansaldo IZ armoured car (Italy) 20

Automotive Industries M-462 Abir light utility vehicle (Israel) 393

Autovettura Fiat 508 C.M. light utility car (Italy) 155–6

BA-10 armoured car (USSR) 98

BA-64 armoured car (USSR) 109, 293

Bahrain 254, 255

Bangalore Torpedo pipe charge (UK) 74, 110

Bangladesh 219, 318

Bantam Car Company *see* Jeep

Bar Minelayer system (UK) 420, *421*

BARV (Beach Armoured Recovery Vehicle) (UK) 433

BAV-485 amphibious truck (USSR) 180, 408, 409

BDX armoured personnel carrier (Belgium) 263–4

Beach Armoured Recovery Vehicle (BARV) (UK) 433

Befehlspanzer Panther command vehicle 54

Befehlspanzer Tiger command vehicle 55

Belgium
    armoured cars 12, 18, 27
    armoured personnel carriers 241, 254, 255, 256, 263–4, 279, 374
    combat engineer vehicles 423, 428
    light vehicles 394, 397
    reconnaissance vehicles 297
    tanks 224

Beobachtungspanzer Panther observation post 54

Bergepanther ARV (Armoured Recovery Vehicle) (Germany) 120, 189

Bergepanzer 2 ARV (Armoured Recovery Vehicle) (Germany) 423

Bergepanzer 38(t) ARV (Armoured Recovery Vehicle) (Germany) 132

Biber armoured vehicle-launched bridge (Germany) 418, *423*, 424

Bishop self-propelled gun (UK) 72

Bison amphibious truck (Germany) 403–4

Blitzkrieg 8, 9

BLR-600 armoured personnel carrier (Spain) 267, 381

BM halftrack (USSR) 196

BMD airborne combat vehicles (USSR) 246–8

BMP-1 mechanised infantry fighting vehicle (USSR) 245, 246, 247, 249, 250, 372

BMP-2 mechanised infantry combat vehicle (USSR) 245, 249–50, 280, 281, 359, 368, 372

BMP-3 mechanised infantry combat vehicle (Russia) 351, 359–60

BMR-600 infantry fighting vehicle (Spain) 267, 306, 381

BMW R-12/R-71/R-75 motorcycle and sidecar combinations (Germany) 166–8

Boeing CH-47 Chinook helicopter (US) *370*

Bofors (Sweden)
    CV 90 infantry combat vehicles 358
    Lyran mortar system 226, 244
    Stridsvagn 122 main battle tank 343

Bolivia 254, 257, 268, 276

Bombardier snowmobiles (Canada) 405

Bosnia 220, 245, 254, 363, 369, 377

Botswana 276

Brazil
    amphibious vehicles 402, 412
    armoured cars 105, 276–7
    armoured personnel carriers 254, 256–7, 381
    light vehicles 392–3
    reconnaissance vehicles 279–80
    tanks 214

BRDM-1 amphibious scout car (USSR) 293, 294

BRDM-2 amphibious scout car (USSR) 269, 293–4

BREM-K armoured recovery vehicle (USSR) 372

Bren Gun Carrier (UK) 197, 200

BRM-23 reconnaissance vehicle (Bulgaria) 280–1

Brückenlegerpanzer Biber armoured vehicle-launched bridge (Germany) 418, *423*, 424

Brunei 377

BSA (UK)
    motorcycles 169, *171*
    Scout Car 100, 101

BT-7 fast tank (USSR) 39

BTR-40 armoured personnel carrier (USSR) 218, 269, 368

BTR-50P armoured personnel carrier (USSR) 241, 249, 251, 252, 294

BTR-60 armoured personnel carrier (USSR) 204, 257, 268, 269, 371, 381

BTR-70 armoured personnel carrier (USSR) 371, 381

BTR-80 armoured personnel carrier (USSR) 371–2

BTR-152 armoured personnel carrier (USSR) 218, 268–9

Buffel armoured personnel carrier (South Africa) 266–7

Bulgaria 48, 49, 280–1

Bulldog armoured personnel carrier (South Africa) 380

Bv 202 tracked oversnow vehicle (Sweden) 406, 407

Bv 206 tracked oversnow vehicle (Sweden) 406, 407

C 44 light vehicle (France) 396, 397

Cadillac Gage (US)
    Commando Ranger armoured personnel carrier 275, 381

LAV-105 light armoured vehicle 308
LAV-150 Commando armoured personnel carrier 273–4, 381
LAV-300 infantry combat vehicle 307
LAV-600 armoured car 307–8
Stingray light tank 300, 307
V-100 armoured personnel carrier 273, 381
V-300 Commando armoured personnel carrier 274–5
Calliope T34 rocket launcher *34*
CAMANF amphibious truck (Brazil) 402
Cambodia 219, 254, 318, 377
Canada
 armoured cars 102
 armoured personnel carriers 254, 255, 378, 379, 434
 combat engineer vehicles 423, 424, 434, 435
 light vehicles 154–5, *165*, 382, 383, 397, 405
 oversnow vehicles 405, 407
 reconnaissance vehicles 301
 special purpose vehicles 75, 282
 tanks 17, 33, 72, 75, 224
Car, 4-seater, 4x2 staff car (UK) 157
Car, Heavy Utility, 4x2, Ford C 11 ADF heavy utility car (Canada) 154–5
Car, Heavy Utility, 4x4 (FWD), Humber staff car (UK) 159
Car, Scout, Daimler (UK) *100,* 101
Carden-Loyd (UK)
 A4E11 amphibious tank 175
 Mk VIII light tank 62, 76
 Universal Carrier 197, 200
Carro Armato P.40 heavy tank (Italy) 78
Castor light river crossing equipment (France) 419
Centaur cruiser tank (UK) 67, 119
Centauro tank destroyer (Italy) 369, 370
Central African Republic 377, 394
Centurion ARV (Armoured Recovery Vehicle) (UK) 211, *213*
Centurion AVLB (Armoured Vehicle-launched Bridge) (UK) 211, *212*
Centurion AVRE (Assault Vehicle Royal Engineers) (UK) 112, 211, *212*, 429–30
Centurion BARV (Beach Armoured Recovery Vehicle) (UK) 211, 433
Centurion main battle tank (UK) 206, 209, 210, 211–13, 217, 226, 227, 228, 237, 238–9, 325
CET (Combat Engineer Tractor) (UK) 430–2
Chad 276, 285, 378, 394
Chaffee light tank M24 (US) 29, 302
Chaimite armoured personnel carriers (Portugal) 381
Challenger 1 main battle tank (UK) 229–31, 327, 333, 425
Challenger 2 main battle tank (UK) 229, 328, 333–4, 364
Challenger cruiser tank (UK) 67
Char B1 heavy tank (France) 86–7
Char d'Assaut St Chamond tank (France) 22
Char d'Assaut Schneider tank (France) 21, 22
Chechnya 246, 338, 339
Chieftain ARRV (Armoured Repair and Recovery Vehicle) (UK) 228, 230
Chieftain AVRE (Armoured Vehicle Royal Engineer) (UK) 228, 428
Chieftain main battle tank (UK) 210, 211, 228, 229, 230, 327, 333
Chile 220, 254, 257, 268, 276, 379, 381
China
 armoured cars 89
 tanks 40, 205, 218–19, 318–22
 tracked infantry fighting vehicles 240–1
Christie, J. Walter 39, 64
Churchill ARK bridging tank (UK) 74, 116–17
Churchill ARV (Armoured Recovery Vehicle) (UK) 74, 119, 120, *121*

Churchill AVRE (Armoured Vehicle Royal Engineers) (UK) 74, 110–12, *117,* 118, *122,* 123–4, 429
Churchill BARV (Beach Armoured Recovery Vehicle) (UK) 120, 121
Churchill Crocodile flamethrower tank (UK) 74, *122,* 124
Churchill Infantry Tank (UK) *10–11,* 73–4, *122*
Citroën (France)
 A FAF light vehicle 396
 C 44 light vehicle 396, 397
 Méhari Armée light vehicle 395–6
CNIM Pont Flottant Motorisé Modèle 1 bridgelayer (France) 419
Cold War
 amphibious vehicles 180, 294
 armoured cars 9, 88, 100, *258,* 265, 271, 276–8, 284–6, 289–91, 295–6, 304–6, 307–8
 armoured personnel carriers 9, 203, 204, 216, 218, 256–75, 279, 291–2, 312, 371
 halftracks 201
 mine-clearing tanks 211, 220, 429–30
 reconnaissance vehicles 9, 260, 276–315, 404
 special purpose vehicles 112, 206, 209, 211, 220, 233, 429
 tank destroyers 276, 351, 353
 tanks 9, 49, 55, 203–39, 276, 278, 294, 300, 302–4, 327
 tracked infantry fighting vehicles 9, 218, 240–55, 361, 362
Colombia 104–5, 254, 257, 276
Combat Engineer Tractor (CET) (UK) 430–2
combat engineer vehicles 233, 417–40
 see also special purpose vehicles
Combat Mobility Vehicle (CMV) (US) 437
Comet cruiser tank (UK) 66
Commando armoured personnel carrier (US) 273–4, 381
Commando Ranger armoured personnel carrier (US) 275, 381
Commercial Utility Cargo Vehicle (CUCV) (US) 385
Condor armoured personnel carrier (Germany) 261
Congo 219, 254, 306, 318
Conqueror ARV (Armoured Recovery Vehicle) (UK) 209
Conqueror heavy tank (UK) 209, 217
Covenanter cruiser tank (UK) 64, 65, 113, 119
Crab flail tank (UK) *31, 114,* 115, 123, 124
Croatia 220, 245, 342, 377
Cromwell ARV (Armoured Recovery Vehicle) (UK) 66, *119*
Cromwell cruiser tank (UK) 66, 67
Cruiser Tank Challenger (UK) 67
Cruiser Tank Mks I-V (UK) 63–4, 65, 68, 69,113, 119
Cruiser Tank Mk VI Crusader (UK) 65, 66, *68, 69,* 119, 142
Cruiser Tank Mk VII Cavalier (UK) 67, 119
Cruiser Tank Mk VIII Centaur (UK) 67, 119
Cruiser Tank Mk VIII Cromwell (UK) 66, 67
Cruiser Tank Ram (Canada) 33, 75, 119
Cruiser Tank Sentinel AC (Australia) 74–5
CUCV (Commercial Utility Cargo Vehicle) (US) 385
Cushman 53 Autoglide motorcycle (US) 170
CV 90 infantry combat vehicles (Sweden) 344, 358–9, 361
CV 90120-T lightweight battle tank (Sweden) 344–5, 359
Cyprus 220, 241, 276, 359, 377
Czechoslovakia
 armoured personnel carriers 250, 251, 257–8, 269
 combat engineer vehicles 426
 reconnaissance vehicles 281
 tanks 48–9, 130, 205, 206, 234, 335

Daimler-Benz G 5 personnel carrier (Germany) 153
Daimler (UK)

armoured cars 100, *101, 108,* 296
 Ferret Scout Car 284, 295, 296
 scout cars *100,* 101
Dardo armoured infantry fighting vehicle (Italy) 355–6, 370
Defender light utility vehicle (UK) 388–9, 391
Denmark 211, 224, 254, 326, 379, 397
Desert Storm, Operation *see* Gulf War, 1991
Djibouti 377, 378
Dodge (US)
 M37 light vehicle 382
 T207 series multi-role 1/2-ton light trucks160
 T214 series multi-role 3/4-ton light trucks 161–2, 382
 T215 series multi-role 1/2-ton light trucks160–1
Dragoon armoured personnel carrier (US) 273, 381
Dubai 221, 222
DUKW amphibious truck (US) 177, 402, 409
Duplex Drive (DD) Sherman tank (UK) *34,* 122, 178–9

Eagle reconnaissance vehicle (Switzerland) 310
East Germany 206, 207
EBR heavy armoured car (France) 277–8
Ecuador 241, 254, 257, 276
EE-3 Jararaca scout car (Brazil) 279–80
EE-9 Cascavel armoured car (Brazil) 276–7, 392, 402
EE-11 Urutu armoured personnel carrier (Brazil) 256–7, 381, 392, 402
EE-12 light utility vehicle (Brazil) 392–3
Egypt
 amphibious vehicles 403, 408
 armoured personnel carriers 251, 254, 255, 368
 combat engineer vehicles 427, 428
 light vehicles 389, 390
 reconnaissance vehicles 293
 tanks 41, 204, 206, *208,* 211, 215, 217, 346, 347
Ehrhardt Panzerkraftwagen 1915/1917 27
EKW Bison amphibious truck (Germany) 403–4
Eland armoured car (South Africa) 265, 284, 306
Enfield motorcycles (UK) 169–70
ENGESA (Brazil)
 EE-3 Jararaca scout car 279–80
 EE-9 Cascavel armoured car 276–7, 392, 402
 EE-11 Urutu armoured personnel carrier 256–7, 381, 392, 402
 EE-12 light utility vehicle 392–3
Engin Blindé du Génie (EBG) combat engineer tractor (France) *417,* 418, 428

Fahd armoured personnel carrier (Egypt) 368
Falklands War, 1982 219, 406, 412, 432
fascines 17, *112,* 117–18, *123,* 124, 211, 429
Fast Attack Vehicle (US) 386–7
FBRV (Future Beach Recovery Vehicle) (UK) 433
Fennek multi-purpose carrier (Dutch/German) 288–9
Ferret scout car (UK) 284, 295, 296
Fiat
 1107 AD Campagnola light vehicle 381, 396, 398–9
 Centauro tank destroyer 369
 Puma armoured personnel carrier 370
 Tipo 6614 armoured personnel carrier 264, 289, 381
 Tipo 6616 armoured car 264, 289
Fiat Ansaldo
 Autovettura 508 C.M. light utility car 155–6
 Carro Armato P.40 heavy tank 78
 L.3 tankette 76, 77, 140
 L.6/40 light tank 76, 140, 141
 M.11/39 and M.13/40 medium tanks 77
 M.14/41 medium tank 77, 78, 141
 M.15/42 medium tank 77, 78, 141
Fieseler Fi 156 Storch reconnaissance aircraft *94*
Finland

armoured personnel carriers 375–6
combat engineer vehicles *426*
oversnow vehicles 406, 407
tanks 344
Winter War 37, 38, 39, 44
Flammpanzer II flamethrower tank 51
Flammpanzer 38(t) flamethrower tank 132
Ford (US)
    Fordor Station Wagon 154
    GPA amphibious Jeep 165, 183, 401
    M151 light vehicle 383, 384, 386–7
    see also Jeep
Fox light armoured car (UK) 295–6, 297
France
    armoured cars
        Cold War *258*, 277–8, 284–6, 290, 306, *381*
        World War I 24–5
        World War II 88
    armoured personnel carriers
        Cold War 241–2, 249, 258–60, 290
        Modern Era 350–1, 372, 376–8, 381
    combat engineer vehicles 417–19
    halftracks 195, 198, 200
    light vehicles 394–6, 397
    oversnow vehicles *407*
    reconnaissance vehicles 284–7
    special purpose vehicles 220
    tanks
        Cold War 54, 214, 219–21, 224, 241, 278, 324
        Modern Era 324–5
        World War I 11, 17, 21–4, 25
        World War II 24, *33*, 82–7, *147*
FT 17 tank (France) 17, 21, 22, 23–4, 25, 83
Future Beach Recovery Vehicle (FBRV) (UK) 433
Future Combat System (US) 435, 437
FV432 armoured personnel carrier (UK)
    252–3, 270, 295, 361, 420, 421
FV433 Abbot 105-mm self-propelled gun (UK) 252

Gabon 244, 258, 276, 285
GAZ (USSR)
    BTR-80 armoured personnel carrier 371
    Model 60 halftrack 196
    Model 67 light utility car 154, 183
    Model 69 light cross-country vehicle 400–1
General Aircraft Hamilcar glider (UK) 63
Germany
    amphibious vehicles 51, 172–4, 179, 403–4
    armoured cars
        Cold War 290–1
        World War I 27
        World War II 49, 88, 89–95, 96, 98, *108*, 109
    armoured personnel carriers
        Cold War 244–5, 249, 254, 260–2, 404
        Modern Era 218, 351–4, 368, 372–3, 381
    combat engineer vehicles 418, 423–5, 428
    halftracks *89*, 184–94, 195, 196, 197, 200
    light vehicles
        Modern Era 383, 396, 397, 405
        World War II 148–53
    motorcycles and sidecars 166–8
    reconnaissance vehicles 260, 287–9, 314–15, 404
    special purpose vehicles 48, 50, 53, 54,
        120, 125–7, 132, 189
    tank destroyers
        Cold War 351, 353
        World War II 49, 51, 54, 61, 83, 128–39,140
    tanks
        Cold War 207, 215, 217, 219, 224–5
        Modern Era 221, 228, 325–8, 343, 352
        World War I 15, 17, 25–6
        World War II 9, 24, 32, 39, 42, 48–61, 78,
        83, 86, 87, 120
Ghana 268, 276, 379
Gillois bridge and ferry system (France) 425

GKN Sankey Saxon armoured personnel carrier (UK)
    272, *380*, 381
GMC 6x6 truck (US) 179
Goat demolition charge (UK) 111, 122
GPA amphibious Jeep (US) 165, 183, 401
Grant medium tank (UK) 30, 75
Greece
    armoured personnel carriers 254, 255, 268, 350
    light vehicles 396
    reconnaissance vehicles 287
    tanks 214, 217, 220, 224
Greyhound M8 light armoured car (US) *94*, 102–5,
    109
Grizzly Combat Mobility Vehicle (CMV) (US) 437
GT-S tracked oversnow vehicle (USSR) 410
Guardian patrol vehicle (Italy) 381, 399
Guderian, Heinz 8
Gulf War, 1991
    armoured personnel carriers *362*, 363, 377, 379
    combat engineer vehicles 438
    light vehicles 385
    reconnaissance vehicles 284, *298*
    tanks 230, 318, 333, 336, 337, 342,*346*, 348
Gulf War, 2003 *385*, *386*, 438
Gun Motor Carriage M10 tank destroyer (US)
    54, 143, 144, 145, *146*
Gun Motor Carriage M18 Hellcat tank
    destroyer (US) 144, 146
Gun Motor Carriage M36 tank destroyer (US) *143*,
    145

H-35, H-38 and H-39 light tanks (France) 82–3,*147*
Haflinger high-mobility light utility vehicle (Austria)
    397–8
halftracks *34*, *89*, 106, 184–201
Harley-Davidson motorcycles (US) 170
Hetzer tank destroyer (Germany) 49, 131–2
Hillman 10 HP light utility car (UK) 157
HMMWV High Mobility Multi-purpose Wheeled
    Vehicle (US) 310, 384, 385–6, 387
Holt tractor (US) 14, 21, 22, 26
Hotchkiss (France)
    AMX VCI infantry combat vehicle 241
    H-35, H-38 and H-39 light tanks 82–3, *147*
    M 201 light vehicle 394, 396
Humber (UK)
    8-cwt Lorry 158
    armoured cars 98, *101*, 102
    Car, 4-seater, 4x2 staff car 157
    Car, Heavy Utility, 4x4 (FWD) staff car 159
    Mk II light reconnaissance car *171*
    'Pig' armoured personnel carrier 270, *380*, 381
    Pullman staff car 157
    Scout Car *100*
    Staff Saloon Mk 2 staff car 157
Hummel self-propelled gun (Germany) *138*
Hungary 48, 49, 262–3, 372, 400, 401
Husky wheeled maintenance and recovery vehicle
    (Canada) 434

IFAV (Interim Fast Attack Vehicle) (US) 387
Iltis light utility vehicle (Germany) 383, 396, 397, 405
IMR combat engineer vehicle (USSR) 428
India
    armoured personnel carriers 246
    light vehicles 382
    tanks 210, 211, 215, 238, 323, 335, 339
Indian motorcycles (US) 170–1
Indonesia 242, 271, 287, 350, 351, 364, 377
Infantry Tank Mks I and II Matilda (UK) *64*, 70–1
Infantry Tank Mk III Valentine (UK) 71–2, 75, 99, 142
Infantry Tank Mk IV Churchill (UK) *10–11*, 73–4, *122*
Interim Fast Attack Vehicle (IFAV) (US) 387
internal security vehicles 279, 380–1, 389, 399
Iran 214, 217, 219, 228, 229, 230, 254, 318

Iraq
    amphibious vehicles 408
    armoured personnel carriers 246, 254, 258, 268,
        350, 378
    reconnaissance vehicles 276
    tanks 219, 220, 228, 318, 336, 339
    see also Gulf War
Ireland 263, 375, 379
IS-2 heavy tank (USSR) 46–7, 129, 135
IS-3 heavy tank (USSR) 47
Israel
    armoured personnel carriers 254, 269, 291–2
    combat engineer vehicles 426
    halftracks 199, 201
    light vehicles 386, 393
    reconnaissance vehicles 291–2
    tanks 41, 204, 206, *208*, 211, *213*, 215, 217,
        222–3, 237–8, 330–1
Italy
    amphibious vehicles 403, 407, 412
    armoured cars 20, 96, 264, 289
    armoured personnel carriers 242, 254, 264,
        355–6, 369–70, 381
    combat engineer vehicles 423, 424
    halftracks 187
    light vehicles 155–6, 398–9
    oversnow vehicles 407
    tank destroyers 76, 140–1, 369
    tanks 76–9, 214, 221–2, 224, 329
Ivory Coast 285, 377

Jagdpanther tank destroyer 54, 135, 137, *139*
Jagdpanzer IV tank destroyer 132–3, *139*, *146*
Jagdpanzer Kanone tank destroyer 351, 353
Jagdpanzer Rakete tank destroyer 351, 353
Jagdtiger tank destroyer 61, 137
James ML collapsible motorcycle (UK) 169
Japan
    amphibious vehicles 176–7
    armoured personnel carriers 243
    combat engineer vehicles 425
    light vehicles 156, 382
    oversnow vehicles 404
    reconnaissance vehicles 292
    special purpose vehicles 81
    tanks 79–81, 176, 177, 225–6, 331
Jeep multi-purpose vehicle (US) 148, 150, 154,
    163–5, 383, 386, 394
Jones Onion demolition device (UK) 74, 110–11,
    124
Jordan
    armoured personnel carriers 254, 255, 257,
        271
    tanks 211, 214, 215, 217, 228, 229, 237, 238

K1 and K1A1 main battle tank (South Korea) 332–3
Karl self-propelled mortar (Germany) 125–6
Kégresse P 107 halftrack (France) 195, 198, 200
kleiner Panzerbefehlswagen SdKfz 265
    command vehicle 50, 126–7
KMM truck-mounted treadway bridge (USSR) 427
Komatsu Type 60 and 61 oversnow vehicles (Japan)
    404
Korean War
    halftracks 199
    light vehicles 164, 382, 383
    tanks 29, 35, 41, 211, 212, 215
Kraftfahrzeug 2 (Stöwer 40) personnel carrier 151,
    153
Kraftfahrzeug 11 (Auto-Union/Horch 830) personnel
    carrier 152
Kraftfahrzeug 15 (Mercedes-Benz 340) personnel
    carrier 152–3
Kübel, Volkswagen 148–50, 174
Kuwait

armoured personnel carriers 254, 255, 263, 271, 359, 361, 374, 377
reconnaissance vehicles 279, 287
tanks 8, 210, 220, 228, 337, 342, 347
KV-1 heavy tank (USSR) 44–5, 52
KV-2 heavy tank (USSR) 45–6
KV-85 heavy tank (USSR) 40, 45, 46

L.3 tankette (Italy) 76, 77, 140
L.6/40 light tank (Italy) 76, 140, 141
L3314 Laplander light vehicle (Sweden) 400
Lanchester armoured car 19–20
Land Rover (UK) 279, 381
    1-Tonne light utility vehicle/artillery tractor 389–90
    Defender light utility vehicle 388–9, 391
    Perentie heavy-duty light truck 391–2
    Special Operations Vehicle 389
Land-Wasser-Schlepper amphibious tractor (Germany) 172–3
LARC-5/15/60 amphibious cargo carriers (US) 402, 411
LAV-25 Coyote reconnaissance vehicle (Canada) 282
LAV-105 light armoured vehicle (US) 308
LAV-150 Commando armoured personnel carrier (US) 273–4, 381
LAV-300 infantry combat vehicle (US) 307
LAV-600 armoured car (US) 307–8
LAV-E light armored vehicle - engineer (US) 435
Lebanon
    armoured personnel carriers 242, 254, 269, 271, 377
    tanks 214, 217, 222, 337
Leclerc main battle tank (France) 324–5, 343
Lee medium tank M3 (US) see M3 Medium Tank
leichter Panzerspähwagen SdKfz 221 light armoured car 89, *94*
leichter Panzerspähwagen SdKfz 222 light armoured car 49, 89, *95*
leichter Panzerspähwagen SdKfz 223 light armoured car 89
leichter Zugkraftwagen U 304(f) 195
Leopard 1 AEV (Armoured Engineer Vehicle) (Germany) 421–4
Leopard 1 ARV (Armoured Recovery Vehicle) (Germany) 423
Leopard 1 main battle tank (Germany) 207, 215, 217, 219, 221, 224–5, 326, 352, 421, 422, 424
Leopard 2 main battle tank (Germany) 221, 228, 244, 324, 328–8, 331, 343, 347, 352
Liberia 268, 379
Libya 254, 257, 271, 276
Light Armored Car M8 Greyhound (US) *94,*102–5, *109*
Light Armored Car T17E1 Staghound (US) 107
Light Strike Vehicle (UK) *387*
Light Tank M2 (US) 28
Light Tank M3 (US) 28, 181
Light Tank M5 (US) 28, 29
Light Tank Mk VII Tetrarch (UK) 63, 178
light vehicles
    Gulf War, 1991 385
    Korean War 164, 382, 383
    Modern Era 310, 382–401, 405
    Vietnam War 382, 384
    World War II 148–71, 382, 386
LT vz 35 light tank (Czech) 48
Luxembourg 389, 390
LVT2, 3 and 4 amphibious tractors (US) 181–2
Lynx command and reconnaissance vehicle (Canada) 301

M1 Abrams main battle tank (US) 217, 232, 308, 324, 327, 328, 332, 347–9, 437
M1A1 Abrams main battle tank (US) 330, 331, 347, 349, 416

M1A2 Abrams main battle tank (US) 330, 331, 343, 347
M2 amphibious bridge and ferry system (Germany) 425
M2 Bradley infantry fighting vehicle (US) 243, 247, 249, *316–17,* 365–7
M2 halftrack (US) 198, 200, 201
M2 Light Tank (US) 28
M3 armoured personnel carrier (France) 258, 259, 284, 285, 381
M3 Bradley Cavalry Fighting Vehicle (US) 365, *367,* 440
M3 halftrack (US) *34,* 106, *196,* 198–9, 200, 201
M3 Light Tank (US) 28, 181
M3 Medium Tank (US) 29–30, 31, 35, 74, 75, 77, 113, 120
M3A1 White Scout Car (US) 106
M4 Sherman Crab flail tank (UK) *31, 114,* 115, 123, 124
M4 Sherman Duplex Drive (DD) tank (UK) *34,* 122, 178–9
M4 Sherman Medium Tank (US) *8,* 31–4, 34, 54, 66, *73,* 75, 113–14, 115, 120, 178–9
M5 halftrack (US) 199, 201
M5 Light Tank (US) 28, 29
M8 Greyhound light armoured car (US) *94,* 102–5, *109*
M9 ACE (Armored Combat Earthmover) (US) 438
M9 halftrack (US) *198,* 199, 201
M10 Gun Motor Carriage tank destroyer (US) 54, 143, 144, 145, *146*
M.11/39 and M.13/40 medium tanks (Italy) 77
M.14/41 medium tank (Italy) 77, 78, 141
M.15/42 medium tank (Italy) 77, 78, 141
M18 Hellcat Gun Motor Carriage tank destroyer (US) 144, 146
M20 Armored Utility Car (US) 103, 105, 109
M22 Locust light tank (US) 63
M24 Chaffee Light Tank (US) 29, 302
M26 Pershing heavy tank (US) 35, 214
M29C Weasel amphibious cargo carrier (US) 182–3, 406
M31 Tank Recovery Vehicle (US) 120
M32 Tank Recovery Vehicle (US) 113, 120
M36 Gun Motor Carriage tank destroyer (US)*143,* 145
M37 light vehicle (US) 382
M38 Truck, Utility, 1/4-ton, 4x4 (US) 164, 383, 384, 397
M41 Walker Bulldog light tank (US) 216, 217, 302, 303
M43 ambulance (US) 382
M46 medium tank (US) 214
M47 medium tank (US) 214, 215, 217, 219, 221
M48 AVLB (Armoured Vehicle-launched Bridge) (US) 215
M48 Patton medium tank (US) 35, 206, 207, 214–17, 223, 232, 237, 402, 436
M60 AVLB (Armoured Vehicle-launched Bridge) (US) 233
M60 main battle tank (US) 207, 214, 217, 221, 223, 232–3, 237, 330, 346–7, 347, 436
M67 flamethrower tanks (US) 215
M-80 mechanised infantry combat vehicle (Yugoslavia) 245
M-84 main battle tank (Yugoslavia) 341–2
M88 ARV (Armoured Recovery Vehicle) (US) 215, 439
M103 heavy tank (US) 217
M113 armoured personnel carrier (US) 217, 242, 243, 244, 252, 254–5, 301, 362, 366, 440
M125 mortar carrier (US) *254,* 255
M151 light vehicle (US) 383, 384, 386–7
M170 ambulance (US) 383
M 201 light vehicle (France) 394, 396
M-325 4x4 truck (Israel) 393
M-462 Abir light utility vehicle (Israel) 393

M551 Sheridan light tank (US) 303–4
M578 ARV (Armoured Recovery Vehicle) (US) *440*
M728 Combat Engineer Vehicle (US) 233, 428, 436, 437
M901 Improved TOW Vehicle (US) 254, 255
M1059 smoke-generating vehicle (US) 440
Macedonia 245, 253, 254
Magach main battle tank (Israel) 237, 238
main battle tanks
    Cold War 9, 203–39, 327
    Modern Era 9, 318–49
    see also tanks
Malawi 295, 306
Malaysia 256, 272, 341, 364
Marder I tank destroyer (Germany) 51
Marder II tank destroyer (Germany) 51, 129, 147
Marder III tank destroyer (Germany) 49, 130, *139, 146*
Marder infantry combat vehicle (Germany) 218, 244, 249, 351–4
Marmon Herrington armoured cars (South Africa) 97–8
Matchless motorcycles (UK) 169
Matilda Baron mine-clearing tank (UK) 70, 114
Matilda Infantry Tank Mks I and II (UK) *64,* 70–1
Matilda Scorpion mine-clearing tank (UK) 70, 114, *115*
Mauritania 271, 278
Medium Tank M3 (US) *see* M3 Medium Tank
Medium Tank M4 (US) *see* M4 Sherman Medium Tank
Medium Tank Mk A 'Whippet' (UK) 15
Méhari Armée light vehicle (France) 395–6
Merkava Mks 1 and 2 main battle tanks (Israel) 222–3, 238, 330
Merkava Mk 3 main battle tank (Israel) 330–1
Mexico 105, 242, 258, 264, 268, 285, 287, 403
MILAN anti-tank missiles *387,* 389, 390, 394, 396, 397
mine-clearing tanks
    Cold War 211, 220, 429–30
    Modern Era *418,* 431
    Vietnam War 217
    World War II *31,* 70, 74, 113–15, 123, 124
Minerva armoured car (Belgium) 12
Modern Era
    amphibious vehicles 374, 401, 402–4, 406–16
    armoured personnel carriers 265, 368–81, 434
    combat engineer vehicles 417–40
    light vehicles 310, 382–401, 405
    main battle tanks 9, 318–49
    mine-clearing tanks 431
    overnsnow vehicles 404–7, 410
    reconnaissance vehicles 365, 386–9
    special purpose vehicles 111
    tank destroyers 369
    tanks 210, 211, 217, 221, 228, 229, 232, 317, 352
    tracked infantry fighting vehicles 9, 241, 243, 249, *316–17,* 350–67
Montgomery, Field Marshal Bernard 157, *164*
Morocco
    armoured personnel carriers 241, 254, 265
    reconnaissance vehicles 276, 278, 284, 306
    tanks 214, 217
Morris 10 HP Series M light utility car (UK) 157
motorcycles and sidecars, World War II 166–71
MOWAG (Switzerland)
    Eagle reconnaissance vehicle 310
    Grenadier armoured personnel carrier 268
    Piranha armoured personnel carrier 268, 308, 371, 378–9, 381, 434
    Piranha IIIC armoured combat vehicle 309
    Roland armoured personnel carrier 268, 381
    SPY reconnaissance vehicle 310
    Tornado infantry combat vehicle 244–5

MRAV multi-role armoured vehicle (Germany/UK) 372–3

MT-LB multi-purpose tracked vehicle (USSR) 251–2

MTU-20 armoured vehicle-launched bridge (USSR) 417–18, 426

Multiple Launc Rocket System (MLRS) (US) 365

Munitionpanzer IV Ausf F Karl ammunition carrier 125–6

Munitions-Schlepper ammunition carrier (Germany) 50

Nashorn tank destroyer (Germany) 133–4

Netherlands
  armoured personnel carriers 255, 265, 272, 373, 375
  combat engineer vehicles 423, 424, 428
  oversnow vehicles 406
  reconnaissance vehicles 288, 301
  tanks 211, 224, 237, 325

New Zealand 72, 254, 379

Nigeria 210, 220, 271, 272, 276, 295, 379

Nissan Q4W73 truck (Japan) 382

North Korea 41, 219, 234, 318, 319

Northern Ireland 270, *380*

Norton motorcycles (UK) 169

Norway 224, 344, 375, 377, 406, 407, 421–2

OF-40 main battle tank 221–2

Olifant main battle tank (South Africa) *212,* 238–9

Oman 228, 272, 290, 333, 334, 364, 377, 379, 397, 436

Opel Typ S/SSM trucks 191

OT-64 armoured personnel carrier (Czech) 257–8, 269

OTO-Melara (Italy)
  Biber armoured vehicle-launched bridge 424
  Centauro tank destroyer 369
  Leopard 1 AEV (Armoured Engineer Vehicle) 423
  Leopard 1 tank 221, 224
  M47 tank 214
  M113 armoured personnel carrier 242, 254
  Puma armoured personnel carrier 370
  Tipo 6614 armoured personnel carrier 264, 289, 381
  Tipo 6616 armoured car 264, 289

oversnow vehicles 404–7, 410

P4 light vehicle (France) 394, 396, 397

Pakistan
  armoured personnel carriers 254, 255
  tanks 211, 214, 215, 217, 219, 318, 322

Pandur armoured personnel carrier (Austria) 374

Panhard (France)
  178 armoured car 88
  AML 90 light armoured car *258,* 265, 284–5, 306
  EBR heavy armoured car 277–8
  ERC Sagaie armoured car 285–6
  M3 armoured personnel carrier 258, 259, 284, 285, 381
  Sagaie 2 armoured car 286
  VBL scout car 287
  VCR armoured personnel carrier 258, 285, 381

Panzerjäger I tank destroyer 50, 128, 138

Panzerjäger Tiger (P) Ferdinand tank destroyer 55, 136, *146, 147*

Panzerkampfwagen I light tank 49–50, 126, *127,* 128

Panzerkampfwagen II light tank 50–1, 76, *109,* 129, 147, 191

Panzerkampfwagen III medium tank 42, 50, 51–2, 133, 138

Panzerkampfwagen III (Tauchfähig) amphibious medium tank 172

Panzerkampfwagen IV medium tank 42, 50, 51–2, 52–3, 87, *119,* 125, 132–3

Panzerkampfwagen V Panther medium tank 32, 53–4, 61, 120, 135

Panzerkampfwagen VI Tiger heavy tank 32, 47, 53, 54–9, 60, 120, 136

Panzerkampfwagen VI Tiger II King Tiger heavy tank 60–1, 135, 145

Panzerkampfwagen 35-H 734(f) light tank 83

Panzerkampfwagen 35-S 739(f) medium tank 86

Panzerkampfwagen 35(t) light tank 48

Panzerkampfwagen 38(t) light tank 48–9, *51,* 130, 131, 139

Panzerkampfwagen 39-H 735(f) light tank 83

Panzerkampfwagen B1-bis 740(f) 87

Panzerkraftwagen Ehrhardt 1915/1917 27

Panzerspähwagen BAF 203(r) armoured car 98

Panzerspähwagen P 204(f) armoured car 88

Patton tank *see* M48 Patton

Pbv 302 armoured personnel carrier (Sweden) 243–4, 358

Pegaso VAP 3550/1 amphibious vehicle (Spain) 402–3

Perentie heavy-duty light truck (Australia/UK) 391–2

Pershing M26 heavy tank (US) 35, 214

Peru 48, 254, 264, 268

Petard spigot mortar (UK) 111–12, 122–3, 124

Peugeot (France)
  504 pick-up truck 396
  Autoblindé armoured car 24–5
  P4 light vehicle 394, 396, 397

Philippines 254, 255

'Pig' armoured personnel carrier (UK) 270, *380,* 381

Pinzgauer utility vehicle (Austria) 388, 397

Piranha armoured personnel carrier (Switzerland) 268, 308, 309, 371, 378–9, 381, 434

Piranha IIIC armoured combat vehicle (Switzerland) 309

PMP heavy floating bridge (USSR) 419, 427–8

Poland
  amphibious vehicles 408
  armoured personnel carriers 257–8, 269
  combat engineer vehicles 426, 427
  tanks 205, 206, 294, 335, 340–1

Pont Automoteur d'Accompagnement (PAA) self-propelled bridge system (France) 419

Pony light vehicle (Greece) 396

Portugal 214, 217, 254, 278, 381

PSZH-IV armoured personnel carrier (Hungary) 262–3

PT-76 amphibious light tank (USSR) 245, 251, 252, 294, 320

PT-91 main battle tank (Poland) 340–1

PTS amphibious vehicle (USSR) 408

Puma armoured personnel carrier (Italy) 370

Puma (Germany) *see* schwerer Panzerspähwagen SdKfz 234

Pz 61 and Pz 68 main battle tanks (Swiss) 226

Qatar 220, 242, 271, 284, 350, 377

Qayd al Ardh tank (Oman) 228

R-12/R-71/R-75 motorcycle and sidecar combinations (Germany) 166–8

R-35 light tank (France) 83–4

R-400 armoured car (Germany) 290–1

Ram cruiser tank (Canada) 33, 75, 119

Ram Kangaroo armoured personnel carrier (Canada) 75

RAM light armoured vehicle (Israel) 291–2

Ranger anti-personnel mine system (UK) 420–1

Ratel 20 infantry fighting vehicles (South Africa) 265–6, 381

reconnaissance vehicles
  Cold War 9, 260, 276–315, 404
  Modern Era 365, 386–9
  see also armoured cars

Reinhardt, General Georg-Hans 172

Renault
  FT 17 tank 17, 21, 22, 23–4, 25, 83
  Panhard 178 armoured car 88
  R-35 light tank 83–4
  TRM 500 light vehicle 396, 399
  VAB armoured personnel carrier 290, 377–8, 381

RG-31 Nyala armoured personnel carrier (South Africa) 312

RG-32 Scout general-purpose patrol vehicle (South Africa) 312–13

Rhino armoured personnel carrier (South Africa) 380

Ribbon Bridge heavy floating bridge (US) 428

Roland armoured personnel carrier (Switzerland) 268, 381

Rolls-Royce armoured car 18, 27

Romania 48, 49, 427

Rommel, Erwin 49, 108

Rooikat armoured car (South Africa) 304–5, 306

RST-V Shadow reconnaissance vehicle (US) *386,* 387

Russia
  armoured cars 12, 13, 19, 20
  armoured personnel carriers 351, 359–60, 371–2
  tanks 335, 338–9, 340
  see also Union of Soviet Socialist Republics

Sabra main battle tank (Israel) 237, 330

Sagaie 2 armoured car (France) 286

Saladin armoured car (UK) 271, 296

SAMO light vehicle (France) 394

Saracen armoured personnel carrier (UK) 252, 265, 270, 271, 296, 381

Saudi Arabia
  armoured personnel carriers 242, 254, 255, 350, 365, 379
  combat engineer vehicles 436
  tanks 8, 214, 220, 346, 347

Saxon armoured personnel carrier (UK) 272, *380,* 381

Scarab reconnaissance vehicle (UK) 311

Schneider (France)
  Char d'Assaut tank 21, 22
  SOMUA S-35 medium tank 85–6

schwerer Panzerspähwagen SdKfz 231 armoured car 90, 91

schwerer Panzerspähwagen SdKfz 231(8-Rad) reconnaissance car 90, 91–2, *95*

schwerer Panzerspähwagen SdKfz 234 (8-Rad) reconnaissance car 91, 92–3, *94–5, 109*

schwerer Wehrmachtsschlepper medium infantry halftrack 189–90

Schwimmwagen light amphibious vehicle (Germany) 173–4

Scorpion reconnaissance vehicle (UK) 295, 297–9, 364

Scout Car M3A1 White (US) 106

SdKfz 2 kleines Kettenrad light halftrack 184

SdKfz 5 Maultier halftrack truck 191

SdKfz 6 mittlerer Zugkraftwagen 5t medium artillery tractor 186

SdKfz 7 mittlerer Zugkraftwagen 8t medium artillery tractor 187

SdKfz 8 mittlerer Zugkraftwagen 12t medium artillery tractor 188

SdKfz 9 schwerer Zugkraftwagen 18t heavy artillery tractor 189

SdKfz 10 leichter Zugkraftwagen 1t light artillery tractor 184–5

SdKfz 11 leichter Zugkraftwagen 3t medium artillery tractor 185

SdKfz 250 leichter Schützenpanzerwagen *89,* 185, 192–3

SdKfz 251 mittlerer Schützenpanzerwagen 193–4, 200

Semovente Comando M.40 command vehicle (Italy) 77

Semovente L.40 da 47/32 light tank destroyer (Italy) 76, 140, 141

Semovente M.41M da 90/53 heavy tank destroyer (Italy) 141

Sentinel AC cruiser tank (Australia) 74–5

Sexton self-propelled gun (Canada) 75

Shadow RST-V reconnaissance vehicle (US) *386*, 387

Sherman M4 ARV (Armoured Recovery Vehicle) (UK) 120, *121*

Sherman M4 BARV (Beach Armoured Recovery Vehicle) (UK) 120, 121

Sherman M4 Crab flail tank (UK) *31*, *114*, 115, 123, 124

Sherman M4 Duplex Drive (DD) tank (UK) *34*, 122, 178–9

Sherman M4 Firefly medium tank (UK) 31–2, 67

Sherman M4 Medium Tank (US) *8*, 31–4, 35, 54, 66, *73*, 75, 113–14, 115, 120, 178–9

Shielder mine-layer (UK) 364

Shorland armoured patrol car (UK) 279, 381

Sho't main battle tank (Israel) 237–8

SIBMAS armoured personnel carrier (Belgium) 256

Sierra Leone 268, 379

Simplex Servi-Cycle motorcycle (US) 171

Singapore 254, 273, 350, 351, 425, 436

Six-Day War, 1967 201, 204, 208, 217, 222, 237, 238

SK 105 light tank/tank destroyer (Austria) 276

SKOT armoured personnel carriers (Poland) 257–8, 269

Slovenia 245, 374

Snezka reconnaissance vehicle (Czech) 281

Somalia 211, 242, 254, 264, 377

SOMUA (France)
  MCG halftrack 200
  S-35 medium tank 85–6

South Africa
  armoured cars 97–8, 265, 284, 304–6
  armoured personnel carriers 265–7, 271, 312, 380, 381
  reconnaissance vehicles 304–6, 312–13
  tanks 211, *212*, 238–9

South Korea 214, 217, 254, 264, 332–3, 412, 438

Spähpanzer Luchs reconnaissance vehicle 260, 287–8, 404

Spain
  amphibious vehicles 402–3, 413
  armoured personnel carriers 254, 267, 356–7, 381
  light vehicles 383
  reconnaissance vehicles 306–7
  tanks 214, 217, 220, 326, 402

Spanish Civil War 37, 39, 50

Special Operations Vehicle (SOV) (UK) 389

special purpose vehicles
  Cold War 112, 206, 209, 211, 220, 233, 429
  Modern Era 111
  World War II 48, 50, 54, 65, 66, 67, 70–1, 72, 74, 110–27, 429
  see also combat engineer vehicles

SPY reconnaissance vehicle (Switzerland) 310

SPz 4K 7FA armoured personnel carrier (Austria) 240

Sri Lanka 271, 318

Staff Saloon Mk 2 staff car (UK) 157

Staghound T17E1 Light Armored Car (US) 107

Standard 12 HP Series UV light utility car (UK) 157

S-tank main battle tank (Sweden) 227

Steyr-Daimler-Puch (Austria)
  ASCOD armoured infantry fighting vehicle 356–7
  Haflinger high-mobility light utility vehicle 397–8
  Pandur armoured personnel carrier 374

Pinzgauer utility vehicle 388

SK 105 light tank/tank destroyer 276

SPz 4K 7FA armoured personnel carrier 240

Stingray light tank (US) 300, 307

Stormer multi-role armoured personnel carrier (UK) 364

Stridsvagn 103 (S-tank) main battle tank (Sweden) 227

Stridsvagn 122 main battle tank (Sweden) 343–4

Stryker Mobile Gun System (US) 283, 435

Stuart M3 light tank (US) 28, 181

Sturmgeschütz III self-propelled gun 132, *138*

Sturmpanzerwagen A7V 17, 25–6

Sturmtiger assault gun 55

SU-76 self-propelled gun (USSR) 37

SU-100 self-propelled gun (USSR) 218

Sudan 219, 242, 254, 271

Surinam 265, 276

Sweden
  amphibious vehicles 406–7
  armoured personnel carriers 243–4, 358–9, 375, 379
  combat engineer vehicles 428
  light vehicles 398, 400
  oversnow vehicles 406–7
  reconnaissance vehicles 309
  tanks 48, 211, 227, 326, 343–5

Switzerland
  armoured personnel carriers 244–5, 254, 268, 309, 361, 371, 378–9, 381, 434
  light vehicles 398
  reconnaissance vehicles 309–10
  tanks 48, 49, 211, 226, 238, 326, 344

Syria
  amphibious vehicles 408
  armoured personnel carriers 251
  reconnaissance vehicles 293, *388*
  tanks 41, 206, 215, 222, 223, 337

T-10 heavy tank (USSR) 204

T17E1 Staghound Light Armored Car (US) 107

T-26 light tank (USSR) 37, 98, 196

T-28 medium tank (USSR) 38

T34 Calliope rocket launcher *34*

T-34 medium tank (USSR) 36, 39–42, 45, 47, 52, 53, 54, 109, 218, 426

T-35 heavy tank (USSR) 43, 44

T-37 light amphibious tank (USSR) 175, 176

T-38 light amphibious tank (USSR) 175–6

T-40 light tank (USSR) 36

T-54/55 main battle tanks (USSR) *202–3*, 204, 205–8, 217, 219, 235, 318, 328, 341, 428

T-60 light tank (USSR) 36, 109

T-62 main battle tank (USSR) 207, 234–5, 327, 328

T-64 main battle tank (USSR) 235–6, 335, 338, 339

T-70 light tank (USSR) 36–7

T-72 main battle tank (USSR) 207, 222, 235, 236, 294, 322, 335–7, 339, 340, 341

T-80 light tank (USSR) 37

T-80 main battle tank (Russia) 338, 339, 349

T-84 main battle tank (Ukraine) 340

T-90 main battle tank (Russia) 335, 339

T207 series multi-role 1/2-ton light trucks (US) 160

T214 series multi-role 3/4-ton light trucks (US) 161–2, 382

T215 series multi-role 1/2-ton light trucks (US) 160–1

Taiwan 214, 217, 254

TAM medium tank (Argentina) 218

tank destroyers
  Cold War 276, 351, 353
  Modern Era 369
  World War II 49, 51, 54, 61, 72, 76, 83, 128–47

Tank Mk I (UK) 14, 16, 17

Tank Mk II (UK) 16

Tank Mk III (UK) 16

Tank Mk IV (UK) 16–17, 26

Tank Mk V (UK) 17

Tank Recovery Vehicle M31 (US) 120

Tank Recovery Vehicle M32 (US) 113, 120

tanks
  Cold War 9, 49, 55, 203–39, 276, 278, 294, 300, 302–4, 327
  Gulf War, 1991 230, 318, 333, 336, 337, 342, *346*, 348
  Korean War 29, 35, 41, 211, 212, 215
  Modern Era 210, 211, 217, 221, 228, 229, 232, 317, 352
  Six-Day War, 1967 201, 204, 208, 217, 222, 237, 238
  Spanish Civil War 37, 39, 50
  Vietnam War 41, 207, 211, *213*, 215, 216–17, 303, 320
  World War I 8, 11, 14–17, 21–4, 25–6, 73, 117, 428
  World War II 8, 9, *10–11*, 24, 28–87, 203, 302
  Yom Kippur War, 1973 208, 238
  see also main battle tanks; mine-clearing tanks

Tanzania 219, 318

Terrapin light amphibious load carrier (UK) 177

Tetrarch Mk VII light tank (UK) 63, 178

Textron Marine & Land Systems *see* Cadillac Gage

Thailand 214, 217, 219, 254, 255, 271, 300, 412

Timoney armoured personnel carrier (Ireland) 263

Tipo 6614 armoured personnel carrier (Italy) 264, 289, 381

Tipo 6616 armoured car (Italy) 264, 289

TM 170 armoured personnel carrier (Germany) 262, 381

TMM truck-mounted treadway bridge (USSR) 426–7

TNH P-S light tank (Czech) 48–9, 130, 131, 139

Tornado infantry combat vehicle (Switzerland) 244–5

TOW anti-tank missiles 104, 314, *315*, 337, 356, 365, 367, 386

Toyota 2FQ15L truck (Japan) 382

tracked infantry fighting vehicles
  Cold War 9, 218, 240–55, 361, 362
  Modern Era 9, 241, 243, 249, *316–17*, 350–67
  see also amphibious vehicles; armoured personnel carriers

Transportpanzer 1 armoured personnel carrier (Germany) 260–1, 287, 404

Trippel 4x4 light vehicle (Germany) 404

Triumph motorcycles (UK) 170

TRM 500 light vehicle (France) 396, 399

Truck, 1/4-ton, Utility, 4x4, Jeep (US) 148, 150, 154, 163–3, 383, 386, 394

Truck, Utility, 1/4-ton, 4x4, M38 (US) 164, 383, 384, 397

Tunisia 214, 254, 257, 276, 278

Turkey 48, 105, 214, 217, 224, 254, 255, 330, 372, 406

Type 1 medium tank (Japan) 81

Type 2 Ka-Mi light amphibious tank (Japan) 176–7

Type 2 light tank (Japan) 79, 80

Type 3 medium tank (Japan) 81

Type 59 main battle tank (China) 205, 218–19, 318, 319

Type 60/61 oversnow vehicles (Japan) 404

Type 62/63 light tanks (China) 319–20

Type 69 main battle tank (China) 219, 318, 319, 320

Type 73 armoured personnel carrier (Japan) 243

Type 74 main battle tank (Japan) 225–6

Type 77 armoured personnel carrier (China) 241

Type 78 ARV (Armoured Recovery Vehicle) (Japan) 226

Type 80 main battle tank (China) 321

Type 85 main battle tank (China) 319

Type 87 reconnaissance vehicle (Japan) 292

Type 89 infantry combat vehicle (Japan) 243

Type 89 light tank (Japan) 79
Type 90 main battle tank (China) 319
Type 90 main battle tank (Japan) 331
Type 95 light tank (Japan) 79, 80, 176, 177
Type 95 Scout Car (Kurogane Black Medal) (Japan) 156
Type 97 medium tank (Japan) 80, 81
Type 98 main battle tank (China) 322

UAZ-69 light cross-country vehicle (USSR) 400–1
UAZ-469B light cross-country vehicle (USSR) 400, 401
Ukraine 338, 340, 372
Unic Kégresse P 107 halftrack (France) 195, 198, 200
Unimog 4x4 truck (Germany) 261, 266, 279
Union of Soviet Socialist Republics
  amphibious vehicles
    Modern Era 401, 408–10
    World War II 175–6, 180, 183, 401, 409
  armoured cars 98, 106, 109, 293
  armoured personnel carriers
    Cold War 9, 204, 218, 241, 245, 246–52, 257, 268–9, 371
    Modern Era 371–2, 381
  combat engineer vehicles 417–18, 419, 426–8
  halftracks 196, 197, 199, 201
  light vehicles 154, 400–1
  oversnow vehicles 410
  reconnaissance vehicles 269, 293–4
  special purpose vehicles 206, 426
  tanks·
    Cold War 202–3, 204–8, 218, 234–6, 251, 294, 327
    Modern Era 207, 335–9
    Spanish Civil War 37, 39
    World War II 36–47, 72, 109, 129, 135
United Arab Emirates
  armoured personnel carriers 242, 257, 258, 271, 272, 350, 359, 377
  tanks 325
United Kingdom
  amphibious vehicles
    Cold War 180
    Modern Era 406, 407
    World War II 34, 177–9, 183
  armoured cars
    Cold War 100, 271, 295–6
    World War I 13, 18–19, 27
    World War II 18, 97–8, 99–102, 103, 105, 107, 108–9, 171, 296
  armoured personnel carriers
    Cold War 249, 252–3, 263, 264, 265, 270–2, 279
    Modern Era 361–4, 372–3, 379, 380, 381
  combat engineer vehicles 420–1, 425, 428, 429–33
  halftracks 187, 197, 198, 199
  light vehicles
    Modern Era 387, 388–90
    World War II 154–5, 157–9, 164–5
  mine-clearing tanks 31, 70, 74, 113, 114–15, 123, 124, 211, 429–30
  motorcycles 169–70, 171
  oversnow vehicles 406, 407
  reconnaissance vehicles 284, 295–9, 311, 313
  special purpose vehicles
    Cold War 112, 209, 211
    World War II 65, 66, 67, 70–1, 72, 74, 110–13, 114–24, 429
  tank destroyers 72, 142, 143
  tanks
    Cold War 206, 209–13, 226, 227, 228–31, 327
    Modern Era 210, 211, 229, 328, 333–4
    World War I 11, 14–17, 25, 26, 73, 117, 428

World War II 10–11, 28, 30, 31–2, 62–74, 77, 178–9, 211
United States
  amphibious vehicles
    Modern Era 402, 407, 411–16, 439
    World War II 165, 177, 401, 402, 406, 409
  armoured cars 94, 102–7, 109, 307–8
  armoured personnel carriers
    Cold War 216, 242, 243, 254–5, 273–5, 362
    Modern Era 243, 316–17, 365–7, 374, 378–9, 381
  combat engineer vehicles 233, 428, 435–40
  halftracks 34, 106, 196, 198–201
  light vehicles
    Cold War 164
    Modern Era 310, 382–7
    Word War II 148, 150, 154, 160–5, 382
  mine-clearing tanks 113–14, 217
  motorcycles 169, 170–1
  oversnow vehicles 407
  reconnaissance vehicles 283, 300–4, 386–7
  special purpose vehicles 113–14, 120, 233
  tank destroyers 54, 143–5, 146
  tanks
    Cold War 206, 207, 214–17, 219, 221, 232–3, 300, 302–4
    Korean War 29, 35
    Modern Era 217, 232, 327, 328, 346–9
    Vietnam War 215, 216–17, 303
    World War I 17, 23, 24
    World War II 28–35, 73, 113–14, 120, 302
Universal Engineer Tractor (US) 438
UR-416 armoured personnel carrier (Germany) 261, 381
Uruguay 254, 276

V-100 armoured personnel carrier (US) 273, 381
V-300 Commando armoured personnel carrier (US) 274–5
VAB armoured personnel carrier (France) 290, 377–8, 381
Valentine Infantry Tank Mk III (UK) 71–2, 75, 99, 142
Valkyr armoured personnel carrier (UK) 263, 264
VBC-90 armoured car (France) 290, 381
VBCI armoured personnel carrier (France) 372, 376–7
VBL scout car (France) 287
VBRG armoured personnel carrier (France) 381
VCC-1 Camillino armoured infantry fighting vehicle (Italy) 242, 254
VCR armoured personnel carrier (France) 258, 285, 381
VCTP infantry fighting vehicle (Argentina) 218
VEC cavalry scout vehicle (Spain) 306–7
Velocette motorcycles (UK) 170
Venezuela 220, 242, 412
Verne Dragoon armoured personnel carrier (US) 273, 381
Vickers (UK)
  6-ton Type E light tank 37
  ABV (Armoured Bridgelaying Vehicle) 210
  ARRV (Armoured Repair and Recovery Vehicle) 210
  ARV (Armoured Recovery Vehicle) 210
  Independent heavy tank 43
  Infantry Tank Mk III Valentine 71–2, 75, 99, 142
  Light Tanks 62–3
  Main Battle Tank 210
  Scarab reconnaissance vehicle 311
  Valkyr armoured personnel carrier 263, 264
Vietnam 214, 219, 254, 294, 318, 320, 382
Vietnam War
  armoured personnel carriers 251, 273
  light vehicles 382, 384
  mine-clearing tanks 217
  tanks 41, 207, 211, 213, 215, 216–17, 303, 320

VM Pikap halftrack (USSR) 196
Volkswagen
  181 light vehicle 397
  Iltis light utility vehicle 383, 396, 397, 405
  Kübel 148–50, 174
  Schwimmwagen light amphibious vehicle 173–4
Volvo
  4140 series light vehicles 400
  L3314 Laplander light vehicle 400
VTP 2 patrol vehicle (Chile) 381
VZ halftrack (USSR) 196

Walid armoured personnel carrier (Egypt) 368
Warrior mechanised combat vehicle (UK) 249, 361–3
Weasel M29C amphibious cargo carrier (US) 182–3, 406
Welbike Mk II collapsible motorcycle (UK) 169
Wespe self-propelled howitzer (Germany) 51
West Germany see Ge`rmany
'Whippet' Medium Tank Mk A (UK) 15
Wiesel multi-purpose carrier (Germany) 314–15
Willys-Overland (US)
  AM7, AM8 and AM10 light vehicles 383
  M38 Truck, Utility, 1/4-ton, 4x4 164, 383, 384, 397
  see also Jeep
World War I
  armoured cars 9, 12–13, 18–20, 24–5, 27
  halftracks 198
  tanks 8, 11, 14–17, 21–4, 25–6, 73, 117, 428
World War II
  amphibious vehicles 34, 51, 165, 172–83, 401, 402, 406, 409
  armoured cars 9, 18, 49, 88–109, 171
  halftracks 34, 89, 106, 184–201
  light vehicles 148–71, 382, 386
  mine-clearing tanks 31, 70, 74, 113–15, 123, 124
  motorcycles and sidecars 166–71
  special purpose vehicles 48, 50, 54, 65, 66, 67, 70–1, 72, 74, 110–27, 429
  tank destroyers 49, 51, 54, 61, 72, 76, 83, 128–47
  tanks 8, 9, 10–11, 24, 28–87, 203, 302

XA series armoured personnel carrier (Finland) 375–6

YaSP halftrack (USSR) 196
Yom Kippur War, 1973 208, 238, 251, 293, 426, 427
YP-408 armoured personnel carrier (Netherlands) 265
YPR-765 armoured personnel carrier (Netherlands) 265
Yugoslavia 214, 245, 335, 341–2, 399, 428
YW 531 armoured personnel carrier (China) 240, 241
YW 534 armoured personnel carrier (China) 241

Zahal halftrack (Israel) 201
Zimbabwe 219, 276, 306, 318
Zis-33/42 halftracks (USSR) 196
Zündapp KS-750 motorcycle and sidecar combination (Germany) 166